AFRICAN BIRDS
IN FIELD & AVIARY
A guide to a mixed collection

by

The Avicultural Research Unit

in cooperation with

DR JOSEF M STEYN
Nest Heating and The Bird Breeder and Medication

DR ARTHUR WRIGHT
Artificial Incubation and Egg Hatching

BARBARA HUCKETT
Nutritional Principles

TONY ROOCROFT
Understanding Welded Mesh

MARTIN WEST
Plants for the Aviary, Poisonous Plants & Plants useful to birds

STEPHEN GREEN
Birdrooms, Construction, Nest boxes & Feeding

TREVOR KONIGKRAMER
Nesting Materials and Linings. Exhibiting Birds & Show Cages

NEVILLE BRICKELL
Species Accounts, Photography, Catching and Handling and Ringing or Banding

Illustrated by
REX M. SHIRLEY AND KAREN DE KLERK

African Bird Book Publishing
Westville, KwaZulu-Natal

Area map of Africa

AFRICAN BIRDS IN FIELD & AVIARY

A guide to a mixed collection

Standard Edition

EDITORS

The Publisher is grateful to the following companies for their generous support:

TEXT PRINTED ON MONDI ENVAPOST 90GSM

Cover and coated paper supplied by First Paper House.

Cover film - Laminated by Pro Bind SA, Durban and Gauteng.

Grateful thanks are due to Ian Askew, J.A. Kriel, Chris Digges AND NATAL BIRD BREEDER'S SOCIETY for their help in the preparation of this book.

Dedicated to the memory of

Ernie Campbell

Cyril "Shorty" Clewlow

Bill Collard

Des Davidson

Des Ferreira

Nick Grobler

George Harrower

Bruce Huntley

Walter Konigkramer

Dudley Nourse

Clive Sandy

Maurice Scotney

Derek Scheicher

Jack Scheepers

Les Unger

Jack Vorster

Ron Vorster

Mervyn Wills

Sid Whittaker

Members of −
Natal Avicultural Society
Natal Bird Breeder's Society
Queensburgh Avicultural Society
(1952-1996)

Contents

Preface

The purpose of this book is to provide a practical guide to the wonderful hobby of birdkeeping. It provides a co-ordinated synthesis of up-to-date information researched from many sources, in a form which has seldom been published before as an avicultural work, but with all the wealth of information here presented, it cannot be complete, for despite the intensive field research and captive observations undertaken in Africa, many species are still inadequately known.

This edition contains the revised texts of volume 1 (1996) and 2 (1989) and now also includes species that cover all Africa from the Mediterranean coast to the Cape, and the off-shore islands from Fernando Pó to Zanzibar. The title has now been changed to *African Birds in Field & Aviary — A guide to a mixed collection.* An attempt has been made to summarise various aspects of avicultural management under clear cut separate headings to allow quick and easy reference to the specific procedures involved. Scientific names: the order of families and nomenclature follow fairly closely though not entirely, Howard and Moore's *A Complete Checklist of the Birds of the World* (1991). To assist those aviculturist perplexed by the many changes, all common names are given as an adjunct to the scientific nomenclature, and have also striven to keep up with changes in territorial names which have taken place in Southern Africa during the preparation of this work in South Africa.

Introduction

The first avicultural guide on the birds of the African continent, *Aviculture in South Africa* was written by Herbert Parker in 1959. This was followed in 1980 with the publication, *The Aviculturist's Handbook, the Management and Treatment of Diseases, Disorders and Ailments of Birds* by Leon Goodman. Six years later in 1986 with volume one and in 1989 with volume two of *Introduction to Southern African Cage & Aviary Birds,* a series of monographic treatments of bird groups to fill some of the gaps in avicultural literature for this region was published. And finally in 1993 a work which concentrates only on the management of exotic bird species, *Keeping and Breeding Birds - A Guide for South Africa* by Vierentia Beukes. The aim of this compact edition is to fill the need of uninterrupted access and brings together in less expensive form and in one volume a complete descriptive text. Besides the compilers this book is truly a cooperative work by both assistants and contributors. While we have done our best to make the guide as complete and accurate as possible, we have no illusions about perfection. We hope that the advice offered in this book will help to answer at least some of the questions a beginner asks the more experienced birdkeeper, and also hope that the latter, in finding errors, should contact:

Avicultural Research Unit
100 Innes Road
Durban
4025
Kwa-Zulu Natal
South Africa
Tel: 031-239701 a/h 031 238918
Fax: 031-239701

Acknowledgements

In the first two volumes of Introduction to Southern African Cage & Aviary Birds, we expressed our indebtedness to a number of individuals whom we sent several sets of rough drafts for comment, namely Messrs Ken Arnold, Mike Balcomb, Fred Barnicoat, Eric Clewlow, Stuart Shillinglaw, Dr Arthur Wright, the late Bruce Huntley and Jack Scheepers, and who made many useful additions, suggestions and criticisms.

To this revised compact edition we include a few more with our gratitude, Messrs Bill Cummings and the Late Nick Grobler.

In the first stages of this work (1982-89), we were kindly assisted in ways too diverse to specify in detail by a number of aviculturists or ornithologists, namely:

A.R. Ali; R.C. Anderson; T.I. Askew; M.L. Balcomb; F.C. Barnicoat; R. Berriman; P. Blom; N. Boshoff; B. Boswell; P.J. Botes; M. Bothma; C.J. Cairns; the late A.E. Campbell; the late W. Clarkson; E. Clohessy; the late W. Collard; K. Cooper; P. Craig-Cooper; D. Crookshank; K.W. Cross; the late A.C. Crowe; the late D.C. Davidson; D. Davis; C.H. de Jongh; C.D. de Klerk; D. de Swardt; I.W. du Preez; P. du Randt; J.A. Edmonds; G.C. Engelbrecht; L.M. Erasmus; J. Finch; I.H. Fletcher; F. Fortgens; C. Fouquereaux; R.K. Fowle; L.K. Grace; G.F.S Gale, A. Green; P.A. Halgreen; B.D. Hall; G. Harrower; J.H. Hearnshaw; C. Hogan; R.C. Hollis; D. Hopkins; F.S. Hylton; B.O. Jenkins; B. Jones; C. A. King;; R. Kotze; J.A. Kriel; A. Lawrence; J. Lagesse; L. L'Homme; F.J. Liebenberg; J.J. Loots; W.J. Lotter; C. Luther; C. Macrae; K. Macguire; Dr D.F. Marais; J.J. Mare; Mrs I. Pocock; Dr J. Mendelsohn; H. Mentz; G. Mortimer; J. Muller; M. Muller; J. Nettman; H. Northwood; the late A.D. Nourse; V. Parker; H. Phillpott; S. Phillipson; C. Podmore; M. Pretorius; C. Quickelberge; J. Ribeiro; B.J. Robertse; W.S. Ross; D. Rubelli; C.H. Russell; Dr W.D. Russell; the late D. Scheicher; M.A. Scotney; H. Scott; H. Smith; P.L. Smith; H. Steiner; P. Strachan; B; Steyn; E. Steytler; E. Taylor; J.C. Taylor; J.W.H. Tischendorf; P.J van der Merwe; V. van Rooyen; C.T. Vermaak; J. Vorster; R. Vorster; E. Warne; F.J. Wessels; the late S. Whittaker; W.A. Wilcox; E.G.K. Williams; the late M. Wills; V.J. Wilson; G. Wood; and G. Zietsman.

To these we must now add many more who contributed information in one form or another, namely:

J. Abbas; A. Abbu; R. Allen; Mrs J. Aumord; A. Aberdein; C. Absolom; J. Ackermann; O. Addinall; P.P. Adendorff; N. Aggett; A. Ahmeh; P. Aitken; J. Akkiah; P. Almeida; J. Andriessen; A. Antzoylatos; I. Arran; M. Alberts; J.A. Adams; P. Ahrens; N. Abbot; T. Allen; R. Ackermann; N. Bircher; Mrs V. Beukes; K. Bezuidenhout; I. Bheem; P. Buck; J. Bryant; N.C. Buchanan; R. Buckley; N. Buckley; C. Brown; T.B. Barman; N. Balie; T. Benson; K. Bruce; M. Botes; M. Biess; K. Blaauw; T. Ballard; A. Becker; K. Buys; H. Brand; L.A. Bartlett; H. Beyer; J. Block; J.J. Booysen; H.A. Bonthuys; A. Cominelli; G.J. Coetzee; D.R. Cruickshank; D. Cunnama; B. Carr; O. Cassim; N. Chambers; M. Cilliers; T. Corneussen; P. Costopoulos; R. Couzens; I. Cuspilli; A. Chetty; L. Cross; N. Cole; V. Cupido; D. Curtis; J.M. Clauss; B. Cronje; P. Campher; E. Cilliers; K. Duminy; A.K. de Wal; D. Dale; W.R.J. Dean; P. de Almeida; J. de Beer; P. de Sousa; M. de Canha; P. de Charmoy; A. Deschamps; M.M. de Villiers; P. Dewhurst; D. Dixon; A. Dolabh; A. dos Santos; M.A. Dunn; P. du Randt; K. du Plooy; S.A. de Beer; W. de Wet; I. Davids; S. da Silva; A. Donough; H.A. de Bruin; M. Dodds; R. Dippenaar; L.M. Erasmus; R.R. Erhart; K. Engelbrecht; T.C. Edwards; W. Esteves; W. Espitalier; T. Evans; J. Els; T. Ellis; D. Edwards; P. Frost; M. Fischer; M. Fick; R. Filip; O. Falowitz; P. Fakir; A. Forbes; K. Fleischer; T. Fine; T.M. Fischer; A.J. Forbes; I. Fish; T. Ferris; O. Friend; S.S. Ferriera; M. France; Mrs M. Gammage; P. Gomes; N. Gaffar; B. Garcia; A.O. Garach; T. Garrib; J. Gomes; A.G. Green; Q. Grimsley; A.A. Grobbler; J. Gilbert; A. Grosskopf; J. Goosen; J. Gerber; H.J. Groenewald; P. Gruhn; C. Hogan; P. Havemann; M. Hamiel; J. Hanif; T.B. Hart; O.A. Haynes; J. Hiran; J.J. Haupt; J. Havanga; J.N. Judson; M. Holtzhausen; I. Hough; K. Horn; T. Hansen; M.I. Heller; J. Herzog; C.A. King; R. Kotze; E, Krugel; P. Koen; A. Kok; S. Kratz; W. Kriess; P. Klein; P. Klaus; K. Kriel; C. Koen; W.J. Lotter; W.A. Laubscher; J. Louwrens; A. Lorentz; B.J. Lottering; K. Laing; I. Luhe; J.B. Loots; A. Mans; G. Maxwell; F. Maartens; T.M. McFarlane; D. Munz; M. Murphy; O. Mace; J.T. Meyer; J. Mohun; T. Muller; W. Nieman; B. Nell; P. Nel; A. Nilssen; H. Naude; D.C. Norval; P. Odekerken; G. Patten; D. Pringle; I. Peters; C. Pereira; R. Peralta; M. Paterson; K. Potgieter; C. Quickelberge; L. Quinton; T. Quail; J. Rough; P.C. Routh; S.W. Rautenbach; M. Rix; P. Sims; S.J. Schutz; A. Sullaphen; R. Schreiber; N. Schubach; K. Schwan; M. Schoon; F. Schroder; N. Schwegmann; S.J. Schutz; L. Stephens; R. Scheepers; K. Small; B. Stein; R. Stander; G. Swarts; L.T. Simond; W. Swanepoel; W. Schnoor; A. Swiel; L. Steffens; B. Stein; W. Stuart; A. Strauss; M. Storm; C. Sage; C.A. Schnelder; I.A.K. Trogisch; T. Thompson; M.P. Teixeira; A. Uurga; S. von Wiechardt; K.L. von Zahn; A.C. von der Meden; J.Q. von Puttkammer; J. Viranna; S.J. van der Merwe; P. van Rensburg; O. van Eck; L. Visagie; N.A. van Heerden; K. van Aswegen; L. Visser; J. Warner; M.C. Weber; W. Wright; M. Woods; A. Wium; P. Waiboer; J. Wassink; T. White; J. Warner; P. Williams; M. Wohler; L. Willemse; H. Wells; W. Walters; K.I. Woermann; S. Wentzel; T. Watt; P.T. Young; Z. Zaneb.

We are indebted also to the following for their generosity in assisting us personally by answering our correspondence.

AUSTRALIA: Mrs R. Anderson, Mrs D. Andersen, Mrs O. Bell, Mrs J. Fernie, Mrs P. Garwood, R. Garwood, Mrs M. Godley, G. Hyde, G.L. Jarick, Mrs E. Macgregor-Davies and Mrs S. Rendell.

GERMANY: Dr D.S. Peters, Dr. R. van den Elzen and Prof. Dr. W. Ziegler.

MADAGASCAR: A. Randrianjafy.

MOZAMBIQUE: Dr. A. Cabral.

NAMIBIA: J. Komen and C.J.V. Rocher.

NEW ZEALAND: D. Brice, A. Benson, Mrs C. Edge and Mrs N. Gates.

SOUTH AFRICA: Dr A.N.S. Abrey, E. Beckx, N. Bircher, L.J. Bunning, Miss B. Eisenhauer, A. Harris, Miss K.A. Herbert, G. Holland, W. Horsfield, Mrs M. Jordaan, P. le Roux, Dr. J.G.H. Londt, Mrs P. Lorber, W. Mangold, Dr. B.S. Noruka, U. Oberprieler, S. Phillipson, C. Quickelberge, Mrs. W. Roos, I. Sinclair, B. Smuts, R. Spector, Dr. B.R. Stuckenberge, Mrs L. Saayman, N. Thomson, J. Vermeulen, Mrs. E. van Hoepen, C.J. Vernon, R. Wilkinson and K. Westphal.

UNITED KINGDOM: P.R. Colston, I.C.J. Galbraith, D. Goodwin and A.J. Mobbs.

UNITED STATES OF AMERICA: G.S. Keith, T.D. Nicholson, T. Silva and Mrs. I. Taylor.

ZIMBABWE: Miss B. Hadebe, P.J. Mundy, Dr. W.K. Nduku and C. Walton.

We wish to express our gratitude to Stephen Green, Barbara Huckett, Tony Roocroft, Dr. Josef Steyn, Martin West and Dr. Arthur Wright who each generously contributed chapters to this work.

We are also grateful to the support of Products Company Directors and Managers, namely: M. Beagle, D. Dennison, Mrs. V. Dennison, D. Hare, Dr. W.B. Hyman, Mrs D. Jarvis, T. Lindsey, R. Martin A. Nuttall.

We are most grateful to the farmers, nurserymen and herbalists who assisted us with the required indigenous wildfoods needed to establish a garden for seed and plant distribution, namely:

P. Adams; J. Aitken; P.P. Albertyn; M. Basson; C. Bekker; J. Bezuidenhout; Z. Bhengu; M. Biyela; W.A. Breytenbach; P. Bloem; P.O. Brown; T. Black; P. Chetty; J. du Plessis; J.J. Fourie; M. Gcabashe; V. Govender; N. Horn; W.A. Hough; O.T. James; J.C. Jansen; A. Jenkins; B. Jwara; T. Jwill; W. Kemp; T. Kleynhans; T. Mzimande; K.L. Norris; K. Nortjie; R. Nzuza; J.W. Oberholzer; J. Schutte; J.N. Schoeder; P. Shezi; A. Smith; P. Stephens; M. Swanepoel; T. Swart; D. van den Berg; G. van der Linde; J. van der Merwe; T. Vumase; C. van Rensburg; O.T. Weston; N. Williams and P. Zulu.

We apologise to anyone who may have been inadvertently omitted.

Citation

The Editors recommend that for references to this work in avicultural publications, the following citation should be used:

BRICKELL, N and KONIGKRAMER, T (eds) (1997) *African Birds in Field & Aviary – A guide to a mixed collection.*

Topography of a bird
showing parts of plumage and body

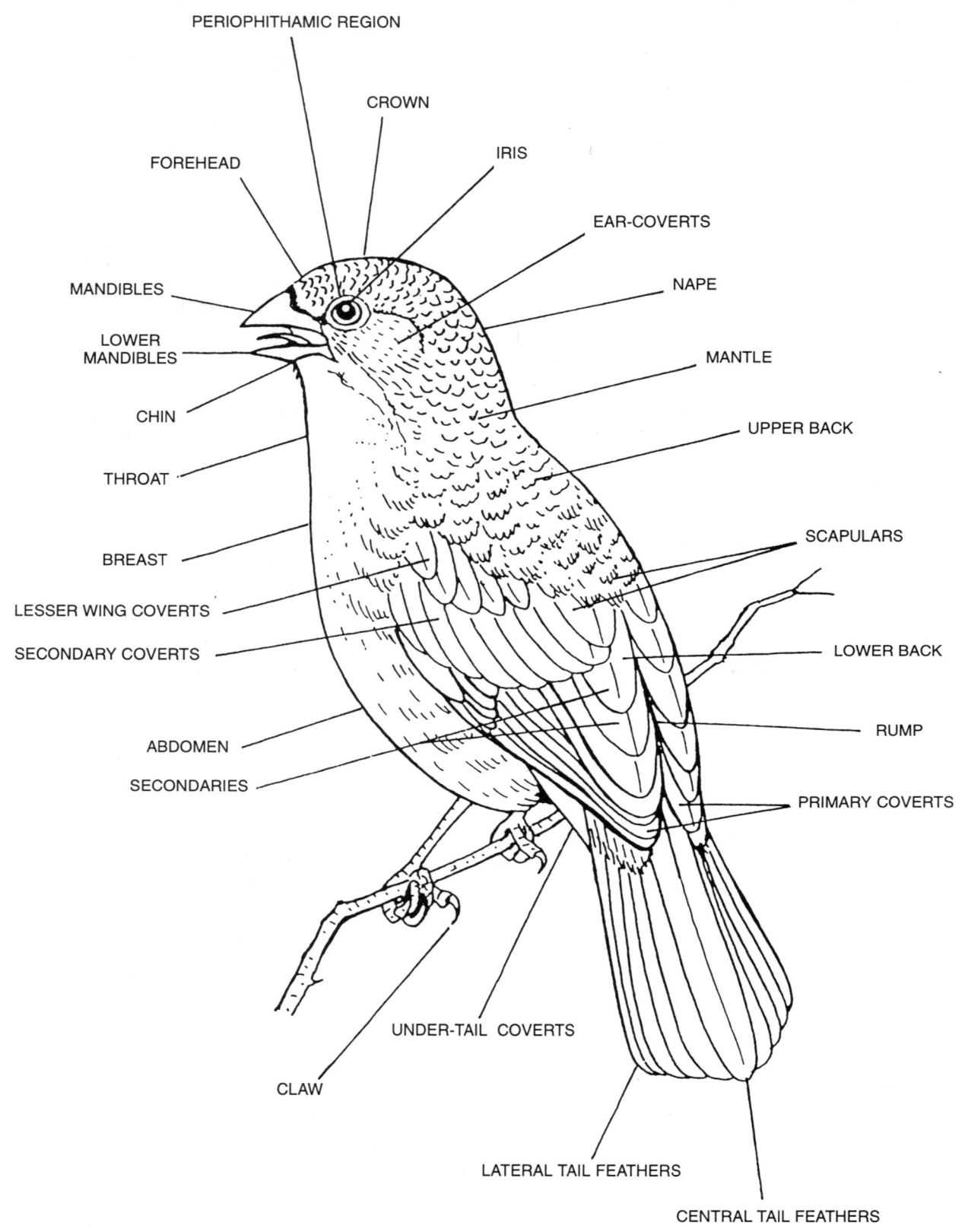

PERIOPHITHAMIC REGION

CROWN

IRIS

FOREHEAD

EAR-COVERTS

NAPE

MANDIBLES

MANTLE

LOWER
MANDIBLES

CHIN

UPPER BACK

THROAT

BREAST

SCAPULARS

LESSER WING COVERTS

SECONDARY COVERTS

LOWER BACK

ABDOMEN

RUMP

SECONDARIES

PRIMARY COVERTS

UNDER-TAIL COVERTS

CLAW

LATERAL TAIL FEATHERS

CENTRAL TAIL FEATHERS

Species accounts

This part of the book features closely related species which are listed together in natural sequence.

Family Phasiaidae – Game Birds: Spurfowl, Guineafowl, Francolin, Partridge, Quail
Turnicidae – Button-Quail, Quail Plover
Pteroclididae – Sandgrouse
Columbidae – Pigeons and Doves
Psittacidae – Parrots, Parakeets and Lovebirds
Ploceidae – Sparrows, Weavers, Widow-Birds, etc
Estrilidae – Waxbills, Mannikins, Twinspots, Fire-Finches, etc
Fringillidae – Finches and Canaries
Emberizidae – Buntings

Barbary Partridge

Alectoris barbara 32-34cm

Description: Sexes similar. Forehead, crown and nape chestnut; hindneck ash-grey; mantle, back, rump and upper tail-coverts dark grey, tinged slate; tail rufous chestnut; wings with greater and primary-coverts cinnamon; under wing-coverts pale grey with buff edges; flanks with vertical bars of rufous cinnamon, black and white; chin and cheeks ash-grey; ear-coverts rufous buff; deep chestnut gorget with white spots from sides of neck to lower throat; breast, belly and rest of underparts pink-buff, tinged grey on sides of vent; iris pale brown or red-brown, bill red or orange-red; legs and feet reddish. Juvenile similar to adult, but paler overall, pale chestnut gorget with buff spots from sides of neck to lower throat, flanks with vertical bars of rufous buff. Chick is pale tawny buff, back barred and streaked blackish; iris dark brown; bill yellow; legs and feet pale yellow or pinkish buff.

Adults *A.b. spatzi* differs from the nominate race in being paler overall, crown rufous brown, flanks less heavily barred.

A.b. keonigi differs from nominate in having upperparts less olive-brown; breasts deeper cinnamon.

Voice: Described by Etchecoper & Hue as a rapid '*kakelik*' followed by slower '*tchouk...tchouk... tchoukor...tchoukor*'.

Habitat: Citrus groves, *Thuja* and *Euphorbia* stands and occasionally in Eucalyptus, also on thorny marquis, broom scrub, along dry riverbeds and in sparse bushes in sandy coastal hills.

Distribution: North-eastern Morocco, northern Algeria and northern Tunisia. *A.b. spatzi* south-western and eastern Morocco, Algeria, and Tunisia south to Atlas Mountains *A.b. koenigi* north-western Morocco.

Feeding: Seeds, shoots, leaves, fruits and insects. Stomach contents of 7 birds revealed seeds and fruits of *Rhus pentaphylla*, *Euphorbia cclytrata*, barley *Hordeum*, leaves and shoots of *Asparagus altisimus*, and *Lycium intricatum*. Chicks observed eating ants.

Breeding: On the ground, usually in shelter of a bush. The shallow scrape is unlined or with a small amount of vegetation. Eggs very pale yellow-buff finely marked red-brown; clutch 6-20, probably laid on consecutive days; incubation period probably 24-25 days as in congeners; capable of flight at 10-12 days, and reach full size at 50-60 days; both parents attend single broods.

Aviculture: Selected Reference CLUTCH 10-14. INCUBATION PERIOD 25 days

Bare-throated Francolin

Francolinus afer 33-38cm

Alternative names: Cape Red-necked Francolin, Red-necked Spurfowl, Red-necked Francolin, Red-throated Francolin, Spur-Fowl.
***F.a.leucoparaeus* Fischer's Red-necked Francolin.**
***F.a. nyanzae* Vermiculated Francolin.**
***F.a. bohmi* Vermiculated Francolin.**
***F.a. humboldtii* Humboldt's Francolin.**

Description: Sexes similar but female unspurred; crown brown; forehead, eye and moustachial stripe white; nape brown mottled black and white, mantle, back and upper tail-coverts brown, feathers edged blackish; tail brown; skin round eye, chin and throat bare, coloured red; underparts creamy white, broadly streaked black; under wingcoverts greyish brown; iris brown; bill, legs and feet red. Juvenile has feathers of underparts edged chestnut; red facial adornment lacking; bill dusky red; legs and feet yellowish orange. Chick has centre of crown and nape brown, edged black, broad dark brown stripe down centre of back vermiculated and edged blackish, flanked by ochre buff; underparts yellowish buff.

Adults *F.a.intercedens* (see Reichenow, 1909, Orn.Monats; p.88 Rukwa).

F.a.castaneiventer differs from *notatus* in having the underparts blackish chestnut.

F.a.loangwae differs from the nominate in having super-cilliary and malar stripe and cheeks and breast to belly black.

F.a.benguellensis differs from *cranchii* in having the feathers of the breast to belly grey.

F.a.punctulatus (see Bowen, Proc.Acad.Nat.Sci.Phila., 82, 1930, p.158).

F.a.humboldtii differs from *swynnertoni* in having less white over the face.

F.a.swynnertoni differs from the nominate in having more white over the face; underparts black; flanks heavily streaked with white.

F.a.lehmanni differs from *castaneiventer* in having broader streaking on the underparts.

F.a.notatus differs from *castaneiventer* in having the underparts blackish, less white streaking.

F.a.bohmi (see Reichenow, 1885, J Orn., p.465 Igonda, Tabora:hybrid, with black striped forms).

F.a.itigi (see Bowen, 1930, Proc.Acad.N.Sci.Phil., p.86 Itigi, Domona:hybrid, with melanogaster).

F.a.harterti differs from *cranchii* but maroon chestnut streaking below.

F.a.cranchii differs from nominate in having forehead black or dark brown; face black mottled whitish.

F.a.leucoparaeus differs from *loangwae* in having face white with little black mottling.

Voice: Described by Chaplin as a hoarse croaking, slowly repeated 'k-rack-k-k, k-rack-k-k'.

Habitat: Evergreen forest and clearings and cultivation.

Distribution: North-western Namibia and western Angola.

F.a.punctulatus central Angola.

F.a.nyanzae Uganda, western Kenya and western Tanzania.

F.a.harterti Rwanda.

F.a.cranchii northern Angola, northern Zambia and western Tanzania.

F.a.leucoparaeus eastern Kenya and northern Tanzania.

F.a.bohmi western Tanzania.

F.a.itigi central Tanzania.

F.a.intercedens south eastern Zaire, southern Tanzania and northern Zambia.

F.a.castaneiventer interior and western KwaZulu-Natal province of South Africa.

F.a. loangwae north-eastern Zambia.

F.a. benguellensis western Angola.

F.a. humboldtii Mozambique (Tete district) to south-western Malawi.

F.a.swynnertoni Mozambique and southern Zimbabwe.

F.a.lehmanni North-West and Northern Province, South Africa and western Swaziland

F.a.notatus southern Cape Province, South Africa.

Feeding: Seeds, roots, bulbs, shoots, fruit, fallen grain, insects and land molluscs. Cultivated crops in the form of beans *Lathyrus* and peas *Pisum*. Livefood such as termites, gleans ticks from grass stalks and also feeds in Rhinocerus and Buffalo dung pats.

Breeding: A scrape in the ground, lined with grass and roots among rank vegetation or beneath a bush. Eggs pinkish buff, yellowish cream or pale brown; clutch 3-9; incubation period 23 days; no information on the role of parental care.

Aviculture: Selected Reference CLUTCH 4-7; INCUBATION PERIOD 22-23 days; first flight after 9 days. Selected Reference WILDFOOD Shoots of young pumpkins, fresh cut Lucerne *Medicago sativa*. Selected Reference ANIMAL FOOD termites, butterfly / moth caterpillars.

Sand Partridge
Ammoperdix heyi nicolli 22-25cm

Description: Male. Forehead, crown, nape and chin pale blue-grey; mantle and back pale cinnamon; wings brown mottled buff; under wing-coverts pale pinkish; breast, belly and flanks sandy buff; throat orange buff; iris hazel, pale brown or red-brown; bill pale orange; legs and feet pale yellow. Female. Paler and more sandy than male and lacks pale patch on ear-coverts. Juvenile similar to adult female, but culmen and tip of bill pale brown.

Male. *A.h.cholmleyi* differs from the nominate race in being darker overall; chin chestnut. Chicks has upperparts sandy buff, mottled on lower back; eyestripe blackish; underparts buffy; iris brown; bill blackish; legs and feet pale buff.

Voice: Described by Hollom *et al*, as variously noted as 'quay', 'teu', 'quake'.

Habitat: Rocky slopes with sparse vegetation.

Distribution: North-eastern Egypt and Lower Nile.

A.h.cholmleyi eastern Egypt and north-eastern Sudan.

Feeding: Seeds, green leaves, corms, bulbs, berries and insects. In Oman 3 stomach contents revealed berries of *Reptonia muscatensis*, *Salvadora persica* and *Lycium shawii*. Also seeds of grasses.

Breeding: Nests on the ground, usually in shelter of rock or bush making a shallow scrape which is not lined. Eggs oval, smooth, glossy, pale sandy buff, grey, tinged pink; clutch 5-7; no information on incubation period or on the role of the sexes in parental care.

Aviculture: No records.

Stone Partridge

Ptilopachus petrosus 27cm

Alternate names: *P.p.florentiae* Kenya Stone Partridge.
P.p.saturatior Dusky Stone Partridge.
P.p.emini Lady Stone Partridge.

Description: Male. Entire head greyish brown, mottled brownish white; nape, mantle and back greyish brown, feathers edged whitish, rump and upper tail-coverts pale greyish brown, heavily vermiculated buffish white; tail dark brown, tinged black; chin and throat greyish brown, mottled brownish white; centre of breast and belly buff; iris brown; naked skin round eye red; bill base red; tip dusky; legs and feet crimson. Female similar to male, but centre of breast and belly creamy white. Juvenile similar to adult female, but having upperparts barred. Chick has forehead and brown blackish chestnut; underparts dark brown, speckled black.

Males *P.p.saturatior* differs from *brehmi* in being darker overall.

P.p.brehmi differs from *florentiae* in being paler overall.

P.p.major differs from nominate in being paler overall; broader chestnut, flanks streaked.

P.p.florentiae differs from the nominate in being more blackish brown.

Voice: Described by Mackworth-Praed & Grant as an unmistakable loud piping cry '*weet-weet-weet-weet*'.

Habitat: Confined to rocky hills and cliffs at 600 - 1500m in East Africa.

Distribution: Gambia to Cameroon.

P.p.saturatior north-central Cameroon.

P.p.brehmi Lake Chad to Sudan.

P.p.major northern Ethiopia.

P.p.florentiae southern Sudan to north-eastern Zaire, Uganda and Kenya.

Feeding: Seeds of grasses, green leaves, buds, fruits and insects.

Breeding: A depression in grass or at the base of a grass tuft, bolder or tree, lined with some grass or leaves. Eggs pale stone or ochre yellow; clutch 4-6; no information

on incubation period or on the role of the sexes in parental care.

Aviculture: No records.

Swainson's Francolin

Francolinus swainsonii 33-38cm

Alternative name: Swainson's Spurfowl

Description: Male. Forehead, crown and nape dark brown; sides of neck dark brown, mottled black and white; ear-coverts greyish brown; mantle, back and upper tail-coverts dark brown, feathers edged buff; tail greyish brown; bare skin, mid-throat and around eye deep pinkish to red; upper breast dark brown streaked black; rest of underparts dark brown, feathers streaked black and buff; under wing-coverts dark brown streaked blackish; iris brown; bill, upper mandible blackish, lower red; legs and feet black. Female similar to male, but upperparts vermiculated dark brown. Juvenile has nape and crown dark brown, feathers tinged greyish or buff; face buffy white with dusky flecking; bill dark, base yellowish; legs and feet yellowish brown. Chick has centre of crown dark brown, flanked by buffy stripes; stripe down centre of back reddish brown, blackish at margins; underparts buffy.

Males *F.s.lundazi* differs from *gilli* in being much darker and greyer overall

F.s.damarensis differs from the nominate race in being paler overall; underparts greyer, less brown.

F.s.gilli differs from *damarensis* in having underparts whitish, less greyish.

Voice: Described by Mackworth-Praed & Grant as a harsh crowing call of '*kwaali*' repeated several times, mainly heard at dawn and in the evening.

Habitat: Rank vegetation bordering vleis, cultivation and woodland.

Distribution: KwaZulu-Natal midlands and western regions, Free State, North-West, Northern Province, Gauteng and Mpumalanga in South Africa to Swaziland, southern Mozambique, Zimbabwe and eastern Botswana.

F.s.lundazi northern Zimbabwe and western Mozambique (Zambezi valley).

F.s.damarensis north-western Namibia.

F.s.gilli northern Namibia, the Caprivi Strip and northern Botswana.

Feeding: Seeds, roots, shoots, bulbs, fallen grain, insects and land molluscs. Green shoots of Kikuyu grass *Pennisetum clandestinum*. Partial to sprouting cereal crops. Fruit of common Taaibos *Rhus pyroides*. Livefood, namely termites and locusthoppers.

Breeding: Nest is a hollow in the ground, lined with grass beneath a shrub or in a rank grass. Two nests recorded in Zimbabwe revealed one near water, the other not, as well as one in a concealed position, the other in a exposed position. Eggs pinkish or buffy cream; clutch 4-8; incubation period 21 days.

Aviculture: Selected Reference CLUTCH 4-8; INCUBATION PERIOD 21 days. Selected Reference WILD-FOOD Seeds of Bulrush millet *Pennisetum americanum*, Monkey bulb *Mariscus capensis*, tubers of Elephant ear *Colocasia antiquorum*, shoots of young pumpkins, leaves of Tree nettle *Urera tenax*, Kikuyu grass *Pennisetum clandestinum*, fresh cut Lucerne *Medicago sativa*.

Selected Reference FRUIT Common taaibos *Rhus pyroides*. ANIMAL FOOD termites, cockroaches, weevils, grasshoppers, crickets, maggots, beetle larvae, including mealworms.

Painted Francolin

Francolinus rufopictus 37cm

Alternative names: Grey-breasted Spurwing, Grey-breasted Francolin.

Description: Sexes similar. Forehead dark brown; crown and nape pale brown; ear-coverts, sides of neck and upper mantle grey, streaked blackish; lower mantle, back, rump and upper tail-coverts chestnut, streaked grey; breast, belly and rest of underparts grey, streaked buffish; iris brown; bare skin round eye and throat orange; legs and feet brownish black. Juvenile similar to adult but upperparts grey. Chick undescribed.

Voice: Described by Urban *et al* as a loud, grating 'ka-waaaak, ka-waaaak, ka-waark' descending towards ends.

Habitat: Thorn bush and dry grassland with thorn trees.

Distribution: North-western Tanzania.

Feeding: Seeds of grasses, weeds and insects, such as termites and grasshoppers. Tubers of sedge *Cyperus* sp.

Breeding: Nest scrape in ground in tall grass, lined with dry grass and feathers. Eggs buff or pale brown; clutch 4-5; incubaion period unrecorded.

Aviculture: No records.

Yellow-necked Francolin

Francolinus leucoscepus 38cm

Alternative names: Yellow-headed Spurwing *F.i.infuscatus* Kenya Yellow-throated Francolin, Yellow-necked Spurwing

Description: Sexes similar, but female not spurred. Forehead and crown olive-brown, streaked cream; nape, mantle and back dark brown, feathers streaked buff; sides of neck blackish brown, feathers edged white; tail brown, vermiculated buff; wings with primaries and secondaries dark brown, broadly edged buff; breast, belly and under tail-coverts pale buff, streaked brown; iris brown; bill black, base reddish; legs and feet blackish brown. Juvenile similar to adult, but upperparts grey buffy; throat and bare facial skin paler yellow. Chick has forehead dark brown; crown pale brown; underparts buffy.

Adults *F.I.infuscatus* differs from the nominate race in being darker overall.

F.I.muhamed-ben-abdullah differs from the nominate in having edges of breast and belly greyish.

Voice: Described by Mackworth-Praed & Grant as having a loud grating cry usually heard in the mornings or evenings.

Habitat: Grasslands, semi-arid bushveld and cultivation.

Distribution: Eastern Ethiopia and northern Somalia.

F.I.infuscatus north-eastern Uganda, southern Ethiopia to northern Tanzania.

F.I.muhamed-ben-abdullah southern Somalia and northern Kenya.

Feeding: Seeds, grain, roots and insects. Tubers of sedges, especially *Cyperus rotundus*. Seeds of herbs and grasses, notably *Commelina*, *Urochloa*, *Oxygonum* and also termites.

Breeding: Simple scrape in ground, unlined or with a few grass stems and feathers. Eggs oval, cream or pale pinkish buff, speckled darker with white; clutch normally 3-8, usually 5; incubation period 18-20 days; young leaves nest 24 hours after hatching.

Aviculture: No records.

Erckel's Francolin

Francolinus erckelii 42cm

Alternative name: Erckel's Spurwing.

Description: Sexes similar, but female unspurred. Forehead black; crown and nape chestnut; mantle and back chestnut, streaked white; rump and upper tail-coverts greyish olive-brown, feathers with chestnut margins; tail brown, barred chestnut; throat white; eye-stripe black; breast grey; belly and flanks creamy white; iris dark brown; bill black; legs and feet olive-yellow. Juvenile upperparts paler grey; heavily streaked and barred. Chick has sides of head buff with black moustachial stripe; underparts plain brownish white.

Adult *P.e.pentoni* differs from the nominate race, being greyer overall.

Voice: Described by Blandford as '*kri-kri-kri-kri-wa-wa-wa-wa*', harsh and creaking at first.

Habitat: Montane bush between 2000-3500m.

Distribution: Ethiopia.

P.e.pentoni north-eastern Sudan.

Feeding: Fallen grain, shoots, berries, seeds of grasses, shrubs and herbs, notably *Rumex* spp., some insects also.

Breeding: A scrape on the ground lined with grass and similar materials. Eggs dirty white to pale brown; clutch 4-10; incubation period is unreported; both parents accompany the brood for some time.

Aviculture: Selected Reference CLUTCH 1-10. Selected Reference FRUIT mulberry *Morus* sp., fig *Ficus* sp., cotoneaster *Contoneaster* sp., pyracantha *Pyracantha* sp., blackberry *Rubus* sp., Rasberry *R.idaeus*. Selected Reference ANIMAL FOOD mealworms, crickets, grasshoppers, cornworms.

Pale-bellied Francolin

Francolinus ochropectus 30cm

Alternative names: Djibouti Francolin, Dadjoura Francolin.

Description: Male. Forehead blackish, streaked white; crown rufous chestnut; nape greyish; eye-stripe white; ear-coverts grey, spotted blackish; mantle, back, rump and upper tail-coverts grey, streaked rufous buff; flight feathers greyish brown; tail rufous; breast, belly and under tail-coverts white, streaked buff; iris brown; bill black, tinged yellow; legs and feet yellow. Female similar to male, but upperparts somewhat vermiculated; more rufous in tail. Juvenile similar to female, but less streaking, more barring with grey and buff. Chick undescribed.

Voice: Described by Welch & Welch as *erk-ka,ka,ka,k k k kkk*, with the *erk* being the dominant sound, and the

ka,ka,ka,' etc., getting faster and quieter as it progressed ending in what can best be described as a chuckle.

Habitat: Primary and secondary forest, with such species as *Juniperus procera*, *Buxus hildebrandti*, *Clutia abyssinica* and *Acacia etbaica*.

Distribution: Somalia.

Feeding: Seeds of grasses, weeds, figs, berries and termites.

Breeding: The nest is a simple scrape hidden in dense herbage such as ferns and around palm fringed wadis. The incubation is probably by the female alone, but unknown length as well as the development of the young.

Aviculture: No records.

Chestnut-naped Francolin

Francolinus castaneicollis 36-38cm

Description: Sexes similar. Forehead black; crown and nape chestnut, spotted blackish; mantle and back chestnut; wings brownish grey; rump and tail grey; under wing-coverts dark brown; throat white; neck tawny; breast chestnut, streaked black and white; under-tail coverts grey, barred black; iris dark brown; bill red; legs and feet coral red. Juvenile similar to adult, but paler rump and tail barred black and buff. Chick undescribed.

Adults *F.c.ogoensis* differs from the nominate race in having wing-coverts, mantle and back greyer.

F.c.bottegi (see id, 1898, ib 38, p.652 Burgil).

F.c.kaffanus differs from the nominate in being paler overall.

F.c.gofanus differs from nominate in having head and neck brighter.

F.c.atrijrons differs from nominate in having belly buffy, lacking strongly marked chestnut and black.

Voice: Described by Mackworth-Praed & Grant as a loud and strident '*kawar-kawar*'.

Habitat: Dense tangled undergrowth.

Distribution: Eastern Ethiopia.

F.s.ogoensis Somalia.

F.c.bottegi southern Ethiopia.

F.c.kaffanus western Ethiopia.

F.c.gofanus south-western Ethiopia.

F.s.atrifrons southern Ethiopia.

Feeding: Seeds and some insects including termites.

Breeding: Nest a scrape in the ground, lined with dead leaves. Eggs cream, smooth and roundish; clutch 5-7 or more; incubation period unrecorded; parents remain with young until fully grown.

Aviculture: No records.

Jackson's Francolin

Francolinus jacksoni 33-38cm

Description: Sexes similar. Forehead, crown and nape greyish brown, feathers tinged rufous, edged buff; ear-coverts light grey; sides of neck white, feathers tinged chestnut; mantle chestnut, feathers edged white; back, rump, upper tail-coverts and tail rufous brown; wings grey-brown; chin and throat white; breast and belly chestnut, feathers edged white; flanks and tail-coverts chestnut, feathers edged black and grey; iris brown; bill coral-red; legs and feet reddish. Juvenile paler overall. Chick undescribed.

Adults *F.j.pollenorum* differs from the nominate race in having margins of breast feathers narrower.

F.j.gurae differs from the nominate in having feathers of underparts edged white.

Voice: Described by Williams & Arlott as having a harsh '*grrr,grrr,grrr*'.

Habitat: Forests of *Podocarpus* and *Juniperus*, including bamboo, *Arundinaria alpina*, *Hagenia*, *Hypericum*, *Erica* and *Stoebe* thickets at 2300-3000m in East Africa.

Distribution: Upper Aberdare Mountains.

F.j.pollenorum Mount Kenya.

F.j.gurae Lower Aberdare Mountains.

Feeding: Seeds of grass, shoots, bulbous roots, berries, insects and snails. Also fallen seed of drying bamboo and *achenes* and some *compositae*.

Breeding: One record at edge of a clump of bamboos. Eggs glossy, pale brown; clutch 3; incubation period is unknown as is the development of the young.

Aviculture: No records.

Handsome Francolin

Francolinus nobilis 33-36cm

Alternative name: *F.n.chapini* Ruwenzori Handsome Francolin.

Description: Male. Forehead, crown and nape dark grey; ear-coverts pale grey; mantle rufous; feathers edged grey; back and wings deep rufous, edged blackish; rump, upper tail-coverts and tail dark brownish grey; throat greyish brown; breast, belly and flanks rufous, feathers edged grey, under tail-coverts blackish brown, edged light brown; iris brown; bare skin round eye, legs and feet bright red. Female similar to male, but paler overall. Juvenile similar to adult female, but upperparts dark grey, barred rufous buff; underparts paler. Chick undescribed.

Male *F.n.chapini* differs from the nominate race in having belly narrowly edged grey.

Voice: Described by Guggisberg as '*cock rick*'.

Habitat: Bamboo and mountain forests, usually near water.

Distribution: Eastern Zaire to south western Uganda.

F.n.chapini Ruwenzori Mountains (eastern Zaire).

Feeding: Seeds.

Breeding: The nest and eggs are still undescribed.

Aviculture: No records.

Cameroon Mountain Francolin

Francolinus camerunensis 32cm

Alternative name: Cameroon Francolin.

Description: Male. Forehead, crown, nape and sides of head dark brown; mantle, back, wings, rump, upper tail-coverts and tail dark greyish brown; chin and throat dark brownish grey, feathers edged buffy grey; breast, belly and rest of underparts greyish, feathers edged whitish; iris brown; bill and patch round eye red; legs and feet dusky red. Female has upperparts mottled and barred black, buff and whitish; underparts black, streaked whitish. Juvenile similar to female, but breast to belly barred whitish and black; bill, legs and feet dusky red. Chick undescribed.

Voice: Described by Urban *et al* as a high pitched musical, triple whistle.

Habitat: Mountain forests between 850-2100m.

Distribution: Cameroon.

Feeding: Grass, grass seeds, berries and insects.

Breeding: The nest and eggs are still undescribed.

Aviculture: No records.

Swierstra's Francolin

Francolinus swierstrai 33cm

Description: Male. Forehead, crown and nape blackish brown; stripe brown; stripe over eye to down side of head and sides of neck white; mantle, back and wing-coverts grey-brown, feathers edged rusty brown; rump and tail dark greyish brown; chin and throat white; breast band and flanks black, the latter with whitish centres; belly and rest of underparts streaked black and white; iris brown; bill, legs and feet red. Female has back reddish brown, blotched pale brown; rump pale brown, vermiculated dusky. Juvenile similar to female, but throat pale buff; upperparts streaked and barred rufous buff. Chick undescribed.

Voice: Described by Mackworth-Praed & Grant as a sort of scythe-sharpening noise.

Habitat: Montane evergreen forest and forest edges.

Distribution: Southern Angola.

Feeding: Seeds of grasses and *Leguminosae* spp, including insects.

Breeding: The nest and eggs are still undescribed.

Aviculture: No records.

Ahanta Francolin

Francolinus ahantensis 35cm

Alternative name: *F.a.hopkinsoni* Gambian Ahanta Francolin

Description: Male. Forehead, crown and nape brown; indistinct black stripe over to behind eye; ear coverts brown; sides of neck brown, streaked white; mantle and back mixed brown, blackish and buff; rump and tail brown, streaked buff; chin and throat white; breast, belly and rest of underparts grey-brown, streaked white; iris brown; bill orange-red; legs and feet orange. Female similar to male, but buff spots on wing-coverts. Juvenile similar to adult female, but underparts ashy, streaked white. Chick has crown, nape and back dark rufous brown; sides of head buffy rufous; underparts buffy, tinged rufous; iris brown; bill brownish horn; legs and feet pinkish.

Male *F.a.hopkinsoni* differs from the nominate race in having underparts paler greyish brown, streaked with black and white.

Voice: Described by Mackworth-Praed & Grant as a raucous 'ka-ka-karar' repeated and occasionally with and added syllable.

Habitat: Forest edges and old plantations.

Distribution: Guinea to Nigeria.

Feeding: Seeds, small beans, cassava, large fruits and insects which includes termites.

Breeding: Nest a depression in the ground, scantly lined with leaves in thick cover. Eggs cream to pinkish buff; clutch 4-6 up to 12; incubation period is unknown as is the development of the young.

Aviculture: No records.

Scaly Francolin

Francolinus squamatus 25-31cm

Alternative names: *F.s.maranensis* Mount Kenya Scaly Francolin, *F.s.zappeyi* Lady Victoria Scaly Francolin

Description: Sexes similar. Forehead and crown grey-brown; supercillium pale grey; sides of head pale grey-brown; mantle and back dark brownish grey, feathers margined with buff; rest of upperparts greyish brown, irregularly barred buff; chin and throat buff; breast grey-brown; rest of underparts greyish buff, vermiculated darker; under tail-coverts dark grey, vermiculated with black, edged buff; iris grey-brown; bill, legs and feet red. Juvenile similar to adult female, but more rufous overall; underparts barred black and white. Chick upperparts dark brown, washed with rufous and mottled with buff; two buff parallel stripes and rufous brown stripe on mid-back; underparts buff.

Adults *F.s.schuetti* differs from the nominate race in having underparts darker and more distinctly marked.

F.s.zappeyi (see *Mearns, 1911, Smiths Misc. Coll. 56, No 20, p.4 East of Lake Victoria*).

F.s.tetraoninus (see *Blundell & Lovat, 1899, Bull B.O.C. 10, p.22 Mendie, Ethiopia*).

F.s.maranensis differs from *schuetti* in having underparts generally much darker.

F.s.usambarae differs from *maranensis* in having ear-coverts and sides of neck mottled black and white.

F.s.uzungwensis differs from *usumbarae* in being paler overall.

F.s.doni differs from *schuetti* in having lower neck to flanks chocolate-brown.

Voice: Described by Guggisberg as a guttural 'kew-koo-kwah, kew-koo-kwah'.

Habitat: Forest and thick bush.

Distribution: Southern Nigeria to northern Zaire.

F.s.schuetti north-eastern Angola to Ethiopia and western Kenya.

F.s.zappeyi Uganda and western Kenya.

F.s.tetraoninus western Ethiopia.

F.s.maranensis southern Kenya.

F.s.usambarae Usambara Mountains, Tanzania.

F.s.uzungwensis Uzungwe Mountains, Tanzania.

F.s.doni Vipya plateau, western Malawi.

Feeding: Seeds, cultivated plants such as cassava, sweets potato, groundnuts, maize, rice, fruit and berries, termites, ants, millipedes and snails.

Breeding: Nest a scrape in the ground, well hidden beneath a low bush and lined with dry grass, leaves and a few feathers. Eggs, oval, pale cream of buff; clutch 3-8 usually 6. In Cameroon one record on top of termite mound; incubation period is unknown as is the development of the young.

Aviculture: No records.

Grey-striped Francolin

Francolinus griseostriatus 32cm

Description: Sexes similar. Forehead buff; crown and nape grey-brown; ear-coverts pale greyish brown; sides of neck, hindneck, mantle and back chestnut, streaked dark brown; rump and upper tail-coverts greyish brown, barred buff; tail rufous brown with indistinct black bars; chin and upper throat whitish; lower throat and breast chestnut, streaked greyish buff; rest of underparts buffy, streaked rufous brown; iris brown; bill, upper mandible black, lower orange-red; legs and feet reddish orange. Juvenile has upperparts chestnut, streaked blackish. Chick undescribed.

Voice: Described by Chapin (in Urban *et al*) as a high pitched, rasping '*kerak*'.

Habitat: Dense undergrowth of gallery forests or dense thickets.

Distribution: North-western Angola.

Feeding: Insects, green shoots and seeds.

Breeding: The nest and eggs are still undescribed.

Aviculture: No records.

Double-spurred Francolin

Francolinus bicalcaratus 30-33cm

Alternative names: Double-spurred Bushfowl
F.b.adamauae **Adamauae Double-spurred Francolin.**
F.b.ogilvie-granti **Olgilvie-Grant's Double-spurred Francolin.**
F.b.thornei **Sierra Leone Double-spurred Francolin.**

Description: Sexes similar. Forehead and ear-coverts black; crown and nape rufous cinnamon; ear-coverts cinnamon; mantle and back dark greyish brown; heavily streaked with buff and white, upper tail-coverts pale grey; tail grey, mottled brown; flight feathers marbled and barred sepia and cinnamon-pink; chin whitish; throat, breast, belly and rest of underparts rufous heavily streaked with white; under-tail coverts grey, feathers broadly edged buff; iris dark brown; bill lemon-horn or yellowish green; legs and feet olive-green. Juvenile similar to adult, but paler, especially upperparts indistinctly barred and streaked buff; flanks barred black. Chick has crown rufous brown; sides of head buff; underparts creamy buff.

Adults *F.b.ayesha* differs from the nominate race in having upperparts and underparts paler.

F.b.thornei, adamauae, ogilvie-granti differ from the nominate in all having upperparts darker brown or more heavily marked with black; underparts variably deeper buff.

Voice: Described by Serle *et al* as a harsh grating '*krrrrak...*', repeated in 2 second intervals.

Habitat: Wadis, cultivation and palm groves.

Distribution: Senegal to Niger and northern Nigeria.

F.b.ayesha western Morocco.

F.b.thornei Sierra Leone to Benin.

F.b.adamauae northern Nigeria, Cameroon.

F.b.ogilvie-granti Cameroon.

Feeding: Seeds, cultivated crops, namely rice, maize, millet, groundnuts and small fruits and berries, roots, green leaves and livefood in the form of caterpillars, ants, beetles, termites and also small frogs. In Senegal favours the grass seeds of *Panicum*, *Echinochloa* and *Dactyloctenium*.

Breeding: On the ground in thick vegetation which consists of only a slight scrape, lined with available materials and a few feathers. Eggs oval, smooth and glossy buff; clutch 5-7; incubation period unrecorded.

Aviculture: No records.

Yellow-billed Francolin

Francolinus icterorhynchus 28-33cm

Alternative name: Heuglin's Francolin.

Description: Sexes similar. Forehead and crown dark rufous brown; ear-coverts chocolate brown; eye and moustachial stripes blackish brown; sides of neck white, feathers edged buff; mantle brownish black, feathers edged buff; back, rump and upper tail-coverts and tail greyish brown, vermiculated buff; chin and throat white; breast and belly buff, feathers streaked dark brown; under tail-coverts irregularly barred brown and whitish; iris dark brown; bill, upper mandle dusky yellow, lower orange yellow; legs and feet orange yellow. Chick has crown rufous-brown; sides of head buffy; underparts buffy with faint rufous wash. Juvenile similar to female, but upperparts has barring more apparent.

Adults *F.i.dybowskii* differs from the nominate race in being darker overall.

F.i.ugandensis differs from the nominate in being somewhat larger.

Voice: Described by Williams & Arlott as having a shrill three note call, uttered usually at dusk.

Habitat: Grassland, bushed cultivation at 500-1400m.

Distribution: Central African Republic to south-western Sudan.

F.i.dybowskii north-eastern Zaire and western Uganda.

F.i.ugandensis central Uganda.

Feeding: Seeds, millet berries, beetles, millipedes, termites and ants.

Breeding: Nest in a scrape beneath a small bush. Eggs pale greyish buff; clutch 6-8; incubation period unrecorded.

Aviculture: No records.

Clapperton's Francolin

Francolinus clappertoni 30-33cm

Alternative name: *F.c.gedgii* Gedge's Francolin

Description: Sexes similar. Forehead, crown, nape and ear-coverts rufous brown; eye stripe and sides of head white; moustachial stripe dark brown; mantle, back and rump pale greyish brown, feathers edged buff; upper tail-coverts and tail grey, barred buff; wing with primaries greyish brown, broadly edged buff, secondaries brownish grey, barred buff; chin and throat white; rest of underparts creamy white, feathers with buff shaft streaks; iris brown; naked skin around eye, legs and feet red; bill black. Juvenile similar to adult, but paler overall. Chick undescribed.

Adults *F.c.heuglini* differs from *gedgii* in having upperparts greyer, and rather darker overall.

F.c.cavei differs from *gedgii* in having upperparts darker.

F.c.gedgii differs form the nominate race in having moustachial stripe black.

F.c.testis differs from *sharpii* in being paler overall.

F.c.nigrosquamatus differs from *sharpii* in being much darker overall.

Voice: Described by Serle *et al* as a blend of a whistle and grating call, after-carrying 'hu-hu-hu-hurror'.

Habitat: Semi-arid savannas and grasslands e.g. *Hyparrhenia* spp. with bushes and trees e.g. *Acacia*, *Terminalia* and *Combretum*.

Distribution: Mali to western Sudan.

F.c.heuglini south-western Sudan.

F.c.cavei south-eastern Sudan.

F.c.gedgii Mount Elgon.

F.c.sharpii eastern Ethiopia.

F.c.testis Ethiopia.

F.c.nigrosquamatus Ethiopia.

Feeding: Seeds, berries, insects and small molluscs.

Breeding: Nest a scrape on the ground, well hidden beneath a small bush. Eggs dusky white or yellowish brown; clutch and incubation period unrecorded.

Aviculture: Selected Reference FRUIT fig *Ficus* sp., mulberry *Morus* sp., cotoneaster *Cotoneaster* sp., pyracantha *Pyracantha* sp., blackberry *Rubus* sp., Raspberry *R.idaeus*. Selected Reference ANIMAL FOOD, mealworms, crickets, grasshoppers, cornworms.

Hilderbrandt's Francolin

Francolinus hilderbrandti 30-32cm

Alternative names: *F.h.altumi* Naivasha Hilderbrandt Francolin.
F.h.helleri Heller's Hilderbrandt Francolin.
F.h.fischeri Fischer's Francolin.
F.h.johnstoni Johnston's Francolin.

Description: Male. Forehead and crown greyish brown; ear-coverts rufous; sides of head white feathers streaked dark greyish brown; mantle black, feathers edged creamy; back, rump, upper tail-coverts and tail dark greyish brown, vermiculated buff, mottled rufous; chin and throat white, mottled black; breast, belly and rest of underparts heavily blotched black; iris brown; bill, upper mandible black, lower red; legs and feet red. Female upperparts paler; underparts rufous buff, feathers edged paler. Juvenile similar to adult female, but upperparts having central dark spotting and shaft stripes. Chick has crown rufous brown; sides of head buffy; underparts rufous buff.

Males *F.h.helleri* (see Mearns, 1915, Proc. US Nat. Mus. 48, p.381. Mt Lolokui).

F.h.fischeri (see Reichenow, 1887, J. Orn, p.51 Wembere Steppes).

Females *F.h.altumi* differs from the nominate race in having breast and neck mottled and spotted blackish.

F.h.grotei similar to nominate, but lacks black mottled on hindneck and breast.

F.h.johnstoni differs from the nominate in having the nape and breast uniform with the rest of the plumage.

Voice: Described by Urban *et al* as a high-pitched crackle 'kek-kekek-kek-kerek'.

Habitat: Bush-covered hillsides, bushed grasslands, bracken-briar and thickets.

Distribution: Eastern Kenya to north-eastern Zambia and western Malawi.

F.h.helleri northern Kenya.

F.h.altumi western Kenya.

F.h.fischeri central Tanzania.

F.h.grotei south-eastern Tanzania.

F.h.johnstoni southern Tanzania, eastern Zambia, southern Malawi and Mozambique.

Feeding: Seeds, bulbs, tubers, insects and their larvae.

Breeding: Nest a well hidden small scrape lined with dry grass, leaves and some feathers. Eggs creamy white to pale brown; clutch 4-8; incubation period unrecorded.

Aviculture: No records.

Natal Francolin
Francolinus natalensis 30-38cm

Description: Sexes similar, but female is unspurred. Forehead and sides of crown blackish brown; centre of brown and nape brown, with dark centres to feathers; mantle, back, rump and upper tail-coverts greyish brown; tail light brown, feathers vermiculated; sides of face, chin and throat spotted with black; breast, belly and flanks white, heavily spotted with black; rest of underparts and under tail-coverts buff, barred with brown; wings with coverts greyish brown; under wing-coverts reddish; iris brown; bill orange, cere greenish; legs and feet orange to reddish. Juvenile similar to adult but paler overall. Chick has forehead and crown rufous brown, tinged with black; down centre of back rufous brown, flanked dark brown; underparts creamy buff.

Males *F.n.thamnobium* differs from the nominate race in having finer streaking on underparts.

F.n.neavei differs from the nominate in being paler on the upperparts.

Voice: Described by Prozesky as a harsh 'kwaali-kwaali-kwaali'; several birds may often be called together.

Habitat: Acacia scrub, rocky terrain, coastal dune forest and to a lesser extent, in sugar cane.

Distribution: Eastern Cape, KwaZulu-Natal, North-West and Northern Province, South Africa, Swaziland, Mozambique (Maputo district).

F.n.thamnobium the provinces of Northern Cape, western Free State, North-West, Northern Province, Gauteng and Mpumalanga regions of South Africa.

F.s.neavei Mozambique (Tete district), north-western Zimbabwe, western Mozambique and north-eastern Zambia.

Feeding: Seeds, roots, bulbs, fruits, fallen grain, insects and molluscs. Seeds of Red Devil *Amaranthus thunbergii*, dry elm eaten on the ground, spilled grain in the form of maize *Zea* and sorghum *Sorghum*. Pinioned birds have been observed feeding on the seeds of Babala *Pennisetum americanum* and sunflower *Helianthus*. Livefood in the form of beetles, assassin bugs, grasshoppers, caterpillars and termites. Recorded also pecking inside a flattened mound of Elephant droppings for insects.

Breeding: Presumably monogamous since usually observed in pairs during breeding. Digs a slight hollow in the ground under cover of thorny tangles or other rank vegetation. Lining consists of grass, stalks and rootlets. Eggs oval, pale, creamy white or yellowish white; clutch 5-8 up to 10, probably laid by two females; incubation period.

Aviculture: Selected Reference CLUTCH 5-8, up to 10; INCUBATION PERIOD 20 days. Selected Reference WILDFOOD. Leaves of dock *Rumex* spp., Red pigwood *Amaranthus thunbergii*, Gladiolus *Gladiolus alatus*, corms of Watonia *Watonia angusta*, young pumpkin shoots, seeds of Babala *Pennisetum americanum*. Selected Reference FRUIT African mulberry *Morus mesozygia*. Selected Reference ANIMAL FOOD termites, grasshoppers, crickets, hairless caterpillars, bugs.

Hartlaub's Francolin
Francolinus hartlaubi 27-28cm

Description: Male. Forehead and crown blackish brown; eye stripe white, offset by black line below it; ear-coverts orange-brown; rest of face white, heavily streaked with black; mantle and back dark brown or blackish brown with dark tawny shaft stripes; rump and upper tail-coverts dark greyish brown; under wing-coverts greyish; tail grey, barred black and white; under tail-coverts tawny, the feathers streaked black and tipped white; chin and throat white, streaked black; breast and flanks pale tawny, streaked black; iris hazel; bill yellowish brown; legs and feet pale yellow to yellow-ochre. Female has face grey-brown; eye stripe orange-brown; chin, throat, breast and rest of underparts tawny, feathers fringed white. Juvenile males paler than adult on upperparts, more narrowly streaked; female similar to adult female. Chick undescribed.

Males *F.h.bradfieldi* differs from the nominate race in being darker; black stripes below broader.

F.s.crypticus differs from the nominate in being more brightly coloured overall.

Voice: Described by Komen as uttering a quiet 'kechar-kechar-kechar' during solicitation of a male when approaching a female.

Habitat: Rocky koppies, mountain and escarpments with mixed grass shrub and sandy soil.

Distribution: Angola.

F.h.bradfieldi central and northern Namibia (intergrades with *crypticus* in the Erongo Mountains).

F.h.crypticus north-western Namibia.

Feeding: Seed, bulbs such as shoots, berries, insects including beetles and land molluscs. Bulbs of *Cyperus edulis*.

Breeding: Monogamous and territorial, 1 pair per koppie. One record of a scrape on ledge of precipice. Eggs cream; clutch 3; incubation period unrecorded; young remain with parents in a family group for some period after the breeding season.

Aviculture: Reference WILDFOOD Seeds of Babala *Pennisetum americanum*.

Harwood's Francolin

Francolinus harwoodi 35cm

Description: Male. Forehead black; crown dark brown; ear-coverts grey; sides of head white, streaked brown; nape and mantle pale greyish brown, barred buff; back, rump and upper tail-coverts brownish grey; chin and throat white, streaked brown; breast pale greyish brown, densely vermiculated buff; belly buff, streaked blackish; iris brown, bare skin around eye, legs and feet red. Female similar to male, but underparts paler and browner. Juvenile similar to female but less distinctly barred. Chick undescribed.

Voice: Described by Urban *et al* as a rasping 'koree', somewhat like that of *clappertoni*.

Habitat: Dense *Typha* beds and also open *Combretum/Terminalia* woodland and cultivation.

Distribution: Central and southern Ethiopia.

Feeding: Tubers *Dioscorea* sp., grass and other seeds including *Echinochloa* spp., berries *Commelinaceae* sp., and *Amaranthus* spp., also sorghum and termites.

Breeding: The nest eggs are still undescribed.

Aviculture: No records.

Red-billed Francolin

Francolinus adspersus 36-38cm

Alternative name: Close-barred Francolin.

Description: Sexes similar, but female is unspurred. Forehead, crown, lower mantle, back, rump and tail dark brown; sides if neck and upper mantle finely barred with blackish brown and white; chin, throat, breast and flanks greyish white; wing feathers dark brown; iris brown; bare skin around eye yellow; bill red or orange; legs and feet orange-red. Juvenile is brighter and browner than adult; yellow eye patch absent; iris greyish brown; legs and feet yellowish brown. Chick has crown rufous brown; sides of head buffy; underparts pale yellowish buff; iris brown; bill brown; legs and feet pale yellow.

Adults *F.s.kalahari* differs from the nominate race in having upperparts grey; bill smaller.

Voice: Described by Maclean as 'chak, chak, chak, CHAK, kachakitty-chak, kachikitty-chak , then stopping abruptly.

Distribution: North-West and northern Cape Province, South Africa to Botswana, north-western Zimbabwe, north-western and northern Namibia and southern Angola.

F.a.kalahari north-eastern Namibia, the Caprivi Strip and north-western Botswana.

Feeding: Seeds, bulbs, shoots, leaves, berries and insects namely, beetles, termites, grasshoppers, bugs and land molluscs. Fruit of Volstruisdubbeltjie *Tribulus terrestris*. In Zambia red arils of Large false mophane *Guibourtia coleosperma*.

Breeding: The nest is usually a scrape in the sand among rank vegetation, under a bush, lined with grass and leaves. Eggs oval, yellowish white or cream-buff; clutch 6-10; incubation period 22 days.

Aviculture: Selected Reference CLUTCH 6-10 INCUBATION PERIOD 22 days. Selected Reference WILDFOOD leaves of Black-jack *Bidens pilosa*, roots of Sweet root commiphora *Commiphora neglecta*, young pumpkin shoots, fresh cut Lucerne *Medicago sativa*. Selected Reference ANIMAL FOOD termites, cockroaches.

Cape Francolin

Francolinus capensis 40-42cm

Alternative name: Cape Pheasant.

Description: Sexes similar. Forehead, crown and nape blackish brown, feathers with greyish fringes; mantle, back, rump and upper tail-coverts blackish brown, feathers with buff fringes; tail dark brown; sides of face dark brown, feathers edged white; chin and throat white; neck to breast brownish black, feathers edged whitish; under wing-coverts slate grey, vermiculated whitish; iris reddish brown; bill dark horn, base orange; legs and feet yellow or orange. Juvenile upperparts browner, the vermiculations more buffy, less whitish. Chick undescribed.

Voice: Described by Urban *et al.* as loud crowing 'kak-keek, kak-keet, kak, keeeeek'.

Habitat: Riverine bush and coastal enviroments. Also recorded taking refuge on rocks beside the sea.

Distribution: Western and south-western Cape Province, South Africa.

Feeding: Seeds, leaves, bulbs, corms, shoots, fallen grain and fruit, usually apple and pears, insects and molluscs. Seeds of Rooi-krans *Acacia cyclops*.

Breeding: Presumably monogamous since usually in pairs during breeding season. Nest, a scrape in the ground among plants, rank grass or rushes. The lining consists of grass, plant stalks and rootlets. One record of a nest lying beside a sandhill close to the sea and screened by a clump of rushes with dry grass as a lining. Eggs pinkish buff, sometimes with a few white spots; clutch 6-8, up to 14, probably laid by two females; incubation period unrecorded.

Aviculture: Selected Reference CLUTCH 6-8 up to 14. Selected Reference WILDFOOD Tubers of Elephant ear *Colocasia antiquorum*, leaves of Tree Nettle *Urera tenex*, fresh cut Lucerne *Medicago sativa*.

Crested Francolin

Francolinus sephaena 30-36cm

Alternative names: Bush Partridge, Crested Partridge.
F.s.rovuma **Kirk's Francolin, Rovuma Crested Francolin.**
F.s.grantii **Colonel Grant's Crested Francolin, Grants Francolin.**

Description: Male. Forehead, crown and nape greyish brown, dark centres to feathers; mantle and back chestnut brown with white shaft stripes; rump and upper tail-coverts olive-grey; tail reddish brown; stripe over eye, lores, chin and upper throat white; lower stripe over eye black; cheeks and side of neck white, freckles with reddish brown; lower throat and upper breast buff; lower breast buff heavily streaked with reddish brown, rest of underparts plain olive-brown; iris brown; bill black; legs and feet pinkish or purplish red. Female differs from male in having the mantle and wing-coverts barred dark brown. Juvenile similar to adult female, but paler; hindneck and mantle more russet; eye stripe buff. Chick has forehead and face creamy white.

Males *F.s.somaliensis* similar to *grantii*, but flanks streaked chocolate.

F.s.grantii differs from the nominate in not having stripes on underparts chocolate-brown, but with more or less distinct cream stripes on the flanks and underparts.

F.s.zuluensis differs from the nominate race in being darker overall.

F.s.zambesiae differs from zuluensis in being paler on underparts.

F.s.thompsoni differs from the nominate in being paler on underparts.

F.s.rovuma differs from the nominate in having the underparts streaked with brown.

Distribution: North-West Province, South Africa to Mozambique (lowlands), Zimbabwe and south-eastern Botswana.

F.s.zuluensis KwaZulu-Natal, South Africa to Swaziland and southern Mozambique.

F.s.zambesiae north-western and north-eastern Zimbabwe, western Mozambique (Tete district), southern Zambia (Kafue River), south, central and western Malawi.

F.s.thompsoni northern Nambia, the Caprivi Strip, northern Botswana and north-western Zimbabwe.

F.s.somaliensis Somalia.

F.s.grantii Ethiopia to central Tanzania.

F.s.rovuma Mozambique (north of Save River), southern Malawi, eastern Zaire to Somalia.

Feeding: Bulbs, seeds, berries, fallen grain, insects including termites and molluscs. Also recorded feeding on gum exuding from the trunk of *Acacia* sp.

Breeding: Nest a shallow depression in sand amongst rank grass or under a thicket, scantily lined with grass or rootlets. Egg white, cream or pinkish buff; clutch 4-9; incubation period about 19 days.

Aviculture: Selected Reference: CLUTCH 4-12; INCUBATION PERIOD 22-23 days; FLEDGING PERIOD 28-30 days; first flight after 14 days. Nest Record Cards CLUTCH 7,9 (ANRC); INCUBATION PERIOD 19, 22 days (ANRC); FLEDGING PERIOD 28,30 days (ANRC). Selected Reference WILDFOOD seeds of Babala *Pennisetum americanum*, leaves of Red pigweed *Amaranthus thunbergii*. Diet Record Cards shoots of young pumpkins, roots of Sweet-root commiphora *Commiphora neglecta* (ADRC). Selected Reference ANIMAL FOOD termites, grasshoppers, crickets, maggots.

Red-necked Francolin
Francolinus streptophorus 32cm

Description: Male. Forehead and crown greyish brown; supercillium white, extending backwards to nape, sides of neck and ear-coverts chestnut; upper mantle barred black and white; lower mantle, back and tail greyish brown; wings uniform brownish grey; chin and throat white; breast barred black and white; belly and rest of underparts rufous buff; iris brown; bill black, legs and feet pale yellow. Female similar to male but upperparts barred pale brown. Juvenile undescribed. Chick has crown brown, stripe back; sides of face buff; underparts yellow-buff.

Voice: Described by William & Arlott as a very loud, far-carrying '*tee-dee-jee*' uttered over and over again.

Habitat: Semi-desert bush and coastal thickets.

Distribution: Cameroon, western Kenya and north-western Tanzania.

Feeding: Seeds and insects.

Breeding: Scrape, under bush or close to a large stone with little or no lining. Eggs greyish buff; clutch 4-5; incubation period unrecorded.

Aviculture: Selected Reference WILDFOOD fresh cut Lucerne *Medicago sativa*. Selected Reference FRUIT Bird's brandy *Lantana rugosa*, African mulberry *Morus mesozygia*. Selected Reference ANIMAL FOOD termites, crickets, weevils.

Montane Francolin
Francolinus psilolaemus 38-40cm

Alternative name: Harris's Francolin, Montane Red-winged Francolin, Moorland Francolin.

Description: Sexes similar. Forehead, crown and nape dark brown, feathers edged rufous buff; ear-coverts brown, mottled brown and black; eye and moustachial stripes black, streaked rufous buff; sides of neck buffy, streaked brown, mantle, back and rump blackish brown, tinged rufous; upper tail-coverts with broad cream shaft streaks; tail dark brown, barred rufous buff; chin and throat buff, streaked brown; upper breast rufous, spotted brownish black; lower breast, belly and flanks buff, barred black; iris brown; bill blackish brown; legs and feet pale yellow. Juvenile undescribed. Chick undescribed.

Voice: Described by Guggisberg as consisting of 3-4 strident notes, heard mainly towards dusk.

Habitat: Mountain grasslands and rocky outcrops.

Distribution: Central and south-eastern Ethiopia.

Feeding: Seeds, bulbs, grass roots, sedges and insects.

Breeding: Nest in rough grass; clutch 3; incubation period unrecorded.

Aviculture: No records.

Shelly's Francolin
Francolinus shelleyi 31-33cm

Alternative names: *F.s.trothae* Trotha's Francolin.
***F.s.elgonensis* Elgon Francolin.**

Description: Sexes similar, but female rather small and unspurred. Forehead, crown and nape brown, feathers edged with buff; mantle, back and rump greyish brown, feathers edged with white; tail light brown; sides of face and neck buff; chin and mid-throat white, encircled with a black line; lower throat, breast and flanks chestnut; rest of underparts buffy white, finely barred with blackish brown; flight feathers chestnut with greyish tips; under wing-coverts buff; iris brown; bill blackish horn, base yellow; legs and feet dull ochraceous or yellowish. Juvenile has breast and belly barred with black; throat buffy white. Chick has centre of crown and nape pale cinnamon, edged with sepia; broad stripe down centre of mid-back rufous brown, edged dark brown; underparts buffy.

Adults. *F.s.elgonensis* differs from the nominate race in being coloured with distinct black spots on chestnut breast.

F.s.theresae differs from *elgonesis* in having underparts paler.

F.s.trothae (*see* Reichenow, *Vog. Afr.*, 1, 1901, p.490 *Ugulla Tanganyika Territory*).

F.s.whytei differs from nominate in having white barring on upper breast often reduced and front of throat buffy.

F.s.sequestris differs from the nominate race in being darker, less greyish on the upperparts.

F.s.canidorsalis differs from the nominate in having considerably less extensive dark tawny on the breast and flanks.

Voice: Described by Maclean as a lilting musical whistle, '*tel-el-ke-BIR,tel-el-ke BIR*' repeated 3-4 times.

Habitat: Savanna interspersed with acacia and at the edges of cultivation.

Distribution: Central and northern Zimbabwe and western Mozambique.

F.s.elgonesis Kenya.

F.s.theresae Mount Kenya.

F.s.trothae western Tanzania.

F.s.whytei northern Malawi, northern Zambia and south-eastern Zaire.

F.s.sequestris KwaZulu-Natal, South Africa to south-eastern Swaziland and southern Mozambique.

F.s.canidorsalis Gauteng, Mpumalanga and Northern Province, South Africa to Mozambique southern and south-eastern Zimbabwe and southern Malawi.

Feeding: Seeds, roots, bulbs, shoots, fallen grain, fruit and insects.

Breeding: The nest is a small scrape in the ground, lined with grass and rootlets, placed in rank grass or under a bush. Egg white or pinkish buff; clutch 4-8; incubation period 22 days.

Aviculture: Selected reference CLUTCH 4-8; INCUBATION PERIOD 22 days. Selected Reference WILDFOOD Stems of Edible-stemmed vine *Cissus quadrangularis*, roots of Sweet-root commophora *Commophora neglecta*, leaves of Calabash *Langenaris siceraria*, Black-jack *Bidens pilosa*, Tree nettle *Urera tenax*, young pumpkin shoots. Selected Reference ANIMAL FOOD termites, locusthoppers, butterflies, moths.

Grey-wing Francolin
Francolinus africanus 30-33cm

Alternative name: *F.a.uluensis* Kenya Grey-wing Francolin.

Description: Sexes similar, but female slightly smaller and unspurred. Forehead, crown and nape brown, feathers edged with yellowish buff, feathers suffused with blackish brown; tail dark brown; sides of nape and hindneck buff, streaked black; lores and area behind eye buffy white, flecked with black; upper and mid-throat white; wing-coverts brown; under wing-coverts reddish brown; iris dark brown; bill blackish; legs and feet dull yellowish brown. Juvenile has under parts pale buffy white, feathers barred with brown; tail greyish brown; base of bill yellowish. Chick has centre of forehead, crown and nape rufous brown; stripe down mid-back dark brown, borded by narrow buffy stripes; underparts buffy.

Adults. *F.a.gutteralis* differs from *uluensis* in having wings more chestnut; underparts streaked with black.

F.a.eritreae (*see Zedlitz, Journ. f. Orn., 58, 1910, p.357, pl.5, figs 4 and 5 Plateau of Asmara, Eritreae*).

F.a.lorti differs from *uluensis* in having upperparts greyer; black spotting more solid on cheeks.

F.a.ellenbecki differs from archeri in having a mixture of greys on underparts.

F.a.archeri differs from ellenbecki in having underparts clear buff with a few sparse black markings.

F.a.uluensis (*see Ogilvie-Grant Ibis, 1892, p.44 Mackakos, Kenya Colony*).

F.a.macarthuri differs from uluensis in being rather darker; underparts with heavier markings,

F.a.proximas differs from the nominate in being darker and more coarsely marked brown on underparts.

Voice: Described by Mackworth-Praed & Grant as a particularly penetrating repeated '*tid-jid-jid-jie*' not unmusical.

Habitat: Semi-arid Karoo-type country where it frequents grass and low scrub; also cultivated lands.

Distribution: Western, south-western and eastern Cape Province and south western Free State, South Africa.

F.a.gutterallis north Ethiopia

F.a.eritreae north-eastern Ethiopia.

F.a.lorti Somalia.

F.a.ellenbecki central Ethiopia.

F.a.archeri south-central Ethiopia.

F.a.uluensis central Kenya

F.a.macarthuri south-eastern Kenya.

F.a.proximus Eastern Cape, eastern Free State, Mpumalanga and western KwaZulu-Natal provinces of South Africa and Lesotho (lowlands).

Feeding: *Monocotyledonous* bulbs (75%), fallen grain, including small potatoes (5%) and insects (20%), butterfly/moth larvae, beetles, termites and locusthoppers. Rushes are recorded, but not identified.

Breeding: Monogamous. There is no real nest, the eggs being laid in a hollow in the ground amongst dry grass and roots. Eggs yellow or pale yellowish brown finely speckled with grey and brown: cluth 4-8; incubation period unrecorded.

Aviculture: Selected Reference WILDFOOD Tubers of Cassava *Manihout esculenta*, Elephant ear *Colocasia antiquorum*. Selected reference ANIMAL FOOD termites.

Archer's Grey-wing Francolin
Francolinus levalliantoides 33-35cm

Alternative name: Acacia Francolin, Orange River Francolin.

Description: Sexes similar. Forehead and crown buff, streaked with black; mantle, back and upper tail-coverts grey-buff with barring blackish; tail blackish; moustachial stripe black; lores, below and behind eye buff overlaid with black spotting; chin and mid-throat white, bordered with black; breast and rest of underparts buff, broadly edged chestnut; wings chestnut; under wing-coverts buff; iris bown; bill blackish horn, base pink or yellow; legs and feet yellowish brown. Juvenile has scupulars have broader buff and blackish bars; collar absent. Chick undescribed.

Males *F.l.jugularis* differs from *palliaor* in being paler overall; neck patch broader.

F.l.cunenensis differs from the nominate race in being paler, breast broad mottled black and white, chestnut spotting on underparts reduced.

F.l.pallidor differs from the nominate in having the crown and hindneck paler buff.

F.l.wattii differs from *pallidor* in that the flight feathers are more reddish; wings and tail a little paler.

Voice: Described by Maclean as having rapid 4-syllabled phase, quickly repeated 2-9 times, '*kibitele, kibitele, kibitele*'.

Habitat: Slopes of grass-covered hills, open fields, edges of pans and cultivated lands.

Distribution: Gauteng, Free State, northern Cape Provinces, South Africa to Lesotho (lowlands) and south-eastern Botswana.

F.i.jugularis north-western Namibia and southern and western Angola.

F.i.cunenensis northern Namibia and southern Angola.

F.i.pallidor northern Namibia and north-eastern Botswana.

F.i.wattii central Namibia.

Feeding: Seeds, bulbs, shoots, corms, fallen grain, berries and insects. Bulbs and corms of Moraea spp. and insects, namely butterfly/moth larvae, beetles, bugs, mites and locusthoppers.

Breeding: Probably monogamous since usually in pairs during breeding season. Nest is a scrape in the ground,

lined with dry grass and situated under a tuft of grass of shrub. Eggs pale yellowish brown, finely speckled with dark brown; clutch 4-8, incubation period ur recorded.

Aviculture: Selected Reference CLUTCH 4-8. Selected Reference WILDFOOD Roots of Wild sweetpea *Vigna vexilata*, Zulu round potato *V.lobatifolia*, young pumpkin shoots, leaves of Nasturtium *Tropaeolum majus*, fresh cut lucerne *Medicago sativa*. Selected Reference ANIMAL FOOD termites, cockroaches, weevils.

Red-wing Francolin

Francolinus levaillantii 32-33cm

Alternative name: *F.i.kikuyuensis* Uasingishu Red-wing Francolin.

Description: Sexes similar. Crown and nape speckled with black; forehead, sides of hindneck buff; mantle, back and upper tail-coverts greyish brown, feathers flecked with black; tail blackish brown; wings with coverts greyish brown with buff overlay; under wing-coverts buff; chin and throat white; upper breast white, feathers flecked with black; rest of underparts buff, feathers speckled with chestnut; iris brown; bill blackish brown, base yellow; legs and feet yellowish brown. Juvenile similar to adult, but paler. Chick has forehead and crown brown, edged with black; stripe down mid-back dark brown, edged blackish; underparts buffy.

Adults *F.l.kikuyuensis* differes from the nominate race in having underparts buff vermiculated and barred broadly with black.

F.l.crawshayi differs from the nominate in having deeper tawny down side of neck, more black spots on belly.

F.l.benguellensis differs from nominate in having some irregular black patches on lower breast to belly.

F.l.clayi differs from the nominate in having rufous band across the nape.

Voice: Described by Van Someren as a loud 'ki-al-de-werk', mostly heard at dawn.

Habitat: Steep grassy slopes of valleys and rank vegetation bordering on swamps and vleis.

Distribution: Southern and eastern Cape Province, KwaZulu-Natal (midlands), Free State, Eastern North-West, Gauteng, Central Northern Province South Africa to Lesotho (lowlands).

F.i.kikuyuensis Uganda and Kenya.

F.i.crawshayi northern Malawi.

F.i.benguellensis southern Angola.

F.i.clayi western Zambia.

Feeding: Seeds, bulbs, shoots, berries, fallen grain, insects and land molluscs. Feeds largely on the bulbs and roots of various veld plants being particularly partial to those of Gladiolus and Watsonia. Also recorded fragmented material not readily identifiable, but probably mostly Amaryilidacious tubers. Live food in the form of termites, ants, grasshoppers, beetles spiders and millipedes.

Breeding: Presumably monogamous since often in pairs during breeding season. Makes practically no nest but scrapes with feet or moulds with breast, a simple hollow in rank grass or sedge which is sparsely lined with grass and rootlets. Eggs brownish yellow, spotted with brownish; clutch 3-8.; incubation period unrecorded.

Aviculture: Selected Reference CLUTCH 3-8. Selected Reference WILDFOOD Monkey bulb *Mariscus capensis*, leaves of Nasturtium *Tropaeotum majus*, tubers of Cape asparagus *Aponogeton distachyos*, young pumpkin shoots. Selected Reference ANIMAL FOOD termites.

Finsch's Francolin
Francolinus finschi 35-38cm

Description: Sexes similar. Forehead, crown and nape brownish grey; ear-coverts and sides of neck rufous; mantle, back and rump dark greyish brown, feathers vermiculated and barred buff; tail brownish grey, barred buff; chin and throat white; breast and belly buff blotched chestnut; under tail-coverts grey, barred buff; iris brown; bill black; legs and feet pale yellow. Juvenile undescribed. Chick undescribed.

Voice: Described by Urban *et al* as a loud '*wit-u-wit*' usually heard at dusk.

Habitat: Grasslands near gallery forests and among *Brachystegia* scrub.

Distribution: South-western Zaire and Angola.

Feeding: Seeds, beetles and other insect larvae.

Breeding: A shallow circular depression is placed in vegetation on the ground. Eggs light brown; clutch 5; incubation period unrecorded.

Aviculture: No records.

Coqui Francolin
Francolinus coqui 27-28cm

Alternative names: *F.c.spinetorum* High-Volta Coqui Francolin.
F.c.ruandae Ankole Coqui Francolin.
F.c.hubbardi Hubbard's Coqui Francolin.

Description: Male. Forehead, crown and nape chestnut; rest of head except throat yellowish or orange; throat white; mantle, black and upper tail-coverts grey-brown, streaked and barred with buff and black; tail blackish; upper breast brown, barred white; rest of underparts buff, each feather barred with black; under tail-coverts deep buff; under wing-coverts reddish brown; iris reddish brown; bill blackish, base yellow; cere, legs and feet yellow. Female similar to male, but two black streaks border the white eye stripe; black streaks border the white throat; chest chestnut. Juvenile similar to adult female, but browner on upperparts and more buff on underparts. Chick has forehead and crown rufous brown; sides of head-top and nape white; supercilliary, eye and moustachial stripes dark brown; centre of back rufous brown, bordered with black.

Males *F.c.spinetorum* similar to *angolensis*, but having breast and belly buffish white.

F.c.maharao differs from the nominate in having breast barring narrower.

F.c.angolensis differs from the nominate in having crown, nape and mantle darker; underparts and under tail-coverts deeper tawny.

F.c.ruahdae differs from the nominate in having broader and blacker breast barring.

F.c.hubbardi differs from the nominate in having underparts pale buff and being unbarred.

F.c.thikae similar to *hubbardi*, but having narrower breast barring.

F.c.kasaicus similar to *angolensis*, but upperparts and wing-coverts much redder; tail less distinctly barred.

F.c.campbelli differs fom the nominate in having the middle of the upperparts mainly black.

F.c.vernayi differs from the nominate in being more sandy on the upperparts; underparts paler with fewer barrings.

F.c.hoeschianus differs from the nominate in being greyer on upperparts; underparts pale buff.

Voice: Described by Newman as a piping '*ko-kwee, ko-kwee...*' or '*be-quick, be-quick...*' repeated continually.

Habitat: *Acacia*-veld, savanna, open grassland and cultivated lands.

Distribution: North-West, Northern Province and northern Free State, South Africa to Zimbabwe, Mozambique, south-eastern Botswana, south-eastern Zambia and Malawi.

F.c.spinetorum Mali to Nigeria.

F.c.maharao southern Ethiopia.

F.c.angolensis Gabon to Angola and Zambia.

F.c.ruahdae southern Uganda.

F.c.hubbardi western Kenya.

F.c.thikae central Kenya.

F.c.kasaicus central Zaire.

F.c.campbelli KwaZulu-Natal, South Africa to eastern Swaziland and southern Mozambique.

F.c.vernayi north-eastern Namibia, northern Botswana east to western Zimbabwe, southern Angola and south-western Zambia.

F.c.hoeschianus northern Namibia.

Feeding: Seeds of grasses and weeds, shoots, fallen grain and insects. Released birds which have been reared in an incubator were never seen to drink from still or running water. All water taken was either dew or raindrops on blades of grass and stalks. Animal food taken were grasshoppers, locusts, mantises, termites, slugs, spiders, earthworms, moths, caterpillars, beetles and small frogs *Kassina* and *Hyperolius spp*. Dead prey was sometimes eaten. The larger livefood such as locusts, Emperor moths, earthworms and cicadas were broken up before being eaten. Gleans ticks from grass stems. Bees caught when walking on the ground.

Breeding: Nest a slight hollow 10-12cm diameter, lined with some grass, stalks and occasionally roots and leaves; usually well concealed under a bush or grass tuft. A female was found sitting on a nest, set in 30m high *paspalum* grass field in KwaZulu-Natal, South Africa. Two days following the discovery of the nest site, the sitting female had been killed by an unknown predator. The 5 eggs were placed in an incubator. On hatching 5 time-related stages were recognized: downy chick (day 1-10), juvenile (day 11-30), immature (day 31) to about (day 106). adult Eggs white, cream or pinkish buff; clutch 3-8, usually 5; incubation period unrecorded.

Aviculture: Selected Reference CLUTCH 3-8, usually 5. Selected Reference WILDFOOD Seeds of Babala *Pennisetum americanum*, tubers of Cape asparagus *Aponogeneton distachyos*, shoots of Nasturtium *Tropaeolum majus* and young pumpkins, leaves of Chickweed *Stellaria media*, Tree nettle *Urera tenax*, fresh cut Lucerne *Medicago sativa*. Selected Reference FRUIT African mulberry *Morus mesozygia*, Bush cherry *Syzgium paniculatum*, African holly *Ilex mitis*. Selected Reference ANIMAL FOOD termites, hairless caterpillars, grasshoppers, crickets, cockroaches, weevils.

White-throated Francolin

*Francolinus albogularis 23*cm

Alternative name: *F.a.buckleyi* **Buckley's White-throated Francolin.**

Description: Male. Forehead, crown and nape grey, tinged rufous; ear-coverts grey; supercillium creamy white; wings with secondaries and primaries tawny, former, streaked white and latter, streaked dusky; chin and throat white; breast buff, streaked chestnut; belly and underparts buff; under tail-coverts rufous buff, barred black; iris brown; bill black, base yellow; legs and feet

orange-yellow. Female has black barring from lower neck in front of breast. Juvenile closely resembles adult female, but paler overall. Chick has crown darker brown; sides of head buff; chin and throat white; underparts buff, tinged rufous.

Males *F.a.buckleyi* differs from the nominate race in having upperparts darker and greyer.

F.a.dewittei differs from the nominate in having underparts reddish buff.

Voice: Described by Serle *et al* as a loud strident distinctive '*kili,kili,kili*', especially at dawn and dusk.

Habitat: Open savanna, disused fields, light scrub, especially burned areas.

Distribution: Senegal and Gambia.

F.a.buckleyi Ghana to Cameroon.

F.a.dewittei south-eastern Zaire.

Feeding: Grass seeds and other plant material as well as grasshoppers, termites, beetles and other insects.

Breeding: Slight depression in ground with a few strands of dry grass or green leaves as lining. Eggs buff to pale brown with slight gloss; clutch 4-7, usually 6; incubation period unrecorded.

Aviculture: No records.

Schlegel's Francolin

*Francolinus schlegelii 20-25*cm

Alternative name: Schlegel's Banded Francolin.

Description: Male. Forehead, crown and nape greyish brown, mottled rufous; supercillium rufous yellow; mantle and back rufous-chestnut, mottled grey; tail rufous, faintly barred black; wing-coverts with secondaries and primaries brown; ear-coverts, chin and throat brownish grey; breast, belly and under tail-coverts buffish white, barred black; iris brown; bill black, base yellow; legs and feet yellow. Female similar to male, but back browner; belly barring irregular. Juvenile similar to female, but mantle barred rufous buff. Chick undescribed.

Voice: Described by Mackworth-Praed & Grant as a soft '*korrr-korrr-korrr*' uttered mostly at dusk.

Habitat: Grasslands, woodland and occasionally in cultivation.

Distribution: Western Cameroon, Central African Republic, southern Chad to south-western Sudan.

Feeding: Grass seeds, grain and insects. Takes caterpillars that feed from the larvae of the 'Ka' tree *Isoberinia doka*.

Breeding: Nest a scrape in the ground often lined with leaves. Eggs smooth and creamy; clutch 2-5.

Latham's Francolin

Francolinus Lathami 30-32cm

Alternative names: Forest Francolin. Latham's Forest Francolin *F.i.schubotzi* Schubotzi's Forest Francolin.

Description. Male. Forehead, crown and nape olive-brown; eye stripe black, bordered with white; ear-coverts pale grey; hindneck and upper mantle black, feathers spotted white; lower mantle and back dark greyish brown; rump and upper tail-coverts dark olive-brown, vermiculated buff and black; tail brownish grey; chin and throat black; breast, belly and rest of underparts black, mottled white; iris brown; bill black; legs and feet yellow. Female has ear-coverts greyish brown; upper mantle brown; rump and upper tail-coverts pale brown. Juvenile similar to female, but crown mottled black and brown. Chick has crown and back dark chestnut brown; underparts dark buff; iris greyish brown; bill, upper mandible horn, lower dusky; legs and feet yellow. Male *F.i. schubotzi* differs from the nominate race in having ear-coverts and sides of neck whiter.

Voice: Described by Serle *et al* as a clucking call.

Habitat: Lowland primary forests.

Distribution: Sierra Leone to Gabon and north-western Zaire.

F.i.schubotzi north-eastern Zaire to south-western Sudan and Uganda.

Feeding: Seeds, green leaves, fruit, insects, especially arthropods which accounts for 90% of food intake. Termites *Basidentitermes* spp. and ants *Psalidomyrmex* spp., also beetles and other insects and their larvae. Also recorded are snails. Fruit of African oil palm *Elaeis guineensis*.

Breeding: Nest a hollow on forest floor, lines with dry leaves at base of tree such as *Piptadeniastrum africanum*. Eggs ovate, reddish brown or light brown; clutch 2, rarely 3; incubation period unrecorded.

Aviculture: No records

Nahan's Forest Francolin

Francolinus nahani 32cm

Alternative name: Nahan's Francolin

Description: Sexes similar. Forehead, crown and nape blackish brown; supercillium white, spotted black; mantle and back rufous buff, feathers edged white; sides of rump and upper tail-coverts brown, barred dusky; tail greyish brown, vermiculated darker; chin white; upper breast black, barred white; lower breast, belly and flanks black, mottled and streaked white; wing-coverts rufous brown, primaries greyish, secondaries black, all barred buff or blackish brown; under tail-coverts black; iris brown; bill black, base red including bare eye patch; legs and feet reddish. Juvenile like adult, but darker overall; legs and feet grey. Chick undescribed.

Habitat: Dense forest up to 1400m.

Distribution: North-eastern Zaire and Uganda.

Feeding: Seed, green shoots, bulbs and small molluscs.

Breeding: A tree hollow 1m from the ground. Eggs smooth, glossy, rich buffish or purplish cream speckled or finely spotted pale brown with paler purplish under-markings; incubation period unrecorded.

Aviculture: No records.

Common Quail

Coturnix coturnix 16-18cm

Alternative names: *C.c.africana* African Painted Quail, African Quail, Cape Quail, Quail

Description: Male. Crown, nape blackish brown, the feathers edged buffy; mantle, back and rump blackish brown mottled and streaked with white; wings light vinaceous brown, under wing-coverts whitish; tail blackish brown barred buffy white; throat and ear-coverts chestnut; breast buff-brown; iris light brown to yellowish brown; bill blackish; legs and feet yellowish pink. Female differs from the male in lacking the strongly patterned face; chin, throat and upper breast buffy white; underparts creamy white. Juvenile similar to adult female, but with blackish edges to breast feathers. Chick is buff and russet above with two black streaks on crown and a black central dorsal stripe.

Males. *C.c.africana* differs too little from nominate race to warrant recognition.

C.c.erlangeri differs from nominate in being more richly coloured above, with chestnut and black throat pattern predominating.

Voice: Described by Maclean as a penetrating high pitched '*whit WHIT tit, whit WHIT tit*' repeated 4-8 times.

Habitat: Lightly wooded savanna, open grassland and cultivation; non-breeding birds occur in Kalahari sandveld and karoo.

Distribution: *C.c.africana* central and northern Namibia, Swaziland, Lesotho (lowlands), and South Africa provinces of Cape, Free State and KwaZulu-Natal.

C.c.erlangeri eastern Zimbabwe and western Mozambique to Malawi, Tanzania, eastern Zaire, Kenya to Ethiopia.

Feeding: Seed, tubers, buds, leaves, berries, fallen grain and invertebrates, comprising mostly insects and small molluscs. Cramp & Simmons inform us that in Europe it feeds on weeds or seeds of dock *Rumex*, chickweed *Stellaria*, hemp-nettle *Galeopsis*, bistorts, notably knotgrass *Polygonum aviculare*, horehound *Ballota,* spurreys *Spergularis, eye* bright *Euphrasia*, stachys *Stachys*, poppy *Papaver,* plantain *Plantago* and grasses of 'Bristle-grass' *Setaria*, 'Ryegrass' *Lolium* and 'Brome' *Bromus*; cereals, namely oats Avena, barley *Hordeum* and wheat *Triticum*; animal material, chiefly true or snout, clock, rove and leaf beetles *Coleoptera*, bugs *Hemiptera*, ants *Hymenoptera*, earwigs *Dermaptera*, locusts and grasshoppers *Orthoptera*, mantises *Dictyoptera*, spiders *Arachnida* and snails *Gastropoda*; in USSR seeds of Black Horehound *Ballota nigra*, Fat Hen *Chenopodium album* and Red shank *Polygonum persicaria*; in the Canary Islands feeds on the berries of *Daphne gnidium*; in North Africa eats Fool's Parsley *Aethusa cynapium*; in southern Africa the seeds of pigweed *Amaranthus* spp., Scotch thistle *Circium vulgare*, black-jack *Bidens pilosa* spp., Prickly apple *Datura stramonium*, panic *Panicum* spp., paspalum *Paspalum* spp., buckwheat *Fagopyrum*, maize *Zea* and rye-grass *Lotium*; fruit of Inkberry *Solanum nigrum*, buds and green leaves (unidentified); livefood includes termites, beetles, including weevils and ladybird, larvae, pupae and adult moths and butterflies, the latter probably mostly African Clouded Yellow *Colas electo*, crickets, locusts and grasshoppers, larger plant bugs, centipedes, millipedes, fly larvae, mites, spiders and molluscs. In India the grubs of *Hypera variabilis* have been identified in stomach contents.

Breeding: The nest is composed of grass and small rootlets, placed in a little hollow scratch in the ground by the female in the shelter of a tuft of grass, thorny shrub, weeds or standing crops. Eggs broad, oval, smooth and glossy, yellowish white or buff to brownish, either speckled or boldly marked with dark brown; clutch 8-13, usually 5-7, laid on consecutive days; normally 1 brood, but 2 may occur, relaying up to twice after egg loss; incubation begins after clutch complete; incubation 16-18 days by female only; male may sit near incubating female; hatching synchronous; cared for by female and brooded while small; fledging period 22-24 days; capable of short flights at 9-10 days; remain in family party for further 30-45 days before becoming independent; sexual maturity and first breeding at age of 1 year.

Aviculture: Selected Reference CLUTCH 2-15; INCUBATION PERIOD 16-18 days; FLEDGING PERIOD 22-24 days; first flight after 9 days. Nest Record Cards CLUTCH 4,5,7 (ARU) 7 (NASNRC); INCUBATION PERIOD 16,17 (ARU) about 17 (ANRC) after 16 days (NASNRC); FLEDGING PERIOD 20,22 (ARU) about 22 days (ANRC).

Selected Reference WILDFOOD Seeds (dried out, beaten off the stalk), Common thatchgrass *Hyperrhenia hirta*, chickweed *Stelleric* sp., Sow thistle *Sonchus oleraceus*. Hay *Chloris virgata*, Broad-leaved panic *Panicum deustum*, Blue panic *P.laevifolium* (NASDRC), Natal panic *P.ratalense*, Johnson grass *Sorghum halpense*, leaves of Devil's thorn *Emex australis*, Red garden sorrel *Oxalis latifolia*, Canary creeper *Seneico temoides*, Smelter's bush *Flaveria bidentis*, Spider's wisp *Cleome gynandra*, chickweed *Stellaris media*, flowers of Gallant soldier *Galinsoga parvifora* (SAADRC). Selected Reference ANIMAL FOOD mealworms. Diet Record Cards termites, maggots, mealworms (NASDRC ADRC), weevils, ladybirds (NASDRC), butterfly / moth caterpillars, millipedes, centipedes (SAADRC).

Harlequin Quail
Coturnix delegorguei 16-18cm
Alternative name: African Harlequin Quail, Black-breasted Quail.

Description: Male crown and nape blackish brown, feathers fringed greyish brown; mantle, rump and upper tail-coverts blackish brown, feathers specked with white; tail blackish, crossed by narrow whitish bars; flanks chestnut, heavily streaked black; lores, ear-coverts and proximal cheek black; below the eye and side of the throat white; chin and upper breast black; iris brown; bill black, base yellowish; legs and feet pink or yellow pink. Female has chin and throat buffy white; upper breast tawny; rest of underparts brown; underparts tawny; bill horn coloured. Juvenile similar to adult female, but with black spots on the breast. Chick has underparts and wings brown; five streaks down centre of back and rump; head brown with a single tawny streak bordered with black.

Male. *C.d.histrionica* differs from the nominate race in being darker overall.

Voice: Described by Mackworth-Praed & Grant as a loud whistling double chirp *'twee-twit-twee-twit'*.

Habitat: Moist grassland, borders of vleis and close to cultivation.

Distribution: Senegal to Somalia, Kenya, Uganda, Tanzania, Angola the Congo, Zambia, Zimbabwe, Mozambique, Swaziland, Botswana, Namibia and South African provinces of eastern Cape, KwaZulu-Natal (breeds), central North-West and Mpumalanga and Free State.

C.d.histrionica São Thomé Island, Gulf of Guinea.

Feeding: Seeds, green shoots, leaves, insects, namely grasshoppers, beetles, bugs, caterpillars, ants, termites and small ground molluscs. Feeds on seeds of setaria *Setaria* spp., signal grass *Brachiaria* spp., and sorghum *Sorghum* sp.

Breeding: Nest, a hollow in the ground, scantily lined with fine grass, situated in rank grass, crops or weeds, with several escape routes. Sometimes in loose colonies. Eggs creamy buff to yellowish, speckled, spotted and blotched with dark chestnut, sepia and black; clutch 3-8 or even 15, the last figure probably the result of laying by two females; incubation period 15-18 days, by female alone; fledging period 22-24 days; short distance flights at 5-7 days, full 11-13 days.

Aviculture: Selected Reference CLUTCH 8-12, may lay more than 20; INCUBATION PERIOD 15-18 days; FLEDGING PERIOD 22-24 days; first flight at 10 days. Nest Record Cards CLUTCH 4,5 (ARU) 7 (SAANRC) 4 (NASNRC) 5 (ANRC); INCUBATION PERIOD 16 17 (ARU) 16 days (SAANRC); FLEDGING PERIOD 20 (ARU) 23 days (SAANRC).

Selection Reference WILDFOOD Seeds of (dried out, beaten off the stalk), Common thatchgrass *Hyparrhenia hirta*, Teff grass *Eragrostis tef*. Diet Record Cards Annual blue grass *Poa annua* (ARU SAADRC), Natal panic *Panicum natalense* (NASDRC), leaves of Kaffir cabbage *Cleome gynandra*, Chickweed *Stellaria media*, Corn spurry *Spergula arvensis*, Parrot leaf *Alternanthera ficoidea*, Nasturtium *Tropaeolum majus* (ADRC). Diet Record Crads termites, beetles larvae, including mealworms (NASDRC ADRC), ants, crickets, hairless caterpillars (ADRC). Selected Reference ANIMAL FOOD ants, cocoons, mealworms.

Blue Quail

Coturnix adansonii 14-15cm

Alternative names: Adanson's Quail, African Blue Quail, African Blue-breasted Quail, African Painted Quail.

Desciption: Male. Forehead, crown and nape bluish slate; mantle, back and rump dark bluish black; tail blackish; chin and throat black; over the lores a narrow line of pale white; breast, belly and under tail-coverts dark slate-grey; wings and flanked chestnut; under wing-coverts brownish; iris red-brown to ruby red; bill black, base tinged blue; legs and feet yellow to orange-yellow. Female has forehead, crown and nape dark brown, streaked with black; chin and throat buff; wings brown, barred black; bill dark horn, base tinged pinkish. Juvenile similar to female, but with distinct light shaft stripes on greater wing-coverts. Chick has throat and belly yellowish brown; upperparts uniform pale brown, streaked blackish.

Voice: Described by Urban *et al* as a trisyllabic piping whistle 'kee kee yew', first note loudest.

Habitat: Moist grasslands, including areas of rank grass, weed and cultivation.

Distribution: Sierra Leone, Mali, Cameroon, southern Chad, southern Sudan, western Ethiopia, Gabon, Zaire, Angola, Zambia, Malawi, north-eastern Kenya, Tanzania, southern Mozambique, eastern Zimbabwe, Swaziland and South African provinces of eastern Cape, eastern KwaZulu-Natal and Mpumalanga.

Feeding: Small seeds, termites, other insects and their larvae and small land molluscs.

Breeding: The nest is a small cavity in the ground, lined with fine grass and usually partly hidden by a tuft of grass. Eggs broad ovals without gloss, pale yellowish brown or olive-brown; clutch 4-9; incubation 16 days by female alone, but males collected showed signs of brood patch suggesting they may also incubate; both parents care for the chicks; family parties remain together until young can fly well.

Aviculture: Selected Reference CLUTCH 4-9; INCUBATION PERIOD 15-16 days. Nest Record Cards CLUTCH 5 (ARU); INCUBATION PERIOD 16 days (ARU). Selected Reference WILDFOOD Seeds (dried out, beaten off the stalk), Natal panic *Panicum natalense*. Diet Record Cards Guinea grass *Panicum maximum*, Broad-leaved panic *P.deustum* (ARU). Diet Record Cards ANIMAL FOOD termites, beetle larvae, including mealworms, ants, maggots, spiders (ARU).

Congo Peafowl

Afropavo congensis -cm

Alternative name: African Peafowl.

Description: Male. Forehead and nape velvety black; long bristly chest black and white; mantle and back bronzy green; tail glossy violet blue and green; bare skin on side of neck and throat red; sides of face bluish grey; breast and belly black; flanks green; wings brown-black, glossy greenish; iris brown; bill blue-grey; legs and feet green, spurs whitish. Female has short bristly crest brown; upperparts glossy iridescent green; underparts chestnut, spotted black. Juvenile similar to adult female, but underparts paler, mantle and back tinged brown; underparts pale and black. Chick has crown and nape black; sides of head tawny yellow; underparts and flanks creamy yellow, tinged rufous; bill, upper mandle dusky, lower buff; legs and feet pinkish buff.

Voice: Described by Urban *et al* with calls 'ko-ko-wa' and female responds with higher pitched 'hi-ho-hi-ho'.

Habitat: Primary rain forest.

Distribution: Central and eastern Zaire.

Feeding: Seeds, fruits, berries and insects. Fruit of *Celtris adolfi-fridericii*, Jumping seed tree *Sapium ellipticum, Ficus* spp., *Strombosia grandifolia*, Lemonwood *Xymalos monospora*, Mauritius thorn *Caealpinia* *delcapentala*, ants, e.g. *Tallothyreus tarsatus*, termites and their larvae, other ground living invertebrates and aquatic insects e.g. *Orecotopyrus* spp.

Breeding: Nest site is a hollow in fork of a large branch of a tree at 1,5-3m above the ground. Eggs rufous brown or cream; clutch 2-4; incubation period 25-28 days by female; male remains near nest during incubation; after hatching brooded for 1-2 days before taking to ground; young cared for by both parents.

Aviculture: Selected Reference CLUTCH 3; INCUBATION PERIOD 30 days.

Black Guineafowl
Phasidus niger -cm

Description: Sexes similar, female not spurred. Bare skin on head and nape pinkish; short crest and neck with feathers black; rest of plumage black, except belly browner and feather bases white; iris brownish grey; bill greyish green; legs and feet greyish brown. Juvenile similar to adult but paler overall and belly white. Keet has forehead and crown blackish; upper back uniform dark rufous, lower dark maroon; throat and ear-coverts rich buff; underparts whitish, tinged rufous; iris brown; bill pale brownish grey; legs and feet pale greyish brown.

Voice: Described by Urban *et al* as a short, musical, high-pitched '*kwee*' repeated monotonously 2-3 times a second.

Habitat: Lowland forests and occasionally in cultivated patches on its borders.

Distribution: Southern Cameroon to central Zaire.

Feeding: Seeds, green leaves, forest fungi, small frogs, millipedes, beetles, ants, termites and fruits.

Breeding: Presumably a scrape in dense vegetation. Eggs pale reddish brown, sometimes washed with yellowish or violet, very deeply pitted; incubation period unrecorded.

Aviculture: No records.

White-breasted Guineafowl
Agelastes meleagrides 45cm

Description: Sexes similar, female lacks spurs; head and neck naked and red; broad white collar on hind-neck and breast; rest of plumage black, finely vermiculated with white; wings, the primaries dark brown, edged with grey on outer webs; iris brown; bill greenish brown; legs and feet brown or greyish black. Juvenile

upperparts black-brown except head paler; belly white. Keet undescribed.

Voice: Described by Pfeffer as a low deep '*kok-kok*'.

Habitat: Lowland forests.

Distribution: Liberia and Ghana.

Feeding: Fallen seeds of forest trees, berries, insects and small molluscs.

Breeding: Presumably a scrape in dense undergrowth. Eggs reddish buff, very deeply pitted; incubation period unrecorded.

Aviculture: No records.

Helmeted Guineafowl
Numida meleagris 60-65cm.

Alternative names: Guineafowl, Crowned Guineafowl, Tufted Guineafowl.

N.m.galeata **Grey-breasted Helmeted Guineafowl.**
N.m.marchei **Gabon Helmeted Guineafowl.**
N.m. strasseni **Ubangi Bristle-nosed Guineafowl.**
N.m.somaliensis **Somali Guineafowl.**
N.m.major **Uganda Guineafowl.**
N.m.intermedia **Ankole Helmeted Guineafowl.**
N.m.macroceras **Baringo Guineafowl.**
N.m.reichenowi **East African Helmeted Guineafowl.**

Description: Sexes similar. Uniform colour slate-grey thickly spotted with white; bare skin and sides of head and neck blue; wattle red with blue tips; head cap red; horny casque yellowish horn; chin and fore-throat dusky; breast normally finely barred with finer spotting; iris brown; bill yellowish horn; legs and feet blackish. Juvenile uniformally browner, darker on underparts; head paler blue and red. Keet has upperparts brown; buffish white below; one blackish strip on centre of crown and two on flanks.

Adults. *N.m.sabyi* similar to nominate race, but facial skin pale bluish white; wattle red; collar violet-red.

N.m.galeata similar to *major* in having lateral wattles scarlet-vermillion; breast and upper mantle vinous grey; chin and throat blackish brown.

N.m.marchei similar to *galeata* in having feathers of lower neck more bluish or purplish; lateral wattles mostly red.

N.m.strasseni differs from the nominate in having the breast in front blue; nasal tufts small and hair-like; lateral wattles blue.

N.m.somaliensis similar to nominate, but cere bristles longer; wattles somewhat pointed and blue, tips red.

N.m.major differs from nominate in being darker overall; nasal tufts shorter, wattles wholly blue.

N.m.tortuensis differs from the nominate in having nasal tufts smaller; wattles wholly blue.

N.m.intermedia differs from the nominate in having nasal tufts barely indicated; wattles with terminal half red.

N.m.mitrara similar to *reichenowi*, but casque smaller; wattles pointed; facial skin bluish grey.

N.m.reichenowi similar to nominate, but facial skin pale bluish white; longer casque; wattles entirely red.

N.m.uhehensis (see Reichenow, Orn., Monatsb; 6 1898, p.88, Uhehe, Tanganyika Territory).

N.m.callewaerte differs from the nominate in having lower neck and breast in front bluish; lateral wattles blue, tips red.

N.m.marungensis differs from *mitrata* in having casque yellow-ochre.

N.m.maxima (see Neumann, Orn. Monatsb., 6, 1898, p.21 Caconda, Benguella).

N.m.rikwae similar to *mitrata* but casque often longer and a tuft of fleshy nasal papillae present.

N.m.papillosa differs from nominate in having fairly broad casque; papillae on cere well developed in males.

N.m.coronata differs from nominate in having larger casque; small feathers of the lower neck not barred.

Voice: Described by McLachlan & Liversidge as a stuttering, rattling 'kek kek' (alarm call); a monotonous '*come back, come back*' (normal call).

Habitat: Open grasslands, cultivation, bushveld and vleis.

Distribution: Chad, Sudan, northern Ethiopia.

N.m.sabyi western Morocco.

N.m.galeata Senegal to Cameroon.

N.m.marchei Gabon and Central African Republic.

N.m.strasseni eastern Cameroon, northern Central African Republic.

N.m.somaliensis south-eastern Ethiopia, Somalia and northen Kenya.

N.m.major north-eastern Zaire and western Uganda.

N.m.intermedia south-western Uganda.

N.m.mitrata southern Kenya, eastern Tanzania, Malawi, Zambia, eastern Botswana, Mozambique, Zimbabwe, eastern Swaziland and North-West, Northern Province and Mpumalanga, South Africa.

N.m.macroceras western Kenya.

N.m.reichenowi south-western Kenya and north-western Tanzania.

N.m.uhehensis south central Tanzania.

N.m.callewaerte northern Angola to south central Zaire.

N.m.marungensis southern Zaire and Zambia.

N.m.maxima southern Angola.

N.m.rikwae south-western Tanzania.

N.m.papillosa southern Angola, Namibia, the Caprivi Strip, northern and north-western Botswana.

N.m.coronata western Swaziland, Lesotho (lowlands and South African provinces of eastern Cape, Gauteng (highveld), Free State and KwaZulu-Natal.

Feeding: Seeds, tubers, bulbs, fruit, fallen grain, insects, arthropods and land molluscs. Seeds of Guineafowl grass *Rottboellia exaltara*, Blackjack *Bidens* sp., Burweed *Achyranthes aspera*, Cat-thorn *Scutia myrtina*, Kuni-bush *Rhus undulate*, Blue-and-white daisy bush *Osteospermum ecklonis*, African marigold *Tagetes erecta*, Sweet thorn *Acacia karroo*, White stinkwood *Celtis africana*, Wild Barley *Hordeum marinum*, acorns *Quercus* sp., blades of Couch grass *Cynodon* sp., lovegrass *Eragrostis* sp., bulbs of Nutgrass *Cyperus rotundas*, fruit of Needle bush *Azima tetracantha*, Cat-thorn *Scutia myrtina*, Hoednderuintjie *Cyperus esculentus*, Slangbessie *Lycium campanulatum*, Common taaibos *Rhus pyroides*, spilled grain in the form of maize *Zea*, oats *Avena*, wheat *Triticum*, Barley *Hordeum*, sorghum *Sorghum*, and livefood, namely termites, grasshoppers, crickets, locust hoppers, cockroaches, mantises, crane fly larvae, leather jackets, robber flies, pill, shield-back and bagrada bugs, the latter probably the species *Bagrada hilaris*, anti lion larvae, butterfly/moth caterpillars especially bagworms, wasps larvae or "grubs", ants, ground, click and tortoise beetles, weevils, ladybirds and chafers, centipedes, millipedes, ticks, pseudoscorpions, spiders, slugs and snails. A small toad also recorded.

Breeding: Nest a scrape in the ground situated in tall grass, under a scrub or hidden in dense cover, measuring 25-32cm across, up to 8cm deep, lined presumably by female with dry grass and feathers. Eggs heavy pitted, cream or yellowish buff; clutch 8-12, up to 20, probably with two birds laying in one nest; incubation starts with complete clutch, by female for 25-30 days; probably one brood; no information on replacements; hatching synchronous; precocial and nidifugous brooded by both parents; first flight after 16 days, strongly at 30 days; casque appears at 32-40 days; fledging period 38-40 days; female can lay at 26-30 weeks.

Aviculture: Selected Reference CLUTCH 6-10; INCUBATION PERIOD 24 days; FLEDGING PERIOD 28-30 days; first flight after 16 days. Nest Record Cards CLUTCH 8,12 (ANRC); INCUBATION PERIOD 24-28 days (ANRC); FLEDGING PERIOD 38-31 days (ANRC). Selected Reference WIDLFOOD Seeds of Black-jack *Bidens* sp., fresh cut Lucerne *Medicago sativa*, young pumpkin shoots. Diet Record Cards Johnson grass *Sorghum halpense*, leaves of Red garden sorrel *Oxalis latifolia*, Chickweed *Stellaris media*, Nasturtium *Tropaeolum majus*, Corn spurry *Spergula arvensis*, Sow-thistle *Sonchus oleraceus*, Gallant soldier *Galinsoga parviflora* (ADRC). Diet Record Cards FRUIT *Latana camara* (no common name), Common taaibos *Rhus pyroides* (ADRC). Diet Record Cards ANIMAL FOOD termites, grasshoppers, crickets, locust hoppers, cockroaches, mantises, cranefly larvae, leather jackets, pill bugs, millipedes, spiders, mealworms (ADRC).

Plumed Guineafowl

Guttera plumifera 50-55cm

Description: Sexes similar. Head and neck slate-grey, largely bare and with pendent wattles; crest of long bristly plumes; rest of plumage black, spotted white; iris brown; bill bluish grey, tip white; legs and feet greyish blue.

Adult. *G.p.schubotzi* differs from the nominate race in having orange patch in front of ear-coverts and on hind-neck. Juvenile upperparts grey, barred blackish; short black feathers on head, latter forming crest; breast dusky with whitish bars and spots. Keet has forehead, crown and nape dark brown; sides of head brown with irregular streaks of rufous buff; iris grey; bill light buff; legs and feet yellow.

Voice: Described by Mackworth-Praed & Grant as a nasal '*kow*' by individuals answered by '*kak*', but when alarmed remains silent.

Habitat: Primary forest and in old overgrown clearings.

Distribution: Cameroon, Gabon and northern Angola.

G.p.schubotzi northern Zaire.

Feeding: Seeds, leaves, fruit, molluscs, insects and arthropods such as slugs, snails, grasshoppers, crickets, beetles, termites, ants, cockroaches, spiders and millipedes.

Breeding: Nest a simple scrape in ground, lined with dried leaves from the forest floor. Eggs pale buff, with numerous pits darkened by soiling and neat straining; clutch 9-10; incubation period unrecorded.

Aviculture: No records.

Crested Guineafowl

Guttera edouardi 50cm

Alternative names: Black Crested Guineafowl
G.e.verreauxi West African Crested.
Guineafowl, Pallas's Black Crested Guineafowl.
G.e.sethsmithi Uganda Crested Guineafowl.

Description: Sexes similar. Crown with curly mop-like feathers bluish black; hind-crown, nape, face and upper neck skin bare, with small wattle at gape and large occipital fold whitish; upper hindneck, lower neck and upper breast black, glossed bluish purple; rest of body black, spotted all over with bluish white spots; wings, the primaries brown with outer webs verrmiculated bluish white, secondaries with logitudinal bluish streaks and white edges; tail black, spotted bluish white; iris red; bill greyish to yellowish; legs and feet dark olive-brown to black. Juvenile upperparts barred with chestnut, grey and black; underparts blackish with buff feather edges. Keet has upperparts brown with crown stripe and cap

rufous buff; central dorsal and lower parallel stripe dark brown, inner buffy.

Adults. *G.e.sclateri* similar to *verreauxi*, but crest less curly; bare skin of face and neck grey-blue.

G.e.sethsmithi similar to *verreauxi*, but having bare skin of throat and foreneck brick-coloured.

G.e.schoutedeni similar to *verreauxi*, but red skin on throat, less extensive, rest of facial skin and neck dark blue.

G.e.kathleenae similar to *schoutendeni* in having cheeks, chin and throat scarlet.

G.e.symonsi differs from the nominate race in having spotting of upper and underparts larger.

G.e.barbata differs from the nominate race in having a shorter crest; body spotting sometimes interspersed with chestnut.

G.e.verreauxi differs from the nominate race in having a longer crest.

G.e.chapini similar to *symonsi* in having the bare skin on the middle of the chin and throat crimson; rest of facial skin and neck steel blue.

Voice: Described by Mackworth-Praed & Grant as when feeding a deep '*tok-a-tok-tok-tok-tok*'

Habitat: Dense scrub and gallery forest.

Distribution: Southern Malawi, northern Mozambique, south-eastern Zambia, eastern and northern Zimbabwe, eastern Swaziland and the provinces of KwaZulu-Natal (north of Durban) and Northern Province in South Africa.

G.e.verreauxi Guinea to Togo.

G.e.sclateri western Cameroon.

G.e.schoutendeni southern Zaire.

G.e.chapini southern Angola.

G.e.sethsmithi eastern Zaire and north-western Tanzania.

G.e.suahelica central Tanzania.

G.e.barbata south-western Tanzania and western Mozambique.

G.e.kathleenae western Zambia.

G.e.symonsi restricted to Karkloof forest near Howick, KwaZulu-Natal, South Africa.

Feeding: Seeds, spilled grain, roots, corms, leaves, stems, berries, fruit, insects and land molluscs. Seeds of Black-jack *Bidens pilosa* and Burweed *Achyranthes aspera*, fruit of *Rubiaceae*, mostly tropical shrubs and trees. Frequently feed on fruits dropped by Vervet Monkey *Cercopithecus aethiops* and in northern KwaZulu-Natal, South Africa feeds in association with Red Duiker *Cephalophus natalensis*, but nature of relationship uncertain. Leaves of *Compositae* characterized by its small ray and disc florets. Livefood taken in the form of termites, grasshoppers, crickets, cranefly larvae, robber flies, pill, shield-backed, twig wilters and assassin bugs, soft scales, antlion larvae, butterfly/moth caterpillars, wasp larvae of "grubs", ground click weevils, chafers, tortoise beetles, millipedes, pseudoscorpions, spiders, slugs and snails.

Breeding: Scrape in ground, scantily lined with dry plant matter, situated under a fallen log or amongst exposed tree roots. Eggs buff or pinkish buff with deep pore marks; clutch 4-6, though often, with two birds laying in one nest, up to 14; incubation period 22-23 days, by female alone; fledging period 28-32 days; first flight after 14 days.

Aviculture: Selected Reference FRUIT Mulberry *Morus* sp., Nana-berry *Rhus dentata*. Selected Reference WILDFOOD chickweed *Stellaria* sp. Selected Reference ANIMAL FOOD beetles, caterpillars, crickets, termites.

Kenya Crested Guineafowl

Guttera pucherani 46-55cm

Description: Sexes similar. Face and upper neck naked with small wattle at gape and large occipital fold; round eye and throat red; rest of head and neck greyish blue; crown with black crest of downy feathers; rest of body black with bluish white spots, except primaries brown and secondaries darker brown; tail blackish blue; iris red; bill reddish brown; legs and feet dark-olive to black. Juvenile differs from adult in being paler overall. Keet has forehead, crown and nape dark brown; sides of head dark brown with irregular rufous buff streaks; throat buffy; rest of underparts rufous buff; legs and feet yellow.

Voice: Described by Mackworth-Praed & Grant as a rattling alarm cry, and also a soft chuckling note while feeding.

Habitat: Scrub or dense thickets and forest edges and in stands of *Cryptosepalum* woodland.

Distribution: South-eastern Somalia, eastern Kenya, north-eastern Tanzania and Zanzibar.

Feeding: Seeds, fruit, green leaves, bulbs and roots, namely *Rubiaceae*, *Compositae*, *Malvaceae*, *Leguminosae* and *Amaranthaceae*. Livefood in the form of molluscs, small snails, termites and grasshoppers.

Breeding: Nest, a scrape among dead leaves in dense cover on ground. Eggs cream, minutely speckled with brown; clutch 3-4; incubation period unrecorded.

Aviculture: No records.

Vulturine Guineafowl

Acryllium vulturinum 58-61cm

Description: Sexes similar. Bare skin on head bluish grey; nape feathers chestnut; upper neck greyish; lower neck extending into long pointed hackles, black with wide white shaft-stripes, edged bright cobalt-blue; mantle, lower rump, tail and flanks black, streaked and spotted with white; wings, with edges of outer secondaries pinkish violet; lower breast and belly cobalt-blue, becoming black centrally; iris red; bill bluish white; legs and feet blackish. Juvenile differs from adult in having blue less intense; primaries brownish black, barred with buff on tips and secondaries darker, barred with buff. Keet has crown dark brown; rest yellowish buff.

Voice: Described by Rutgers and Norris as something like '*tee-tee-tee-teet*' while the female also utters a soft, enticing call, '*Who-Hee*'.

Habitat: Desert thorn scrub and forages in tall riverine *acacia* woodland.

Distribution: Eastern Uganda, southern Somalia, eastern Kenya and north-eastern Tanzania.

Feeding: Seeds and leaves of grasses and herbs, fruit, berries, insects, also spiders and scorpions and small molluscs. Fruit of Mustard Tree *Salvadora perisca*, *Commiphora* spp. and *Ficus* spp.

Breeding: Nest, a scrape amid tall grass, and consists of only a hollow in the ground lined with some trampled grass. Eggs creamy white or pale brown, broad, oval and slightly pointed; clutch 13-15; incubation 24 days by female alone.

Aviculture: Selected Reference CLUTCH 8-12; INCUBATION PERIOD 23-28, 23-25 days by domestic chicken; FLEDGING PERIOD 25-30 days; first flight after 14 days. Nest Record Cards CLUTCH 9 (ANRC); INCUBATION PERIOD 25 days (ANRC); FLEDGING PERIOD 28 days (ANRC). Personal Communication leaves of Shepherd's purse *Capsela bursapastoris*, Sow thistle *Sonchus oleraceus*. Diet Record Cards Gallant soldier *Galinsoga parviflora*, Red garden sorrel *Oxalis latifolia*, Chickweed *Stellaria media* (ADRC). Selected Reference WILDFOOD dandelion *Taraxacum* sp., chickweed *Stellaria* sp., Comfrey *Symphytum officinale*. Diet Record Cards ANIMAL FOOD termites, mealworms, crickets, grasshoppers, locust hoppers, spiders (ADRC). Selected Reference FRUIT mulberry *Morus* sp., Nana-berry *Rhus dentata*.

Kurrichane Button Quail

Turnix sylvatica 13-14cm

Alternative names: Adalusian Hemipode, Button Quail, Kurrichane Bustard Quail, Little Button-Quail.
***T.s.lepurana* African Button-Quail.**

Description: Male. Forehead and crown black, mottled with russet; nape russet, feathers edged paler; mantle, rump and tail barred black and russet; feathers edged creamy; wings with coverts pale pinkish brown, spotted blackish brown, outer vane creamy white; chin and upper fore-throat white; lower throat and breast deep buff; iris cream; bill blue-grey; legs and feet pink. Female similar to male, but larger and brighter. Juvenile differs from adult in having spots over the breast and smaller spots on the wings. Chick is tawny coloured with two white strips down centre of back; lores and eyebrow whitish; underparts pale brownish white.

Males. *T.s.alleni* differs from *lepurana* in having the crown, mantle, rump and tail much darker; breast more russet.

T.s.lepurana differs from the nominate race in having feathers chestnut, barred blackish and edged greyish buff.

Voice: Described by Maclean, the female calls deep hooting *'hoom hoom hoom'* at about 2-second intervals; male calls like sparrowhawk.

Habitat: Grasslands, woodland and fallow lands. In North Africa principally Dwarf palm or Palmetto *Champerops humilis* scrub, or found among *Asphodels* sp. In southern Iberia also in low thickets and sugar-beet fields.

Distribution: Southern Iberia, Morocco, Algeria and Tunisia.

T.s.lepurana Senegal to Sudan, northern and north-western Namibia and Botswana (Nana River); in non-breeding season occurs in South Africa to Zimbabwe, Zambia and south-western and southern Angola.

T.s.alleni eastern Cape, North-West, Northern Province, Gauteng, Mpumalanga and KwaZulu-Natal, South Africa to Swaziland, Mozambique and Zimbabwe.

Feeding: Seeds of grasses and weeds, insects and their larvae including ants and other invertebrates.

Breeding: Nests on the ground in a shallow depression lined with seedheads and usually situated beneath a tuft of thick grass or other vegetation. Eggs smooth, glossy, pale cream, greyish white or pinkish buff, spotted at the thick end with greyish yellow and brown; clutch 2-4,7 on record; lays again if clutch destroyed before incubation starts which lasts for 13-15 days by the male only; fed first 4-6 days by male; fledging period 34-38 days; capable of flight at 10 days.

Aviculture: Selected Reference CLUTCH 2-7; INCUBATION PERIOD 12-15 days; FLEDGING PERIOD 34-38 days; first flight after 9 days. Nest Record Cards CLUTCH 5 (SAANRC) 7 (ARU); INCUBATION PERIOD 13 (SAANRC) 14 days (ARU); FLEDGING PERIOD 33 (SAANRC) about 30 days (ARU). Selected Reference WILDFOOD Seeds of (dried out, beaten off the stalk) Wolvoet panicum *Panicum lanipes*. Diet Record Cards Guinea grass *Panicum maximum* (ARU), Blackseed panicum *P.novemerve*, Berg grass *Setaria appendiculata* (SAADRC). Selected Reference ANIMAL FOOD mealworms, ants' eggs. Diet Record Cards termites, beetle larvae, including mealworms (SAADRC) (ARU), spiders, millipedes (ARU).

Hottentot Button Quail

Turnix hottentotta 13-14cm

Alternative names: Black-rumped Button Quail. *T.h.nana* Natal Button Quail.

Description: Male. Headtop blackish brown, edged white, mantle and scapulars broadly barred black and deep buff, feathers whitish edged; wing-coverts and secondaries sandy, barred with blackish brown and broadly tipped whitish; rump black; tail dark brown; sides of face; stripe over eye, chin and upper throat tawny; breast, sides of belly and flanks tawny, spotted with black; rest of underparts white; iris brown; bill pale greyish to horn; legs and feet pinkish white. Female similar to male, but larger and brighter. Juvenile spotted over the whole breast. Chick undescribed.

Males *T.h.nana* differs from the nominate race in being a brighter chestnut on the breast and throat; rump more blackish.

T.h.luciana differs from *nana* in having breast deeper and tawny.

Voice: Described by Maclean as having low-pitched hooting *'hoom hoom hoom'* (female).

Habitat: Open grasslands, moist fringes or marshes and fallow lands. In Zimbabwe on dark clay soil with 25-50 cm grass mixed with *Thesium brevibarbatum*.

Distribution: South-western and southern Cape Province, South Africa.

T.h.nana eastern Cape, eastern Mpumulanga and eastern Northern Province and KwaZulu-Natal, South Africa to Swaziland, southern Mozambique (Sul-do-Save).

T.h.luciana Zimbabwe, western Mozambique, Angola, Zaire, Kenya, Uganda and Sudan, then west to north of lower Guinea forest to Sierra Leone.

Feeding: Grass and weed seeds, insects and their larvae and other invertebrates.

Breeding: Solitary nester and possibly polyandrous. Nests on the ground under an overhanging tuft of grass in a scrape or natural hollow, which is lined with fine grass. Eggs yellowish grey, blotched with light and dark grey; clutch 2-6; incubation 12-14 days by male.

Aviculture: Selected Reference CLUTCH 3-5; INCU-BATION PERIOD 12-13 days; FLEDGING PERIOD 32-35 days; first flight after 12 days. Nest Record Cards CLUTCH 3 (ARU) 5 (SAANRC) 3 (NASNRC); INCU-BATION PERIOD 13 (ARU) 14 (SAANRC) 14 days (NASNRC); FLEDGING PERIOD 30 (ARU) 35 (SAANRC) about 33 days (NASNRC). Selected Reference WILDFOOD Seeds (dried out, beaten off the stalk). Rescue grass *Bromus unioloides*, Guinea grass *Panicum maximum*. Diet Record Cards Natal panic *Panicum natalense* (ARU) Hay *Chloris virgata* (NASDRC), Teff *Eragrostis tef*, Common thatchgrass *Hyparrhenia hirta* (SAADRC). Diet Record Cards ANIMAL FOOD termites (SAADRC) (NASDRC).

Quail Plover

Ortyxelos meiffrenii 15cm

Alternative names: Bush-lark Quail, Lark Quail.

Description: Male. Forehead, crown, nape, hindneck and streak behind eye rufous brown; streak above eye yellowish; ear-coverts pale rufous brown; mantle and back rufous brown feathers broadly fringed cream; rump and upper tail-coverts pale rufous; shoulder white; flight feathers black with broad white tips and tawny patch through middle of primaries; breast golden-buff; rest of underparts white, iris brown; bill yellowish; legs and feet pale flesh coloured. Female differs from the male in having the breast deeper rufous brown. Juvenile paler overall, more sandy less rufous; wings marking less regular.

Voice: Described by Urban *et al* as a very soft low whistle, uttered on the ground; silent when flushed.

Habitat: Dry sandy scrub, usually in association with a burr-bearing grass *Cenchrus catharticus*.

Distribution: Senegal to Mali, central Sudan and northern Kenya.

Feeding: Grass seeds, and insects, notably termites.

Breeding: Nest, a scrape in bare ground with sparse lining of available grass stalks and with a rim of small pebbles. Eggs stone or cream, spotted and blotched with black, brown and grey; clutch 2; incubation by male.

Aviculture: No records.

Pin-tailed Sandgrouse

Pterocles alchata caudacutus 31-39cm

Description: Male. Forehead and crown greenish yellow; face chestnut yellow, with black line through eye; throat chestnut-brown; mantle and back greenish yellow mottled with yellow; upper tail coverts barred black; tail boldly barred yellow and black; upper breast greenish ochre, lower deep rufous buff bordered above and below by narrow black bands; rest of underparts white; wings, primaries grey, secondaries greenish yellow and under wing-coverts white; iris brown; bill brown or grey; legs and feet dusky yellow. Female lacks black on throat, but has an additional collar in front of the other two. Juvenile resembles female, but lacking grey on upperparts; eyebrow, throat and underparts white. Chick has crown rufous with black edges to forehead feathers and whitish line down mid-crown; underparts creamy; iris brown; bill pale yellowish; legs and feet pale yellowish.

Voice: Described by Hollom *et al* as frequently uttering 'kar' or 'kar-tar' in flight.

Habitat: Stony waste with stones of various sizes and sparse vegetation. Often near areas of cereal cultivation.

Distribution: Morocco, Algeria, Tunisia and Libya. Egypt accidental.

Feeding: Seeds, grain, shoots, green leaves, and insects, mainly beetles. Seeds of Shepherd's purse *Capsella bursa-pastoris*, dandelion *Taraxacum* spp., Hops *Humulus lupulus*, sorrel *Rumex* spp., shoots of grasswort *Salicornia*, wormwood *Artemisia* sp., Camel thorn *Acacia* sp., *Arthraterum pungens*, leaves of Asphodel *Asphodelus fistulosus*, *A.alba*, flowers of *Mesembryanthemum nodiflorum*. Feeding data not restricted to Africa only.

Breeding: Nest, shallow depression on ground in open or at base of low scrub, 10-12cm in diameter, 1-4cm in depth. Unlined, but sometimes contains a few small stones. Eggs elliptical, smooth and glossy, shades of buff, variably spotted, blotched or speckled with brown and pale grey; clutch 2-3 usually 3; incubation period 19-25 days; both sexes incubate, female by day, male by night; cared for by both parents; fledging period 30 days.

Aviculture: Selected Reference CLUTCH 2-3; INCU-BATION PERIOD 21-23 days; FLEDGING PERIOD 25 days.

Namaqua Sandgrouse

Pterocles namaqua 25-27cm

Alternative name: Namaqua Partridge.

Description: Male. Forehead and crown yellowish olive, mottled with brown; nape and upper mantle brownish olive; lower mantle yellowish olive; rump and upper tail-coverts light brownish olive; tail wedge-shaped, olive-brown, broadly tipped with white; sides of face, chin and throat buff; breast band white; lower breast chestnut mottled with dark brown; wings with lesser median-coverts brownish olive; iris dark brown, orbital skin yellow; bill greyish horn; legs and feet greyish or buffish. Female has forehead, crown and nape tawny olive, streaked with black; sides of face yellowish olive; rest of underparts brown and buff, streaked and mottled with black. Juvenile similar to adult female, but more finely mottled and barred. Chick has crown and nape yellowish brown; rest of upperparts buff; underparts pale buff, breast darker.

Males. P.n.furvus differs from the nominate race in being darker overall and less buff over the throat and breast.

P.n.ngami differs from the nominate in having the crown and nape tinges greenish; upperparts paler, more sandy.

Voice: Described by Maclean as a nasal 3-note flight call 'ki-ki-keeu' or 'kelkiewyn' accented and higher-pitched on the last syllable.

Habitat: Semi-desert sparsely covered with shrubs and grasstufts.

Distribution: Western and northern Cape Province, South Africa, Namibia, south-western Angola and south-western Botswana.

F.n.furvus south-western Cape Province, Free State, Gauteng (highveld) and northern KwaZulu-Natal, South Africa, Lesotho (lowlands) and northern Namibia and Botswana in winter.

P.n.ngami northern Namibia and northern Botswana.

Feeding: Small hard seeds of desert grass and other plants.

Breeding: Nest a simple scrape in bare ground, lined with a little grass, situated among pebbles, side of sand clods or near a small shrub of grasstuft. Eggs greyish green, buffish green or pinkish grey, speckled and blotched with brown, reddish brown or slate-grey; single brooded; clutch 2-3; incubation period 21-23 days; incubation by male at night, female by day; fledging period about 28 days; young dependant on parents for 14-21 days after first flight.

Aviculture: Selected Reference CLUTCH 2-3; INCUBATION PERIOD 21-23 days; FLEDGING PERIOD about 28 days. Selected Reference WILDFOOD Shepherd's purse Capsella bursa-pastoris, clover Trifolium sp., Wolvoet panicum Panicum lanipes, Blackseed panicum P.novemnerve, Bulrush millet Pennisetum americanum, Napier (fodder) grass P.purpureum, Black-jack Bidens pilosa, Khaki weed Alternanthera pungens. Selected Reference ANIMAL FOOD termites.

Chestnut-bellied Sandgrouse

Pterocles exustus 31-33cm

Alternate names: Somaliland Pin-tailed Sandgrouse.
***P.e.polivascens* Kenya Pin-tailed Sandgrouse.**

Description: Male. Forehead, crown and nape brownish sandy to olive-grey; ear-coverts golden ochre; mantle and back olive-grey to brownish sandy; rump and upper tail-coverts olive-brown; chin, throat and breast bright ochre-yellow washed rusty; thin back line across breast; underparts chestnut merging to black in centre of belly; iris dark brown; bill pale bluish grey; legs and feet yellowish grey to bluish grey. Female has crown, forehead and nape sandy, heavily streaked with brown; ear-coverts yellow buff; rest of upper and underparts heavily streaked with brown. Juvenile similar to adult female but somewhat more heavily streaked.

Males. P.e.floweri differs from the nominate race in being darker and greyer.

P.e.ellioti differs from the nominate in having underparts more rufous.

P.e.olivascens differs from the nominate in having upperparts more olive-brown. Chick has patch round eye golden-buff, edged black; line down centre of back white; underparts creamy white with brownish patch on upper breast; iris reddish brown; bill bluish slate; legs and feet dusky pink.

Voice: Described by Hollom et al as a deep short 'whit-gerut' 'whit-gerut', 'ke-rep,'ke-rep,'ke-rup' with stress on the last syllable.

Habitat: Semi-desert with sparse vegetation.

Distribution: Senegal to Ethiopia.

P.e.floweri Egypt.

P.e.ellioti northern Ethiopia, south-eastern Sudan and Somalia.

P.e.olivascens south-eastern Ethiopia Kenya and Tanzania.

Feeding: Mainly seeds and plucks off parts of growing plants such as leaves of mustard and thistle. In Chad recorded taking ants. Seeds of Amogia *Tephrosia apollinea*, *Pseudanthispteria hispida*, *Eleusine aristata*, *Cyperus congolomeratus*, Umbrella thorn *Acacia tortillis*, Purse *Phaseolus radiatus*, *Panicum turgidum*, Indigo *Indigofera*, Peliotrope *Heliotropium strigosum*, *Tephrosia*, *Chrozophora*, *Trianthema*, *Alysicarpus*, *Amaranthus*, *Crotalaria*, *Cyamoposis psoralioides*, *Desmodium*, Kaffir cabbage *Gynandropsis gynandra*. Feeding data not restricted to Africa only.

Breeding: Nest, shallow unlined depression. Eggs elliptical, smooth and glossy, cream buff, greyish to light olive, heavily spotted and blotched with purplish grey and brown, incubation 20 days by both sexes, female during day, male at night; young cared for by both parents; first breeding at 1st year. Clutch 3, rarely 2.

Aviculture: No records.

Spotted Sandgrouse
Pterocles senegallus 30-35cm

Description: Male. Forehead and crown cinnamon-buff; stripe over and below eye, including nape, sides of neck and breast silver-grey; sides of face and chin orange-yellow; mantle and back sandy or pinkish buff; belly and rest of underparts buffy grey, centre of belly spotted with dark brown; iris brown; bill bluish grey; legs and feet pale grey. Female has forehead and crown, streaked and spotted with black; stripe over and below eye, including nape, sides of neck and breast golden-ochre, finely spotted with brown. Juvenile similar to adult female, but paler overall. Chick undescribed.

Voice: Described by Hollom *et al* as a bubbling guttural *'whit-oo'* or *'kwut-al'* also a single *'whilp'*.

Habitat: Sandy deserts with sparse vegetation.

Distribution: Mauritania, Mali, Morocco, Tunisia, Libya, Egypt, western Sudan to Somalia.

Feeding: Seeds and other plant material including grain. In Morocco ants recorded. Seeds of *Euphorbia guyoniana*, Amioga *Tephrosia apollinea*, Crucifer *Sisymbrium cinereum*, *Salicornia* sp. and *Asphodela tenuifolia*.

Breeding: Nest, shallow depression on ground in natural hollow such as animal foot print. Eggs elliptical, smooth and glossy, pale buff, sparingly spotted and scrawled with light brown and pale purplish grey; clutch 2-3, usually 3; incubation 29-31 days by both sexes, female during the day and male at night; young cared for by both parents.

Aviculture: Selected Reference CLUTCH 2.

Black-bellied Sandgrouse
Pterocles orientalis 33-35 cm

Description: Male. Forehead, crown, nape and hind-neck grey, tinged chestnut; mantle and back buff grey; sides of head paler grey; chin and sides of throat black; breast pink-buff followed by black line; upper belly cinnamon rufous; lower belly and rest of underparts black; iris brown; bill grey, tip darker; legs and feet greyish brown. Female has forehead, crown, nape and hind-neck cinnamon-buff, tinged blackish brown; chin and sides of throat cream; breast buff; lower belly and rest of underparts blackish. Juvenile similar to adult female but

less distinctly patterned. Chick upperparts ochre-buff, feathers tipped black; underparts pinkish buff, except throat and neck whitish; bill light grey; legs and feet buffy pink.

Voice: Described by Hollom *et al* as deep, purring *'currru'*, or *'Tschurr-rurr-rurr.'*

Habitat: Arid regions with sparse vegetation and on edges of cultivation.

Distribution: Morocco, Algeria, Tunisia and Libya; north-eastern Egypt winters.

Feeding: Mostly seeds, including melilot *Melilotus*, milk vetch *Astrangalus*, sainfoin *Onobrychis*, Indigo *Indigofera*, Linifolia, *l.cordifolia*, Purse *Phaseolus radiatus*, *P.acontifolius*, *Tephrosia purpurea*, *Cyamopsis psoraliodes*, panic *Panicum*, Heliotrope *Heliotropium strigosum*, Kaffir cabbage *Gynandropsis gynandra*, grasswort *Salicornia*, *Sisymbrium cinerium*, *Ammodendron*, *Polygonum*, shoots of wormwood *Artemisia*, Camel thorn *Alhagi camelorum* and thistle *Salsala*. Grain, including barley and wheat; berries, termites, beetles and their larvae. Feeding data not restricted to Africa only.

Breeding: Nest, shallow depression on ground in the open, unlined or a little dried grass and sometimes in a circle of stones. Eggs elliptical, smooth and glossy, greyish green or cream buff, heavily spotted and blotched with brown and grey; clutch 2-3, usually 3; incubation 21-22 days by both sexes, female by day, male at night; young cared for by both parents; age of first breeding 1 year.

Aviculture: Selected Reference: CLUTCH 2-3; INCUBATION PERIOD 23-28 days.

Crowned Sandgrouse
Pterocles coronatus 52-63 cm

Description: Male. Centre of forehead buff; sides of forehead, lores and chin black forming a mask around bill; sides of face white; cheeks and hindneck ochre-gold; mantle and back rufous buff; underparts sandy, washed grey on breast, rufous or pinkish on belly; wings with primaries dark grey-brown, greater coverts rufous buff with pale brown inner webs, median and lesser coverts rufous with pale buff wedge at tip, bordered dark grey; iris dark brown to black; bill pale bluish grey, tip grey; legs and feet greenish grey. Female has chin, throat and cheek-patch ochre-yellow; crown rufous buff, streaked with dark grey; rest of underparts pale buff to cream-white. Juvenile similar to adult female, but throat whitish; underparts rufous buff, streaked greyish brown. Chick has upperparts rufous buff; underparts whitish.

Voice: Described by Hollom *et al* as a gutteral chatting *'ch-chok-choker'* or *'chuk-a-chuck-a-chuck'*.

Habitat: Dry rocky deserts.

Distribution: Niger and Algeria to Egypt.

Feeding: Seeds and shoots of grasses. In Sudan favours Amioga *Tephrosia apollinea*. In North Africa seeds of *Asphedala tenuifolia*. Insects may be taken (confirmation required).

Breeding: Nest, shallow depression on ground in the open without lining and sometimes with ring of small stones around rim. Eggs elliptical, smooth, fairly glossy, cream, spotted and blotched pale brown and purplish grey; clutch 2-3, usually 3; females incubates by day, male by night; young cared for by both parents.

Aviculture: No records.

Yellow-Throated Sandgrouse

Pterocles gutturalis 29-31cm

Alternative names: Turf Quail, Yellow-throated Partridge.

P.g.saturatior **Kenya Yellow-throated Sandgrouse**

Description: Male. Forehead, crown and nape olive-buffy; mantle and back slate-grey; rump and upper tail-coverts greyish olive; wedge-shaped tail black, broadly tipped with buffy white; ear coverts cream-buff; throat band black; breast greyish lilac; rest of underparts chestnut, lightly barred with black; wings with lesser coverts greyish; primary-coverts blackish brown; iris brown, orbital skin grey; bill bluish grey; legs and feet pinkish brown. Female has forehead, crown and nape blackish brown; ear-coverts creamy buff; rest of underparts mottled blackish and buff; underparts chestnut, heavily barred with black. Juvenile similar to female, but with buff tips to flight feathers. Chick similar to that of Namaqua Sandgrouse but more reddish brown above.

P.g.saturatior differs from the nominate race in having the edges of wing-coverts more cinammon-brown.

Voice: Described by Newman as a harsh *'tweet'* or *'tweet-tweet'*.

Habitat: Short grasslands, newly burnt areas and poorly cultivated land.

Distribution: Northern Cape, North-West and Northern Province, South Africa, the Caprivi Strip, western Zimbabwe, eastern and northern Botswana, Zambia to southern Tanzania.

P.g.saturatior northern Ethiopia to northern Tanzania.

Feeding: Seeds of fallen grain. In Zambia, ramely oats, wheat, barley and sorghum. Seeds of *Achytranthes exaltata, Sesbania, Crotolaria, Cassia, Leersia hexandra*, Guineafowl grass *Rottboelia cochinchinensis* and *Bidens* sp. Crop contents of 2 specimens have the seeds of *Hibiscus trionum, Sesbania, Amaranthus* and *Sesamum*.

Breeding: Monogamous, solitary nester. The nest is a shallow scrape about 11cm across and less than 2,5cm deep in open ground among grasstufts. In the North-West Province, South Africa, nesting on old lands has at least one negative consequence as many fields are ploughed over in winter. Of thirteen nests found, six were ploughed over with two others being pillaged and one accidently trodden on by a researcher.

Eggs light brown, speckled and spotted with reddish brown and violet-slate; clutch 3, nest is usually covered by one of the pair from the laying of the first egg to prevent temperature fluctuations from the night chill and the sun; both incubating and complete clutch for 27 days, single brooded young can fly short distances at about 4 weeks and well at 6 weeks.

Aviculture: Selected Reference CLUTCH 2.

Variegated Sandgrouse

Pterocles burchelli 24-26cm

Alternative names: Burchell's Sandgrouse, Spotted Partridge, Spotted Sandgrouse.

Description: Male. Forehead, crown and nape olive-brown, streaked with black; mantle, back, rump and upper tail-coverts olive-brown, spotted with buff; tail rounded, slate, tipped with white; sides of face, chin and throat lilac-grey; breast and upper belly chestnut, spotted with white; lower belly and rest of underparts buff; wing lesser-coverts light olive-brown, primary coverts blackish brown; iris brown; bill blackish; legs and feet yellowish slate. Female has sides of face, chin and throat buff; breast and upper belly pinkish cinnamon, spotted with white. Juvenile similar to female, but with buff tips to the primaries. Chick similar to that of Namaqua Sandgrouse.

Male *P.b.makarikari* differs from the nominate race in being paler overall.

Voice: Described by Newman as '*chock-lit, choc-lit, choc-lit*' in flight.

Habitat: A species associated with Kalahari sand with grass standing 30-50cm high; also *acacia* veld.

Distribution: Northern Cape, North-West and western Free State, South Africa to southern Botswana.

P.b.makarikari Namibia, south-eastern Angola, northern Botswana and north-western Zimbabwe.

Feeding: Small dry seeds of grasses and shrubs. In the Kalahari mainly seeds of Sandaarbossie *Lophiocarpus burchelli*.

Breeding: Monogamous, solitary nester. The nest, which consists of no more than a shallow scrape, is excavated by the female using her feet as she pivots on her breast. The scrape is sparsely lined with grass or bits of dry vegetation beneath a shrub or grasstuft. Eggs creamy white or olive, spotted with underlying greyish mauve markings; single brooded; clutch 3.

Aviculture: Selected Reference CLUTCH 3.

Black-faced Sandgrouse

Pterocles decoratus 28cm

Alternative names: *P.d.ellenbecki* **Pale Black-faced Sandgrouse.**
P.d.loveridgei **Tanganyika Black-faced Sandgrouse.**

Description: Male. Forehead, chin and throat black; crown and nape khaki, streaked with black; white and black stripe over eye; ear-coverts yellowish buff; mantle khaki; back, rump and upper tail-coverts khaki, boldly barred brownish black; breast plain khaki, below with band black; breast white; belly and flanks black; iris brown; bill yellowish; legs and feet dull orange-yellow. Female similar to male, but lacks black and white facial adornment; breast buff. Juvenile similar to female, but black belly broken with white.

Males *P.d.ellenbecki* differs from the nominate race in being paler overall.

P.d.loveridgei differs from *ellenbecki* in being more greyish sandy, less rusty.

Habitat: Desert thorn scrub and dry bush country.

Voice: Described by Williams *et al* as a series of chuckling whistles of three notes '*chucker, chucker, chucker*'.

Distribution: South-eastern Kenya.

P.d.ellenbecki southern Somalia, southern Ethiopia, north-eastern Kenya and north-eastern Uganda.

P.d.loveridgei south-western Kenya and central Tanzania.

Feeding: Dry seeds, mainly of legumes. *Trianthema salsoloides, Indigofera* spp., and *Heliotropium undulatifolium*.

Breeding: Nest, shallow depression on ground and unlined. Eggs oval and glossy, buff, spotted or blotched with reddish brown with mauve-grey undermarkings.

Aviculture: No records.

Lichtenstein's Sandgrouse

Pterocles lichtensteinii 48-52cm

Alternative name: *P.l.sukensis* Suk Sandgrouse

Description: Male. Forehead and forecrown white; above and in front of eye black; hindneck, nape and sides of neck rufous buff streaked with black; mantle, back and rump rufous buff heavily barred with black; broad yellow-buff chest-band, with narrow black line across centre, and thick black line across lower; rest of underparts whitish barred black; under tail-coverts yellow-ochre; iris brown; bill yellow to orange; legs and feet chrome-yellow. Female lacks back facial adornment and breast lines; forehead and forecrown yellow-buff. Juvenile similar to adult female, but upperparts more closely barred.

Males. *P.l.targius* differs from the nominate race in being paler overall, and more barring on underparts.

P.l.sukensis differs from the nominate in being darker overall. Chick has upperparts pale brown with ear-coverts and under eye light chocolate brown.

Voice: Described by Sellar as a suckling, whistling '*qu wheeto*' give on the ground and in flight.

Habitat: Wadi beds, wooded rocky slopes, thornbush notably *acacia*.

Distribution: Ethiopia, northern Sudan and Egypt.

P.l.targius southern Algeria and Niger.

P.l.sukensis Kenya.

Feeding: Seeds, including White-gall acacia *Acacia sayal, Asphodel tenuifolius*, Kandi *Prosopis spicigera, Cassia* spp. and *Salsola* sp, livefood in the form of beetles, ants and ant-lions.

Breeding: Nest, shallow depression on the ground in the open or in shelter of a low shrub. Eggs elliptical, smooth and glossy, pinkish to buff, blotched, spotted or sparsely marked with reddish brown or purplish grey.

Aviculture: No records.

Double-banded Sandgrouse

Pterocles bicinctus 24-25cm

Alternative name: Double-banded Partridge.

Description: Male. Base of bill and forecrown white; nape olive, streaked black; mantle and back olive-buff; rump and upper tail-coverts buff, barred with brown; tail buff, banded with blackish brown; sides of face, chin and throat olive; breast band black; belly and rest of underparts barred black and whitish; lesser and median wing-coverts olive; under wing-coverts greyish brown; iris dark brown, orbital skin yellow; bill yellow to reddish; legs and feet yellowish brown. Female has forehead, crown and nape cinnamon-buff, streaked black; sides of face creamy buff; rest of upperparts including wing-coverts and innermost secondaries mottled and barred with black. Juvenile similar to adult female, but upperparts more pinkish fawn. Chick. Similar to that of Namaqua Sandgrouse, but somewhat darker brown; bill black, tip greyish black.

Males. *P.b.ansorgei* differs from the nominate in being paler overall.

P.b.chobiensis differs from the nominate race in having the nape and upperparts less rufous and with more conspicuous white spotting.

P.b.multicolor differs from the nominate in being brighter overall; upperparts barred with chestnut and black.

P.b.usheri differs from *multicolor* in size only, being smaller.

Voice: Described by Newman as 'chuck-chuck', coming to drink 'Don't weep so Charlie'.

Habitat: Acacia-veld, stony patches, grassy plains and along desert edge.

Distribution: Central and northern Namibia. *P.b.ansorgei* southern Angola.

P.b.chobiensis northern Namibia, the Capriv. Strip, northern and north-eastern Botswana, western Zimbabwe, southern Angola and south-western Zambia.

P.b.multicolor north-eastern Cape, North-West, Northern Province and Mpumalanga, South Africa to Mozambique and south-eastern Botswana.

P.b.usheri north-western Mozambique, northern Zimbabwe, southern Malawi and eastern Zambia.

Feeding: Small dry seeds of grasses and shrubs. Seeds of Black-jack *Bidens bidentata*.

Breeding: A shallow scrape, which may be lined with pebbles or bits of plant material, is placed beneath a small bush or grass tuft, with one being recorded beneath some strands of rusty barbed wire. Eggs pinkish buff, spotted with purplish slate to reddish brown; clutch 2-3; female incubates at night, male by day; young are able to run about as soon as they have dried out, and are tended by both parents.

Aviculture: Selected Reference CLUTCH 2-4; INCUBATION PERIOD 23-24 days; FLEDGING PERIOD 33 days.

Four-banded Sandgrouse

Pterocles quadricinctus 28cm

Alternative name: *P.q.lowei* Lowe's Four-banded Sandgrouse.

Description: Male. Forehead black and white; nape chestnut streaked black; sides of face and nape sandy buff with olive wash; mantle and black yellow-buff broadly marked with chestnut and black; rump and tail barred black; chin whitish; upper breast chestnut, middle breast white, lower breast black; belly and underparts barred black and white; iris brown; bill yellowish, tip black; legs and feet yellowish olive. Female lacks black and white facial adornment; hindneck barred, with chestnut. Juvenile similar to adult female, but black barring finer. Chick has crown brown; rest of upperparts chestnut-brown except chin whitish; underparts buffy.

Male *P.q.lowei* differs from the nominate race in being darker overall.

Voice: Described by Serle *et al* as a shrill piping note uttered at dusk when flighting out to watering places.

Habitat: Sandy or stony ground, in short grass plains and cultivated areas.

Distribution: Senegal, Mauritania, Ivory Coast, Ghana, northern Nigeria and Central African Republic *P.q.lowei* Chad to Sudan, Uganda and north-western Kenya.

Feeding: Seeds.

Breeding: Nest, slight depression on ground at base of shrub or bush, often laid among fallen leaves of *Bauhinia* sp. Eggs blunt and oval, salmon-buff, spotted with orange-brown and underlying mauve; clutch 2-3, usually 3.

Aviculture: No records.

Rock Dove

Columba livia 31-34cm

Alternative name: *C.I.'domestica'* **Feral Pigeon, Feral Rock Dove.**

Description: Sexes similar. Entire head, nape and upper mantle dark blue-grey; sides of neck blue-grey, slightly glossed green of purple; lower mantle and upper back pale grey; wing-coverts ash grey, greater coverts with broad subterminal black bar forming, with secondaries, two black bars across wing; lower back and rump white; lower rump and upper tail-coverts dark bluish grey; tail slate-grey, feathers tipped black; throat dark blue-grey, strongly glossed green or deep purple; breast and belly bluish grey; under tail-coverts dark bluish grey; iris orange; red or golden-orange; skin round eye bluish grey; pink *'domestica'*; bill black or greyish black; legs and feet dark pink to reddish purple. Juvenile paler than adult with wing bars less conspicuous, feathers with little or no iridescence.

Adults *C.I.gymnocyclus* differs from the nominate in having head, mantle and back slate-grey; neck iridescence more green, less violet; bare skin around eye red.

C.I.targia differs from *gymnocyclus* in having upperparts blue-grey

C.I.daklae differs from the nominate in being paler overall; rump pure white; lower breast and belly greyish white.

C.I.schimperi differs only from *gaddi* in being smaller.

C.I.gaddi differs from nominate in having mantle, back and rump pale grey; upper tail-coverts mid grey; legs and feet partly feathered.

C.I.canariensis differs from the nominate in having rump grey.

C.I.'domestica' main morphs are blue-grey, pale cinammon and blackish.

Voice: Described by Goodwin, the advertising *'coo'* is a moaning *'oorh'* or *'oh-oo-oor'* subject to some variation.

Habitat: Arid or semi-arid and nearly treeless country.

Distribution: Morocco to Maghreb in northern Libya and north-western Egypt.

C.I.gymnocyclus Senegal, Mali, Ghana and Nigeria.

C.I.targia Ahaggar in Algeria, Tibesti and Ennedi in Chad to central Sudan.

C.I.daklae Dakla and Kharga Oasis in Libya south to central Egypt.

C.I.schimperi Nile delta south to northern Sudan.

C.I.canariensis Essaouira Island.

C.I.gaddi North-western Egypt.

C.I.'domestica' not mapped.

Feeding: Seeds of cereal, legumes, weeds, green leaves, fruits, flowers and invertebrates. Feral birds also take variety of artificial foods including cereals. Seeds of Mustard tree *Salvadora persica, Schowia purpurea, Colocynthis* spp. Desert melon *Coloquintus vulgaris* and broken or rotten oak *Quercus* sp., legumes of *Pisum, Vicia, Phaseolus* and *Melilotus*, seeds of weeds such as crucifers *Raphansus, Capsella, Sinapsis, Brassica*, docks *Rumex* spp., fumitory *Fumaria*, goosefoots *Chenopodium, Atriplex*, knotgrass *Polygonum*, buttercup *Ranunculus* and chickweed *Stellaria*, pieces of potato, seaweed, fruit and seeds of plane *Platanus*, privet *Ligustrum*, nightshade *Solanum, Prunus*, ivy *Hedera, Vibrunum*; and poison ivy *Rhus*, green leaves of tulip *Tulipa*, primrose *Prumula* and sea-stock *Matthiola*, flowers of *Ulmus* and sycamore *Acer*, feral birds take seeds of clover *Trifolium*, crucifers *Erysium, Sisymbrium, Barbarea*, corn surrey *Spergula*, hempnettle *Galeopsis* and garlic *Allium*, livefood such as cocoons of earthworms, moth larvae, slugs *Agriolimax, Arion*, and small snails *Helix, Helicella, Bulimus* and *Trichia*. Domestic scraps namely meat, fat, bread, biscuits, apple peel, fish, cheese and chocolate. Feeding data not restricted to Africa only.

Breeding: Nest a loosely constructed cup of roots, stems and leaves. Also may contain seaweed, small pieces of driftwood and feathers. No true lining. Built by both sexes. Placed on base rock or artificial ledge, or hole inside a cave. Eggs sub-elliptical, smooth and slightly glossy white; clutch 1-3, usually 2; incubation period 16-19 days; by both sexes; nestling period 23-25 days.

Aviculture: Selected Reference CLUTCH 2; INCUBATION PERIOD 14-19 days; NESTLING PERIOD 20-37 days. Personal cmmunication CLUTCH 2,2; INCUBATION period 16,19 days, NESTLING PERIOD 27,30 days. Selected Reference WILDFOOD Comfrey *Symphytum officinale*, vetch *Rumex* sp., clover *Trifolium* sp. Personal Commincation Guinea corn *Sorghum caffrorum*.

Speckled Pigeon

Columba guinea 32-33cm

Alternative names: African Rock Pigeon, Guinea Pigeon, Hackled Pigeon, Red-eyed Pigeon, Rock Pigeon, Triangular Spotted Pigeon, Triangular Spotted Dove, Bush Dove, Rock Dove.
C.g.phaeonota & bradfieldi; **Cape Rock Pigeon, Roussard Pigeon.**

Description: Sexes similar but males more powerfully built; entire head slate-grey except eye surrounded by large area of bare red skin; wide collar of chocolate-brown encircles the neck; mantle and wing chocolate-brown with the coverts having many small white triangular white spots; back, rump and upper tail-coverts slate-grey; underparts grey; iris yellow; outer ring orange to purple; bill black, cere whitish; legs and feet red. Juvenile paler than adult, but wing-spots less pronounced; iris cream, outer ring ashy; legs and feet grey. Adults. *C.g.phaeonota* differs from the nominate race in having crown slate-grey; mantle and wings chocolate-brown; rump dark grey.

C.g.bradfieldi paler overall from *phaeonota*, less tawny.

Voice: Described by Maclean as about 10-20 deep mellow *'coos,doo,doo,doo'* increasing in volume, then falling away.

Habitat: Mountain kranzes, sea cliffs, tall buildings, bridges and mine shafts as well as off-shore islands.

Distribution: Senegal to Ethiopia and Tanzania.

C.g.phaeonota south-eastern Botswana, Zimbabwe, Swaziland, Lesotho and South Africa in North-West, Gauteng, Mpumalanga and Northern Province, Cape, Free State and KwaZulu-Natal.

C.l.bradfieldi. Namibia, western Botswana, western Zimbabwe and north-western Cape Province in South Africa.

Feeding: Seeds, including cultivated grains. Seeds of *Amaranthus* spp., (mostly herbaceous annuals with coloured leaves); Wild buckwheat *Fadopyrum esculentum*, panic *Panicum* spp. Fruit of Devilthorn *Tribulus terrestris*. Cultivated crops in the form of Maize *Zea*, wheat *Triticum*, sorghum *Sorghum* groundnuts (in pods) *Arachis hypogoea*, lentils *Lens*, barley *Hordeum*. Observed perched on sunflower *Helianthus* heads, showing a preference for black seeds rather than striped seeds varieties. Attracted to salt lick. Snails recorded in Ethiopia.

Breeding: The nest may vary from being fairly substantial to a few scattered sticks and may be found on building ledges, in roof-gutterings and beside chimneys; also in barns, windmills, water tanks, bridge supports, recesses in cliffs, caves, dongas, crown of wild date palm *Phoenix* sp., nest boxes, stables, boat shelters and on the ground amongst rocks or in niches of walls on off-shore islands; also below ground level in mine shafts. Known to utilise the nests of crown and egret. The same nest site may be used for periods of two to four years. Laying on bare earth or rock is also recorded. Building materials are variable and include sticks, rootlets, weeds and grasses. One nest in South Africa found contained one 16 bore shotgun shell (unused), 37g; 1 cigarette lighter, 11g; 1 steel nail; 26 pieces of wire, average length 10cm (6-23); 1 large black fruit; 42 twigs, average length 11cm (5-28); total weight nest 148g. A second nest examined consisted of 345 sticks and 97 pieces of grass; total weight of nest 72g. Nest sites include trees (Blue gums *Eucalyptus* sp.). Eggs white; clutch 2; incubation 15-17 days, by both sexes; nestling period 25-27 days; fed by both parents; double-brooded; previous young still being fed while incubating second clutch.

Aviculture: Selected Reference CLUTCH 2; INCUBATION PERIOD 15-17 days; NESTLING PERIOD 23-26 days. Nest Record Cards CLUTCH 2 (ARU) 2,2 (SAANRC) 2 (NASNRC) 2,2 (ANRC); INCUBATION PERIOD 15 (ARU) 14,16 (SAANRC) 14 days (ANRC); NESTLING PERIOD 15 (ARU) 22,24 (SAANRC) 24 days (ANRC). Selected Reference WILDFOOD Comfrey *Symphytum officinale*, vetch *Rumex* sp., clover *Trifolium* sp., Cockscomb *Amaranthus hybridus*. Diet Record Cards Red pigweed *A.thunbergii*, (SAADRC), Bulrush millet *Pennisentum americanum* (ARU, NASDRC), Johnson grass *Sorghum halepense* (ADRC).

White-collared Pigeon
Columba albitorques 36cm
Alternative name: Abyssinian Rock Pigeon.

Description: Male. Forehead, crown and sides of head dark grey; collar across nape white; sides of neck pale greenish iridecscence, tipped silvery; mantle greyish brown; back and rump bluish grey; upper tail-coverts greyish black; tail blackish with subterminal slate-grey band; chin dark grey; breast, belly and rest of underparts slate-grey; iris dark brown; bill black, cere white; legs and feet red. Female similar to male but collar narrower. Juvenile has forehead and crown feathers, edged buff; sides of neck lacks iridescence.

Voice: Described by Pitwell as having an advertising call as "a long soft drawn-out cooing *'coo-oo'*."

Habitat: Rocky mountain areas and old cultivation.

Distribution: Central and eastern Ethiopia.

Feeding: Grain, notably wheat and barley.

Breeding: Nests in rocks, caves, cliffs, ledges and attics of buildings. Eggs slightly glossed, creamy white; clutch 2.

Aviculture: Selected Reference CLUTCH 2; INCUBATION PERIOD 16 DAYS; NESTLING PERIOD 27-31 days. Nest Record Cards CLUTCH 2 (ARU); INCUBATION PERIOD 17 days (ARU); NESTLING PERIOD 28 days. Diet Record Cards WILDFOOD Guinea corn *Sorghum caffrorum* (ARU).

Stock Dove
Columba oenas 32-34cm
Alternative name: Rock Dove.

Description: Sexes similar. Forehead, crown, nape and sides of head bluish grey; sides of neck bluish grey; glossed green and purple; mantle dark bluish grey; black and rump light bluish grey; tail dark greyish blue, tipped black; chin and throat bluish grey; breast and upper belly greyish blue, glossed green and purple; rest of underparts light bluish grey; wing-coverts dark bluish grey; iris dark brown to dark red-brown; bare skin round eye blue-grey; cere bright red or purplish red; bill yellowish horn; legs and feet pinkish mauve. Juvenile similar to adult, but paler; wing bar less conspicuous, feathers with little or no iridescence.

Voice: Described by Wilson as '*ooo-uh*' or '*ooo-er*' given 10 times in an accelerating sequence.

Habitat: Oak, pine and cedar forests at altitudes between 1000-2300m.

Distribution: Northern Algeria and northern Egypt, Tunisia accidental.

Feeding: Seeds, grain, green leaves, buds and flowers. Seeds of goosefoots *Chenopodium, Atriplex,* turnip *Brassica,* charlock and mustard *Sinapis,* corn surrey *Spergula,* campion *Silene,* spurge *Euphorbia,* knotgrass *Polygonum,* buttercup *Ranunculus,* bedstraw *Galium,* pansy *Viola,* milkwort *Polygala,* cowherb *Vaccaria,* dock *Rumex,* Scarlet pimpernel *Anagallis,* fluellen *Kickxia,* speedwell *Veronica,* Field madder *Sheradia arvensis, Helianthus, Centaurea,* sedge *Carex* and *Schoenoplectus,* fumitory *Fumaria,* acorns *Quercus,* beech-mast *Fagus,* pine *Pinus,* hornbeam *Carpinus,* currants and gooseberries *Ribes,* bilberries *Vaccinium,* leaves of swede, kale, cabbage, brussels sprouts, turnips *Brassica,* clover *Trifolium,* dandelion *Taraxacum,* grain namely, wheat *Triticum,* barley *Hordeum,* oats *Avena,* rye *Secale,* maize *Zea,* millet *Panicum* and buckwheat *Fagopyrum* livefood in the form of snails (*Pulilla, Succinea, Vallonia, Limax, Monacha, Cochlicopa, Fruiticicola, Hyalina*), aquatic molluscs *Valvata, Planorbis sphaerium,* slugs, cocoons of earthworms, centipedes, larvae of gall-midges, weevils and potato beetles. Feeding data not restricted to Africa only.

Breeding: Nests in old tree holes, buildings or cliffs and even under a bush. Also recorded using rabbit burrow and drey of squirrel. In sub-desert in the branches of pistachio trees. Both sexes construct a platform of small twigs with sometimes adding grass and leaves. Eggs elliptical, smooth and glossy, white; clutch 2, occasionally 1; incubation 16-18 days by both sexes; nestlings cared for and fed by both parents; nestling period 20-30 days; age of first breeding 1 year.

Aviculture: Personal Communication CLUTCH 2; INCUBATION PERIOD 16 days; NESTLING PERIOD 25 days. Personal Communication WILDFOOD Guinea corn *Sorghum caffrorum.*

Somali Stock Dove
Columba oliviae 26cm

Alternative names: Somaliland Pigeon, Somali Rock Pigeon.

Description: Sexes similar. Forehead, crown, nape and upper hindneck pale purplish; sides of neck and face, lower hindneck and upper mantle dark pink, tinged green; lower mantle and wing-coverts isabelline; back and rump pale bluish grey; upper tail-coverts dark bluish grey; tail greyish blue, tipped blackish; chin, throat, breast, belly and rest of underparts pale grey; iris yellowish; bill black, cere white; purple-red naked area round eye; legs and feet pink. Juvenile undescribed.

Voice: Described by North as displaying coos as '*wuk-wuk-wuk-oh, wuk-ow*', the 'wuks' being short 'coos' and the 'oh' and 'ow' deep growls.

Habitat: Barren sandstone hills and escarpments in the maritime desert or desert regions at altitudes up to 800m.

Distribution: North and north-eastern Somalia.

Feeding: Seeds, grains and berries.

Breeding: Nest in a recess in the roof of caves on hillsides, site almost dark. Clutch 1.

Aviculture: No records.

Wood Pigeon
Columba palumbus excelsa 40-42cm

Description: Sexes similar. Entire head and nape bluish grey, slightly glossed green or purple on latter; sides of neck strongly glossed green with conspicuous white patch; mantle grey-brown, back, rump and upper tail-coverts greyish blue; tail dark grey, broad band black; primaries dark brown, outer webs broadly edged white, secondaries brown, washed grey; sides of breast brownish purple; belly and under tail-coverts pale grey; iris yellowish white; bill yellow, tip horn; legs and feet mauve-pink. Juvenile similar to adult, but paler overall; lacks iridescence patch on sides of neck.

Voice: Described by Goodwin as a deep intense sounding '*coo-coo,cu-cu,coo*' or '*coo,cu-cu-cu-cu-coo*'.

Habitat: Deciduous oak, pine, cedar and thuja forests, groves of olives and Argan *Argania sideroxylon* and Thuja *Terraculinus articulata.* In Tunisia Aleppo pines.

Distribution: Northern Morocco, northern Algeria and northern Tunisia. Accidental Mauritania.

Feeding: Seeds, leaves, flowers, root crops, berries and occasionally invertebrates. Fruits and seeds of oak *Quercus,* beech *Fagus,* elder *Sambucus,* hawthorn *Crataegus,* hazel *Corylus,* ivy *Hedera, Viburnum,* pivet *Lingustrum,* holly *Ilex,* black thorn, apple *Malus,* buckthorn *Rhamnus,* dogwood *Cornus,* spindle *Euonymus,* yew *Taxus,* pine *Pinus,* maple *Acer,* rose *Rosa,* crowberry *Ribes,* mulberry *Morus,* mistletow *Viscum,* rape, linseed *Linum,* blackberry and raspberry *Rubus,* vetch *Vicia,* knotgrass *Polygonum,* pansy *Viola,* fat-hen *Chenopodium,* wild strawberry *Fragaria,* buckwheat, roots, rhizomes or bulbs of potato *Solanum,* sugarbeet, turnip, silverweed *Potentilla*, *Oxalis*, figwort *Scxophularia*, wood anemone *Anemone*, pignut *Colopodium*. Flowers and buds of ash, beech, cherry, plum, elder, elm *Ulmus*, plane *Platanus*, hawthorn, hazel, oak, walnut *Juglans*, willows *Salix*, also pines; also galls, fungus and moss. Leaves of clover *Trifolium*, rape, cabbage, brussels sprouts, turnip, kale, cauliflower, lettuce, ash *Fraxinus*, ivy *Hedera*, peas, sugarbeet, lucerne and medick *Medicago*, mustard *Sinapsis*, surry *Spergula*, raddish, buttercup and *Ranunculus*, chickweeds *Stellaria*, mouse-ears *Cerastium* sainfoin *Onobrychis*, speedwell *Veronica*, plantain *Plantago*, dandelion *Taraxacum*, nettle *Urtica*, mallow *Malva*, grain in the form of wheat *Triticum*, barley *Hordeum*, oats *Avena*, maize *Zea*, rye *Secale*. Livefood in the form of earthworms and their cocoons, gall wasps, beetles, larvae and pupae of butterflies, scale insects, feather lice, spiders, slugs and snails. Also pecks at salt licks for cattle. Feeding not restricted to Africa only.

Breeding: In the fork of branch, in thickets, creepers, under bush on ground and on ledge of building. A flimsy platform of twigs, measuring 17-23cm across, lined with finer twigs and may or may not include leaves and grasses. Nests usually take between 8-12 days to construct, male carrying, female arranging materials which may number up to 99 twigs in upperparts and 112 twigs forming lower part. Eggs sub-elliptical, smooth and glossy, white; clutch 1-2 rarely 3-4; incubation 17 days, by both sexes; cared for and fed by both parents; nestling period 33-34 days; age of first breeding 1 year.

Aviculture: Selected Reference CLUTCH 2; INCUBATION PERIOD 15-17 days; NESTLING PERIOD 20-34 days. Nest Record Cards CLUTCH 2,2 (ANRC); INCUBATION PERIOD 16-17 days (ANRC); NESTLING PERIOD about 31,33 days (ANRC). Personal Communication WILDFOOD vetch *Rumex* sp., clover *Trifolium* sp., chickweed *Stellaria* sp. Diet Record Card FRUIT mulberry *Morus* sp. (ADRC).

African Wood Pigeon

Columba unicincta 36cm

Alternative names: Afep Pigeon, Congo Wood Pigeon, Grey Pigeon, Grey Wood Pigeon, Scaly Grey Pigeon.

Description: Male. Forehead, crown nape, sides of face and neck pale grey; mantle grey; back, rump and upper tail-coverts slate-grey, edged pale grey, producing a scale-like effect; tail grey, tipped blackish; wing-coverts slate, feathers edged pale grey; chin and upper throat white; lower throat and breast vinous pink; belly, flanks and under tail-coverts whitish; bill slate-grey; iris orange-red, legs and feet bluish grey.

Voice: Described by Chapin, advertising 'coo' "as a series of 7-12 'coo's' delivered rather slowly".

Habitat: Moist evergreen and riparian forests.

Distribution: Liberia to Zaire and Uganda.

Feeding: Seeds and fruits. Fruit of *Solanum torvum*, *Sapioum mannianum*. Termites recorded in Zaire.

Breeding: A stick nest in forest tree, usually at some height from the ground. Eggs white; clutch 1.

Aviculture: Personal Communication CLUTCH 11; INCUBATION PERIOD 16,17,19 days: NESTLING PERIOD 30, about 29-32 days. Personal Communication FRUIT Marula *sclerocaryo birrea*. Personal Communication ANIMAL FOOD termite alates.

Rameron Pigeon

Columba arquatrix 38-40cm

Alternative names: Forest Pigeon, Olive Pigeon, Speckled Wood Pigeon, Yellow-eyed Pigeon.

Description: Sexes similar. General colour purple and grey. Crown and nape silvery grey; forehead, ear-coverts and chin mauve; breast and belly dark vinous mauve, the former profusely spotted with white. mantle blackish mauve; tail black; under tail-coverts dark grey; wing-coverts purple; iris pale yellow to light brown; bare skin around eye; bill, legs and feet. Juvenile browner and less greenish; feathers of belly edged with greyish white.

Voice: Described by Goodwin as a very deep, muffled, throbbing 'coo-coo, croo-croo, croo-croo, croo-croo...' first two notes loudest the other more throbbing and 'dying away'.

Habitat: Highland forests and less often exotic wattle and conifer plantations.

Distribution: Ethiopia, eastern Kenya, eastern Zimbabwe, Mozambique, Swaziland and the South

African provinces of Mpumalanga south-western Cape to KwaZulu-Natal; also Zaire and Angola.

Feeding: Seeds, fruits and berries. Seeds or fruit of Wild olive *Olea africana*, Forest olive, *O.woodiana*, Ironwood, *capensis*, Hard pear *Olinia ventosa*, Mountain olina *O.emarginata*, Cape plane *Ochna arborea*, Large-flowered ochna *O.tropurprea*, Outeniqua yellowood *Podocarpus falcatus*, Wild peach *Kiggelaria africana*, Red saffronwood *Casine crocea*, Bastard saffronwood *C.peragua*, Cape beech *Rapanae melanophloeos*, White milkwood *Sideroxylon inerme*, Thorny bone-apple *Xeromphis obovata*, Pigeonwood *Trema orientalis*, Large-leaved guarii *Euclea natalensis*, Red pear *Scolopia mundii*, White ironwood *Veprus undulata*, Cape chestnut *Colodendrum capense*, Rare forest fig *Ficus craterostoma*, Bugwood *Solanum mauritanum*, Poison-peach *Diospyros dichrophylla*, Blue guarri *Euclea crispa*, Comman *Dovyalis rhamnoides*, Thorn pear *Scolopia zeyheri*, Cape ash *Ekebergia capensis*, African holly Ibex mites, Dune taaibos Rhus laevigata, African mulberry *Morus mesoxygia*, White stinkwood *Celtis africana*, Red stinkwood *Prunis africanus*, Inkberry *Phytolocca dodecandra*, Stinkwood *Ocotea bullata*, seeds of Croton *macrostachys* (E.afr. no known common name), Fine-leaved ironwood *Chionanthus foveolata*, Pokeweed *Phytolacca dodecandra*, Cape Chestnut *Calendendrum capense*, Stone Pine *Pinus pinea*, Black Wattle *Acacia mearnsii*, Rooikrans *cyclops* and *Candelabra* tree *Euphorbia ingens*, cultivated cereals usually comprising of maize *Zea* and sorghum *Sorghum* as observed at a feeding tray; at times may take the larvae of caterpillars as recorded in Malawi; attracted to cattle salt lick.

Breeding: The nest is usually a platform of twigs taken from trees, rarely from the ground with one observation of dry heather twigs and three green leaves as lining being used. Situated low down at 1m, situated at the foot of a large waterfall, and 1,5m in shrubby evergreens to 14m above ground in the fork of a forest tree and among creepers. Both sexes take part in nest construction, male carrying, female building. Two nests measured 13 and 19cm across, but up to 30cm may occur. Eggs creamy white, slightly glossed, and rather cylindrical; clutch 1, rarely 2; incubation period 16-17 days, by both sexes; nestling period 19-23 days.

Aviculture: Selected Reference CLUTCH 1-2; INCUBATION PERIOD 16-20 days; NESTLING PERIOD 19-20 days. Nest Record Cards CLUTCH 1,1 (ARU) 1 (ANRC) 2 (NASNRC). Selected Reference FRUIT Black nightshade *Solanum nigrum*, Bugweed *S.mauritianum*, Inkberry tree *Phytolacca dodecandra*, Cape beech *Rapenae melonophloeos*, Cape gooseberry *Physalis edulis*, Appleberry *Billardiera longiflora* (ARU), Bush cherry *Syzgium paniculatum*, Common wild fig *Ficus natalensis*, Strawberry-guava *Psidium littorale*, Cape ash *Ekebergia capensis* (ADRC).

Cameroon Olive Pigeon

Columba sjostedi 40cm

Alternative names: Cameroon Mountain Olive Pigeon, Cameroon Rameron Pigeon, Mountain Olive Pigeon, Sjostedt's Pigeon.

Description: Sexes similar. Entire head dark bluish grey; mantle, back, rump, upper tail-coverts and wings rich dark maroon with some white spots on latter; tail slaty black; breast, belly and rest of underparts mauve profusely spotted white; iris yellow; bill yellowish, base red; legs and feet purple. Juvenile has upperparts dark earth brown; underparts warm rufescent brown.

Voice: Described by Eisentraut as a deep 'uur' irregularly repeated.

Habitat: Highland forests up to 2 500m in West Africa.

Distribution: South-eastern Nigeria and Cameroon.

Feeding: Fruit, especially *Podocarpus Ficus* and berries.

Breeding: A scanty platform of sticks in trees and creepers. One nest was almost flat on top, and had a diameter of 18cm and depth of 5cm, placed in a horizontal fork, 8m above the ground near the upper branch of a forest tree. Eggs glossy, white; clutch 1.

Aviculture: Selected Reference CLUTCH 1,1. Personal Communication CLUTCH 2; INCUBATION PERIOD 16 days; NESTLING PERIOD 19 days. Selected Reference FRUIT Kaffir apple *Harpephyllum caffrum*, mulberry *Morus* sp., Common wild fig *Ficus burkei*.

São Thomé Olive Pigeon

Columba thomensis - cm

Alternative names: Maroon Pigeon, São Thomé Maroon Pigeon, São Thomé Pigeon.

Description: Male. Entire head, nape, chin and throat slate-grey; mantle maroon; back and rump blackish slate; upper tail-coverts and tail brown; white spots on wing-coverts; breast and belly maroon; under tail-coverts slate-grey; iris brown; bill yellowish; legs and feet red. Female similar to male but paler overall. Juvenile similar to adult, but maroon replaced by dark brown; lacks white spots on wing-coverts.

Voice: Described by Snow as a short rolling 'crrrr'.

Habitat: Primary forests.

Distribution: São Thomé Island.

Feeding: Fruit. Montane tree *Scheffleria mannii* recorded in 3 crops.

Breeding: Not known.

Aviculture: No records.

White-naped Pigeon

Columba albinucha 36cm

Description: Male. Forehead maroon; hind crown and nape white; upper mantle purple, fringed pale grey; lower mantle purple; back, rump and upper tail-coverts slate-grey; tail slate-grey; tip paler; sides of face, chin and throat ash-grey; breast and belly dark purple, spotted white; iris yellow; bill, legs and feet brownish red. Female has upper mantle greyish purple; breast vinous grey. Juvenile has upperparts earth-brown; upper-tail coverts blue-grey; tail grey.

Voice: Described by Goodwin, advertising coo as a deep, rather quavering deliberate '*tuu-uu*' followed by 3 to 4 '*tuu-tu tu tu*'.

Habitat: Dense lowland forests.

Distribution: Eastern Zaire and western Uganda.

Breeding: Not known.

Aviculture: No records.

Delegorgue's Pigeon

Columba delegorguei 28-33 cm

Alternative names: Bronze-naped Pigeon, Crimson-winged Pigeon, Eastern Bronze-naped Pigeon, C.d.sharpi Elgon Bronze-naped Pigeon.

Description: Male. Entire head slate-grey; sides of neck iridescent pink and green, a broad opaque white collar on upper back; lower back, mantle and wing-coverts black, washed maroon; rump dark bluish grey; tail black; tipped dark grey; chin grey; breast dark greyish pink or purple; belly reddish brown; rest of underparts dark greyish, tinged pink; iris dark brown; bill slate-grey; legs and feet purplish pink. Female paler overall; lacks white collar. Juvenile. Upperparts dark greyish brown; underparts dark rufous; lacks white collar.

Male. *c.d.sharpi* differs from the nominate race in lacking purple tinge on lower mantle; belly and flanks slate-grey.

Voice: Described by Mackworth-Praed & Grant as a distinctive '*coo-co-coo*' followed by four or five low '*coos*'.

Habitat: Evergreen forest, occasionally forages in gardens.

Distribution: KwaZulu-Natal (interior and coast), Mpumalanga, Northern Province and Eastern Cape, South Africa, eastern Zimbabwe and southern Mozambique.

C.d.sharpi southern Sudan, Kenya and Tanzania.

Feeding: Fruit of Real Yellowwood *Podocarpus latifolius*, Wild poplar *Macaranga capensis*, *Phialodiscus*

zambesianus, wild figs *Ficus* spp., berries of Pigeon-wood *Trema orientalis* and stomach contents of a single bird revealed the larvae of a small *Cicada* sp

Breeding: Nest a thin platform of twigs placed 7-10m above the ground in a tree. Eggs slight gloss, white; clutch 2.

Aviculture: No records.

Western Bronze-naped Pigeon

Columba iriditorques 25cm

Alternative names: Bronze-naped Pigeon, Gabon Bronze-naped Pigeon.

Description: Male. Forehead, crown and sides of face dark bluish grey; nape greyish blue; glossed green; upper mantle copper-green, glossed pink; lower mantle golden-green, glossed violet; back, rump and upper tail-coverts black, tinged grey; tail blackish slate, except central feathers, tipped chestnut-buff; chin and throat bluish grey; breast and belly dark mauve-pink; under tail-coverts chestnut; bill bluish grey; tip whitish; cere dark red; iris pinkish, reddish, golden, grey, blue or greenish; orbital ring red; legs and feet reddish. Female has forehead, crown, nape and belly rufous; under tail-coverts rufous-chestnut. Juvenile unrecorded.

Voice: Described by Mackworth-Praed & Grant as a sonorous deep repeated '*coo-coo*' or something with a prelimary soft '*coo*' or two, then drop in its voice and another series of softer '*coo-oos*'.

Habitat: Forest, both primary and second growth.

Distribution: Sierra Leone, western Ivory Coast, southern Ghana, south-western Nigeria, southern Cameroon, eastern Zaire and Angola.

Feeding: Seeds, berries and fruit. Fruit of *Musanga, Eisterya* and *Haronga*.

Breeding: Flimsy platform of sticks at 1,2m above ground in dense thicket (Zambia), and in Haronga tree (Cameroon). Eggs pale cream, smooth, slightly glossy; clutch 1.

Aviculture: No records.

São-Thomé Bronze-naped Pigeon

Columba malherbii 25cm

Alternative name: São Thomé Grey Pigeon.

Description: Male. Forehead, chin and throat grey; nape slate-grey, washed with green; hindneck and upper mantle pink; lower mantle and back blackish brown; tail blackish slate; breast and belly grey; rest of underparts and under tail-coverts buffy white; iris pale grey; bill slate-grey, tip greyish white; legs and feet red. Female similar to male but lacks adornment on nape, hindneck and upper mantle; rest of underparts more brownish less blackish; underparts less brownish. Juvenile similar to adult female, but underparts darker and heavily speckled with rufous.

Voice: Described by Mackworth-Praed and Grant as a monotonous guttural cooing at all hours of the day.

Habitat: Deep forests and plantations at 400-500m altitude.

Distribution: São Thomé, Principé and Annobon Islands.

Feeding: Not known.

Breeding: Nest, substantial platform at 5-12m above the ground in *Erythrina* and cacao trees. Eggs oval, glossy and white.

Aviculture: No records.

European Turtle Dove
Streptopelia turtur arenicola 26-28cm

Alternative names: *S.t.isabellina* Isabelline Turtle Dove.

Description: Sexes similar. Forehead and crown bluish grey, tinged cream-buff on former; sides of face cream-buff; sides of neck white, feathers tipped black; mantle olive-brown, feathers having black centres tinged bluish grey; back bluish grey; rump greenish blue, mottled pale brown; upper tail-coverts pale greyish blue, tipped pale rufous; tail greyish; flight feathers greyish black, tips of secondaries tinged olive-brown; chin and throat pinkish buff; breast vinous pink; belly and under tail-coverts white; iris orange-red, orange-yellow, golden-yellow or golden-brown; bare skin round eye reddish purple; bill blackish brown; legs and feet reddish purple. Juvenile similar to adult, but paler overall; lacks black neck patch.

Adults. *S.t.hoggara* differs from the nominate race in having crown buffy; mantle and back more rufous.

S.t.isabellina brown; wing-coverts broadly edged rufous.

Voice: Described by Goodwin, the advertising coo is purring '*Coorr-coorr*' or '*Turr-turr*'.

Habitat: Open country with bushes and scattered trees and date palm oasis; common in juniper and cork forests; winter habitat *acacia* and *combretum* savannas coastal *suaedia* bush.

Distribution: Morocco to northern Libya and southern Algeria.

S.t.hoggara mountains of central Sahara from Ahaggar, Algeria to Air, northern Niger.

S.t.isabellina Kufra oasis in Libya, Egypt, northern Sudan and north-western Ethiopia.

Feeding: Seeds, grain, fruit, leaves and snails. In Senegambia feeds on *Panicum laetum*, Volstruis-dubbeltjie *Tribulus terestris* and *Cyperus rhizomes*, also on Scots pine *Pinus sylvestris*, fumitory *Fumaria*, millet *Setaria*, cornflower *Centaurea*, vetch *Vicia*, medick *Medicago*, leaves of chickweed *Stellaria media*, sainfoin *Onybrychis*, fruit of mulberry *Morus*, grain, namely sunflower *Helianthus*, wheat *Triticum*, and livefood in the form of cocoons of earthworms and occasionally small snails. Feeding data not restricted to Africa only.

Breeding: Nest, flimsy platform of small twigs, lined with finer material, including roots, grass stems and leaves with a diameter of 20-24cm, depth 3-7cm. One nest contained rusty wire. Both sexes build in *Aleppo* pines, date palms, olive, *Eucalyptus*, *Argan*, *Carob* and *Juniper* trees. Eggs oval, smooth and slightly glossy white; clutch 2; incubation 13-16 days, by both sexes; young cared and fed by both parents; nestling period 20 days.

Aviculture: Selected Reference CLUTCH 2; INCUBATION PERIOD 13-16 days; NESTLING PERIOD 18-23 days. Personal Communication CLUTCH 2; INCUBATION PERIOD 13, 15 days; NESTLING PERIOD about 17, 19 days. Selected Reference WILDFOOD chickweed *Stellaria* sp., persicaria *Polygonum* sp. Personal Communication vetch *Rumex* sp., sunflower *Helianthus* sp. Personal Communication FRUIT Black mulberry *Morus nigra*.

Dusky Turtle Dove
Streptopelia lugens 28cm

Alternative names: Black Dove, Pink-breasted Dove, Pink-breasted Pigeon.

Description: Sexes similar. Forehead, crown and nape dark grey; sides of face and neck light grey-brown; patch on side of neck black; mantle and upper tail-coverts earth-brown, edged pale brown with greater primary-coverts dark brown, edged bluish grey; chin and throat buff; breast pinkish buff; belly and under tail-coverts dark grey; iris orange, orbital ring purplish; bill blackish; legs and feet reddish purple. Juvenile similar to adult, but paler and browner overall.

Voice: Described by Curry-Lindahl as an advertising coo.

Habitat: *Eucalyptus* and *Juniperus* plantations and cultivation, wooded country, forest edges, bamboo and gardens.

Distribution: Ethiopia, Somalia, Uganda, Tanzania and Malawi.

Feeding: Seeds, grain, rhizomes, berries, insects and molluscs. Recorded feeding on *Salvadora* berries.

Breeding: A frail platform of twigs, lined with rootlets is situated at 2-7m above the ground in a tree, once in leafless thorn bush and in a creeper. Eggs oval, white; clutch 2; both sexes incubate for 20 days.

Aviculture: Nest Record Cards CLUTCH 2,2; INCU-BATION PERIOD 13, 14 days (ANRC); NESTLING PERIOD about 17, 19 days (ANRC) Diet Record Cards WILDFOOD sunflower *Helianthus* sp., Guinea corn *Sorghum caffrorum* (ADRC). Diet Record Card FRUIT Real mustard tree *Salvadora persica*. Diet Record Cards ANIMAL FOOD small slugs, termite alates (ADRC).

Pink-bellied Turtle Dove

Streptopelia hypopyrrha 26cm

Alternative name: Adamawa Turtle Dove.

Description: Sexes similar. Forehead pale grey; crown and nape bluish grey; half collar black; mantle, back, rump and upper tail-coverts earth-brown; tail blackish; tipped pale grey; wings dusky, edged white; sides of face bluish grey; ear-coverts bluish grey, tinged rufous; chin silvery grey; throat, breast and belly vinous brown; under tail-coverts grey; iris red; bill black; legs and feet purplish red. Juvenile similar to adult, but upperparts more brownish; less bluish grey.

Voice: Described by Bates, advertising coo as a 'low heavy-toned cooing'.

Habitat: Wooded or shrub-covered banks of streams, cultivation and gardens.

Distribution: Eastern and central Nigeria, northern Cameroon and south-western Chad.

Feeding: Seeds and grain.

Breeding: A slight platform of twigs with a diameter of 15cm, usually 4-5m above ground in dense foliaged tree, notably Mango *Magnifera indica* and once recorded on palm frond. Eggs white, elliptical; clutch 2.

Aviculture: Nest Record Cards CLUTCH 2 (ANRC); INCUBATION PERIOD 16 days (ANRC); NESTLING PERIOD 18 days (ANRC). Diet Record Cards WILD-FOOD Guinea corn *Sorghum caffrorum*, Black wild sorghum *S.versicolor* (ADRC).

African Collared Dove

Streptopelia roseogrisea 29-30 cm

Alternative names: Pink-headed Turtle Dove, Pink-headed Dove, Rosy-Grey Dove.

Description: Sexes similar. Forehead, crown and nape greyish rose, former paler; half collar on hindneck black, edged above with white; sides of neck and face pinkish mauve; mantle, back, rump and upper tail-coverts earth brown; tail pale brown, tipped blackish; chin whitish; throat, breast and belly pale pinkish mauve; rest of underparts white; iris red; bill blackish; legs and feet purplish red. Juvenile similar to adult, but collar not well defined; iris pale brown; legs and feet pale pink.

Adults: *S.r.borneensis* differs from the nominate race in being darker overall; iris red.

S.r.arabica differs from the nominate in having the under wing-coverts tinged grey.

Voice: Described by Urban *et al* as 2 notes, a short 'coo' or 'Hoo' and a lower and longer 'rrroo', each note followed by a 'wa'.

Habitat: In Somalia found in coastal gardens. At wells and other drinking places around tamarisk *Tamarix* sp., also *acacia* thorn-bush.

Distribution: Mauritania, Senegal, northern Sudan and western Ethiopia.

S.r.borneensis Mali, northern Nigeria and Chad *S.r.arabica* eastern Ethiopia, Sudan and Somalia.

Feeding: Seeds of grasses, spilled grain and berries. In Sahara mainly seeds of *Euphorbia*, dicotyledons of Volstruisdubbeltjie, *Tribulus terrestris, Gisekic pharnacioides, Colocynthis, Arachis, Cocculus, Tinospora, Boscia, Salvadora, Commiphora* and *Panicum laetum*.

Breeding: Nest a scanty platform of twigs in trees or bushes usually 4-5m above the ground. In Senegamiba 219 nests were mainly in *Bulanites aegyptiaca, Acacia raddiana*, Bastard brandy bush *Grewia bicolor* and Poison-grub commiphora *Commiphora africana*. Also uses old nests of other species. Eggs oval, white; clutch 1-2.

Aviculture: Selected Reference CLUTCH 2: INCUBATION PERIOD 15 DAYS; NESTLING PERIOD 15 days. Nest Record Cards CLUTCH 2 (ARU); Incubation period 15 days (ARU); NESTLING PERIOD 17 DAYS (ARU) Selected Reference WILDFOOD chickweed *Stellaria* sp. Diet Record Cards Guinea corn *Sorghum caffrorum*, Sunflower *Helianthus annuus* (ARU). Diet Record Card FRUIT Kooboo berry *Casine aethiopica* (ADRC). Diet Record Cards ANIMAL FOOD termite alates.

White-winged Collared Dove

Streptopelia reichenowi 24cm

Alternative names: African White-winged Dove, Reichenow's Dove, White-winged Ringdove, White-winged Dove.

Description: Male. Forehead, crown and nape grey-brown; half collar brown-black; mantle earth-crown; back light blue-grey; rump and upper tail-coverts brown; tail greyish white; flanks pale grey, tinged brown; belly and under tail-coverts greyish white; wings with primaries dark brown, outer and greater coverts pale bluish grey, edged whitish; sides of face and breast light grey-brown; chin whitish; iris pale yellow-brown; bill brown-black; legs and feet reddish. Female similar to male, but paler overall. Juvenile similar to female but feathers fringed buff.

Voice: Described by Brown as a deep-toned *'kok-kooorrr-kok-kooorrr'* repeated rapidly.

Habitat: In Somalia *riparian* woodland dominated by Doum Palm *Hyphaene coriacea* and Fan Palm *Borassus aethiopicum*; in Ethiopia broad-leaved trees and over-grazed former *acacia* woodland.

Distribution: South-eastern Ethiopia, Southern Somalia and north-eastern Kenya.

Feeding: Red berries found in the crops of 4 birds.

Breeding: A frail semi-transparent platform of twigs with a diameter of 15cm, sited 2,5m high in *Parkinsonia*, a small tree up to 6m tall with branchlets being armed with spines, leaves bi-pinnate composed elongated flattened green rhacides of up to 30cm. Eggs white; clutch 2; both sexes incubate.

Aviculture: Nest Record Cards CLUTCH 2 (ANRC). Diet Record Cards WILDFOOD Jimson weed *Oxalis corniculata*, Bulrush millet *Pennisetum americanum*, Guinea corn *Sorghum caffrorum* (ADRC). Diet Record Card FRUIT Koobooberry *Cassine aethiopica* (ADRC).

Mourning Collared Dove

Streptopelia decipiens 29-30cm

Alternative names: African Mourning Dove, Mourning Dove, White-bellied Turtle Dove. *S.d.shelleyi* Niger Mourning Dove.

Description: Sexes similar. Forehead and crown grey; nape and ear-coverts grey, shading to pink; black half-colour across hindneck, edged above with pinkish white; upper parts scapulars and lesser wing-coverts earth brown; breast pinkish; centre of belly white; under tail-coverts grey, edged with white; tail dark brown, lighter in centre with white tips; iris orange-red or red with narrow yellow inner ring; bill black; legs and feet wine-red. Juvenile browner than the adult with buffish tips to the wing-coverts; iris pale brown.

Adults *S.d.shelleyi* differs from nominate race in having upperparts paler; belly and under tail-coverts grey.

S.d.perspicillata differs from nominate in having belly, flanks and under tail-coverts white; iris pale yellow.

S.d.logonesis similar to *shelleyi* but breast vinous grey.

S.d.ambigua differs from *logonesis* in having under tail-coverts darker grey.

Voice: Described by Maclean as a resonant 3-syllabled *'wuwu-woo'*, dropping in pitch on last note.

Habitat: Riverine woodland, especially *acacia* and palms, *Borassus* spp. and *Hyphaene* spp., also close to cultivation, around villages and gardens. In West Africa roosts in great numbers in *Aeschynomene elaphroxylon* standing in water.

Distribution: Sudan, Ethiopia and north western Somalia.

S.d.shelleyi southern Mauritania, Senegal, southern Niger and southern Nigeria.

S.d.perspicillata western Kenya and southern Tanzania.

S.d.logonesis Chad, southern Sudan, northern and eastern Zaire and western and northern Uganda.

S.d.ambigua Zambia, south eastern Zaire, Malawi, Angola, Zimbabwe, northern Botswana, northern Namibia and Northern Province, South Africa.

Feeding: Seeds, berries, grain and insects. Seeds of Bulrush millet *Pennisetum americanum*, *Panicum laetum*, Crowfoot *Dactyloctenium aegyptium*, *Acacia* sp. In West Africa recorded feeding on the seeds of berries of Mustard tree *Salvadora persica*, Confetti tree *Maytenus senegalensis*, Volstruisdubbeltjie *Tribulus terrestris*, *Grisekia pharnacoides*, *Cocculus pendulus*, and *Boscia senegalensis*. Also consumes sorghum on standing stalks. Livefood, namely termites alates and beetles.

Breeding: A scanty, shallow saucer of twigs and a few grass stems is built 1,5-15m above ground in the fork of a tree. In West Africa uses mainly Scented thorn *Acacia nilotica*, *A.raddiana* and Simple-thorned torchwood *Balanites aegyptiaca*. Eggs white, oval, matt or with slight gloss; clutch 2; incubation 13-14 days, by both sexes; nestling period 17-20 days; fed by both parents; dependant on parents for a further 10-14 days after leaving the nest.

Aviculture: Selected Reference CLUTCH 2; INCUBATION PERIOD 13-14 days; NESTLING PERIOD 17-21 days. Nest Record Cards CLUTCH 2 (ANRC); INCUBATION PERIOD 14 days; NESTLING PERIOD 19 days (ANRC). Selected Reference WILDFOOD Guinea corn *Sorghum caffrorum*. Diet Record Cards Japanese millet *Echinochloa frumentacea* (ADRC). Diet Record Card FRUIT Mustard tree *Salvadora persica* (ADRC). Diet Record Cards ANIMAL FOOD termite alates.

Red-eyed Dove

Streptopelia semitorquata 33-36 cm

Alternative names: Big Ring Dove, Black Dove, Damara Dove, Red-eyed Half-collared Dove, Lesser Red-eyed Dove, Red-eyed Turtle Dove.

Description: Sexes similar. Forehead, forecrown and sides of face ashy grey; nape grey, with a black half collar, edged above and below with white; mantle, back and upper tail-coverts greyish brown; tail blackish;

throat silvery grey; rest of underparts mauve-pink; wings, flanks and side of rump blue-grey; iris orange, reddish or yellow; bill black; orbital skin red; legs and feet reddish purple. Juvenile lacks the black half collar and is overall paler and browner.

Adult. *S.s.australis* differs from the nominate race in being smaller and paler.

Voice: Described by Newman as '*coo-coo,coo-koo-cuk-coo*'.

Habitat: Woodland, plantations of exotic trees, mangroves, cultivated land, parks and gardens.

Distribution: North-eastern Namibia, the Caprivi Strip, northern Botswana, north Zimbabwe, southern Mozambique, eastern Kenya, north-eastern Tanzania and southern Somalia.

S.s.australis South-western, northern and eastern Cape Province, Free State, North-West, Gauteng, Mpumalanga, Northern Province, Free State, KwaZulu-Natal, South Africa to Swaziland, Southern Mozambique, south-eastern Botswana and southern Zimbabwe.

Feeding: Seeds and insects. Seeds of Castor oil plant *Ricinus communis*, Bulrush millet *Pennisetum americanum, Croton* spp. (evergreen shrubs and trees, usually with stellate hairs or rounded scales), dry elm eaten on the ground. Fruits of Pigeonwood *Trema orientalis*, White Ironwood *Vepris undulata*. Recorded feeding on discarded apple pulp at a factory in the Cape Province, South Africa. Berries of Confetti bush *Lantana camara*, fruit of *Maytenus* sp. Partial to cultivated mulberries. Bulbs of Nut Grass *Cyperus esculentus* are eaten mainly during the wet season when easily extracted from the ground. Flower petals of the Toon tree *Cedrella toona*. Cultivated crops in the form of maize *Zea*, sunflower *Helianthus*, groundnuts (in shell) *Arachis hypogaea*, sorghum *Sorghum*, cowpeas *Vigna unguiculata*. Much artificial food and domestic scraps eaten. Attracted to salt lick. Livefood in the form of termite alates and millipedes.

Breeding: A fairly substantial platform of twigs is made, sometimes with the dead leaves still attached, and lined with fine grass blades or pine needles Situated in a tree or bush usually at 2-3m above ground or water. The female constructs the nest while the male collects material. The disused nests of egrets, thrushes, and crows have also been utilized. Eggs white to creamy white; clutch 2; incubation 15-17 days, by both sexes, nestling period 16-21 days; nestlings fed by both parents.

Aviculture: Selected Reference CLUTCH 2; INCUBATION PERIOD 16-17 DAYS; NESTLING PERIOD 16-21 days. Nest Record Cards CLUTCH 2,2,2 (ARU) 2 (SAANRC) 2,2 (NASNRC): INCUBATION PERIOD 16,17 (ARU) 15 (ARU) 17 (SAANRC) 15,17 days (NASNRC). Selected Reference WILDFOOD Guinea corn *Sorghum caffrorum* (ARUSAADRC NASDRC), Johnson grass *Sorghum halepense* (ARU), Sunflower *Helianthus annus* (SAANRC). Selected Reference FRUIT African mulberry *Morus mosozygia*. Diet Record Cards mulberry *Morus* sp. (ARU SAADRC NASDRC).

Diet Record Cards ANIMAL FOOD termite alates (SAADRC), small slugs (ARU).

Ring-necked Dove
Streptopelia capicola 26-28cm

Alternative names: Cape Ring-necked Dove, Cape Turtle Dove *S.c.damarensis* Damara (Turtle) Dove.
S.c.tropica East African Ring-neck Dove.

Description: Sexes similar. Forehead and crown blue-grey; sides of face and upper breast lavender-grey; half-collar across hindneck black; mantle and back brownish; belly lavender-grey becoming white on under tail-coverts; wings dusky, secondaries edged with pale grey; iris dark brown; bill slate-grey to black; legs and feet reddish purple. Juvenile paler than adult with tawny edges to wing-coverts, scapulars and breast.

Adults *S.c.abunda* differs from the nominate race in being slightly larger in size and in having the crown lighter grey; neck ring less prominent.

S.c.damarensis differs from the nominate in being paler overall.

S.c.ongauti differs from *damarensis* in being paler overall.

S.c.tropica differs from *damarensis* in being more vinous, less grey on the breast.

S.c.electa differs from *tropica* in having greyer face and belly.

S.c.somalica differs from *tropica* in being paler overall.

Voice: Described by Newman as a harsh '*work harder, work harder...*' much repeated.

Habitat: Woodland, savanna, cultivated land, towns, parks and gardens.

Distribution: Western, south-western and eastern Cape Province, South Africa.

S.c.electa southern Ethiopia.

S.c.somalica central Ethiopia, southern Somalia and eastern Kenya.

S.c.tropica North-West, eastern KwaZulu-Natal, South Africa to eastern Swaziland, Mozambique, Zimbabwe, northern Namibia, Angola, Zaire, Kenya and western Tanzania.

S.c.onqouati north-western Namibia.

S.c.abunda eastern Cape Province, Gauteng (high-veld), Free State and western KwaZulu-Natal, provinces of South Africa to Lesotho (lowlands) and western Swaziland.

Feeding: Seeds, fruits, nectar, grain and insects. Seeds of Milkbush *Euphorbia* spp., panic *Panicum* spp., conifers and wattles, oak *Quercus* sp., (usually broken or rotten), Blue Lupins *Lupinus angustifolius*, dry elm eaten on the ground, fruit of Pigeonwood *Trema orientalis*, Bird's Brandy *Lantana rugosa, Pyrenacantha* sp., Common taaibos *Rhus pyroides*, nectar of Flat-flowered aloe *Aloe marlothii*, bulbs of Nut grass *Cyperus esculentus*, red stems of Rooi-krans *Acacia cyclops*, leaves of *Mesembryanthemum* and cultivated crops in the form of oats *Avena*, sorghum *Sorghum*, maize *Zea*, sunflower *Helianthus*. Much artificial food and domestic scraps eaten, namely mealie pap and water, bread crumbs, cheese, raw minced meat. Attracted to salt-lick. Livefood, namely termite alates, aphids, earthworms, weevils, locusthoppers. Also recorded are Harvester termites *Hodotermes mossambicus* and "Bulb Weevils" *Brachycerus scelestus*.

Breeding: The nest is a platform of small twigs and rootlets in the fork of a tree, bush, tangle of creepers at 0,5m to 9m above the ground, occasionally up to 15m, and there is a record of a nest on the ground on a small island. Constructed in 3-8 days, working for a few hours each day. Indigenous trees recorded as nest site, 81% of 244 nests in Zimbabwe and exotic trees recorded of 844 nests in south western Cape Province, South Africa. *Acacia* spp., and *Eucalyptus* spp., most favoured. One pair nested on a tower standing in the sea, and another on an electric light pole. May utilise the same site many times, and may occupy nests of thrushes, sparrows, egrets and other doves. The female constructs the nest with the male collecting the materials. Eggs oval, white, slight gloss, white; clutch 2 (rarely 1-3); incubation period 12-16 days; nestling period 15-22 days; fed by both sexes.

Aviculture: Selected Reference CLUTCH 2; rarely 3: INCUBATION PERIOD 12-16 days; NESTLING PERIOD 15-22 days. Nest Record Cards CLUTCH 2 (ANRC) 2,2 (ARU) 2 (SAANRC); INCUBATION PERIOD 13 (ANRC) 13,14 days (ARU); NESTLING PERIOD 19 (ANRC) 17 days (SAANRC). Selected Reference WILDFOOD. Seeds of Guinea corn *Sorghum caffrorum*, Bulrush millet *Pennisetum americanum*. Diet Record Cards Guinea corn *Sorghum caffrorum* (ARU SAADRC ADRC), Sunflower *Helianthus annuus* (ARU). Selected Reference ANIMAL FOOD termite alates, weevils, aphids.

Vinaceous Dove
Streptopelia vinacea 20cm

Alternative names: Vinaceous Ring Dove, Vinaceous Turtle Dove.

Description: Sexes similar. Forehead and crown pale pink; nape greyish pink, tinged brown; half collar on hindneck black; sides of neck and face pale vinous pink, mantle, back and rump brown, slightly washed bluish grey; tail black, tipped white; chin, throat and breast pale vinous pink, merging to whitish on belly; under tail-coverts white; flanks pale bluish grey; wing-coverts pale greyish blue; iris dark brown; bill black; legs and feet red. Juvenile similar to adult, but wing-coverts edge buffish overall.

Adults *S.v.grotei* differs from the nominate race in being paler overall.

S.v.savannae differs from the nominate in being darker overall; wing-coverts edged whiter.

Voice: Described by Harwin as having an advertising '*coo*' as '*coo-coo-coo-coo*'.

Habitat: Dry savanna, thorn scrub country and old cultivation below 1200m in East Africa.

Distribution: Senegal to Sudan.

S.v.grotei Chad and northern Cameroon.

S.v.savannae Sierra Leone to northern Zaire.

Feeding: Seeds, grain, fruit stones, insects and snails. Seeds of *Panicum laetum*, animal food in the form of termites and caterpillars, fruit stones of *Maytenus, Boscia* and *Tribulus* and legumes of *Zornia, Alysicarpus, Colocynthis, Arachis* and *Gisekia pharnacioides*.

Breeding: Nest flimsy circular saucer of twigs built 1,5-7,6m from the ground. In Senegambia 111 nests were recorded in *Acacia raddiana, Sclerocarya, Commiphora and Balanties*. Eggs glossy, oval, white; clutch 2.

Aviculture: Selected Reference CLUTCH 2; INCUBATION PERIOD 13 days; NESTLING PERIOD 13-14 days. Nest Record Cards CLUTCH 2 (ARU) 2,2,2 (ANRC); INCUBATION PERIOD 13 (ARU) 13,13 about 14 days (ANRC); NESTLING PERIOD 15 (ARU) 14, 16 (ANRC). Diet Record Cards WILDFOOD seeds of sorghum *Sorghum* sp. (ARU), Common millet *Panicum milliaceum* (ADRC). Diet Record Cards ANIMAL FOOD termite alates (ARU ADRC).

Laughing Dove
Streptopelia senegalensis 24-25cm

Alternative names: Cape Laughing Dove, Garden Dove, Lemon Dove, Little Brown Dove, Palm Dove, Pink-breasted Dove, Senegal (Turtle) Dove, Town Dove, Village Dove.

Description: Male. Head, neck and breast lilac; mantle, back and upper tail-coverts grey; tail dark grey; feathers of underside of neck black, broadly tipped tawny and feathers bifurcated; underparts grey; under tail-coverts white; wing-coverts reddish brown, primaries greyish brown; iris dark brown; bill black; legs and feet purplish red. Female has plumage slighter paler and less reddish. Juvenile similar to adult female, but duller, more brownish, less greyish.

Males. *S.s.phoenicophila* differs from nominate race in being larger and browner.

S.s.aegyptiaca differs from nominate in being darker overall.

S.s.divergens differs from nominate in having the sides of the head and neck more violaceous, less ruddy brown.

Voice: Described by Hollom *et al* as usually five-syllables 'doo,doo,dooh,dooh,doo', third and fourth notes slightly longer and higher in tone.

Distribution: South-western and eastern Cape Province, KwaZulu-Natal, South Africa to southern Mozambique, northern Namibia, the Caprivi Strip, northern Botswana, Zimbabwe, northwards to Zambia, Malawi, Tanzania, Kenya, Uganda, Somalia, Ethiopia westwards to north-western Sudan, north-western Niger, northern and eastern Chad, Mali to Senegal.

S.s.phoenicophila Morocco, Algeria, Tunisia and Libya.

S.s. aegyptiaca Egypt. Introduced to São Thomé and Principé islands.

S.s.divergens North-West and the northern Cape Province, South Africa to Namibia, Botswana, western Zimbabwe and Zambia.

Feeding: Seeds, fruits, nectar, insects and molluscs. Seeds of Sunflower *Helianthus annuus, Croton* spp., *Celosia* spp., *Amaranthus* spp., Jimson weed *Oxalis corniculata*, Common taaibos *Rhus pyriodes*, September bush *Polygala myitifolic*, *Acacia* spp., *Cleome* spp., Annual bluegrass *Poa annua*, Goose grass *Eleusine indica*, dry elm eaten on the ground, fruits of White-berry bush *Securinega virosa*, Mustard tree *Salvadora persica*, Sycamore Fig *Ficus sycamorus,*

Common taaibos *Rhus pyriodes*. Cultivated fruit such as Paw Paw *Carina papaya* and olives *Olea* spp., nectar of Flat-flowered aloe *Aloe marlothii*, red stems of Rooikrans *Acacia cyclops*, cultivated crops in the form of maize *Zea*, wheat *Triticum*, sunflower *Helianthus*, sorghum *Sorghum* and fodder plant Lucerne *Medicago sativa* Feeds at bird table on mealie pap and water. Much artificial food and domestic scraps eaten. Attracted to salt lick. In India takes Bajra *Pennisetum typhoides* and Jowar *Sorghum vulgare*. Livefood namely, termite alates, Argentine ants *Iridomyrmex humilis*, Harvester termites *Hodotermes mossambicus* and the larvae and pupae of the house fly *Musca domestica*, Snails *Succinea straita* has also been recorded.

Breeding: A typical dove nest being a flimsy platform of small sticks and grass stalks sited at 0,5-15m above the ground in bushes or trees. One nest contained 80 rootlets, while another contained 85 twigs and 6 grass bents. In West Africa favours *Acacia raddiana*, Simple-thorned torchwood *Balanites aegyptaca* and *Zizyphus mauritiana* (exotic) as nest sites. Also uses the old nests of bulbuls and thrushes. Individual nesting sites have been used up to 8 times. Artificial nest sites recorded were on rafters or in the thatch of a hut, on electric light poles, trolley-bus wires, in window boxes, in flower pots, on verandahs and also on the windscreen wiper of a car. The construction of the nest takes 2-4 days with the female building and the male carrying materials. Multi-brooded breeding throughout the year, each making 5-6 attempts. Eggs white, oval slightly glossy; clutch 2 (rarely 1-4); incubation period 12-16 days; cared for and fed by both parents; nestling period 14-17 days.

Aviculture: Selected Reference CLUTCH 2, rarely 1-4; INCUBATION PERIOD 12,12 14 (ARU) 12, 14 (SAANRC) 15 days (ANRC); NESTLING PERIOD 14,14,16 (ARU) 14 17 (SAANRC) 13 days (ANRC). Selected Reference WILDFOOD Seeds of Guinea corn *Sorghum caffrorum*, Bulrush millet *Pennisetum americanum*. Diet Record Cards Guinea corn *Sorghum caffrorum* (ARU SAADRC ADRC), Jimson weed *Oxalis corniculata* (ADRC), Japanese millet *Echinochloa frumentacea* (ARU). Diet Record Cards ANIMAL FOOD termite alates (ARU ADRC), weevils (SAADRC).

Lemon Dove
Aplopelia larvata 25-30cm
Alternative names: Cinnamon Dove, Cinnamon Wood Dove, Forest Dove, Olive Dove, Rufous-breasted Wood Dove.
A.l.principalis **Princes' Island Lemon Dove.**
A.l.jacksoni **Ruwenzori Lemon Dove.**

Description: Male. Forehead, sides of face and throat white; chin greyish white; breast pink, shading to cinnamon on the underparts and the under wing-coverts; hindneck and upper mantle iridescent green, bronze and pink; wings dark greenish brown; iris variable brown to red, rim pinkish; bill black; legs and feet red. Female like the male but forehead, sides of face and throat less white and lacking much of the iridescent sheen. Juvenile is dark rich russet-brown with black bars on the breast, wing-coverts and upper tail-coverts.

Males. *A.l.bronzina* differs only from the nominate race in being smaller overall.

A.l.jacksoni upperparts darker with breast grey or greyish brown.

A.l.plumbescens having wings and rump black.

A.l.samaliyae having hindneck and upper mantle iridescent vinous red.

A.l.inornata having underparts darker.

A.l.poensis similar to *hypoleuca*, but female having upperparts darker.

A.l.principalis having breast vinous.

A.l.simplex having underparts brownish.

A.l.hypoleuca similar to *inornata* in having back, rump and wing-coverts greyish brown.

A.l.inornata similar to *jacksoni* but upperparts darker and lower belly; under tail-coverts clear grey and white.

Voice: Described by Rowan the 'advertising call' is a deep soft 'coo' that slurs upwards.

Habitat: A forest species, favouring shaded areas with dense undergrowth, but also found in exotic plantations of pine and oak in South Africa and cacao on Principé Island.

Distribution: Western Cape to KwaZulu-Natal and Mpumalanga, South Africa, Swaziland, Mozambique and eastern Zimbabwe to south-eastern Sudan.

A.l.bronzina Ethiopia.

A.l.jacksoni eastern Zaire, Uganda and western Tanzania.

A.l.plumbescens southern Cameroon.

A.l.samaliyae Angola and north-western Zambia.

A.l.inornata Cameroon Mountains and eastern Nigeria.

A.l.poensis Fernando Pó Island

Po.A.l.principalis Principé Islands.

A.l.simplex São Thomé Island.

A.l.hypoleuca Annobon Island.

Feeding: Seeds, bulbs, tubers, berries, insects and molluscs. Seeds of Wild Peach *Kiggelaria africana* Cape Chestnut *Calodendron capense*. Livefood in the form of termites and a snail *Gullela* sp., has also been recorded.

Breeding: Monogamous, territorial, solitary. Nest, a fairly substantial flat platform of twigs and rootlets is built in the fork of a tree or amongst matted creepers mostly in deep shade at about 1,20m above ground. One record showed nest material to consist entirely of pine needles. Re-use old nests with one record on frond of *Encephalarctos* for three successive summers.

Construction of nests by both sexes in 7-9 days. Eggs creamy to yellowish white; clutch 1-3, mostly 2; incubation 14-16 days mainly or entirely by female; nestling period 21-23 days; young cared and fed by both parents; remain in company of adults for 55-61 days.

Aviculture: Selected Reference CLUTCH 2, rarely 1; INCUBATION PERIOD 21-23 days. Nest Record Cards CLUTCH 2 (SAANRC) 2 (ARU); INCUBATION PERIOD 16 (SAANRC) 15 days (ARU); NESTLING PERIOD 21 (SAANRC) 19 days (ARU). Selected Reference WILDFOOD Bulbs of Broad-leaf plantain *Plantago major*. Diet Record Cards tubers of Yellow nutsedge *Cyperus esculentes* (SAADRC), Jerusalem aritchoke *Helianthus tuberosus*, chickweed *Stellaria media* (ARU). Diet Record Cards FRUIT Cape cranberry *Dovyalis rhamnoides*, Cape cherry *Cassine aethiopica* (SAADRC), Num-Num berry *Carissa bispinosa*, African mulberry *Morus mesozygia* (ARU). Diet Record Cards ANIMAL FOOD termite alates (ARU), small slugs (SAADRC).

Emerald-spotted Wood Dove

Turtur chalcospilos 19-20cm

Alternative names: Green-spotted Dove, Metallic-spotted Wood Dove, Rufous-winged Turtle Dove, River Dove.

Description: Sexes similar. Forehead, crown and hindneck slate-grey; mantle and upper tail-coverts grey-brown; two broad black bands across rump; underparts mauvy pink; flanks pale chestnut; emerald-green spots on the inner secondaries; under wing-coverts cinammon; iris brown; bill blackish; legs and feet purplish red. Juvenile similar to Blue-spotted Dove, but secondaries blacker; no bands on rump.

Adults. *T.c.zambesiensis* differs from the nominate race in having brown, rather than greyish underparts.

T.c.volkmanni differs from the nominate in being paler and greyer above.

Voice: The fullest description of the voice of this species that I have read, is by Newman, a soft descending cooing '*du,du...du-du...du...du-dudu-du-du-du*'..tailing off at the end.

Habitat: Mostly woodland and thornveld.

Distribution: Eastern Cape Province, KwaZulu-Natal, South Africa.

T.c.zambesiensis Northern Province, north-eastern KwaZulu-Natal, South Africa to western Swaziland, Mozambique and central and eastern Zimbabwe.

T.c.volkmanni North-West Province, South Africa to western Zimbabwe, northern and eastern Botswana and northern Namibia.

Feeding: Grass and weed seeds, berries, insects and small molluscs. Insects in the form of termite alates.

Breeding: The nest is a platform and is composed of twigs, rootlets and grass stems. Usually situated no more than 6m above ground in a bush, small tree, creeper or aloe. The same nest may be used for several years. Eggs creamy of buff; clutch 2; incubation 15-17 days, by both sexes; nestling period 16-19 days; fed by both parents.

Aviculture: Selected Reference CLUTCH 2; INCUBATION PERIOD 16-17 DAYS; NESTLING PERIOD 16-19 days. Nest Record Cards CLUTCH 2,2 (NASNRC) 2 (SAANRC) 2 (ARU); INCUBATION PERIOD 16, 17 (NASNRC) 17 days (SAANRC); NESTLING PERIOD 18 (NASNRC) 17 days (SAANRC). Selected Reference WILDFOOD Seeds of Bulrush millet *Pennisetum americanum* (NASDRC) A, Hay *Chloris vigata*, Rescue grass *Bromus unioliodes* (NASNRCARU), Guinea grass *Panicum maximum*, Blue panic *P.laevifolium*, chickweed *Stellaria media* (SAADRC). Selected Reference FRUIT Blackberry *Ribes fruiticosus*. Diet Record Cards ANIMAL FOOD termite alates (ARU SAADRC), small slugs (SAADRC).

Black-billed Wood Dove

Turtur abyssinicus 20cm

Alternative names: Abyssinian Wood Dove, Black-billed Blue-spotted Wood Dove, Nile Black-billed Blue-spotted Dove, Nile Black-billed Blue-spotted Wood Dove.

Description: Sexes similar. Forehead whitish; crown and nape bluish grey; hindneck brown, tinged grey; sides of neck greyish pink; sides of face greyish; mantle, back and wing-coverts pale earth brown; upper tail-coverts and rump paler brown, latter two conspicuous blackish bars; tail slate-grey, tip blackish; chin and throat whitish; breast and belly pale greyish pink; under tail-coverts black; bill black; iris brown; legs and feet purplish red. Juvenile similar to adult, but tips to feathers of upperparts are usually buffy white.

Voice: Described by Urban as like that of Blue-spotted Wood Dove, but rather longer, with 24-27 'coos' lasting 15-18 seconds.

Habitat: Dry thickets and wooded watercourses in East Africa.

Distribution: Senegal to northern Ethiopia.

Feeding: Seeds of *Brachiaria*, Crowfoot *Dactyloctenium aegyptium*, sorghum *Sorghum* sp., *Pennisetum*, *Oryza* and *Panicum laetum*.

Breeding: Nest of platform of twigs and roots, more or less concealed in foliage of *Balanites, Acacia nilotica*, Scented thorn, *Ziyphus mauritiaca* (exotic), *Salvadora*,

Boscia and *Maytenus* at 1,0-2,5m above the ground. Eggs brownish cream; clutch 2.

Aviculture: Selected Reference CLUTCH 2; INCUBATION PERIOD 12-14 days. Nest Record Cards CLUTCH 2,2 (ANRC); INCUBATION PERIOD 15,16 days (ANRC); NESTLING PERIOD 17,29 days (ANRC). Selected Reference WILDFOOD Guinea corn *Sorghum caffrorum*. Diet Record cards Guinea corn *Sorghum caffrorum*, Common wild sorghum *S.verticilliflorum* (ADRC).

Blue-spotted Wood Dove

Turtur afer 22cm

Alternative names: Blue-spotted Dove, Bronze-spotted Dove, Metallic-spotted Dove, Red-billed Wood Dove, Red-billed Blue-spotted Wood Dove, Sapphire-spotted Dove, West African Red-billed Wood Dove.

Description: Sexes similar. Forehead and crown grey; mantle, black, upper tail-coverts earth brown; two broad black bands across rump; tail earth brown, edged with black; underparts warm pink, paler on chin; under tail-coverts blackish brown; flanks pale chestnut; inner secondaries blue-black with purple sheen; under wing-coverts cinnamon; iris brown; bill red with purplish red, tip orange or yellow; legs and feet red. Juvenile resembles the young of the Tambourine Dove, but belly buff, not white.

Voice: Described by Maclean as hooting phrase, starting of slowly and speeding up only slightly towards end, ending abruptly after only 6-9 quick notes.

Habitat: Lowland evergreen forest, riverine woodlands, gardens, farms, mangroves and *Eucalyptus* plantations.

Distribution: Northern Province, South Africa, eastern Zimbabwe, Mozambique, Kenya, Tanzania, Ethiopia, Nigeria, Chad, Senegal, Gabon to Southern Angola.

Feeding: Small seeds and insects. Seeds of Castor oil plant *Ricinus communis* may be eaten. Insects namely termite alates.

Breeding: The nest is usually placed 2-3m above the ground in the fork of a small tree. Nest a small platform constructed of twigs and rootlets. Recorded utilizing old nests of thrushes. Eggs cream; clutch 2.

Aviculture: Selected Reference CLUTCH 2; INCUBATION PERIOD 12-16 days; NESTLING PERIOD 12-18 days. Nest Record Cards CLUTCH 2 (ARU) 2,2 (ANRC); INCUBATION PERIOD 17 (ARU) 16,17 days (ANRC); NESTLING PERIOD 16 (ARU) 18 days (ANRC). Selected Reference WILDFOOD Seeds of Bulrush millet *Pennisetum americanum*. Teff grass *Eragrostis tef* (ARU), Giant millet *Sorghum dochna*, chickweed *Stellaria media* (ADRD). Diet Record Cards ANIMAL FOOD termite alates (ADRC).

Tambourine Dove

Turtur tympanistra 21-23cm

Alternative names: African White-breasted Dove, Tambourine Ground Dove, White-breasted Forest Dove, White-breasted Wood Dove, White-breasted Dove, White-breasted Pigeon. *T.t.fraseri* West African Tambourine Dove.

Description: Male. Forehead, throat, breast and belly snow white; nape, ear-coverts and black ashy brown; tail dark brown, the outer feathers with subterminal markings in black; under tail-coverts and flanks ashy brown; iridescent wing spots blackish purple; under wing-coverts cinnamon; iris brown; bill purplish, with black tip; legs and feet reddish purple. Female differs from the male in having the white parts suffused with grey. Juvenile has sides of the chest and flanks barred, the feathers edged with greyish white.

Male. *T.f.fraseri* differs from the nominate race in having darker and warmer brown upperparts.

Voice: Described by Newman as 'coo,cu,cu-du-du-du-du-du'.

Habitat: Occurs in mistbelt evergreen forest, coastal dune bush and mixed woodland; also rubber, cacao and kola plantations in West Africa and coconut groves in East Africa.

Distribution: Western and eastern Cape Province, KwaZulu-Natal, and Mpumalanga, South Africa to Swaziland, Mozambique and Zimbabwe.

T.f.fraseri Tanzania, south-eastern Kenya, northern Uganda, southern Somalia, west-central Ethiopia, western Sudan to Sierra Leone and western and northern Angola.

Feeding: Weed seeds, fruit, grain and insects. Seeds of Castor oil plant *Ricinus communis*, African finger millet *Eleusine coracana*, *Albizia*, *Celtis*, *Solanum*, *Croton*, *Neoboutonia*, *Polyscias*, fruits of African mulberry *Morus mesozygia*, Wild strawberry *Fragaria vesca*, Red currant *Ribes sativum*, *Syzygium*, cultivated sorghum *Sorghum* spp., and frequently eats termites and small molluscs.

Breeding: Nest may be from 1-10m, above ground and occurs in trees or tangled branches of creepers. The male carries twigs to the nest site while the frail platform of twigs and roots is constructed by the female. A pair has been recorded utilising a nest originally built by a Laughing Dove *Streptopelia senegalensis*. Eggs creamy white; clutch 2, occasionally 1; incubation 17-20 days, by both sexes; nestling period 19-22 days; egg shells are usually removed by the male soon after hatching; both adults feed the young.

Aviculture: Selected Reference CLUTCH 2; INCUBATION PERIOD 17-20 days; NESTLING PERIOD 19-22 days. Nest Record Cards CLUTCH 2,2,2 (ARU) 2,2 (SAANRC) 2 (NASNRC) 2 (ANRC); INCUBATION PERIOD 17, 18 (ARU) 18 (SAANRC) 16 (NASNRC) 18 days (ANRC); NESTLING PERIOD 19,21 (ARU) 19 (SAANRC) close to 22 (NASNRC) about 20 days (ANRC). Selected Reference WILDFOOD Seeds of Castor oil plant *Ricinus communis*. Diet Record Cards. Bulrush millet *Pennisetum americanum* (SAADRC), Koda millet *Paspalum scrobiculatum* (ARU), Chickweed *Stellaria media* (ARU SAADRC ADRC NASDRC). Selected Reference FRUIT Common Privet *Lingustrum vulgare*, elder *Sambucus nigra*, mulberry *Morus* sp. Diet Record Card Wild Strawberry *Fragaria vesca*, Red currant *Ribes sativum* (ADRC), African mulberry *Morus mesozygia* (ARU NASDRC). Selected Reference ANIMAL FOOD mealworms. Diet Record Cards termite alates (SAADRC), ants, flies, spiders, small slugs (ARU).

Blue-headed Wood Dove

Turtur brehmeri 25cm

Alternative names: Blue-headed Dove, Gold Coast Blue-headed Dove, Maiden Dove.

Description: Sexes similar. Forehead bluish white; crown blue-grey; nape blue; hindneck chestnut, tinged light blue; mantle and back chocolate brown; rump brown; upper tail-coverts and tail dark rufous; forehead and chin light blue; throat, breast and belly deep rust brown; under tail-coverts chocolate; iris dark brown; bill dark red; tip greenish; legs and feet dark red. Juvenile has upperparts cinnamon-brown with indistinct black barring.

Male. *T.b.infelix* differs from the nominate race in having upperparts paler; wingspots metallic green.

Voice: Described by Serle *et al* as a plaintive cooing louder and more abrupt than the cooing of the the Tambourine Dove.

Habitat: Lowland primary forest and old secondary growth.

Distribution: Southern Cameroon, Gabon and Zaire.

T.b.infelix Sierre Leoné to Mt. Cameroon.

Feeding: Seeds, namely Castor oil plant *Ricinus communis*, insects, including termites and their larvae.

Breeding: Nest, constructed of sticks, twigs and rootlets forming a shallow cup deposited on top of dry leaves, placed at 2,5-5,5m above ground on a horizontal branch of a forest tree. Eggs buff; clutch 1-2.

Namaqua Dove

Oena capensis 24-27cm

Alternative names: Black-throated Dove, Cape Dove, Harlequin Dove, Masked Dove, Long-tailed Dove.

Description: Male. Forehead, in front of eye, chin, throat and upper breast black; crown and nape grey; mantle and upper tail-coverts earth brown; two black bands across rump; long graduated tail blackish; breast to belly white; wing-coverts grey; violet-blue on inner secondaries; under wing-coverts chestnut; iris dark brown; bill purple, tip orange; legs and feet purplish red. Female differs from the male in lacking the black facial mask; upperparts more greyish, less brownish; bill reddish black. Juvenile similar to adult female, but the feathers of the upperparts sub-terminally barred with black and tipped with buffish white.

Male. *O.c.anonyma* differs from the nominate race in being paler grey above.

Voice: Described by Urban *et al* as having an advertising song, a quiet, frequently repeated, very short double 'hoo', followed by longer, plaintive 'wooooo'.

Habitat: *Acacia* thornveld, riverine bush, gardens and cultivated lands.

Distribution: Northern and western Cape Province, Gauteng (highveld), Free State, KwaZulu-Natal, South Africa to Lesotho and Swaziland.

O.c.anonyma Northern Province and northern Cape, South Africa to Namibia, Botswana, Zimbabwe, Mozambique, Zambia, Malawi, Kenya, Uganda, Tanzania, Somalia and Ethiopia. Also Chad, Mali, Nigeria, Togo and Sierre Leone. Algeria (breeding). Accidental in Morocco, Mauritania and Egypt.

Feeding: Seeds of grasses and weeds, grain, insects and molluscs. Seeds of Teff *Eragrostis tef*, Rain Grass *E.pilosa*, 'proso' (as commonly known) *Panicum milliaceum*, Pearl millet *Pennisetum glaucum*, finger millet (racemes arranged digitately or sub-digitately. Other important seeds are dicotyledons *Cleome* and *Heliotropium*. Cultivated crops sorghum *Sorghum* spp., and rice *Oryza* spp. Insects picked from cattle and horse dung. Snails recorded in the droppings of two immature birds.

Breeding: The nest is a tiny frail structure of fine rootlets and dry grasses, usually less than 1,5m above the ground. Sites vary from low bushes, in dead branches, in reeds, grass tufts, hedges, on top of a low mound or anthill, on broken maize stalks and on the ground beneath a small shrub. Recorded nesting in piles of dead wood and low branches of the following species, namely Three-thorned acacia, *Acacia senegal*, *A.raddiana*, *Commiphore*, *Balanites*, *Lycium* and *tamarisks*. Unusual sites recorded are in an old tin lying in the veld, in a mist net over a shrub and on a railing adjacent to a building. Eggs creamy yellow or deep buff; clutch 2, sometimes 1 and even 3 recorded; incubation period 14-17 days; fed by both parents; nestling period 16-18 days.

Aviculture: Selected Reference CLUTCH 2; INCUBATION PERIOD 12-17 days; NESTLING PERIOD 12-21 days. Personal Communication CLUTCH 2,2,2; INCUBATION PERIOD 13,14,14 days; NESTLING PERIOD 16, about 17 days. Nest Record Cards CLUTCH 1,2,2,2; INCUBATION PERIOD 13,14, (ANRC) 14 (ARU) 15 days (SAANRC); NESTLING PERIOD 16,16 (ANRC) 14 (ARU) 17 days (SAANRC). Selected Reference WILDFOOD Seeds of Teff grass *Eragrostis tef*, Bulrush millet *Pennisetum americanum* Personal Communication Napier (fodder) grass *P.purpureum*. Diet Record Cards Guinea grass *Panicum maximum* (SAADRD), Hay *Chloris virgata* (ARU ADRC). Diet Record Cards ANIMAL FOOD beetle larvae, including mealworms (ARU), termites (ARU ADRC).

Yellow-bellied Green Pigeon

Treron waalia 30cm

Alternative names: Bruce's Green Pigeon, Waalia Fruit Pigeon.

Description: Male. Entire head, sides of neck, nape and upper mantle light grey; lower mantle, back, rump and upper tail-coverts olive-green; tail greyish; flanks grey, washed olive; chin and throat light grey; breast and belly bright lemon-yellow; under tail-coverts chestnut, edged cream; wing-patch mauve, primaries brown, edged pale yellow; iris blue, outer ring red; bill whitish, cere blue; legs and feet orange. Female differs from the male in having mauve wing patch smaller. Juvenile differs from adult female in having wing patch incomplete.

Voice: Described by Goodwin as a 'quarrelsome chatter' and a 'crooning whistle' a 'long soft call followed by two shorter ones, and a 'sort of clucking whistling yap.'

Habitat: Dry savanna thorn scrub and densely wooded valleys where there are fig trees.

Distribution: Senegal to southern Arabia.

Feeding: Fruit of Sycamore fig *Ficus sycamous*, *F.platyphylla*, *Gutta percha*, *Podocarpus* and *Zizyphyus*.

Breeding: Nest, a loosely made platform of twigs and a concealed or exposed position, often at end of wide spreading branch, such as *Acacia* spp., at least 3m above the ground. Eggs glossy, white; clutch 1-2.

Aviculture: Selected Reference CLUTCH 1-2; INCUBATION PERIOD 16-18 days. Nest Record Card CLUTCH 1 (ANRC); INCUBATION PERIOD 15 days (ANRC); NESTLING PERIOD 14 days (ANRC). Selected Reference FRUIT blueberry *Vaccinium* sp., blackberry *Rubus* sp. Diet Record Card mulberry *Morus* sp., Herero wild melon *Acanthosicyos naudiniana* (ADRC).

African Green Pigeon

Treron calva 28-30cm

Alternative names: African Fruit Pigeon, Barefaced Green Pigeon, Green Pigeon, Green Fruit Pigeon.
T.c.wakefieldii Wakefield's Green Pigeon.
T.c.granviki Uganda Green Pigeon.
T.c.brevicera Moshi Green Pigeon,
Kenya Green Pigeon.
T.c.delalandii Delalande's Green Pigeon.
T.c.granti Coastal Green Pigeon.

Description: Sexes similar. Entire head bright yellow-green merging into hind-neck of grey; mantle, back, rump and upper tail-coverts olive-green; chin and throat dark yellowish olive; rest of underparts greyish yellow-green; flanks olive, the feathers broadly edged laterally with white; under tail-coverts olive-green grading to cinnamon; tail pale grey, same viewed dorsally olive-green, tipped with greyish cream; wing shoulder dark vinaceous grey or mauve; primaries and secondaries black; iris bluish white; bill silvery bluish white, cere ans scarlet; legs and feet orange. Juvenile paler than adult and lacking lilac wing-shoulder.

Adults. *T.c.nudirostris* differs from the nominate in having underparts more yellowish green; bare skin more extensive on forehead.

T.c.sharpei differs from the nominate in having head brighter yellowish green; mantle and rump paler.

T.c.peonsis differs from nominate in having upper and underparts brighter.

T.c.virescens differs from the nominate in having underparts deeper and duller tone of green.

T.c.uellensis differs from *granviki* in having head less bright yellow-green; lacking or almost lacking grey on hindneck and collar.

T.c.brevicera similar to *granviki* but under tail-coverts grey, feathers edged with yellow; bill orange-red, salmon-pink or vermillion.

T.c.gibberifrons similar to *sharpei* but more yellower; more pronounced grey hindneck collar.

T.c.wakefieldii similar to *gibberifrons* but tail grey.

T.c.orientalis differs from nominate in having small pinkish shoulder patch.

T.c.schalowi differs from the nominate in having grey collar ill-defined or absent; mantle, rump and upper tail-coverts more grey, less olive-green.

T.c.ansorgei similar to *gibberifrons* but greener.

T.c.damarensis differs from *schalowi* in having head and upperparts brighter yellowish green.

T.c.vylderi similar to *gibberifrons* but greyer.

T.c.granti similar to *delalandii* but belly yellower.

Voice: Described by Mackworth-Praed & Grant as a piping cry 'tweti-tweti-tweti' followed by several popping clicks.

Habitat: *Brachystegia*, in mixed woodland, especially coastal dune forest, open cultivated country in vicinity of fruit trees.

Distribution: South-eastern Nigeria, western Zaire, Gabon and northern Angola.

T.c.nudirostris Senegal to Guinea.

T.c.sharpei Guinea, Sierre Leone, western Nigeria and northern Cameroon.

T.c.peonsis Fernando Pó Island.

T.c.virescens Principé Island.

T.c.uellensis north-eastern Zaire, southern Central African Republic, south-western Sudan, western Uganda and south-western Ethiopia.

T.c.brevicera southern Kenya and north-eastern Tanzania.

T.c.gibberifrons south-eastern Sudan, southern Zaire, western Kenya and north-western Tanzania.

T.c.wakefieldii eastern Kenya, north-eastern Tanzania.

T.c.orientalis south-eastern Tanzania, northern Mozambique, eastern Zambia, Malawi and eastern Zimbabwe.

T.c.schalowi south-eastern Zaire, Zambia, eastern Angola, north-western Zimbabwe and northern Botswana.

T.c.ansorgei southern Angola.

T.c.damarensis northern Namibia and northern Botswana.

T.c.vylderi north-eastern Namibia.

T.c.granti eastern Tanzania.

T.c.delalandii Mozambique, Swaziland and South African provinces of eastern Cape and KwaZulu-Natal.

T.c.glauca eastern Botswana, Zimbabwe and South African province of western and northern Mpumalanga.

Feeding: Fruits, mainly figs *Ficus* spp., Waterbessie *Syzgium cordatum*, Transvaal Ebony *Doispyros mespili-formis*, Persian lilac *Melia azederach*. Forget-me-not tree *Duranta repens*, Lance-leaf waxberry *Myrica serrata*, Transvaal red-milkwood *Mimusops zeyheri*, Large-leaved cassine *Caccine schlecterana*, Dopprium *Pappea capensis*, African mulberry *Morus misozygia*, Wild peach *Kiggelaria africana*, Veld fig *Ficus burt-davyi*, Umbrella tree *Musanga smithii*, yellowoods *Popocarpus* spp. Buds of mangroves. Reputed to attack cultivated peaches and other fruit in Gauteng, South Africa. Recorded to feed on sorghum *Sorghum* sp., and Common Russet grass *Loudetia simplex* in Zimbabwe. Also consumes mound termites.

Breeding: Nest is a flat flimsy platform of interlaced twigs and leaf petioles on a horizontal or gently sloping branch or in a fork. Forty eight nesting sites revealed that 41 nests were sighted in leafy growth and 7 in bare trees; sometimes in Mistletoe *Viscum* spp., or *Loranthus* spp. or on old pigeon nest. Sited 2-21m above ground in *acacia, brachystegia*, mopane and other woodland with Marula *Sclerocarya caffra* recorded. They are inclined to nest in country gardens, in tourist camps and around villages. It is suggested that close proximity to man enables improved security against predators. Nests built solitary or in loose aggregations at 18-20m apart by both sexes. The nest measurements are 13-15cm in diameter and 3-4cm in depth, but vary considerably. Eggs white, oval, smooth, matt or slightly glossy; clutch 1-2; incubation carried out by both sexes for 13-14 days; additional material is brought to the nest during this period; nestling period 11-13 days.

Aviculture: Selected Reference CLUTCH 1-2; INCUBATION PERIOD 13-14 days; NESTLING PERIOD 11-18 days. Nest Record Cards CLUTCH 2,2 (ARU) 1 (SAANRC) 2 (ANRC); INCUBATION PERIOD 13 (ARU) 13 (SAANRC) 13 days (ANRC); NESTLING PERIOD 12 (ARU) 12 (SAANRC) 13 days (ANRC). Selected Reference FRUIT blueberry *Vaccinium* sp., mulberry *Morus* sp., blackberry *Rubus* sp. Diet Record Cards mulberry *Morus* sp., (SAADRC), Custard apple *Annona reticulata*, (ADRC), Pomegranate *Punica granatum* (ARU).

Pemba Island Pigeon

Treron pembaensis 27cm

Alternative name: Pemba Green Pigeon.

Description: Sexes similar. Entire head, nape, chin, throat and breast greyish green; mantle and back olive-yellow; mauve patch on wing-shoulder; under tail-coverts rufous; iris blue; bill whitish; legs and feet yellow. Juvenile undescribed.

Voice: Described by Pakenham as a soft '*kui-riu-kiu-tiu,kiwrikekwrikek*'.

Habitat: Forests with Kapok tree *Ceiba pentandra* (exotic), Mango *Mangifera indica*, a dense evergreen tree, medium sized or large reaching 18-20m in height.

Distribution: Pemba Island.

Feeding: One crop contained 106 young fruit of Betal Palm *Areca catechu*. The fruit is also ovoid to oblong, narrow at the apex, 4-5cm long. When mature, yellow to orange or scarlet.

Breeding: Slight platform of twigs, namely of *Tamarindus*, a medium to large evergreen tree with dense rounded crown and dropping leaves reaching 20-24m in height, *Pteroparpus, Millingtonia, Cassia siamese* and *Cassis javanica* often at the end of a bough; clutch 2.

Aviculture: No records.

São Thomé Green Pigeon

Treron sanctithomae 31cm

Description: Sexes similar. Entire head, nape, chin, throat and breast dark greenish grey; mantle and back dark olive-green; mauve patch on wing-shoulder; under tail-coverts rufous, edged buff; iris blue; bill whitish; legs and feet red. Juvenile undescribed.

Voice: Described by Alexander (in Bannerman) as a bi-syllabic '*crooning rattle*'.

Habitat: Plantations and forest canopy.

Distribution: São Thomé Island.

Feeding: Not known.

Breeding: Nest, loosely constructed platform of slender twigs. One nest which held one fresh egg was built in a cacao tree at 2,5m above the ground.

Aviculture: No records.

Grey Parrot

Psittacus erithacus 33cm

Alternative names: African Grey Parrot, Congo Parrot, King Grey Parrot, African Silver Congo Grey Parrot and Silver African Grey (not mutant form).
***P.r.timneh* Timneh Parrot, Timneh African Grey.**

Description: Male. General colour grey with feathers of the crown, nape, hindneck and mantle edged paler grey, giving a silvered effect; rump and underparts even paler, almost whitish; tail and upper tail-coverts red; facial area whitish; iris pale yellow; bill blackish; legs and feet dark grey. Female similar in colouring except smaller and the naked periophthalmic ring rounded instead of obtusely pointed behind; head more rounded, less flat. Juvenile similar to adult female, but tail dark red towards tip; iris black, turning to grey after a year and finally to pale yellow.

Males. *P.e.princeps* similar to nominate race but general to plumage darker and feathers of the underparts tipped with purple.

P.e.timneh differs from nominate in being smaller and having general plumage slate-grey; tail maroon; bill, upper mandible reddish tipped with black, lower mandible black.

Voice: Described by Forshaw as a medley of high-pitched screams and prolonged whistling notes.

Habitat: Primary a lowland forest dweller, but does visit woodland and savanna to feed; also to be found in coastal mangroves, African Oil Plams *Elaeis guineensis* plantations and gardens.

Distribution: South-eastern Ivory Coast to western Kenya and northern Angola.

P.e.timneh southern Guinea to Ivory Coast.

P.e.princeps Fernando Pó and Principé Islands.

Feeding: Seeds, fruits, berries, nuts and grain. Especially favouring the African Oil Palm *Elaeis guineensis* which it strips to extract the kernal. Also feeds on banana *Musca cavendishii*, Red Stinkwood *Prunus africanum* and *Cola tragacantha*. Attacks Maize *Zea mays* doing considerable damage. African girls are employed all day to beat drums in an effort to drive the parrots from their crops. They enjoy a little white fish as these birds have been known to wait in trees along a river where Africans are fishing in the hope that fish will be tossed to them.

Breeding: Nests in holes 10-30m above the ground in a large tree with a knot hole in *Terminalia* sp; also recorded were eggs laid on decayed wood dust 60-200cm from the entrance. Eggs white, rounded, ovate, slightly glossy; clutch 2-4, 4 usually, rarely 5; incubation is carried out by the female; young leave nest at 2-3 months and can feed themselves although still fed and attended to by parents for about 4 months.

Aviculture: Selected Reference CLUTCH 2-5; INCUBATION PERIOD 28-30 days; NESTLING PERIOD 10-13 weeks. Personal Communication CLUTCH 3,4,4,4; INCUBATION PERIOD 27, about 28 days; NESTLING PERIOD 11 weeks. Nest Record Cards CLUTCH 4,4 (SAANRC) 3,4 (NASNRC) 4,4 (ANRC); INCUBATION PERIOD 28 days (SAANRC) 28, about 30 days (ARU), 28 days (ANRC); NESTLING PERIOD 12 weeks (SAANRC) 11,12 weeks (ARU) 13 weeks (ANRC). Selected Reference WILDFOOD, chickweed *Stellaria* spp., Sowthistle *Sonchus oleraceus*, dock *Rumex* sp., dandelion *Taraxacum* spp., fresh green twigs of Hawthorn *Crataegus monogyna*, willow *Salex* sp., Ash *Fraxinus excelsior*. Personal Communication chickweed *Stellaria* sp., fresh green twigs of Hawthorn *Crataegus monogyna*. Nest Record Cards chickweed

Stellaria sp., (ARU ADRC SAADRC). Selected Reference FRUIT Hawthorn *Crataegus monogyna*, Elder *Sambucus nigra*, blackberry *Rubus* sp., Diet Record Cards Marula *Sclerocarya caffra* (ARU SAADRC), Dinya *Vitex clenkowskii* (ADRC), Bird Plum *Berchemia discolor* (ARU ADRC). Pomegranate *Punica granatum* (SAADRC).

Cape Parrot
Poicephalus robustus 33-35cm

Alternative names: Amatola Parrot, Brown-necked Parrot, Green Parrot, Knysna Parrot, Levailiant's Parrot, Pirie Parrot, Red-crowned Parrot, Red-shouldered Parrot.
P.r.fuscicollis **West African Brown-necked Parrot.**

Description: Male. Forehead and cheeks tinged reddish brown; rest of neck and head silvery olive-green, the feathers with dusky centres, streaked and fleckled; reddish frontal patch sometimes present; mantle, scapulars and wing-coverts dusky black with a greenish wash and dark green edges to the feathers; bend of wing and thighs orange-red; under wing-coverts greenish black, edged with olive-green; upper breast pale green; tail blackish brown; iris reddish brown; bare skin around eye whitish; bill whitish brown; legs and feet greyish blue (plumage variable). Female resembles the male except that forehead and crown are deep red. Juvenile has head and wings brownish olive, sometimes tinged with pink; lacks red on thighs and wings; tail greenish black.

Adults. *P.r.sauhelicus* differs from the nominate race in having the head and neck silvery grey; reddish frontal band rarely displayed.

P.r.fuscicollis similar to *sauhelicus* but more bluish mostly on lower back and rump.

Voice: Described by Skead as a high pitched 'zzkeek' or a disyllabic 'zzk-eek'; also a variety of notes such as 'zwee-ank' or 'zwee-enk'.

Habitat: Evergreen and riverine forests and mangroves.

Distribution: Cape, Mpumalanga and KwaZulu-Natal, provinces of South Africa to western Swaziland.

P.r.suahelicus Northern Province and Mpumalanga, South Africa to Mozambique, Zimbabwe, the Caprivi Strip, northern Botswana, central Tanzania, south-eastern Zaire and Angola.

P.r.fuscicollis Gambia to northern Ghana and Togo.

Feeding: Fruit kernels, seeds and to a large extent grain. The kernel is cracked open after the skin and flesh have been split and discarded, only the pip is retained. Kernels from the following trees are eaten in southern African; Outeniqua yellowood *Popocarpus falcatus,* Real yellowood *P.latifolius,* Wild Plum *Harpephyllum caffrum,* Ironwood *Olea capensis,* Coast red-milkwood *Mumusops caffra,* Cape Chestnut *Calendendrum capense,* Forest comminphora *Commiphora woodii,* Coast erythrina *Erythina caffra,* Narrow-leaved mahobohobo *Uapaca nitdula,* Kuduberry *Pseudo-lachnostylis maprouncifolia,* Pale-fruited monotes *Monotes glaber,* White stinkwood *Celtis africana,* Transvaal Ebony *Diospyros mespiliformis,* Marketti tree *Ricinodendron rautanenii,* Persian lilac *Melia azedrach,* Black wattle *Acacia mearnsii,* fruit of Wild fig *Ficus* spp., Boabab *Adansonia digitata,* Mobala Plum *Parinari curateillifolia* and nectar of Coast erythrina *Erythrina caffra.* On occasions raid apple orchards and Pecan nut plantations. Also recorded taking sorghum while perched on the plant. In Gambia raids harvested groundnuts left in heaps to dry.

Breeding: Nests in cavities in trees, namely the Boabab *Adansonia digitata* and *Brachystegia.* Situated at up to 12m above ground with natural hollows being preferred, but may also utilise a disused hole of the barbet or woodpecker. On record utilising that of an Olive Woodpecker *Mesopicos griseocephalus.* Holes are often deepened by the birds to suit their needs. The only material used to deposit the eggs on is the chips of which happen to accumulate in the nest chamber during the excavation process. Nest cavities have been recorded at 19cm deep and 18cm across with an access hole 8cm in diameter. Eggs white, glossy, rounded; clutch 2-4; incubation 24-28 days by both sexes; nestling period 67-72 days.

Aviculture: Selected Reference CLUTCH 2-4; INCUBATION PERIOD 25-28 days; NESTLING PERIOD 55-57 days. Personal Communication CLUTCH 3. Nest Record Cards CLUTCH 3,3,4 (SAANRC) 4 (ANRC); INCUBATION PERIOD 26, about 28 days (SAANRC) 28 days (ANRC); NESTLING PERIOD 9 weeks (SAANRC) 10 weeks (ANRC). Selected Reference WILDFOOD. Seeds of Wild grain sorghum *Sorghum bicolor,* Giant millet *S.dochna.* Diet Record Cards Natal plum *Carissa grandilora,* Star apple *Chrysophyllum cainito.* Common wild fig *Ficus natalensis* (SAADRC),

Mobola plum *Parinari mobola,* Kaffirboom *Erythrina caffra.* Wild olive *Olea capensis,* Black wattle *Acacia mearnsii,* Pomegranate *Pucina grandatum,* Prickly pear *Opuntia bulgaris,* Herero wild melon *Acanthosicyos naudiniana,* Bread fruit *Artocarpus incisus,* Wild grain *Sorghum bicolor,* Giant millet *S.dochna* (ADRC). Diet Record Cards FRUIT. Natal plum *Carrisa grandiflora.* Mobola plum *Parinari mobola* (SAADRC), Wild olive *Olea capensis,* Pomegranate *Pucina grandatum,* Prickly pear *Opuntia vulgaris,* Herero wild melon *Acanthosicyos naudiniana,* Star apple *Chrysophyllum cainito,* Common wild fig *Ficus natalensis* (ADRC).

Jardine's Parrot
Poicephalus gulielmi 28cm

Alternative names: Congo Red-crowned Parrot, Red-headed Parrot, Red-crowned Parrot.
***P.g.fantiensis,* Gold Coast Orange-crowned Parrot, The Fantee.**
***P.g.massaicus,* Masai Red-headed Parrot.**
***P.g.permistus,* Eldoma Red-headed Parrot.**

Description: Sexes similar. Plumage mainly dark green; forehead, crown, bend and lower edge of wings and thighs orange-red; lores blackish; mantle, back and scapulars blackish brown; each feather edged with green; rump yellowish green; wing primaries secondaries and tail blackish; iris reddish brown, orbital ring pinkish white; bill, upper mandible whitish, lower blackish; legs and feet greyish brown. Juvenile is paler than adult and lacks the orange red on the forehead, edge of wings and thighs.

Adults. *P.g.fantiensis* differs from the nominate race in having the forehead, crown and edges of wings orange instead of orange-red

P.g.permistus is a doubtful sub-species which is said to be intermediate between nominate and *massicus* and differs in having rump and upper tail-coverts lighter and more yellowish green; mantle, back and scapulars more brownish, less blackish and less orange-red on forehead and crown.

Voice: Described by Brown (in Forshaw) as a conversational, screeching chatter in flight and while feeding.

Habitat: *Podocarpus* forests and in tall trees adjacent to coffee plantations.

Distribution: Southern Cameroon, Central African Republic to northern Angola.

P.g.fantiensis Cameroon, Ghana to Liberia,

P.g.massaicus southern Kenya and north-eastern Tanzania.

P.g.permistus central Kenya.

Feeding: Seeds, nuts, fruits and berries with the contents of one stomach revealing pieces of insects. Also recorded feeding on the flowers or seeds of Australian

Silver Oak *Grevillea robusta*, pods of *Spathodea* spp. *Cedrus* spp., including wild olives and oil palm nuts.

Breeding: Eighteen nests were investigated on Mount Meru in northern Tanzania during the breeding season 1971-72 and of these 13 (72%) were found in Muhonde *Hagenia abyssinica*; four (22%) in *Podocarpus* and one (6%) in *Juniper* at an average height of 9m in natural hollows of live trees with a terminal nesting chamber of (7,5-12,5cm) in diameter. Eggs white, oval, glossy; clutch 2,4.

Aviculture: Selected Reference CLUTCH 4; INCUBATION PERIOD 28, about 26 days; NESTLING PERIOD 10-11 weeks. Nest Record Cards CLUTCH 4 (SAANRC), 3,4 (ARU); INCUBATION PERIOD 26 days (ARU), 26,26 days (ANRC); NESTLING PERIOD after 7 weeks (ARU). Diet Record Cards, Seeds of fruit of Star apple *Chrysopyllum cainito*, Climbing Raisin *Grewia caffra*, Bird Plum *Berchemia discolor*, Sand Jackalberry *Diospyros batocana*, Nana Berry *Rhus dentata*, African Cranberry *Vaccinium exul* (ARU), Tassel Berry *Antidesma venosum* (ADRC). Diet Record Cards FRUIT Tassel berry *Antidesma venosum*, Live-Long *Lannea discolor*, Green Monkey Orange *Strychnos spinosa*, Waterberry *Syzgium guineense*, White-berry bush *Securinega virosa*, Tree Strawberry *Caphalanthus natalensis* (ARU), Giant Raisin *Grewia hexamita*, African cranberry *Vaccinium exul*, Nana berry *Rhus dentata*, Sand Jackalberry *Diospyros batocana*, Bird Plum *Berchemia discolor*, Climbing Raisin *Grewia caffra*, Star apple *Chrysopyhllum caintito*, Pomegranate *Punica granatum*, Custard apple *Ammona recticulata* (ADRC).

Brown-headed Parrot
Poicephalus cryptoxanthus 22-24cm

Alternative names: Brown-hooded Parrot, Concealed Yellow Parrot.

Description: Sexes similar. Head and neck dusky brown with a yellowish wash; sides of head, throat and upper breast light buffy olive; mantle and back yellowish green, the feathers laced with deep green; wing-coverts and secondaries olive-green; under wing-coverts bright yellow; primary-coverts and primaries greenish brown, tinged on outer webs with blue, upper tail-coverts and rump olive-green; tail olive-brown, tipped with green; iris pale yellow; bill, upper mandible greyish blue becoming darker towards tip, lower mandible whitish; legs and feet greyish black. Juvenile paler than adult with the upper breast suffused with dull yellow.

Adult. *P.c.tanganyikae* differs from the nominate race in having head more olive-brown; rump and underparts brighter and more yellowish.

Voice: Described by Maclean, giving usual calls as a strident '*chree-oo*'...and a sharp '*Kreek*', with variations.

Habitat: Woodland and dry thornveld and sparsely timbered grasslands.

Distribution: Gauteng (lowlands), and eastern KwaZulu-Natal, South Africa to eastern Swaziland and south-eastern Zimbabwe

P.c.tanganyikae Mozambique (north to Save River), southern Malawi, eastern Tanzania and coastal Kenya, Zanzibar and Pemba Islands.

Feeding: Seeds, nuts, fruits, berries and nectar. Seeds of Baobab *Adansonia digitata*, Knob-thorn *Acacia nigrescens*, Umbrella-thorn *A.tortillis*, Smooth-bark flat-crown *Albizia gummifera*, Kaffirboom *Erythrina* sp., fruit of Mkwata *Ficus* spp., Nyala tree *Pseudocadia zambesica*, berries of cultivated cassava *Manihot esculenta*, flower petals of Kiaat tree *Pterocarpus angolensis*, young green shoots of various trees and nectar by probing the blooms of the Flat-flowered aloe *Aloe marlothii*. Record attacking millet, ripening maize and sorghum, as well as nuts laid out to dry in the sun. Feeds on the inflorescences of coconut palms in Zanzibar.

Breeding: Nest site is a natural hole in a dead or living tree up to 10m above ground, the baobab being a favourite tree. A record exists of a discarded woodpecker's nest being utilized. Nest cavities 50-90cm deep and 12cm in diameter have been recorded. Eggs white, glossy, rounded; clutch 3-4; incubation period 26-30 days by female only, male feeds female on nest.

Aviculture: Selected Reference CLUTCH 3-4; INCUBATION PERIOD 26-30 days; NESTLING PERIOD 12 WEEKS. Personal Communication CLUTCH 3. Nest Record Cards CLUTCH 3; INCUBATION PERIOD 26 days (ANRC) 28 days (ARU); NESTLING PERIOD 11 WEEKS (ANRC) 12 weeks (ARU). Selected Reference WILDFOOD. Seeds of Guineafowl grass *Rottoellia exaltata*, flowers of Weeping boer-bean *Schotia brachypatala*. Diet Record Cards fruit of Baobab *Adansonia digitata*, Common wild fig *Ficus natalensis* (ARU ADRC), Custard apple *Annona reticulata*, Natal plum *Carissa grandatum*, Shepherd's tree *Bosicia albitrunia* (ADRC), Cape fig *F.capensis* (ARU).

Niam-Niam Parrot
Poicephalus crassus 25cm

Description: Sexes similar. General plumage colour green, darker on back and wings; while head and nape brown, tinged with olive-yellow; ear-coverts silvery grey; mantle and back brownish, the feathers broadly marked with dark green, upper tail-coverts bright green; tail dusky, tinged dark green; throat and breast olive-brown; rest of underparts bright green; iris red; bill greyish brown, upper mandible, becoming black towards tip, lower pale yellowish horn; legs and feet greyish black. Juvenile: Crown and nape greyish brown, marked with olive-yellow; underparts yellowish green; bill yellowish, tip dark grey on upper mandible.

Habitat: Mountain forests and gallery forest in savanna.

Distribution: Eastern Cameroon to south-western Sudan.

Feeding: Stomach contents revealed partly digested millet and pale yellow seeds.

Breeding: Not known.

Aviculture: Selected Reference CLUTCH 4; INCUBATION PERIOD 27 days; NESTLING PERIOD 13 WEEKS. Nest Record Cards CLUTCH 4 (ANRC); INCUBATION PERIOD 27 days (ANRC); NESTLING PERIOD 13 weeks (ANRC).

Senegal Parrot
Poicephalus senegalus 23-24cm

Alternative names: Grey-headed Parrot, Yellow-bellied Senegal, Yellow-vented Senegal Parrot.
***P.s.mesotypus* Kano Yellow-vented Senegal Parrot, Orange-bellied Senegal Parrot.**
***P.s.versteri* Red-vented Senegal Parrot, Scarlet-bellied Senegal Parrot.**

Description: Sexes similar. Crown, nape, chin and throat dark grey; cheeks, sides of face and ear-coverts silvery grey; hindneck, mantle, back and wing-coverts bright green; tail brownish green; wing primaries blackish brown, with outer webs washed with bright green; lower breast and belly orange-yellow; under tail-coverts yellow; iris yellow; bill, legs and feet blackish. Juvenile paler with brownish head and ear-coverts less silvery-grey; lacks the yellow breast; iris dark brown, changing gradually to grey, later greyish yellow; bill greyish brown, tinged pink.

Adults. *P.s.versteri* differs from the nominate race in having the belly red; flanks yellow; upperparts deeper green.

P.s.mesotypus differs from the nominate in having upperparts paler green; belly orange.

Voice: Described by Forshaw as a series of short screeches and rather high-pitched whistles.

Habitat: Open forest and savanna, woodland, preferring areas where Baobab *Adansonia digitata*, Locust Bean *Parkia filicoidea* and Borassus Palms *Borassus* sp. are numerous.

Distribution: Senegal to Guinea and southern Mali.

P.s.versteri Ivory Coast, Ghana to Nigeria.

P.s.mesotypus eastern and north-eastern Nigeria, south-western Chad and northern Cameroon.

Feeding: Seeds, leaf buds, fruits and grain. Recorded feeding on the seeds of Locust Bean *Parkia filicoidea*, Mahogany *Khaya senegalensis*, Shea Butter *Butyrosperum parkii*, Dinya *Vitex cienkowskii* and Madobia *Pterocarpus erinaceua*, pods of Ana tree *Acacia abida*, *Kassia* sp., fruit of figs *Ficus* spp., Marula *Selerocarya birrea*, Baobab *Adansonia digitata*, Small sourplum *Ximenia americana*. Raiding parties visit cultivated areas to feed on maize, millet and groundnuts.

Breeding: Nests in tree holes with Baobab *Adansonia digitata* and Locust Bean *Parkia fillicoidea* being known sites most favoured. Woodland Kingfishers *Halcyon senegalensis* were observed showing aggression to these parrots who ventured too close to their intended nest holes. Eggs white, rounded; clutch 2-4.

Aviculture: Selected Reference CLUTCH 2-4; INCUBATION PERIOD about 22-28 days; NESTLING PERIOD 9-11 weeks. Personal Communication CLUTCH 2; INCUBATION PERIOD 25 days; NESTLING PERIOD after 9 weeks. Nest Record Cards CLUTCH 3,3,4 (ANRC); INCUBATION PERIOD 27 days (SAANRC) 27, 28 days (ARU); NESTLING PERIOD 9 weeks (SAANRC) about 9,10 weeks (ARU). Selected Reference WILDFOOD. Fresh cut Lucerne *Medicago sativa*. Personal Communication fresh cut lucerne *Medicago sativa*. Diet Record Cards Star apple *Chrysophyllum cainito*, Bird Plum *Berchemia discolor*, Sand Jackalberry *Diospyros batocana* (ARU), Climbing Raisin *Grewia hexamita*, Tree Strawberry *Cephalanthus natalensis*, White-berry Bush *Securinega virosa*, Waterberry *Syzygium guineense*, Green Monkey Orange *Strychnos spinosa*, Live-long *Lannea discolor*, Tassel Berry *Antidesma venosum* (ADRC). Diet Record Cards FRUIT. Custard apple *Annona reticulata*, Pomegranate *Punica granatum*, Star apple *Chrysophyllum cainito*, Climbing Raisin *Grewia caffra*, Bird Plum *Berchemia discolor* (ARU), Sand Jackalberry *Diospyros batocana*, Nana berry *Rhus dentata*, African cranberry *Vaccinium exul*, Giant Raisin *Grewia hexamita*, Tree Strawberry *Cephalanthus natalensis*, White-berry bush *Securinega virosa*, Waterberry *Syzygium guineense* (ADRC), Green Monkey Orange *Strychnos spinosa*, Live-long *Lannea discolor*, Tassel berry *Antidesma venosum* (SAADRC).

Red-bellied Parrot
Poicephalus rufiventris 22cm

Alternative names: Abyssinian Parrot, African Orange-bellied Parrot, Orange-bellied Parrot, Red-breasted Parrot.
***P.r.pallidus* Somaliland Orange-bellied Parrot, Somalil and Red-bellied Parrot.**

Description: Male. Forehead, crown and nape greyish brown; ear-coverts paler; chin to upper breast pale brown, tinged reddish; lower breast, under wing-coverts and rest of underparts orange; mantle, back and wings ashy brown, latter faintly tinged bluish; rump yellowish green, tinged bluish; iris orange-red; bill, cere and orbital skin black; legs and feet greyish black. Female differs from the male in having lower breast and rest of underparts green; under wing-coverts greyish. Juvenile is like adult female, but males have under wing-coverts orange and orange markings on upper belly.

Male. *P.r.pallidus* differs from the nominate race in having head and upper breast paler brown.

Voice: Described by Mackworth-Praed & Grant as a shrill screech in flight.

Habitat: Dry woodland with large flat-topped *acacia* trees and *commiphora* thornbush and especially where Baobab trees are present.

Distribution: Central Ethiopia to north-eastern Tanzania.

P.r.pallidus Somalia and eastern Ethiopia.

Feeding: Seeds, fruits and cultivated grain, notably maize. In Somalia, the fruits of *Ficus* sp. and *acacia* seeds are taken. In Kenya fruit of *Commiphora* sp., Simple-thorned torchwood *Balanites aegyptica*, and Tanzania Sandpaper cordia *Cordia ovalis* and Blackwood dalbergia *Dalbergia molanoxylon* are taken.

Breeding: Nests in tree holes 2-3m above ground, often in a Baobab or in an arboreal or terrestrial termite's mound. Eggs ivory white, clutch 1-2; two nests were found in Somalia with one containing two advanced chicks and the other a fresh egg.

Aviculture: Selected Reference CLUTCH 3; INCUBATION PERIOD 28 days; NESTLING PERIOD after 12 weeks. Personal Communication CLUTCH 3. Nest Record Card CLUTCH 3, INCUBATION PERIOD 28 days, NESTLING PERIOD 12 WEEKS (ANRC). Personal Communication FRUIT Baobab *Adansonia digitata*, Elder *Sambucus nigra*, Hawthorn *Crataegus monogyna*, blackberry *Rubus* sp. Diet Record Cards Bird Plum *Berchemia discolor* (ADRC).

Meyer's Parrot
Poicephalus meyeri 21-23 cm

Alternative names: Brown Parrot, Meyer's Brown Parrot, Sudan Brown Parrot. *P.m.matschiei* East African Brown Parrot. *P.m.transvaalensis* South African Parrot, South African Brown Parrot. *P.m.saturatus* Uganda Brown Parrot.

Description: Sexes similar. Forehead and nape brown; crown bright yellow; edge and bend of wing, under wing-coverts and thighs yellow; lower back, rump and upper tail-coverts greenish blue; tail olive-brown with greenish tips; foreneck, chin and throat brown; breast to under tail-coverts bluish green; iris orange, red, brown or brown around the pupil with a yellow outer rim; bill dark brown to black; legs and feet greyish black. Juvenile lacks yellow on crown and thighs; under wing-coverts greenish brown with less or no yellow visible; underparts olive- green; iris dark brown.

Adults. *P.m.saturatus* differs from the nominate race in having darker brown upperparts; rump green washed with cobalt blue.

P.m.matschiei differs from the nominate race in having darker underparts; rump bright blue.

P.m.transvaalensis similar to *matschiei,* but has upperparts paler brown.

P.m.reichenowi differs from the nominate in lacking yellow on crown; upperparts dark brown.

P.m.damarensis differs from the nominate in also lacking yellow on crown; upperparts paler brown.

Voice: Described by McLachlan & Liversidge as a high-pitched 'chee-chee-chee'.

Habitat: Savanna woodland, dry *acacia* thornveld country interspersed with baobab trees and belts of timber bordering watercourses.

Distribution: Southern Chad, north-eastern Cameroon to western Ethiopia.

P.m.saturatus Uganda, Kenya and western Tanzania.

P.m.matschiei south-eastern Kenya to Zambia and Malawi.

P.m.transvaalensis North-West and Northern Province, South Africa to Mozambique (north of Save River), Zimbabwe and eastern and northern Botswana.

P.m.reichenowi northern and central Angola and south-western Zaire.

P.m.damarensis northern Namibia and southern Angola.

Feeding: Seeds, nuts, fruits, berries and grain. Feeds on the fruits, pods or nuts of Narrow-leaved mahobohobo *Upapaca nitidula*, Pale-fruited monotes *Monotes glaber*, Russet bushwillow *Combretum hereroensis*, Cross-berry *Grewia occidentalis*, Marula *Sclerocarya caffra*, Kudu-berry *Pseudolachnostylis maprouneifolia*, Buffalo-thorn *Ziziphus mucronata*, Persial lilac *Melia* azedarach, Rough-leaved raisin *Grewia flavescens*. Flowers of Weeping boer-bean *Schotia brachypetala*, Pod mahogany *Afzelia quanzensis*, Sycamore fig *Ficus sycomorus*, Sausage tree *Kilgelia africana*. Known to raid orange orchards and maize from cobs of living plants.

Breeding: The nest is made in a hole in a dead or living tree, or amongst thick creepers or tangles. May also utilize holes of barbets and woodpeckers. Two records exist, one of a nest recently vacated by a Bearded Woodpecker *Tripias namaquus* and the second in the Nylsvley Nature Reserve in Gauteng, South Africa which contained young birds which were thought to be two-thirds grown with the parents making infrequent visits from one to three hour intervals; they remained at the nest site for half and hour in which time both fed the chicks by swopping places at the entrance hole. Nest trees recorded are Baobab *Adansonia digitata*, White-thorn *Acacia polyacantha*, Mukwa *Pterocarpus angolensis*, Msasa *Brachystegis speciformis* and Mopane *Colophospermum mopane*. Nest holes are 4-10m above ground, with entrance hole about 5cm in diameter and cavities 40-46cm deep. Eggs white, glossy and slightly ovate; clutch 2-4; deposited on bare wood or a layer of decayed wood chips; incubation period about 30 days, by female only; nestling period about 56 days.

Aviculture: Selected Reference CLUTCH 2-4; INCUBATION PERIOD 29-30, about 29, approximately 30 days; NESTLING PERIOD 8-9 weeks. Personal Communication INCUBATION PERIOD 27, 30 days; NESTLING PERIOD 8,9 weeks. Nest Record Cards CLUTCH 2,3,4,4 (ANRC) 3 (ARU); INCUBATION PERIOD 28,29 days (ANRC); NESTLING PERIOD 8,8 weeks (ANRC). Diet Record Cards FRUIT Marula *Sclerocarya caffra*, Persian lilac *Melia azedarach*, Natal plum *Carissa grandiflora* (ADRC), Jackal-berry *Diospyros mespiliformis*, Common wild fig *Ficus burkei*, Cape fig *F.capensis*, Sycamore fig *F.sycamorus*, Bird's brandy *Lantana rugosa* (ARU). Selected Reference WILDFOOD groundsel *Senecio* sp., chickweed *Stellaria* spp., Jungle rice *Echinocloa colonum*, seeds of Common wild sorghum *Sorghum verticilliformus*. Diet Record Cards chickweed *Stellaria* sp. (ADRC ARU), seeds of fruit of Marula *Sclerocarya caffra*, Jackal-berry *Diospyros mespiliformis*, Cherimoya *Annona chermilia*, Common wild fig *Ficus burkei*, Cape fig *F.capensis*, Sycamore fig *F.sycamorus*, Bird's brandy *Lantana rugosa*, leaves of fresh cut Lucerne *Medicago sativa* (ADRC).

Rüppell's Parrot
Poicephalus rueppellii 22-23cm
Alternative names: Brown Parrot, Damara Parrot.

Description: Male. Crown, nape, hindneck and mantle dusky brown; sides of head and cheeks silvery grey; rump and upper tail-coverts dusky brown and faintly glossed with blue; breast, belly and under tail-coverts dusky brown; bend and front edge of wing, thighs and under wing-coverts yellow; iris orange-red; bill, legs and feet greyish black. Female has rump and upper tail-coverts bright blue; vent and under tail-coverts pale blue. Juvenile with both sexes resemble the female, but with only a faint tinge of yellow on the shoulder; lighter blue rump; under wing-coverts yellowish white; iris brownish; bill, legs and feet black.

Voice: Described by Mackworth-Praed & Grant as a sharp 'quaw'; when alarmed a continuous, shrill screech increasing in pitch and volume.

Distribution: Northern Namibia and southern Angola.

Habitat: Mainly thornveld where there are baobabs and also in the taller trees along the Kunene River.

Feeding: Seeds, fruits, berries, buds, young shoots and insect larvae. Seeds of Sweet thorn *Acacia karoo*. Ana tree *A.albida*, Blue thorn *A.erubescens*, Mosquito tree *Prosopis julifora*, Leadwood *Combretum imberbe*, Eland's bean *Elephantorrhiza elephantina*. Blossoms of Sweet thorn *Acacia karoo*. Shoots of Eland's bean *Elephantorrhiza elephantina*. Fruit of wild figs *Ficus* spp. Insect larvae unidentified.

Breeding: Three records, one nest in a hole about 5m high in a Baobab *Adansonia digitata* one in a dead branch of a *Brachystegia* tree, and one in an acacia, the latter appeared to be discarded by woodpeckers. Eggs ivory-white; clutch 3-4; incubation period 28 days by female only.

Aviculture: Selected Reference CLUTCH 3-4; INCUBATION PERIOD 28-30. Personal Communication CLUTCH 3,3. Nest Record Cards CLUTCH 3 (SAANRC), 3 (NASNRC), 4 (ARU) 3, 4 (ANRC); INCUBATION PERIOD 28,28 days (ARU) 29 days (ANRC); NESTLING PERIOD 8,8 weeks (ARU) 9 weeks (ANRC). Diet Record Cards Sycamore fig *Ficus sycomorus* (ARU), Herero wild melon *Acanthosicyos naudiniana* (ADRC), Transvaal milk plum *Bequaertiodendron megalismontanum*, Marula *Sclerocarya caffra*, African holly *Ilex mitis* (SAADRC). Selected Reference WILD-FOOD. Diet Record Cards Seeds of fruit of Sycamore fig *Ficus sycomorus* (NASDRC), Cashew apple *Averrhoe carambola* (ARU), Marula *Sclerocarya caffra*, African holly *Ilex mitis*, leaves of fresh cut Lucerne *Medicago sativa* (ADRC). Selected Reference ANIMAL FOOD wasp larvae.

Yellow-faced Parrot

Poicephalus flavifrons 26-28cm

Alternative names: Yellow-front Parrot, Shoa Parrot.

Description: Sexes similar. The general plumage colour is green; forehead, crown, around eyes and upper cheeks yellow; in some birds a touch of yellow on the thighs and edge of wings is visible; nape, mantle, back and wings green; primaries dark green, tipped with greenish brown; tail greenish black; iris orange-red; bill, upper mandible greyish black, lower greyish white; legs and feet blackish grey.

Adult. *P.f.aurantiiceps* differs from the nominate race in having orange on the forehead, cheeks and ear-coverts in place of yellow. Juvenile has crown and upper cheeks yellowish olive.

Voice: Described by Mackworth-Praed & Grant as a shrill, unmusical whistle.

Habitat: *Hagenia* forests at an altitude of about 1000-3000m.

Distribution: North-central Ethiopia.

P.f.aurantiiceps south-western Ethiopia.

Feeding: Reported to raid cultivation belonging to African tribesmen to take their grain and millet in season. Fruit and seeds are procured from forest trees, the parrots being partial to avoid fruit of the Baobab *Adansonia digitata*.

Breeding: Nothing is known of the parrot's nesting habits, but is suspected that the site is a tree hole.

Aviculture: No records.

Red-faced Lovebird

Agapornis pullaria 14cm

Alternative names: Angola lovebird, Red-headed lovebird, A.p.ugandae Uganda Red-headed Lovebird. A.p.guineensis West African Lovebird.

Description: Male. Facial mask including chin red; rump bright blue; flight features and wing-coverts black; rest of plumage green; bill red; iris dark brown; legs and feet grey. Female has facial mask including chin orange-red; under wing-coverts green. Juvenile has facial mask including chin yellow; under wing-coverts black in males, green in females; bill reddish with black near base of upper mandible.

Males. *A.p.guineensis* differs from the nominate in having facial mask richer red; rump more extensive blue.

A.p.ugandae differs from the nominate in having rump paler blue.

Voice: Described by Mackworth-Praed & Grant as a twittering 'si-si-si-si' in flight or when perched.

Habitat: Secondary forest, savanna woodland and in vicinity of cultivation.

Distribution: Southern Ethiopia, southern Sudan to north-western Tanzania.

A.p.guineensis, Guinea to northern Zaire and south to Angola.

A.p.ugandae south-western Ethiopia to north-western Tanzania and eastern Zaire.

Feeding: Seeds, fruits, berries and leaf buds. Figs, and sometimes attack guavas and grain.

Breeding: Probably monogamous, nesting solitarily. Nests in a hole excavated by the birds in an aboreal termitarium, but also on rare occasions in a terrestrial termitarium. A spherical chamber is excavated at the end of a tunnel which leads from a rounded entrance hole in an occupied termitarium attached to a bole of a tree 4,2m from the ground; the hard earthy ant's nest had no nesting materials but the floor was covered by a circular pad of hardened excrement 90mm in diameter and 15mm thick.

Aviculture: Selected Reference CLUTCH 3-7; INCUBATION PERIOD about 23, 22-25 days; NESTLING PERIOD 6-7 weeks. Personal Communication CLUTCH 7,5; INCUBATION PERIOD 24 days; NESTLING PERIOD 47 days. Nest Record Cards CLUTCH 4,6 (SAANRC), 4,5 (ARU); INCUBATION PERIOD 22,24 days (SAANRU) 23,25 days (ARU) 24 days (ANRC); NESTLING PERIOD 43,45 days (SAANRC) 45,48 days (ARU) 45 days (ANRC). Selected Reference ANIMAL FOOD ants' eggs, mealworms.

Black-winged Lovebird

Agapornis taranta 16,5 cm

Alternative names: Abyssinian Lovebird, Ethiopian Lovebird, Omo Lovebird, Sobat Black-winged Lovebird.

Description: Male. Forehead, lores and a narrow ring around the eye carmine-red; flight feathers, under wing-coverts and subterminal band on black tail; rest of plumage rich green; iris brown; bill red; legs and feet grey. Female similar to male but lacks red facial adornment; under wing-coverts green, often marked with black. Juvenile similar to adult female, but males have under-wing coverts black; bill dusky yellow, blackish at base.

Voice: Described by Mackworth-Praed & Grant as a shrill twittering call.

Habitat: Highland forests being fairly common in *Juniperus* or *Podocarpus* forests and at low elevations in savanna grasslands with *acacias*.

Distribution: Ethiopia.

Feeding: Seeds, berries and fruits. Recorded are juniper berries and Sycamore fig *Ficus sycamous* and seeds of *Euphorbia* sp.

Breeding: The nest is a cavity in hollow limb or hole in tree, lined with small twigs, grass or leaves. Also uses holes in walls, and may also utilize weavers' nests. Eggs rounded, white; clutch 5-6.

Aviculture: Selected Reference CLUTCH 3-5; INCUBATION PERIOD about 23,24-26 days; NESTLING PERIOD 6-7 weeks. Nest Record Cards CLUTCH 3 (SAANRC) 3 (NASNRC) 4 (ARU); INCUBATION PERIOD 24 days (ARU), 23,24,24 days (ANRC); NESTLING PERIOD 42 days (ARU), 43,45,47 days (ANRC). WILDFOOD Personal Communication Giant millet *Sorghum dochna*. Diet Record Cards unripe heads of Finger millet *Eleusine coracana*, Jungle rice *Echinochloa colona*. (ANRC). FRUIT Selected Reference African mulberry *Morus mesozygia*. Personal Communication Common Wild Fig *Ficus natalensis*. Diet Record Card Litchee *Litchi chinensis* (ARU).

Black-collared Lovebird

Agapornis swinderniana 13cm

Alternative names: Cameroon Black-collared Lovebird, Liberian Lovebird, Swindern's Black-collared Lovebird, Swindern's Lovebird. Ghanaian Black-collared Lovebird.
***A.s.zenkeri* Zenkeri's Lovebird.**
***A.s.emini* Emin's Lovebird.**

Description: Sexes similar. General plumage colour green, head darker; narrow collar on hindneck black followed by reddish band extending to sides of breast; mantle, upper back and under wing-coverts dark green; lower back, rump and upper tail-coverts mauve-blue; tail green, lateral feathers marked with orange and subterminally barred with black as is in wings, outer webs of flight feathers; iris yellow; bill greyish black; legs and feet dusky greenish yellow. Juvenile similar to adult, but lacks collar on hindneck.

Adults. *A.s.zenkeri* differs from the nominate race in having the neck, below the collar, of a reddish brown.

A.s.emini differs from the nominate in having area of reddish brown much narrower.

Voice: Described by Williams as a relatively subdued twittering notes; shriller calls in flight.

Habitat: Lowland moist, evergreen forests.

Distribution: Liberia and Ghana.
A.s.zenkeri Cameroon, Gabon to central Zaire.
A.s.emini eastern Zaire and western Uganda.

Feeding: Almost exclusively on figs *Ficus* spp., also *Rauwolfia, Harungana* and *Mascaranga*, grain, especially millet and visits the blossoms of flame trees *Spathodea*. Crops contents taken in the Congo revealed a caterpillar and some white insect larvae.

Breeding: No records.

Aviculture: Selected Reference FRUIT wild fig *Ficus* sp.

Fischer's Lovebird

Agapornis fischeri 14-15cm

Description: Sexes similar. Forehead red; crown olive-brown; cheeks, chin and throat orange-red; nape, sides of neck and breast dull golden-yellow; underparts dull green; under tail-coverts pale blue; mantle to rump green; upper tail-coverts washed with pale blue; under wing-coverts blue and green; naked periophthalmic ring white; iris brown; bill coral red; legs and feet pale grey. Juvenile similar to the adult, but paler, more noticeable on the head; blackish streaks on the base of the upper mandible.

Voice: Described by Forshaw as a shrill whistle and a high pitched twittering.

Habitat: Frequents savanna dominated by *Commiphora, Acacia* and *Balanites* trees and in cultivation scattered with Baobab *Adansonia digitata*. In Serengeti National Park occurs in stands of Borassus palms *Borassus* sp.

Distribution: Southern Kenya and northern Tanzania. A population recorded from the Isiolo district of Kenya were probably originated from aviary escapees. Introduced some time prior to 1928 to the Tanga district of Tanzania.

Feeding: Seeds of trees and also forages on the ground. In cultivated areas resorts to feeding on crops surrounding native villages.

Breeding: Build in colonies in a tree hole, notably Baobab *Adansonia digitata*, among the bases of palm fronds and in cavities in buildings. In the two latter sites a bulky dome-shaped nest with a side entrance is roughly lined with twigs, grasses, leaves and other available materials. On occasions utilizes swallow's nests and known to roost in the nests of the Rufous-tailed Weaver *Histurgops ruficauda*. Eggs white; clutch 5-8.

Aviculture: Selected Reference CLUTCH 3-8; INCUBATION PERIOD 21-23 days; NESTLING PERIOD 35-38 days. Personal Communication CLUTCH 5;

INCUBATION PERIOD 21,22 days; NESTLING PERIOD 35-37 days. Nest Record Cards CLUTCH 3,4,8 (SAANRC) 3,4,4,6 (ARU) 4,5 (ANRC); INCUBATION PERIOD 21,21 days (ARU) 21,21,23,23,23 days (ANRC); NESTLING PERIOD 35,37 days (ARU) 34,36,36,38,days (ANRC). Personal Communication WILDFOOD Twigs of willow sp., Beech *Fagus sylvatica*, Hawthorn *Crataegus monogyna*, Blackthorn *Prunus spinosa*.

Masked Lovebird

Agapornis personata 14-15cm

Alternative names: Black-faced Lovebird, Black-headed Lovebird, Black-masked Lovebird, Yellow-collared Lovebird.

Description: Sexes similar. Forehead, crown and cheeks brownish black; remainder of head dusky olive; nape, sides of neck, throat and upper breast yellow; mantle, rump and tail green, lateral feathers are subterminally barred with black; upper tail-coverts pale blue; under wing-coverts greyish blue and green; naked periophthalmic ring white; iris dark brown; bill red; legs and feet grey. Juvenile like adult, but duller and small black markings at base of upper mandible.

Voice: Described by Forshaw as a high-pitched twittering.

Habitat: Frequents grasslands and open woodland which is dominated by *acacia*.

Distribution: Northern and central Tanzania and possible south-eastern Kenya. Feral populations in Dar es Salaam and Tanga in Tanzania and in Mombasa, Nairobi and Naivasha in Kenya.

Feeding: Seeds of grasses and weeds. Seeds of *Cassia* sp.

Breeding: Colonial nesters which utilize tree holes, notable Baobab *Adansonia digitata*. Also recorded using the discarded nest holes of barbets and woodpeckers. The nest is a bulky dome shaped construction and lined with stripped bark with entrance tunnel usually being blocked with thorn branches. The bark plays an important part in maintaining the required humidity throughout the incubation period. Also records of conventional sites such as beneath corrugated iron roofs of houses, in crannies of buildings or seafront cliff (Mombasa), and occasionally in an old swift's nest. Eggs white; clutch 4-6.

Aviculture: Selected Reference CLUTCH 3-6; INCUBATION PERIOD 21-23 days, about 25 days; NESTLING PERIOD 37-45 days; Personal Communication CLUTCH 3,4,6,6; INCUBATION PERIOD 21,24 days; NESTLING PERIOD 41,42 days. Nest Record Cards CLUTCH 3,4,4,6 (SAANRC) 3,3,5,6 (ARU); INCUBATION PERIOD 23 days (SAANRC) 21,22,24 days (ARU) 21,23 days (ANRC); NESTLING

PERIOD 40 days (SAANRC) 42,40,41 days (ARU) 40,43 days (ANRC). Selected Reference WILDFOOD dandelion *Taraxacum* spp., Milk thistle *Sonchus oleraceus*, Shepherd's purse *Capsella bursa-pastoris*, chickweed *Stellaria* spp., Personal Communication Twigs of maple *Acer* sp., Blackthorn *Prunes spinosa*, Sycamore *Acer pseudoplatanus*, Mountain ash *Sorbus aucuparia*. Diet Record Cards Leaves of Small-leaved Kiaat *Pterocarpus stevensoni* (ARU), Silver oak *Grevillea robusta* (ADRC) seeds of Johnson grass Sorghum halepense (SAADRC).

Nyasa Lovebird

Agapornis lilianae 13-14cm

Alternative name: Lilian's Lovebird.

Description: Sexes similar. General colour green, more yellowish on underparts, forehead and crown orange-red; sides of face, throat and upper breast salmon pink; hindneck washed with gold; flights greenish black; underwing-coverts green; tail pale red at base with a subterminal dark bar; iris brown; bill red; legs and feet grey. Average weight of birds in captivity, males 38g, females 43g; a single wild bird caught weighed only 29,2g. Juvenile similar to adult, but with a blackish suffusion over the cheeks; bill reddish yellow with blackish spots at the base of the upper mandible.

Voice: Described by Benson *et al* as a shrill chatter, reminiscent of the rattling of a metal chain, though more high pitched.

Habitat: *Mopane* and *acacia* woodland.

Distribution: Central and northern Mozambique, north-eastern Zimbabwe, eastern Zambia, Malawi and southern Tanzania.

Feeding: Seeds of indigenous grasses and trees, buds, fruits and ripening sorghums and finger millet. Flowers of Ana tree *Acacia albida*, Ordeal tree *Erythrophleum africanum*, Wild mango *Cordyla africana* and Black plum *Vitex doniana*.

Breeding: A bulky, dome-shaped nest with tubular entrance is built of stalks and bark strips by the female, the material being carried in her bill. The nest may be situated under the eaves of buildings and in hollow trees and in Zambia breed in discarded nests of the Red-billed Buffalo Weaver *Bulalornis albirostris*. Eggs white; clutch 3-5; incubation period 22-23 days; nestling period 35-44 days; fed by both parents.

Aviculture: Selected Reference CLUTCH 3-6, up to 8; INCUBATION PERIOD 21-23 days. Personal Communication CLUTCH 3. Nest Record Cards CLUTCH 3,5 (ANRC). Nest Record Cards WILDFOOD unripe heads of Finger millet *Eleusine coracana*, Giant millet *Sorghum dochna*, Wild grain sorghum *S.bicolor*, Buffalo grass *Setaria sphacelata*, Rescue grass *Bromus unioloides*, Guineafowl grass *Rottboellia exaltata*, leaves of Stinging nettle *Urtica diocica*, Silver oak *Grevillea robusta*, Morning glory *Ipomoea acuminata, Eucalyptus* spp., flowers of Weeping boerbean *Schotia brachypetala, Gladiolus* sp. (ANRC). Diet Record Cards FRUIT. African mulberry *Morus mesozygia* (ADRC).

Black-cheeked Lovebird

Agapornis nigrigenis 13-14cm
Alternative name: Black-faced Lovebird.

Description: Sexes similar. Forehead and forecrown reddish brown; hind-crown and nape olive-green; mantle, rump and upper tail-coverts green; flight feathers blackish with green edges; tail green with tips to feathers red; cheeks and throat black; breast reddish brown; abdomen and under tail-coverts green; more yellowish on the vent; iris red-brown; bill red; white at base; legs and feet grey. Juvenile similar to adult, but with duller plumage; blackish markings visible at base of bill.

Voice: Described by Mackworth-Praed & Grant as a thrill and rapidly repeated, uttered on the wing

Habitat: *Mopane* woodland, *acacia* savanna and river valleys between 600m and 1000m above sea level.

Distribution: North-eastern Namibia, south-western Zambia and north-western Zimbabwe.

Feeding: Seeds, ripening grain, leaf buds of indigenous trees, fruits and berries. Seeds of Woodland waterberry *Syzygium guineese*, River rhus *Rhus quartiniana*, thatch *Hyparrhenia* sp., Fruit of Koobooberry *Cassine aethiopica*, African allophylus *Allophylus africanus* and Bird plum *Berchemia discolor*. Young leaves of the Small-leaved Kiaat *Pterocarpus stevensoni*. Occasionally troublesome in agricultural areas due to feeding on sorghum and finger millet.

Breeding: Little is known of nesting in the wild state. A nest hole which contained three eggs was found in a dead vertical branch of a mopane tree. A bulky dome-shaped nest is constructed from twigs and strips of bark carried by the female in her bill. Eggs white; clutch 3-6.

Aviculture: Selected Reference CLUTCH 2-8. INCUBATION PERIOD 16-24 days; NESTLING PERIOD after 30,44 days. Personal Communication CLUTCH 3; INCUBATION PERIOD 21,23 days; NESTLING PERIOD 41,42 days. Nest Record Cards CLUTCH 3,4,4,6 (SAANRC) 4,5 (ARU) 4,4,6 (ANRC); INCUBATION PERIOD 20,23, 23,24 days (NASNRC) 24,24 days (ARU); NESTLING PERIOD 38,40 days (NASNRC), 39,43 days (ARU); NESTLING PERIOD 38,40 days (NASNRC), 39,43 days (ARU). Diet Record Cards WILDFOOD unripe heads of finger millet *Eleusine coracana*, Johnson grass *Sorghum halepense*, Rescue grass *Bromus unioloides*, chickweed *Stellaria* spp., leaves of Silver oak *Grevillia robusta, Eucalyptus* spp.,

Morning glory *Impomoea acuminata*, Stinging nettle *Urticc dioica*, buds of Red garden sorrel *Oxala latifolia*, flowers of Kiaat tree *Pterocarpus angolensis*, Weeping boer-bean *Schotia brachypetala* (NASDRC ARU ADRC). Diet Record Cards Fruit African mulberry *Morus mesozygia* (ARU NASDRC SAADRC).

Rose-ringed Parakeet

Psittacula krameri 38-42cm
Alternative names: African Ring-necked Parakeet, African Ringneck, Green Parakeet, Ring-necked Parakeet, Senegal Long-tailed Parakeet, Senegal Parakeet.
***P.k.borealis* Northern Rose-ringed Parakeet.**

Description: Male. General colour green, becoming slightly lighter and more yellowish on the crown and underparts; forehead, lores and cheeks yellowish green; line from nostrils to eye black; broad black band runs from the chin along the lower edge of the cheeks narrowing to the nape, followed by a rose-red collar; nape variably suffused with blue; mantle, back, wing-coverts, rump and upper tail-coverts bright green; under wing-coverts and under tail-coverts pale yellowish green; long graduated tail feathers bluish, tipped with yellowish green; lateral feathers green; iris pale straw colour, eye lids orange; bill, upper mandible dark red, tip black, lower mandible black with reddish markings at base; legs and feet olive-grey. Female resembles male but has only indistinct emerald neck-ring; lacks blue bloom on nape. Juvenile similar to adult female, but yellower edges to flight feathers; neck-ring indistinct or lacking; adult plumage attained only after second complete moult at about 3 years old.

Males. *P.k.parvirostris* differs from the nominate race in having head and cheeks darker green, less yellowish; collar markings more distinct; bill smaller, upper mandible brighter red.

P.k.borealis differs from the nominate in having more blue on the head and hind-neck; underparts greyish green; bill larger, coral red, lower mandible marked with black.

Voice: Described by Mackworth-Praed & Grant as a distinctive shrill screeching note '*chai-chai-chai-chai*'.

Habitat: Lightly wooded country, cultivation and in the vicinity of human habitations. Also to be found in orchards and gardens.

Distribution: Southern Sudan to Senegal.

P.k.parvirostris north-western Somalia to Sudan.

P.k.borealis introduced to KwaZulu-Natal, South Africa.

Feeding: Seeds, grain, berries, fruits, blossoms, buds and nectar, and are pests in some part of their range. Seeds of African Oil Palm *Elaeis guineese*, Ana tree *Acacia albida*, fruits of wild figs *Ficus* spp., Baobab *Adansonia digitata*, Tamarind *Tamarindus irdicata*,

Jujube *Ziziphus abyssinica*, African Wild Date *Phoenix reclinata*, blossoms of Fiddlewood tree *Citharexylum quadrangulare* and Bomax *Rhodognaphalon* sp. In Pujab, India much damage to maize, average loss of 20%, guavas 30% and sunflower 22% and to a lesser extent also coffee, groundnuts, sorghum, sesame, wheat, sarson, pomegranates, gram, barley, mangoes, mustard, rice, lentils and millet. In Asia also recorded feeding on the fruit of *Dalbergia sissoo, Azadirachta indica, Albizia lebbek, Capparis aphylla*, seeds of *Prosops spicigera, Casuarina equisetifolia*, Rambutan *Nephelium lappaceum*, beans of Blackwood *Dalbergia latifolia*, chillies, blossoms or nectar of *Salmalia malabarica, Erythrina indica, Butea monosperma* and *Bassia latifolia*. In the Middle East on the seeds of *Acacia arabica* and Peacock tree *Caesalpina pulcherrima*. In the U.K. (feral state) the seeds or fruit of Hornbeam *Carpinus betulus*, Ash *Fraxinus excelsior*, Pine *Pinus* sp., Horse-chestnut *Aesculus hippocastanum*, Beech *Fagus sylvatica*, Danework *Sambucus ebulus* and Holly *Ilex aquifolium*. Cotoneaster *Cotoneaster* sp., Hawthorn *Crataegus monogyna*, Rose *Rosa* spp., Pear *Pyrus communis*, Crab apple *Malus sylvestris*, Raspberry *Rubus idaeus*, Strawberry *Fragaria* sp., Pea *Pisum sativum*, Barley *Hordeum secalinum* and Maize *Zea mays*.

Breeding: Nests in tree holes at a considerable height from the ground, usually up to 10m. Sites may be natural knot-hole in soft wooded trees decayed palm trucks or expropriated old barbet or woodpecker holes, enlarging them to an appropriate size, about 11cm in diameter. In Gauteng, South Africa a flock of 5-8 birds (escapees) were observed attending 2 nest cavities in willow trees, one at 8m and the other at 10m above the ground. The entrance holes were both 70mm in diameter, one cavity was 500mm deep by 150mm wide; the other 300mm deep contained at least 2 eggs; both chambers were lined with bark chips. Also reported to use a Weeping Willow *Salix babylonica* in South Africa, Indian Mahogany *Terminalia catappa* in Mauritius and in a Jacaranda tree *Jacaranda mimosifoila* in India. The latter was previously occupied by Brahminy Mynahs *Sturnus pagodarum*. In the same country use holes in rock crevices, earth moulds, cavity under house roof, in walls such as ancient forts and in noisy congested market bazaars. In the U.K. (feral state) observed to compete for nest holes with Starlings *Sturnus vulgaris*, Great Tit *Parus major*, Jackdaw *Corvus monedula* and may use those of Green or Grey-headed Woodpeckers *Picus* spp. In the Nairobi National Park, Kenya, escapees nested in a dead limb of a *Brachylaena butchsii*. Nest chamber copiously lined with bark chips. Eggs white, broad-oval, smooth without gloss; clutch 2-6, single brooded if successful in rearing young; incubation by female only, seldom beginning until clutch near completion; male feeds female in nest hole; nestlings brooded more or less continuously while small; cared for and fed by both parents.

Aviculture: Selected Reference CLUTCH 4-5, occasionally 6; INCUBATION PERIOD 23-24 days. Personal

Communication CLUTCH 4,4; INCUBATION PERIOD 23 days; NESTLING PERIOD 8 weeks. Nest Record Cards CLUTCH 4,5,5 (ARU) 5 (ANRC); INCUBATION PERIOD 22,23,23,24 days (ARU); NESTLING PERIOD 7,8 weeks (ARU). Selected Reference FRUIT Elder *Sambucus nigra*. Diet Record Cards Natal Plum *Carissa grandiflora*, Prickly Pear *Opuntia vulgaris*, Indian Jujube *Ziziphus mauritiania*, Nana-berry *Rhus pentheri* (ARU), Wild Plum *Harpephyllum caffrum*, Shepherd's tree *Boscia albitrunca*, Mustard tree *Salvadora persica*, Kapok tree *Ceiba pentandra*, Red-bitter Apple *Solanum giganteum*, Litchee *Litchi chinensis*, African mulberry *Morus mesozygia* (ADRC). Selected Reference WILD-FOOD. Seeds of Blue thorn *Acacia erubescens*, Black wattle *A.mearnsii*. Diet Record Cards Johnson grass *Sorghum halepense* (ARU), Jungle rice *Echinochloa colona* (ADRC).

Black-eared Finch Lark

Eremopterix australis 12-13cm
Alternative names: Black-eared Sparrow-lark, Black Finch-lark.

Description: Male. Head-top, lores, ear-coverts black; mantle, back, rump, wing-coverts and inner most secondaries dark brown; tail black; chin, throat and underparts black; iris orange-red to red-brown; bill bluish white; legs and feet brownish to greyish white. Female has head, breast and mantle brownish, mottled with buff; throat, breast and underparts white, streaked and spotted with black. Juvenile similar to female, but breast and flanks off-white.

Voice: Described by Newman as 'cht-cht-cht' in flight.

Habitat: Kalahari sandveld, associated with spiny shrub or small tree species particularly *Rhigozum* and *Galenia*.

Distribution: Western and northern Cape Province and western Free State, South Africa to southern Botswana and southern and central Namibia.

Feeding: Seeds and insects.

Breeding: Nest is a ground scrape containing a cup of fine grass and rootlets which is covered with spider's web on the outer rim. Collection of nesting materials is by the male, the nest construction by the female. Eggs white, finely speckled with pinkish brown; clutch 2; incubation 11-13 days, by both sexes; nestling period 8-10 days; young fed by both parents; first flight after 12 days.

Aviculture: Selected Reference CLUTCH 2; INCUBATION PERIOD 11-13 days; NESTLING PERIOD 8-10 days. Personal Communication CLUTCH 2,2,3; INCUBATION PERIOD 12,12,12,13 days; NESTLING PERIOD 8,10,10 days. Selected Reference WILDFOOD

Seeds of Silky Bushman grass *Stipagrostis uniplumis*, Tall Bushman grass *S.ciliata*, Guinea grass *Panicum maximum*, Buffalo grass *P.stapfianum*. Personal Communication Guinea grass *Panicum maximum*. Selected Reference ANIMAL FOOD termites.

Chestnut-backed Finch-lark

Eremopterix leucotis 12-13cm

Alternative names: Chestnut-backed Sparrow-lark.

E.I.smithi **Smith's Finch-lark.**

Description: Male. Entire head black except for white ring round lower neck and ear-coverts; mantle and wing-coverts chestnut; iris brown; bill bluish to whitish horn; legs and feet pale grey. Female has head-top, mantle and breast brown, streaked with black; centre of belly black; flanks streaked black or chestnut. Juvenile similar to adult female, but paler, male more dusky above.

Males. *E.I.melanocephala* differs from the nominate race in having wing-shoulders chestnut and white, instead of black.

E.I.madaraszi differs from the nominate in having rump more dusky, not whitish.

E.I.hoeschi differs from the nominate in being a little whiter on the upper tail-coverts.

E.I.smithi differs from the nominate in having rump greyish white.

Voice: Described by MacLachlan & Liversidge as a sharp rattling call '*chip-chee-w*'.

Habitat: Open stony or sandy ground, in the vicinity of burnt grasslands, roadside verges and airstrips.

Distribution: Ethiopia.

E.I.melanocephala Senegal to Nile valley.

E.I.madaraszi Kenya, Tanzania and Mozambique.

E.I.smithi South African provinces of KwaZulu-Natal, North-West Gauteng, northern Cape to eastern Swaziland, Mozambique and eastern Botswana, Malawi and Zambia.

E.I.hoeschi central and northern Namibia, northern and north-eastern Botswana and north-western Zimbabwe, southern Angola and south-western Zambia.

Feeding: Grass and weed seeds and insects.

Breeding: Nest is a shallow cup-shaped depression in soil, lined with dry roots and grass, situated at the base of a clod, stone or grasstuft. In one observation found breeding on old lands with short dead grass, 3 on an air-field, 1 on a recently reaped maize field, 2 in groundnut plantation and 3 in lands presently being cleared for cultivation, amongst grass stubble. In 14 observations nests were found to be sited on the south, south-east or eastern side. Material continues to be added to the nest by the female after the complete clutch has been laid. Eggs greyish white, freckled with brown especially at the thick end; clutch 2; incubation period 11 days, by both sexes, female also sits at night; fed by both parents; first flight after 12 days.

Aviculture: Selected Reference CLUTCH 2; INCUBATION PERIOD 12 days; NESTLING PERIOD 8-10 days. Nest Record Cards CLUTCH 2,2 (ARU) 2,2,2 (SAANRC); INCUBATION PERIOD 12,12 (ARU) 11,12,12 days (SAANRC); NESTLING PERIOD 8,10 (ARU) 8, about 8, 10 days (SAANRC). Selected Reference WILDFOOD Seeds of Blue panic *Panicum laevifolium*, Guinea grass *P.maximum*, Natal redtop *Rhynchelytrum repens*, Teff grass *Eragrostis tef* Annual blue grass *Poa annua*, Hay *Chloris virgata*. Diet Record Cards Guinea grass *Panicum maximum* (ARU SAADRC), Teff grass *Eragrostis tef* (ARU), Blue panic *Panicum laevifolium* (SAADRC). Diet Record Cards ANIMAL FOOD termites (ARU SAADRC), mealworms, aphids, wasp larvae (ARU).

Chestnut-headed Finch-lark

Eremopterix signata 12cm

Description: Male. Crown, ear-coverts and flanks white; rest of head, chin and breast black; underparts and under tail-coverts brown; mantle and back greyish brown; rump dusky; iris brown; bill whitish; legs and feet pinkish brown. Female is buffish brown, streaked and mottled with blackish brown. Juvenile similar to adult female, but underparts whitish buff.

Voice: Described by Williams & Arlott as various '*tsssp*' type flock calls.

Habitat: Sandy semi-desert country and areas of open bush up to 1500m.

Distribution: Ethiopia, Somalia and Kenya.

E.s.harrisoni south-eastern Sudan and northern Kenya.

Feeding: Not known.

Breeding: Nests among short grass with stalks drawn together about it. Eggs pale ashy, thickly spotted violet, grey and brown.

Aviculture: Personal Communication CLUTCH 2,2; INCUBATION PERIOD 11,12 days; NESTLING PERIOD 8,9 days. Personal Communication WILDFOOD African bush buffalo grass *Panicum aequinerve*, Reed panicum *Panicum deustum*, African finger millet *Eleusine coracana*. Personal Communication mealworms, termites, aphids.

Grey-backed Finch-lark

Eremopterix verticalis 13cm

Alternative name: Grey-backed Sparrow-lark.

Description: Male. Headtop, lores, ring around *eye*, hindneck and ear-coverts white; chin, throat and underparts black; mantle, scapulars and wing-coverts dark grey, mottled dusky; flight feathers and tail ashy; iris brown; bill bluish to greyish; legs and feet pinkish grey. Female has head, breast and mantle brownish, mottled with pale grey; centre of belly black; bill whitish. Juvenile similar to adult female, but feathers of upperparts tipped buff.

Males. *E.v.damarensis* differs from the nominate race in being paler above, more sandy, the feathers margined with sandy buff.

E.v.harti differs from the nominate in having a darker, more blackish mantle; wing-coverts not so broadly margined with white. *E.v.khama* differs from the nominate in having upperparts greyish white; wing-coverts secondaries and broadly margined with white.

Voice: Described by Maclean as a sharp tinkling song '*twip twip twip chik*' in flight.

Habitat: Sandy ground, burnt grasslands and cultivation.

Distribution: Northern and south-western Cape, western Free State and North-West province, South Africa to eastern Botswana.

E.v.damarensis north-western and northern Cape Province, South Africa to western and northern Namibia and western Angola.

E.v.harti northern Namibia, Angola and south-western Zambia.

E.v.khama north-eastern Botswana.

Feeding: Seeds 91% with plant material 1% and insects 8%.

Breeding: Nest a depression in the ground, the cup lined with dry grass and rootlets, situated against a shrub, grasstuft or stones on the south, south-eastern or eastern side as protection against fierce sun. Nest construction by female. Eggs pale white, speckled with brownish yellow, grey and brown, particularly at the thick end; clutch 2-3; incubation 11-13 days, by both sexes; fledging period 8-10 days; young fed by both parents; first flight after 13 days.

Aviculture: Selected Reference CLUTCH 2-3; INCUBATION PERIOD 11-13 days; NESTLING PERIOD 8-10 days. Nest Record Cards CLUTCH 2 (ARU) 2,2 (SAANRC) 3 (NASNRC) 2 (ANRC); INCUBATION PERIOD 12 (ARU) 12,13 (SAANRC) 12 (NASNRC) 12 days (ANRC); NESTLING PERIOD 9 (ARU) 8,10 (SAANRC) 10 (NASNRC) about 9 days (ANRC). Selected Reference WILDFOOD Seeds of Guinea grass *Panicum maximum* (ARU ADRC NASDRC SAADRC), Napier fodder *Pennisetum purpureum* (ADRC), Millet grass *Setaria woodii* (ARU). Diet Record Cards ANIMAL FOOD termites (ARU ADRC NASDRC SAADRC), mealworms (ARU), ants (ADRC).

Black-crowned Finch-lark

Eremopterix nigriceps 10-11cm

Alternative name: White-fronted Sparrow-lark.

Description: Male. Forehead white; cheeks, sides of neck and nape greyish white; mantle sandy grey, tinged cinnamon-pink; tail blackish brown, with sandy brown central feathers and black outer feathers; flight feathers dark grey, narrowly fringed with white; lores, chin, throat, breast, belly and rest of underparts black; iris brown; bill bluish white; legs and feet greenish white. Female upperparts rufous brown; lores, sides of neck pinkish buff; ear-coverts cinnamon-buff. Juvenile similar to adult female but indistinct dusky spots on rump and upper tail-coverts.

Male. *E.n.melanauchen* differs from the nominate race in being darker and more grey, less sandy; black on crown extends further back.

Voice: Described by Hollom *et al* as '*chee, dee-vee*' or '*pooo, pee-voo-pee*'.

Habitat: Semi-desert savanna, cultivation and on aircraft runways.

Distribution: Cape Verde Island

E.n.albifrons Mauritania to Nile valley. (Accidental) Algeria.

E.n.melanauchen Egypt, Ethiopia and Sudan.

Feeding: Seeds and insects. Livefood in the form of spiders, grasshoppers, small locust hoppers, small beetles, caterpillars and Assassin bugs. In Chad recorded also feeding on the seeds of *Panicum turgidum*.

Aviculture: Nest Record Cards CLUTCH 2 (ANRC); INCUBATION PERIOD 12 days; NESTLING PERIOD 9 days. Selected Reference WILDFOOD Guinea grass *Panicum maximum, P.parvifolium*. Selected Reference ANIMAL FOOD termites.

Fischer's Finch-lark

Eremopterix leucopareia 11cm
Alternative name: Fischer's Sparrow-lark.

Description: Male. Crown and nape buff-brown; ear-coverts, band across hindneck white; chin and centre of breast black; rest of underparts white, tinged with buff; mantle and back greyish brown; tail blackish; iris brown; bill whitish; legs and feet blackish brown. Female lacks the facial adornment of the male; rest of underparts greyish brown. Juvenile similar to adult female, but has whitish tips to the feathers of the upperparts.

Voice: Described by Williams & Arlott as a low *'tweet,ess'* flock call.

Habitat: Short grass plains from sea-level to 1800m.

Distribution: Uganda, Kenya and Malawi.

Feeding: Seeds and insects.

Breeding: Nest, a shallow scrape in the ground lined with dry grass. Eggs creamy white, spotted and blotched brown with mauve-grey under markings; clutch 2-3.

Aviculture: Personal Communication CLUTCH 2; INCUBATION PERIOD 13 days; NESTLING PERIOD 12 days. Nest Record Cards CLUTCH 2,2,2 (ARU) 2 (ARU); INCUBATION PERIOD 12,13 (ANRC) 12 days (ARU); NESTLING PERIOD 9,10 days (ANRC). Diet Record Cards WILDFOOD Guinea grass *Panicum maximum* (ARU ADRC), Black seed finger grass *Digitaria ternata*, Foxtail millet *Setaria italica* (ADRC). Diet Record Cards ANIMAL FOOD termites (ARU ADRC).

Corn Bunting

Emberiza calandra 17,5cm

Description: Sexes similar. Upperparts pale brown, streaked with blackish; white on tail; underparts whitish; iris brown; bill yellowish; legs and feet yellowish. Juvenile similar to adult, but upperparts more heavily streaked.

Voice: Described by Gallagher & Woodcock as a long *'kwit'* or *'pit'* or *'kwit-it-it'*; the song is like the rattling of a bunch of keys.

Habitat: Cultivation, slopes with scattered bushes and damp grasslands.

Distribution: Morocco, coastal Libya to Egypt (winters).

Feeding: Weed and grass seeds, cereals, leaves and invertebrates namely adult and larval beetles, ants, earwigs, damsel flies, grasshoppers, bugs, spiders, millipedes, earthworms, snails, seeds of dock *Rumex*, rape *Brassica*, Knotgrass *Polygonum*, sycamore *Acer*, grasses, wheat *Triticum*, oats *Avena*, barley *Hordeum* and rye *Secale.*; in India also rice. Feeding data not confined to Africa.

Breeding: Female builds nest of dried grass in long grass or similar vegetation or on the ground. Eggs pale grey or pale brown, streaked with blackish brown; clutch 4-7; incubation 12-13 days, by female only; nestling period 9-11 days; usually 2 broods.

Aviculture: Selected Reference INCUBATION PERIOD 12-13 days; NESTLING PERIOD 9-11 days.

Yellowhammer

Emberiza citrinella 16-17cm
Alternative name: Yellow Bunting (nominate).

Description: Male. Entire head lemon-yellow, streaked dusky; mantle and back reddish brown, streaked dusky; rump and upper tail-coverts chestnut; tail greyish, outer feathers white; chin, throat, breast and underparts lemon-yellow, streaked reddish brown on breast and flanks; iris brown; bill bluish horn; legs and feet colour deep pinkish. Female is pale reddish brown streaked dusky; entire head and belly paler yellow. Juvenile similar to adult female, but almost lacks all yellow.

Voice: Described by Lockley as *'bit-o-bread-and-no-chee-eeese'*.

Habitat: Cultivation and open country with bushes.

Distribution: Algeria and Tunisia (migrant) Morocco (vagrant).

Feeding: Seeds of weeds, grain, grass shoots, fruit and invertebrates, namely seeds of spruce *Picea*, beech *Fagus*, chickweed *Stellaria*, crowberry *Empetrum*, mouse-ear *Cerastium*, fleabane *Coryza*, dandelion *Taraxacum*, plantain *Plantago*, grasses, including cereals, *Festuca*, *Poa* and *Lolium*, grasshoppers, lacewings, caddis flies, adult and larval beetles, earwigs, bugs, spiders, woodlice, earthworms and snails.

Breeding: Female constructs a bulky structure of grass stalks, roots and moss, lined with hair or fine vegetable matter, on the ground, in the grass, bush, ivy, bank or on a wall. Eggs white or pale pinkish with brown or purple brown streaking; clutch 3-5; incubation 12-14 days, by female only; nestling period 11-13 days, nestling fed by both sexes; 2 broods, sometimes 3.

Aviculture: Selected Reference INCUBATION PERIOD 12-14 days; NESTLING PERIOD 12-13 days. Selected Reference WILDFOOD Coltsfoot *Tussilago farfara*, dandelion *Taraxacum* sp., dock *Rumex* sp., Sow-Thistle *Sonchus oleraceus*, chickweed *Stellaria* sp.,

Meadowsweet *Filipendula ulmaria*, plantain *Plantago* sp. Personal Communication chickweed *Stellaria* sp., Shepherd's purse *Capsella bursa-pastoris*, Sow-Thistle *Sonchus oleraceus*, Alyssum *Alyssum* sp. Selected Reference ANIMAL FOOD mealworms, caterpillars, beetles, spiders, earthworms earwigs, millipedes, slugs. Selected Reference ANIMAL FOOD slugs, spiders, millipedes, earthworms, brandlings.

Rock Bunting
Emberiza cia africana 16cm

Description: Male. Entire head, chin, throat and breast greyish; thin black stripes on crown and through and below the eye; mantle, back and wings brown, streaked dusky; rump chestnut; tail blackish brown; belly and rest of underparts chestnut; iris brown; bill slate-grey; legs and feet brownish straw. Female paler with underparts more or less streaked, but some resemble males. Juvenile upperparts, crown brownish buff, streaked black; mantle more chestnut-brown and broadly streaked; throat buff; upper breast and flanks rufous buff, spotted and streaked blackish brown.

Voice: Described by Keith & Gooders as high-pitched and buzzy, several short notes followed by a longer one, 'zi-zi.zirr'.

Habitat: Rocky districts with scattered trees.

Distribution: Morocco, Algeria, Tunisia, Libya and Chad.

Feeding: Seeds of grasses and other parts of plant and invertebrates, namely damselflies, dragonflies, bugs, earwigs, ants, bees, adult and larval beetles, spiders, millipedes, earthworms, snails, seeds of pine *Pinus*, grasses including *Elymus*, rye *Secale*, wheat *Triticum*, oats *Avena* and millet *Panicum*. Feeding data not confined to Africa.

Breeding: Nests on the ground in amongst loose stones or in steep banks, small quarries, rarely in small bushes, heath and loose stone walls. Constructed of grasses and bark strips and a little moss, then lined with fine roots and horse hair. Eggs light brown, tinted grey, olive or more rarely pink; clutch 3-6, usually 4; incubation period 12-14 days by female only; nestling period 10-13 days.

Aviculture: No records.

Cinererous Bunting
Emberiza cineracea 16,5cm

Description: Male. Entire head, chin and throat olive-yellow; rest of upperparts olive-grey, streaked dusky; tail olive grey, outer feathers white; breast and flanks darker olive; rest of underparts lemon yellow; iris dark brown; bill dark bluish horn; legs and feet pale flesh brown.

Female is greyer, finely streaked head paler and less extensive yellow on throat. Juvenile similar to female, but head greyer; throat pale sulphur yellow, and more extensive streaking on head and breast.

Voice: Described by Hollom *et al* as short metallic 'kjip'; song consists of 5-6 notes, 'drip-srip-srip-srip-drie-drieh'.

Habitat: Broken rocky ground with sparse vegetation.

Distribution: Ethiopia. Tunisia and Egypt (Vagrant).

E.c.semenowi north-eastern Africa.

Feeding: Seeds of weeds and grasses, grain, fruit and small invertebrates, namely small beetles, weevils, moths, maggots, spiders, earthworms, millipedes and small snails. Feeding data not confined to Africa.

Breeding: Open cup nest of dead leaves and grasses, lined with small roots and hair placed on sloping ground up against a stone and concealed by vegetation. Eggs blue or beige, spotted blackish; clutch usually 3-4, sometimes 5 or 2 only, very rarely 6; incubation chiefly by female for 12-14 days with both sexes feeding young; nestling period 12-13 days; 2 or 3 broods per year.

Aviculture: Selected Reference CLUTCH 4-5; INCUBATION PERIOD about 14 days; NESTLING PERIOD 12-14 days. Selected Reference WILDFOOD Sow-Thistle *Sonchus oleraceus*, chickweed *Stellaria* sp., Charlock *Sinapis arvensis*.

Ortolan Bunting
Emberiza hortulana 15-17cm
Alternative name: European Ortolan Bunting.

Description: Male. Entire head olive-green, except chin and moustachial stripes yellow; mantle and back streaked with black; tail chestnut brown, streaked blackish, outer feathers edged with white; breast, belly and rest of underparts buffish chestnut; iris brown; bill, legs and feet reddish. Female upperparts brown, streaked blackish; underparts creamy buff with dark moustachial streaks and also on breast and flanks. Juvenile similar to female, but heavily streaked blackish.

Voice: Described by Peterson *et al* as a soft 'tsee-ip' and 'tsip' and a piping 'tseu'.

Habitat: Open hilly country and cultivated areas with trees.

Distribution: Senegal and Sudan. Formerly only regarded as a passage migrant.

Feeding: Seeds of grasses, cereals, mainly invertebrates, namely damselflies, dragonflies, bugs, earwigs, ants, bees, adult and larval beetles, spiders, millipedes, earthworms, snails, seeds of hemp *Cannabis*, pine *Pinus*, grasses including *Elymus*, rye *Secale*, wheat *Triticum*, oats *Avena* and millet *Panicum*. Feeding data not confined to Africa.

Breeding: Nest, slight hollow of dried grasses, roots and leaves, lined with finer roots and hair, placed on the ground under vegetation. Eggs pale blue or pinkish grey with dark scattered spots; clutch 4-6; incubation chiefly, if not entirely by female for 11-13 days; nestling period 11-13 days; two broods.

Aviculture: Selected Reference CLUTCH 4-5; INCUBATION PERIOD 11-14 days; NESTLING PERIOD 12 days. Personal Communication CLUTCH 4; INCUBATION PERIOD 13 days; NESTLING PERIOD 13 days. Selected Reference WILDFOOD Charlock *Sinapis arvensis*. Personal Communication Groundsel *Senecio vulgaris*. Selected Reference ANIMAL FOOD beetles, crickets, moths.

Cretzschmar's Bunting
Emberiza caesia 16cm

Description: Male. Entire head, sides of neck and upper breast bluish grey; chin, upper throat and moustachial stripes rufous; mantle, back and wings brown, streaked with black; rump and upper tail-coverts chestnut-brown; tail dark brown, edged chestnut, outer feathers white; lower breast, belly and underparts chestnut; iris brownish; bill pinkish; legs and feet dusky pink. Female upperparts brown, streaked blackish; underparts pale chestnut, spotted on lower breast. Juvenile similar to adult female, but underparts rufous brown.

Voice: Described by Keith & Gooders as a loud '*tyup or tyip*'.

Habitat: Dry rocky slopes with scrub, gardens and cultivation.

Distribution: North-eastern Egypt. vagrant: Libya, taken in Chad.

Feeding: Seeds, cereals and small invertebrates. Growing oats *Avena* (on Fair Isle) and flying ants and pupae in Arabia.

Breeding: Constructs a nest of plant stems lined with grass and hair and placed among vegetation on the ground. Eggs pale grey, blue or purplish with fine and heavy spotting; clutch 4-5; incubation period 12-14 days; nestling period 12-13 days; young fed and cared for by female.

Aviculture: Selected Reference CLUTCH 4-5; INCUBATION PERIOD about 14 days; NESTLING PERIOD 12-13 days. Selected Reference WILDFOOD Charlock *Sinapis arvensis*.

Cirl Bunting
Emberiza cirlus 16-17cm

Description: Male. Forehead, crown and nape olive-green, streaked blackish; stripe above and below eye yellow; stripe through eye; chin and throat black; under throat is a yellow pectoral band; sides of breast chestnut; rest of underparts yellow; mantle and back chestnut; wings and tail olive-yellow, streaked blackish; iris dark brown; bill bluish; legs and feet brownish flesh. Female is distinguished from the Yellowhammer by olive-brown rump. Juvenile similar to adult female, but paler overall.

Voice: Described by Lockley as '*zit-zit-zit*'.

Habitat: Bushy and rocky hillsides and clearings in palm groves.

Distribution: Morocco, Algeria, Tunisia, Egypt (vagrant).

Feeding: Seeds of grasses and weeds, cereals, berries and invertebrates, namely mayflies, bugs, beetles, wasps, sawflies, grasshoppers, moths, spiders, earthworms, snails, seeds of couch grass *Elymus*, rye grass *Lolium*, meadow grass *Poa*, nettle *Urtica*, bindweed *Fallopia*, bittersweet *Solanum*, groundsel *Senecio* and chickweed *Stellaria*. Feeding data not confined to Africa.

Breeding: Female constructs an untidy, bulky nest of grass and roots on a foundation of moss, in tall hedgerows, gorse-bushes, brambles, bank-sides and at times in ricks or on the ground. Lining consists of fine grasses and horse hair. Eggs pale blue or pale green with dark streaking and scribbling; clutch 3-4; incubation by female alone for 12-13 days with male feeding at the nest; young fed chiefly by female, quite exceptionally by male; nestling period 11-13 days; two broods, sometimes three.

Aviculture: Selected Reference INCUBATION PERIOD 11-13 days; NESTLING PERIOD 11-13 days.

Striped Bunting
Emberiza striolata 13-14cm

Alternative name: House Bunting.

Description: Male. Entire head slate-grey, streaked black and white, including moustachial supercilliary stripes white; mantle and back dark brown, streaked with black; rump, upper tail-coverts and wings chestnut, streaked with black; tail black; chin whitish; throat uniform pale chestnut; iris brown; bill pinkish; legs and feet orange. Female upperparts grey, streaked with slate-grey; underparts slighter paler chestnut. Juvenile paler grey-brown with dark streaks and indistinct head streaks.

Male. *E.s.sahari* differs from the nominate race in having upperparts darker; underparts less greyish.

E.s.sanghae similar to *sahari*, but more chestnut.

E.s.saturatior similar to *sanghae*, but less redder and more streaked.

E.s.jebelmarrae similar to *saturatior*, but larger.

Voice: Described by Guggisberg as having a chirpy call and a wheezy tri-syllabic song.

Habitat: Desert edges and in villages, even entering houses and shops.

Distribution: Tunisia, Mauritania. Breeds Morocco, Algeria. Egypt (accidental).

E.s.sanghae southern Mali.

E.s.saturatior western Sudan, Ethiopia and north-western Kenya.

E.s.jebelmarrae Darfur, Kordofan.

E.s.sahari western Sahara and Morocco.

Feeding: Seeds, mostly grasses, berries and invertebrates namely, ants and spiders, seeds of jujube *Ziziphus*, Toothbrush tree *Salvadora persica*, reed, *Phalaris*, *Phragmites* and *Bromus*, millet *Panicum* and barley *Hordeum*. Feeding data not confined to Africa.

Breeding: A cup-shaped nest is constructed in a wall crack, rock crevices or a hole in a building. Eggs whitish, spotted with rufous brown and mauve; clutch 2-4; incubation period 13-14 days; nestling period 17-19 days.

Aviculture: No records.

Lark-like Bunting
Emberiza impetuani 13-14cm

Alternative names: Lark-like; Pale Rock Bunting.

Description: Sexes similar. Forehead, crown, nape, mantle, back and upper tail-coverts buffy brown, streaked dark brown; ear-coverts buffy; stripe over and below eyes whitish; wings with primaries brown, edged cinnamon, secondaries brown, edged pinkish cinnamon; chin and throat whitish buff; breast, belly and underparts tawny buff; iris brown; bill blackish brown; legs and feet brown. Juvenile paler, with less streaking on the upperparts.

Adult. *E.i.sloggetti* differs from the nominate race in being paler overall.

Voice: Described by Maclean as repeated shortish phase of somewhat canary-like trilled notes, '*chiriririri chippy-chirpy-chirip*'.

Habitat: Arid savanna, rocky slopes and dry water courses.

Distribution: Western and north-western Cape and North-West provinces, South Africa to Namibia, western Zimbabwe, Botswana, Angola, Zimbabwe and southern Zaire.

E.i.sloggetti south-western and south-eastern Cape, Gauteng and Free State, South Africa to Lesotho and Transkei.

Feeding: Seeds and invertebrates, notably hairless caterpillars.

Breeding: A loose cup-shaped nest of twigs, fine rootlets and grass form the framework which is placed in the open or in the shelter of a grass tuft. Building by female, although male stays near her during the

building. Eggs white, pale bluish or pale greenish white, with spots and blotches of reddish brown; clutch 2-4, usually 3; incubation period 12-13 days, by female alone, parental duties are shared; nestling period 12-14 days.

Aviculture: Selected Reference CLUTCH 3-4; INCUBATION PERIOD 12-13 days; NESTLING PERIOD 12-13 days. Nest Record Cards CLUTCH 3,3 (ARU); INCUBATION PERIOD 12,13 days (ARU); NESTLING PERIOD 13,13 days (ARU). Selected Reference WILD-FOOD. Seeds of Hay *Chloris virgata*, Natal redtop *Rhynchelytrum repens*, Guinea grass *Panicum maximum*, Weeping lovegrass *Eragrostis curvula*, Buffaloquick *Paspalum sistichum*, Garden setaria *Setaria pallide-fusca*. Nest Record Card Guinea grass *Panicum maximum* (ARU). Diet Record Cards ANIMAL FOOD mealworms, hairless caterpillars, thrips-nymphs, termites, gnats, millipedes, spiders (ARU).

Cinnamon-breasted Rock Bunting
Emberiza tahapisi 14-16cm

Alternative names: Rock Bunting, Seven-striped Bunting.

Description: Male. Entire head, nape and chin black with a white stripe down the centre of the crown and nape; stripe over and below the eye which extends to the nape white; chin and throat whitish; mantle, back and upper tail-coverts russet-brown, streaked black; tail blackish; breast, belly and rest of underparts warm russet brown; wing-coverts blackish brown, edged tawny; iris brown; bill, upper mandible blackish, lower yellow; legs and feet crome-yellow. Female had entire head and nape tawny, streaked black; chin and throat blackish; rest of underparts pale russet brown. Juvenile similar to adult female, but stripe down centre of crown and nape tawny; chin and throat dusky.

Males. *E.t.nivenorum* differs from the nominate race in being paler and yellower, especially on the underparts.

E.t.septemstriata differs from the nominate in having throat greyer and extensive rufous inner webs of wing primaries.

E.t.goslingi differs from the nominate in having throat greyer; rest of plumage paler overall.

Voice: Described by Maclean as a repeated shrill '*chirp chrree-rippity-peep*' uttered quickly with pauses between.

Habitat: Rocky, hilly country and occasionally in orchard bush.

Distribution: Eastern Cape, KwaZulu-Natal (interior), North-West, Gauteng, Mpumalanga and Free State, province of South Africa, Transkei, Swaziland, southern Mozambique, Zimbabwe, eastern and northern Botswana, northern Namibia, Angola, southern Zaire to southern Ethiopia.

E.t.nivenorum north-western Namibia and perhaps western Angola.

E.t.septemstriata eastern Sudan and north-western Ethiopia.

E.t.goslingi Sierra Leone to Sudan and northern Zaire.

Feeding: Seeds and insects. Seeds of lovegrass *Eragrostis* spp. Stomach contents have revealed grits. Invertebrates in the form of grasshoppers and hairless caterpillars. A small *Melolonthid* chafer beetle also recorded.

Breeding: Constructs a loose shallow cup of twiglets, pieces of bark, grass and occasionally dry seed pods. The lining is of fine grass or rootlets. It may be located in a tuft of grass, shrub or low bank, beneath a stone, amongst rocks or on a ledge. Nests have also been found against a wall at the bottom of a cement pit and inside old laternware smelting pots which were lying on the ground at a mine dump. Eggs whitish, pale bluish or pale green, rather thickly spotted and blotched with reddish brown; clutch 2-4; normally 3; incubation period 12-14 days, by both sexes; nestling period 14-16 days; young fed by both parents.

Aviculture: Selected Reference CLUTCH 2-5 INCUBATION PERIOD 12-14 days; NESTLING PERIOD 14-16 days. Nest Record Cards CLUTCH 3,3 (ARU) 3,4 (ANRC); INCUBATION PERIOD 12,13 (ARU) 13 days (ANRC); NESTLING PERIOD 14.16 (ARU) about 15 days (ANRC). Selected WILDFOOD Seeds of Hay *Chloris virgata*, Teff grass *Eragrostis tef*, Berg grass *Setaria appendiculata*, Popo grass *Hyparrhenia cymbaria*, Common thatchgrass *H.hirta*. Nest Record Cards Teff grass *Eragrostis tef* (ARU), Common thatchgrass *Hyparrhenia cymbaria* (ADRC). Selected Reference WILDFOOD chickweed *Stellaria* sp. Diet Record Cards ANIMAL FOOD mealworms, termites, grasshoppers, maggots, gnats, wasp larvae (ARU), thrips-nymphs, hairless caterpillars (ADRC).

Cape Bunting
Emberiza capensis 13cm
Alternative names: Cape Rock Bunting, Southern Rock Bunting.

Description: Sexes similar. Forehead, crown and nape blackish brown; mantle and back russet brown, streaked black; rump and upper tail-coverts russet brown; tail blackish brown; greater wing-coverts brown, tipped chestnut, lesser wing-coverts chestnut; stripe over and below eye and chin buff; stripe through eye and moustache stripe black; breast, belly and flanks greyish olive; under tail-coverts buff; iris brown bill, legs and feet blackish brown. Juvenile is paler than adult with dusky streaking on the breast.

Adults. *E.c.cinnamomea* (see *Fringilla cinnamomea* Lichtenstin, Samml. Sang. Vog., Kaffernl., 1842. p.16: Vaal River).

E.c.reidi differs from the nominate race in having the mantle and back brown; breast, belly and flanks greyish brown.

E.c.basutoensis differs from the nominate in being darker on the upperparts; breast and belly greyer

E.c.limpopoensis differs from the nominate in having greater wing-coverts chestnut.

E.c.vinacea differs from the nominate in having the mantle and back lighter and redder, less heavily streaked.

E.c.bradfieldi differs from the nominate in being generally paler especially on the chin, throat and breast.

E.c.plowesi differs from the nominate in having the chin white; underparts creamy white.

E.c.smithersii differs from the nominate in having the chin whitish; underparts deep greyish olive.

E.c.vincenti differs from the nominate in having upperparts dusky brown and underparts sooty grey.

E.c.nebularum similar to *plowesi*, but paler; bill considerably longer.

Voice: Described by Newman as '*cheep, cheep, tip, cheeucheeu, tip-cheeu-tip-cheeu*'.

Habitat: Frequents hilly or coastal regions where there is an abundance of rocks.

Distribution: Namibia and the South African province of northern, south-western and western Cape.

E.c.cinnamomea western, eastern and central regions of the Cape and western Free State, provinces of South Africa.

E.c.reidi northern Lesotho (lowlands), western Swaziland and eastern Free State, Gauteng, western KwaZulu-Natal and south-eastern Mpumalanga, South Africa.

E.c.basutoensis Lesotho (highlands) and adjacent regions of South Africa in KwaZulu-Natal.

E.c.limpopoensis south-eastern Botswana and in South Africa in Gauteng (highveld).

E.c.vinacea northern Cape Province, South Africa.

E.c.bradfieldi Namibia.

E.c.plowesi Zimbabwe and north-eastern Botswana.

E.c.smithersii eastern Zimbabwe and in adjacent Mozambique.

E.c.vincenti north-eastern Zambia, Malawi and northern Mozambique.

E.c.nebularum South-western Angola.

Feeding: Seeds, insects and spiders. Red arils of Rooi-krans *Acacia cyclops*. Livefood in the form of grasshoppers, beetle and fly larvae and termites.

Breeding: Nest, a cup of twigs, grass and roots, on or near ground in bus; clutch 2-3; eggs white, cream or pale blue, spotted or blotched.

Aviculture: Selected Reference CLUTCH 2-4; INCUBATION PERIOD 13-14 days; NESTLING PERIOD 17-19 days; Nest Record Cards CLUTCH 3 (SAANRC) 2,3 (ARU) 3 (ANRC); INCUBATION PERIOD 13,13 (SAANRC) about 13 (ARU) 13 days (ANRC); NESTLING PERIOD 17 (SAANRC) 17,18 (ARU) about 18 days (ANRC). Selected Reference WILDFOOD seeds of Hay *Chloris virgata*, Hartseed lovegrass *Eragrostis capensis*, Narrow-heart lovegrass *E.racemosa*, Speckled vlei grass *E.bicolor*, Weeping lovegrass *E.Curvula*, Teff grass *E.tef*, Guinea grass *Panicum maximum*, Blue panic *P.laevifolium*. Nest Record Cards Hay *Chloris virgata* (ARU), Teff grass *Eragrostis capensis* (ARU SAADRC ADRC). Diet Record Cards ANIMAL FOOD mealworms (ARU SAADRC ADRC), termites, hairless caterpillars (ARU), moths, fishmoths, grasshoppers (SAADRC), thrips-nymphs, maggots, wasp larvae, spiders (ADRC).

Somali Golden-breasted Bunting

Emberiza poliopleura 14cm

Description: Male. Stripe on forehead, crown and nape white; stripe starting narrowly at the bill, stripe through eye, cheeks and sides of neck black; stripe above and below eye white; mantle and back dark brown, feathers edged with white or pale buffish white; rump pale grey; tail sooty brown; wings with primaries olive-brown, edged cinnamon-buff, median wing-coverts from a striking white band across the wing; chin white; throat yellow; breast yellowish; belly and rest of underparts yellowish olive; under tail-coverts white; iris dark sepia; bill flesh coloured; legs and feet dusky red. Female similar to male, but paler overall; facial stripes buffy. Juvenile similar to adult female, but much paler overall.

Voice: Described by Guggisberg as '*tizekh-tizekh*' repeated over and over again.

Habitat: Wooded grasslands and open bush in arid country.

Distribution: Sudan, north-eastern Uganda, Ethiopia, Somalia, Kenya to northern Tanzania.

Feeding: Not known.

Breeding: Nest a ragged cup of dry grass or other stems with centre lining of finer grasses, placed on a horizontal fork of a small bush. Eggs whitish or whitish with a few spots and many lines of blackish brown with paler undermarkings.

Aviculture: Nest Record Cards CLUTCH 2,2 (ARU) 2 (ANRC); INCUBATION PERIOD 13,13 (ARU) 12 days (ANRC); NESTLING PERIOD 16,18 (ARU) 17 days (ANRC). Diet Record Cards WILDFOOD Hay *Chloris virgata* (ARU), Chickweed *Stellaria media* (ADRC). Diet Record Card ANIMAL FOOD mealworms, termites, moth, fishmoths (ADRC).

Golden-breasted Bunting

Emberiza flaviventris 15-16cm

Alternative names: Red-backed Yellow Bunting, Red-backed Bunting, Yellow-bellied Bunting.

Description: Male. Striped white down centre of crown to nape, above and below eye; rest of head black; mantle and back chestnut, streaked greyish brown; rump and upper tail-coverts grey; tail blackish, edged white; chin and throat yellow; breast cinnamon; belly and flanks yellow; under tail-coverts white; iris brown; bill, upper mandible blackish, lower horn; legs and feet pale brown. Female is uniformly paler than male with facial stripes blackish brown. Juvenile similar to adult female, but paler yellow with centre of crown to nape buff.

Males. *E.f.flavigaster* differs from the nominate race in being paler overall; flanks more extensive white.

E.f.carychroa differs from the nominate in having mantle darker and more reddish; throat, breast and underparts darker; flanks overlaid with pinkish cinnamon.

E.f.princeps differs from the nominate in having mantle paler; flanks white; tail longer.

E.f.kalaharica differs from the nominate in having a lighter and greyer hindneck; mantle paler and redder; breast paler cinnamon.

Voice: Described by Mackworth-Praed & Grant as a typical bunting-like '*zizi-zizi*'; also a pleasant little song of '*chwee-chi-it-twee*'.

Habitat: Open grasslands, woodland, plantations and gardens in small towns.

Distribution: Eastern Swaziland, southern Mozambique and South African provinces of western and eastern Cape to KwaZulu-Natal.

E.f.flavigaster Niger to Ethiopia.

E.f.carychroa southern Sudan, Uganda, Kenya, eastern and southern Zaire, Tanzania, Malawi, Mozambique, northern Zambia and central and northern Angola.

E.f.princeps Namibia and south-western Angola.

E.f.kalaharica southern Zambia, south-eastern Angola, north-eastern Namibia, northern Mozambique, Zimbabwe, Botswana and South Africa in Nort-West, Gauteng, Mpumalanga and Northern Province, west to northern Cape.

Feeding: Seeds, buds and insects. Seeds of Hay *Chloris virgata*. Livefood in the form of termites, beetles, fly larvae, grasshoppers, crickets and small mantis.

Breeding: The nest is a frail untidy shallow cup made of rootlets and dry grass stems which is lined with fine rootlets and a thin layer of cow or horse-tail hair. Placed in a small tree or bush 40-150cm above ground. Eggs white, pale cream, bluish or greenish white with a zone of black round the thick end; clutch 2-4; incubation period 12,5-13 days by female alone; young cared for and fed by both parents; nestling period 16-17 days; fed for another 10-12 days; mostly by the male, before becoming independant; host to caprious the Diederik Cuckoo, *Chrysococcyx*.

Aviculture: Selected Reference CLUTCH 2-4; INCUBATION PERIOD 13, 12-13 days; NESTLING PERIOD 14-17 days. Nest Record Cards CLUTCH 2,3,3 (NASNRC) 3 (ARU); INCUBATION PERIOD 13,13,13 days (NASNRC) 15,17, about 17 (NASNRC) 16 days (ARU). Selected Reference WILDFOOD Seeds of Hay *Chloris virgata*, Teff grass *Eragrostis tef*, Weeping lovegrass *E.curvula*, Dew grass *E.obtusa*, Guinea grass *Panicum maximum*, Blue panic *P.'aevifolium*. Diet Record Cards Lucerne *Medicago sctiva* (NASDRC), Teff grass *Eragrostis tef* (ARU). Selected Reference WILDFOOD chickweed *Stellaria* sp. Diet Record Cards *Stellaria media* (NASDRC ARU). Selected Reference ANIMAL FOOD mealworms, ants' eggs, whiteworms. Diet Record Cards mealworms (ARU NASDRC), termites, thrips-nymphs, springtails (ARU, fishmoths, hairless caterpillars, moths, wasp larvae (NASDRC)

Brown-rumped Bunting

Emberiza affinis 15cm

Alternative name: *E.a.nigeriae* Nigerian Little Bunting.

Description: Male. Entire head and chin white, heavily streaked with black; mantle, back, rump and upper tail-coverts chestnut-brown; tail brown, washed blackish; throat, breast, belly and rest of underparts pale yellowish brown; iris brown; bill dark horn; legs and feet brownish grey. Female undescribed. Juvenile undescribed.

Males. *E.a.vulpecula* differs from the nominate race in having mantle and back deeper reddish brown.

E.a.nigeriae differs from the nominate in being paler overall; entire head more whitish.

Voice: Described by Mackworth-Praed & Grant as a typical bunting song, not very loud but vigorous and well modulated.

Habitat: Open woodland and cultivation.

Distribution: Southern Sudan, south-western Ethiopia, northern Uganda and north-eastern Zaire.

E.a.vulpecula Cameroon and Central African Republic.

E.a.nigeriae Gambia to western Cameroon.

Feeding: Seeds and insects.

Breeding: Not known.

Aviculture: Nest Record Cards CLUTCH 3,4 (ANRC); INCUBATION PERIOD 12,12 days (ANRC); NESTLING PERIOD 14,17 days (ANRC). Diet Record Card WILDFOOD Shepherd's purse *Capsella bursa-pastoris*, Guinea grass *Panicum maximum*, White buffalo grass *P.coloratum* (ADRC). Diet Record Card ANIMAL FOOD mealworms, crickets, spiders (ADRC).

Cabanis's Yellow Bunting

Emberiza cabanisi 16cm

Alternative names: Cabanis's Bunting, Three-streaked Bunting, Yellow Bunting.

Description: Male. Centre of forehead, crown and nape grey; rest of headtop, sides of face and ear-coverts black; stripe over eye extending to the nape white; mantle and back brown, streaked black; rump greyish white; tail black, edged white on the outermost feathers; flight feathers black, edged grey; chin and throat white; breast, belly and flanks yellow; under tail-coverts white; iris brown; bill horn; legs and feet flesh coloured. Female has stripe down centre of head less distinct; tail blackish brown. Juvenile has stripe over eye brownish; belly and flanks pale yellow.

Males. *E.c.orientalis* differs from the nominate race in having upperparts lighter and warmer brown feather edges, giving more marked pattern.

E.c.cognominata differs from *orientalis* in having the throat yellow; mantle and back more heavily streaked; flanks greyish.

Voice: Described by Maclean as a sweet penetrating whistled '*wee chidder-chidder-chidder wee*'.

Habitat: Well developed *Brachystegia* and *Montane* grasslands.

Distribution: Western and north-central Africa.

E.c.cognominata south-western Zaire and northern Angola.

E.c.orientalis eastern Zimbabwe, Mozambique (north of the Limpopo River), Zambia, Malawi, Tanzania and south-eastern Zaire.

Feeding: Seeds, grain and insects.

Breeding: Nests are well hidden in a tree or bush 1-3m from the ground. A loose shallow cup is constructed by the female of grass and twiglets and lined with finer grass. Eggs white to pale green, scrawled and blotched with brown and grey; clutch 2-3; host to Klaas's Cuckoo *Chrysococcyx klaas*.

Aviculture: Personal Communication CLUTCH 3; INCUBATION PERIOD 14 days; NESTLING PERIOD 16 days. Selected Reference WILDFOOD Seeds of Natal redtop *Rhynehelystrum repens*, Natal panic *Panicum natalense*, Guinea grass *P.maximum*. Selected Reference ANIMAL FOOD mealworms, grasshoppers, crickets.

Reed Bunting
Emberiza schoeniclus 15-19cm

Alternative name: Northern Reed Bunting (nominate).

Description: Male. Entire head, chin, throat and upper breast black; moustachial stripes and collar on the back of neck white; mantle and back rufous brown, streaked blackish; rump greyish; tail blackish brown, outer feathers white; lower breast and belly buffish; iris brown; bill greyish white; legs and feet pinkish. Female is brown like the male in winter plumage, with chestnut lesser wing-coverts, sides of breast and flanks, streaked blackish brown. Juvenile lacks black on head, which is streaked; similar mottling on the breast.

Voice: Described by Flint as a soft '*Tsees-tseek*', song, loud '*shree-shree-tee-ree-teeree*'.

Habitat: Margins of streams, reed beds and rushes.

Distribution: Morocco (breeds). Egypt (vagrant).

Feeding: Seeds and other plant materials and invertebrates namely mayflies, stoneflies, dragonflies, springtails, grasshoppers, bugs, beetles, ants, spiders, ticks and snails, seeds and shoots of bur-marigold *Bidens*, hawksbeard *Crepis*, Gold of Pleasure *Camelina*, pennycress *Thlaspi*, mouse-ear *Cerastium*, chickweed *Stellaria*, basil *Chinopodium*, rushes, grasses, including maize *Zea*, millet *Panicum*, reed *Lolium* and *Phragmites*. Feeding data not confined to Africa only.

Breeding: Nests on marshy ground in the tussocks, osier stumps and saplings in plantations. Female constructs an untidy structure of leaves and stems of aquatic plants and grasses, which is then lined with finer grasses, roots and hair. Eggs pale olive-brown, spotted with dark and light brown; clutch 4-5, occasionally 6, rarely 7; incubation by female, but male also shares duties for 13-14 days; nestling period 10-13 days; fed by both parents; fly after 12 days; 2, occasionally 3 broods.

Aviculture: Selected Reference CLUTCH 3-5; INCUBATION PERIOD 13-14 days; NESTLING PERIOD 10-13 days. Selected Reference WILDFOOD Marram grass *Ammophila arenaria*, bent grass *Agrostis* spp., Charlock *Sinapis arvensis*. Selected Reference ANIMAL FOOD waxmoth larvae, mealworms, crickets, Buffalo worms, green aphids.

Chaffinch
Fringilla coelebs 15cm

Alternative names: British Chaffinch, Continental Chaffinch, (nominate)
***F.c.spodiogenys* Algerian Chaffinch**
***F.c.africana* Green-backed Chaffinch.**

Description: Male. Forehead black; crown and nape slate-grey; hindneck and upper mantle greyish blue; lower mantle chestnut-brown; back and rump yellowish green; upper tail-coverts blue-grey, tinged green; tail dark grey, fringed green; wings with primaries and secondaries blackish brown, fringed greenish white, greater wing-coverts blackish brown, tipped white; sides of face, ear-coverts, chin, throat and breast pinkish brown; flanks pinkish brown, tinged greenish buff; centre of belly white; under tail-coverts creamy; iris brown; bill lead-blue; legs and feet pale brown. Female upperparts brownish olive; wings paler; underparts buffy olive; bill whitish horn. Juvenile has ground colour as adult female, but rump brownish green; underparts paler and tinged yellowish.

Males. *F.c.spodiogenys* similar to *africana* but paler overall.

F.c.africana differs from the nominate race in having the back more greener.

F.c.gengleri (see *Kleinschmidt, 1909, Falco, p.13 Hampstead*).

Voice: Described by Maclean as repeated cascades of about 12 tumbling notes, '*tee-tee-tee-tee-wi-wi-wi-woo treeeer*'.

Habitat: Pine and oak plantations, parks and gardens (nominate).

Distribution: North Africa (migrant).

F.c.gengleri south-western Cape Province. South Africa (introduced).

F.c.spodiogenys Tunisia (breeds).

F.c.africana Morocco to western Tunisia (breeds).

Feeding: Seeds, grain, small fruit, leaf buds spiders, caterpillars, worms and snails. Seeds of chickweed *Stellaria* spp. and Beechmast *Fagus* sp. Feeding not restricted to Africa only.

Breeding: Cup-shaped nest is usually very finely built of rootlets, moss and lichen, bound with spider web, lined with wool, hair and feathers. Outside diameter 9-10cm, depth 7-8cm, inside diameter about 5cm, depth 4-5cm. Placed either in the twigs of a small tree, fruit favoured such as apple, but even palms at 3-10m above ground. Eggs stone-coloured with a few spots and streaks of dark purplish brown; clutch 3-6; incubation 12-14 days by female only; nestling period 12-15 days; young fed by both parents.

Aviculture: Selected Reference CLUTCH 2-8; INCUBATION PERIOD 11-14 days; NESTLING PERIOD 12-15 days. Personal Communication CLUTCH 5; INCUBATION PERIOD 14 days; NESTLING PERIOD 15 days. Nest Record Cards CLUTCH 3 (ARU) 5 (ANRC); INCUBATION PERIOD 13 (ARU) 13 days (ANRC); NESTLING PERIOD 14 (ARU) 15 days (ANRC). Selected Reference WILDFOOD. Seeds of Newcastle grass, thistle *Silybum* sp., dandelion *Taraxacum* sp., chickweed *Stellaria* sp., Charlock *Sinapis arvensis*, Hardheads *Centuarea nigra*, Persicaria *Polygonum persicaria*, Teazle *Dipsacus fullonum*, Gold of Pleasure *Camelina sativa*. Personal Communication Newcastle grass, chickweed *Stellaria* sp., Gold of Pleasure *Camelina sativa*. Diet Record Cards Corn spurry *Spergula arvensis* (ARU), Red garden sorrel *Oxalis latifolia*, Chickweed *Stellaria media* (ADRC). Selected Reference ANIMAL FOOD whiteworms, spiders, caterpillars, Buffalo worms, mealworms, termites, moths, maggots.

Brambling

Fringilla montifringilla 14.5cm

Alternative names: Bramble-finch, Mountain Finch, Royal Chaffinch.

Description: Male. Forehead and crown glossy blackish blue; nape and mantle bluish black, fringed buff; back and rump black; upper tail-coverts black, tipped buff; tail black, edged yellowish; wings black,

fringed yellowish; sides of neck and ear-coverts glossy blue-black; chin, throat and breast chestnut buff; belly white, under tail-coverts pale buff; iris brown; bill blue-black; legs and feet brownish flesh. Female similar to male, but paler overall. Juvenile similar to female, but rump and belly tinged yellow.

Voice: Described by Beven as having a hoarse, rather metallic '*tsweek*'.

Habitat: Mixed woodland and edge of conifer forest, in winter beech woods and plantations.

Distribution: Morocco, Algeria, Tunisia and Egypt (migrant).

Feeding: Seeds of grasses and weeds, grain, berries and insects. Seeds of Knotgrass *Polygonum aviculare*, berries of Rowan *Sorbus aucuparia* and Elder *Sambucus nigra*. Also caterpillars, butterfly/moth larvae, craneflies and aphids. Feeding not restricted to Africa only.

Breeding: Nest, deep cut of grasses, pieces of bark, lichens and moss, lined with feathers, hair and sometimes down. Placed in a conifer or birch. Eggs greenish blue to olive-brown; clutch 6-7 but 4-8 and 9 recorded, occasionally only 5; incubation 12 days by female only; nestling period 14 days; young fed by both parents; single brooded.

Aviculture: Selected Reference CLUTCH 6-7; INCUBATION PERIOD 12 days; NESTLING PERIOD after 14 days. Nest Record Cards CLUTCH 6,2 addled (ANRC); INCUBATION PERIOD 13 days (ANRC); NESTLING PERIOD 16 days (ANRC). Selected Reference WILDFOOD Nipplewort *Lampsana communis*, Alder *Alnus glutinosa*, Persicaria *Polygonum persicaria*. Diet Record Cards Chickweed *Stellaria media*, Shepherd's purse *Capsella bursa-pastoris*, buds of Dwarf marigold *Schkuhria pinnata* (ADRC). Selected Reference ANIMAL FOOD mealworms, maggots. Diet Record Cards mealworms (ADRC).

Serin

Serinus serinus 11-12cm

Alternative names: Common Serin, European Serin, The Serin.

Description: Male. Forehead yellow; mantle and back yellow, streaked greenish black; rump bright greenish yellow; upper tail-coverts greenish brown, tinged grey; tail blackish brown, tipped yellowish green; wings with inner secondaries brown, tipped white, greater-coverts tipped yellowish buff and lesser-coverts, tipped yellowish green; eye stripe yellow; nape greenish, streaked blackish brown; hindneck yellow; chin, throat and centre of breast blackish brown; iris blackish brown; bill dark horn; legs and feet dark brown. Female resembling male, but paler yellow; crown and nape, tinged yellow, streaked dark greenish brown; throat and breast paler yellow. Juvenile upperparts brownish buff, streaked dark brown; underparts pale yellowish buff, streaked brown.

Voice: Described by Etchecopar & Hüe, resembles that of the domestic canary, a 'tuit'.

Habitat: Palm groves to the edge of the desert.

Distribution: Morocco, Algeria and Tunisia (breeds), Egypt (migrant).

Feeding: Seeds and buds from a wide variety of plants, namely dock *Rumex*, dandelion *Taraxacum*, and ragwort *Senecio*.

Breeding: Nest built by female of dry stalks, roots and moss interwoven with lichens and spiders' web and lined thickly with hair, vegetable down, occasionally feathers, string and cotton. Sited in evergreen tree, vines, heath or brambles, also recorded in conifers, cedars, cypress, junipers, ivy on rose pergola and in bare recess on main trunk of a date palm. Eggs pale bluish, spotted and streaked with purplish and reddish brown; clutch 4, sometimes 5 or only 3; incubation 13 days by female, occasionally male covers the eggs; nestling period 13-17 days; young fed by both parents.

Aviculture: Selected Reference CLUTCH 3-5; INCUBATION PERIOD 13-14 days; NESTLING PERIOD 14 days. Nest Record Cards CLUTCH 4 (ANRC); INCUBATION PERIOD 14 days (ANRC); NESTLING PERIOD 15 days (ANRC). Selected Reference WILDFOOD. Seeds of Teasel *Dipsacus fullonum*, Gold of Pleasure *Camelina sativa*, Sow-Thistle *Sonchus oleraceus*, dandelion *Taraxacum* sp., Mugwort *Artemisia vulgaris*, Sorrel *Rumex acetosa*, Birch *Betula pubescens*, Alder *Alnus glutinosa*. Selected Reference WILDFOOD Ragwort *Senecio jacobaea*, dandelion *Taraxacum* sp., dock *Rumex* sp. Diet Record Cards Chickweed *Stellaria media*, Shepherd's purse *Capsella bursa-pastoris*, Sow-thistle *Sonchus oleraceus* (ADRC).

Syrian Serin

Serinus syriacus 12,5cm
Alternative name: Tristram' Serin.

Description: Male. Forehead, round eyes and sides of neck lemon-yellow; crown, nape and ear-coverts pale grey; mantle and back olive-yellow, faintly streaked darker; rump yellow; tail blackish, feathers edged and tipped olive-yellow; wings golden-yellow, greater-coverts yellowish forming broad band wing-bar; chin, throat and belly yellowish; flanks greyish; iris brownish; bill greyish horn; legs and feet dusky grey. Female upperparts olive-grey, faintly streaked greyish on head and round eyes; upperparts greyish yellow, greyer on flanks. Juvenile upperparts sandy brown, tinged yellow on wings; underparts whitish.

Voice: Described by Hollom *et al* as a very low, soft 'tree-dar-dee', or 'tree-der-doo'.

Habitat: Mountain trees, such as cedars and junipers, but also deciduous including orchards.

Distribution: Northern Egypt (migrant).

Feeding: Seeds and insects.

Breeding: Nests may be constructed in Acer bush, oak *Quercus*, maple, cedar *Cedrus*, hawthorn *Crataegus*, juniper *Juniperus* and Almond *Prunus dulcis* at 1-2m above the ground. Eggs sub-elliptical to oval, smooth and glossy, pale blue, sparesly speckled purplish-brown. Clutch 4; incubation 12-14 days, probably by female only; nestling period 14-16 days.

Aviculture: No records.

Cape Canary

Serinus canicollis 13cm
Alternative names: Grey-necked Serin.
***S.c.flavivertex* Yellow-crowned Canary.**

Description: Male. Forehead, crown, nape, sides of face, chin, throat and breast golden-green; hindneck and sides, including ear-coverts grey; mantle, wing-coverts and rump yellowish green; tail black; flight feathers blackish, edged green; underparts yellow; iris brown; bill horn; legs and feet blackish. Female has chin, throat and breast greyish, with distinctive streakings. Juvenile is paler than adult female and streaked with black on upperparts, underparts buff and black.

Males. *S.c.thompsonae* differs from the nominate race in having the mantle, lesser wing-coverts and sides of throat mid-grey; greater wing-coverts blackish brown.

S.c.griseitergum differs from the nominate in having the forehead paler and greener; hindneck and sides of neck more extensively grey.

S.c.flavivertex similar to *sassii*, tail feathers mainly black with less buffy yellow.

S.c.sassii differs from the nominate in having hindneck and side of neck greenish.

S.c.huillensis differs from the nominate in being brighter and paler yellow, less streaked on nape.

Voice: Described by Newman as a series of loud, rolling warbles and trills.

Habitat: Frequents grassland with scattered bushes and in the vicinity of orchards and plantations.

Distribution: Western and south-western Cape, western Free State provinces of South Africa.

S.c.thompsonae Swaziland, Lesotho and the South African provinces of Mpumalanga and Northern Province, eastern Free State, KwaZulu-Natal (midlands).

S.c.griseitergum Zimbabwe and Mozambique (highlands).

S.c.flavivertex Ethiopia to northern Tanzania.

S.c.sassii southern Zaire to northern Malawi.

S.c.hullensis central Angola.

Feeding: Seeds, especially of weeds, also flower and tree buds. Seeds of Black-jack *Bidens pilosa* Khaki-weed *Alternanthera pungens*, Guava *Psidium guajava*. Loquat *Eriobotrya japonica*, green achenes of compositae plants, *Ursinia, Senecio, Osteospermum* and *Venidium*, buds and petals of Scarlet Salvia *Salvia splendens*. Afrikaans salie *S.chamelaeagnea* and *Buddleia sp.*

Breeding: The site is usually in stands of exotic trees, namely pines and oaks, but recently recorded on Ouhout trees *Leucosidae sericea*. Nests singly or colonially at 2-20m from the ground. The construction of the nest may take up to two weeks with only the female doing the work. The neat cup-shaped nest comprises of long tendrils of *Helichrysum* and numerous other materials, namely lichens, mosses, pine needles, leaves, rootlets, twigs, stringwool, cotton etc. Lined with fur, feathers, wooly seed-covers etc. Eggs white to pale greenish white, plain or sparingly speckled with reddish brown and occasionally greyish purple. Clutch 3-4; incubation by female alone for 12-16, usually 12-14 days; male feeds female on the nest; both parents feed the young at hatching; nestling period 15,5-18,5 days.

Aviculture: Selected Reference CLUTCH 3-4; INCUBATION PERIOD 12-14 days; NESTLING PERIOD 14-19 days. Personal Communication CLUTCH 4; INCUBATION PERIOD 14 days; NESTLING PERIOD 17 days. Selected Reference WILDFOOD. Seeds of Khaki-weed *Alternanthera pungens*, Black-jack *Bidens pilosa*, Milk thistle *Sonchus oleraceus*, Bird grass *Poa trivialis*, Berg grass *Setaria appendiculata*, leaves of Canary creeper *Senecio tamoides*, Dwarf marigold *Schkuhria pinnata*, Smelter's bush *Flaveria bidentis*. Personal Communication Shepherd's purse *Capsella bursa-pastoris*, Chickweed *Stellaria media*. Diet Record Cards buds of marigold *Schkuhria* sp., Red garden sorrel *Oxalis latifolia*.

Black-headed Siskin

Serinus nigriceps 11,5cm

Description: Male. Entire head black; nape, mantle and back pale olive-green; tail white and pale olive-green; rump and upper tail-coverts yellowish green; wings with primaries and secondaries edged and tipped with white and pale olive-brown; chin throat, breast and upper belly pale olive-green; lower belly and rest of underparts whitish; iris dark brown; bill blackish; legs and feet blackish, tinged yellow. Female has entire head pale olive-green; chin, throat, breast washed blackish. Juvenile similar to adult female, but upperparts browner, streaked dusky.

Voice: Utters a typical canary-like song of a series of musical trills (João pers.comm.)

Habitat: Montane forests and grasslands.

Distribution: Northern Ethiopia.

Feeding: Seeds from a variety of plant species.

Breeding: Nest usually placed below 2m from the ground in a small tree or bush. A neat compact cup, noticeably deeper than *canicollis* and composed of fine grass and rootlets with lining of very fine grass materials, sometimes mixed with down. Eggs bluish white, finely spotted brown; clutch 2-3.

Aviculture: Nest Record Cards CLUTCH 3 (ANRC) 3 (ARU) 5 (SAANRC); INCUBATION PERIOD 14 (ANRC) 14 (ARU) 15 days (SAANRC); NESTLING PERIOD 17 (ANRC) about 17 (ARU) 18 (SAANRC). Diet Record Cards WILDFOOD Guinea grass *Panicum maximum* (ARU), Shepherd's purse *Capsella bursa-pastoris*, thistle heads *Sonchus* sp., Chickweed *Stellaria media* (SAADRC), buds of Yellow sorrel *Oxalis pes-caprae* (ADRC).

African Citril Finch

Serinus citrinelloides 11,5cm

Alternative name: African Citril.

Description: Male. Forehead, ear-coverts and chin black; nape, mantle and back yellow-green, streaked black; wings and tail dusky, edged green; throat, breast, belly and underparts bright yellow, slightly washed with greenish on breast and flanks; iris brown; bill whitish horn; legs and feet brown. Female has forehead, ear-coverts and chin dusky green; throat and breast yellow, streaked blackish. Juvenile: Similar to adult female, but paler overall.

S.c.hypostictus differs from the nominate race in having chin and sides of face sooty grey.

S.c.frontalis differs from the nominate in having chin and sides of face black.

S.c.kikuyensis differs from the nominate in being darker overall. eyes stripe more distinct.

S.c.martinsi (see *N. Wirbelt. Vog.* pg. 95, pl. 34, fig 1, 1840).

Voice: Described by Williams & Arlott as a soft cheeping call and a sustained whistling song.

Habitat: Woodland, forest edges, bamboo, cultivation and gardens. In Malawi partial to *Eucalyptus* and *Cupressus* plantations.

Distribution: Ethiopia and south-eastern Sudan.

S.c.kikuyensis western Kenya.

S.c.frontalis western Uganda, eastern Zaire and north-western Tanzania.

S.c.hypostictus southern Kenya, eastern Zambia to Mozambique.

S.c.martinsi Angola.

Feeding: Seeds, in Malawi ripe Cosmos and insects, notably termites alates.

Breeding: A neat shallow cup of dead grass, rootlets, cocoons and cobwebs with a soft lining. placed in the fork of a tree or bush at no great height from the ground. Nesting has been observed in *Pinus caribea* plantations. Eggs white or cream with reddish or purplish brown spots and blotches; clutch 2-3.

Aviculture: No records.

Black-faced Canary

Serinus capistratus 13cm

Description: Male. Forehead, crown and nape yellowish green, streaked black; mantle yellowish green, streaked black; mantle and back greenish yellow, streaked black; rump and upper tail-coverts yellow; tail and wings blackish, edged green; lores, round eye, ear-coverts and chin black; sides of neck, throat, breast, belly and under tail-coverts yellow; iris brown; bill greenish horn; legs and feet dark brown. Female is greenish all over, yellowish on underparts, streaked blackish on upperparts with chin to breast dusky; lacks black face. Juvenile resembles female, but more heavily streaked.

Male. *S.c.hildegardae* differs from the nominate race in having underparts olive-yellow.

Voice: Described (João pers. comm) as a loud canary-like piping whistle.

Habitat: Papyrus swamps.

Distribution: Gabon to northern Angola and Zambia.

S.c.hildegardae southern Angola.

Feeding: Grass and plant seeds.

Breeding: Nests in a bush or tree, not differing from other species. Eggs probably 3, very pale slate coloured, speckled with reddish brown.

Aviculture: Nest Record Cards CLUTCH 3,4 (ANRC); INCUBATION PERIOD 12 days (ANRC); NESTLING PERIOD 15 days (ANRC). Diet Record Cards WILD-FOOD Chickweed *Stellaria media*. Little seeded canary grass *Phalaris minor* (ADRC). Diet Record Card FRUIT South African blackberry *Rubus pinnatus* (ADRC). Diet Record Cards ANIMAL FOOD termites (ADRC).

Van Someren's Canary

Serinus koliensis 11cm

Alternative name: Papyrus Canary.

Description: Male. Forehead, crown, nape, mantle and back yellowish green, distinctly streaked blackish; rump and upper tail-coverts yellowish olive-green; tail blackish, tinged olive-green; wings black, edged yellowish olive-green; chin, throat, breast and belly dark olive-green; iris brown; bill horn, lower mandible paler; legs and feet pinkish brown. Female lower forehead and ear-coverts grey; throat pale yellow; flanks heavily

streaked brown. Juvenile similar to female but upperparts having wing edged pale buffish white; underparts buffish, streaked brownish.

Voice: A quite, plantive flute-like call.

Habitat: Papyrus and adjacent bananas *Musa* sp. plantations and cultivation.

Distribution: Uganda and western Kenya.

Feeding: Seeds of papyrus and other seeds.

Breeding: Not known.

Aviculture: No records.

Forest Canary

Serinus scotops 13cm

Alternative names: Grass Shelly, Natal Linnet, Striped Canary.

Description: Male. Forehead, crown, nape, mantle and back bright olive-green, heavily streaked with blackish green; rump and upper tail-coverts olive-green; tail olive-green, edged black; stripe over the eye yellow; ear-coverts green; chin blackish; wings with greater and lesser-coverts blackish brown, edged yellow; throat yellow; breast and belly green, streaked blackish green; under tail-coverts yellow; iris brown; bill horn; legs and feet brownish. Female has ear-coverts and chin greyish. Juvenile similar to adult female, but paler.

Males. *S.s.umbrosus* differs from the nominate race in having the upperparts darker green; rump olive-green, streaked blackish green.

S.s.transvaalensis differs from the nominate in having lower throat and breast darker; flanks more heavily streaked.

Voice: Described by Maclean as a quiet *tsik, tsip-tsip* or stuttered *tsit-itit* callnotes.

Habitat: Dense evergreen forest and adjacent bush and exotic vegetation.

Distribution: South African provinces of eastern Cape and KwaZulu-Natal (coastal and lower midlands).

S.s.umbrosus southern Cape Province (coastal regions), South Africa, Mpumalanga, western KwaZulu-Natal.

S.s.transvaalensis eastern and northern Mpumalanga Province (highlands) and probably also western Swaziland.

Feeding: Seeds of weeds, small fruits and the bases of leaf petioles. Fruit of *Rubiaceae* sp. and leaf petioles of Sneezewood *Ptaeroxylon obliquum*.

Breeding: The nest site is a bush or small tree 1-5m above ground, usually in dense cover. The cup nest consists of moss and various sorts of vegetable down, then lined with stringy lichen. Eggs white to pale blue, spotted reddish to slate-grey, chiefly at the thick end; clutch 2-4, usually 3; young cared for and fed by both parents.

Aviculture: Selected Reference CLUTCH 2-4; INCU-BATION PERIOD 13-14 days; NESTLING PERIOD 15-21 days. Nest Record Cards CLUTCH 3,4,4 (ANRC) 3 (ARU) 3,4 (NASNRC) 4 (SAANRC); INCU-BATION PERIOD 13,14 (ANRC) 14 (ARU) 14 days (SAANRC); NESTLING PERIOD 17,18 (ANRC) 15 (ARU) 17 days (SAANRC); Personal Communication CLUTCH 3; INCUBATION PERIOD 14; NESTLING PERIOD 17 days. Selected Reference WILDFOOD Seeds of Khaki-weed *Alternanthera pungens*, Black-jack *Bidens pilosa*, Milk thistle *Sonchus oleraceus*, Cape pigweed *Amaranthus thunbergii*, Bird grass *Poa trivialis*, Guinea grass *Panicum maximum*, Blue panic *P.laevifolium*. Diet Record Cards *thistle* sp. (ADRC), chickweed *Stellaria* sp. (SAADRC), Shepherd's purse *Capsella bursa-pastoris*, Little seeded canary grass *Phalaris minor* (ARU).

White-rumped Seedeater

Serinus leucopygius 10cm

Alternative names: African Songbird, Grey Canary, Grey Singing Finch, White-rumped Serin.

Description: Sexes similar. Forehead, crown and nape ash-grey, streaked brown; mantle and back greyish brown; wings blackish, feathers edged white; chin and throat white; breast buff shading to white, mottled brown; rump and rest of underparts white; iris brown; bill pale brown; legs and feet brown. Juvenile similar to adult, but upper and underparts more heavily streaked.

Adults. *S.l.riggenbachi* differs from the nominate race in having throat and breast whitish, spotted dusky.

S.l.pallens differs from the nominate in having upper-parts paler with narrower streaking.

Voice: Described by Serle *et al* as a pleasant, varied, resonant song '*too-ee-ee*'.

Habitat: Grasslands and savanna woodland, cultivated lands and gardens.

Distribution: Eastern Sudan and northern Ethiopia.

S.i.riggenbachi Senegal to Chad and Central African Republic.

S.l.pallens Zaire to northern Niger.

Feeding: Seeds, including millet.

Breeding: A tiny compact nest cup in slender outer fork of a bough of a soft leaved or thorny tree, or lashed between two twigs, made of fine grass stems, hair, lined with vegetable down and a few feathers. Eggs white, tinged grey or blue sparingly spotted blackish brown; clutch 3-4.

Aviculture: Selected Reference CLUTCH 3-4; INCU-BATION PERIOD 12-14 days; NESTLING PERIOD 14-21 days. Nest Record Cards CLUTCH 3 (ARU) 3 (ANRC); INCUBATION PERIOD 13 (ARU) 13 days (ANRC); NESTLING PERIOD 15 (ARU) 17 days (ANRC). Diet Record Cards WILDFOOD Chickweed *Stellaria media*, Common dandelion *Taraxacum officinale* (ARU), Ragwort *Senecio consanguineus*, buds of Gallant soldier *Galinsoga parviflora* (ADRC). Selected Reference ANIMAL FOOD maggots. Diet Record Cards aphids (ADRC), wasp larvae (ARU).

Yellow-rumped Seedeater

Serinus atrogularis 10-12cm

Alternative names: Black-throated Canary, Peach Canary, Yellow-rumped Serin. *S.a.lwenarum* Angolan Singing Finch.

Description: Sexes similar. Forehead, crown, nape, mantle and back ashy brown, streaked black; rump yellow; upper tail-coverts yellow, edged white; tail ashy brown; wings with greater and lesser-coverts ashy brown, streaked black; ear-coverts dusky; chin and throat dusky, spotted blackish; belly and flanks buffish white; under tail-coverts dusky; iris brown; bill horn; legs and feet flesh coloured. Juvenile is blackish brown on the chin, throat and rest of underparts.

Adults. *S.a.xanthopygius* differs from *somereni* in being paler overall.

S.a.reichenowi differs from *xanthopygius* in having upperparts browner, supercilliary stripe white; ear-coverts dusky white.

S.a.somereni differs from *reichenowi* in having upper and underparts darker; throat having more black.

S.a.lwenarum differs from the nominate in having upperparts greyer; neck blackish brown.

S.a.impiger differs from the nominate in having upper-parts darker, more buffish; rump bright yellow; underparts washed with pinkish buff.

S.a.deserti differs from the nominate in being paler overall; chin and throat broken into black spots.

S.a.semideserti differs from the nominate in having forehead white; tail ashy brown; edged white.

Voice: Described by Serle *et al* as the usual canary-type song and double '*tsssp*' calls.

Habitat: Woodland, cultivation and open bush grasslands.

Distribution: Gauteng (highveld), northern Free State, South Africa to south-eastern Botswana and Zimbabwe.

S.a.xanthopygius northern Ethiopia.

S.a.reichenowi southern Sudan to north-eastern Tanzania.

S.a.somereni eastern Zaire, western Uganda and western Kenya.

S.a.lwenarum southern Zaire, Angola, and Zambia.

S.a.semideserti northern Namibia, Botswana, Zimbabwe, southern Angola, south-western Zambia and western North-West Province, South Africa.

S.a.impiger north-eastern Cape, western Free State, Mpumalanga and northern KwaZulu-Natal, South Africa to Lesotho.

S.a.deserti north-western Namibia, south-western Angola and northern and north-western Cape, South Africa.

Feeding: Grass and weed seeds, buds and insects. Seeds of Annual Signal grass *Urochloa panicoides*, Sunflower *Helianthus annus*, buds and petals of Blue Lupin *Lupinus augustifolius*.

Breeding: Nests 1-15m from the ground in dry cone of a protea flower, fork of tree, often conifer or at base of palm frond, on rafter of shed, in notch of tree trunk and in fruit trees. The nest with a cup diameter of about 4,5cm, depth 3,2cm is constructed of dry grass, rootlets and other plant matter which is all bound with cobwebs. The lining is of protea down and a few feathers. Both sexes become involved in nest building. Eggs white or pale green, plain or speckled with black or spotted with brown, chiefly at the thick end; clutch 3-5, usually 3; incubation period 12-13 days, by female only; male feeds female at nest; nestling period 15-17 days; parental duties towards young shared, but male plays a greater part in feeding for some considerable time.

Aviculture: Selected Reference CLUTCH 3-5; INCUBATION PERIOD 12-14 days; NESTLING PERIOD 14-17 days. Nest Record Cat Cards CLUTCH 3 (ARU) 3 (SAANRC); INCUBATION PERIOD 13 (ARU) 14 (SAANRC); NESTLING PERIOD 15 (ARU) 16 days (SANRC). Selected Reference WILDFOOD Seeds of Annual meadow grass *Poa annua*, Khaki-weed *Alternanthera pungens*, Black-jack *Bidens pilosa*, Milk thistle *Sonchus oleraceus*, Annual signal grass *Urochloa panicoides*, Bushveld signal grass *U.mosambicensis*, Blue panic *Panicum laevifolium*, Guinea grass *P.maximum*, buds, flower petals and leaves of Canary creeper *Senecio tamoides*, Parrot leaf *Alternanthera ficoidea*, Smelter's bush *Flaveria bidentis*. Diet Record Cards thistle heads *Sonchus* sp., chickweed *Stellaria* sp., Shepherd's purse *Capsella bursa-pastoris*, Ragwort *Senecio cosanguineus* (ARU SAADRC). Diet Record Cards FRUIT African mulberry *Morus mesozygia* (ARU), Raspberry of the men *Rubus rigidus* (SAADRC). Selected Reference ANIMAL FOOD mealworms, beetles, caterpillars.

Lemon-breasted Canary
Serinus citrinipectus 12cm

Alternative names: Lemon-breasted Seedeater, Variegated Singing Finch, Scheeper's Canary.

Description: Male. Forehead, crown and nape grey, mottled with black; mantle and back dark olive-buff, streaked black; rump yellow; under tail-coverts olive, broadly edged and tipped yellow; lores white; sides of face and ear-coverts yellow; stripe behind the eye and throat blackish; chin white; lower throat and breast lemon-yellow; flanks brownish buff, lightly streaked grey; centre of lower breast and under tail-coverts white; wing-coverts olive-brown, edged white; outer webs of primaries and secondaries edged yellow; iris dark brown; bill dark flesh to horn; legs and feet brown. Female lacks the yellow on the sides of the face and ear-coverts; lores pinkish white; flanks pinkish buff; spots on lower throat grey. Juvenile similar to adult female, but more heavily streaked.

Habitat: Dry savanna, woodland and cultivation.

Voice: Described by Maclean as canary-like with sparrowy tone.

Distribution: Mozambique, southern Malawi, south-eastern Zimbabwe, Mpumalanga to north-eastern KwaZulu-Natal, South Africa.

Feeding: Seeds.

Breeding: A nest recorded in northern KwaZulu-Natal was concealed within the fold of a Lala Palm leaf *Hyphaene natalensis* about 1,6m above the ground. It was constructed of a base about 160mm long x 65mm and consisted of fibres and dead creeper stems, bits of leaf which were covered in short soft hairs, chewed bark bound with caterpillar silk tubes from Umdoni *Syzygium cordatum*. The nest cup was lined with hair-like fibres stripped from Lala Palm leaves. Eggs white, lightly streaked brown; clutch 3-4.

Aviculture: Selected Reference CLUTCH 3-4; INCUBATION PERIOD 12-14 days. Personal Communication CLUTCH 3; INCUBATION PERIOD 14 days; NESTLING PERIOD 15 days. Selected Reference WILDFOOD. Seeds of Black-jack *B.dens pilosa*, Milk thistle *Sonchus oleraceus*, Bird grass *Poa trivialis*, Crab finger grass *Digitaria sanguinalis*, buds and leaves of Smelter's bush *Flaveria bidentis*. Personal Communication thistle *Sonchus* sp., chickweed *Stellaria* sp., buds of Gallant soldier *Galinsoga parviflora*. Selected Reference ANIMAL FOOD termites.

Yellow-eyed Canary

Serinus mozambicus 12-13cm

Alternative names: African Canary, Green Singing Finch, Little Singer, Little Green Singer, Icterine Canary, Yellow-fronted Canary, Small Green Singing Finch, *S.m. granti*, Mozambique Serin.

Description: Male. Forehead, crown and nape green, streaked black; broad streak over eye yellow mantle and back green, streaked black; upper tail-coverts yellow; tall greenish black, tipped white; lores blackish; cheeks, chin, breast, belly and under tail-coverts yellow; moustachial stripe blackish; wings and wing-coverts dusky, edged greenish yellow; iris brown; bill horn; legs and feet dusky. Female is paler overall. Juvenile similar to adult female, but less yellow on forehead; sides of breast and flanks streaked.

Males. *S.m.caniceps* differs from *punctigula* in being paler on upperparts and with crown grey.

S.m.punctigula similar to *barbatus*, but upperparts yellowish green; underparts olive-green.

S.m.barbatus differs from the nominate in having head and mantle brighter green.

S.m.santhome similar to *caniceps*, but upperparts without tinge of grey on head and less streaking on back and mantle.

S.m.tando differs from the nominate in having the upperparts brighter green.

S.m.samaliyae similar to *santhome*, but upperparts more yellowish green.

S.m.vansoni differs from the nominate in having upperparts more olivaceous green.

S.m.granti differs from the nominate in having upper parts darker green.

S.m.gommaensis differs from the nominate in having forehead paler yellow; stripe over eye does not extend far back.

Voice: Described by Guggisberg as a sharp 'twsstp'; also soft warbling song.

Habitat: Tree savanna and bushveld. Also near human habitation on farms, villages, towns and gardens.

Distribution: South-eastern Tanzania, Zambia, Malawi, south-eastern Botswana, Zimbabwe, Mozambique, Swaziland and North-West, Gauteng, Mpumalanga Northern Province and Free State, South Africa.

S.m.caniceps Senegal to northern Cameroon.

S.m.punctigula Cameroon.

S.m.barbatus Central African Republic, south-western Sudan, northern and eastern Zaire, Uganda, central and eastern Kenya.

S.m.santhome São Thomé Island.

S.m.tando south-western Zaire and northern Angola.

S.m.samaliyae south-eastern Zaire and Zambia.

S.m.vansoni south-western Zambia, southern Angola, north-eastern Botswana and north-eastern Namibia.

S.m.granti eastern Swaziland, southern Mozambique and the South African provinces of Cape, Gauteng (highveld) and KwaZulu-Natal.

S.m.grotei eastern and south-eastern Sudan and western Ethiopia.

S.m.gommaensis western Ethiopia.

Feeding: Seeds, flower petals, fruit, leaves and insects. Seeds of *Eucalyptus* spp., Sunflower *Helianthus annuus*, Sorghum *caffrorun*, Guinea grass *Panicum maximum*, Beefwood tree *Casuarina equisetifolia*, petals of red-hot poker (*Kniphofia*), leaves of Chinese hibiscus *Hibiscus rosa-sinensis* and soft achenes of small *Composites* such as *Ursinia* and *Veronia*. Probes for nectar at the base of flower tubes, namely Flat-crowned aloe *Aloe marlothii*, Candelabra aloe *A.candelabrum*, Kranz aloe *A.arborescens*, fruit of Dull-leaved mukwakwa *Strychnos innocua*. Attracted to salt lick left on farms for cattle. Live food in the form of fly larvae, aphids, beetles, termites and hairless caterpillars.

Breeding: The nest is placed in horizontal forks of trees, shrubs and bushes and may vary in position from 1-6m from the ground. A shallow compact cup of dead grass, seedheads and rootlets is constructed and then bound with cobwebs. The centre lining consists of finer grass and hair-like vegetation. The brim is thinly laid with animal hair notably cow and horse, but when scarce, fine wool and feathers may be used as a substitute. Building by both sexes. Occasionally breeds in loose colonies.

Eggs white or pale blue, plain or sparsely and faintly marked with pink or brown; clutch 3-4; female incubates while fed by male; incubation period 13-14,5 days; young brooded by female when small; male assists with feeding after a few days; young leave the nest at 16-24 days; male feeds the fledglings for some time afterwards; independant at 9-10 weeks.

Aviculture: Selected Reference CLUTCH 2-5; INCUBATION PERIOD 12-14 days, NESTLING PERIOD 14-25 days. Nest Record Cards CLUTCH 3,3,3,4,4 (ANRC) 2 (ARU); INCUBATION PERIOD 12,12,13,13 (ANRC) 13 days (ARU); NESTLING PERIOD 16,17 (ANRC) 17 days (ARU). Selected Reference WILD-FOOD. Seeds of Khaki-weed *Alternanthera pungens*, Black-jack *Bidens pilosa*, Milk thistle *Sonchus oleraceus*, Bird grass *Poa trivialis*, Guinea grass *Panicum maximum*, Blue panic *P.laevifolium*, buds, flower petals and leaves of Canary creeper *Senecio tamoides*, Parrot leaf *Alternanthera ficoidea*, Smelter's bush *Flaveria bidentis*. Diet Record Cards thistle *Sonchus* sp., chickweed *Stellaria* (ARU ADRC), Shepherd's purse *Capsella bursa-pastoris*, Ragwort *Senecio consanguineus*, buds of Gallant soldier *Galinsoga parviflora*.

Grosbeak Canary
Serinus donaldsoni 14cm

Alternative names: Abyssinian Grosbeak Canary, Ethiopian Grosbeak Canary, Northern Grosbeak Canary, Somaliland Grosbeak Canary, *S.d.buchanani* Kenya Grosbeak Canary, Southern Grosbeak Canary.

Description: Male. Forehead, crown and nape green, streaked blackish; mantle, back, rump and upper tail-coverts yellow; tail dusky, tinged greenish; wings dusky with pale edges; ear-coverts greenish; chin, throat, breast, belly and rest of underparts bright yellow, streaked blackish on breast and flanks; iris brown; bill horn; legs and feet greyish black. Female is ash-brown with dark streaking and bright yellow rump; underparts yellowish white with dark streaking on breast and flanks. Juvenile closely resembles adult female, but paler.

Male. *S.d.buchanani* differs from the nominate race in having upperparts greener; underparts more greenish yellow.

Voice: Described by Guggisberg as short song with higher finale note, '*kiki-kiki-kiki-kiki-kiki-hirrer*'.

Habitat: Semi-desert areas, dry bush country at 200-1600m.

Distribution: Ethiopia and northern Kenya.

S.d.buchanani southern Kenya and northern Tanzania.

Feeding: Seeds and other vegetable matter including *acacia* fruit.

Breeding: Nest is rather flat, of twigs, rootlets, cobwebs and vegetable down, placed in a tree fork. Eggs pale blue with dots and lines or purplish black; clutch 3.

Aviculture: No records.

Yellow Canary
Serinus flaviventris 13-14cm

Alternative names: Giant Green Singing Finch, St Helena Seedeater, Swainson's Canary, Yellow Seedeater, Yellow-bellied Seedeater. *S.f.marshalli* Shelley's Seedeater

Description: Male. Forehead, crown, nape, mantle and back olive-green, streaked with blackish; rump and upper tail-coverts greenish yellow; stripe above eye and ear-coverts yellow; malar stripe, below ear-coverts olive-green; chin, throat, breast, belly and under tail-coverts chrome yellow; flanks grey; iris brown; bill horn; legs and feet black. Female paler overall; upperparts streaked with blackish brown; stripe above eye buffish white. Juvenile similar to adult female with spots on the underparts.

Males. *S.f.hesperus* differs from the nominate in having throat and underparts uniform yellow without the greenish band.

S.f.aurescens differs from the nominate in being more yellowish, less greenish; forehead, crown, nape and mantle less distinctive streaking.

S.f.quintoni differs from the nominate in having underparts orange-yellow.

S.f.guillarmodi differs from the nominate in having crown, mantle and back more heavily streaked.

S.f.marshalli differs from the nominate in having upperparts brighter green.

S.f.damarensis differs from the nominate in having upperparts more greenish yellow.

Voice: Described by Maclean as a sustained jumble of fast trilling and warbling notes.

Habitat: Montane shrub, semi-arid savanna and coastal bush.

Distribution: South-western Cape Province, South Africa.

S.f.hesperus western Cape Province, South Africa and south-west in Namibia.

S.f.aurescens north-western Cape Province, South Africa and southern and central Namibia.

S.f.quintoni Cape (highlands), South Africa.

S.f.marshalli north-eastern Cape Province, Gauteng North-West, Free State and KwaZulu-Natal (interior) South Africa to Lesotho (lowlands).

S.f.damarensis northern Cape Province, South Africa to central and northern Namibia, Botswana and Zimbabwe.

Feeding: Seeds, flowers, nectar, insects and small crustaceans. Small seeds of achenes *graminoid*, also *Arctotheca, Bidens, Senecio, Elytropappus, Stoebe, Eriocephalus, Dorotheanthus, Diascia, Cannomis, Cliffortia, Erica, Chenopodium, Melalasia*, Tumbleweed *Amaranthus angustifolius*, Cape Pigweed *A.thunbergii* and Milk Thistle *Sonchus oleraceus*.

Breeding: The nest site is usually low down at a height of 30cm-3m in a bush or tree, notably pines and firs. Recorded also as nesting on the ground. A shallow cup of stems, rootlets, soft weeds and heaths, then lined with soft materials such as seedheads. Eggs white, sometimes pale green or blue, plain or spotted or streaked at the thick end with dark brown or black; clutch 3-4, occasionally 5, usually 3; incubation period about 12 days by female only; male feeds her on the nest; nestling period 14; young cared for by both partners; brooded by female when small.

Aviculture: Selected Reference CLUTCH 2-5. INCUBATION PERIOD 12-14 days; NESTLING PERIOD 14-17 days. Nest Record Cards CLUTCH 4 (ARU) 4,5 (ANRC); INCUBATION PERIOD 12 (ARU) 13,13 (ANRC); NESTLING PERIOD 15 (ARU) 15,17 days (ANRC). Selected Reference WILDFOOD thistle *Silybum* sp., Comfrey *Symphytum officinale*, buds and leaves of Smelters's bush *Flaveria bidentis*, seeds of Khaki-weed *Alternanthera pungens*, Black-jack *Bidens pilosa*, Golden setaria *Setaria sphacelata*, Milk thistle *Sonchus oleraceus*, Guinea grass *Panicum maximum*, Blue panic *P.laevifolium*. Diet Record Cards thistle *Sonchus* sp., Guinea grass *Panicum maximum* Chickweed *Stellaria media* (ARU), Common dandelion *Taraxacum officinale* Ragwort *Senecio consanguineua*, buds of Cape wild mustard *Sisymbrium capense* (ANRC). Diet Record Cards FRUIT African mulberry *Morus mesozygia* (ARU ADRC). Selected Reference ANIMAL FOOD termites, mealworms, maggots.

White-bellied Canary
Serinus dorsostriatus 12-13cm
Alternative names: White-bellied Serin.
S.d.maculicollis **Somali White-bellied Canary.**

Description: Male. Forehead and ear-coverts yellow; crown and nape yellowish green, streaked black; mantle and back olive-green; rump yellow; uppper tail-coverts greenish yellow; chin, throat and breast yellow; flanks and belly white; under tail-coverts pale yellow; bill, upper mandible blackish horn, lower pale horn; iris brownish; legs and feet greyish black or greysh horn. Female upperparts dark brown, streaked dusky; lower rump yellow; tail dusky black, edged yellowish white; underparts pale brown, somewhat paler on belly to under tail-coverts. Juvenile similar to female with breast and flanks more streaked and spotted dusky; males having less yellowish, more greenish, with broader streaking.

S.d.maculicollis female as nominate, but breast and belly white.

Voice: Described by Mackworth-Praed & Grant as a shrill '*whee*', and a sweet quite loud song.

Habitat: Arid and semi arid bush, woodland and grassy savannas.

Distribution: Northern Tanzania (Mount Meru).

S.d.maculicollis southern Ethiopia, Kenya and Somalia.

Feeding: Grass seeds.

Breeding: Constructs a twig foundation nest placed in the fork of a tree or bush. Eggs pale blue plain or spotted and streaked sepia and black; clutch 2-4.

Aviculture: Personal Communication CLUTCH 3,4; INCUBATION PERIOD 12,12; NESTLING PERIOD 15,16; Personal Communication Guinea grass *Panicum maximum*, Chickweed *Stellaria media*, Common dandelion *Taraxacum officinale*, Khaki-weed *Alternanthera pungens*.

Brimstone Canary
Serinus sulphuratus 15-16cm
Alternative names: Bully Canary, Bully Seedeater, Sulphury Seedeater, Sulphur-coloured Seedeater.
S.s.sharpii **Uganda Brimstone Canary.**

Description: Male. Forehead, crown and nape yellow-green, streaked blackish brown; stripe above eye yellow; ear-coverts yellowish olive-green; mantle, back, rump and upper tail-coverts yellow-green, streaked brownish black; tail black, edged olive yellowish green; wing coverts blackish brown, edged olive-green; chin and throat lemon-yellow; breast and flanks olive-green;

iris brown; bill horn; legs and feet brownish. Female is paler and more heavily streaked on the upperparts. Juvenile similar to female, but even paler.

Males. *S.s.sharpii* differs from the nominate race in having upperparts yellowish olive-green, streaked dusky; upper tail-coverts not streaked.

S.s.wilsoni upperparts brighter yellow-green.

S.s.languens more yellowish on the mantle and back.

S.s.loveridgei paler yellowish green on the upperparts including the ear-coverts.

Voice: Described by MacLachlan & Liversidge as a deep 'sqeerk'; song deep and rather undistinguished.

Habitat: Frequents mixed woodland, riverine thickets, mountain valleys and cultivation including parks and gardens.

Distribution: South-western Cape Province, South Africa.

S.s.sharpii Angola to Kenya and Mozambique.

S.s.wilsoni eastern Cape Province, central and western KwaZulu-Natal, Free State, Mpumalanga (lowveld) and eastern to Northern Province, South Africa to western Swaziland.

S.s.languens eastern KwaZulu-Natal and Mpumalanga, provinces of South Africa, to eastern Swaziland, southern Mozambique and Zimbabwe.

S.s.loveridgei northern Zimbabwe.

Feeding: On relatively large seed types, chiefly seed kernels in developed fleshy fruit and also seeds of grasses, weeds, shrubs and insects. Seeds of Swaziland grass *Digitaria horizontalis*, Sunflower *Helianthus annuus*, Wild radish *Raphanus rapanistrum*, Cat-thorn *Scutia myrtina*, Cape spinach *Emex australis*, Candelabra tree *Euphorbia ingens*, *Lycium*, Chinese privet *Ligustrum lucidum*, Veld fig *Ficus burtt-dayvi*.

Breeding: Nest site is the fork of a tree or bush, usually 2-6m from the ground. It is not uncommon to find a nest in a bunch of bananas. The cup consists of grass and rootlets, with the possibility of fibre strands of string, pieces of paper, knitting wool and cow tail hair being incorporated into the structure. Lining may consist of fine grass fibres, rags, string and plant down. Lining completed before laying. Eggs white, pale green or pale blue, streaked and spotted with dark brown or black; clutch 2-4; incubation period 12,5-17 days; only female incubates, male feeds her on the nest; nestling period 15-21 days; parental duties are shared.

Aviculture: Selected Reference CLUTCH 2-4; INCUBATION PERIOD 12,5-17 days; NESTLING PERIOD 15-22 days. Nest Record Cards CLUTCH 3,3,4,5 (ARU); INCUBATION PERIOD 13,15 (ARU); NESTLING PERIOD 17,19 days (ARU). Selected Reference WILDFOOD. Seeds of Khaki-weed *Alternanthera pungens*, Black-jack *Bidens pilosa*. Milk thistle *Sonchus oleraceus*, Bird grass *Poa trivialis*, Golden setaria *Setaria, sphacelata*, Millet grass *S.woodii*, Guinea grass *Panicum maximum*, Blue panic *P.laevifolium*, flower petals of Scarlet salvia *Salvia splendens*, African

marigold *Tagetes erecta*, buds and leaves of Canary creeper *Senecio tamoides*, Smeltersbossie *Flaveria bidentis*. Diet Record Cards chickweed *Stellaria* sp., Sow-thistle *Sonchus oleraceus*, buds of Cape wild mustard *Sisymbrium capense* (ARU). Diet Record Cards FRUIT Nana-berry *Rhus dentata*, Wild plum *Harpephyllum caffrum*, African cranberry *Vaccinium exul*, Common forest grape *Rhoicissus tomentosa*, Giant raisin *Grewia hexamita*, Mallow raisin *G.villosa*, Tree strawberry *Caphalanthus natalensis*, African mulberry *Morus mesozygia*, Strawberry-guava *Psidium cattleianum*, White-berry bush *Securinega virosa*, Waterberry *Syzgium guineense*, Climbing raisin *Grewia caffra*, Black monkey orange *Strychnos madagascariensis*, Bird plum *Berchemia discolor*, Bastard forest grape *Rhoicissus rhomboidea*, Sand jackal-berry *Diospyros batocana*, Raspberry of the men *Rubus rigidus* (ARU). Diet Record Cards ANIMAL FOOD mealworms, moths, termites, earthworms (ARU).

White-throated Seedeater
Serinus albogularis 15cm

Alternative names: Thick-billed Seedeater, White-throated Canary.

Description: Male. Forehead, crown, mantle and back ashy brown, the feathers edged black; rump and upper tail-coverts pale olive-green; tail and flight feathers ash brown, edged pinkish buff; sides of face and ear-coverts pale ash-brown; stripe above eye, chin and throat white; breast and flanks pale ash-brown; belly silvery grey; under tail-coverts white; iris brown; bill, upper mandible pale brown, lower pale horn; legs and feet blackish brown. Female has rump and upper tail-coverts paler olive-green. Juvenile upperparts browner with indistinct dusky streaks on breast.

S.a.hewitti differs from the nominate race in having the upper and underparts darker; rump and upper tail-coverts pale yellow.

S.s.orangensis differs from the nominate in having the rump bright yellow.

S.a.crocopygius differs from the nominate in having forehead, crown, nape, mantle and back brown, feathers edged ash-brown; chin, throat and upper breast white; rump and upper tail-coverts bright yellow.

S.a.sordahlae differs from the nominate in having upper and underparts paler; conspicuous white eyebrows.

Voice: Described by MacLachlan & Liversidge as powerful and tuneful.

Habitat: Frequents dry savanna and thorn scrub along river valleys and bush adjacent to the sea.

Distribution: Western Cape Province, South Africa.

S.a.hewitti south western to eastern Cape north of the Orange River in South Africa.

S.a.orangensis north-eastern Cape, Free State and Gauteng, South Africa and Lesotho (lowlands).

S.a.crocophgius Namibia and south-western Angola.

S.a.sordahlae north-western Cape Province, South Africa and Namibia (northern limits currently uncertain).

Feeding: Seeds of weed and grasses, berries, buds and insects. Plant parts of *Zygophyllum, Erodium Kleinia, Relhania, Othonna, Euryops, Chrysanthemoides, Sonchus, Steobe, Emex, Eriocephalus, Microloma, Salsola, Chenopodium, Raphanus, Acacia, Olea, Protea* and *Senecio*, berries of Kraal honey-thorn *Lycium afrum*. Large honey-thorn *L.austrinum* Bastard brandy bush *Grewia bicolor*, Cross-berry *G.occidentalis*, Kalahari Sand raisin *G.retinervis*, Spekboom *Portulacaria afra* and buds of Yellow milk bush *Euphorbia mauritanica*.

Breeding: The nest is a loosely made cup of rootlets and twigs lined with vegetable down, 1-3, above ground in a fork of a bush or low tree. Eggs white, pinkish cream or greenish blue, sparingly spotted with purplish black; clutch 2-4, usually 3; incubation by female alone, male feeds at nest; young cared for and fed by both parents.

Aviculture: Selected Reference CLUTCH 2-4 INCUBATION PERIOD 13-14 days; NESTLING PERIOD 16-19 days. Personal Communication CLUTCH 3,4; INCUBATION PERIOD 13,13 days; NESTLING PERIOD 17,18 days. Nest Record Cards CLUTCH 3; INCUBATION PERIOD 13 days; NESTLING PERIOD 17 days (ANRC). Selected Reference WILDFOOD Seeds of Khaki-weed *Alternanthera pungens*, Black-jack *Bidens pilosa*, Milk thistle *Sonchus oleraceus*, Berg grass *Setaria appendiculata*, Bird grass *Poa trivialis*, Guinea grass *Panicum maximum*, Blue panic *P.laevifolium*, Natal redtop *Rhynchelytrum repens*, Weeping love grass *Eragrostis curvula*, Dropseed grass *Sporobolus fimbriatus*, Kuri millet *Urochloa panicoides*, buds and flower petals of Canary creeper *Senecio tamoides*, Smelter's bush *Flaveria bidentis*. Personal Communication Thistle *Sonchus* sp., chickweed *Stellaria* sp., Shepherd's purse *Capsella bursa-pastoris*. Little seeded canary grass *Phalaris minor*. Diet Record Card Shepherd's purse *Capsella bursa-pastoris* (ADRC). Diet Record Cards ANIMAL FOOD mealworms, termites (ADRC).

Streaky-headed Seedeater

Serinus gularis 15cm

Alternative names: Streaky-headed Canary.
S.g.reichardi Reichard's Seedeater,
Stripe-breasted Seedeater.

Description: Sexes similar. Forehead, crown and nape sooty brown, streaked white; sides of face and ear-coverts light greyish brown; mantle, back, rump and upper tail-coverts greyish black, streaked brown; tail dusky edged yellowish; chin, throat and upper breast white; lower breast buffy grey; belly, flanks light buff; under tail-coverts olive-buff; iris brown; bill horn; legs and feet pale brown. Juvenile similar to adult, but mantle and back heavily streaked black; tail dusky.

Adults. *S.g.canicapilla* differs from the nominate race in having crown ashy brown; under tail-coverts white.

S.g.montanorum differs from nominate in having upperparts warmer brown.

S.g.uamensis very doubtfully distinct from *elongensis*.

S.g.elgonensis differs from *reichardi* in having upperparts browner; streaks on upperparts very indistinct.

S.g.reichardi differs from nominate in having more pronounced streaking on breast.

S.g.benguellensis differs from nominate in that body mass slightly greater.

S.g.mendosus differs from nominate in having less streaking on the mantle and back; under tail-coverts white.

S.g.endemion differs from nominate in having upperparts darker and greyer.

S.g.humilis differs from nominate in being darker and more buffy on underparts, chin white, spotted with black; under tail-coverts greyish buff.

S.g.striatipicus more diffusely streaked on throat and breast.

Voice: Described by Newman as 'wit-chee-chee-chee-cha,cha,cha,cha,chip', rising to a crescendo.

Habitat: Savanna, open woodland and cultivation including gardens.

Distribution: South African provinces of northern Cape, western Free State, North-West and Northern Province to Botswana.

S.g.canicapilla Senegal to northern Cameroon.

S.g.montanorum Cameroon.

S.g.uamensis western Central African Republic.

S.g.elongensis northern Zaire, southern Sudan and western Kenya.

S.g.striatipectus south-western, Uganda and western and central Kenya.

S.g.reichardi Tanzania to northern Mozambique, Malawi, southern Zaire and Zambia.

S.g.benguellensis northern Namibia, central Angola and western Zambia.

S.g.mendosus north-eastern Botswana and central and western Zimbabwe, perhaps also Mozambique (highlands).

S.g.endemion Cape Province, eastern Free State, south-eastern Transvaal, KwaZulu-Natal, Lesotho, Swaziland and Mozambique.

S.g.humilis eastern and western Cape Province, South Africa.

Feeding: Seeds, berries, buds, flowers, nectar and insects. Seeds of Silver *Protea roupelliae*, White Stinkwood *Celtis africana*, Sweet thorn *Acacia karoo*, Bulrush millet *Pennisetum glaucum*, Paw Paw *Carica papaya*, Thatch grass *Hyparrhenia hirta*, Tobacco *Nicotiana tabacum*, Pine *Pinus* spp., *Casuarina* and *Opuntia*, cultivated crops, namely Sunflower *Helianthus annuus* and Sudan grass *Sorghum bicolor*. In the south-western Cape Province recorded feeding on *Maytenus, Aspalathus, Aloe, Nymania, Lampranthus, Salsola, Chenopodium* and *Olea*. Probing the base of flowers to extract the nectar from the red-hot poker *Kniphofia*, Flat-flowered aloe *Aloe marlothii*, Candelabra aloe *A.candelabrum*, Krantz aloe *A.arborescens*, Cape Honeysuckle *Tecomaria capensis*, Bitter aloe *Aloe ferox*, Dwarf Hedgehog aloe *A.humilis*, Partridge aloe *A.variegata*, Hibiscus, buds and petals of Peach tree *Prunus persica*, Apricot tree *P.armeniaca*, Scarlet salvia *Salvia africana, Erythrina*, Cockscomb *Amaranthus hybridus*, African marigold *Taretes erecta*, French marigold *T.patula*, fruit of Taaibos *Rhus pyroides*, African mulberry *Morus mesozygia*, Kraal honey-thorn *Lycium afrum*, Large honey-thorn *L.austrinum*. Bird's Brandy *Lantana rugosa* and figs *Ficus* spp. Livefood in the form of termites, hairless caterpillars and hover flies.

Breeding: The nest site is usually 1-15m above ground and placed in the horizontal or vertical fork of a tree. A bulky cup-shaped nest consists of grasses, twigs and leaves, then bound with cobwebs and lined with vegetable matter and wool. A single nest in Zimbabwe contained guineafowl feathers. Eggs white, or pale blue, plain or speckled with brown or black at the thick end; clutch 2-4; incubation period 12,5-15 days, by female only; male feeds female on the nest; young cared for by both parents; brooded by female when small; nestling period about 17 days.

Aviculture: Selected Reference CLUTCH 2-5; INCUBATION PERIOD 12-15 days; NESTLING PERIOD 14-17 days. Nest Record Cards CLUTCH 2 (ARU); INCUBATION PERIOD 14 days (ARU); NESTLING

PERIOD 18 days (ARU). Selected Reference WILD-FOOD. Seeds of Khaki-weed *Alternanthera pungens*, Black-jack *Bidens pilosa*, Millet grass *Setaria woodii*, Golden setaria *S.sphacelata*, Common thatch grass *Hyparrhenia hirta*, Tef grass *Eragrostis tef*, Bird grass *Poa trivialis*, buds and leaves of Canary creeper *Senecio tamoides*, Smelter's bush *Flaveria bidentis*. Diet Record Cards Canary creeper *Senecio tamoides*, Chickweed *Stellaria media*, Khaki-weed *Alternanthera pungens*, buds of Corn spurry *Spergula arvensis* (ARU). Diet Record Cards FRUIT Wild raspberry *Rubus ludwigii*, Sand jackal-berry *Diospyros batocana*, Bird plum *Berchemia discolor*, Strawberry-guava *Psidium cattleianum*, Common forest grape *Rhoicissus rhomboidea*, Nana-berry *Rhus dentata*, Climbing raisin *Grewia caffra*, White-berry bush *Securinega virosa* (ARU). Diet Record Cards ANIMAL FOOD termites (ARU).

Black-eared Canary
Serinus mennelli 13-14cm

Alternative names: Black-eared Seedeater, Black-eared Streaky Seedeater, Mennell's Seedeater.

Description: Male. Forehead white, speckled blackish brown; crown and nape blackish brown, streaked white; sides of face and ear-coverts blackish brown; chin and throat white, streaked black; mantle and back sooty brown; rump and upper tail-coverts blackish, feathers edged brown; tail blackish, tinged yellowish at tips; breast and flanks pale pinkish buff; rest of underparts blackish; iris brown; bill brownish; legs and feet slate-grey. Female similar to male but paler. Juvenile has plumage pattern basically as adult female, but paler.

Voice: Described by Maclean as twittering whistled 'de-ree-te-rue-se-ree-sue' or 'twee chip, chio-chip pre-eeu pilly twee pilly' rapidly repeated over and over.

Habitat: A highland species belonging to *Brachystegia* woodland and *Mopane* thornveld.

Distribution: Northern Mozambique, Zimbabwe, north-eastern Botswana, Angola, Zambia, south-eastern Zaire and Malawi.

Feeding: Seeds, leaves, flowers, nectar, small fruits and insects. Seeds of Sunflower *Helianthus annuus*, flowers of *Brachystegia* spp., ripe fruit of *Uapaca* and berries of Mistletoe *Viscum capanse*.

Breeding: The site is usually the fork of a *Brachystegia* sapling 1-9m above ground. The cup-shaped nest is constructed of grass and decorated with bark and a few feathers which are bound with cobwebs. The interior consists of rootlets, lichens or moss. Eggs pale greenish or bluish white, spotted and speckled with brown, purple or black; clutch 2-3; incubation by female, male feeds at the nest.

Aviculture: Selected Reference CLUTCH 2-3; INCU-BATION PERIOD 12-14 days; NESTLING PERIOD 15-19 days. Selected Reference WILDFOOD. Seeds of Blue panic *Panicum laevifolium*, Guinea grass *P.maximum*, Khaki-weed *Alternanthera pungens*, Black-jack *Bidens pilosa*, buds, flower petals and leaves of Smelter's bush *Flaveria bidentis* and Canary creeper *Senecio tamoides*. Personal Communication. Canary creeper *Senecio tamoides*, Chickweed *Stellaria media*, buds of Smelter's bush *Flaveria bidentis*. Selected Reference FRUIT Bird plum *Berchemia discolor*, African cranberry *Vaccinium exul*, Wild plum *Harpephyllum caffrum*, African mulberry *Morus mesozygia*, Nana-berry *Rhus dentata*, Raspberry of the men *R.rigidus*. Selected Reference ANIMAL FOOD termites.

Brown-rumped Seedeater
Serinus tristriatus 13cm

Description: Sexes similar. Forehead, crown and nape ashy brown, streaked blackish; mantle, back, rump and upper tail-coverts brown, heavily streaked blackish; tail brown, feathers edged ashy; superciliary stripe and chin white, latter spotted; throat, belly and rest of underparts ashy brown; iris dark brown; bill horn; legs and feet pale reddish. Juvenile similar to adult, but heavily streaked overall.

Voice: Described by Clement *et al* as a shrill '*Tscoee*' or '*swee*'.

Habitat: Scrub and forest margins.

Distribution: Eastern Ethiopia.

Feedings: Seeds of shrubs.

Breeding: Nest, a neat cup of fine grass stems and spider's web forms the outer rim while animal wool forms the inner lining. Placed in a horizontal fork of a bush or juniper at any height from the ground. Eggs pale bluish green, spotted brown, violet or blackish; clutch 3-4.

Aviculture: No records.

Streaky Seedeater
Serinus striolatus 15cm

Description: Sexes similar. Upperparts brown, heavily streaked buff and black; superciliary stripe buff or whitish; ear-coverts and moustachial stripe blackish brown; underparts buff, heavily streaked brown; iris brown; bill horn; legs and feet dusky brown. Juvenile similar to adult, but with narrower streaking.

Adults. *S.s.graueri* differs from the nominate in having underparts warmer buff.

S.s.whytii differs from the nominate in having crown and sides of face lemon-yellow.

S.s.affinis (see *Peters Checklist of Birds of the World p.227, vol. 14, 1968*).

Voice: Described by Williams & Arlott as a high-pitched three-note call and a bubbling canary type song.

Habitat: Grassland, forest edges, cultivation and gardens.

Distribution: Ethiopia and northern Kenya.

S.s.affinis Kenya and northern Tanzania.

S.s.graueri Uganda, western Kenya and western Tanzania.

S.s.whytii southern Tanzania and northern Malawi.

Feeding: Seeds and fruits. In Malawi observed feeding on bramble berries *Rubus* sp.

Breeding: Nest, a shallow cup of rootlets and twigs woven together with grass and moss, lined with vegetable down, fibres and hair. Placed in a bush, creeper or small tree at any height from the ground. Eggs creamy or greenish white, marked with speckles and blotches of dark brown; clutch 3-4, occasionally 5.

Aviculture: Nest Record Cards CLUTCH 3,5 (ANRC); INCUBATION PERIOD 14,15 days (ANRC); NESTLING PERIOD 17,20 days (ANRC). Diet Record Cards WILDFOOD Buds of Smelter's bush *Flaveria bidentis*, young shoots of Chicory *Cichorium intybus* (ADRC). Diet Record Cards FRUIT mulberry *Morus* sp., South African blackberry *Rubus pinnatus* (ADRC).

Thick-billed Seedeater
Serinus burtoni 18cm

Description: Sexes similar. Forehead, crown, nape, mantle and back dark brown, indistinct blackish streaking; wings and tail brown, edged green; forehead white; underparts brownish grey, mottled on breast, paler on belly; chin blackish; throat mottled dusky and white; iris dark brown; bill dark horn; legs and feet brown. Juvenile upperparts browner; wings edged buffish; bill darker horn.

Adults. *S.b.tanganjicae* differs from the nominate race in having underparts more uniform in colour.

S.b.kilimensis differs from albifrons in lacking while on forehead; upperparts darker.

S.b.albifrons differs from the nominate in having underparts deeper buff.

S.b.melanochrous differs from *kilimensis* in having throat whitish or yellowish underparts heavily streaked black.

Voice: Described by Williams & Arlott as a silent, unobtrusive bird, sometimes utter a soft 'pleet'; song a brief soft warble.

Habitat: Highland forest and bamboo at 1700-3000m.

Distribution: Cameroon.

S.b.tanganjicae eastern Zaire and western Uganda.

S.b.kilimensis northern Kenya and northern Tanzania.

S.b.albifrons eastern Kenya.

S.b.melanochrous southern Tanzania.

Feeding: Seeds of shrubs and trees.

Breeding: Not known.

Aviculture: No records.

Principé Seedeater
Serinus rufobrunneus 12cm

Description: Sexes similar. Forehead, crown, nape, mantle, back and upper tail-coverts rufous brown, heavily streaked blackish; tail blackish brown; wings blackish, edged rufous; ear-coverts and sides of face blackish brown; chin, throat, breast and belly rufous finely streaked blackish; iris brown; bill, upper mandible dark horn, lower paler; legs and feet brown.

S.r.thomensis differs from the nominate race in having head distinctly streaked black; underparts buff-brown; lower belly white. Juvenile similar to adult, but paler brown overall.

Voice: Described by Mackworth-Praed & Grant as a clear 'tweet' often part of a trill.

Habitat: Not confined to any one habitat.

Distribution: Principé Island.

S.r.thomensis São Thomé Island.

Feeding: Seeds.

Breeding: Not known.

Aviculture: No records.

White-winged Canary
Serinus leucopterus 15cm

Alternative names: Dusky-faced Seedeater, Layard's Seedeater, Protea Canary, Protea Seedeater, White-winged Seedeater.

Description: Sexes similar. Forehead and crown sooty brown; mantle, back and rump sooty brown, tinged greenish; tail blackish; ear-coverts and chin black; throat white; spotted black; wing-coverts blackish brown; edged and tipped white; breast, belly and flanks brown, washed olive; centre of belly and under tail-coverts white; iris brown; bill pinkish to whitish; legs and feet blackish brown to grey. Juvenile upperparts ashy; underparts sandy. Juvenile upperparts more blackish, less brownish; underparts buff.

Voice: Described by McLachlan & Liversidge as a soft 'tree-lee-loo'.

Habitat: Strongly associated with mature fynbos on mountain slopes; Blue sugarbush *Protea nerifolia* and Cluster *Pine Pinus pinaster* appear to be important plants in its restricted environment.

Distribution: Western Cape Province, South Africa.

Feeding: Seeds, grasses, sedges, nectar, fruits, flowers, buds and young pine needles. Plant parts of *Protea, Restio, Senecio, Erica, Rhus, Maytenus, Diosma* and *Othonna*. Seed kernels in fleshy fruit of *Oftia* (exotic), *Olea, Rhus, Phylica, Cassytha, Maytenus*, large seeds of *Phylica, Raphanus, Psoralea, Hakea, Leucadendron, Diosma, Rhus*, small seeds of *Pelargonium Chenopodium, Anthospermum, Erica, Salvia*, nectar of *Erica, Halleria, Protea*, fruit-pulp of *Diospyros, Maytenus*, fresh floral parts of *Euryops, Senecio, Gymnodisus*, foilage buds of *Cliffortia, Olea, Pinus*, Graminoid seed of *Tertaria, Ficinia, Elegia, Leptocarpus, Restoio, Thamnochortus* and *Cannomois*. Also the seeds of Blue Sugarbush *Protea nerifolia*, Sugarbush *R.repens*, flowers of Wild *Fuchia Halleria elliptica*, fruit of Wild Peach *Kiggelaria africana*.

Breeding: Cup-shaped nest with outer shell of dry plant stems, and inner shell densely rimmed with fluff or Blue Sugarbush *Protea nerifolia* and then lined with fine dry grass; cup diameter 5,3-5,8cm, depth 3,5-4,7cm. The nest site is a vertical fork of a protea or pine 3,5m from the ground. Eggs ivory white or very pale blue, spotted with reddish brown; clutch 2-4; incubation 17 days by female only, male feeds her at nest; nestling period at least 14 days; young fed by both parents.

Aviculture: No records.

Cape Siskin
Serinus totta 13cm

Alternative Names: Brown Canary
Totta Siskin, South African Siskin.

Description: Male. Forehead, crown and nape brownish olive, streaked olive-brown; mantle and back blackish brown; rump olive-green; upper tail-coverts brown, edged with whitish; tail black; tipped white; wings with primaries and secondaries blackish brown; sides of face and ear-coverts olive-brown; chin and throat lemon-yellow; breast and belly yellow-green; under tail-coverts yellowish buff; flanks pale brownish olive; iris brown; bill brownish; legs and feet light brown. Female paler overall; tall blackish brown. Juvenile similar to adult female, but throat and breast heavily streaked.

Voice: Described by Skead with such phrases as "... a pretty little song" and "... of some merit" which are meaningless.

Habitat: Scrub on mountain slopes and pine plantations.

Distribution: Western Cape Province, South Africa.

Feeding: Seeds, buds and possibly insects. Seeds of *Athanasia*, *Metalasia*, *Stoebe*, *Elytropappus*, *Chenopodium*, *Ficinia*, *Protea*, *Thamnochortus*, *Leucadendron*, *Erica*, *Cliffortia*, *Urticaceae*, *Restio* and nectar of Hangertjie *Erica plukenetii*.

Breeding: Nests in crevices of rocks or on secluded rock-ledges amongst vegetation such as maiden-hair fern. A hole in a large tree trunk has also been recorded. A shallow cup with a diameter of 5,1cm and a depth of 2cm is constructed of dry grass and rootlets, then lined with very fine grass and sometimes mixed with wool or down. Popular lining is furry from the protea when available. Only the female builds with the male accompanying her as she collects material. Eggs white; clutch 3-5; incubation by female alone for 16-17 days; male feeds female at nest; both parents feed young; nestling period 20 days.

Aviculture: Selected Reference CLUTCH 3-5 days; INCUBATION PERIOD 15-17 days; NESTLING PERIOD 16-20 days. Nest Record Cards CLUTCH 2-3 (ARU) 3 (SAANRC) 5 (ANRC); INCUBATION PERIOD 15 days (ANRC); NESTLING PERIOD about 16 (ANRC) 17 days (SAANRC). Selected Reference WILDFOOD. Seeds of Khaki-weed *Alternanthera pungens*, Black-jack *Bidens pilosa*, Crab finger grass *Digitaria sanguinalis*, Blue panic *Panicum laevifolium*, Guinea grass *P.maximum*, Bird grass *Poa trivialis*, Milk-thistle *Sonchus oleraceus*, chickweed *Stellaria* sp., buds, flower petals and leaves of Canary creeper *Senecio tamoides*, Smelter's bush *Flaveria bidentis*. Diet Record Cards Khaki-weed *Alternanthera pungens* (SAADRC), Canary creeper *Senecio tamcides* (ADRC). Pepperweed *Lepidium africanum* (ARU). Selected Reference ANIMAL FOOD termites.

Drakensberg Siskin

Serinus symonsi 12cm

Alternative names: Symond's Cape Siskin, Symond's Mountain Siskin.

Description: Male. Forehead, crown and nape, streaked olive-yellow; mantle, back and rump russet brown; upper tail-coverts dusky, feathers tipped grey; tail blackish; wings dusky, edged greyish; sides of face and ear-coverts dusky, streaked olive-yellow; eye stripe yellow; chin, throat, breast and belly bright olive-yellow; under tail-coverts dusky, feathers edged white; flanks dark brown; iris brown; bill brownish horn; legs and feet brown. Female had forehead, crown and nape uniform with the mantle; chin, throat, breast and belly paler; chin and throat, streaked dusky. Juvenile similar to adult female, but underparts more heavily streaked.

Voice: Described by Maclean as quiet '*chink*' or '*tweet*' callnotes.

Habitat: High elevations in grass lands and riverine scrub in valleys of mountain slopes.

Distribution: Lesotho, and the South African provinces of northern Cape, western KwaZulu-Natal and Free State.

Feeding: Seeds of *Protea* spp., and *Leucodendron* sp., soft bases of Kaffirboom *Erythrina* sp.

Breeding: The nest is a shallow cup of grasses and rootlets, lines with very fine grass and hair. Building by female only, accompanied by male. Placed in a sheltered position on rock ledge, sometimes concealed by grass or small shrub. Also nests in tufts of grass and shrubs at 0,6-1,2m, above the ground. Eggs white to pale greenish blue, spotted with purplish brown; clutch 2-4; incubation by female only, fed on nest by male; care of young by both parents.

Aviculture: Selected Reference CLUTCH 2-4; Selected Reference WILDFOOD Seeds of Black-jack *Bidens pilosa*, Bird grass *Poa trivialis*, buds and leaves of Canary creeper *Senecio tamoides*, Smelter's bush *Flaveria bidentis*.

Black-headed Canary

Serinus alario 12-15cm

Alternative names: Alario Finch, Blackhead S.a.leucolaema Blackhead Canary, Damara Black-head Canary, King Black-head Canary Mountain Canary.

Description: Male. Entire head, nape and chin black; mantle, back rump and upper tail-coverts chestnut; sides of neck and breast, flanks and under tail-coverts white; iris brown; bill greyish brown; legs and feet slate-grey. Female has entire head, nape and chin brown, streaked dusky; wing-coverts russet-brown; sides of breast, flanks and under tail-coverts buff lightly streaked with brown.

Male. *S.a.leucolaema* differs from the nominate race in having the chin, throat, ear-coverts and stripe over eye white. Juvenile similar to adult female, but more heavily streaked with black.

Voice: Described by Maclean as a musical '*tweet*' and '*pee-chee*', call-notes, rising in pitch.

Habitat: *Miombo* woodland.

Distribution: Lesotho (highlands) and South African provinces of north-eastern, northern and western Cape and southern Free State.

S.a.leucolaema southern Botswana, central and northern Namibia and north-western Cape, western Free State and south-western North West provinces of South Africa.

Feeding: Seeds.

Breeding: A small cup nest of dry grasses and vegetable down with a lining of wool or similar soft material is placed in a bush, usually no more than a metre from the ground. Building by female, though male often stays during building. Eggs pale blue-green with a few speckles of brown chiefly at the wide end; clutch 3, occasionally 5; incubation period 13 days by female only; male feeds female on the nest; young cared for by both parents; brooded by female when small; nestling period 20-21 days.

Aviculture: Selected Reference CLUTCH 2-5; INCUBATION PERIOD 13-14 days; NESTLING PERIOD 20-21 days. Personal Communication CLUTCH 3; INCUBATION PERIOD 14 days; NESTLING PERIOD 19 days. Nest Record Cards CLUTCH 3,4 (ARU) 4 (SAADRC); INCUBATION PERIOD 13,13 (ARU) 13 days (SAANRC); NESTLING PERIOD 19,20 (ARU) 20 days (SAADRC). Selected Reference WILDFOOD. Seeds of Khaki-weed *Alternanthera pungens*, Black-jack *Bidens pilosa*, Guinea grass *Panicum maximum*, Blue panic *P.laevifolium*, buds, petals of Canary creeper *Senecio tamoides*, Smelter's bush *Flaveria bidentis*. Diet Record Cards chickweed *Stellaria* sp. (ARU), thistle heads *Sonchus* sp., buds of black-jack *Bidens* sp. (SAADRC). Diet Record Cards FRUIT African mulberry *Morus mesozygia* (ARU SAADRC). Diet Record Cards ANIMAL FOOD termites (ADRC).

São Thomé Grosbeak Weaver

Neospiza concolor 19cm

Alternative names: Grosbeak Bunting, Grosbeak Weaver, São Thomé Grosbeak, São Thomé Canary.

Description: Sexes similar. Forehead, crown and nape blackish brown; mantle, back, rump and upper tail-coverts chocolate-brown, tinged blackish; tail blackish chocolate; wings blackish brown, feathers edged whitish; chin, throat, breast, belly and under tail-coverts chocolate; iris pale brown; bill dark horn, paler below; legs and feet brown. Juvenile undescribed.

Voice: Canary like series of thin whistles.

Habitat: Primary forests.

Distribution: São Thomé Island.

Feeding: Not known but suspected of taking shelled seeds.

Breeding: Not known.

Aviculture: No records

Oriole-finch

Linurgus olivaceus 13cm

Alternative name: Olive-finch.

Description: Male. Entire head black; mantle, back and tail olivaceous moss green; wings black, edged white, tipped pale yellow; rump and upper tail-coverts more yellow; sides of neck, breast, belly and underparts bright yellow; iris brown; bill orange-yellow; legs and feet orange-brown. Female olive-green overall, shading to greenish yellow on belly. Juvenile has plumage pattern basically as adult female, but paler and wing-coverts, tipped greenish.

Males. *L.o.prigoginei* differs from the nominate race in being yellower on mantle and back; underparts deeper yellow, tinged orange-brown.

L.o.elgonensis differs from *kilimensis* in having upper and underparts more golden-yellow.

L.o.kilimensis differs from *elgonensis* in having mantle, back and rump more greenish, less yellowish.

Voice: Described by Williams & Arlott as being silent birds, sometimes utter a soft '*tsssp*' call.

Habitat: Highland mountain and bamboo forests.

Distribution: North-eastern Nigeria, Cameroon and Fernando Pó Island.

L.o.prigoginei eastern Zaire.

L.o.elgonensis south-eastern Sudan and northern Kenya.

L.o.kilimensis Tanzania and northern Malawi.

Feeding: Seeds, relishes and unripe seeds of cultivated tobacco, of a *saprophyric* orchid, and animal food such as termite alates and occasionally caterpillars.

Breeding: Nest a rather shallow cup of moss, lichens and rootlets, lined with softer lichen plant down, usually in low bush. Eggs white, sparsely speckled with reddish brown with occasional hair lines; clutch 2.

Aviculture: No records.

Orange-winged Grosbeak

Rhynchostruthus socotranus louisae 14,5cm

Alternative names: Gold-winged Grosbeak, Golden-winged Grosbeak.

Description: Male. Forehead, crown and nape brown; mantle and back brownish grey; rump greyish; upper tail-coverts greyish, tinged yellowish; tail greyish. feathers edged yellow; ear-coverts greyish; lores and area around base of bill and chin blackish brown; breast and upper belly chestnut; lower belly and underparts greyish; wings black with bright yellow fringes; iris black; bill slate grey to blackish; legs and feet dusky red. Juvenile has forehead, crown and nape ashy brown; ear-coverts pale grey, streaked brown; upper and underparts, streaked brown. Female similar to male but paler especially black area.

Voice: Described by Hollom *et al* as liquid, musical and discordant.

Habitat: Wooded hills and wadis with *Acacia, Juniper* and *Euphorbia* at 1200-2000m.

Distribution: Northern Somalia.

Feeding: Buds of *Euphorbia* sp., fruit and seeds.

Breeding: Not known.

Aviculture: No records.

Greenfinch

Carduelis chloris 12,5cm

Alternative names: Green Linnet, European Greenfinch (nominate).

Description: Sexes similar. Crown, nape, mantle and back greyish brown, tinged greenish; rump yellowish green; upper tail-coverts grey, tinged green; sides of head, ear-coverts and sides of neck brownish grey, tinged green; chin, throat and breast yellowish green; upper tail-coverts grey, tinged green; sides of head, ear-coverts and sides of neck brownish grey, tinged green; chin, throat and breast yellowish green, tinged grey; belly and under wing-coverts bright greenish yellow; under-tail coverts pale yellowish grey; iris brown; bill whitish flesh, tip dark brown; legs and feet pale flesh. Female paler and browner, and with less yellow. Juvenile resembles adult female on upperparts, but much more streaked dark brown.

Adults. *C.c.aurantiiventris* differs from the nominal race in having upperparts more greener and underparts more yellower.

C.c.chlorotica differs from *aurantiiventris* in having upperparts paler.

Voice: Described by Witherby as '*chichichichichit-teu-teu-teu-teu*'.

Habitat: Parks, gardens, olive groves and oasis.

Distribution: *C.c.aurantiiventris* Algeria, Morocco and Tunisia (breeds)

C.c.chlorotica Egypt (winters).

Feeding: Seeds of grasses and weeds, grain berries, flower and leaf buds, green plant material and insects. Recorded feeding on Wild Blackberry *Rubus ulmifolius*, Yewberry *Taxaceae baccata*, Hops *Humulus lupulus*, Sainfoin *Onobrychis vicifolia*, clover *Trifolium* sp., and live food, namely beetles, ants, aphids and spiders.

Breeding: A cup-shaped nest is built of grass, twigs and moss, lined with hair and feathers and placed 2-20m above ground level in a tree, bush or hedge. Building by female only, accompanied by male. Eggs dirty white to pale greenish blue, sparingly spotted and streaked reddish brown and pale violet; clutch 4-6, rarely 3,7 or 8; incubation 13 days by female only, fed on nest by male; care of young by both sexes; nestling period 13-16 days; 2 broods.

Aviculture: Selected Reference CLUTCH 3-8; INCUBATION PERIOD 12-14 days; NESTLING PERIOD 12-16 days. Selected Reference WILDFOOD. Groundsel *Senecio vulgaris*, dandelion *Taraxacum* sp., Teasel *Dipsacus fullonum*, Gold of Pleasure *Camelina sativa* Nipplewort *Lapensana communis*, Broom *Cytisus scoparius*, Burdock *Arctium ailoa*, Dog's Mercury *Mercurialis annua*, Curled dock *Rumex crispus*, Campion *Silene* sp., Hemp *Cannabis sativa*, chickweed *Stellaria* sp., Sow-Thistle *Sonchus oleraceus*, Persicaria *Polygonum persicaria*. Personal Communication Persicaria *Polygonum persicaria*, plantain *Plantago* sp., mustard *Sinapsis* sp. Diet Record Cards Chickweed *Stellaria media*, Shepherd's purse *Capsella bursa-pastoris* (ARU), buds of Gallant soldier *Galinsoga parviflora* (ADRC). Selected Reference FRUIT Wild rasberry *Rubus ludwigii*, Raspberry of the men *R. rigidus*, mulberry *Morus* sp. Selected Reference ANIMAL FOOD mealworms, termites, maggots.

Siskin

Carduellis spinus 12cm

Alternative names: European Siskin; Spruce Siskin

Description: Male. Forehead and crown black; mantle and back yellowish green; rump greenish yellow; upper tail-coverts green, tipped grey; tail blackish brown, fringed yellow; chin black, feathers tipped grey; ear-coverts yellow, tinged greyish green; stripe behind eye, throat and breast greenish yellow, tinged greyish; belly greyish white, tinged yellow; wings black-brown, fringed yellow; iris black; bill dark brown; legs and feet dark brown. Female upperparts buffish brown, streaked greenish; stripe behind eye and throat white; wings brownish, fringed pale buff. Juvenile plumage pattern basically as adult female, but paler.

Voice: Described by Witherby as having a "sweet, lively and tolerably varied twittering terminating in a prolonged creaking note".

Habitat: Frequents birches and alders and in breeding season conifers and spruce.

Distribution: Morocco, Libya, Tunisia and Egypt (Migrant).

Feeding: Seeds of trees, notably conifers, alders and elms, juniper berries and aphids.

Breeding: Female constructs a compact nest of dead twigs, lichens, moss and wool, lined with down, hair and feathers. Situated in conifers, spruce and firs, but also in pines and larch. Eggs pale blue, spotted and streaked with purplish-red; clutch 3.5, rarely 6; incubation 11-12 days by female only, fed by male; nestling period 15 days; young fed by both parents, except by female only for first few days after hatching; 2 broods.

Aviculture: Selected Reference CLUTCH 3-5; INCUBATION PERIOD 11-14 days; NESTLING PERIOD 12-15 days. Nest Record Cards CLUTCH 4,5 (ARU); INCUBATION PERIOD 12,12 days; NESTLING PERIOD 13,14 days (ARU). Selected Reference WILDFOOD thistle *Silybum* sp., dock *Rumex* sp., Persicaria *Polygonum persicaria*, Groundsel *Senecio vulgaris*, chickweed *Stellaria* sp., Milk thistle *Silybum marianum*. Diet Record Cards Corn spurry *Spergula arvensis*, Ragwort *Senecio consangiuneus*, buds of Cape wild mustard *Sisymbrium capense* (ARU).

Goldfinch
Carduelis carduelis 12cm

Alternative names: British Goldfinch, King Harry, Many-coloured Finch, Seven-coloured Linnet, Teazle Finch (nominate).

Description: Sexes similar. Forehead and crown glossy crimson; nape white; mantle and back tawny; rump buff; upper tail-coverts blackish; tail black, tipped white; lores black; chin and upper throat glossy crimson; lower throat and sides of neck white; breast and flanks greyish buff; under tail-coverts white, tinged buff; wings with primaries and secondaries black; fringed white, greater coverts bright yellow; iris dark brown; bill pinkish white; legs and feet pale flesh. Juvenile upperparts greyish buff; chin, throat, breast and flanks more whitish.

Male. *C.c.parva* differs from the nominate race in being greyer, less warm brown on mantle.

Voice: Described by Witherby as a pleasing liquid twittering elaboration of call-notes of variations and modulations.

Habitat: Gardens, orchards, cultivated areas, also scrub and tree covered valleys.

Distribution: *C.c.niediecki* Egypt (breeds).
C.c.parva Morocco, Algeria, Tunisia and Libya (breeds).

Feeding: Seeds of weeds, flowers, cones, fruits and insects. Seeds of thistle *Carduus* sp., dandelion *Taraxacum* sp., burdock *Arctium*, knapweed *Centuarea*, cones of Alder *Alnus glutinosa*, birches of *Betula* and livefood, namely beetles, butterfly/moth, fly and wasp larvae.

Breeding: Female builds a neat deep cup of roots, bents, moss and lichens, interwoven with wool, lined with vegetable down and wool. Placed in fruit or chestnut trees and occasionally also in hedges. Eggs bluish white, streaked and spotted reddish brown; clutch 5-6, 3-4 and 7 also on record; incubation 12-13 days by female alone, fed by male; nestling period 13-14 days; young fed by both parents, normally 2 broods.

Aviculture: Selected Reference CLUTCH 3-7; INCUBATION PERIOD 12-14 days; NESTLING PERIOD 12-15 days. Personal Communication CLUTCH 4.5; INCUBATION PERIOD 13,13 days; NESTLING PERIOD 14,15 days. Selected Reference WILDFOOD. Knot-grass *Polygonum aviculare*, thistle *Silybum* sp., Sow-Thistle *Sonchus oleraceus*, chickweed *Stellaria* sp., dandelion *Taraxacum* sp., Cape pigweed *Amaranthus thunbergii*, Hemp *Cannabis sativa*, Groundsel *Senecio vulgaris*, Teazle *Dipsacus fullonum*, Hardheads *Centaurea nigra*, Birch *Betula pubescens*, Alder *Alunus glutinosa*, Shepherd's purse *Capsella bursa-pastoris*, Cornflower *Centaurea cyanus*, Greater Knapweed *C.scabiosa*, Ragwort *Senecio jacobaea*, Personal Communication Meadow-sweet *Filipendula ulmaria*, pine *Pinus* sp., elm *Ulmus* sp., Rye-grass *Lolium perenne*. Diet Record Cards Chickweed *Stellaria media*, heads of Common dandelion *Taraxacum officinale* (ARU).

Linnet
Acanthis cannabina 13cm

Description: Male. Forehead crimson; crown, nape and hindneck brownish grey; mantle and back chestnut; rump brown; tail blackish brown, edged buff; wings blackish, edged white; flanks chestnut-buff; upper tail-coverts blackish brown, edged yellowish green; chin whitish; breast crimson; belly greyish white; iris blackish brown; bill dark brown; legs and feet brownish pink. Female lacks crimson adornment; darker, more heavily streaked blackish brown overall. Juvenile resembles adult female, but uniformly buffish white.

Male. *A.c.bella* differs from the nominate race in having underparts paler.

Voice: Described by Peterson *et al* as a varied, musical twitter, interspersed with pure and nasal notes, delivered from top of a bush.

Habitat: Open and often uncultivated areas from coast to mountains of 3000m.

Distribution: Egypt (migrant), Morocco, Algeria and Tunisia (breeds).

A.c.bella northern Egypt (migrant).

Feeding: Seeds of weeds, flax *Linum* spp , Hemp *Cannabis sativa*, Wild Cabbage *Brassica oleracea*, Turnips *B.rapa* and livefood, namely spiders, flies, beetles, butterfly/moth larvae and caterpillars.

Breeding: Female constructs a nest of grass and moss, lined with wool and hair, and sometimes down or feathers, usually close to the ground in low bush, vine hedge and *Salicornia* sp. Eggs pale bluish or bluish white, spotted and occasionally streaked with purplish red; clutch 4-6, occasionally 7; incubation 10-12, chiefly by female, male only relieving for short periods nestling period 11-12 days; fed by both parents; 2 or 3 broods.

Aviculture: Nest Record Cards CLUTCH 4,5 (ARU); INCUBATION PERIOD 12,12 days (ARU); NESTLING PERIOD 12,14 days (ARU). Selected Reference WILD-FOOD Charlock *Sinapis arvensis*. Meadow-sweet *Filipendula ulmaria*, Hemp *Cannabis sativa*, chickweed *Stellaria* sp., Groundsel *Senecio vulgaria*, Sow-Thistle *Sonchus oleraceus*, Shepherd's purse *Capsella bursa-pastoris*, plantain *Plantago* sp., Cornflower *Centaurea cyanus*, Fat Hen *Chenopodium album*, dock *Rumex* sp., thistle *Carduus* sp., flax *Linum* sp., mustard *Sinapis* sp., garlic *Allium* sp., Personal Communication chickweed *Stellaria* sp., Fat Hen *Chenopodium album*. Diet Record Cards Red garden sorrel *Oxalis latifolia*, Chickweed *Stellaria media*, Shepherd's purse *Capsella bursa-pastoris* (ARU).

Warsangli Linnet

Acanthis johannis 13cm

Alternative name: Somalia Linnet.

Description: Male. Forehead and superciliary stripe white; eye stripe blackish grey; crown, nape, mantle and back dusky grey; rump chestnut; tail black, central feathers white; flanks chestnut; ear-coverts white, tinged blackish grey; chin, throat, breast, belly and rest of underparts white; iris dark brown; bill dark greyish; legs and feet blackish horn. Female has mantle, tinged brown; forehead having less extensive white; chin, throat, upper breast and flanks tinged white. Juvenile upperparts pale greyish buff; underparts brownish buff, streaked on side of breast and flanks.

Voice: Described by Godman & Archer as a high pitched '*tssp*' or '*chip*'.

Habitat: Juniper and other woodland scrub.

Distribution: North-eastern Somalia.

Feeding: Grass and salvia *Salvia* sp. seeds.

Breeding: It is claimed by A.R. Tribe (in *Ash & Miskell 1981*) that they nested in the hollows formed by branches on the trunks of Junipers.

Aviculture: No records.

Crimson-winged Finch

Rhodopechys sanguinea aliena 15cm

Alternative name: Crimson-winged Desert Finch.

Description: Male. Forehead, crown and nape black; ear-coverts, ring around the eye sandy buff, tinged rosy pink; nape ashy; mantle and back dark brown feathers edged buff; rump and upper tail-coverts rosy pink; tail dusky, edged pink, tipped white; chin, throat, breast and flanks whitish buff; rest of underparts whitish; wing-coverts pale pink, primary coverts tipped black; under wing-coverts white; iris brown; bill pale yellow, in breeding season, greyish horn in non-breeding season. Female has forehead, crown and nape dark brown; mantle greyish brown; back brown; chin, throat, breast and flanks whitish; wing-coverts brown, primary-coverts tipped blackish; bill buffish horn in breeding season. Juvenile closely resembles adult female, but paler.

Voice: Described by Hollom *et al* as a soft '*cnee-rup*', '*tureep, tureep*', or '*dy-lit-di-lyt*'.

Habitat: Amongst bushes and scrub in dry mountain regions at altitudes of 2800m. In winter descend to lower levels.

Distribution: Morocco and Algeria.

Feeding: Grass seeds. Also *Alyssum granatense* and *Houndstonge cynoglossum*.

Breeding: Nest in bush, with one record in a clump of dwarf broom which contained 5 nestlings.

Aviculture: No records.

Trumpeter Finch

Rhodopechys githaginea 12,5cm

Alternative names: Trumpeter Bullfinch, Trumpeter Desert-finch.

Description: Male. Forehead pinkish red, crown, nape, sides of face and ear-coverts pearl-grey; mantle and back earth brown; rump pinkish red; tail dusky, tinged pinkish; wings salmon-pink, secondaries black, edged pink; lores and chin pinkish red; throat, breast, belly and underparts pink; iris black; bill coral-red; legs and feet pale orange. Female similar to male, but without pink tinge and only faint tinge on underparts; bill pale yellowish brown. Juvenile males are more buff, females slightly more brown in tone.

R.g.zedlitzi differs from the nominate race in being darker pink overall.

Voice: Described by Hollom *et al* as a drawn out wheezing nazal buzz '*cheeee*'; shorter conversational '*chee*' or '*chit*'.

Habitat: Stony deserts and arid wadis.

Distribution: Southern Egypt and northern Sudan.

R.g.zedlitzi southern Morocco, Algeria, Tunisia and Libya.

Breeding: Nest amongst rocks, in stone walls or the shelter of bushes. Consists of an untidy ball of stalks, roots, strong grass and then lined with plant down, hair, wool and rarely a few feathers. Eggs sub-elliptical to short oval, slightly glossy, pale blue, spots of purplish black; clutch 4-6; incubation period 13-14 days by female only, starting with last egg; nestling period 13-14 days.

Feeding: Seeds, leaves, buds of desert plants and insects. Nymphs of grasshoppers, etc,. Buds of grass-wort *Salicornia*, mugwort *Artemisia*, grasses *Bromus* spp., seeds of *Salvia aegyptiaca*, *Rumex vesicarius* and *Nicotiana glauca*.

Aviculture: Selected Reference CLUTCH 4-5. Selected Reference WILDFOOD, chickweed *Stellaria* sp., Speedwell *Veronica officinalis*, Shepherd's purse *Capsella bursa-pastoris*.

Ankober Serin
Serinus ankoberensis 12-13cm

Description: Sexes similar. Crown dark brown, streaked blackish; nape buff, streaked blackish; mantle brown with pale buff edges to feathers; back, rump and tail dark brown, edge to feathers greyish on outer webs; chin and throat greyish white, spotted brown; breast, belly and under tail-coverts greyish brown, spotted buff; iris dark brown; bill, upper mandible greyish horn, lower greyish white; legs and feet pale brownish pink. Juvenile is said to be similar to adult.

Voice: Described by Ash & Gullick as a double note, '*chree*' and '*treet-treet*'.

Habitat: Grass and low bush vegetation and also amongst lichen-covered rocks.

Distribution: Ethiopia (Shoa Province).

Feeding: Grass and other local seeding plants. Sometimes feeds in small patches of barley stubble. The gizzard of two birds contained grit and few fruit remains of Dock *Rumex bequaertii* and mericarps of *Sida ternata*.

Breeding: Nest, consists largely of fine rootlets with the cup lined with animal hairs. One nest was situated inside a vertical hole on the underside of a overhanging earth bank about 3m above the base of the bank; a strand of bright green wool over 15cm long was recorded. Eggs white; clutch 3.

Aviculture: No records.

Red Crossbill
Loxia curvirostra poliogyna 16-17cm
Alternative names: Crossbill, Common Crossbill, Spruce Crossbill (nominate).

Description: Male. Forehead, crown and nape scarlet-pink; mantle brown; rump and upper tail-coverts dark brown, tinged orange; chin and ear-coverts brown; tail blackish brown, belly greyish white; under tail-coverts greyish; throat and breast brown; tinged pink; wings with primaries and secondaries blackish brown with very narrow pinkish fringes on outer webs; iris dark brown; bill, legs and feet dark brown. Female is olive with yellowish on rump and underparts. Juvenile is greenish grey, strongly streaked on underparts.

Voice: Described by Witherby *et al* as '*chip-chip-chip-jee-jee-jee-jee*'.

Habitat: Coniferous woods, chiefly spruce, but also larch and pine.

Distribution; Northern Morocco (Migrant).

L.c.poliogyna eastern Morocco, Algeria and Tunisia. (breeds)

Feeding: Seeds of cones, of Scots Pine *Pinus sylvestris*, European Larch *Larix decidua*, spruce *Picea* sp., and other conifers, but also Hawthorn *Crataegus monogyna*, Ivy *Hedera helix*, apple-pips *Malus* spp., thistle *Carduus* spp., and livefood in the form of aphids, caterpillars, beetles and flies.

Breeding: Female constructs a cup-shaped nest of pine twigs, grasses and wool, then lined with finer grass, rabbit's fur, hair and feathers. Eggs green, tinged with purplish red; clutch usually 4, sometimes 3 only, rarely 5 or 2; incubation by female for 12-13 days; fed by male on nest; nestling period 18-22 days; young fed by both parents.

Aviculture: Selected Reference CLUTCH 3-5; INCUBATION PERIOD 13-16 days; NESTLING PERIOD 17-22 days. Selected Reference WILDFOOD Hemp *Cannabis sativa*, buds of larch *Larix* sp., pine *Pinus* sp. Personal Communication Khaki-weed *Tagetes minuta* (1 male).

Hawfinch
Coccothraustes coccothraustes 17,5-18cm
Alternative names: Common Hawfinch, European Hawfinch (nominate).

Description: Male. Forehead and ear-coverts yellowish brown; crown rufous brown; nape deeper rufous brown; hindneck pinkish grey; mantle and back brown; tail black; with a white tip; lores, chin and centre of throat black; breast pinkish brown; belly greyish white;

under tail-coverts white; wings with primaries black, tipped purplish, with a white wing-bar; iris red-brown; bill lead blue; blackish at tip; legs and feet brownish flesh. Female paler, less rufous on crown, chin and throat pale buffish yellow; bill yellowish horn, dark brown tip. *C.c.burryi* differs from the nominate race in having the rump pure grey.

Voice: Described by Witherby *et al* as a halting rather bunting-like '*deek-waree, ree, ree*' or '*Tchee-tchee-turr-wee-wee*'.

Habitat: Orchards, gardens, parks and groves

Distribution: Algeria, Tunisia and lower Egypt (migrant)

C.c.burryi in Morocco, Algeria and Tunisia (breeds).

Feeding: Seeds, berries, kernels of fruit stones such as Elm *Ulmus* sp., Hornbeam *Carpenus betulus*, Beech *Fagus sylvatica*, Sycamore *Acer pseudoplatanus*, Common Maple *A.campestre*, Hawthorn *Crataegus monogyna*, buds of oak *Quercus robur*, shoots of Yew *Texaceae baccata*, caterpillars, beetles and cockshafers. Also consumes cherries, olives, apples and pears rotting on the ground. Said to be partial to peas.

Breeding: Nest, an untidy structure consisting of grasses, rootlets and lichens and lined with fine material such as hair. Placed on the main stem of a sapling or on horizontal branch of a tree or in a bush at 2-6m above ground. Eggs pale bluish or greyish green, sometimes pale slate or warm buff, marked irregularly with purple-brown; clutch 4-5, rarely 3,6 or 7; incubation 12-13 days, by female only, fed on nest by male; nestling period 10-11 days; young fed by both parents; sometimes 2 broods.

Aviculture: Selected Reference CLUTCH 3-7; INCUBATION PERIOD after 9-14 days; NESTLING PERIOD about 20 days. Selected Reference WILDFOOD Hardheads *Centaurea nigra*, Burdock *Arctium lappa*, Persicaria *Polygonum persicaria*, Mountain ash *Pyrus aucaparia*, pods from *Brassica* sp., Wych Elm *Ulmus glabra*, Sycamore *Acer pseudoplatanus*, Blackthorn *Prunus spinosa*. Personal Communication Khaki-weed *Tagetes minuta* (2 males). Selected Reference FRUIT African mulberry *Morus mesozygia*. Selected Reference ANIMAL FOOD beetles, moths, crickets, grasshoppers, cotton worms, mealworms, waxmoth larvae.

Flowerpecker Weaver Finch

Parmoptila woodhousei 10-11cm

Alternative names: Antpecker, Woodhouse's Antpecker, Flower-pecking finch.

Description: Male. Forehead reddish brown; crown and nape brown, finely spotted with buff mantle, back, wings and tail dark brown; sides of face and throat

chestnut; breast, belly and rest of underparts pale buff, spotted black; under wing-coverts golden-buff; iris reddish brown; bill blackish; legs and feet greyish brown. Female has forehead brown, spotted with buff. Juvenile upperparts paler, underparts darker.

Habitat: Forest canopy, but may occur in bushes on open land.

Distribution: South-eastern Nigeria, Cameroon and western Zaire.

P.w.ansorgei northern Angola.

Feeding: Small spiders and soft-bodied insects but particularly small ants, especially driver.

Breeding: Constructs a large roundish nest composed of dried grass, dead leaves, with moss worked into the exterior. Lined with fine fibres and plantain leaves. Side entrance sometimes with portico above it. Eggs white; clutch 3-4.

Aviculture: Personal Communication CLUTCH 3. Nest Record Cards CLUTCH 3,3 (ANRC). Selected Reference ANIMAL FOOD Wood ant *Formica rufa*, spiders, beetles, moths, green aphids. Personal Communication spiders, small black ants.

Red-fronted flower-pecker Weaver-finch

Parmoptila jamesoni 9cm

Alternative names: Jameson's Hylia-Finch; Red-fronted antpecker

Description: Male. Forehead bright red; crown, nape, sides of neck and ear-coverts olive-brown, spotted with white; mantle and back olive-brown with pale feather tips; tail blackish, streaked with olive brown; chin white; throat, belly, breast and rest of underparts chestnut; iris reddish brown; bill dusky; legs and feet yellowish buff. Female had forehead and crown dusky, spotted with buff; mantle, back and tail dark brown; ear-coverts pale grey, spotted with white; rest of underparts whitish, spotted with brown. Juvenile undescribed.

Male. *P.r.rubrifrons* differs from the nominate race in having ear-coverts chestnut, spotted buff; nape and sides of neck chestnut.

Voice: Described by Williams & Arlott as a weak 'zee'-call note.

Habitat: Foliage, mainly in trees at forest edge.

Distribution: Eastern Zaire and western Uganda.

P.j.rubrifrons Ghana.

Feeding: Insects, namely ants, their larvae and pupae including small beetles.

Breeding: Not known.

Aviculture: No records.

White-breasted Negro Finch

Nigrita fusconota 10cm

Alternative name: *N.f.uropygialis* Gold Coast Negro Finch.

Description: Male. Forehead, crown, nape, sides of face glossy bluish black; mantle and back earth brown; lower rump, upper tail-coverts and tail glossy bluish black; wings pale brown, tinged yellowish; under wing-coverts white; chin, throat and rest of underparts white or buffish white; iris dark brown; bill black; legs and feet slate-grey or greenish grey. Female underparts greyish white. Juvenile underparts buff.

Male. *N.f.uropygialis* differs from the nominate race in having mantle and back paler.

Voice: Described by Marchant as a descending trill becoming slowed down to a separate note.

Habitat: Associated with palms, particularly the African Oil Palm *Elaeis guineensis* and coastal forests. In East Africa forest edges at 700-1800m.

Distribution: Fernando Pó Island, Gabon, Cameroon to Angola, Uganda and Kenya.

N.f.uropygialis Guinea to southern Nigeria.

Feeding: Oily epicarp of the orange fruit of the African Oil Palm *Elaeis guineensis*, berries, small caterpillars and other small insects.

Breeding: Nest, large globular structure of bast, dry grass, dead leaves and moss, including banana fibres in East Africa, and one constructed entirely of fine bark fibres of a vine. Placed in the angle of a shrub or palm frond. Eggs white; clutch 3-6.

Aviculture: Selected Reference CLUTCH 4-6; INCUBATION PERIOD 12-13 days. Personal Communication CLUTCH 4,4; INCUBATION PERIOD about 13 days. Personal Communication WILDFOOD Seeds of Mulberry *Morus alba*, Common wild fig *Ficus natalensis*, Sycamore fig *F.sycomorus*. Selected Reference ANIMAL FOOD mealworms, waxmoth larvae. Personal Communication ANIMAL FOOD spiders.

Chestnut-breasted Negro Finch

Nigrita bicolor 11cm

Alternative names: Chestnut Negro Finch. *N.b.brunnescens* Principe Chestnut-breasted Negro Finch.

Description: Male. Crown, nape, mantle and back slate-grey; tail and upper tail-coverts blackish; forehead, sides of face, chin, throat, breast, belly and under tail-coverts chestnut-maroon; wings dark brown; under wing-coverts pale silvery grey; iris brown, red or reddish; bill black; legs and feet dark brown. Female upperparts brownish slate; underparts more chestnut less maroon. Juvenile upperparts dark brown; underparts paler brown.

Male. *N.b.brunnescens* differs from the nominate race in having upperparts sooty greyish brown; underparts dark maroon.

Voice: Described by Bates as having a sweet little song as '*kiya-kiya-weh-weh-weh*'.

Habitat: Associated with palms, particularly the African Oil Palm *Elaeis guineensis* in West Africa. Coastal forests at 700m in East Africa.

Distribution: Guinea to Ghana.

N.b.brunnescens southern Nigeria to western Uganda and northern Angola.

Feeding: Oily epicarp fruit of the African Oil Palm *Elaeis guineensis*, small caterpillars and other small insects. Also recorded taking the white eggs of the Tree Frog *Chiromantis rufescens*.

Breeding: Nest of grasses, dried leaves and moss, then lined with seeding grassheads. Placed in a small bush at no great height from the ground. Eggs white; clutch 4-5; incubation period 11-12 days.

Aviculture: No records.

Pale-fronted Negro Finch

Nigrita luteifrons 10cm

Description: Male. Forehead, crown and nape silvery grey; mantle and back slate-grey; rump silvery grey; tail black; chin, line above eye white; throat, breast, belly and underparts black; wing-coverts dark blackish grey; under wing-coverts silvery grey; iris red, pale grey, brownish white or cream; bill black; legs and feet greyish brown. Female differs from the male in having underparts grey; sides of face black; iris pale grey or greyish white. Juvenile upperparts pale grey; underparts brownish grey.

Male. *N.i.alexanderi* differs from the nominate race as having more yellow on forehead; iris black.

Voice: Described by Fry as simple but melodious, quite loud and given throughout the year.

Habitat: Forest edges at 700-800m in East Africa.

Distribution: Southern Nigeria to northern Zaire and Gabon.

N.i.alexanderi Fernando Pó Island.

Feeding: Insects, namely scale insects and oily epicarp fruit of African Oil Palm *Elaeis guineensis*.

Breeding: Nest, a large globular structure built of dry moss, grass stems and then lined with green grassheads. Entrance hole is situated in one side. One nest measured about 130mm in diameter and entrance hole about 35mm across. Placed 2,7-3,6m above ground in a tree, often an exotic such as the *Mango Magnifera indica*. Eggs white; clutch 4.

Aviculture: No records.

Grey-crowned Negro Finch

Nigrita canicapilla 12cm

Alternative names: Grey-headed Negro Finch. *N.c.emilae* Ashanti Grey-crowned Negro Finch.

Description: Sexes similar. Forehead, chin, throat and sides of face black; sides of face bordered with whitish line; crown and nape silvery grey; mantle and back slate-grey; rump pale grey, sometimes almost whitish; tail black; breast, belly and rest of underparts blackish; under wing-coverts white; iris red or orange-red; bill black; legs and feet dark brown or blackish. Juvenile is sooty black overall, except paler on rump and wing-coverts blackish, spotted buffish.

Adults. *N.c.emilae* differs from the nominate race in having rump greyer.

N.c.angolensis differs from the nominate in having crown and rump darker grey; iris orange red; legs and feet dark brown.

N.c.schistacea differs from the nominate in having head and mantle darker grey.

N.c.diabolica similar to *schistacea*, but wing averaging smaller; underparts sooty grey.

N.c.candida similar to *schistacea*, but crown and nape whitish grey.

Voice: Described by Williams & Arlott as a soft three-note whistle.

Habitat: Open forests and in undergrowth from 1,800m to 2,750m on Kilimanjaro, below 1,500m in East Africa; coastal forests and associated with African Oil *Palm Elaeis guineensis* in West Africa.

Distribution: Southern Nigeria, Cameroon and Zaire.

N.c.emilae Guinea to Ghana.

N.c.angolensis north-western Angola and south-western Zaire.

N.c.schistacea southern Sudan, Uganda, Kenya and northern Tanzania.

N.c.diabolica central Kenya.

N.c.candida western Tanzania.

Feeding: Oily epicarp fruit of African Oil Palm *Elaeis guineensis*, fruit such as *Ficus* spp., berries, said to be mulberry-like, caterpillars and other insects.

Breeding: Nest, untidy and built of fibres, dead leaves, grasses and moss, sometimes of strips of fine bark, then lined with fine grassheads. Placed 3-15m above ground in thick foliage, such as in oil-bean *Poinciana* and mango *Magnifera* in compounds near houses in West Africa. Eggs pinkish white; clutch 4-6.

Aviculture: No records.

Shelley's Olive-back

Nesocharis shelleyi 8,5cm

Alternative names: Fernando Pó Olive-back. *N.s.bansoensis* Banso Little Weaver, Little Olive Waxbill

Description: Male. Entire head black; thin collar extending to hindneck white; nape grey; mantle and back golden-olive; upper tail-coverts golden-yellow; tail black; chin, throat and breast golden-olive; rest of underparts bluish-grey; iris brown; bill bluish grey; legs and feet grey to greyish brown. Female underparts bluish grey. Juvenile paler overall; iris black; bill bluish black; legs and feet slate-grey.

Male. *N.s.bansoensis* differs from the nominate race in having underparts paler bluish grey.

Voice: Described by Mackworth-Praed & Grant as a continuous high-pitched twittering.

Habitat: Mountain forests and savanna.

Distribution: Fernando Pó Island and Cameroon Mountains.

N.s.bansoensis south-eastern Nigeria and Cameroon.

Feeding: Seeds and insects.

Breeding: Weaver-like nest with long hanging side entrance which may not have been constructed by the birds themselves, but commandeered. Also may utilize the abandoned nest of sunbirds. Lining consists of moss and similar vegetable down. Eggs white; clutch 3.

Aviculture: Nest Record Cards CLUTCH 4 (ARU). Nest Record Cards seeds of figs *Ficus* spp. *Luanaea cornuta, Melanthera scandens, Vernonia cinerea* (ARU). Selected Reference WILDFOOD chickweed *Stellaria* sp. Selected Reference ANIMAL FOOD green aphids, wax-moth larvae, spiders. Diet Record Card small red ants (ARU).

White-collared Olive-back

Nesocharis ansorgei 10cm

Alternative name: Olive Weaver-finch.

Description: Male. Entire head black; broad collar white shading to grey on hindneck; mantle and back olive-green; wings yellowish olive; under wing-coverts silvery white; breast olive-green; belly and under tail-coverts grey; iris dark brown; bill black; legs and feet blackish slate. Female has narrow white collar. Juvenile has plumage pattern basically as adult female, but paler.

Voice: Described by Williams & Arlott as a soft sunbird-like 'tsssp'.

Habitat: Marshy places along forest margins.

Distribution: Eastern Zaire and western Uganda.

Feeding: Shelled seeds of *Melanthera scandens*.

Breeding: Mostly makes use of old, deserted or commandeered nests of weavers. One record of a bird carrying material into drooping head of a dead *Hagenia abyssinica* which when in flower have inflorescence 30-50cm long, which are orange-buff or white with plume-like appearance. Eggs white; clutch 2-3.

Aviculture: No records.

Grey-headed Olive-back

Nesocharis capistrata 11,5-12 cm.

Alternative names: White-cheecked Olive-back, White-cheecked Waxbill.

Description: Sexes similar. Forehead and ear-coverts greyish white; crown and nape grey; mantle, back, rump and tail olive-green; flanks yellow; chin and throat black; breast, belly and underparts grey; iris red; bill black; legs and feet blackish slate. Juvenile closely resembles adult, but paler and having legs and feet greyish.

Voice: Described by Williams & Arlott as a soft 'tssp' call but silent.

Habitat: The undergrowth of degraded and secondary riparian growth.

Distribution: Gambia to Sudan and Uganda.

Feeding: Seeds of grasses, wild fig *Ficus* spp., Livefood in the form of ants and small snails.

Breeding: Nest, a rather large dome structure with side entrance and made of dry stems of weeds and grasses. One nest measured about 18cm deep and unlined was placed in a thick bush at 3m above the ground. Eggs white.

Aviculture: Nest Record Cards CLUTCH 3; INCUBATION PERIOD 14 days; NESTLING PERIOD 23 days (ARU).

Crimson-winged Pytilia

Pytilia phoenicoptera 13cm

Alternative names: Aurora Finch, Aurora Waxbill, Red-winged Waxbill.
***P.p.lineata* Abyssinian Aurora Finch, Red-billed Aurora Finch, *P.p.emini* Crimson-winged Waxbill.**

Description: Male. Forehead, crown, nape, mantle and back brownish grey; rump, upper tail-coverts and tail crimson-red; wings dark brownish grey, edged crimson-red; chin, throat and belly pale grey, feathers delicately barred with dull white; under tail-coverts dark grey, broadly tipped white; iris red; bill black; legs and feet pale brown. Female upperparts and underparts more brownish, less greyish. Juvenile similar to adult female, but still more browner; bill brown.

Males. *P.p.lineata* differs from the nominate race in being slightly darker bill.

P.p.emini differs from the nominate in having under wing-coverts darker.

Voice: Described by Mackworth-Praed & Grant as an "occasional chirping call".

Habitat: Bushed and wooded country.

Distribution: Senegal to Cameroon.

P.p.lineata northern Ethiopia.

P.p.emini Cameroon to Uganda and southern Sudan.

Feeding: Grass seeds and insects.

Breeding: Nest globular, being built of grass seedheads and then thickly lined with feathers also having a side entrance. Placed at about 2m from the ground in a bush or small tree. Eggs white; clutch 3-4.

Aviculture: Selected Reference CLUTCH 3-6; INCUBATION PERIOD 12 days; NESTLING PERIOD 18-20 days. Personal Communication CLUTCH 3,4,4,6; INCUBATION PERIOD 12,12,13,14; NESTLING PERIOD 18,20,20,21 days. Nest Record Cards CLUTCH 3,3,4 (ARU) 4 (SAANRC) 4,5 (ANRC); INCUBATION PERIOD 12, 14 (ARU)1 4 (SAANRC) 12,12 days (ANRC); NESTLING PERIOD 18,21 (ARU) 18 (SAANRC) 18,20 days (ANRC). Personal Communication WILDFOOD Guinea grass *Panicum maximum*, Cockspur *Echinochloa crus-galli*. Diet Record Cards Guinea grass *Panicum maximum* (ARU ADRC SAADRC), Golden setaria *Setaria sphacelata* (ARU), *African finger millet Eleusine coracana* (ADRC), Broad-leaved panic *Panicum deustum* (SAADRC). Selected Reference ANIMAL FOOD mealworms, grasshoppers, termites. Diet Record Cards termites, mealworms (SAADRC) (ARU), spiders (ADRC).

Yellow-winged Pytilia

Pytilia hypogrammica 12cm

Alternative names: Golden-winged Pytilia, Red-faced Aurora Finch, Red-faced Pytilia, Red-faced Aurora Waxbill.

Description: Male. Forehead, forecrown, sides of face and chin red; mantle and back brownish grey; rump and upper tail-coverts red; tail blackish, tinged red; flight feathers and wing-coverts dusky, edged yellowish; throat and breast grey; belly and rest of underparts brownish grey, barred white; iris red; bill black; legs and feet pale brown. Female lacks facial adornment; underparts pale brown, barred white. Juvenile similar to adult female, but paler overall.

Voice: Described by Goodwin as a repeated 'vee-vee-vee'

Habitat: Savanna woodland and neglected cultivation.

Distribution: Sierra Leone to Cameroon.

Feeding: Grass and insects, such as termites and ants.

Breeding: Nest a spherical structure with the usual side entrance. The loosely made outer layer consists of broad grass blades, middle layer of grass stems and the inner layer of soft seeding heads and a few guineafowl feathers placed in the fork of a tree, bush or shrub at 0,5-4m above the ground. Eggs ovate, smooth, slightly glossy white; clutch 3-4; incubation period 12-14 days; nestling period 16-17 days.

Aviculture: Selected Reference CLUTCH 3-4; INCUBATION PERIOD 12-14 days; NESTLING PERIOD 15-17 days. Nest Record Cards CLUTCH 3,4,5 (NASNRC) 4,4 (ARU); INCUBATION PERIOD 12,12 (NASNRC) 12,13 (ARU); NESTLING PERIOD 15,17 (NASNRC) 15 days (ARU). Nest Record Cards WILDFOOD Guinea grass *Panicum maximum* (ARU NASDRC), Broad-leaved panic *P.deustum*, Blue panic *P.laevifolium* (ARU), Rhodes grass *Chloris gayana*, Black Seed finger grass *Digitaria ternata*, Natal panic *Panicum natalense*, Barnyard millet *Echinochloa crusgalli* (NASDRC). Selected Reference WILDFOOD. Chickweed *Stellaria* sp. Diet Record Cards ANIMAL FOOD termites, mealworms (ARU NASDRC).

Orange-winged Pytilia

Pytilia afra 11cm

Alternative names: Red-faced Finch, Red-faced Waxbill, Yellow-backed Pytilia, Yellow-backed Melba Finch.

Description: Male. Forehead, sides of face, upper throat, upper tail-coverts and central tail feathers red; crown, mantle and lesser wing-coverts olive-brown; neck grey; breast olive-green washed with orange; rest of underparts whitish, barred with olive-green; iris reddish brown; bill brown, tip and lower mandible red; legs and feet flesh coloured. Female has ear-coverts greyish; mantle olive-green; bill, upper mandible brown, lower orange. Juvenile resembles adult female, but rump orange.

Voice: Described by Guggisberg as a single flat 'saaa'; sometimes a piping whistle of two notes.

Habitat: Frequents thorny thickets and long grass near water. Occasionally occuring neat cultivation and villages.

Distribution: Sudan, Ethiopia, Zaire Zambia, Zimbabwe, Mozambique, Angola to Northern Province and Mpumalanga South Africa.

Feeding: Grass seeds and termites.

Breeding: The nest is a rather frail or at least frail-looking roundish structure of dried grass stems, and sometimes other vegetation, usually lined with only a slight pad of feathers. Placed in a tree, bush shrub or palm about 1-3m above ground. Eggs white; clutch 3-5, usually 4; incubation period 12-13 days; nestling period about 21 days; red specks on the face of young males is in evidence at this age.

Aviculture: Selected Reference CLUTCH 3-5; INCUBATION PERIOD 12-13 days; NESTLING PERIOD 21 days. Personal Communication CLUTCH 3,4,4; INCUBATION PERIOD 12,12,12,13,13 days; NESTLING PERIOD 19, about 20 approximately 20,22 22 days (ARU) Diet Record Cards WILDFOOD. Seeds of Natal redtop *Rhynchelytrum repens*, Bur-bristle grass *Setaria verticillata*, Guinea grass *Panicum maximum*, Blue panic *P.laevifolium*, Bushveld signal grass *Urochloa mosambicensis*, Buffalo-quick paspalum *Paspclum distichum* (ARU). Personal Communication WILDFOOD Guinea grass *Panicum maximum*, Natal Buffalo grass. *P.natalense*. Selected Reference ANIMAL FOOD termites, mealworms. Diet Record Cards termites, spiders (ARU).

Melba Finch

Pytilia melba 13cm

Alternative names: Common Melba Finch, Crimson-faced Waxbill, Green-winged Pytilia, Melba Waxbill, Red-faced Weaver-finch.
***P.m.grotei* Uganda Melba Finch,**
***P.m.soudanensis* Sudan Melba Finch,**
***P.m.citerior* Senegambian Melba Finch.**

Description: Male. Forehead, forecrown and chin coral-red; throat pale red; hindcrown, lores, around eye, ear-coverts and sides of neck dark grey; mantle and back olive-green; rump and upper tail-coverts coral-red; tail brownish red; breast pale olive; belly and flanks barred or spotted black and white; flight feathers olive-green; under tail-coverts buff; iris reddish brown; bill red; legs and feet brownish. Female has forehead, crown, nape and ear-coverts grey; throat, breast and belly barred or spotted grey and white. Juvenile similar to adult female, but darker on upperparts and lacks the barred or spotted underparts; bill sepia.

Males. *P.m.criteria* Differs from the nominate race in having the lores and round the eyes not extending behind the eye; barring on underparts paler.

P.m.soundanensis differs from *criterior* in having the red of the lores and round the eyes not extending behind the eye; barring on underparts darker.

P.m.percivali differs from the nominate in having red of the lores and round the eyes paler; chest paler olive.

P.m.belli differs from the nominate in having the red of the throat extending onto the chest.

P.m.grotei differs from *damarensis* in having paler red face; chest with pinkish red overlay.

P.m.thamnophilus differs from the nominate in having mantle greener with little or no golden overlay.

P.m.damarensis differs from the nominate in having grey throat paler.

Voice: Described by Mackworth-Praed and Grant as a low single '*wick*', also a long plaintive whistle.

Habitat: Dry thornveld, thickets, neglected cultivation near water.

Distribution: The Congo, Zaire, Zambia, western Malawi, Zimbabwe, Botswana, southern Namibia and Central South Africa.

P.m.citerior Senegal to the Sudan.

P.m.soundanensis southern and eastern Sudan, Ethiopia, Somalia and northern and eastern Kenya.

P.m.percivali south-western Kenya and northern Tanzania.

P.m.belli eastern Zaire, Uganda, Tanzania and Malawi.

P.m.grotei north eastern Tanzania, southern Malawi and northern Mozambique.

P.m.hygrophila northern Zambia and northern Malawi.

P.m.thamnophilus Zimbabwe, Mozambique, eastern Swaziland and northern and eastern regions including KwaZulu-Natal in South Africa.

P.m.damarensis Namibia, southern Angola, south-western Zambia, north-western Zimbabwe, Botswana and the northern Cape, western Free State and North-West provinces of South Africa.

Feeding: Seeds and insects. Seeds of Guinea grass *Panicum maximum*, Bushveld signal grass *Urochloa mosambicensis*, Natal redtop *Rhynchelytrum repens*, Burbristle grass *Setaria verticillata*, Khaki-weed *Alternanthera pungens*.

Breeding: The nest is built of dry grass stems with a side entrance and a low porch, in a tree 2-4m from the ground. The lining consists of vegetable down or feathers, mostly guineafowl and domestic fowl. Eggs white; clutch 2-5, occasionally 6; incubation period 12-13 days; both sexes incubate in turns by day, the female at night, but the male may spend the night in the nest; both parents feed the young; nestling period 21 days.

Aviculture: Selected Reference CLUTCH 2-6; INCUBATION PERIOD 12-14 days; NESTLING PERIOD 20-21 days. Personal Communication CLUTCH 3,3, 3,4,4,4,4,5,6,6; INCUBATION PERIOD 12,12,12, 12,13,14,14; NESTLING PERIOD 18,18,20,20,21 days. Nest Record Cards CLUTCH 3,3,3,4,4,4,4,5,5 (SAANRC) 3,5,5 (NASNRC) 3,3,4,5 (ARU) 3,5 (ANRC); INCUBATION PERIOD 12,12,12,13,13,14 days (SAANRC) 13,13 (NASNRC) 12,13,13 (ARU) 13 (ANRC); NESTLING PERIOD 17,18,20,20,22,23 (SAANRC) 18,20 (NASNRC) 20,22 (ARU) 21 days (ANRC). Diet Record Cards WILDFOOD. Chickweed *Stellaria* sp., seeds of Black-jack *Bidens pilosa*, Teff grass *Eragrostis tef*, Lehmann's love grass. *E.lehmanniana*, Small finger grass *Digitaria argyrograpta*, Rolling grass *Trichoneura grandiglumis*, Blue buffalo grass *Cenchrus* cilliaris, Blue seed grass *Tricholaena monachne*, Blue panic *Panicum laevifolium*, Guinea grass. *P.maximum*, Bushveld signal grass *Urochloa mosambicensis*, Natal redtop *Rhynchelytrum repens*, Bur-bristle grass *Setaria verticillata* (ARU SAADRC NASDRC). Personal Communication WILDFOOD Common comfrey *Symphytum officinale*, Guinea grass *Panicum maximum*, Rhodes grass *Chloris gayana*, Summer grass *Digitaria sanguinalis*, Weeping lovegrass *Eragrostis parviflora*. Selected Reference ANIMAL FOOD mealworms, whiteworms, termites, spiders. Diet Record Cards mealworms, termites, fishmoths (ARU SAADRC ADRC), fly larvae of "maggots" (ARU), grasshoppers, crickets (SAADRC), wasp larvae or "grubs" (ADRC).

Green-backed twinspot

Mandingoa nitidula 11cm

Alternative names: Green Twinspot, *M.n.schlegeli* Schlegel's Twinspot, Schlegel's green-backed Twinspot. *M.n.chubbi* Chubb's Twinspot, Chubb's green-backed Twinspot.

Description: Male. Lores, sides of face and chin crimson; forehead, crown, nape and mantle olive-green; rump golden-olive; tail black, edged with olive-green; sides of neck, throat and breast olive-green; wings olive-green, edged with brownish black; belly black, densely spotted with white; under tail-coverts olive-green; iris brown; bill black, tip orange; legs and feet brown. Female paler than male with lores and around eye to chin pale orange. Juvenile paler than adult female with underparts greyish olive; sides of face and chin buff.

Males. *M.n.schlegeli* differs from the nominate race in having lores, round eye to chin rich tomato red; bill larger.

M.n.virginiae differs from *schlegeli* in having mantle and back heavily swashed with orange.

M.n.chubbi differs from the nominate as having throat and breast washed with olive-yellow.

Voice: Described by Mackworth-Praed & Grant as various squeaking calls and a chirping '*tzeet*'.

Habitat: Moist evergreen forests, thick coastal bush and exotic plantations.

Distribution: Northern and central Tanzania, eastern Zambia, Malawi, northern Mozambique, eastern Zimbabwe, Swaziland and South Africa in eastern Cape, KwaZulu-Natal and Northern Province

M.n.schlegeli differs from the nominate race in having lores, round eye to chin rich tomato red; bill larger.

M.n.virginiae Fernando Pó Island.

M.n.chubbi southern Ethiopia, south-eastern Sudan, Kenya to south-eastern Uganda, Tanzania, Zanzibar and Pemba Islands.

Feeding: Grass and weed seeds, including rice fragments when available. Also feeds on scraps of cassava and oil palm husks. Insects, especially wooly aphids.

Breeding: A large oval shaped nest about 15cm long, 12,5cm deep and side entrance 4-7cm in diameter, with or without tube. Placed 3-5cm from the ground in a tree, bush or creeper. Constructed by both sexes, the male carrying while the female arranging the materials. It consists of grass stems, rootlets, twigs, lichens and moss. A nest on Pemba Island was found to be partly covered with the cast-off skin of a snake and built in a mangrove tree at the edge of a swamp. Eggs white; clutch 3; both sexes incubate and roost in the nest at night; incubation period 12-14 days; nestling period 17 days.

Aviculture: Selected Reference CLUTCH 3-6; INCUBATION PERIOD 12-14 days; NESTLING PERIOD 18-21 days. Nest Record Cards CLUTCH 3 (NASNRC) 3 (NASNRC) (ARU); INCUBATION PERIOD 12 (NASNRC) 12 days (ARU); NESTLING PERIOD 17 (NASNRC) 20 days (ARU). Nest Record Cards WILDFOOD Guinea grass *Panicum maximum* (ARU NASDRC), Jungle rice *Echinochloa colona* (NASDRC). Selected Reference ANIMAL FOOD winged termites, Meadow ants *Lasius* spp., whiteworms, mealworms, spiders. Diet Record Cards mealworms, termites (ARU NASDRC), aphids, fishmoths (ARU), springtails (NASDRC).

Red-faced Crimson-wing

Cryptospiza reichenovii 12cm

Alternative names: Forest Finch, Malawian Crimson-wing, Nyasa Crimson-wing, Red-eyed Crimson-wing, Red-eyed Finch, Reichenow's Crimson-wing.

Description: Male. Lores and patch encircling the eye crimson-red; crown, nape and upper matle olive; lower mantle, back, rump, upper tail-coverts and wing-coverts red; flights and tail blackish; chin and throat pale olive; breast, belly and flanks dark olive; iris brown; bill black; legs and feet olive brown. Female lacks the crimson-red

facial markings, with the lores and ear-coverts pale olive; lower mantle, back, rump, upper tail-coverts and wing-coverts reddish brown; tail olive-brown. Juvenile resembles female with less reddish brown on the rump and upper tail-coverts; mantle olive-brown; bill black.

Males. *C.r.australis* differs from the *homogenes* in having crown and hindneck darker green; bill less robust.

C.r.homogenes differs from *australis* in having crown and hindneck paler green; bill more robust.

Voice: Described by Williams & Arlott as high pitched 'tzeeet'.

Habitat: Dense undergrowth in high plateau country.

Distribution: Cameroon to Uganda and northern Angola.

C.r.australis southern Uganda, Tanzania and Malawi.

C.r.homogenes eastern Zimbabwe and Mozambique.

Feeding: Grass seeds, namely Buffalo grass *Setaria chevaleri*, fragments of pounded maize, small green bean-like seeds of balsams *Impatiens* sp., and *Pinus patula* (exotic).

Breeding: Nests are mostly placed quite low down, often 5-7m from the ground in bushes, tree ferns or saplings, but particularly in Forest Paw Paw *Cycliomorpha parviflora* and Common spike-thorn. Occasionally nests alongside the Red ant *Pheidole* sp. A spherical ball of seedheads and leaves form the outer shell. A wide porch protrudes over a slightly raised side entrance. The lining consists of fine grass and the horse hair-like *mycelium* of a fungus, probably a species of *Merasmius*. Eggs white; clutch 3-4.

Aviculture: Personal Communication CLUTCH 4; INCUBATION PERIOD about 14 days; NESTLING PERIOD about 20 days. Personal Communication chickweed *Stellaria* sp., seeds of Broadleaved setaria *Setaria chevalieri*, Guinea grass *Panicum maximum*, Popo grass *Hyparrhenia cymbaria*. Selected Reference ANIMAL FOOD whiteworms, gnat larvae, mealworms. Personal Communication mealworms.

Ethiopian Crimson-wing

Cryptospiza salvadorii 11,5cm

Alternative names: Abyssinian Crimson-wing, Crimson-backed Forest Finch, Salvadori's Crimson-wing.

Description: Male. Entire head, nape and upper mantle greyish olive; lower mantle, back, flanks and wings crimson-red; tail blackish; chin, throat, belly, breast and under tail-coverts greyish olive; under wing-coverts buffish; iris dark brown; bill black; legs and feet dark brown. Female has lower mantle, back, flanks and wings duller crimson-red.

Males. *C.s.ruwenzori* differs from the nominate race in having underparts paler.

C.s.kilimensis differs from the nominate in having underparts more greyish olive.

Voice: Described by van Someren as a low pitched 'chip-chip'.

Habitat: Forest edges and stands of bamboo and other grasses which bear seeds.

Distribution: Southern Ethiopia.

C.s.ruwenzori eastern Zaire and western Uganda.

C.s.kilimensis south-eastern Sudan, Kenya and northern Tanzania.

Feeding: Grass seed, *Setaria* sp., grain and balsams of *Impatiens* sp.

Breeding: Nest an oval ball of grass covered with moss, lined with finer grass and a few feathers, and having a side entrance near the top, placed amongst dense creepers or tree fork at 2-4m above the ground. Eggs white, occasionally with minute grey spots; clutch 3-5.

Aviculture: Selected Reference: ant pupae.

Dusky Crimson-wing

Cryptospiza jacksoni 11,5cm

Alternative names: Jackson's Crimson-wing, Jackson's Hill finch.

Description: Male. Forehead, crown, sides of face, mantle, back and rump crimson-red; tail blackish; nape, collar on hindneck, chin, throat, breast belly and wings slate-grey; under wing-coverts buff; iris dark brown; bill black; legs and feet olive-brown. Female has crown, nape and hindneck dark grey; crimson-red parts paler. Juvenile similar to adult female, but crimson parts even paler.

Voice: Described by Burkard (in Goodwin) as incorporation a high-pitched 'peeee' and a rather deep but not loud drawn-out 'gay' or 'gooayoo'.

Habitat: Dense undergrowth with bamboo in highland forests.

Breeding: No information. Probably similar to that of the Red-faced Crimson-wing.

Distribution: Eastern Zaire and western Uganda.

Feeding: Seeds, including grasses. Small green, bean-like seeds of balsam *Impatiens* sp.

Aviculture: Personal Communication CLUTCH 4; INCUBATION PERIOD 14 days; NESTLING PERIOD 21 days. Selected Reference ANIMAL FOOD mealworms, whiteworms. Personal Communication gnats, mealworms, aphids.

Shelley's Crimson-wing

Cryptospiza shelleyi 13cm

Alternative name: Red-billed Crimson-wing.

Description: Male. Forehead, crown, nape, sides of face, mantle, back, rump and upper tail-coverts red; tail and wings blackish; chin, throat and breast olive; belly and under tail-coverts black; iris dark brown; bill pinkish red; legs and feet brown. Female has entire head olive; bill horn. Juvenile has plumage pattern basically as adult female, but paler.

Voice: Described by Williams & Arlott as a series of rapid twittering notes, not unlike the call of some small sunbird.

Habitat: Dense underground.

Distribution: Eastern Zaire and western Uganda.

Feeding: Tiny seeds of balsams *Impatiens* sp., and insects.

Breeding: Not known.

Aviculture: Selected Reference WILDFOOD. Seeds of *Impatiens* sp.

Crimson Seedcracker

Pyrenestes sanguineus 13cm

Description: Male. Entire head, nape and sides of neck crimson-red; mantle, back, upper rump and wings earth brown; lower rump and upper tail-coverts crimson-red; tail, central crimson-red, outer webs of others pale crimson; chin, throat, breast and flanks crimson-red; belly earth brown; iris dark brown; bill bluish grey; legs and feet brownish olive. Female has entire head orange-red; rest of upper and underparts dark pale olive, except rump and tail dark rusty orange. Juvenile has rump and tail dark olive-brown; iris greyish brown; bill blackish.

Male. *P.s.coccineus* differs from the nominate in having a distinctly smaller bill.

Voice: Described by Rand as 'singing merrily' in flight.

Habitat: Swampy areas, including flooded paddy fields and adjacent cultivation.

Distribution: Senegal to Ivory Coast.

P.s.coccineus Sierra Leone and Gabon.

Feeding: Not known, but presumably hard seeds.

Breeding: An untidy nest constructed mostly of reeds and lined with grassheads and with a side entrance. Usually in a shrub at no great height from the ground. Eggs white; clutch 3.

Aviculture: Selected Reference CLUTCH 3-4; INCUBATION PERIOD 16 days; NESTLING PERIOD 24 days. Nest Record Cards CLUTCH 3 (ANRC) 4 (SAANRC); INCUBATION PERIOD 15 (ANRC) 16 days (SAANRC); NESTLING PERIOD 22 (ANRC) 24 days (SAANRC). Diet Record Cards WILDFOOD Guinea grass *Panicum maximum* (ADRC SAADRC), Jungle rice *Echinochloa colona*, Johnson grass *Sorghum halepense* (ARU), False barley *Hordeum murinum* (SAADRC). Selected Reference ANIMAL FOOD whiteworms, mealworms, ant pupae. Diet Record Cards mealworms (SAADRC ADRC).

Black-bellied Seedcracker

Pyrenestes ostrinus 15cm

Alternative names: Notch-billed Weaver, Seedcracker.
***P.o.frommi* Great-billed Seedcracker, Large-billed Seedcracker, Urungu Seedcracker.**
***P.o.rothschildi* Rothschild's Seedcracker.**

Description: Male. Entire head, nape, upper mantle, breast and flanks crimson; lower mantle, back and wings black; rump and upper tail-coverts crimson; tail black, edged crimson; belly and rest of underparts black; iris brown; bill black; legs and feet dusky yellow. Female is black is replaced by brown; red less bright. Juvenile is brown overall; tail paler red.

Feeding: Seeds on one occasion of a sedge *Scleria* sp., pieces of green leaves, unripe rice and spiders.

Males. *P.o.frommi* differs from the nominate race in having a larger and heavier bill.

P.o.rothschildi differs from the nominate in having bill smaller, especially at base of lower mandible.

Voice: Described by Serle with the call note as a sharp 'zeet'.

Habitat: Dense forest, undergrowth in old forest clearings.

Distribution: Ghana to Togo.

P.o.frommi central Togo, northern Nigeria Central African Republic, Cameroon and northern Zaire.

P.o.rothschildi Ghana, Cameroon, Zaire, Uganda and Angola.

Breeding: Nest, large globular mass of grass stems, palm leaf and fern fronds with side entrance and lined with finer grass. Placed from 1-8m from the ground in a tree, creeper or screw pine *Pandanus* spp., which is rather palm-like, the leaves making it strongly reminiscent of a tree pineapple and occurring along river banks. Eggs white, without gloss; clutch 3-5; both sexes incubate.

Aviculture: Selected Reference CLUTCH 3-5; INCUBATION PERIOD 10-16 days; NESTLING PERIOD 21-23 days. Nest Record Cards CLUTCH 3,3,4 days (ANRC); INCUBATION PERIOD 12,12,13 days (ANRC); NESTLING PERIOD 20,21,24 days (ANRC). Selected Reference: WILDFOOD dandelion *Taraxacum* sp., Milk-Thistle *Silybum marianum*, Knapweed *Centaurea* sp. Diet Record Cards Jungle rice *Echinochloa colona*, Wild rye *Secale africanum*, Yellow sorrel *Oxalis pes-caprae*, Shepherd's purse *Capsella bursa-pastoris* (ADRC). Selected Reference ANIMAL FOOD mealworms, grasshoppers. Diet Record Cards mealworms, termites, spiders (ADRC).

Nyasa Seedcracker

Pyrenestes minor 14cm

Alternative names: Lesser Seedcracker, Nyasaland Seedcracker.

Description: Male. Crown, forehead, sides of face, throat crimson; nape, mantle, wings, breast and rest of underparts earth brown; upper tail-coverts and central pair of tail feathers crimson; iris dark brown; bill black; legs and feet dark brown. Female similar to male, but throat and chest earth-brown. Juvenile earth brown replaces crimson; bill blackish horn.

Voice: Described by Newman as '*tzeet*', plus a sharp clicking when alarmed.

Habitat: Tall rank grass and other dense scrub along wooded streams.

Distribution: Northern Mozambique, eastern Zimbabwe, Malawi and Tanzania.

Feeding: Grass seeds and rice.

Breeding: A large untidy globular nest is constructed of dried grass, ferns or leaf strips and lined with the flowering heads of grass, usually situated in a small tree or bush in dense shade at 2-8m from the ground. Eggs white; clutch 3-6.

Aviculture: Selected Reference CLUTCH 3-5; Personal Communication CLUTCH 3; INCUBATION PERIOD 13 days; NESTLING PERIOD 23 days. Personal Communication WILDFOOD. Seeds of Blue panic *Panicum aequinerve*, Broad-leaved panic *P.deustum*. Personal Communication ANIMAL FOOD spiders, aphids, termites.

Grant's Blue-bill

Spermophaga poliogenys 14cm

Alternative name: Grant's Forest Weaver.

Description: Male. Forehead, crown and sides of face scarlet-red; nape, mantle and back bluish black; rump, upper tail-coverts and flanks scarlet-red; tail blackish; chin, throat and belly scarlet-red; under tail-coverts black; iris brown; bill bluish white, tip red; legs and feet greenish brown. Female has forehead, crown and sides of face dark grey; throat and breast orange-red; rest of underparts spotted white. Juvenile has forehead, crown and sides of face brownish grey; upper tail-coverts red; rest of underparts indistinctly spotted buffish white.

Voice: Described by Mackworth-Praed & Grant as having a chirping note (Juvenile).

Habitat: Primary forest.

Distribution: Eastern Zaire and western Uganda.

Feeding: Seeds and insects.

Breeding: Not known.

Aviculture: No records.

Western Blue-bill

Spermophaga haematina 15cm

Alternative names: Blue-billed Weaver, Blue-bill, Crimson-breasted Weaver, Red-breasted Blue-bill, Red-breasted Forest Weaver.

Description: Male. Forehead, crown, nape, mantle, back and tail black; rump and upper tail-coverts, chin, throat, breast and flanks scarlet-red; belly and under tail-coverts black; iris reddish brown; bill bluish silver or blue; legs and feet blackish brown, greenish black or olive. Female upperparts blackish slate, except rump and upper tail-coverts dull crimson; underparts dull crimson, except belly and under tail-coverts blackish, spotted with white. Juvenile upperparts dusky slate, except rump and upper tail-coverts dull red; underparts rufous brown.

Male. *S.h.togoensis* differs from the nominate race in having cutting edge of bill red.

S.h.pustulata differs from the nominate in having sides of the face suffused with red; breast paler scarlet-red.

Voice: Described by Fry as having a quiet, simply structured series of irregular jingling notes, rather like that of a sunbird.

Habitat: Forest edges and depressions in cultivation.

Distribution: Gambia to Ghana.

S.g.togoensis Togo to south-western Nigeria.

S.h.pustulata southern and central Nigeria, southern Cameroon, northern Zaire and northern Angola.

Feeding: Seeds, rice, the husks of oil palm, insects and spiders.

Breeding: The nest is a roundish structure placed near the forest floor in a bush or shrub, made of grass, dry leaves, fern fronds and then lined with vegetable down and sometimes a few feathers are added. The entrance hole is to one side and incorporates some protruding grass stems. Eggs white; clutch 3-6.

Aviculture: Selected Reference CLUTCH 4; INCUBATION PERIOD 12-16 days; NESTLING PERIOD 21 days. Nest Record Cards CLUTCH 4,4 (ARU) 3 (SAANRC); INCUBATION PERIOD 14,14 (ARU) 14 days (SAANRC); NESTLING PERIOD 19,21 (ARU) 21 days (SAANRC). Selected Reference WILDFOOD chickweed *Stellaria* sp., Diet Record Cards Guinea grass *Panicum maximum* (ARU SAADRC), Jungle rice *Echinochloa colona* (ARU), Johnson grass *Sorghum halepense* (SAADRC). Selected Reference ANIMAL FOOD whiteworms, crickets, wax moth larvae, ant pupae. Diet Record Cards fly larvae or "maggots" (SAADRC), green hairless caterpillars (ARU).

Red-headed Blue-bill

Spermophaga ruficapilla 15cm

Alternative names: Red-headed Blue-billed Weaver, Red-headed Forest Weaver.

Description: Male. Entire head and nape scarlet-red; mantle, back and wings black; upper tail-coverts and flanks scarlet-red; tail black; chin, throat and breast scarlet-red; belly and under tail-coverts black; iris brown; bill silvery blue, light blue or purplish blue; legs and feet greenish black. Female has mantle and back slate-grey;

belly blackish densely spotted with white. Juvenile similar to female, but belly sooty black.

Male. *S.r.cana* differs from the nominate in having black replaced by slate-grey.

Voice: Described by Williams & Arlott as a series of barely audible clinking notes.

Habitat: Dense forest undergrowth.

Distribution: Northern Angola to eastern Zaire, Uganda, southern Sudan and western Kenya.

S.r.cana Tanzania.

Feeding: Seeds of *Ipomoea* (*Covolvulaceae*), *Olyra latifolia* (inflorescence a scanty whitish grass panicle), *Indigofera* (*Leguminosae)* and also small tarelike seeds of another unidentified leguminous plant. Livefood, namely weevils, termites and other small insects.

Breeding: One incomplete nest was at the base of an oil palm, a second nest was about 2,5m high in a tree that contained 3 nestlings. The first nest was undescribed as a large untidy structure of coarse grass and feathers, lined with finer grass. The second nest was domed, untidy of course and covered with a loosely hanging dry tree fern. Eggs white; clutch 3-4.

Aviculture: Selected Reference CLUTCH; INCUBATION PERIOD 17-18 days; NESTLING PERIOD 20 days. Nest Record Cards CLUTCH 3 (ARU) 3,4 (ANRC); INCUBATION PERIOD 17 (ARU) 17,18 (ANRC); NESTLING PERIOD 19 (ARU), approximately 21 days (ANRC). Selected Reference WILD-FOOD. Seeds of *Tithonia diversifolia*, chickweed *Stellaria* sp. Diet Record Cards WILDFOOD Jungle rice *Echinochloa colona*, Wild rye *Secale africanum*, (bamboo-like) *Olyra latifolia*, Cotton wool grass *Imperata cylindrica* (ARU ADRC). Selected Reference ANIMAL FOOD whiteworms, crickets, waxworm, ant pupae. Diet Record Cards spiders (ARU ADRC), termites (ARU), aphids (ARU).

Brown Twinspot

Clytospiza monteiri 13cm

Alternative name: Monteiro's Twinspot.

Description: Male. Entire head slate-grey; nape, mantle, back and wings dark brown; rump and upper tail-coverts reddish orange; tail blackish brown; sides of neck slate-grey; chin and throat red; breast, belly and rest of underparts chestnut-brown, spotted and barred with white; iris red; bill greyish blue; legs and feet brown. Female has throat white; underparts paler. Juvenile has underparts and iris brown.

Voice: Described by Goodwin, close contact call is repeated 'vay-vay-vay...' which is intensified and tends to be uttered in longer series as a distance contact call.

Habitat: Forest clearings, moist thickets and edges of cultivation.

Distribution: Cameroon to Sudan and Uganda.

Feeding: Grass seeds, termites and spiders.

Breeding: Nest loosely built of grass, domed and placed in fork of trees. The old nest of a Bronze Mannikin *Lonchura cucullata* has been relined with hair, feathers, soft vegetable material and with some cast snake skin. may also reline old weavers' nests. Eggs white; clutch 4-6.

Aviculture: Selected Reference CLUTCH 4-6; INCUBATION PERIOD 13 days; NESTLING PERIOD 19-21 days. Nest Record Cards CLUTCH 4,4 (ARU) 3 (ANRC) 4 (SAANRC); INCUBATION PERIOD 12,13 (ARU) 13 days (SAANRC); NESTLING PERIOD 18,20 (ARU) 21 days (ANRC). Selected Reference WILD-FOOD chickweed *Stellaria* sp. Personal Communication Guinea grass *Panicum maximum*. Nest Record Cards Guinea grass *Panicum maximum* (ARU ADRC). Selected Reference ANIMAL FOOD whiteworms, ant pupae. Diet Record Cards termites (ADRC SAADRC), spiders (ADRC).

Rosy Twinspot

Hypargos margaritatus 13cm

Alternative names: Pink-throated Twinspot, Verreaux's Twinspot.

Description: Male. Headtop, mantle, rump, fight feathers and wing-coverts russet brown; tail and order tail-coverts black; breast to belly black with pinkish white spots; lores, sides of face, ear-coverts, chin to breast pinkish red; iris brown; bill black; legs and feet blackish. Female has lores, sides of face, ear-coverts and chin pale grey; flanks and sides of breast black with white spots; centre of belly white. Juvenile similar to adult female, but males have the throat faintly washed with pinkish red.

Voice: Described by Maclean, the song 2-6 soft fluty notes.

Habitat: Forests of the Lebombo Mountains, and adjacent thickets; also found in savanna with scattered trees or palms.

Distribution: Eastern KwaZulu-Natal and Mpumulanga, South Africa to Swaziland and southern Mozambique.

Feeding: Seeds and insects.

Breeding: Nest oval of leaf ribs and skeletons. mixed with grasses, leaves and spider's web, with short circular tunnel towards the top may or may not be included in the construction. Lined with palm fibre, finer grass and a few feathers. Built in a low bush, in a clump of drooping grass or at base of palm frond. Eggs white; clutch 3.

Aviculture: Selected Reference CLUTCH 4. Personal Communication CLUTCH 4. Selected Reference WILDFOOD. Chickweed *Stellaria* sp. Selected Reference ANIMAL FOOD ant pupae. Personal Communication aphids, fishmoths, Thrips-nymphs, termites, beetle larvae, including mealworms.

Peter's Twinspot

Hypargos niveoguttatus 13cm

Alternative names: Peter's Ruddy waxbill, Peter's Spotted Firefinch, Red-throated Twinspot

Description: Male. Forehead, crown and nape greyish brown; mantle to rump russet brown; upper tail-coverts deep crimson; tail blackish crimson; sides of face and neck crimson; wings russet brown; underparts black; flanks black with large white spots; iris dark brown; bill blue-black, legs and feet slate-grey. Female has head and sides of face greyish; chin, throat and upper tail-coverts buff, washed with crimson; underparts grey or brownish grey with each spot encircled with black. Juvenile similar to adult female, but paler head, chin and breast; rest of underparts greyish brown.

Males. *H.n.idius* (see *Peters Checklist of the Birds of the World p.323, vol. 14, 1968*).

H.n.interior differs from the nominate race in having the headtop greyish olive; mantle paler and warmer brown; sides of face and neck paler crimson.

H.n.macrospilotus differs from the nominate in averaging richer red.

Voice: Described by Goodwin as a soft and very variable '*tseet*' of '*tseet*'.

Habitat: Bushes near water on the outskirts of forests.

Distribution: Eastern Zimbabwe and Mozambique. Visually recorded in north-eastern South Africa.

H.n.interior northern Zimbabwe (Zambesi River valley) east to Mozambique (Tete district).

H.n.idius Zambia.

H.n.macrospilotus eastern Zaire, Kenya, Tanzania, Malawi and eastern Angola.

Feeding: Weed and grass, seeds and insects.

Breeding: Nests are globular in shape with a short tunnel at one side and are built of grass, vegetable fibre and moss, then lined with a few feathers. A nest recorded in Zimbabwe was well camouflaged and positioned on sloping ground between the exposed roots of a tree growing out of an embankment. Nest constructed of small maiden hair fern stalks, fine hair, roots, decomposed "skeletonised" leaflets and dry moss, the latter used mainly as lining and the whole exterior covered with soft decomposing leaves giving a superb camouflage effect. Eggs white; clutch 3-6; incubation period 12-13 days; both sexes incubate; nestling period 21 days.

Aviculture: Selected Reference CLUTCH 3-6; INCUBATION PERIOD 12-14 days; NESTLING PERIOD 18-21 days. Personal Communication CLUTCH 3. Nest Record Cards CLUTCH 3,4,4 (ARU) 5 (NASNRC) 4 (ANRC); INCUBATION PERIOD 12,13,13 (ARU) 13 (NASNRC) 13 days (NASNRC); NESTLING PERIOD 20,23 (ARU) 20 (NASNRC) 18 days (ANRC). Diet Record Cards WILDFOOD. Seeds of Blue panic *Panicum laevifolium*, Guinea grass *P.maximum*, Blue seed grass *Tricholaena monache*, Bushveld signal grass *Urochloa mosambicensis*, Millet grass *Setaria woodii* (NASDRC ADRC). Selected Reference ANIMAL FOOD Diet Record Cards beetle larvae, including mealworms, termites, fly larvae or "maggots" (ARU NASDRC), fishmoths, springtails (ARU), aphids, hairless caterpillars, moths (NASDRC).

Dybowski's Twinspot

Euschistospiza dybowskii 10,5cm

Alternative names: Dybowski's Dusky Twinspot, Red-backed Twinspot.

Description: Male. Entire head, nape, sides of neck and upper mantle slate-grey; lower mantle, back and upper tail-coverts crimson-red; tail black, fringes red; wings dusky brown, tipped white; under wing-coverts slate-grey, barred and speckled darker; chin, throat and breast slate-grey; belly and under tail-coverts black with white spots; iris red; bill black; legs and feet greyish brown. Female paler overall. Juvenile has spots on back and rump rusty brown; iris grey; bill slate-grey; legs and feet greyish white.

Voice: Described by Goodwin with the alarm call being a loud, '*tset-tset*' or '*tset-tset-tset*'.

Habitat: Grasslands, edge of gallery forests and cultivation.

Distribution: Sierra Leone to Sudan.

Feeding: Grass seeds and small insects.

Breeding: Not known.

Aviculture: Selected Reference CLUTCH 3-6; INCUBATION PERIOD 12-14 days; NESTLING PERIOD approximately 23 days. Nest Record Cards CLUTCH 3,4,5,5 (ARU) 4 (SAANRC); INCUBATION PERIOD 12,13,13,13 (ARU) 13 days (SAANRC); NESTLING PERIOD 18,20 (ARU) 21 days (SAANRC). Selected Reference WILDFOOD chickweed *Stellaria* sp., seeds of Rye grass *Lolium perenne*, Annual meadow grass *Poa annua* Diet Record Guinea grass (ARU SAADRC),

Natal panic *P.natalense* (ARU). Selected Reference ANIMAL FOOD mealworms, crickets, green aphids, bee grubs, ant pupae. Diet Record Cards spiders, mealworms (SAADRC).

Dusky Twinspot

Euschistospiza cinereovinacea 11,5cm

Alternative names: Grey Twinspot.
E.c.graueri **Dusky Firefinch.**

Description: Sexes similar. Entire head, nape, mantle, back and upper rump blackish slate; lower rump and upper tail-coverts maroon-red; tail blackish slate; chin, throat, sides of neck and upper breast slaty black; lower breast and under tail-coverts black; flanks maroon-red, with white spots; wings brownish slate; iris reddish brown; bill slate-grey; legs and feet greyish black. Juvenile paler overall; bill blackish horn.

Adult. *E.c.graueri* differs from the nominate race in having wings more brownish, less slate.

Voice: Described by Goodwin, with contact call as '*tsyip tsyip*'.

Habitat: Tall marsh grasses and forest edge.

Distribution: Western Angola.

E.c.graueri eastern Zaire and western Tanzania.

Feeding: Grass seeds and insects.

Breeding: Not known.

Aviculture: Selected Reference CLUTCH 3; INCUBATION PERIOD 13 days; NESTLING PERIOD 21 days. Personal Communication CLUTCH 3,4. Nest Record Cards CLUTCH 3,4 (ARU); INCUBATION PERIOD 12,12 days; (ARU); NESTLING PERIOD about 18,20 days (ARU). Diet Record Cards Guinea grass *Panicum maximum*, Blue panic *P.laevifolium*, Natal panic *P.natalense* (ARU). Diet Record Cards ANIMAL FOOD termites, spiders (ARU).

Black-bellied Firefinch

Lagonosticta rara 10cm

Alternative name: Black-bellied Waxbill.

Description: Male. Entire head, nape, mantle and back deep mauvish wine-red; rump and upper tail-coverts wine-red; tail black, edged wine-red; chin, throat, sides of throat and upper breast dark mauvish pink; lower breast, belly and under tail-coverts black; under wing-coverts silvery buff; iris black; bill, upper mandible black, lower red; legs and feet brown. Female has entire

head brownish grey; throat buffish; mantle and back pale brown suffused with reddish. Juvenile sooty brown suffused with pale red.

Male. *L.r.forbesi* differs from the nominate race in being considerably brighter overall.

Voice: Described by Harrison as having contact call as a single, rather nasal '*keeyl*' or '*squeer*'.

Habitat: Grasslands interspersed with bush and overgrown cultivation.

Distribution: Northern Cameroon to southern Sudan, Uganda and Kenya.

L.r.forbesi Sierra Leone to Nigeria.

Feeding: Small seeds and insects, especially termites.

Breeding: Nest roundish with side entrance, built of grass seedheads, sometimes also rootlets or other vegetable matter and lined with feathers. Usually placed low down in grass tuft, but also in a shrub, tree or in the thatch of a hut. Eggs slightly glossy, white; clutch 3-4.

Aviculture: Selected Reference CLUTCH 3-4. Nest Record Cards CLUTCH 3,4,4,4 (ARU); INCUBATION PERIOD 11,11,11,12 days (ANRC); NESTLING PERIOD approximately 17,17,19 days (ANRC). Diet Record Cards Blue panic *Panicum laevifolium*, Burbristle grass *Setaria verticillata*, African finger millet *Eleusine coracana* (ADRC). Selected Reference WILDFOOD chickweed *Stellaria* sp. Selected Reference ANIMAL FOOD ant pupae. Diet Record Cards termites (ADRC).

Bar-breasted Firefinch

Lagonosticta rufopicta 11cm

Alternative name: Speckled Firefinch.

Description: Sexes similar. Forehead, crown, nape, mantle and back greyish earth brown, rump and upper tail-coverts crimson; tail black; sides of face, chin and throat crimson-wine; breast crimson-wine, feathers tipped white; belly dusky under tail-coverts buff; iris greyish; bill crimson; legs and feet dark brown. Juvenile underparts earth brown, washed with crimson from breast to belly; upper tail-coverts pale crimson; bill dusky.

L.r.lateritia differs from the nominate race in having upperparts more greyish, less brownish.

Voice: Described by Mackworth-Praed & Grant as a musical twittering.

Habitat: Savanna and riverine bush.

Distribution: Senegal to northern Cameroon and Central African Republic.

L.r.lateritia Sudan, north-eastern Zaire and western Uganda.

Feeding: Seeds and insects, mostly termites.

Breeding: Loosely-built ball of grass stems and coarse blades, with side entrance. Scantily lined with seeding grass-heads and feathers. One nest at 60cm high in tall grass. Eggs white; clutch 4.

Aviculture: Selected Reference CLUTCH 3-5. Nest Record Cards CLUTCH 3 (ARU) 3 (ANRC); INCUBATION PERIOD 12,12 (ARU) 12,12 days (ANRC); NESTLING PERIOD 15,16 (ARU) 15,17 days (ANRC). Diet Record Cards Guinea grass *Panicum maximum* (ARU), African Buffalo grass *P.aequinerve, P.atrosanguineum*, Natal panic *P.natalense*, Blue panic *P.laevifolium* (ADRC), wasp larvae or "grubs" (ARU).

Brown Firefinch

Lagonosticta nitidula 10cm

Alternative name: Dark little Ruddy Waxbill.

Description: Male. Forehead, crown, nape, mantle, back and upper tail-coverts earth brown; tail earth brown washed with black; sides of face, ear-coverts, chin and throat reddish pink, spotted white; belly and tail-coverts pale dusky earth brown; flight feathers and wing-coverts earth brown; iris brown; bill red, purple at base; legs and feet slate-grey. Female similar to male, but reddish pink on upperparts paler. Juvenile wholly earth brown with chin to breast greyish; bill purplish.

Voice: Described by Maclean as having the song variable tsee-kee-dee-tswee, sometimes with trills; not bell-like as in other firefinches.

Habitat: Grassy or shubby places at forest edges, riparian fringing forests, or in a small clearing in forest.

Distribution: Eastern Angola, southern Zaire and northern Zambia.

L.n.plumbaria north eastern Zambia, the Caprivi Strip, northern Botswana, north-western Zimbabwe and southern Zambia.

Feeding: Seeds, millet and insects.

Breeding: A dome-shaped nest with side entrance, lined with domestic fowl feathers, was 'built' into the inside of the grass shelter of a pit-latrine. A brood of 3 were found in the old nest of a sunbird. Nests are placed in the thatch of a hut, in a wall hole, low bush or disused nest of a weaver. Eggs white; clutch 3-7; incubation period 12-13 days; nestling period 18-19 days.

Aviculture: Selected Reference CLUTCH 3-7; INCUBATION PERIOD 12-13 days; NESTLING PERIOD 18-19 days. Nest Record Cards CLUTCH 4,4 (ARU); INCUBATION PERIOD 12,12 days (ARU); NESTLING PERIOD 18-21 days (ARU). Diet Record Cards WILDFOOD chickweed *Stellaria* sp., seeds of Teff grass *Eragrostis tef*, Bur-bristle grass *Setaria verticullata*, Golden setaria *S.sphacelata*, Natal redtop *Rhynchelytrum*

repens (ARU). Selected Reference ANIMAL FOOD whiteworms, ant pupae. Diet Record Cards termites, mealworms, small black ants (ARU).

Red-billed Firefinch

Lagonosticta senegala 12cm

Alternative names: Common Firefinch
***L.s.rendalli* Little Ruddy Waxbill, Little Firefinch, Rosy Senegal Firefinch.**

Description: Male. Crown, nape, mantle, back and rump earth brown, washed with pale red. Upper tail-coverts red; tail black; edged with red; lores, ear-coverts, chin, throat and breast pinkish red; belly, flanks and upper tail-coverts pale brown; wings brown; iris red; bill red, ridge of culmen black; legs and feet brownish. Female has lores, ear-coverts, chin, throat and breast earth brown; belly, flanks and under tail-coverts pale brown, finely spotted with white; forehead pinkish red. Juvenile similar to adult female, but lacks the pinkish red on the forehead and white spots on the underparts.

Males *L.s.somaliensis* differs from *brunneiceps* in being paler carmine.

L.s.ruberrima differs from the nominate in being a rich reddish purple; lower belly and under tail-coverts dark greyish brown.

L.s. rendalli differs from *somaliensis* in being pale brown on belly extending up towards the breast.

L.s. pallidicrissa differs from *ruberrima* in being paler overall, especially underparts *L.s. rhodopsis* differs from the nominate in being paler overall with mantle washed with yellowish.

L.s.confidens differs from *rendalli* in having upperparts paler; rump and upper tail-coverts paler red.

L.s. brunneiceps differs from the nominate in being overall brighter red; fewer, and in some individuals no white spots on sides of breast.

Voice: Described by Newman as a slightly nasal 'fweet, fweet'.

Habitat: Thornveld, where in West Africa occurs in areas dominated by Scented thorn *Acacia nilotica*, Umbrella thorn *A.tortilis*. Three-thorned acacia *A.senegal*, White-gali acacia *A.seyal*, Buffalo thorn *Zizyphus mucronata*, Mustard tree *Salvadora persica* and on lakeside with *Tarmarix* sp., and *Typha* sp.

Distribution: Gambia, Senegal south and east to Sierra Leone, Ghana and Nigeria.

L.s.rhodopsis northern Nigeria, northern Cameroon, south-western Sudan to Chad.

L.s.brunneiceps Ethiopia.

L.s.somaliensis Somalia, Kenya and Tanzania.

L.s.ruberrima Uganda, south-eastern Zaire, Zambia and western Tanzania.

L.s.pallidiscrissa south-western Zambia, southern Angola, northern Namibia, north-eastern Botswana and in the South African provinces of North-West and north-eastern Cape.

L.s.confidens Zimbabwe, Mozambique (south to the Save River), Swaziland and Gauteng, Northern Province (except dry west), Free State and Kwa-Zulu-Natal, South Africa.

L.s.rendalli southern Malawi, northern Zimbabwe, east to Tete and Manica district, Mozambique.

Feeding: Seeds, grain and small insects. The food of netted birds was sampled by inserting a flexible plastic tube through the mouth into the crop, then drawing the plunger of a small syringe attached to the tube. The main foods taken at all times of the year were seeds of the seasonal grasses, Bur-bristle grass *Setaria verticillata*, Teff grass *Eragrostis tef*, *Panicum apharonum*, Elbow buffalo grass *P.subalbidum*, Elbow grass *P.longijubatum*, *Pennisetum asperifolion*, *P.violaceum*, Long-plumbed finger grass *Digitaria veluntina*, Crowfoot *Dactylocetium aegyptium*, Jungle rice *Echinochloa colona* *Chloris pilosa*, *C.pulsa*, *C.prieuri*, Small dropseed *Sporobolus coromandelianus* and Khaki-weed *Alternanthera pungens*. Partial to spilled cultivated grains, especially millet. Also consumes termites when available.

Breeding: Nest, an untidy grass dome of dried grass, roots, leaves and rags, lined with feathers and animal hair. A large entrance hole is made on one side at the top with a small grass canopy above it. Nests are placed beneath thatch roofs, in crowns of palms, bushes, in low wall holes or on the ground in a depression among luxuriant vegetation. Eggs white; clutch 2-4; incubation period 11-12 days, by both sexes; young cared for by both parents; nestling period 14-19 days; feeding continues for 8-10 days more, mostly by the male. Host to Village indigobird *Vidua chalybeata* which may enter the nest and lay her egg while the firefinch is incubating with very little opposition being aimed towards the intruder.

Aviculture: Selected Reference CLUTCH 3-6; INCUBATION PERIOD 11-14 days; NESTLING PERIOD 18-21 days. Personal Communication CLUTCH 3,3,4,4,4,6; INCUBATION PERIOD 11,11,11,12,12 days; NESTLING PERIOD 17,17,18,18,20 days. Nest Record Cards CLUTCH 3,4,4 (SAANRC) 3,4 (NASNRC) 3 (ARU) 4,4 (ANRC); INCUBATION PERIOD 11,11 (SAANRC) 12 (NASNRC) 11 (ARU) 11, about 12 days (ANRC); NESTLING PERIOD 16,18 (SAANRC) 19 (NASNRC) 16 (ARU) 17,18 days (ANRC). Diet Record Cards WILDFOOD Chickweed *Stellaria media*, dandelion *Taraxacum* sp., seeds of Burbristle grass *Setaria verticillata*, Teff grass *Eragrostis tef*, Broad-leaved panic *Panicum deustum*, Blue panic *P.laevifolium*, Guinea grass *P.maximum*, Natal redtop *Rhynchelytrum repens*, Catstail dropseed *Sporobolus pyramidalis* (ARU ADRC NASDRC SAADRC). Selected Reference ANIMAL FOOD mealworms, termites, spiders, whiteworms, ant pupae. Diet Record Cards termites, mealworms, aphids (ARU SAADRC), thrips-nymphs, fishmoths, gnats (NASDRC), small brown ants (ARU).

Kuli Koro Firefinch
Lagonosticta virata 10cm
Alternative name: Grey-backed Firefinch.

Description: Male. Forehead, crown and nape greyish brown; mantle, back and wings brownish grey; rump and upper tail-coverts scarlet; tail blackish brown, tinged pale scarlet; under wing-coverts silvery grey; sides of face, chin, throat, breast and belly pinkish crimson; white spots on sides of breast and upper flanks; under tail-coverts black; iris dark brown, bill slate-grey, lower mandible blackish; legs and feet brownish black. Female similar to male, but pinkish crimson parts paler. Juvenile similar to female, but paler overall; bill blackish.

Voice: Described by Harrison with contact call a low-pitched nasal, slightly harsh 'kyew' or 'kyah'.

Habitat: Grasslands and scrub growing along streams.

Distribution: Mali.

Feeding: Grass seeds.

Breeding: A domed nest with a hole in one side at the top is usually situated low in, or at the base of a small bush or grass tuft. Strongly built of grassheads and a few feathers as lining. Eggs white; clutch 3-4.

Aviculture: Selected Reference CLUTCH 4, Personal Communication CLUTCH 4; INCUBATION PERIOD 12 days; NESTLING PERIOD 17 days. Nest Record Cards CLUTCH 4 (ARU) 4 (NASNRC); INCUBATION PERIOD 12 days (ARU) 11 (NASNRC); NESTING PERIOD 18 (ARU) 18 days (NASNRC). Diet Record Cards Guinea grass *Panicum maximum* (ARU NASDRC). Bur-bristle grass *Setaria verticillata*, Rhodes grass *Chloris gayana* (ARU), African finger millet *Eleusine coracana* (NASDRC). Diet Record Cards ANIMAL FOOD termites, gnats (NASDRC).

Blue-billed Firefinch
Lagonosticta rubricata 12cm
Alternative names: South African Ruddy Waxbill.
L.r.polionota **African Firefinch, African Crimson Finch, Brown-backed Firefinch, Dark Firefinch, Lilac Firefinch, Ruddy Waxbill.**

Description: Male. Crown and hindneck greyish brown; mantle and wings earth brown; upper tail-coverts claret-rose with a few small white pin-spots on side of breast; centre of abdomen blackish brown; iris brown; bill blue-black; legs and feet slate-grey. Female upperparts paler earth brown; underparts brown. Juvenile upperparts brownish; belly dusky; bill, upper mandible blackish, lower horn.

Males. *L.r.polionota* differs from the nominate race in having mantle darker greyer brown.

L.r.haematocephala differs from the nominate in having upperparts clearer earth brown; crown and nape washed with claret-red; underparts less brownish.

L.r.congica differs from nominate in being browner on upperparts.

Voice: Described by Newman as '*wink-wink,wink*,' but it also has a clear bell-like trill.

Habitat: Undergrowth of low bushes, partly cleared and cultivated lands and forest fringes.

Distribution: Swaziland, southern Mozambique and in the South African provinces of western and eastern Cape, Gauteng, Free State, and KwaZulu-Natal.

L.r.polionota Guinea to Nigeria.

L.r.haematocephala south eastern Zaire, Tanzania, Zambia, Malawi, northern Mozambique and eastern Zimbabwe.

L.r.congica Gabon to southern Zaire and north-western Zambia.

Feeding: Seeds of Bur-bristle grass *Setaria verticullata*, and insects, particularly ants and termites

Breeding: The site is a tree, thick bush or grass tuft usually no more than 2m from the ground. The nest is well concealed as a rule, and consists of a flimsy dome-shaped structure with an outer shell of course grass and an inner shell of finer dried grass. Both adults construct the nest, the male the outer shell, the female the inner shell. The egg chamber is lined with feathers. Eggs white; clutch 3-5 usually 3; both sexes incubate; incubation period 11-12 days; nestling period 13-16 days; fed by both parents; host to Black Widowfinch *Vidua funerea*.

Aviculture: Selected Reference CLUTCH 3-5; INCUBATION PERIOD 12 days. Personal Communication CLUTCH 3,4,4; INCUBATION PERIOD 11,11,12 days; NESTLING PERIOD 14,17,19 days. Nest Record Cards CLUTCH 4,4,4 (ARU) 4,4 (SAANRC) 4,4 (ANRC); INCUBATION PERIOD 11,12 (SAANRC) 12 (NASNRC) 12 (ARU) 11,12 (ANRC); NESTLING PERIOD 16,18 (SAANRC) 18 (NASNRC) 16 (ARU) 17, about 18 (ANRC). Diet Record Cards WILDFOOD Seeds of Bur-bristle grass *Setaria verticullata*, Popo grass *Hyparrhenia cymbaria*, Common thatch grass *H.hirta*, Teff grass *Eragrostis tef*, Blue panic *Panicum laevifolium*, Guinea grass *P.maximum*. Lehmann's love grass *Eragrostis lehmanniana* (ADRC ADRC NAS-DRC). Selected Reference ANIMAL FOOD green aphids, whiteworms. Diet Record Cards termites (ARU NASDRC SAADRC), mealworms (ARU SAADRC), aphids and moths (ARU).

Pale-billed Firefinch
Lagonosticta landanae 10cm
Alternative name: Landana Firefinch.

Description: Male. Forehead, crown and nape brown; mantle, back, rump and wings greyish brown; upper tail-coverts crimson-red; tail black, edged crimson; chin, throat, sides of face, breast and belly crimson-red; flanks crimson, spotted white; iris brown; bill upper mandible slate-grey, lower purplish red; legs and feet greyish green. Female has entire head greyish brown; underparts brown, tinged red. Juvenile similar to adult female, but belly brown.

Voice: Not known.

Habitat: Savanna and edge of secondary forests.

Distribution: Western and northern Angola and southern Congo.

Feeding: Small seeds.

Breeding: Not known.

Aviculture: Nest Record Cards CLUTCH 3,3,4 (ARU) 3 (ANRC); INCUBATION PERIOD 11,12,12 (ARU) 12 days (ANRC); NESTLING PERIOD 15,16 (ARU) 16 days (ANRC). Diet Record Cards ANIMAL FOOD termites (ARU ADRC), wasp larvae or "grubs" (ADRC).

Jameson's Firefinch
Lagonosticta rhodopareia 12cm
Alternative names: Pink-backed Firefinch.
L.r.jamesoni, Jameson's Ruddy Waxbill,

Description: Male. Crown, mantle and wings brown, washed with pinkish red; underparts pinkish red, with little contrast between breast and mantle; small white spots on underpart of flanks; iris brown; bill bluish grey; legs and feet pinkish grey. Female slightly less vividly coloured; flanks very sparingly spotted white. Juvenile resemble the female, but lacks the pink on the breast and lores.

Males. *L.r.taruensis* differs from the nominate race in having a distinct reddish wash to mantle, nape, crown, centre of abdomen; under tail-coverts black; bill bluish grey.

L.r.ansorgei differs from the nominate in having the head strongly washed with crimson; bill slate-grey.

L.r.jamesoni differs from *ansorgei* in having the top of the head less strongly washed with claret-red.

Voice: Described by Maclean as a tinkling '*trrr trr trt*' alarm notes; sharp '*zik-zik-zik-zik.*'

Habitat: Prefers thorn tree scrub with tall grass, but can also be found in thick bush along water courses.

Distribution: Ethiopia, Chad and northern Kenya.

L.r.taruensis Northern Zimbabwe (Kariba), eastern Zambia, Zaire, Malawi, northern Mozambique, Tanzania (absent north-west) and southern and south-eastern Kenya.

L.r.ansorgei North-western Namibia (lower Cunene River), western Angola and lower Congo.

L.r.jamesoni KwaZulu-Natal, Northern Province, eastern North-West, South Africa, central to eastern Swaziland, Mozambique (excluding Tete district), Zimbabwe (highlands), eastern and northern Botswana, the Caprivi Strip, northern Namibia, southern Angola and south-western Zambia.

Feeding: Seeds and insects, mostly ants.

Breeding: The site is usually in a tree or bush in tall grass 0,6-1,5m from the ground. The nest is a spherical ball of dried grass, with the flowering heads in particular forming the inner shell, the outer shell consisted of coarser leaf strands. The lining is mostly feathers. Green plant material may be visible protruding through the nest. The entrance hole is at one side near the top. Eggs white; clutch 3-4, occasionally 5; host to Purple Widowfinch *Vidua purpurascens*.

Aviculture: Selected Reference CLUTCH 3-5; INCUBATION PERIOD 11-12 days. Personal Communication CLUTCH 3; INCUBATION PERIOD 12 days; NESTLING PERIOD 19 days. Nest Record Cards CLUTCH 3,3,4 (SAANRC); INCUBATION PERIOD 12,2 days; NESTLING PERIOD 18, about 19 days (ARU). Diet Record Cards WILDFOOD Seeds of Burbristle grass *Setaria verticillara*, Natal redtop *Rhynchelytrum repens*, Guinea grass *Panicum maximum*, Bushveld signal grass *Urochloa mosarr bicensis*, Teff grass *Eragrostis tef* (ARU SAADRC). Selected Reference ANIMAL FOOD ant pupae. Diet Record Cards termites (ARU SAADRC), mealworms, moths, fishmoths, aphids (ARU).

Masked Firefinch
Lagonosticta larvata 11,5cm
Alternative names: Black-faced Firefinch, Masked Waxbill.

Description: Male. Forehead, crown, nape, mantle and upper back dark brownish grey, tinged maroon-red; lower back, rump and upper tail-coverts maroon-red; tail maroon, tinged blackish; face mask and throat black; breast and upper belly maroon-red; lower belly and rest of underparts dark greyish brown; iris brown; bill bluish black, lower mandible paler; legs and feet dark bluish grey. Female upperparts dark brownish slate with rump and upper tail-coverts reddish brown; underparts greyish buff with under tail-coverts greyish black. Juvenile has plumage pattern basically as adult female, but paler.

Voice: Described by Serle as a series of two clear whistled notes sung together, the first one low and slurred down and the second high and slurred up.

Habitat Edges of thickets, tall grass, abandoned cultivation with scattered trees.

Distribution: Ethiopia and Sudan.

Feeding: Small seeds, millet, small insects and spiders.

Breeding: Not known.

Aviculture: No records.

Vinaceous Firefinch
Lagonosticta vinacea 11,5cm
Alternative names: Vinaceous Waxbill.
L.v.togoensis **Togo Black-faced Firefinch.**
L.v.nigricollis **Grey Firefinch.**

Description: Male. Forehead, crown and nape dark grey; hindneck grey, tinged rosy mauvish pink; mantle and back paler mauvish pink; rump and upper tail-coverts rosy crimson; tail black, edged rosy crimson; wing-coverts mauvish pink, primaries and outer secondaries greyish brown; under wing-coverts silver grey; face mask and throat black; breast and upper belly rosy mauvish pink; lower belly and under tail-coverts white; flanks mauvish pink, spotted white; iris reddish brown; bill dark olive-grey; legs and feet olive-green. Female has entire head greyish brown; rest of upperparts brownish except rump and upper tail-coverts pale pink; underparts buff except flanks paler rosy pink. Juvenile paler brown overall, with red on rump and tail paler.

Males. *L.v.togoensis* differs from *nigricollis* in having upperparts browner.

L.v.nigricollis upper parts dark grey, except rump crimson; underparts pale lavender with small white spots on flanks.

Voice: Described by Bannerman as uttering a 'loud, clear song'.

Habitat: Bamboo thickets.

Distribution: Senegal to Guinea.

L.v.nigricollis Central African Republic to Sudan.

L.v.togoensis Ghana, Togo to northern Cameroon and western Sudan.

Feeding: Grass seeds and insects, notably termites.

Breeding: A single nest was found to be roundish and loosely built of withered grass with side entrance and lined with fine grass tops and a few feathers, placed in a pile of brushwood. Eggs white; clutch 3-4.

Aviculture: Selected Reference CLUTCH 2,3,5; INCUBATION PERIOD 11,11,12 days; DIET Personal Communication ANIMAL FOOD termites.

Cordon-bleu

Uraeginthus angolensis 12cm

Alternative names: Angola Cordon-bleu
U.a.niassensis **Southern Blue Waxbill, Blue-breasted Waxbill, Blue Waxbill.**

Description: Male. Forehead, crown, nape, mantle and back earth brown; rump, upper tail-coverts and tail blue; sides of face, ear-coverts, chin and throat dark blue, breast and flanks blue; centre of breast and under tail-coverts buff; iris red; bill lilac; legs and feet brown. Female upperparts light blue; underparts pinkish buff. Juvenile similar to adult female, but paler; bill blackish.

Males.*U.a.cyanopleurus* differs from the nominate race in having upperparts paler; underparts darker blue.

U.a.niassensis differs from nominate in having upperparts darker; underparts paler.

U.a.natalensis differs from the nominate in having the mantle and back darker brown; belly pale bluish green.

Voice: Described by Maclean as having song of sibilant and harsh notes interspersed, '*chreu chreu chittywood weeoo wee*', etc; harsh stuttering rattling alarm notes.

Habitat: Thornveld, mixed woodland, cultivated areas and in the vicinity of human dwellings.

Distribution: Angola and northern Namibia.

U.a.cyanopleurus south-western Zambia, north and north-eastern Botswana, north-western Zimbabwe, southern Angola and north-eastern Namibia.

U.a.niassensis eastern Tanzania, south eastern Zaire to Zimbabwe.

U.a.natalensis Zimbabwe, south-eastern Botswana, Swaziland and South Africa in KwaZulu-Natal, Northern Province, central and southern North-West, northern Gauteng and Mpumalanga (except north-eastern lowlands).

Feeding: Small seeds and insects. Seeds of Blue Panic *Panicum laevifolium*, Guinea grass *P.maximum*, Bushveld signal grass *Urochloa mosambicansis*, Blue seed grass *Tricholaena monachne*, Natal redtop *Rhynchelytrum repens*, Bur bristle grass *Setaria verticullata*, Hay *Chloris vigata*, Blue waterbush *Verbena bonariensis*, Khaki-weed *Alternanthera pungens* and fallen fruit of Sheperd's tree *Boscia albitrunca*. Livefood, namely termites, beetle larvae and spiders.

Breeding: Constructs a rough dome of grass with a side entrance in a bush, tree or palm, but most often in an *acacia* up to 3m above the ground. Preferred lining is light coloured feathers, but sometimes dark or spotted feathers are used. Frequently nests within a few centimetres of wasp or hornet nest, with 19 nests found in Malawi, wasps of the genera *polistes, icuria* and *belanogaster* were recorded. Observed also nesting on iron telegraph poles and old nests of the other birds, namely Masked Weaver *Ploceus velatus* and Scarlet-chested Sunbird *Nectarinia senegalensis*. Eggs white; clutch 4-5; incubation period 11-12 days, by both sexes which also feed and care for their offspring; nestling period 17-21 days.

Aviculture: Selected Reference CLUTCH 3-6; INCUBATION PERIOD 11-14 days; NESTLING PERIOD 17-21 days. Personal Communication CLUTCH 3,3,4,4,6; INCUBATION PERIOD 11,12,12,12,13 days; NESTLING PERIOD 17,18,18,19 days. Nest Record Cards CLUTCH 3,3,4 (SAANRC) 4,4 (NASNRC) 4 (ARU) 4,4 (ANRC); INCUBATION PERIOD 11,11,12,12 (SAANRC) 12,12 (NASNRC) 12, about 12 days (ANRC); NESTLING PERIOD 18,19 (SAANRC) 17,19 (NASNRC) 19 (ARU) 18,21 days (ANRC). Diet Record Cards WILDFOOD Seeds of Guinea grass *Panicum maximum*, Blue panic *P.laevifolium*, Small Buffalo grass *P.coloratum*, Buffalo grass *P.stapfianum*, Bushveld signal grass *Urochloa mosambicensis*, Kuri millet *U.panicoides*, Natal redtop *Rhynchelytrum repens*, Blue seed grass *tricholaena monachne*, Bur-bristle grass *Setaria verticillata*. Small creeping foxtail *S.flabellata*, Hay *Chloris virgata*, Common thatch grass

Hyparrhenia hirta, Bird grass *Poa trivialis* (SAADRC ARU ADRC NASDRC). Personal Communication Red Natal grass *Rhynchelytrum repens*, Annual Veldt grass *Ehrharta loniflora*, Knot-grass *Polygonum aviculare*, Annual Meadow grass *Poa annua*. Selected Reference ANIMAL FOOD mealworms, spiders. Diet Record Cards termites, mealworms (ARU ADRC NASDRC), thrips-nymphs, moths, aphids (ADRC), moths (ARU), fly larvae or "maggots" (NASDRC).

Red-cheeked Cordon-bleu

Uraeginthus bengalus 11,4-12,7cm

Alternative names: Cordon-bleu Finch, Crimson-eared Waxbill, Red-cheeked Blue Waxbill.
***U.b.littoralis* Giant East African Cordon-bleu.**

Description: Male. Forehead, crown and nape earth brown; round eyes and sides of face blue; ear-coverts red; mantle and back earth brown; rump, upper tail-coverts and tail blue; chin, throat and sides of breast blue; centre of breast and under tail-coverts buff-brown; iris reddish; bill mauve, tip black; legs and feet brown. Female paler overall; ear-coverts blue. Juvenile similar to adult female, but chin and breast blue; rest of underparts buff-brown.

Males. *U.b.brunneigularis* differs from the nominate race in averaging a little larger.

U.b.littoralis differs from the nominate in averaging a little smaller and red facial patch smaller.

U.b.ugogoensis differs from the nominate in having upperparts paler tawny brown.

U.b.katangae differs from the nominate in having darker red facial patch.

Habitat: Savanna woodland, with Neem *Azadirachta indica*, Date Palm *Phoenix regia* and Simple-thorned torchwood *Balanites aegyptiaca*, abandoned cultivation and gardens.

Distribution: Senegal, Sudan, Ethiopia south to Kenya and Uganda.

U.b.brunneigularis Kenya.

U.b.littoralis eastern Kenya and Tanzania.

U.b.ugogoensis northern and western Tanzania.

U.b.katangae eastern Angola, southern Zaire and Zambia.

Feeding: Seeds of grasses and insects. The crops contents of 6 individuals taken in the Sudan contained the seeds of Jungle rice *Echinochloa colonum*, Crowfoot *Dactyloctenium aegyptium*, *Setaria verticillata* and some contained small quantities of the remains of the termite *Odontotermes* spp.

Breeding: Nest spherical or oval-shaped, roughly made of green stems of flowering heads of *Boerhaavia repens*, *Sporobolus humifusus* and *Panicum hygrocharis* which were recorded in the Sudan. Nest chambers were usually lined with feathers and flower-heads of grasses of *Sporobolus humaris* and *Panicum hygrocharis*. Also other vegetable matter including feathers which are mostly white or pale coloured. Nest lining in continued to be added to the chamber until the nestlings hatch. Nests are sited from 83-500cm above the ground, often near a hornet's nest. less so with *brunneigularis*. In the Sudan nests in bunches of ripe bananas. The survey revealed 63 out of 112 nests were in banana plants *Musa* sp., 32 in ripening bunches and 31 near the bases of the leaves of these plants. Other sites were 18 in Tontub shrubs *Capparis decidua*, 6 in Hook thorn *Acacia mellifera*, 3 in White-gall acacia *A.seyal*, 5 in Lime tree *Citris paradisi,* 4 in Palm tree *Phoenix regia*, 3 in Neem tree *Azadirachta indica*, 1 in Balanite tree *Balanites aegyptiaca*, 1 in hira shrub *Lawsonia* sp., and 1 in Mango tree *Maniferc indica*. In addition 6 nests were built under the roof of a hut which used to house animals and 1 was in a box of switches on a electricity pole. They also reline old nests of weavers. Both sexes become involved in nest construction with females being observed apparently arranging materials in them. Eggs white, oval; clutch 4-6, up to 7; nestling period for 1 nest in Sudan 18,9 + 0,7 days.

Aviculture: Selected Reference CLUTCH 3-7. INCUBATION PERIOD 11-14 days; NESTLING PERIOD 19-22 days. Personal Communication CLUTCH 4,5,5; INCUBATION PERIOD 11,12 days; NESTLING PERIOD 18,29 days. Nest Record Cards CLUTCH 3,5 (SAANRC) 4,4 (ARU); INCUBATION PERIOD 12,12 (SAANRC) 11,13 days (ARU); NESTLING PERIOD 18,19 (SAANRC) 18,21 days (ARU). Selected Reference WILDFOOD Annual meadow grass *Poa annua*, Knot-grass *Polygonum aviculare*, Chickweed *Stellaria media*, dandelion *Taraxacum* sp. Personal Communication Red Natal grass *Rhynchelytrum repens*, Guinea grass *Panicum maximum*, Blue panic *P.laevifolium*. Diet Record Cards Guinea grass *Panicum maximum*, Bur-bristle grass *Setaria verticullctc*, Blue-seed grass *Tricholaena monachne* (ARU SAADRC). Selected Reference ANIMAL FOOD wax moth and fruitfly larvae, pupae, larvae and winged males and females of Meadow ants *Lasius fuscus* and *L.niger,* green aphids, centipedes, whiteworms. Diet Record Cards termites, aphids (ARU SAADRC).

Blue-capped waxbill

Uraeginthus cyanocephala 11-12cm.

Alternative names: Abyssinian Cordon-bleu, Blue-capped Cordon-bleu, Blue-headed Cordon-bleu.

Description: Male. Entire head blue; mantle, back and wings earth-brown; rump and upper tail-coverts blue; belly to under tail-coverts buff-brown; iris reddish; bill red or deep link, tip black; legs and feet pinkish. Female is paler overall; forehead, crown and nape buff-brown. Juvenile similar to adult female, but paler.

Voice; Described by Goodwin as *'Teu, skuur' 'tsee-ee-wee-see-see, skurr, teh-teh'*.

Habitat: Savanna with *acacia* or similar thornveld.

Distribution: Southern Somalia, Ethiopia, northern Kenya to Tanzania.

Feeding: Seeds and insects, notably termites.

Breeding: The nest is placed low down in fork of shrub or tree. It is oval or barrel-shaped, loosely built of dry grass stems with a large entrance at one side, lined with soft grassheads or feathers, closely by the converging ends of the grass stems. Frequently built near a hornet's nest and seldom shows much attempt at nest concealment. Eggs white; clutch 4-6; building by male who gathers material by carrying one piece at a time to nest and placing it there for the female to arrange; incubation by both sexes, but more by female who sits through night and during part of the day; brooded while small and fed by regurgitation; adult plumage at about 4-5 months of age.

Aviculture: Selected Reference CLUTCH 4-6; INCUBATION PERIOD 11-14 days; NESTLING PERIOD 18 days. Personal Communication CLUTCH 3,5,5,7; INCUBATION PERIOD 11,13,13 days; NESTLING PERIOD 17,18 days. Nest Record Cards CLUTCH 4,5,5 (SAANRC)4 (NASNRC) 3,7 (ARU) 4,4,6 (ANRC); INCUBATION PERIOD 11,12,12 (NASNRC) 12,13 (ARU) 11,12,12 days (ANRC); NESTLING PERIOD 17,18 (SAANRC) 17 (NASNRC) 17,19 (ARU) 18,19 days (ANRC). Personal Communication Hairy panic *Panicum effusum*, African veld grass *Ehrharta calycina*, Crab finger grass *Digitaria sanguinalis*. Diet Record Cards Guinea grass *Panicum maximum*, Blue panic *P.laevifolium*, Blue-seed grass *Tricholaena monachne*, Khaki-weed *Alternanthera pungens*, Annual blue-grass *Poa annua*, Wild rice grass *Leersia hexandra*, Weeping lovegrass *Eragrostis culvula*, Nile grass *Acroceras macrum* (ARU ADRC SAADRC). Selected Reference WILDFOOD Chickweed *Stellaria* sp. Selected Reference ANIMAL FOOD mealworms, termites. Diet Record Cards termites (ARU ADRC SAADRC NASDRC), mealworms (ARU NASDRC), aphids (ARU).

Violet-eared Grenadier

Uraeginthus granatina 14cm

Alternative names: Common Grenadier Waxbill, Common Grenadier, South African Grenadier Waxbill, Violet-eared Cordon-bleu, Violet eared Waxbill.

Description: Male. Forehead blue; sides of face and ear-coverts purplish violet; crown, nape, mantle, rump and rest of underparts chocolate-brown; chin and centre of belly black; Flight feathers light brown, upper and under tail coverts dark blue; tail black; iris red with red or orange eyelid; bill red; legs and feet purplish. Female has forehead light blue; sides of face and ear-coverts pale purplish violet; crown, nape, mantle, rump and rest of underparts tawny; upper tail-coverts light blue, tail blackish. Juvenile male resembles adult female, except sides of face, ear-coverts, chin and belly as in the adult; female resembles adult female, but sides of face and ear-coverts buffy. Male attains violet, blue and black adornment as early as 22 days after leaving the nest, but full adult plumage is attained only many months later after a complete moult.

Males. *U.g.siccata* differs from the nominate race in having the crown, nape, mantle and upper rump russet brown; lower rump upper and under tail-coverts light blue, occasionally suffused more with violet and less purple; chin and centre of belly sooty black.

U.g.retusa pale overall; mantle much lighter with a greyish olive wash on underparts; less black over the chin and upper throat.

Voice: Described by Mackworth-Praed & Grant as a thin thrilling note and a weak Canary-like tinking song.

Habitat: Arid thorn woodlands, especially tangles in tall grass.

Distribution: Southern Angola, north-eastern Namibia, the Caprivi Strip, northern and eastern Botswana, Zimbabwe, Mozambique (escapees) and South Africa in North-West, Gauteng, Mpumalanga and Northern Province, Free State and northern Cape. Observed in KwaZulu-Natal (rare).

U.g.siccata western Angola, western Namibia to northern Cape Province in South Africa, western and south-western Botswana.

U.g.retusa southern Mozambique.

Feeding: Seeds, fruits and insects. Seeds of Carrotseed grass *Tragus berteronianus*, Blue panic *Panicum laevifolium*, Guinea grass *P.maximum*, Bushveld signal grass *Urochloa mosambicensis*, Sweet grass *Brachiaria nigropedata*, Small finger grass *Digitaria argyrograpta*, Blue seed grass *Tricholaena monachne*, Natal redtop *Rhynchelytrum repens*, Blue buffalo grass *Cenchrus ciliaris*, Stick grass *Aristida curvata*, Tassel bristle grass *A.congesta*, Spiderweb grass *Chloris pycnothrix*, Lehmann's love grass *Eragrostis lehmanniana*, Rolling grass *Trichoneura grandiglumis*, Khaki-weed *Alternanthera pungens*. Small undeveloped fruit of the Shepherd's tree *Bosicia albitrunca*. It has been suggested that it also feeds on the fruit of the Num-Num tree *Carissa bispinosa*. Livefood in the form of beetles, termites and ants.

Breeding: A solitary nester, choosing a site 1-2m from the ground in a thorn bush. An oval shaped nest is loosely constructed of strong grass and leaves attached, including vegetation which forms the outer shell, the inner shell consisting of fine grass and inflorescences. The entrance is to one side with a slight porch of protruding grass stems. The innermost lining consists of fine grass varying numbers of feathers, mostly from guineafowl or domestic fowl, but Crested Francolin *Francolinus sephaena*, Grey Loerie *Corythaixoides concolor* and Cattle egret *Ardeola ibis* have been recorded. Both sexes continue to bring feathers to the nest during incubation and when young are newly hatched. Eggs white; clutch 3-6, usually 4, incubation period 12-13 days; both sexes incubate; nestling period 16 days; both parents feed the young; host to Shaft-tailed Whydah *Vidua regia*; pair bonds are developed as early as 8 weeks, long before sexual maturity.

Aviculture: Selected Reference CLUTCH 2-6; INCUBATION PERIOD 11-13 days; NESTLING PERIOD 21-25 days. Personal Communication CLUTCH 3; INCUBATION PERIOD 13 days; NESTLING PERIOD 22 days. Nest Record Cards CLUTCH 2,3,3,5 (ARU) 4 (SAANRC) 4,5 (ANRC); INCUBATION PERIOD 11,12 (ARU) 13 (SANRC)) 11,13 days (ANRC); NESTLING PERIOD 21,22 (ARU) 20 (SAANRC) 20,22 days (ANRC). Diet Record Cards WILDFOOD Seeds of Common thatch grass *Hyparrhenia hirta*, Blue panic *Panicum laevifolium*, Guinea grass *P.maximum*, Natal panic *P.natalense*, Broadleaved panic *P.deustem*, Bush panic *P.aequinerve*, Catstail dropseed *Sporobolus pyramidalis*, Annual blue grass *Poa annua*, Carrot seed grass *Tragus berteronianus*, Blue seeds grass *Tricholaena monachne*, Natal redtop *Rhynchelytrum repens*, Lehmann's love grass *Eragrostis lehmanniana*, Berg grass *Setaria appendiculata* (ARU SAADRC ADRC). Personal Communication Guinea grass *Panicum maximum*, Blue buffalo grass *Cenchrus ciliaris*, Natal redtop *Rhychelytrum repens*, Khaki-weed *Alternanthera pungens*. Selected Reference ANIMAL FOOD mealworms, mites. Diet Record Cards Beetle larvae including mealworms (ARU SAADRC ADRC), moths, aphids (ARU), termites (ADRC), wasp larvae or "grubs" (SAADRC).

Purple Grenadier

Uraeginthus ianthinogaster 14cm

Alternative names: Purple Waxbill, Purple-bellied Waxbill.

Description: Male. Forehead, crown, nape chestnut-brown; mantle and back reddish earth-brown; facial mask blue; rump and upper tail-coverts deep mauvish blue; tail black, tinged with mauve; breast, belly and rest of underparts mixed with chestnut-brown and mauvish blue. Female paler overall; facial mask whitish, pale mauve hue; mantle and back greyish brown; underparts tawny grey. Juvenile has plumage pattern basically as adult female, but lacks facial mass.

Males. *U.i.hawkeri* differs from the nominate race in having mantle and wings more russet.

U.i.roosevelti differs from the nominate in having the mantle and wings more darker.

Voice: Described by Williams & Arlott as a weak chirping note.

Habitat: Thick bush, thorn scrub and cultivation.

Distribution: Somalia, northern Kenya and northern Uganda.

U.i.hawkeri south-eastern Sudan, Uganda and northern Kenya.

U.i.roosevelti Kenya.

Feeding: Grass seeds, probably also alate termites.

Breeding: Nest spherical, loosely woven of fine grass, with side entrance, lined with feathers and placed in fork of low bush or shrub. Eggs white; clutch 5.

Aviculture: Selected Reference CLUTCH 3-5; INCUBATION PERIOD 12-14; NESTLING PERIOD 20-22 days. Nest Record Cards CLUTCH 3,4,4 (ARU) 4 (SAANRC) 4 (ANRC); INCUBATION PERIOD 12,12,13 (ARU) 12 (SAANRC) 13 days (ANRC); NESTLING PERIOD 19,21 (ARU) 22, about 21days (SAANRC). Diet Record Cards Guinea grass *Panicum maximum*, Stapf's buffalo grass *P.stapfianum*, White buffalo grass *P.coloratum*, Carrot seed grass *Tragus berteronianus*, Small finger grass *Digitaria argryographta*, Lehmann's love grass *Eragrostis lehmanniana* (ARU SAADRC). Selected Reference ANIMAL FOOD termites. Diet Record Cards termites (ARU SAADRC).

Lavender Waxbill

Estrilda caerulescens 11cm

Alternative names: Bluish Waxbill, Grey-blue astrid, Grey Waxbill, Lavender Finch, Lavender Firefinch, Red-tailed Waxbill, Red-tailed Lavender Waxbill, Vinegar-tail.

Description: Sexes similar. Forehead, crown, nape, mantle and upper back pearl grey; lower back, rump and upper tail-coverts deep rich crimson; tail pale crimson; feathers edged dark grey; flanks dark grey with occasional white spots at ends of feathers; eye stripe black; sides of face, ear-coverts, chin and throat pale grey becoming darker on breast and very dark on belly; under tail-coverts pale crimson; iris dark brown; bill slate-grey; tip black; legs and feet blackish brown. Juvenile paler overall; lacks white spots on flanks.

Voice: Described by Goodwin as a short shrill high-pitched 'squee' or 'tsee'.

Habitat: Short grass in scattered bush and sometimes in cultivation and gardens.

Distribution: Senegal, Central African Republic, Mali, northern Ghana, northern Nigeria, northern Cameroon and south-western Chad.

Feeding: Seeds, mainly of grasses, also of small fruits and insects.

Breeding: Nest a somewhat untidy woven dome shaped construction of seeding grassheads. Five nests examined were about 20cm in diameter with an entrance hole on one side, the funnels were about 5cm long and 3,5cm in diameter which pointed downwards; sited in the forks of trees, three in citrus and two in exotic shrubs. Eggs white; clutch 4-6.

Aviculture: Selected Reference CLUTCH 3-6; INCUBATION PERIOD 11-12 days; NESTLING PERIOD 14-20 days. Personal Communication CLUTCH 3-5; INCUBATION PERIOD 12,12 days; NESTLING PERIOD 18,19 days. Nest Record Cards CLUTCH 4,4,5 (ARU) 3,4,4 (SAANRC) 4,4,5 (ANRC); INCUBATION PERIOD 11,12,12 (ARU) 12,12,12, (SAANRC) 11,12 days (ANRC); NESTLING PERIOD 18,19, about 19 (ARU) 18,19 SAANRC 18,20 days (ANRC). Selected Reference WILDFOOD chickweed *Stellaria* sp., seeds of turf grass *Ehrharta calycina*, Finger Crabgrass *Digitaria sanguinalis*, Johnson grass *Sorghum halepense*, Rye grass *Lolium perenne*, Personal Communication WILDFOOD Foxtail Bristle grass *Setaria italica*, Crab grass *Digitaria sanguinalis*. Nest Record Cards Guinea grass *Panicum maximum* (ARU ADRC). *P.astrosanguineum* (SAADRC). Selected Reference ANIMAL FOOD termites, fresh ants' eggs.

Grey Waxbill
Estrilda perreini 10,5cm

Alternative names: Black-tailed Lavender, Black-tailed Waxbill, Black-tailed Grey Waxbill, Perrein's Waxbill.

Description: Sexes similar. Crown, nape, mantle, sides of face, breast and upper belly grey; stripe behind eye and chin black; lower belly and under tail-coverts blackish slate; lower rump and upper tail-coverts red; tail black; iris red; bill blue, grey tip; legs and feet black. Juvenile similar to adult, but lacks stripe behind eye; rump paler red.

Adults. *E.p.incana* differs from nominate race in being pale overall.

E.p. torrida differs from nominate in having crown, nape, mantle, sides of face, breast and upper belly light grey; lower rump and upper tail-coverts cherry-red.

Voice: Described by Maclean as a thin, slightly explosive pseeu, pseeu.

Habitat: The edges of moist evergreen forest and mixed woodland.

Distribution: Gabon to northern Angola to Tanzania.

E.p.incana coastal regions and lower midlands of KwaZulu-Natal and Mpumalanga, South Africa to Swaziland, southern Mozambique and eastern Zimbabwe.

E.p.torrida Mozambique and Malawi (Shire River).

Feeding: Seeds of grasses, fruits and small insects, notably termites. Seeds of Guinea grass *Panicum maximum*, Casuarina *Casuarina equisetifolia* and fruit of Marula *Schlerocarya caffra*.

Breeding: Nests are placed 3-5m from the ground in a tree, bush or bamboo stand. The roughly constructed retort shaped nest is composed of dried grasses and seedheads and lined with fine grasses and feathers. A short entrance tunnel protrudes from the top of the nest. Recorded utilizing a Sweet thorn *Acacia karoo* as a nesting site. Also recorded utilizing and relining the nest of other waxbills and weavers, for example the Forest Weaver *Symplectes bicolor*. Both birds share the work of nest building, the male collecting the materials and the female arranging the lining. Eggs white; clutch 2-5, usually 4-5; both parents feed the young; nestling period 19-21 days.

Aviculture: Selected Reference CLUTCH 2-8; INCUBATION PERIOD; NESTLING PERIOD about 21 days. Personal Communication CLUTCH 2,5; INCUBATION PERIOD 12,12 days; NESTLING PERIOD 19,20 days. Nest Record Cards CLUTCH 4,5 (ARU) 4 (SAANRC); INCUBATION PERIOD 12,12 (ARU) 12 days (SAANRC); NESTLING PERIOD 18,21 (ARU) close to 20 days (SAANRC). Diet Record Cards WILDFOOD Seeds of Blue panic *Panicum laevifolium*, Guinea grass *P.maximum*, Bushveld signal grass *Urochloa mosambicensis*, Blue seed grass *Tricholaena monachne*, Natal redtop *Rhynchelytrum repens*, Popo grass *Hyparrhenia cymbaria*, Bird grass *Poa trivialis* (SAADRC ARU), aphids, wasp larvae or "grubs", termites (ARU).

Cinderella Waxbill
Estrilda thomensis 11cm

Alternative names: Neumann's Waxbill, Red-flanked Lavender Finch, São Thomé Waxbill.

Description: Sexes similar. Crown, nape and sides of face pale grey with pinkish wash; mantle and upper back grey; lower back, rump and upper tail-coverts crimson; tail black, outer webs crimson; chin and throat whitish, turning to greyish white on upper breast, washed with pink; lower breast grey; flanks crimson; iris reddish brown; bill red, tip black; legs and feet black. Juvenile similar to adult, but lacks stripe behind the eye, upper tail coverts, flanks and lower abdomen paler scarlet; bill greyish white.

Voice: Described by Maclean as a soft thrilling 'tree' or 'kerr'.

Habitat: Low dense scrub and bushes in savanna country.

Distribution: Cunene River (Lower Valley) on Angola/Namibian border. São Thomé (originally introduced and possibly now extinct).

Feeding: Grass seeds and insects, mainly small ants.

Breeding: Not known.

Aviculture: Selected Reference CLUTCH 4-6; INCUBATION PERIOD 13-15 days; NESTLING PERIOD 18-20 days. Personal Communication CLUTCH 4; INCUBATION PERIOD 13 days; NESTLING PERIOD 18 days. Personal Communication WILDFOOD Rye grass *Lolium perenne*, seeds of Blue panic *Panicum laevifolium*, Natal redtop *Rhychelytrum repens*, Guinea grass *Panicum maximum*, Small Panicum *P.coloratum*, Volvoet Panicum *P.lanipes*. Selected Reference ANIMAL FOOD pupae of Meadow ants *Lasius* sp., spiders, termites, aphids, mealworms.

Swee Waxbill

Estrilda melanotis 9cm

Alternative names: Black-faced Swee, Dufresne's Waxbill.
***E.m.quartinia* Yellowbellied Waxbill.**
***E.m.kilimensis* East African Swee, Green Waxbill.**

Description: Male. Forehead, crown, nape and upper mantle grey; lores, ear-coverts, side of face and upper throat black; mantle and wing-coverts olivaceous green; rump and upper tail-coverts red; tail blackish; lower throat, breast and flanks pale grey; belly and under tail-coverts grey, washed with pale yellow; iris red; bill, upper mandible black, lower red; legs and feet blackish. Female lacks the facial mask in male; chin and upper throat pale grey. Juvenile similar to adult female, but paler in colour; rump green; bill blackish.

Males. *E.m.bocagei* differs from the nominate race in being more distinctly barred on the mantle scapulars and wing-coverts; belly and under tail-coverts lemon-yellow.

E.m.quartinia Forehead, crown, nape and sides of face grey; chin and throat pale grey; rump and upper tail-coverts scarlet; underparts greenish yellow, deeper on centre of belly.

E.m.kilimensis differs from *quartinia* in being slightly more olivaceous on the mantle.

E.m.stuartirwini similar to *kilimensis*, but crown, nape and hindneck are markedly paler and more bluish grey; mantle and wing-coverts pale green rather than olive-brown; rump and upper tail-coverts less crimson; flanks less dusky.

Voice: Described by Maclean as soft 'swee swee' call notes; sharp teerrr alarm note.

Habitat: Thick low undergrowth on the forest edge; in bush along riverine forest at higher elevations; also found in gardens and cultivation.

Distribution: South-eastern Zimbabwe, Mozambique (Lebombo Mountain Range), Lesotho, Swaziland and South Africa in North-West, Gauteng, Mpumalanga, Northern Province (scattered), western Cape, eastern Free State and KwaZulu-Natal.

E.m.bocagei western Angola and northern Namibia.

E.m.quartinia Highlands of Eritrea, Ethiopia and south-eastern Sudan.

E.m.kilimensis northern Tanzania (Pare Mountains), highlands of Kenya, Uganda and eastern Zaire.

E.m.stuartirwini eastern Zimbabwe (highlands) and Mozambique.

Feeding: Feeds largely on grass seeds, including Natal redtop *Rhynchelytrum repens*, Blue finger grass *Digitaria stentiana* and Guinea grass *Panicum maximum*.

Breeding: Constructs a rather flimsy, pear-shaped nest of dry grass with the entrance hole at one and thickly lined with grass seedheads and feathers. The nest may be sited in the fork of a tree or shrub, often in a conspicuous location in the garden around houses. A pair were observed being victimized by Bronze Mannikins *Lonchura cucullata* who completed the nest with long grass stems. The nest of Yellow-bellied Waxbills was built in a wild ginger bush about 2m above the ground. The entrance at the one side was not concealed They also observed nesting in a fir tree. Eggs white; clutch 3-5, up to 9 recorded, probably due to 2 females laying in the same nest; both sexes incubate; both adults feed the young; host to the Pin-tailed Whydah *Vidua macroura.*

Aviculture: Selected Reference CLUTCH 3-5, up to 10, probably due to 2 females laying; Personal Communication CLUTCH 4,4; INCUBATION PERIOD 12,13 days; (NASNRC); INCUBATION PERIOD 11,12,12 (ARU) 12,12 days (SAANRC); NESTLING PERIOD 18,20 (ARU) after 16,19 days (SAANRC). Selected Reference WILDFOOD Sow Thistle *Sonchus oleraceus*, dandelion *Taraxacum* sp., chickweed *Stellaria* sp., Chicory *Cichorium intybus*, seeds of Natal redtop *Rhynchelytrum repens*, Guinea grass *Panicum maximum*, Blue panic *P.laevifolium*, Hay *Chloris virgata*, Golden setaria *Setaria sphacelata*, Dropseed grass *Sporobolus fimbriatus*, Blue finger grass *Digitaria stentiana*. Diet Records Cards WILDFOOD Seeds of Natal redtop *Rhynchelytrum repens*, Guinea grass *Panicum maximum*, Blue panic *P.laevifolium*, Hay *Chloris virgata*, Golden setaria *Setaria sphacelata*, Dropseed grass *Sporobolus fimbriatus*, Blue finger grass *Digitaria stentiana*, Crab finger grass *Digitaria sanguinalis* (ARU SAADRC ANRC). Personal Communication WILDFOOD Guinea grass *Panicum maximum*, Natal redtop *Rhynchelytrum repens*. Selected Reference ANIMAL FOOD whiteworms, spiders, green aphids. Diet Record Cards termites, mealworms (SAADRC ARU), moths, aphids (SAADRC) fishmoths, Thrips-nymphs (ARU).

Anambra Waxbill
Estrilda poliopareia 12cm

Description: Male. Forehead yellowish buff; crown and nape greyish brown; mantle pale brown; back, rump and upper tail-coverts pale orange-red; tail blackish, tinged reddish; flanks buffish yellow, tinged pale reddish; sides of face and ear-coverts light buffish brown; throat buffish white; breast and belly yellowish buff, centre richer buff; iris cream to yellowish; bill red; legs and feet greyish brown. Female has underparts greyish yellow; flanks plain buffish yellow; rump and upper tail-coverts paler, more orange, less red. Juvenile similar to adult female, but underparts greyish, less yellow; bill dusky horn.

Voice: Described by João as a soft *'tyep'*; also sharp *'thick'.*

Habitat: Open deciduous forest with rank grass.

Distribution: South-eastern Nigeria (Onitsha and Asaba districts.)

Feeding: Grass seeds and insects, notably gnats.

Breeding: Not known.

Aviculture: Personal Communication CLUTCH 4; INCUBATION PERIOD 13 days; NESTLING PERIOD

19 days. Personal Communication ANIMAL FOOD gnats, termites.

Fawn-breasted Waxbill
Estrilda paludicola 10-11cm

Alternative names: Buff-bellied Waxbill; Marsh Waxbill.
E.p.ochrogaster **Abyssinian Fawn-breasted Waxbill, Ethiopian Fawn-breasted Waxbill.**

Description: Sexes similar. Forehead and crown dark grey; nape, mantle and back reddish brown; lower rump and upper tail-coverts red; tail black, feathers edged whitish; ear-coverts pale grey; chin and throat yellowish buff; breast pale greyish brown; centre and lower belly patch wine-red; rest of underparts yellowish buff; iris red; bill orange-red; legs and feet dark brown. Juvenile similar to adult, but paler overall; bill blackish. Adults. *E.p.ochrogaster* differs from the nominate race in having underparts heavily suffused with rich golden-buff.

E.p.roseicrissa differs from the nominate in having upperparts warmer russet brown; belly reddish purple.

E.p.marwitzi differs from the nominate in having rump less bright red.

E.p.benguellensis differs from the nominate in having crown washed with olive-yellow.

E.p.ruthae differs from the nominate in having upperparts paler; underparts white.

Voice: Described by Rutgers & Norris as *'teck-teck-tech.'*

Habitat: Moist grasslands, forest edges and overgrown cultivation.

Distribution: Northern Zaire, northern Uganda and southern Sudan

E.p.ochrogaster Ethiopia and south-eastern Sudan

E.p.roseicrissa southern Uganda, north-western Tanzania.

E.p.marwitzi western Tanzania.

E.p.benguellensis Angola and northern Zambia.

E.p.ruthae central Zaire.

Feeding: Grass seeds and insects.

Breeding: A spherical nest built of grass and sometimes with short projecting porch and occasionally a 'cock' nest above the roof of the real nest. Placed on or just off the ground in tall grass, *benguellensis* in thick growth such as the Bracken fern *Pteridium aquilinum* and Wild Ginger *Aframomum* sp. Eggs white; clutch usually 5-6 *benguellensis* 4.

Aviculture: Personal Communication CLUTCH 4,4; INCUBATION PERIOD 13,13 days; NESTLING PERIOD 20,21 days. Nest Record Cards CLUTCH 4

Swee Waxbill (male)

Pin-tailed Whydah (male)

Cutthroat Finch (pair)

Lemon-breasted Canary (male)

Zebra Waxbill (male)

Yellow-eyed Canary

Dybowski's Twinspot

Red-backed Mannikin

Blue-capped Waxbill (male)

Red-billed Firefinch (male)

Red-cheeked Cordon-Bleu (male)

Red-eared Waxbill

Rosy-rumped Waxbill

Crimson-winged Pytilia (male)

Red-bellied Parrot (male)

Pied Mannikin (male)

Yellow Canary (male)

Meyer's Parrot

Black-winged Lovebird (male)

Red Bishop (male)

Black-cheeked Waxbill (male)

Red-billed Quelea (male)

Orange-cheeked Waxbill

Lavender Waxbill

Jardine's Parrot

Cape Parrot (pair)

Golden Bishop (male)

Black-crowned Waxbill

Bronze Mannikin (pair)

Cordon-bleu (male)

Melba Finch (male)

Namaqua Dove (male)

Grey-headed Olive Back

Green-backed Twinspot (male)

Peter's Twinspot (male)

Violet-eared Grenadier (male)

Common Waxbill

Tambourine Dove (pair)

Black-cheeked Lovebird

Black-bellied Firefinch (male)

Peach-faced Lovebird

Red-shouldered Widow (male)

Red-headed Finch (pair)

Brown-headed Parrot

Sudan Golden Sparrow (male)

White-rumped Seedeater (pair)

Orange Bishop (pair)

(ARU) 4 (ANRC); INCUBATION PERIOD 13 (ARU) 12 days (ARU); NESTLING PERIOD 20 (ARU) 19 days (ANRC). Diet Record Cards WILDFOOD Guinea grass *Panicum maximum* (ARU ADRC), Blue panic *P.laevifolium* (ADRC). Selected Reference ANIMAL FOOD ant pupae, termites. Diet Record Cards termites (ARU ADRC), wasp larvae or "grubs", gnats (ADRC).

Orange-cheeked Waxbill

Estrilda melpoda 8-10cm

Alternative names: Orange-cheeked Finch, Red-cheeked Waxbill.

Description: Sexes similar. Forehead, crown and nape grey; hindneck, mantle, wing-coverts with scapulars and upper rump brown; lower rump and upper tail-coverts crimson; lores, round eyes, sides of face and ear-coverts reddish orange; wings dusky, edged brown; tail blackish; chin and throat whitish; centre of belly whitish or buffish yellow; iris brown; bill pale yellow; legs and feet brown. Juvenile upperparts pale greyish brown; underparts paler buffish; bill blackish.

Adult. *E.m.tschadensis* differs from the nominate race in having paler cheek patches.

Voice: Described by Mackworth-Praed & Grant as a shrill sort of 'see-whee-zee-whee'.

Habitat: Savanna, forest clearings and cultivation.

Distribution: Senegal to northern Zaire, northern Angola and Zambia.

E.m.tschadensis Cameroon and Chad.

Feeding: Grass seeds and insects, notably aphids.

Breeding: Constructs an untidy bottle-shaped nest with a diameter of 10-20cm, and with a short tubular side entrance tunnel. Grass stems, blades and the seeding heads being the main materials used and then lined with feathers. Often a 'cock's' nest is built above the roof of the real nest. Both partners share in the construction, the male collecting, the female arranging. Nests are usually well hidden on or near the ground. Eggs white; clutch 3-7, usually 4-6; both sexes incubate in turn, at night female only, but male may spend the night in the nest as well.

Aviculture: Selected Reference CLUTCH 3-7; INCUBATION PERIOD 12 days; NESTLING PERIOD 20-21 days. Personal Communication CLUTCH 3,4,4; INCUBATION PERIOD 11,11,12 days; NESTLING PERIOD 20,20, before 22 days. Nest Record Cards CLUTCH 3,3,5,7(ARU) 4,4,6 (SAANRC) 4,4,5 (NASNRC) 4,7 (ANRC); INCUBATION PERIOD 11,11,12,12,12 (ARU) 11,12 (SAANRC) 12,12 days (NASNRC);

NESTLING PERIOD 18,20 (ARU) 20,20,21 (SAANRC) 20 days (ANRC). Personal Communication WILDFOOD African Veldt grass *Ehrharta calycira*, Guinea grass *Panicum maximum*, Blue panic *P.laevifolium*, Natal panic *P.natalense*, Small finger grass *Digitaria argyrograpta*, Bushveld signal grass *Urochloa mosambicensis*, Carrotseed grass *Tragus berteronianus*, Bushveld dropseed *Sporobolus fimbiatus*, Annual bluegrass *Poa annua*. Diet Record Cards Guinea grass *Panicum maximum* (ARU SAADRC NASDRC), Broadleaved panic *P.deustum* (SAADRC), Blue panic *P.laevifolium*, Dropseed grass *Sporobolus fimbiatus* (NASDRC), Buffalo grass *Panicum stapfianum* (ARU SAADRC). Selected Reference ANIMAL FOOD termites, green aphids, mealworms. Diet Record Cards aphids, termites (ARU), Driver Ants (ADRC), fishmoths (SAADRC).

Rosy-rumped Waxbill

Estrilda rhodopyga 10cm

Alternative names; Crimson-rumped Waxbill, Rosy-winged Waxbill, Sundevall's Waxbill.

Description: Sexes similar. Forehead, crown and nape greyish brown; sides of face creamy buff; mantle and back brownish grey, throughout closely and narrowly barred with brown; rump and upper tail-coverts and central tail feathers crimson; under wing-coverts pinkish buff; chin and throat creamy buff; breast and belly buff with indistinct barring on flanks; iris reddish brown; bill blackish, base reddish; legs and feet dark brown.

E.r.centralis differs from the nominate race in being darker overall.

Juvenile similar to adult, but lacks barring on feathers and crimson parts paler.

Voice: Described by Williams and Arlott as a weak 'tssp' call.

Habitat: Grasslands, abandoned cultivation, small marshes with thick grass and undergrowth.

Distribution: Sudan, Ethiopia and northern Somalia.

Feeding: Small grass seeds and insects and ant larvae.

Breeding: A single nest was found to be built on grassheads, with a lateral entrance, on the ground in short grass. The male was incubating 6 eggs of which 2 were bigger than the others.

Aviculture: Nest Record Cards CLUTCH 4,4,6 (ANRC); INCUBATION PERIOD 11,12 days (ANRC); NESTLING PERIOD 18,19 days (ANRC). Selected Reference WILDFOOD Annual meadow grass *Poa annua*, Knot-grass *Polygonum aviculare*. Selected Reference ANIMAL FOOD mealworms, spiders. Diet Record Card termites (ADRC).

Red-eared Waxbill

Estrilda troglodytes 10cm

Alternative names: Black-rumped Waxbill, Coralbeak, Grey-cheeked Waxbill, Pink-cheeked Waxbill, Red-cheeked Waxbill, Senegal Waxbill.

Description: Sexes similar. Forehead, crown, nape, mantle and back greyish tawny, with very indistinct close narrow barring; rump, upper tail-coverts and tail black; under wing-coverts pale buffish; eye stripe scarlet; ear-coverts white, tinged pinkish; chin and throat, tinged pinkish; breast, belly and flanks buffish, tinged pinkish; a small crimson patch in centre of lower belly; under tail-coverts buffish white; iris reddish brown; bill red; legs and feet blackish brown or purplish brown. Juvenile ground colours as adult, but lacks eye stripe; bill black.

Voice: Described by Serle as a characteristic drawn-out 'tsooeet' frequently uttered.

Habitat: Savanna woodland, riparian thickets and rice cultivation.

Distribution: Senegal to Ethiopia.

Feeding: Grass seeds and insects, especially midges.

Breeding: Nest oval or pear-shaped with lateral entrance and 'cock's' nest, which has no concealed entrance tube is built on top or on one side of the breeding nest. Constructed of dry grassheads on the ground or in a tuft of grass. Eggs white; clutch 3-6.

Aviculture: Selected Reference CLUTCH 2-7; INCUBATION PERIOD 11-14 days; NESTLING PERIOD 17-21 days. Personal Communication CLUTCH 4-6; INCUBATION PERIOD 11,12 days; NESTLING PERIOD 18,19 days. Nest Record Cards CLUTCH 3,3,4,4,4,5,6 (ARU) 4,4 (SAANRC) 4,5 (NASNRC) 4,4,5 (ARU) 3,5,5 (ANRC); NESTLING PERIOD 17,19,20 (SAANRC) 17 (NASNRC) about 20 (ARU) 19,20 days (ANRC). Selected Reference WILDFOOD Seeds of Annual meadow grass *Poa annua*, Chickweed *Stellaria media*, Knot-grass *Polygonum aviculture*, dandelion *Taraxacum* sp., Sheperd's purse *Capsella bursa-pastoris*. Selected Reference ANIMAL FOOD green aphids, Buffalo worms, pupae of Meadow ants *Lasius* sp., termites, whiteworms, daphnias. Diet Record Cards termites (SAADRC ARU ADRC).

Common Waxbill

Estrilda astrild 13cm

Alternative names: Barred Waxbill, Brown Waxbill, Common African Waxbill, Astrild
E.a.jagoensis Cape Verde Island Waxbill, St Helena Waxbill.
E.a.rubriventris Gabon Waxbill.

E.a.kempi Kemp's Sierra Leone Waxbill.
E.a.occidentalis Cameroon Waxbill, Pheasant Finch, Red-bellied Waxbill.

Description: Male. Forehead and nape pale greyish brown, closely and narrowly barred with black; mantle, back, upper tail-coverts, tail and wings greyish, more coarsely barred; lores and through eye streaked bright crimson; throat and ear-coverts greyish white; breast and flanks greyish white; tinged with buff and finely barred with brown; centre of breast and belly pale crimson red; under tail-coverts blackish; iris and bill red; legs and feet black. Female similar to male, but centre of breast and belly paler crimson-red. Juvenile similar to adult female, but indistinctly barred on underparts; streaked through eye, centre of breast and belly pinkish red.

Males. *E.a.kempi* nearest to *occidentalis*, but less rufous; barring and more sharply distinct.

E.a.sousae nearest to *angolensis* and quite possible identical.

E.a.peasei similar to *cavendishi*, but longer tailed; flanks darker; breast pink with little or no barring; belly paler red.

E.a.macmillani similar to *occidentalis*, but upperparts paler and clear pinkish breast and belly.

E.a.cavendishi similar to *minor*, but upperparts browner; larger black patch on lower belly.

E.a.angolensis similar to *cavendishi*, but flanks more heavily washed with pink.

E.a.occidentalis differs from the nominate race in having throat and ear-coverts white to whitish; centre of breast and belly pinkish red.

E.a.minor throat and ear-coverts greyish white; belly rose-red.

E.a.ngamiensis ear-coverts whitish; throat whitish or pinkish white.

E.a.rubriventris throat and ear-coverts pink; breast and belly suffused with deep rose-red.

E.a.damarensis upperparts paler, especially the forehead, crown and upper tail-coverts; throat and upper breast also paler; centre of breast and belly paler red.

E.a.tenebridorsa mantle and back darker, less marked by barring, and strongly washed with olivaceous brown.

Voice: Described by Maclean as a somewhat nasal ching ching ching call notes.

Habitat: Frequents savanna, woodland, rank vegetation in damp localities, cultivation, gardens and in the vicinity of human dwellings.

Distribution: South-eastern Botswana and the South African provinces of North-West (western and south-western), Cape (north and south of Orange River) and western Free State.

E.a.kempi Sierra Leone and Liberia.

E.a.soursa São Thomé Island.

E.a.peasei Ethiopia.

E.a.macmillani southern Sudan and Ethiopia.

E.a.cavendeshi central and south-eastern Tanzania, Zambia, Zimbabwe, Malawi, Mozambique and the South African provinces of eastern Mpumalanga and north-eastern KwaZulu-Natal.

E.a.angolensis western Angola and southern Zaire.

E.a.occidentallis Fernando Pó Island, Cameroon to northern Zaire.

E.a.minor eastern Kenya to north-eastern Tanzania, Mafia and Zanzibar Islands.

E.a.ngamiensis eastern Angola, northern and north-eastern Namibia, the Caprivi Strip and northern Botswana east to north-western Zimbabwe.

E.a.rubriventris Gabon to the Congo mouth.

E.a.damarensis Namibia (absent in north-east) and south African province of north-western Cape (on lower Orange River).

E.a.tenebridorsa southern Mozambique, Swaziland, Lesotho (highlands), and the provinces of Gauteng, Mpumalanga, eastern Free State and KwaZulu-Natal, South Africa.

Feeding: Grass seeds, fruit and small insects. Oren & Smith report that birds introduced to Brazil feed mainly on seeds of Guinea grass *Panicum maximum*, *P.purpurreum*, Vlei grass *Sporobolus indictus*, *Digitaria horozontalis* and *Echinochloa* spp., a sedge *Cyperus surinamensis* and *Amaranthus spinosus*. Southern African records include Blue panic *Panicum laevifolium*, Bushveld signal grass *Urochloa mosambicensis*, Blue seed grass *Tricholaena monachne*, Natal redrop *Rhynchelytrum repens*, Bur-bristle grass *Setaria verticillata*, Blue water bush *Verbena bonariensis*, *Casuarina Casuarina equisetfolia* and ripe fruit of Sycamore fig *Ficus sycamorus*.

Breeding: A large pear-shaped loosely woven dried grass nest is constructed with a well concealed entrance hole, placed mostly low down at about 1-4m from the ground in a bush, creeper or tuft of grass, often over water. On top of the main nest an additional chamber known as the "cock's nest" is constructed which is used as a dormitory for nearly-fledged young to roost in. It is reported that a bare patch of ground is usually visible in front of the main nest, suggesting that harmful elements, notably small biting ants can be controlled before reaching the nest entrance. Both sexes construct the nest, but the female confines her duties to the lining with the placing of soft down and a few feathers. Eggs white; clutch 4-6, 9 on record, probably 2 females laying in the same nest; both sexes incubate; incubation period 11-12 days; nestling period 17-21 days; parasitised by Pin-tailed Whydah *Vidua macroura*.

Aviculture: Selected Reference CLUTCH 3-7; INCUBATION PERIOD 11-12days; NESTLING PERIOD 21 days. Personal Communication CLUTCH 4,4,5; INCUBATION PERIOD 12,12,12, days; NESTLING PERIOD 18,20,20 days. Nest Record Cards CLUTCH 4,6,6 (ARU) 3,4,4,5 (SAANRC); INCUBATION PERIOD 11,12,12 (ARU) 11,12,12,12 (SAANRC) 11,12,12,

12,12 days (ARU); NESTLING PERIOD 17,19,20 (ARU) 17,19 days (SAANRC). Diet Record Cards WILDFOOD Seeds of Blue panic *Panicum laevifolium*, Guinea grass *P.maximum*, Bushveld signal grass *Urochloa mosambicensis*, Blue seed grass *Tricholaena monachne*, Natal redtop *Rhynchelytrum repens*, Bur-bristle grass *Setaria verticillata*, Golden setaria *S.sphacelata*, Popo grass *Hyparrhenia cymbaria*, Teff grass *Eragrostis tef*, Lehmann's love grass *E.lehmanniana*, Hay *Chloris virgata* (ARU SAADRC) Personal Communication Couch grass *Cynodon dactylon*, Natal panic *Panicum natalense*, Guinea grass *P.maximum*. Selected Reference ANIMAL FOOD mealworms, termites. moths, maggots. Diet Record Cards thrips-nymphs (SAADRC), moths, mealworms, termites, fly larvae or "maggots" (ARU).

Black-faced Waxbill

Estrilda nigriloris 10cm

Alternative name: Black-lored Waxbill.

Description: Male. Forehead, crown and nape greyish brown; mantle, back and rump dark brown, tinged with pink and finely barred light brown; flight feathers and wing-coverts dark brown, edged olive-brown; ear-coverts, chin and throat pale pinkish white; narrow upper pale pink and lower broad eye-stripe black; throat and upper breast, tinged pinkish mauve; under tail-coverts black; iris brown; bill scarlet-red; legs and feet brown. Juvenile paler overall, indistinct barring; bill, legs and feet blackish. Female similar to male, but paler brown throat and upper breast, tinged pink.

Voice: Described by João pers.comm. as a loud 'terree' when alarmed, normally 'teep'.

Habitat: Damper parts of grasslands and matted bush.

Distribution: Southern Zaire.

Feeding: Small grass seeds.

Breeding: Not known.

Aviculture: Nest Record Cards CLUTCH 4,4 (ARU); INCUBATION PERIOD 12,12 days (ARU); NESTLING PERIOD 17,20 days (ARU). Diet Record Cards Guinea grass *Panicum maximum*, Broadleaved panic *P.deustum* (ARU). Diet Record Cards ANIMAL FOOD termites, aphids, mealworms (ARU).

Black-crowned Waxbill

Estrilda nonnula 10cm

Alternative names: Black-capped Waxbill, White-breasted Waxbill.

Description: Male. Forehead, crown, nape and around eyes black; hindneck and sides of face greyish white;

mantle, upper back and wing-coverts bluish grey, barred dark grey; lower back, rump and upper tail-coverts rosy crimson; underwing-coverts silvery white; tail black; chin, throat, breast and belly slate-grey; iris dark brown; bill, upper mandible black, lower red; legs and feet blackish. Female similar to male, but upperparts paler and usually less crimson on flanks. Juvenile upperparts buffish brown; bill black.

E.n.elizae differs from the nominate race in having underparts greyer and darker.

E.n.eisentrauti as *elizae* but smaller.

Voice: Described by Goodwin as having the contract call '*tseee-tseee*' or '*tseee-tseee-tseee*'.

Habitat: Grasslands, neglected cultivation and gardens

Distribution: Eastern Cameroon to Sudan, Kenya and Tanzania.

E.n.elizae Fernando Pó Island.

E.n.eisentrauti Mount Cameroon.

Feeding: Grass seeds *Setaria* sp., buds, cultivated millet and tiny insects including red ants.

Breeding: Nest is placed in a shrub, creeper, hedge, tree or in grass tuft, up to 6m above the ground. The oval nest is built of grasses and other plant stems with small porch at lateral entrance and then lined with feathers and other soft materials. More than one pair may nest in some location. A cock's nest is usually built on top of the real nest. Eggs white; clutch 3-6.

Aviculture: Selected Reference CLUTCH 3-6; INCUBATION PERIOD 11-15 days; NESTLING PERIOD 17-21 days. Nest Record Cards CLUTCH 3,6,6 (ANRC); INCUBATION PERIOD 11, about 12,12,13 (ANRC); NESTLING PERIOD 17,18 after 18,20 days (ANRC). Selected Reference WILDFOOD. Persicaria *Polygonum persicaria*, Wood melock *Melica uniflora*. Rye grass *Lolium perenne*, Chickweed *Stellaria media*, dandelion *Taraxacum* sp., Annual meadow grass *Póa annua*, Knot-grass *Polygonum avicuture*. Diet Record Cards Guinea grass *Panicum maximum*, Natal panic *P.natalense*, Blue panic *P.laevifolium*, Creeping setaria *Setaria flabellata*, Golden setaria *S.sphacelata*, Chickweed *Stellaria media* (ADRC). Selected Reference ANIMAL FOOD green aphids, mealworms, water fleas *Drosophila*. Diet Record Cards termites aphids, mealworms, wasp larvae or "grubs" (ADRC).

Black-headed Waxbill

Estrilda articapilla 10cm

Alternative names: Grey-breasted Waxbill.
E.a.kandti **Kandt's Waxbill**

Description: Male. Forehead, crown, nape, sides of face and round eye black; sides of neck white; mantle, back and wing-coverts dark bluish grey, barred black; rump and upper tail-coverts black; flanks crimson; iris

dark brown; bill black, base red; legs and feet blackish. Female has mantle and back browner, crimson parts paler. Juvenile has mantle and back dusky brown; lacks crimson parts; bill black.

Males. *E.a.kandti* differs from the nominate in having more narrowly spaces barring on back; rump darker crimson.

E.a.marungensis similar to *avakubi*, but sides of face greyer.

E.a.avakubi differs from the nominate in being paler, particularly on sides of face and throat; rump brighter red.

Voice: Described by Guggisberg as having a twittering call.

Habitat: Forest edges, grassy clearings in forest belt and bamboo.

Distribution: South-eastern Nigeria, southern Cameroon, Gabon and north eastern Zaire.

E.a.marungensis Marunga.

E.a.avakubi north-eastern Angola.

E.a.kandti eastern Zaire, Uganda and Kenya.

Feeding: Seeds of grasses and sedges. The contents on one crop contained small ants.

Breeding: An untidy 'water bottle shaped' nest made entirely of seeding grassheads and line with feathers is placed about 2-3 above the ground in the fork of a leafy shrub of tree. Eggs pinkish white; clutch 2-5.

Aviculture: Personal Communication CLUTCH 3; INCUBATION PERIOD 12 days; NESTLING PERIOD 19 days. Nest Record Card CLUTCH 4; INCUBATION PERIOD 12 days; NESTLING PERIOD 20 days.

Black-cheeked Waxbill

Estrilda erythronotos 13 cm

Alternative names: Black-eared Cordon-bleu, Black-faced Waxbill, Black-cheeked Grenadier.

Description: Male. Forehead, crown, nape and sides of neck, mantle and back pinkish grey; tail black; rump and upper tail-coverts claret-red lores, round eyes, sides of face and ear-coverts black; sides of belly and flanks claret-red; centre of belly and under tail-coverts black; throat and belly pinkish grey, indistinctly barred dusky; iris red; bill, legs and feet black. Female slightly paler overall, especially belly and flanks. Juvenile has throat and belly greyish; iris brown.

Males. *E.e.delamerei* differs from the nominate race in being darker overall.

E.r.soligena differs from the nominate in having the forehead, crown, nape and mantle paler grey and more strongly washed with claret; rump and upper tail-coverts paler claret; wing-coverts barred brownish of buffy; throat and upper breast grey, finely barred with black, washed with claret; less black on centre of belly.

Voice: Described by Newman as a ascending 'fwooee'.

Habitat: Largely confined to dry acacia thornveld.

Distribution: South-western Zambia, northern Botswana, Zimbabwe, south-eastern Angola and South Africa in northern Cape, western Free State and western Northern Province.

E.e.delamerei southern Uganda to Kenya and Tanzania.

E.e.soligena northern Cape, South Africa, Angola, north-western Botswana and central and northern Namibia.

Feeding: Seeds and insects, namely by termites, caterpillars and small beetles. Seeds of Blue panic Panicum laevifolium, Guinea grass P.maximum, Bushveld signal grass Urochloa mosambicensis, Bur-bristle grass Setaria verticillata, Blue buffalo grass Cenchrus cillaris. Removes flower petals from Apricot Prunus armeniaca and Australian silky oak Grevillea robusta.

Breeding: The site is usually in dense thorn bush between 4-6m above the ground. The nest is a large untidy grass ball with a long entrance tunnel facing downwards with dry grass culms protruding from the entrance. One nest contained mostly Guinea grass Panicum maximum as the outer shell and thickly lined with bristle grass Aristida sp., and Natal redtop Rhynchelytrum repens. The nest chamber is well lined with Eragrostis barbinodis, Natal redtop and Blue seed grass Tricholaena moncahane. In one observation the tunnel entrance contained a few grey feathers with four guineafowl feathers inside. The "cock's" nest was attached to the roof of the breeding nest, and contained bits of snail shell. Only the male was observed carrying nestling materials, the female sat in a tree nearby. Eggs white; clutch 3-6; both sexes incubate; incubation period 12 days; nestling period 22 days; young cared for by both parents.

Aviculture: Selected Reference CLUTCH 3-6; INCUBATION PERIOD 12 days; NESTLING PERIOD 22 days. Personal Communication CLUTCH 4,6; INCUBATION PERIOD 12,12 days; NESTLING PERIOD 21,22 days. Nest Record Cards CLUTCH 4 (ARU) 4,6 (ANRC); INCUBATION PERIOD 12 (ARU) 12,12 days (ANRC); NESTLING PERIOD 21 (ARU) 21, about 20 days (ANRC). Diet Record Cards WILDFOOD Seeds of Guinea grass Panicum maximum, Blue Panic P.laevifolium, Carrot seed grass Tragus berteronianus, Blue seed grass Tricholaena monachne, Rolling grass T.grandiglumis, Tassel bristle grass A.congesta, Teff grass Eragrostis tef (ARU ADRC). Personal Communication Guinea grass Panicum maximum, Blue buffalo grass Cenchrus cillaris. Selected Reference ANIMAL FOOD aphids, blowfly pupae. Diet Record Cards small black beetles, including larvae and also mealworms (ADRC), fly larvae or "maggots", termites (ARU).

Pink-bellied Black-cheeked Waxbill
Estrilda charmosyna 13cm

Alternative name: Pink-bellied Black-faced Waxbill.

Description: Male. Forehead whitish; crown, nape, mantle and back pinkish grey; rump and upper tail-coverts claret-red; tail black, tinged golden; wings greyish barred black and white; breast, belly and under tail-coverts rose-pink; lores, round eyes; sides of face and ear-coverts black; flanks claret-red; iris red or reddish brown; bill pale bluish grey; legs and feet black. Female slightly paler overall, especially the rump and upper tail-coverts. Juvenile similar to adult female, but darker.

Males C.c.pallidior differs from the nominate race in being paler overall.

C.c.kiwanukae differs from the nominate in being more greyer, less pinkish.

Voice: Described by Macworth-Praed & Grant as a 'loud sweet whistle of two cadences and a pretty warbling song'.

Habitat: Rocky scrub country and acacia woodlands.

Distribution: Somalia, southern Ethiopia, southern Sudan, Uganda and northern Kenya.

C.c.pallidior central Kenya.

C.c.kiwanukae southern Kenya and northern Tanzania.

Feeding: Grass seeds and small insects.

Breeding: Nest, rather large pear-shaped structure with side entrance tunnel built of seeding grassheads, lined with finer grass and feathers. A cock's nest, smaller than the real nest is built on top. Usually nests at 2-3m above the ground in bushes or trees. In Kenya uses Prickly acacia Acacia brevispeca, Glossy-leaved commonphora Commiphora schimperi and Woolly cape-bush Capparis tomentosa. Eggs white; clutch 4.

Aviculture: Diet Record Card WILDFOOD Guinea grass Panicum maximum, Black seed panicum P.novemerve (ADRC). Diet Record Cards ANIMAL FOOD termites, aphids (ADRC).

Zebra Waxbill
Amandava subflava 9cm

Alternative names: Goldbreast, Golden-breasted Waxbill, West African Orange-breasted Waxbill.
A.s.clarkei Clarke's Waxbill, Cape Orange-breasted Waxbill, Giant Waxbill, Orange-breasted Waxbill, Orange Waxbill, South African Golden-breasted Waxbill.

Description: Male. Forehead, crown, nape, mantle, rump and wings earth brown; from lores a crimson stripe extends over and behind eye; upper tail-coverts red; tail blackish; outer webs on underside of tail feathers white; ear-coverts yellowish green; chin, breast and belly orange; flanks yellow-green barred with darker green; iris orange-red; bill red, with culmen and underside of lower mandible black; legs and feet brownish. Female lacks crimson stripe over and behind eye; rest of upper and underparts paler overall. Juvenile upperparts earth brown; upper tail-coverts pale brown, washed with crimson; flanks not barred.

A.s.niethammeri differs from nominate in having the throat paler yellow; underparts more golden-yellow.

Voice: Described by Mackworth-Praed & Grant as a metallic twittering.

Habitat: Open grasslands, marshes, rank grass and cultivation.

Distribution: Senegal to Ethiopia and Uganda.

A.s.clarkei eastern Cape, KwaZulu-Natal, Free State, central North-West, Gauteng, Mpumalanga, provinces of South Africa to Lesotho (lowlands), Swaziland, Mozambique, Zimbabwe, south-eastern Botswana, south-eastern Zambia, southern Malawi, Tanzania and Kenya.

A.s.niethammeri north-eastern Namibia, north-western Botswana and the Caprivi Strip.

Feeding: Small seeds and tiny insects.

A.s.clarkei seeds of Golden setaria *Setaria sphacelata*, Natal redtop *Rhynchelytrum repens*, Popo grass *Hyparrhenia cymbaria* and livefood, namely termites, beetle larvae, small black ants, the latter probably *Pheidole megacephala*.

Breeding: Nest, barrel-shaped, loosely constructed and composed of dried grasses, leaves and culms in tall grass or in a small bush no more than 2m above ground. Growing grass often protrudes from the nest. Also recorded nesting on the ground. Lining consists of fine grass and a few feathers.

A.s.clarkei mostly of the Crowned Guineafowl, though other feathers used are of the domestic fowl, and breeds almost exclusively in the abandoned nests of other species, namely Red Bishop, Red-collared Widow, Yellow-backed Widow, Golden Weaver, Red-billed Quelea, White-winged Widow, Golden Bishop, Fire-crowned Bishop, Cape Widow, Masked Weaver, Le Vaillant's Cisticola, Tawny-flanked Prinia, Red-faced Cisticola and Locust Finch. Males continue to add feathers during the incubation period or early part of the nesting period. Eggs white; clutch 4-6; both birds participate in brooding; incubation period 13 days; young cared for and fed by both parents; nestling period 17-19 days.

A.s.clarkei is host to the Pin-tailed Whydah *Vidua macroura*.

Aviculture: Selected Reference CLUTCH 3-6; INCUBATION PERIOD 11-14 days; NESTLING PERIOD 21 days. Personal Communication CLUTCH 3,4,4; INCUBATION PERIOD 12,12 days; NESTLING PERIOD 19-20 days. Nest Record Cards CLUTCH 3,4,5 (ARU) 3,4,4,6 (ANRC) 4,5 (NASNRC); INCUBATION PERIOD 12,12 (ARU) 11,12 (ANRC) 13 days (NASNRC); NESTLING PERIOD 18, about 20,21 (ARU) 19,20 (ANRC) 19 days (NASNRC). Nest Record Cards WILDFOOD Milk-Thistle *Silybum marianum*, seeds of Crab finger grass *Digitaris sanguinalis*, Guinea grass *Panicum maximum*, Blue panic *P.laevifolium*, Burbristle grass *Setaria verticilliata*, Golden setaria *S.sphacelata*, Natal redtop *Rhynchelytrum repens*, Popo grass *Hyparrhenia cymbaria* (ARU NASDRC ADRC). Personal Communication WILDFOOD Guinea grass *Panicum maximum*, Bermuda grass *Cynodon dactylon*, Popo grass *Hyparrhenia cymbaria*, Golden setaria *Setaria sphacelata*. Selected Reference ANIMAL FOOD mealworms, Buffalo worms, whiteworms, ants' eggs. Diet Record Cards termites, mealworms (ARU NASDRC ADRC), ants (ARU) aphids (ADRC).

African Quail Finch

Ortygospiza atricollis 10cm

Alternative names: Bar-breasted Weaver-finch, Ground Finch, Quail Finch, Partridge Finch
O.a.digressa **Giant Quail-finch, South African Quail-finch.**

Description: Male. Forehead, crown, sides of face and throat black; lores, stripe above and below eye and chin white; nape, mantle, back and upper tail-coverts greyish brown; tail slate-grey, tipped with white; wings greyish brown; breast and flanks barred with black and white; belly buffy; under tail-coverts slate-grey; iris brown; bill in breeding, upper mandible brown, lower pinkish; legs and feet pale brown. Female similar to male, but paler and lacking the black adornment on the face. Juvenile similar to female, but breast unbarred; flanks barred dirty white.

Males. *O.a.ansorgei* differs from the nominate race in being darker overall, ear-coverts and upper breast black.

O.a.ugandae paler overall, eye ring white and chin patch larger.

O.a.fuscocrissa flanks mainly black, larger eye ring.

O.a.muelleri similar to *fuscocrissa*, but paler and greyer on underparts.

O.a.smithersi similar to *muelleri* but darker, with a blackish face; thin eye ring.

O.a.pallida differs from *bradfieldi* in having upper parts paler grey.

O.a.bradfieldi differs from *pallida* in being generally darker.

O.a.digressa similar to *pallida* but underparts darker and browner.

Voice: Described by Newman as a querulous, metallic '*terrilink*' given in flight.

Habitat: Open grasslands, cultivation and the margins of swamps and marshes.

Distribution: Senegal to Chad and northern Zaire.

O.a.ansorgei Guinea to Ivory Coast.

O.a.ugandae southern Sudan, Uganda and western Kenya.

O.a.fuscocrissa Ethiopia.

O.a.muelleri southern Kenya, Tanzania and Malawi.

O.a.smithersi north-eastern Zambia.

O.a.pallida north-eastern Botswana (Makgadikgadi Salt Pan) and Zimbabwe (Wankie Game Reserve).

O.a.bradfieldi central and northern Namibia, the Caprivi Strip, Botswana, western Zimbabwe, Angola, western Zambia and the South African provinces of northern Cape and North-West.

O.a.digressa western, eastern and northern Cape, Free State, KwaZulu-Natal, Gauteng, Mpumalanga and Northern Province, South Africa to Lesotho, Swaziland, southern Mozambique and eastern Zimbabwe

Feeding: Forages on the ground for seeds, insects and spiders; catches termites in flight.

Breeding: The nest is built on the ground under a grasstuft or between two tufts. It may vary in shape in different localities always being roundish or dome-shaped with side entrance. The nest is formed with dry grass blades and stems and usually well concealed with a porch or a short entrance tube. Thickly lined with soft grass and feathers. A small patch of bare ground usually occurs in front of the entrance. Eggs white; clutch 4-6; apparently only the female feeds the young; incubation period 14 days; both sexes incubate and roost together in the nest at night; fledging period 17-21 days.

Aviculture: Selected Reference: CLUTCH 4-5; INCUBATION PERIOD 11-14 days; NESTLING PERIOD 19-21 days. Nest Record Card CLUTCH 4,5 (ANU) 5 (ANRC); INCUBATION PERIOD 13,13 days; NESTLING PERIOD 20,21 (ARU) 20 days (ANRC). Diet Record Cards WILDFOOD Seeds of Teff grass *Eragrostis tef*, Guinea grass *Panicum maximum* (ARU ADRC). Selected Reference ANIMAL FOOD whiteworms, mealworms, weevils, red gnat larvae, including mealworms, termites, gnats, aphids (ADRC), wasp larvae or "grubs" (ARU).

Red-billed Quail-finch
Ortygospiza gabonensis
Alternative names: Black-chinned Quail-finch, Gabon Quail-finch.

Description: Male. Forehead black; mantle, back and wings greyish olive-brown; under wing-coverts buffy white; chin, lores, round eye and upper throat black; lower throat and upper breast finely transversely barred black and white; lower breast cinnamon; under tail-coverts russet brown and black; iris brown; bill crimson-red; legs and feet flesh coloured.

Males. *O.g.dorsostriata* differs from the nominate in being larger and darker.

O.g.fuscata differs from the nominate race in being darker overall.

Voice: Described by Mackworth-Praed & Grant as short rasping cries heard on the ground or when alarmed.

Habitat: Moist or swampy grasslands and sedge at 900-1500m in East Africa.

Distribution: Gabon to central Zaire.

O.g.fuscata Angola, southern Zaire and Zambia.

O.g.dorsostriata eastern Zaire and Uganda.

Feeding: Grass seeds, small insects and spiders.

Breeding: A single nest found in Zambia consisted of a ball of old fine stemmed grass with its base in a tussock of coarse grass. The entrance was to one side and the lining consisted of finer green grass and the feathers of Helmet Guineafowl *Numida meleagris*. The nest stood 11cm high and 9cm in diameter and with an entrance of 5cm across. A second nest was completely surrounded by water, in places 2cm deep. It is suggested that both sexes incubate. Eggs white, rounded, smooth and somewhat glossy; clutch 2-3.

Aviculture: Personal Communication CLUTCH 4; INCUBATION PERIOD 15 days; NESTLING PERIOD 20 days. Personal Communication ANIMAL FOOD termites, aphids.

Locust Finch

Ortygospiza locustella 9-10cm

Alternative names: Marsh Finch, Red-Quail finch.

Description: Male. Forehead, lores, sides of face, chin to breast crimson; crown and nape brown, streaked black; mantle, back and rump blackish, spotted white; tail blackish, washed crimson; flight feathers and wing-coverts pale crimson; under wing-coverts buff; belly and flanks black; iris yellow; bill red; legs and feet brown. Female has forehead, crown, nape, sides of face blackish; chin, throat and belly buffish white; flanks evenly barred black and white. Juvenile upperparts brown, streaked black, spotted white on mantle, back and rump; flight feathers and wing-coverts edged brown; bill blackish.

Male. *O.l.uelensis* differs from the nominate race in lacking white spotting on back.

Voice: Described by Maclean as having a squeaky quarelous chip chip flight call.

Habitat: Grasslands, especially on the borders of vleis and a preference for sandveld rather than black soil for permanently swampy ground.

Distribution: Eastern Zimbabwe, Mozambique, north-western Bostwana, eastern Zambia, Zaire, Malawi and southern Tanzania.

O.l.uelensis northern Zaire.

Feeding: Grass seeds.

Breeding: A well concealed domed nest, comprised of grassheads and lined with fine green grass and a few feathers, is placed on the ground in a tussock of grass. Eggs white; clutch 2-8, usually 4-7; both sexes incubate, the female playing the greater part; both birds roost in the nest at night; female feeds for the first few days, after which the male also helps.

Aviculture: Diet Record Cards ANIMAL FOOD aphids, mealworms, termites, wasp larvae or "grubs" (ADRC).

African Silverbill

Lonchura cantans 13cm

Alternative names: Black-rumped Silverbill, Silverbill, Warbling Silverbill, West African Silverbill. *L.c. orientalis* Arabian Silverbill

Description: Sexes similar, forehead and crown brown, feathers fringed with buffish; face and throat pale sandy brown, feathers fringed with yellowish buff; mantle and back ashy brown; rump, upper tail-coverts and tail black; under wing-coverts buff; breast barred buffish white; rest of underparts whitish; iris brownish black, rims bluish grey; bill silvery grey; legs and feet mauvish grey. Juvenile has feather fringes paler and tail shorter.

Male. *L.c.orientalis* differs from the nominate race in having the breast buffish, heavily barred brownish; face and throat darker sandy brown.

Voice: Described by Serle *et al* as soft twittering warble; little sharp cries in flight.

Habitat: Savannas, *acacia* woodland and in the vicinity of human dwellings.

Distribution: Senegal to western Sudan.

L.c.orientalis Somalia, Ethiopia to Tanzania.

Feeding: Grass seeds and weed including small insects when feeding nestlings.

Breeding: Nest, built of grass, verticle side entrance lined with seeding grassheads, sometimes perched, in tree or long grass; also utilize weaver's old nest which are relined; two instances of wasp's nest association has been recorded; eggs white; clutch 5-6; incubation period 11-12 days; nestling period 21-22 days.

Aviculture: Selected Reference CLUTCH 3-8; INCUBATION PERIOD 12-15 days; NESTLING PERIOD 19-21 days. Nest Record Cards CLUTCH 4,6 (ARU) 4,5 (ANRC) 7 (NASNRC); INCUBATION PERIOD 12,12 (ARU) 12,13 (ANRC) after 11 days (NASNRC); NESTLING PERIOD 18,20 (ARU) 20, about 21 (ANRC) about 18 days (NASNRC). Personal Communication WILDFOOD Rhodes grass *Chloris gayans*, Phalaris grass, New Guinea Pit Pit, Green panic *Panicum* sp., Barnyard grass *Echinochoa crus-galli*. Diet Record Cards Guinea grass *Panicum maximum* (ARU ADRC NASDRC). Selected Reference WILDFOOD chickweed *Stellaria* sp. Diet Record Cards Guinea grass *Panicum maximum* (ARU NASDRC ADRC).

Grey-headed Silverbill

Lonchura griseicapilla 11,5cm.

Alternative names: Pearl-headed Silverbill, Pearl-headed Mannikin.

Description: Sexes similar, crown, nape, hindneck and sides of neck pearl-grey; forehead finely speckled with silver; lores blackish; sides of face and chin are covered with tiny white spots; upper throat blackish; mantle and back pinkish chestnut; rump and upper tail-coverts creamy white to white; tail black, tipped with creamy white; wing-coverts dark brown, tinged with pink; under wing-coverts pale pinkish chestnut; breast, belly and rest of underparts rich pinkish chestnut; iris blackish; bill bluish black, lower mandible silvery grey; legs and feet blackish. Juvenile lacks white speckles on the sides of the face and chin.

Voice: Described by Williams as a high-pitched weak trill.

Habitat: Grasslands with scattered thorn trees in the vicinity of water.

Distribution: Southern Ethiopia, Uganda, Kenya and Tanzania.

Feeding: Seeds of grasses and weeds, including insects when feeding nestlings.

Breeding: Nest. Large untidy structure or grassheads, lined with feathers, placed in the upgrowing shoots of pollarded trees or at the end of boughs in tall trees; eggs white; clutch 4-5; incubation period 13-14 days; nestling period 24-28 days.

Aviculture: Selected Reference CLUTCH 4-5; INCUBATION PERIOD 12-13 days; NESTLING PERIOD 20-28 days. Nest Record Cards CLUTCH 4,4,6 (ARU) 4,5 (ANRC); INCUBATION PERIOD 12,12,12 (ARU) 12,13 days (ANRC); NESTLING PERIOD 23, before 26 (ARU) 22, about 23 days (ANRC). Diet Record Cards WILDFOOD Guinea grass *Panicum maximum* (ARU), Goose grass *Eleusine indica* (ADRC). Selected Reference WILDFOOD chickweed *Stellaria* sp. Diet Record Cards Guinea grass *Panicum maximum* (ARU NASDRC ADRC). Selected Reference ANIMAL FOOD mealworms. Diet Record Cards mealworms, termites (ADRC).

Bronze Mannikin

Lonchura cucullata 9cm

Alternative names: Bronze-wing, Bronze-shouldered Mannikin, Bronze-winged Mannikin, Bronze-headed Bengally. *L.c.scutata* Southern Bronze-winged Mannikin, Hooded Finch. Hooded Weaver-finch.

Descriptions: Sexes similar. Head, throat and shoulder patch blackish brown, glossed green, mainly on the forehead and crown; sides of lower neck, mantle back and wing greyish brown; rump and upper tail-coverts white, barred blackish; tail black; lower breast and underparts white; under tail-coverts white barred blackish; iris brown; bill black, lower mandible greyish; legs and feet browner overall.

L.c.tessellatus lateral greenish black patches are more prominent. Juvenile uniformly pale brown, paler below; tail brownish.

Voice: Described by Maclean as a high-pitched rapid 'tsree-tsree-tsree-tsree'; sharp 'chuk-chuk-chuk-chuk' alarm call.

Habitat: Open bush, edge of forest, cultivation, parks and gardens.

Distribution: Senegal eastwards to the Sudan and Uganda.

L.c.scutata Ethiopia westwards to Zaire and Angola, southwards to lower Zambesi River and north-eastern Zimbabwe.

L.c.tessellatus eastern Cape, KwaZulu-Natal, North-West, Gauteng, Mpumalanga and Northern-Province, South Africa to Swaziland, Mozambique, Zimbabwe, eastern Caprivi Strip and northern Botswana. Introduced into Fernando Pó Island where they are now fairly common.

Feeding: Seeds, insects and rice fragments. Recorded feeding on the following grasses, namely Goose grass *Eleusine indica*, Catstail dropseed *Sporobolus pyramidalis*, Guinea grass *Panicum maximum*, Antelope grass *Echinochloa pyramidalis,* Sweet grass *Brachiaria nigropedata*, Giant paspalun *Paspalum urvillei*, Natal redtop *Rhynchelytrum repens*, Bristle-leaved redtop *R.setifolium* Red grass *Themeda triandra*, Common thatchgrass *Hyparrhenia hirta*, Grazaland finger grass *Digitaria gazensis*, Golden bristle grass *Setaria anceps*, Fan leaf bristle grass *S.homonyma* and Garden setaria *S.pallide-fusca*. Recorded pecking the leaves and pulling strands of filamentous algae frog spittle *Spirogyra* from a small dry pond and eating it. Termites of the genus *Microcerotermes*.

Breeding: Constructs a large untidy spherical ball of grass, lined with flowering heads. An entrance hole is situated on the side with a few stalks protruding giving the impression of a short tunnel. The building procedure with breeding nests is for one bird of the pair collecting with the other remaining at the site to position the material. Roosting nests are much thinner and more flimsy than breeding nests. The mean dimensions of four nests are as follows: height 163mm (140-180), width 125mm (110-130), depth 155mm (130-170), entrance height 39mm (38-40), entrance width 42mm (40-45). To analyse the materials used seven nests were pulled apart and yielded 540, 610, 640, 800 pieces of grass (Breeding nests (+-10 pieces), 210, 360, 400 pieces of grass (roosting nests) 1-10 pieces). The following plant species have been recorded, namely Platula Pine *Pinus patula*, Catstail dropseed *Sporobolus pyrimadalis*, Guinea grass *Panicum maximum*; Gazaland finger grass *Digitaria gazensis*; Natal redtop *Rhynchelytrum repens*; Bristle-leaved redtop *R.setifolium*; Tambuki grass *Hyparrhenia dichroa*; Red grass *Hyperthelia dissoluta*; asparagus *Asparagus* sp. (wild). A wide variety of nest sites have been recorded at heights of between 0,6m - 12,2m in trees, bushes, in the thatch of huts, on security lights and relined nest of Red Bishop *Euplectes orix*, Red-headed Weaver *Anaplectes rubriceps*, African Masked Weaver *Ploceus velatus*; Blue Waxbill *Uraeginthus angolensis*. In West Africa recorded building close to nest of the vivious Red Tree Ant *Oecophylla*, apparently for protection. Eggs 2-4, 8-9 usually 3-6; white; incubation period 14-16 days by both sexes; nestling period 18-21 days.

Aviculture: Selected Reference CLUTCH 4-6; INCUBATION PERIOD 12-13 days; NESTLING PERIOD 17-23 days. Personal Communication CLUTCH 4,4,4,4,5,6,6; INCUBATION PERIOD 12,12,12,13,13 days (ARU); NESTLING PERIOD 18,18,19,20 about 22 days (ARU). Diet Record Cards WILDFOOD. Seeds of Guinea grass *Panicum maximum*, Blue panic *P.laevifolium*, Black-jack *Bidens pilosa*, Teff grass *Eragrostis tef*, Hay *Chloris virgata*, Common thatch grass *Hyparrhenia hirta*, Popo grass *H.cymbaria*, Bird grass *Poa trivialis*, Garden setaria *Setaria pallide-fusca*, Berg grass *S.appendiculata*, Golden bristle grass *S.anceps*, Fan-leaf bristle grass *S.homonyma*, Natal redtop *Rhynchelytrum repens*, Bristle-leaved redtop *R.setifolium*, Catstail dropseed *Sporobolus pyramidalis* (ARU). Selected Reference WILDFOOD Goose grass *Eleusine indica*, Catstail dropseed *Sporobolus pyramidalis*, Guinea grass *Panicum maximum*, Antelope grass *Echinochloa pyramidalis*, Sweet grass *Brachiaria nigropedatas*, Natal redtop *Rhynchelytrum repens*, Bristle-leaves redtop *R.setifolium*, Red grass *Themeda triandra*, Common thatchgrass *Hyparrhenia hirta*, Gazaland finger grass *Digitaria gazensis*, Golden bristle grass *Setaria anceps*. Fan leaf bristle grass *S.homonya*, Garden setaria *S.pallide-fusca*. Selected Reference ANIMAL FOOD mealworms. Diet Record Cards mealworms, termites, spiders (ARU).

Red-backed Mannikin
Lonchura bicolor nigriceps 9-10cm
Alternative names: Brown-backed Weaver finch, Rufous-backed Mannikin, Rufous-flanked Mannikin.
L.b.woltersi Wolter's Brown-backed Mannikin.
L.b.minor Lesser Brown-backed Mannikin.

Description: Sexes similar Entire head, breast and nape black, glossed with green; mantle, back and rump chestnut-brown; upper tail-coverts black, speckled with white; tail black; wings with lesser-coverts chestnut-brown; under wing-coverts, breast and underparts white; flanks, scaled with white; iris brown; bill bluish grey; legs and feet slate-grey. Juvenile has back brown faintly washed with chestnut; flanks brown; underparts dirty white.

Adults. *L.b.woltersi* differs from *nigriceps* in having mantle and back darker brown.

L.b.minor differs only from *nigriceps* in being slightly smaller.

Voice: Described by Williams as variour chirping calls.

Habitat: Coastal forest, scrub and open woodland to cultivation and gardens.

Distribution: Eastern Cape, KwaZulu-Natal (coast) and Mpumalanga (Kruger National Park), South Africa to Swaziland, eastern Zimbabwe and Mozambique, Malawi, Zambia, Tanzania, Pemba, Zanzibar and Mafia Islands, eastern Kenya, eastern Zaire to central and southern Somalia but limits currently indefinite.

L.b.woltersi south-eastern Zaire and north-western Zambia.

L.b.minor southern Somalia.

Feeding: Seeds of grasses, nectar and small insects. Petals of Weeping Boerbean *Schotia brachypetala* and leaves of the water weed Frog-spittle *Spirogyra*.

Breeding: The site is usually in a tree, bush or stand of reeds at 3-5m from the ground. The breeding nest constitutes a large globular structure composed of both green and dried grass and lined with flowering heads and the occasional feather or two. A well concealed entrance hole is situated to one side. In the building of the roosting nests up to 6 birds may be involved in the construction of each. Eggs white; clutch 4-6, usually 5.

Aviculture: Selected Reference CLUTCH 3-6; INCUBATION PERIOD 12-15 days; NESTLING PERIOD 17-21 days. Personal Communication CLUTCH 4; INCUBATION PERIOD 13 days; NESTLING PERIOD 19 days. Nest Record Cards CLUTCH 4,5 (ARU) 4 (SAANRC) 3 (ANRC); INCUBATION PERIOD 12,12 days (ANRC). Personal Communication WILDFOOD Seeds of panic *Panicum* spp., Rhodes grass *Chloris gayana*, Summer grass *Digitaria sanguinalis*. Diet Record Cards Gazaland finger grass *Digitaria gazensis*,

Common thatch grass *Hyparrhenic hirta*, Guinea grass *Panicum maximum*, Natal redtop *Rhynchelytrum repens*. Fan-leaf bristle grass *Setaris homonyma*, Garden setaria *S.pallide-fusca*. Antelope grass *Echinochloa pyramidallis*, Bird grass *Poa trivialis* (ARU ADRC SAADRC). Selected Reference WILDFOOD Seeds of Gazaland ginger grass *Digitaria gazensis*, Common thatch grass *Hyparrhenia hirta*, Guinea grass *Panicum maximum*, Natal redtop *Rhynchelytrum repens*, Fan leaf bristle grass *Setaria homonyma*, Garden setaria *S.pallide-fusca* Antelope grass *Echinochloa pyramidallis*, Small Canary grass *Phalaris minor*. Selected Reference ANIMAL FOOD whiteworms, ant pupae. Diet Record Cards mealworms, termites, gnat larvae (ADRC ARU) moths, fishmoths (ADRC).

Black & White Mannikin

Lonchura bicolor 10cm

Alternative names: Black-backed Mannikin, Chequered Mannikin, Black-breasted Mannikin, Blue-billed Mannikin, Two-coloured Mannikin.
L.b.poensis Fernando Pó Mannikin.
L.b.liberiae Liberian Blue-billed Mannikin.

Description: Sexes similar. Entire head, breast, nape, mantle and back black, glossed with green; rump, tail and wings black, with only a faint trace of white barring; under wing-coverts white; flanks black with white edges to feathers; belly and underparts white; iris brown; bill bluish grey; legs and feet blackish.

Adults. *L.b.poensis* differs from the nominate race in having the rump, upper tail-coverts and wings black, outer webs of flight feathers barred black and white.

L.b.stigmatophora mantle and back brownish black; upperparts black, tinged with purple.

L.b.liberiae differs from the nominate in having three white dots on the innermost tertiary.

Juvenile has upperparts sooty brown; underparts greyish buff.

Voice: Described by Mackworth-Praed & Grant as a faint plaintive little '*kip*'.

Habitat: Secondary growth, cultivation and damp forest clearings.

Distribution: Guinea to eastern Nigeria and Cameroon.

L.b.poensis Cameroon, northern Angola, eastern Zaire, southern Sudan, Ethiopia, Kenya and Tanzania; also Fernando Pó.

L.b.stigmatophora south-eastern Ethiopia to Uganda.

L.b.liberiae Liberia.

Feeding: Seeds of grasses *Panicum maximum* and Goose grass *Eleusine indica*, rice, half-ripe sorghum and insects. In western Sierra Leone crop contents revealed fibrous bits of ripe fruits of the oil-palm *Elaeis guineensis*. Termite *Macrotermes bellicosus* and ants *Myrmicinae* and *Oecophylla longinoda*.

Breeding: Large untidy round or oval nest is constructed with grass, mixed dry leaves and beard lichen and then lined with grassheads, sited at about 2-8m high in a bush, tree, creeper or bamboos. Eggs white; clutch 4-6; incubation period 13 days; nesting period 14 days.

Aviculture: Selected Reference CLUTCH 3-6; INCUBATION PERIOD 12-13 days; NESTLING PERIOD 14 days. Nest Record Cards CLUTCH 4,5 (ARU) 4 (SAANRC) 4,5 (NASNRC) 4 (ANRC); INCUBATION PERIOD 12,12 (ARU) 13 (SAANRC) 12,13 (NASNRC) 13 days (ANRC); NESTLING PERIOD 17,18 (ARU) 20 (SAANRC) after 18,21 (NASNRC) about 18 days (ANRC). Personal Communication WILDFOOD Guinea grass *P.maximum* (ARU), Blue panic *P.laevifolium* (NASDRC), Small panic *P.coloratum*, Black wild sorghum (unripe) *Sorghum versicolor* (ADRC). Diet Record Cards ANIMAL FOOD termites, mealworms (SAADRC ADRC ARU).

Magpie Mannikin

Lonchura fringilloides 12cm

Alternative names: Giant Mannikin, King Zanzie, Northern Magpie Mannikin, Pied Weaver-finch, Pied Mannikin.

Description: Sexes similar. Entire head and throat black, glossed greenish; mantle and back earth-brown; upper tail-coverts and rump black, glossed purplish; tail black; wing-coverts dusky; under wing-coverts buff; breast, belly and underparts white; flanks reddish brown; under tail-coverts cream; iris reddish brown; bill slate-grey, lower mandible silvery grey, tip blackish; legs and feet bluish grey to blackish. Juvenile uniformly dusky brown above and buff below; upper tail-coverts and tail black; bill blackish horn.

Voice: Described by Williams as having soft chirping calls but usually silent.

Habitat: Evergreen bush along streams in woodland clearing, bamboo and reedbeds and in the vicinity of native villages, exotic conifers, cultivation and gardens.

Distribution: Senegal eastwards to southern Sudan, Cameroon, Gabon, northern Zaire and western Uganda, Coastal KwaZulu-Natal, and Mpumalanga provinces of South Africa, southern Mozambique, Swaziland, eastern Zimbabwe, Zambia, Malawi, Tanzania, Kenya and eastern Uganda.

Feeding: Grass seeds including those of Bindura Bamboo *Oxytenanthera abyssinica* and cultivated rice. Observed feeding on green algae (Frog-spittle) *Spirogyra* from dry ponds.

Breeding: Nest, a spherical ball of dried grass and leaves, lined with grassheads and feathers with an entrance situated at the top and facing west. Nests may be built for two purposes, namely breeding or roosting, which may account for 3 or 4 individuals assisting carrying material which is arranged in place to form the structure by a female. Nests may be solitary or colonial comprising 3 or 4 built together. The breeding site is usually about 3-5m from the ground in a bush, tree, conifer or bamboos. Eggs white; clutch 4-6. A nest observed in northern KwaZulu-Natal, South Africa was constructed of the seed heads of Common reed *Phragmites australis*, White Ironwood leaves *Vepris lanceolata* and Weeping love grass *Eragrostis curvula* and stood 1,2m above the ground in a Splendid acacia *Acacia robusta*, which was covered with the parasite *Viscum* sp. The nest chamber contained two feathers which were rich brown in colour and thought to have been those of a Burchell's Coucal *Centropus susperciliosus*. The nest contained 4 near fully fledged young.

Aviculture: Selected Reference CLUTCH 4-6; INCUBATION PERIOD 11-16 days; NESTLING PERIOD 20-21 days. Nest Record Cards CLUTCH 4,4,4,6 (ARU) 4,5 (SAANRC) 4,6 (NASNRC); INCUBATION PERIOD 14,14,16 (ARU) 16 (SAANRC) 14,15,16 days (NASNRC); NESTLING PERIOD 19,20,22 (ARU) 21 (SAANRC) about 19,21 days (NASNRC). Selected Reference WILDFOOD Seeds of Dropseed grass *Sporobolus fimbriatus*, Weeping lovegrass *Eragrostis curvula*, Natal panic *P.laevifolium*, Annual bluegrass *Poa annua*, Black-jack *Bidens pilosa*. When fed grass seed with the complete stalk intact the birds would ignore the seedheads and immediately begin to extract the sap from the stems. The leaves of the Giant leaved fig *Ficus vogelli* had only the dying leaves stripped and pieces eaten. No attempt was made to strip living leaves. Diet Record Cards Guinea grass *Panicum maximum* (ARU SAADRC NASDRC), Johnson grass (unripe) *Sorghum halepense* (NASDRC), Black wild sorghum *S.versicolor* (SAADRC). Diet Record Cards ANIMAL FOOD mealworms, termites (ARU NASDRC SAADRC).

Red-headed Finch

Amadina erythrocephala 13cm

Alternative names: Aberdeen Finch, Paradise Sparrow, Red-headed Weaver-finch, Red-head Cut-throat, Red-headed Rice Bird, Red-headed Amadina.

Description: Male. Entire head and throat crimson, sides of neck, hindneck, mantle and back brown; upper tail-coverts greyish brown, feathers tipped with buffish white; rump brown, barred with grey; tail greyish brown, tipped white, wing-coverts brownish grey; under wing-coverts and lower neck buff; breast, belly and flanks buff, barred blackish, giving a spotted appearance; centre of belly chestnut and white; under tail-coverts barred with buff and brown and white tips; iris brown; bill horn, tinged pinkish; legs and feet flesh coloured. Female has entire head and throat earth brown; crown and nape faintly washed with pink; paler barred appearance over the breast and belly; centre of belly creamy buff. Juvenile has upperparts paler, males have faint pinkish wash on crown and nape.

Male. *A.e.dissita* differs from the nominate race in having the head a dark more crimson red; white spots on ventral surface larger and whiter; the blackish barring and fringing broader; wings and tail darker and greyer.

Voice: Described by Maclean as a nasal *'chink chink'* call and alarm note (also in flight).

Habitat: Dry open savannas, thornveld and in the neighbourhood of farm dwellings.

Distribution: North-western Angola, Namibia, Botswana (except north), South-western Zimbabwe to South Africa.

A.e.dissita KwaZulu-Natal (interior), Free State to eastern Cape, provinces of South Africa, Lesotho (lowlands).

Feeding: Grass and other seeds and insects, such as termites.

Breeding: It is perfectly capable of constructing its own nest which is an untidy dome composed entirely of grasses, and lined with feathers, cotton and various other soft materials, placed in a hole in a building. However, it prefers to utilize and reline deserted nests of other species, namely the Cape Sparrow *Passer melanurus*, Little Swift *Apus affinus*, Social Weaver *Philetairus socius*, Red-billed Buffalo Weaver *Bubalornis albirostris niger* and Masked Weaver *Ploceus velatus inustus*. Eggs white clutch 3-6, usually 4, occasionally 7; both sexes incubate,; incubation period 12-14 days; nestling period 15-22 days.

Aviculture: Selected Reference CLUTCH 3-7; INCUBATION PERIOD 11-14 days; NESTLING PERIOD 15-24 days. Personal Communication CLUTCH 5; INCUBATION PERIOD 14 days; NESTLING PERIOD 19 days. Nest Record Cards CLUTCH 3,5,7 (SAANRC) 3,5 (ARU) 5 (NASNRC) 5 (ANRC); INCUBATION PERIOD 12,12,13 (SAANRC) 12,13, (ARU) about 12 (NASNRC) 12 days (ANRC); NESTLING PERIOD 17, after 19 (SAANRC) 21, about 23 (ARU) 20 (NASNRC) 21 days (ANRC). Diet Record Cards WILDFOOD. Diet Record Cards ANIMAL FOOD mealworms (ARU), termites (NASDRC). Seeds of Guinea grass *Panicum maximum*, Blue panic *P.laevifolium*, Broad-leaved panic *P.deustum*, Weeping love grass *Eragrostic curvula*, Common thatch grass *Hyparrhenia hirta* (SAADRC ADRC ARU NASDRC).

Cut-throat Finch

Amadina fasciata 12cm

Alternative names: Cut-throat Weaver, Cut-throat Amadina, Cut-throat, Flame-throated Amadina, Flame-throated Finch, Red-collared Bengaly, Ribbon Weaver, Ribbon Finch, Cut-throat Mannikin.
***A.f.alexanderi* Abyssinian Cut-throat, Alexander's Cut-throat, East African Cut-throat, Giant African Cut-throat.**

Description: Male. Forehead, crown and nape greyish fawn; mantle, back and upper tail-coverts cinnamon, barred with black; tail greyish fawn, tipped with white, chin buff; broad red band across throat extending to ear-coverts, breast and flanks cinnamon, irregularly barred with black; centre of belly russet brown; iris red, bill bluish grey; legs and feet flesh-coloured. Female lacks the buff chin and red throat band; centre of belly white or cinnamon. Juvenile has paler throat band and belly, female resembles adult female but paler.

Males. *A.f.alexanderi* differs from the nominate race in having a broader barring on upper and underparts.

A.f.meridionalis is similar to *alexanderi*, but darker and has a smaller bill.

A.f.contigua differs from *meridionalis* in being warmer and redder brown on upperparts; little or no buff on the chin; breast and flanks more washed with russet buff.

Voice: Described by Williams as having sparrow-like chirping calls.

Habitat: Dry *acacia* savanna and low elevations, but the bird may occur near native villages, cultivated land and dams but absent from forest and desert terrain.

Distribution: Senegal, Gambia, northern Nigeria, southern Sudan to north-western Kenya.

A.f.alexanderi southern and western Eritrea, Ethiopia, Somalia, eastern Kenya and Tanzania.

A.f.meridionalis western Zimbabwe, northern and north-eastern Botswana, the Caprivi Strip and northern Namibia; extralimitally to southern Angola, Zambia, Malawi and northern Mozambique.

A.f.contigua north-western Free State, North West, Mpumalanga and Northern Province and northern KwaZulu-Natal, South Africa to eastern Swaziland, southern Mozambique and Zimbabwe (midlands).

Feeding: Seeds, insects (especially termites).

Breeding: Do not often build nests of their own, but are perfectly capable of constructing an untidy ball of dry grass with a short tunnel entrance at the side when choosing a tree, shrub or bush, or in a hole in a building. The nest chamber is lined with feathers, wool and other available soft materials. More often they utilize the nests of other species. Recorded robbing the lining from one Buffalo Weaver's nest and taking it into another; also a female repeatedly trying to enter the nest of an incubating weaver; they commonly use the abandoned nests of the Social Weaver *Philetarus socius*, Lesser Masked Weaver *Ploceus intermedius* Spotted-backed Weaver *P.cucullatus* and Red-billed Quelea *Quelea quelea*, adding soft lining inside. A record of a disused woodpecker's nest, almost certainly that of a Cardinal Woodpecker *Dendropicos fusescens*. Eggs white; clutch 3-5, sometimes up to 9, which suggest two females laying in the same nest; incubation period 12-13 days, nestling period 21-24 days.

Aviculture: Selected Reference CLUTCH 3-9; INCUBATION PERIOD 12,13 days; NESTLING PERIOD 20-23 days. Personal Communication 4,5; INCUBATION PERIOD 12,12 days; NESTLING PERIOD 19-22 days. Nest Record Cards CLUTCH 4,4,5 (ARU) 4,4 (ANRC) 4,6 (SAANRC); INCUBATION PERIOD 12,12,12,13 (ARU) 12 about 13 (ANRC) 11, after 12 days (SAANRC); NESTLING PERIOD 19,29 near 20,21 (ARU), near 21 (ANRC) 19,22 days (SAANRC). Diet Record Cards WILDFOOD. Selected Reference ANIMAL FOOD whiteworms, mealworms, maggots. Diet Record Cards fishmoths (SAADRC), thripsnymphs, springtails (ADRC), mealworms, termites (ARU). Seeds of Common thatch grass *Hyparrhenia hirta*, Millet grass *Setaria woodii*, Guinea grass *Panicum maximum*, Blue panic *P.laevifolium*, Hay *Chloris virgata* (ARU SAADRC ADRC).

Tit-hylia

Pholidornis rushiae 8cm

Alternative names: Tiny Tit-weaver.
***P.r.bedfordi* Fernando Pó Tiny Tit-weaver.**
***P.r.ussheri* Gold Coast Tiny Tit-weaver.**

Description: Sexes similar. Entire head and mantle brown, streaked dusky; rump and upper tail-coverts greenish yellow; tail and wings blackish; chin, throat and breast dusky brown; belly and under tail-coverts greenish yellow; iris red or reddish brown; bill blackish; legs and feet yellow.

Adults. *P.r.bedfordi* differs from the nominate race in having underparts more heavily streaked.

P.r.ussheri differs from the nominate in having underparts less heavily streaked.

P.r.denti differs from the nominate in having rump more yellowish less greenish.

Voice: Described by Mackworth-Praed & Grant as a scarcely audible little twitter.

Habitat: Forest.

Distribution: Southern Nigeria to Angola.

P.r.bedfordi Fernando Pó Island.

P.r.ussheri Sierra Leone to Ghana.

P.r.denti eastern Zaire and Uganda.

Feeding: Seeds and insects.

Breeding: Globular spout-like nest, with a downward pointing neck, untidy and built chiefly of cotton plant down and attached to the outer branches of a tree or vine. Eggs white; clutch 2.

Aviculture: No records.

Village Indigobird
Vidua chalybeata 11,5cm

Alternative names: Combassou, Green Indigobird, Indigo Finch, Steelblue Widowfinch, Senegal Indigobird, Senegal Combassou, Sengeal Indigo Finch, Red-billed Firefinch Indigobird, Village Combassou.
V.c.neumanni Neumann's Blue Combassou.
V.c.ultramarina Purple Indigobird.
V.c.amauropteryx South African Indigobird, Steel Finch, Steel-green Widowfinch.

Description: Male. General colour black with violet-blue sheen; head and wings greenish blue; tail washed with ash-brown; patch on side of rump white; iris brown; bill, legs and feet red. Female upperparts pale buffish brown, streaked dark brown; underparts buffish brown, except belly and throat whitish. Juvenile upperparts darker with crown plain dusky; underparts paler.

Males. *V.c.okavangoensis* differs from the nominate race in having the tail brown to dark brown.

V.c.neumanni differs from the nominate in being less violet and very slightly more glossy.

V.c.ultramarina differs from the nominate in being more violet blue-black and very slightly more glossy.

Voice: Described by Guggisberg as a sharp '*tk,tk*'.

Habitat: Savanna, open woodland, cultivation and gardens.

Distribution: Senegal to Sierra Leone.

V.c.neumanni Mali to Sudan.

V.c.ultramarina Ethiopia.

V.c.centralis Kenya, Uganda and western Tanzania.

V.c.amauropteryx eastern KwaZulu-Natal, western Gauteng and Free State, South Africa to Swaziland, Mozambique, Angola, Zambia, Malawi and southern Tanzania.

V.c.okavangoensis central and northern Namibia, southern Angola, north-eastern Botswana and south-western Zambia.

Feeding: Seeds.

Breeding: Host Red-billed Firefinch *Lagonostica senegala*. Eggs white; clutch 4, each female laying 1 egg or more in different host nest; up to 26 eggs may be laid in a season; incubation period about 10-11 days; nestling

period unrecorded.

Aviculture: Selected Reference CLUTCH 1, may lay about 26 eggs in a season; INCUBATION PERIOD 10-11 days. Selected Reference WILDFOOD Seeds of Hay *Chloris virgata*, Guinea grass *Panicum maximum*, Common thatch grass *Hyparrhenia hirta*, Common paspalum *Paspalum dilatatum*. Selected Reference WILDFOOD chickweed *Stellaria* sp. Selected Reference ANIMAL FOOD mealworms, termites.

Dusky Indigobird
Vidua purpurascens 11-12cm

Alternative names: Jameson's Firefinch Indigobird, Purple Widowfinch, Purple Indigobird, Purple Widowfinch, Pink-backed Firefinch Indigobird.

Description: Male. General colour black with violet-purple sheen; wings and tail washed with ash-brown; patch on sides of rump white; iris dark brown; bill, legs and feet whitish, tinged pink. Female upperparts boldly striped rufous buff and black; underparts whitish, except breast washed greyish. Juvenile upperparts tipped rufous, except brown blackish; underparts dark tawny.

Voice: Described by Maclean as a mixture of harsh notes and imitates call of Jameson's Firefinch.

Habitat: Mixed woodland and edges of cultivation.

Distribution: Northern KwaZulu-Natal, Northern Province (sparse), northern Mpumalanga, South Africa to eastern Swaziland, Mozambique, north-eastern Botswana, Zimbabwe, Malawi, Zaire, Tanzania and Kenya.

Feeding: Seeds.

Breeding: Host Jameson's Firefinch *Lagonosticta rhodopareia*. Eggs white; clutch 1-4; incubation and nestling period unrecorded.

Aviculture: Selected Reference CLUTCH 1-4. Selected Reference WILDFOOD Seeds of Hay *Chloris virgata*, Guinea grass *Panicum maximum*, Blue panic *P.laevifolium*. Selected Reference ANIMAL FOOD termites.

Variable Indigobird
Vidua funerea 11-12cm

Alternative names: Black Widowfinch, Brown-backed Indigobird, Brown-backed Firefinch Indigobird, Combassou.
V.f.nigerrima, Black Finch, Black Indigobird.

Description: Male. General colour violet-purple; wings and tail washed with ash brown; patch on side of rump white; iris brown; bill whitish; legs and feet coral-red. Female is buff, boldly streaked with blackish; underparts white; flanks greyish. Juvenile has ground colours as adult female, but not streaked; crown dark.

Males. *V.f.codringtoni* differs from the nominate race in being greener; legs and feet orange.

V.f.lusituensis differs from the nominate in being bluer; legs and feet red-orange.

V.f.nigerrima differs from the nominate by the pale blackish appearance with very dark violet-purple sheen.

Voice: The fullest description of this species that we have read, is by Maclean as a harsh rapid '*chichichichi*' call notes; song short variable phrases of chirping notes, *chip cheepy, chirpy, chippy, chippy sweepy*, repeated several times.

Habitat: Cultivation, grasslands and the edges of dams and vleis.

Distribution: Mozambique and South Africa in Mpumalanga, south-eastern Gauteng, Northern Province, eastern Free State and KwaZulu-Natal.

V.f.codringtoni eastern Zambia, Malawi, Zimbabwe (highlands) and adjacent Mozambique, but precise limits still not known.

V.f.lusituensis south-eastern Zimbabwe and adjacent Mozambique.

V.f.nigerrima, Angola, Zambia and southern Tanzania.

Feeding: Seeds.

Breeding: Host Blue-billed Firefinch *Lagonosticta rubricata*. Eggs white; clutch 1-4, but usually only 1 in each host nest; incubation and nestling periods unrecorded.

Aviculture: No records.

Pale-winged Indigobird

Vidua wilsoni 12cm

Description: Male. General colour black with violet-purple sheen, head, wings and tail greyish brown; patch on sides of rump white; iris brown, bill whitish, tinged pinkish; legs and feet brown. Female upperparts rufous buff streaked dark brown, except crown blackish brown; underparts pale brown, except centre of belly white. Juvenile unrecorded.

Males. "*V.f.camerunensis*" differs from the nominate race in having general colour black with blue sheen, wings brown; legs and feet a pale purplish.

"*V.f.nigeriae*" differs from the nominate in having general colour black with greenish blue sheen; legs and feet whitish.

Distribution: Northern Nigeria to western Sudan.

"*V.f.camerunensis*" Gambia to Ethiopia.

"*V.f.nigeriae*" southern Nigeria, Cameroon and southern Sudan. (These constitute groups rather than true sub-species).

Feeding: Not known.

Breeding: Hosts Bar-breasted Firefinch *Lagonosticta rufopicta*, Brown Firefinch *Lagonosticta nitidula* and Masked Firefinch *Lagonosticta larvata*. Eggs white; clutch, incubation and nestling periods unrecorded.

Aviculture: No records.

Violaceous Indigobird

Vidua incognita 12cm

Alternative names: Brown Firefinch Indigobird, Violet Widowfinch, Violaceous Widowfinch.

Description: Male. General colour dark violet-black; iris brown; bill white (?); legs and feet light pinkish. Female undescribed. Juvenile undescribed.

Voice: Described by Maclean as imitating the call of the Brown Firefinch *Lagonosticta nitidula*.

Habitat: Woodland.

Distribution: North-eastern Namibia, the Caprivi Strip, northern Botswana, Angola, Zambia and southern Zaire.

Feeding: Not known.

Breeding: Not known.

Aviculture: No records.

Steel-blue Whydah

Vidua hypocherina male 30cm, female 10cm

Alternative names: Long-tailed Combassou, Resplendent Combassou.

Description: Male. Wholly violet-blue including long central pairs of tail feathers; under wing-coverts, edges of flight feathers and spots on side of rump white; iris dark brown; bill grey; legs and feet blackish. Female has head boldly streaked buff and blackish; back buff, streaked black; underparts ash-brown. Juvenile similar to female, but paler ash-brown.

Voice: Described by Williams and Arlott as chirping calls and a sustained soft warbling song.

Habitat: Dry bush country near water in low and medium rainfall areas below 1400m in East Africa.

Distribution: Ethiopia and Somalia to Tanzania.

Feeding: Seeds.

Breeding: Host Black-faced Waxbill *Estrilda erythronotos*. Eggs white, clutch, incubation and nestling period unrecorded.

Aviculture: No records.

Fischer's Whydah

Vidua fischeri male 28cm, female 10cm

Alternative names: Fischer's Straw-tailed Whydah, Straw-tailed Whydah.

Description: Male. Forehead, crown and nape buff; sides of face, mantle and back black; rump and upper tail-coverts buff, streaked black; four central elongated tail feathers buff; wings dusky black; under wing-coverts dusky black and white; chin, throat and upper breast black; lower breast, belly and rest of underparts buff; iris reddish brown; bill red; legs and feet orange. Female upperparts tawny, streaky dusky; underparts buffish white; bill red. Juvenile similar to adult female, but paler overall; bill dusky.

Voice: Described by Williams and Arlott as a sharp '*tssp*' and a brief three or four note song, repeated over and over again.

Habitat: Bushed grassland in medium and low rainfall areas below 1600m in East Africa.

Distribution: Somalia to Uganda and northern Tanzania.

Feeding: Seeds, insects and their larvae.

Breeding: Host Purple Grenadier *Uraeginthus ianthinogaster*. Eggs white; clutch 1-3; incubation period 12 days; nestling period unrecorded.

Aviculture: Selected Reference CLUTCH 3. Selected Reference ANIMAL FOOD mealworms.

Shaft-tailed Whydah

Vidua regia male 30-34cm, female 12cm

Alternative names: Shaft-tailed Widow bird, Queen Whydah.

Description: Male. Forehead, crown and nape black; collar on hindneck tawny; mantle, back, upper tail-coverts black; tail blackish with white tips; ear-coverts, breast and belly tawny; wing-coverts and innermost secondaries black; under wing-coverts white; iris brown, legs and feet red-orange. Female similar to male in non-breeding plumage, but much paler. Juvenile similar to adult female, but russet brown upperparts; dusky streaks on underparts.

Male. *V.r.woltersi* differs from the nominate race in having mantle blackish, less bluish, underparts paler.

Voice: Described by Maclean as '*tsip-tsreepy-tsri-trii-trripy-tsrreepy*'.

Habitat: Thorny scrub and open grassland.

Distribution: South-western Zambia, southern Angola, western Zimbabwe, Botswana, Namibia and South African in northern Cape, western Free State, North-West and Northern Province.

V.r.woltersi southern Mozambique.

Feeding: Seeds.

Breeding: Host Violet-eared Waxbill *Uraeginthus grnatina*. Eggs white; clutch 3-4, but usually only 1-2; incubation period 12-13 days; nestling period 16 days.

Aviculture: Selected Reference; CLUTCH 1-2, rarely up to 5. Selected Reference WILDFOOD Seeds of Hay *Chloris virgata*, Common thatchgrass *Hyparrhenia hirta*, Natal redtop *Rhynchelytrum repens*, Guinea grass *Panicum maximum*, Blue panic *P.laevifolium*.

Pin-tailed Whydah

Vidua macroura male 26-34cm, female 12-13 cm

Alternative names: King-of-six, Pied Widow-bird, Pin-tailed Widow-bird.

Description: Male. Forehead, crown and nape black; collar on hindneck white; mantle and back black; rump and upper tail-coverts white, streaked black; tail black; sides of face and ear-coverts white; chin black; lesser and secondary wing-coverts white; breast, belly and under tail-coverts white; iris brown; bill red; legs and feet brownish black. Female upperparts tawny, streaked black; underparts white; throat and breast washed buff; flanks streaked black. Juvenile similar to adult female, but upperparts paler brown; underparts paler buff; bill dusky.

Male. *V.m.arenosa* differs from the nominate race in having pale tawny crown; underparts pale sandy yellow.

Voice: Described by Newman as '*tsee-tseet-tseet*' (in flight).

Habitat: Open savanna, thornveld, neglected cultivation and round native dwellings.

Distribution: Senegal to south-eastern Sudan, Ethiopia, north-eastern Uganda, Kenya, Tanzania, southern Zaire, Botswana, Zambia, eastern Zimbabwe, Mozambique (except Tete district), Angola, Swaziland and South African provinces of south-western, and eastern Cape, in Mpumalanga and KwaZulu-Natal.

V.m.arenosa southern Angola, southern Namibia, north-western Bostwana, Zimbabwe, Mozambique (Tete district), south-western Zambia and north and north-eastern Cape, western Free State and adjacent (plateau) of South Africa.

Feeding: Mainly seeds, also insects. Seeds of Hay *Chloris virgata*. In Ghana *Boraria*, *Scaloricia*, *Brachiaria* and *Chloris*. Termites *Tetrapagogon mosambicensis*.

Breeding: Hosts Common Waxbill *Estrilda astild*, Zebra Waxbill *Amandava subflava* Red-billed Firefinch *Lagonosticta senegala*, Bronze Mannikin *Lonchura cucullata*, Swee Waxbill *Estrilda melanotis*, Black-rumped Waxbill *E.trogoldytes*, Neddicky *Cisticola fulvicapilla* and Tawny-flanked Prinia *Prinia subflava*. Eggs white; clutch 2-4, usually 2; incubation period unrecorded; nestling period about 20 days.

Aviculture: Selected Reference CLUTCH 3; NESTLING PERIOD about 20 days. Selected Reference WILDFOOD Seeds of Black-jack *Bidens pilosa*, Hay *Chloris virgata*, Teff grass *Eragrostis tef*, Blue panic *Panicum laevifolium*, Guinea grass *P.maximum*, Large seed setaria *Setaria nigrirostris*. Selected Reference ANIMAL FOOD mealworms, wasp larvae of "grubs".

Paradise Whydah

Vidua paradisaea male 33-39cm, female 15cm

Alternative names: Acacia Paradise Whydah, Long-tailed Paradise Whydah, Paradise Widow-bird, Sharp-tailed Paradise Whydah

Description: Male. Entire head and throat black; broad collar on hindneck golden buff; mantle, back, rump, upper tail-coverts, tails, wings and under tail-coverts black; throat patch chestnut; breast tawny; belly tawny with centre whitish; iris brown; bill, legs and feet black. Female similar to male, but much paler. Juvenile similar to adult female, but upperparts earth brown; underparts white; bill horn.

Voice: Described by Mackworth Praed & Grant as a sharp '*chip*' and occasionally a short chattering song.

Habitat: Open woodland, dry thornveld, cultivation and gardens.

Distribution: Eastern Sudan, Ethiopia, south-eastern Zaire, north-eastern Uganda, Kenya, Angola, Zimbabwe, Botswana, Mozambique, Swaziland and South African coast in KwaZulu-Natal (rare), including east, northern Free State, North-West, Mpumalanga and Northern Province.

Feeding: Seeds and insects.

Breeding: Hosts Melba Finch *Pytilla m.melba*, Uganda Melba Finch *P.m.grotei* and Sudan Melba Finch *P.m.soundanesis*. Eggs white; clutch 3-4, but only 1-3 parasite eggs / host nest; one female may lay as many as 2 eggs / season; incubation period 12-13 days; nestling period 16 days.

Aviculture: Selected Reference CLUTCH 1-4, a female may lay up to 22 eggs in a season. Selected Reference WILDFOOD Seeds of Hay *Chloris virgata*, Common thatchgrass *Hyparrhenia hirta*, Natal redtop *Rhynchelytrum repens*, Guinea grass *Panicum maximum*, Blue panic *P.laevifolium*, dandelion *Taraxacum* sp., dock *Rumex* sp. Sowthistle *Sonchus oleraceus*, Comfrey *Synphytum officinale*. Selected Reference ANIMAL FOOD mealworms, moths, fly larvae of "maggots", earthworms, spiders.

Broad-tailed Paradise Whydah

Vidua orientalis male 35 cm, female 15 cm

Alternative names: Broad-tailed Paradise Widow-bird, Yellow-naped Paradise Whydah. *V.o.togoensis* Togo Paradise Whydah. *V.o.acupum* West African Paradise Whydah. *V.o.interjecta* Cameroon Paradise Whydah, Uelle Paradise Whydah, West African Broad-tailed Paradise Whydah.

Description: Male. Forehead, crown and sides of face black; nape and sides of neck ochraceous buff; mantle, back, rump and tall black; wings black, flight feathers margined whitish; throat black; breast deep burnt sienna; belly pale buff; under-tail-coverts black; iris brown; bill blackish; legs and feet horn. Female has forehead, crown and nape buff-white; rest of upperparts light buff-brown, boldly streaked dark brown; underparts white washed with buff, streaked dusky. Juvenile upperparts buff-grey instead of buff-white. Female similar to the male, but much paler.

Male. *V.o.acupum* differs from the nominate race in having hindneck browner.

V.o.togoensis differs from the nominate in having nape and hindneck dark golden-chestnut.

V.o.obtusa differs from the nominate in having breast very dark brown.

Voice: Not known.

Habitat: Savanna and woodland.

Distribution: Chad to Ethiopia.

V.o.acupum Senegal to northern Nigeria

V.o.togoensis Sierra Leone to Togo.

V.o.interjecta northern Cameroon to southern Sudan.

V.o.obtusa Mpumalanga (Tzaneen region), South Africa to eastern Zimbabwe, Mozambique (north of Save River), Angola, eastern and southern Zaire, Tanzania and Kenya.

Feeding: Seeds.

Breeding: Host Orange-winged Pytilia *Pytilia afra(obtusa)*, Senegambian Melba Finch *P.m.citerior (acupum)*, Crimson-winged Pytilia *P.phoencoptera (interjecta)* and Yellow-winged Pytilia *P.hypogrammica (togoensis)*. Eggs white: clutch 2-3; incubation period 12-13 days, nestling period 21 days.

Aviculture: Selected Reference CLUTCH 3. Selected Reference ANIMAL FOOD mealworms, termites. Selected Reference WILDFOOD Seeds of Hay *Chloris virgata*, Common thatchgrass *Hyparrhenia hirta*, Guinea grass *Panicum maximum*, Blue panic *P.laevifolium*.

Red-billed Buffalo Weaver

Bubalornis niger 23-24cm

Alternative names: Buffalo Weaver, South African Buffalo Weaver.

Description: Male. Wholly black with white bases to feathers; outer webs of primaries edged white; inner webs of flight feathers whitish; iris dark brown; bill coral red to orange; legs and feet pinkish brown to pale orange. Female more brownish, less black; throat, breast and rest of underparts mottled buffish white. Juvenile similar to adult female but more mottled below; bill yellowish horn coloured.

Female. *B.n.militaris* differs from the nominate in having an almost entirely fuscous throat with little or no visible mottling of white on the breast.

Voice: Described by Williams *et al* as having a variety of loud, falsetto croaking and chattering calls.

Habitat: Wooded grassland, especially with large trees like the Baobab *Adansonia digitata* and Camel-thorn *Acacia erioloba*. In Zimbabwe absent from country dominated by *Baikiaea* and *Brachystegia* woodland on Kalahari sand.

Distribution: North-west and northern Cape Province, South Africa to Zimbabwe, Botswana, central and northern Namibia, south-western Zambia and Angola.

B.a.militaris South African provinces Mpumalanga and north-eastern KwaZulu-Natal to eastern Swaziland. Mozambique (Sul do Save), south-eastern and western Zimbabwe and Zambia.

Breeding: Male polygamous. Nest is a large untidy mass of thorns and sticks with two entrances facing in different directions sited in the branches of trees, namely Camel-thorn *Acacia erioloba*, Knob-thorn *A.nigriscens,* Baobab *Adansoni digitata* or on windmills. Nests may be built in close proximity to villages with a record of a small colony almost touching that of the White-backed Vulture *Gyps africanus*. Nests are constantly being tended in readiness for the next season and many seasons to follow. Several nests may be found in one tree. The male constructs the shell of sticks while the female lines the chamber with grass, roots and leaves. Eggs greyish white, spotted and mottled with olive and grey; clutch 3-4; incubation 11 days, by female only, starting with first egg; nestling period 20-24 days; young fed by female alone.

Feeding: Seeds, grain, fruit and insects. Recorded pecking around cattle, examining excrement and also pecking flies and parasites from the animals. Livefood in the form of beetles, ants, crickets, locust-hoppers, termites and spiders.

Aviculture: Selected Reference CLUTCH 3-4; INCUBATION PERIOD 11 days; NESTLING PERIOD 20-24 days. Nest Record Cards CLUTCH 4 (ANRC); INCUBATION PERIOD 12 days (ANRC); NESTLING PERIOD 22 days (ANRC). Diet Record Cards WILD-FOOD Seed of Wolvoet panicum *Panicum lanipes*; Whether love grass *Eragrostis nindensis* (ANRC). Diet Record Card FRUIT berries of Black nightshade *Solanum nigrum* (ADRC). Selected Reference ANIMAL FOOD mealworms. Diet Record Cards termites, beetle larvae, including mealworms, grasshoppers, crickets, hairless caterpillars, aphids, spiders (ADRC).

White-billed Buffalo Weaver

Bubalornis albirostris 25cm

Alternative names: Black Buffalo Weaver, Buffalo Weaver.
B.a.intermedius Kenya Buffalo weaver, Somali Buffalo Weaver.

Description: Male. Wholly black with white bases to the feathers; no white at base of flight feathers; bill white, swollen in breeding dress, black in non-breeding dress; iris dark brown; legs and feet brown. Female. Slaty black; bill blackish. Juvenile similar to adult female; but more mottled below; bill horn coloured.

Male. *B.a.intermedius* differs from the nominate in having primaries with a trace of white basally on the inner webs; bill red.

Voice: Described by Serle *et al.* as a variety of harsh guttural and explosive high pitched cries.

Habitat: Acacia woodland, especially where there are Baobab *Adansonia digitata* and in cultivated areas.

Distribution: Southern Mauritania, Senegal, Mali, Upper Volta, northern Nigeria, Chad to northern Ethiopia, north-eastern Uganda and north-western Kenya.

B.a.intermedius southern Ethiopia, Somalia, South-eastern Kenya and southern Tanzania.

Breeding: The nest is a rough untidy structure of sticks, thorns and grass. The chamber is lined with finer grasses and a few feathers. Nests may be built in close proximity to villages with a record of a small colony almost touching that of a White-backed Vulture *Gyps africanus*. Nests are constantly being tended in readiness for the next season and many seasons to follow. Eggs whitish or pale green, blotched, mottled and streaked with ashy grey and brown; clutch 2-3; incubation and nestling periods unrecorded.

Feeding: Seeds, grain, locusts and other insects.

Aviculture: No records.

White-headed Buffalo Weaver

Dinemellia dinemelli 20cm

Alternative names: Dinemelli's Weaver, Dinemelli's Buffalo Weaver, White-headed Weaver, *D.d.boehmi* Boehm's Buffalo Weaver.

Description: Sexes similar. Entire head white; mantle, back and tail dusky brown; rump and upper tail-coverts orange-red; wings, dusky brown, basal parts of primaries white; chin, throat, breast, belly and underparts white; under tail-coverts orange-red; iris yellowish brown; bill blackish horn; legs and feet blackish brown. Juvenile similar to adult, but rump, upper and under tail-coverts pale-orange.

Adult. *D.d.boehmi* differs from the nominate race in having mantle, wings and tail black.

Voice: Described by Mackworth-Praed & Grant as a harsh trumpet-like cry, freely uttered, also a bubbling twittering call.

Habitat: Dry wooded grasslands and cultivation.

Distribution: Southern Sudan, southern Ethiopia, Somalia and northern Kenya.

D.d.boehmi south-eastern Zaire and Tanzania.

Feeding: Seeds, grain, berries, insects and their larvae. Livefood in the form of beetles, ants, mole crickets, termites and spiders.

Breeding: Large untidy communually-built mass of thorny twigs and sticks with colonies seldom having less than 10 clusters, built 3-10cm up in a savanna tree, often Baobab *Adansonia digitata* and less common in *acacia, balanites* or palms. Nests are dome-shaped with two or more verticle entrance tunnels of the sides. The stick shell is put together by a dozen or so adult males and juveniles, the latter from the last brood working co-operatively. Each nest chamber is shaped by a single female who lines the cavity with grasses, roots and leaves. Eggs greenish blue, streaked and blotched with black, brown, grey, olive or sepia; clutch 2-4; incubation 12 days by female only; nestling period 20-24 days; fed by female only.

Aviculture: Selected Reference CLUTCH 2-4. Nest Record Cards CLUTCH 4 (ARU) 4 (ANRC); INCUBATION PERIOD 11 (ARU) 12 days (ANRC); NESTLING PERIOD 22 (ARU) 23 days (ANRC). Aviculture Personal Communication CLUTCH 4; INCUBATION PERIOD 13 days; NESTLING PERIOD about 18 days. Nest Record Cards CLUTCH 3,4 (ANRC); INCUBATION PERIOD near to 13 days; NESTLING PERIOD about 17 days (ANRC). Diet Record Cards FRUIT Nana-berry *Rhus dentata*, Common taaibos *R.pyroides* (ADRC). Diet Record Cards ANIMAL FOOD termites (ARU ADRC).

White-browed Sparrow Weaver

Plocepasser mahali 16-18cm

Alternative names: Black-billed Sparrow Weaver, Black-billed Mahali Weaverbird, Mahali Weaver. *P.m.melanorhynchus* Sparrow Weaver, Striped breasted Sparrow Weaver, White-browed Weaver.

Description: Sexes similar. Forehead, lores and moustachial stripe blackish brown; sides of head, nape, mantle and back brown; rump white; tail blackish; chin, throat, breast, belly and rest of underparts white; wings blackish, edged and tipped white; iris reddish brown; bill black; legs and feet brownish. Juvenile similar to adult, but paler overall; bill pinkish horn.

Adults. *P.m.propinquatus* differs from *melanorhynchus* in being smaller.

P.m.pectoralis differs from nominate in having black markings on breast.

P.m.ansorgei differs from the nominate in having white tips to tail broader.

P.m.stentor differs from the nominate in being paler and underparts more rusty or buffy.

Voice: Described by Guggisberg as having a harsh chattering call, bubbling whistles and an alarm note "chuk-chuk".

Habitat: Open wooden grasslands. Typically in semi-arid areas and often near villages at 400-1900m in East Africa.

Distribution: The South African provinces of north-eastern Cape, Free State, Gauteng (highveld) and KwaZulu-Natal (interior) and south-eastern Botswana.

P.m.melanorhynchus southern Sudan, southern Ethiopia, northern Uganda and Kenya.

P.m.propinquatus southern Somalia.

P.m.pectoralis northern Mozambique (Tete district) northern Zimbabwe, northern Botswana, eastern Zambia and Malawi.

P.m.ansorgei southern Angola and northern Namibia.

P.m.stentor northern and north-western Cape Province, South Africa to Namibia (except north-east) and western and south-western Botswana.

Feeding: Seeds, grain and insects. Mealiepap and water from feeding tray. Seeds of *Digitaria velutina*, *Eragrostis papposa*, *Chenchrus ciliaris* and *Dactyloctenium aegyptium*.

Breeding: Nests are usually 2-8m above ground in the outer branches of a tree. In Zambia the following tree species were utilized as nesting sites, namely Pink Jacaranda *Stereosperum kunthianum*, Mopane *Colophospermum mopane*, Stocklebush *Dichrostachys cinerea*, Knob-thorn *Acacia nigriscens*, Scented thorn *A.nilotica*, White-thorn *A.polyacantha*, Common commiphora *Commiphora pyrachanthoides*, Spiny monkey orange *Strychnos spinosa* and Worm-cure albizia *Albizia anthelmintica*. The large untidy bundle of dried grass may measure about 24cm long, 15cm wide and 18cm high. The entrance which is difficult to distinguish measures up to 30cm long and 7cm diameter. The chamber is thickly lined with feathers and soft grassheads. Stalks protruding forward in the entrance form protection for the incubating bird by making in very difficult to enter the nest. One observation revealed that a colony entered their nests with a piece of nesting material 688 times, an average of about 22 times an hour. Four nests were built from start to finish within 8-10 days, the shortest was 5 days and the longest 5-6 weeks. Telephone poles are occasionally utilized in treeless locations. The Pygmy Falcon *Polihierax semitorquatus* and Ashy Tit *Parus cinerascens* have been observed roosting in their nests. One tunnel is later closed and the nest lined prior to egg laying, or a "one tunnel" nest may be newly constructed for breeding. Eggs white to pink, sometimes speckled with a ring at the thick end or marked with pink to red, brown or grey; clutch 2-3; incubation period 13-14 days; nestling period 20-24 days; young fed by all members of group, more by females than by males. Fledglings known to beg for food up to 3 months after leaving the nest, though they are able to feed themselves by this time. One observation revealed 4 fledglings each being fed an average of 14 times per hour.

Aviculture: Selected Reference CLUTCH 2-3; INCUBATION PERIOD 13-14 days; NESTLING PERIOD 20-24 days. Personal Communication CLUTCH 2-3; INCUBATION PERIOD 14,14 days; NESTLING PERIOD 19,22 days. Nest Record Cards CLUTCH 3,3 (ANRC); INCUBATION PERIOD 13,13 days (ANRC); NESTLING PERIOD 19,21 days (ANRC). Personal Communication ANIMAL FOOD termites. Diet Record Cards termites, beetle larvae, including mealworms, hairless caterpillars.

Chestnut-crowned Sparrow Weaver
Plocepasser superciliosus 15,5cm

Alternative name: *P.s.brunnescens* Cameroon Sparrow weaver.

Description: Sexes similar. Forehead, crown and ear-coverts chestnut; supercilliary stripe, sides of neck, chin and throat white; malar strip black; mantle, back and rump earth brown, washed with chestnut; tail earth brown, tinged blackish; breast, belly and underparts greyish white; wings earth brown, coverts tipped with white; iris chestnut brown; bill pinkish horn; legs and feet pale brown. Juvenile similar to adult, but paler overall, especialy on forehead and crown adult. *P.s.brunnescens* differs from the nominate race in having a warmer wash of chestnut on mantle and back.

Voice: Described by Serle *et al* as a short ringing cry.

Habitat: In East Africa in dry bushveld hillsides and wooded grassland at 600-1800m.

Distribution: Senegal, Gambia, northern Nigeria, Chad and central Sudan.

P.s.brunnescens Central African Republic to south-western Sudan, Uganda and north-western Kenya.

Feeding: Seeds, insects and their larvae.

Breeding: Nest loose and untidy, of dry coarse yellowish grass resembling straw and leaves. Domed, with usually two entrance tunnels, one at each end, which are used as sleeping roosts and lined with feathery grass tops and feathers. Placed at extremity of an *acacia* thorn branch at 3m above ground, singly or in colonies. Eggs pinkish cream, profusely spotted and blotched with mauve-brown or brownish pink and lilac under markings; clutch 2; incubation period 14 days; nestling period 19-24 days.

Aviculture: Nest Record Cards CLUTCH 3,3 (ARU) 2 (ANRC); INCUBATION PERIOD 13,13 (ARU) 13 days (ANRC); NESTLING PERIOD 20,21 (ARU) 19,20 (ANRC) about 21 days (ANRC). Diet Record Cards ANIMAL FOOD beetle larvae, including mealworms, hairless caterpillars (ARU), termites alates (ADRC).

Chestnut-mantled Sparrow-weaver
Plocepasser rufoscapulatus 18cm

Alternative names: Red-mantled Sparrow-weaver, Rufous-backed Sparrow-weaver.

Description: Male. Forehead, broad stripe each side of crown, under and behind eye, front parts of ear-coverts black; nape, sides of neck grey; mantle and back chestnut; rump and upper tail-coverts grey; tail greyish brown; wing-coverts black, edged white; sides of chin to sides of neck black; centre of chin and throat white; breast, belly and rest of underparts paler buffish grey; iris red; bill whitish; legs and feet pale flesh. Female has bill black. Juvenile undescribed.

Voice: Not known.

Habitat: *Brachystegia* woodland.

Distribution: Southern Angola, south-eastern Zaire to Malawi.

Feeding: Not known.

Breeding: Nest, large round untidy structure of whitish grass stems which projects forward and forms an opening that points downwards with the birds flying up vertically in the antechamber, perching on a ledge before entering the main chamber. Lined with seeding grassheads and feathers. Eggs whitish, spotted at large end; clutch 2-3.

Aviculture: Nest Record Cards CLUTCH 4 (ANRC); INCUBATION PERIOD 13 days (ANRC). Diet Record Cards ANIMAL FOOD termites, hairless caterpillars (ADRC).

Rufous-tailed Weaver

Histurgops ruficauda 22cm

Description: Sexes similar. Entire head and nape tawny grey, mottled brownish; mantle and back dusky grey, feathers edged tawny, giving scaly appearance; flight feathers chestnut, wing-coverts tawny grey; chin and breast buffy, mottled pale brown; tail rufous, central feathers blackish brown; belly and rest of underparts creamy white; iris pale bluish white; bill dusky horn; legs and feet dusky horn. Juvenile differs from the adult in having underparts browner.

Voice: Described by Guggisberg as uttering harsh "*shwee, ur*" or "*phweezee*".

Habitat: Dry *acacia* woodland and wooded grasslands.

Distribution: Tanzania.

Feeding: Grass and tree seeds, grain notably wheat when available and insects.

Breeding: Large untidy globular structure 45 x 22,9cm in size made of course grasses, mainly Bamboo grass *Pennisetum mezianum, P.straminium,* Angle grass *Themeda triandra, Urochloa nubica* and some *Sporobolus* spp., joined together at 1,52-3,05m from the ground. Thorny trees are selected, namely the Umbrella thorn *Acacia tortilis* and *A.drepanclobium.* Eggs very lightly to pale blue, long streaks, scraws and scribblings; clutch 3.

Aviculture: Selected Reference CLUTCH 3-4. Selected Reference ANIMAL FOOD crickets, locusthoppers.

Grey-headed Social Weaver

Pseudonigrita arnaudi 13cm

Alternative name: Grey-capped Social Weaver.

Description: Sexes similar. Forehead and crown pale greyish white; nape, mantle, back and upper tail-coverts greyish buff; tail greyish buff, band blackish; wings with primaries black, wing-shoulder blackish and greyish white; chin, throat, breast, belly and under tail-coverts buffish grey; iris crimson; bill blackish; legs and feet dusky flesh. Juvenile has forehead and crown buffy white; rest of underparts more buffy, less greyish.

Adults. *P.a.australoabyssinicus* differs from the nominate race in having crown darker, more grey, less white.

P.a.dorsalis differs from the nominate in having centre of mantle grey; tail greyish.

Voice: Described by Elliot as a very distinct short pip in flight and a bleating squeak in the vicinity of nesting colonies.

Habitat: Sandy bush country.

Distribution: South-western Sudan, Kenya, Uganda and northern Tanzania.

P.a.australoabyssinicus southern Ethiopia.

P.a.dorsalis central Tanzania.

Feeding: Seeds of grasses and trees.

Breeding: Breeds in colonies with 10,000 nests being observed in Kenya, amongst the galls of Whistling thorn *Acacia* sp. Nests are built of coarse dry grass and attached on the long leafless thorny emergent branches. There are two openings, one directed downwards, used as roosting places between breeding seasons, with the other slanting upwards which serves as an entrance. Eggs pale bluish with darker grey and brown spots; clutch 3-5; incubation period 11 days; nesting period 12 days.

Aviculture: Nest Record Cards CLUTCH 3,3,5 (ANRC); INCUBATION PERIOD 12,13 days (ANRC); NESTLING PERIOD 17,18 days (ANRC). Diet Record Cards ANIMAL FOOD termites (ADRC).

Black-capped Social Weaver

Pseudonigrita cabanisi 13cm

Description: Sexes similar. Forehead, crown, nape and sides of face black; mantle, back and upper tail-coverts pale brown; tail black; chin, throat, belly, breast and rest of underparts white; flanks tinged black and pale brown; iris dark brown; bill whitish horn; legs and feet dusky white. Juvenile upperparts mottled dusky brown; underparts buffish white.

Voice: Described by Mackworth-Praed & Grant as a harsh not unmusical chattering.

Habitat: Frequents bushed and wooded grasslands in arid and semi-arid country at 200-1300m in East Africa.

Feeding: Seeds.

Breeding: Nest in colonies numbering 40-60 in acacias. They are cone-shaped being built of dry grass, without lining and suspended from the top by a grass rope at any height from the ground. Eggs white or pinkish, marked with violet and brown; clutch 3-4.

Aviculture: Nest Record Cards CLUTCH 3,3 (ANRC); INCUBATION PERIOD 12 days (ANRC); NESTLING PERIOD 19 days (ANRC). Diet Record Cards ANIMAL FOOD mealworms, termites (ADRC).

Sociable Weaver

Philetairus socius 13-14cm

Alternative name: Social Weaver.

Description: Sexes similar. Head-top and nape brown; mantle, back and scapulars blackish, edged with buff to give a scaly appearance; upper tail-coverts buffy brown; tail buffy brown, tipped blackish; flanks black with white edges to feathers; lores and bib black; breast, belly and underparts deep buff; iris dark brown; bill, legs and feet blue-grey. Juvenile lacks the black lores and bib before first moult; more spotted on mantle and lighter on flanks.

Adults. *P.s.eremnus* differs from the nominate race in having the head-top darker brown; wings and tail darker; chin and throat deeper black; rest of underparts slightly browner.

P.s.geminus differs from the nominate in having flanks less greyish brown and somewhat brighter.

Habitat: Semi-desert, associated with Camel thorn *Acacia erioloa*, and arborescent plants, namely Quiver tree *Aloe dichotoma*, Shepherd's tree *Boscia albitrunca* and bristle grass *Aristida* spp.

Distribution: Northern and western Cape Province, South Africa and southern Botswana and central and northern Namibia.

P.s.eremnus northern Cape Province (middle Orange River Valley), Free State and southern North-West provinces of South Africa.

P.s.geminus northern Namibia.

Feeding: Seeds (about 20%) and insects (80%). Seeds of bristle grass *Aristida* spp., lovegrass *Eragrostis* spp., and Small dropseed *Sporobolus coromandelianus* and flower ovaries of Driedoring *Rhigozum trichotomum*. Livefood, namely beetles, grasshoppers, wasp larvae or "grubs", moths, including Brown-veined White Butterfly *Belenois aurota*, termites, including Harvester *Hodotermes mossambicus*.

Breeding: Nest an enormous dome shaped structure built in trees strong enough to support it, or on water tank stands, windmill towers or telephone poles. There is a record of one structure built on a buttress of rock protruding from the lower portion of a rock face. Trees mostly commonly used are the Grey camel thorn *Acacia haematroxylon*, Camel thorn *A.eriolola*, Quiver tree *Aloe dichotoma* and Shepherd's tree *Boscia albitrunca*. The super structure consists of dry grass straws, mostly Tall Bushmen grass *Aristida ciliata* but also Gha grass *Centropodis giauca*, Kalahari coach *Stripagrostis amabilis* and Small Bushmen grass *O.obtusa*. Dried springs of Khaki bush *Schkuharia bonariensis*, sticks of Camel thorn *Acacia eriola* and plant parts of Candle acacia *A.hebeclada*, Grey camel thorn *A.haematoxylon*. Black thorn *A.mellifera*, Driedoring *Rhigozum trichotomun*, Koffieboontjie *Aptosimum marlothii* and Mexican poppy *Argemone mexicane* are also included. The chamber is usually formed of green grass stems of Tall Bushmen grass *Aristida ciliata*, Small Bushman grass *Stipagrostis amabilis* and Ringwindhalmgrass *Eragrostis annualata*. The chamber is lined with seedheads, furry leaves of Wild Everlasting flower *Helichrysum argyrosphaerum*, with occasional feathers, cotton or pieces of cloth. When not breeding the birds roost and sleep in the compartments. Many species utilize the nests for roosting and/or breeding, namely the Ashy Tit *Parus cinerascens*, Rosyfaced Lovebird *Agapornis roseicollis*, Pygmy Falcon *Polihierax semitorquantus*, Scalyfeathered Finch *Sporopipes squamifrons*, Redheaded Finch *Amadina erythrocephala*, Pied Barbet *Lybuis leucomelas*, Familiar Chat *Cercomela familiaris* and Greyheaded Sparrow *Passer diffuses*. The Giant Eagle Owl *Bubo laeteus*, Barn Owl *Tyto alba*, Egyptian Goose *Alopochen aegyptiaca*, Yellowbilled Hornbill *Tochus flavirostris* and Lilac breasted Roller *Coracius caudata* roost and/or breed on the upper section or on top of the nest. Eggs, white covered with olive-grey; clutch 2-6, usually 3-4; incubation period

13-14 days, by both sexes; nestling period 20-24 days; young fed by both adults; adult plumage achieved at 16-18 weeks.

Aviculture: Selected Reference CLUTCH 2-6; INCUBATION PERIOD 13-14 days; NESTLING PERIOD 20-24 days. Nest Record Cards CLUTCH 4,4,5 (ARU); INCUBATION PERIOD 13,13 (ARU); NESTLING PERIOD 19,22 days (ARU). Diet Record Cards WILD-FOOD Seeds of Wolvoet panicum *Panicum lanipes*, Guinea grass *P.maximum* (ARU). Selected Reference ANIMAL FOOD mealworms. Diet Record Cards grasshoppers, crickets, termites, mealworms, spiders (ARU).

Donaldson-Smith's Sparrow Weaver
Plocepasser donaldsoni 15cm

Description: Sexes similar. Crown, nape and mantle paler brown, former mottled dusky; rump and upper tail-coverts white; tail brown, edged dusky; ear-coverts blackish; narrow moustachial stripe black; lower cheeks and throat white; breast, belly and underparts pale buff, mottled on breast with brown; iris brown; bill black; legs and feet brownish. Juvenile upperparts browner, feathers edged with tawny on mantle and wings.

Voice: Described by Mackworth-Praed & Grant as a soft double cluck, a loud parrot-like '*chink-chink*'.

Habitat: Arid and semi-arid country at 400-1500m in the south, endemic to grasslands and rocky semi-desert area and trees in the north.

Distribution: South-western Ethiopia and north-eastern Kenya.

Feeding: Mainly grass seeds.

Breeding: Breeds in colonies, a number of nests being usually placed in the outer branches of a tree, usually an acacia thorn. A round untidy dome of yellow or whitish grass resembling a bundle of straw with a short entrance hole and lined with feathers. Eggs pinkish or greyish brown, finely and diffusely speckled with mauve and reddish brown; clutch 2-3.

Aviculture: Nest Record Cards CLUTCH 3 (ANRC); INCUBATION PERIOD 13 days (ANRC); NESTLING PERIOD 19 days (ANRC). Diet Record Cards ANIMAL FOOD mealworms, termites alates (ADRC).

Spanish Sparrow
Passer hispaniolensis 14cm
Alternative name: Black-breasted Sparrow.

Description: Male. Crown and nape chestnut mantle black, streaked and edged buff; rump and upper tail-coverts ashy brown, feathers with dark edges; stripe through eye black, stripe over eye, ear-coverts and sides of neck white; chin, throat and breast black; sides of breast and flanks streaked black and white; rest of underparts creamy white; iris brown, bill brown; legs and feet brownish. Female indistinguishable from female House Sparrow. Juvenile plumage closely resembles adult female, but less clearly marked on mantle.

Voice: Described by Peterson as having a full rich notes resembling a House Sparrow, but somewhat richer in tone.

Habitat: Semi-arid regions, olive groves, plantations, villages, towns and around human settlement.

Distribution: Morocco to Egypt, eastern Chad and northern Sudan.

Feeding: Seeds, green shoots, buds and fruit of trees, cultivated grain and some live food. Hemp *Cannabis, persicaria, Polygonum*, goosefoot *Chenopodium*, mouse-ear *Cerastium*, spurry *Spergula* campion *Silens*, wall-rocket *Diplottaxis*, cress *Lepidium* mignonette *Reseda*, apple *Malus*, pear *Pyrus*, grape *Vitis* fig *Ficus*, rest-harrow *Ononis*, clover *Trifolium*, storksbill *Erodium*, sow-thistle *Sonchus* and prickly pear *Opuntia*. Grasshoppers, earwigs, mantises, bugs larval and adult lacewings, flies, wasps, bees, ants, beetles, centipedes, spiders and small snails.

Breeding: Nesting occurs in huge colonies with the building of bulky ball-shaped structure with a side entrance, placed in acacias, tamarisks, ujubes or palms and also in holes in walls and occasionally rock crevices from a few hundred to a few thousand nests, of which some are often found in the base of a bird of prey's nest. Eggs bluish white with grey or dark purple spots and blotches; clutch 4-8, 1-2 per season; incubation period 11-12 days, chiefly by female; nestling period 15-18 days.

Aviculture: Nest Record Cards CLUTCH 4 (ANRC); INCUBATION PERIOD 12 days (ANRC); NESTLING PERIOD 17 days (ANRC). Selected Reference WILD-FOOD seeds of Common thatch grass *Hyparrhenia hirta*. Diet Record Cards buds of Smelter's bush *Flaveria bidentis* (ADRC). Diet Record Cards ANIMAL FOOD crickets, mealworms (ADRC).

Somali Sparrow
Passer castanopterus 14cm

Alternative names: Chestnut-winged Sparrow
***P.c.fulgens*, South Somali Sparrow.**

Description: Male. Crown, nape and upper mantle chocolate-brown; lower mantle, back and rump grey, former streaked black; tail blackish; wings with primaries blackish and secondaries chocolate-brown; chin, throat and round eyes black; sides of face, breast, belly and rest of underparts pale yellow; iris brown, bill black; legs and feet reddish brown. Female upperparts earth-brown, mantle streaked black; stripe above and behind eye buff; underparts whitish across the belly, washed pale yellow. Juvenile similar to adult female, but paler with little yellow.

Male. *F.c.fulgens* differs from the nominate race in having ear-coverts and underparts brighter yellow.

Voice: Described by Mackworth-Praed & Grant as a chirruping note not distinguished from that of other sparrows.

Habitat: Semi-arid country, rocky and broken ground and often in the vicinity of human dwellings.

Distribution: Somalia.

P.c.fulgens Ethiopia and northern Kenya.

Feeding: Mainly seeds, grain and insects. Recorded feeding on camp litter and the droppings of pack animals.

Breeding: Not known.

Aviculture: No records.

Great Sparrow
Passer motitensis 15-16cm
Alternative name: *P.m.shelleyi* Rufous Sparrow.

Description: Male. Forehead, crown, nape and upper mantle grey; lower mantle and back tawny, streaked with black; tail blackish; flight feathers and wing-coverts blackish with buff edges; wing-stripe white; sides of face breast, belly and rest of underparts white; chin, throat and eye stripe black; iris dark brown; bill black (breeding) horn (non-breeding); legs and feet brownish. Female similar to male, but paler and lacks black bib. Juvenile similar to adult female, but males show blackish bibs.

Males. *P.m. subsolanus* differs from the nominate race in having crown darker grey; back and rump redder;

breast and rest of underparts heavily overlaid with grey.

P.m.benguellensis differs from the nominate in being paler overall.

P.m.cordofanicus differs from *shelleyi* in having upperparts paler; underparts dusky.

P.m.shelleyi differs from *cordofanicus* in having upperparts darker; underparts duskier.

P.m.benguellensis differs from the nominate in being paler overall.

Voice: Described by Maclean as harsh '*twittering cheep, cheep*' and '*chirititit*' call-notes.

Habitat: Arid to semi-arid savannas.

Distribution: North-West and the northern Cape Provinces of South Africa to Namibia and Botswana.

P.m.subsolanus Northern KwaZulu-Natal northern Free State, Gauteng and Northern Province, South Africa to Swaziland and southern Zimbabwe.

P.m.cordofanicus eastern Chad and north-western Sudan.

P.m.shelleyi southern Sudan, southern Ethiopia, north-western Somalia and northern Uganda.

P.m.benguellensis southern Angola and Namibia.

Feeding: Seeds, grain, nectar and insects. Nectar of Common Coral Tree *Erythrina lysistemon*. Also recorded taking mealie pap at a feeding table.

Breeding: The nest is a large thick-walled ball of grass, green leaves and seeding grassheads, lined with soft grass and a few feathers, placed 3-4m above ground in a thorn tree or bush. Eggs white, spotted and blotched with grey and lavender; clutch 2-4.

Aviculture: Selected Reference CLUTCH 2-4. Selected Reference WILDFOOD Seeds of Guinea grass *Panicum maximum*, Blue-seed grass *Tricholaena monachne*, Bur-bristle grass *Setaria verticillata*. Selected Reference ANIMAL FOOD termites, mealworms.

Cape Sparrow
Passer melanurus 14-16cm

Description: Male. Forehead, crown, nape, lores, sides of face, chin, throat and breast band black; broad circular eye stripe white; mantle and back earth brown; lower back, rump and wing-coverts chestnut; tail blackish; wingbar, rest of breast, belly and under tail-coverts white; iris brown; bill black; legs and feet brown. Female has mantle back, rump and upper tail-coverts earth brown; pale eye stripe; underparts buffish. Juvenile similar to adult female, male with darker head.

Males. *P.m.vicinus* differs from the nominate race in having the brown, throat, ear-coverts and breast band a more glossy black; underparts purer white.

P.m.damarensis differs from the nominate in being more sooty, less black; centre of nape and mantle pale olive-brown.

Voice: Described by Maclean as a rolling musical cheep, chirreep, chirrchreep callnotes.

Habitat: Thornveld, cultivation, exotic plantation, parks, gardens, towns and cities, usually in the vicinity of water.

Distribution: Western and eastern Cape Province, southern Free State and KwaZulu-Natal (interior), South Africa.

P.m.vicinus Gauteng (highveld), northern KwaZulu-Natal, central and eastern Free State, South Africa to northern Lesotho (lowlands).

P.m.damarensis North-West province, South Africa to Namibia, southern and south-western Angola, south-western Zimbabwe and southern and western Botswana.

Feeding: Seeds of soft plant parts, fruit, grain and insects. Seeds of Rooikrans *Acacia cyclops*, Gazania hybrids, and dry elms are eaten on the ground, fruit of Mistletoe *Viscum capense*, Common taaibos *Rhus pyroides*, buds and ovaries of prunes (peaches & apricots) including Satsuma Plum *P.salicina*. Live food in the form of hairless caterpillars, grasshoppers, termites, aphids, mantises and spiders.

Breeding: Nest, a large untidy mass of grass, dry weeds, string, old rags and cotton, lined with feathers and other soft materials. A female has been observed removing the linen fabric insulation from the telephone line, and birds have been recorded collecting old scraps of knitting wool left in the garden for them. The lighter coloured wool was preferred to the darker colours. Nests are placed in thorn bushes, trees, creepers, under the eaves of buildings, in hollow fence poles, on telegraph poles or in swallows nests and a record of nestling in a fig tree *Ficus* sp. Eggs white, bluish or greenish, usually blotched and mottled with earth brown or grey-brown; clutch 3-6; incubation 12-14 days, by both sexes; nestling period 16-25 days; young fed by both parents; host to Diederick Cuckoo *Chysococcyx caprius*.

Aviculture: Selected Reference CLUTCH 3-6; INCUBATION PERIOD 12-14 days; NESTLING PERIOD 16-25 days. Nest Record Cards CLUTCH 4; INCUBATION PERIOD 12 days; NESTLING PERIOD 21 days (ARU). Selected Reference WILDFOOD Seeds of Guinea grass *Panicum maximum*. Diet Record Cards Guinea grass *Panicum maximum*, Broadleaved panic *P.deustem*, buds of Wild radish *Raphanus raphanistrum* (ARU). Diet Record Cards ANIMAL FOOD butterfly/moth caterpillars, aphids, termites, crickets, mealworms (ARU).

Kenya Rufous Sparrow
Passer rufocinctus 15-16cm

Description: Male. Forehead, crown and ear-coverts grey; mantle and back tawny; rump rufous as well as stripe over eye, down side of neck and wing-shoulder; chin and throat black; rest of underparts buff; iris pale brown; bill black; legs and feet tawny. Female has forehead and upper mantle duskier. Juvenile similar to adult female, but paler, males having blackish throat.

Voice: Described by Mackworth-Praed & Grant as a high chirp like that of a sparrow, but apparently differing in pitch locally.

Habitat: Grasslands with abundance of Whistling thorn *Acacia drepanolobium*; also around cattle sheds and human settlements.

Distribution: Central Kenya and north-eastern Tanzania.

Feeding: Generally gleans on the ground, hopping stiffly, scratching for seeds; insects taken from low foliage, but occasionally catches termites on the wing.

Breeding: The nest is an untidy affair of dry grass with side entrance placed in a Whistling tree *Acacia drepanolobium* or in the thatch of huts and once among bananas. Lining consists of feathers and any other soft material found in the immediate vicinity. Eggs bluish white, heavily blotched and streaked with brown and grey; clutch 3-4; incubation period 11-12 days by both birds during the day, but longer spells by female; young birds vacant the nest 15-17 days after hatching; cared for and fed by both parents for a further 7-10 days.

Aviculture: Personal Communication CLUTCH 4; INCUBATION PERIOD 12 days; NESTLING PERIOD 16 days. Nest Record Cards CLUTCH 4; INCUBATION PERIOD 11 days; NESTLING PERIOD 17 days (ANRC). Personal Communication WILDFOOD seeds of Common thatch grass *Hyparrhenia hirta*. Diet Record Cards seeds of Guinea grass *Panicum maximum* (ADRC). Personal Communication ANIMAL FOOD aphids. Diet Record Cards termites (ADRC).

Grey-headed Sparrow

Passer griseus 15-16 cm

Alternative names: *P.g.diffusus* Southern Grey-headed Sparrow.
P.g.ugandae Uganda Grey-headed Sparrow.

Description: Sexes similar. Forehead, crown, nape and sides of face grey; mantle, back and wing-coverts tawny; rump rufous; tail earth brown; chin and throat pale grey; breast, belly and rest of underparts whitish; iris brown; bill black; legs and feet brownish. Juvenile similar to adult, but paler with streaked mantle.

Adults. *P.g.ugandae* differs from the nominate race in having head and neck paler grey; underparts remarkably whiter.

P.g.luangwae differs from *stygiceps* in having crown greyer.

P.g.mosambicus differs from nominate in being more richly coloured, especially on mantle and back.

P.g. diffusus differs from nominate in having mantle browner, less tawny.

P.g. stygiceps differs from the nominate in having upperparts warmer and darker.

Voice: Described by Serle *et al* as a loud '*cheerp*' or succession of 'cheerps'.

Habitat: Acacia savanna, exotic plantations, villages and towns with *luangwae* found only in mopane woodland, while *ugandae* strictly associated with African villages.

Distribution: Senegal, southern Mali, northern Ghana, northern Niger, Chad to western and central Sudan.

P.g.ugandae Ivory Coast, Cameroon to Sudan and northern and western Somalia, south to Uganda, Kenya and Tanzania, Zaire, the Congo, Angola, Zambia and Malawi.

P.g. laeneni eastern Chad.

P.g. luangwae eastern Zambia.

P.g. mosambicus eastern Tanzania, Malawi and Mozambique.

P.g. diffusus northern Cape , western Free State and North-West provinces, South Africa to Namibia, the Caprivi Strip, western Zimbabwe, Botswana, western and southern Angola and Zambia.

P.g. stygiceps eastern Cape, North-West, Gauteng, western Northern Province, KwaZulu-Natal and Free State (except west South Africa to Swaziland, Zimbabwe) (except west, southern Mozambique, southern Malawi and Zambia).

Feeding: Seeds and insects.

Breeding: Nest site is a natural hole in a tree, sometimes the disused nests of a woodpecker or barbet, or those of a Little Swift *Apus affinis* and Striped Swallow *Cecropis* sp., in hollow fence posts, under the eaves of buildings or beneath thatched roofs. Lined with feathers, wool and fibres. Eggs white, greenish or bluish, heavily mottled and blotched olive-brown; host of Diederik Cuckoo *Chrysoccyx caprius.*

Aviculture: Selected Reference 3-4; INCUBATION PERIOD 12-14 days; NESTLING PERIOD 17-23 days. Selected Reference WILDFOOD seeds of Common thatch grass *Hyparrhenia hirta*, Guinea grass *Panicum maximum*. Selected Reference ANIMAL FOOD mealworms.

Swainson's Sparrow

Passer swainsonii 15cm

Alternative names: Dusky-headed Sparrow, Abyssinian Grey-headed Sparrow.

Description: Sexes alike. Head, nape and upper mantle dusky grey; lower mantle dusky chestnut-brown; rump chestnut; wings dusky chestnut, median tipped with white, shoulder chestnut; underparts dusky grey; iris brown; bill black; legs and feet brown. Juvenile like adult in non-breeding attire, but mantle having dusky streaks.

Voice: Described by Stephens as a typical sparrow's chirping chatter, similar to the Grey-headed Sparrow.

Habitat: Acacia bushes, woodlands, cliffs, caves, towns and villages.

Distribution: Somalia, eastern and southern Ethiopia and northern Kenya (Moyale).

Feeding: Usually stays on or near ground hopping about seeking seeds and soft plant parts, berries, grain and insects, the latter especially when breeding.

Breeding: Nest, bulky, untidy domes structure with side entrance, of coarse dry grass and lined with feathers in any situation, either in thorn trees, in holes or thatch or in weavers' nest which are often unstriped and furbished to taste. Eggs blue-green, heavily mottled and blurred with deep lavender and brown; clutch 3-4;

incubation period 12-14 days, by both sexes; young tended by both parents; leaves nest at 16-23 days.

Aviculture: Personal Communication CLUTCH 4. Personal Communication WILDFOOD buds of Red garden sorrel *Oxalis latifolia*.

Parrot-billed Sparrow
Passer gongonensis 18cm

Description: Sexes alike. Head greyish brown; mantle, back and rump earth brown; tail blackish brown; chin, throat, breast and underparts greyish tawny; iris brown; large heavy bill black; legs and feet brown. Juvenile ground colours as adults, but paler.

P.g.jubaensis differs from nominate race in having brighter mantle; underparts paler; bill smaller. According to Britton birds with small bills at Liktaung 4' 16N 35' 45E) have been assigned to the nominate race, but they are more likely intergrades with *swainsonii*.

Voice: Described by Williams as a typical sparrow chirping.

Habitat: Open country with scattered trees and bushes.

Distribution: Kenya, north-eastern Uganda and north-eastern Tanzania.

P.g.jubaensis southern Somalia (Juba River Valley).

Feeding: Seeds.

Breeding: In a tree hole or placed amongst its branches and sometimes disused nests of other birds. The nest is an untidy accumulation, mainly of grasses lined with feathers. Eggs greenish white, thickly covered with grey and rufous-brown markings.

Aviculture: Personal Communication CLUTCH 2-3.

Swahili Sparrow
Passer suahelicus 14cm

Description: Sexes similar. Head, nape and mantle dusky grey; scapulars and wing-coverts tawny; rump rufous; tail earth brown; chin and throat white; breast and rest of underparts dusky grey; iris brown; bill black; legs and feet brown. Juvenile plumage pattern basically as adult, but paler, especially throat.

Voice: Described by Stephens as having various chirping notes.

Habitat: Open acacia and bush country.

Distribution: Southern Kenya and north-central Tanzania.

Feeding: Feeds in pairs and family groups hopping over ground often exposing food by scratching. Mainly seeds of weeds, some grain; also insects and larvae.

Breeding: Large untidy spherical nest of grass, lined with feathers etc., with side entrance placed in thorn bushes at 2-5m above the ground.

Aviculture: No records.

Desert Sparrow
Passer simplex 13cm

Description: Male. Head, nape, mantle and rump pale grey; tail blackish brown with broad pale edges at sides; chin, throat, lores black; rest of face, breast and underparts whitish or buff white; there is also some black on the wing-coverts, primaries and inner secondaries; iris dark brown; bill black in (breeding), horn coloured in (non-breeding) season; legs and feet dusky yellow. Female has upperparts sandy buff; chin, throat, lores, breast and underparts buffish white; there is also some dusky brown on the wing-coverts, primaries and inner secondaries; bill yellowish horn. Juvenile drab like the female, except males develop some adult markings by mid-summer.

Male. *P.s.saharae* flanks more whitish, less buff; crown and nape paler grey.

Habitat: Thin grass desert, oasis, tamakisks, cultivation and around human dwellings.

Distribution: South-eastern Morocco, Mauritania, Algeria, Tunisia, Libya and northern Sudan.

P.s.saharae western Sahara.

Feeding: Seeds of Awn grass, *Aristida* (staple food), and desert plants, saxual *Haloxylon*, saltwort *Salso* tragacanth *Astragalus*, *Raetama* flowers, cultivated grain, namely barley *Hordeum* and millet *Panicum* as well as livefood such as adult, larval and pupal beetles, grasshoppers, locusts, flies and spiders.

Breeding: Nest, a globular structure of dry grass and other soft material stuffed in wall hole or in a tree with side entrance, edge of well, crown of palm or within the large bowl of sticks and twigs of raven's nest etc. Eggs white, marked with shades of pale brown or cream and dark brown; clutch 2-5; incubation period 12-14 days by both sexes, mainly by female; nestling period 16-22 days; fed by both parents.

Aviculture: Nest Record Cards CLUTCH 4; INCUBATION PERIOD 14 days (ANRC); NESTLING PERIOD 18 days (ANRC). Diet Record Cards WILDFOOD green seeds of Rescue grass *Bromus unioloides*, Barnyard grass *Echinochloa crus-galli* and ripe seeds of Guinea grass *Panicum maximum* (ADRC). Diet Record Cards ANIMAL FOOD termites (ADRC).

Sudan Golden Sparrow

Auripasser luteus 13cm

Alternative names: Golden Sparrow, Golden Song Sparrow, Yellow Sparrow.

Description: Male. Head lemon-yellow; mantle and back chestnut; upper tail-coverts and rump paler yellow; tail greyish, narrowly edged with whitish buff; chin, throat, breast, belly and rest of underparts lemon-yellow; wings chestnut, two wing-bars whitish on black coverts; iris brown; bill blackish; legs and feet yellowish brown. Female paler having head, mantle, back and rump buffish brown with a few black streaks on mantle; underparts buffish yellow; bill paler horn-brown. Juvenile similar to adult female, but underparts paler.

Voice: Described by Mackworth-Praed & Grant as a sparrow-like chirp, also a twittering call on the wing.

Habitat: Arid thorn bush country visting villages and cultivation.

Distribution: Northern Nigeria, Chad, Sudan and northern Ethiopia.

Feeding: Seeds of *Panicum* grasses, cultivated grains namely millet *Pennisetum*, rice *Ozyza* and sorghum *Sorghum*. Livefood in the form of grasshoppers, termites, bugs, flies, ants, spiders and snails.

Breeding: Colonial nester, in low thorn tree of bush. Nest is an untidy oval structure with a side entrance, lined with fine grass and a few feathers. Eggs greenish white, spotted with greyish brown; clutch 3-4; incubation period 10-13 days; nestling period 14-16 days.

Aviculture: Selected Reference CLUTCH 3-4; INCUBATION PERIOD 10-13 days; NESTLING PERIOD 14 days. Nest Record Cards CLUTCH 3,3,4,4 (ANRC); INCUBATION PERIOD 11,12,12,12 days (ANRC); NESTLING PERIOD 13,14,14,14,15 days (ANRC). Diet Record Cards WILDFOOD Guinea grass *Panicum maximum* (ADRC). Diet Record Cards ANIMAL FOOD termites (ADRC).

Arabian Golden Sparrow

Auripasser euchlorus 13cm

Description: Male. Mainly golden-yellow with tail feathers whitish, tipped blackish; wings whitish, broadly fringed sandy buff; iris blackish; bill black; legs and feet dusky yellow. Female upperparts pale buffish grey; underparts buffy white; bill fleshy horn. Juvenile resembles adult female, but mantle slightly mottled.

Voice: Described by Hollom *et al*, with the flock uttering constant twittering, recalling House Sparrow.

Habitat: *Acacia* thorn country and *Tamarix* savannas and in cultivation.

Distribution: Somalia.

Feeding: Seeds, some grain, insects and their larvae.

Breeding: Builds an untidy dome nest of grass amongst the thorny twigs of *acacia* trees. Lined with any soft materials available within the vicinity of the nesting tree.

Aviculture: No records.

Chestnut Sparrow

Sorella eminibey 11,5cm

Description: Male. Uniform deep chestnut; wings and tail brown, edged pale buff; iris dark brown; bill black in (breeding) and horn-coloured in (non-breeding) season; legs and feet blackish brown. Female has crown ash-grey; mantle brown, streaked blackish; underparts buff. Juvenile similar to adult female, but upperparts ash-brown.

Voice: Described by Williams as subdued chirping.

Habitat: Acacia country, grasslands papyrus, swamps, cultivated tracts away from habitation, parks and gardens.

Distribution: Western and southern Sudan, Ethiopia, eastern Uganda, Kenya and northern Tanzania.

Feeding: Feeds on seeds of grasses and weeds, while young are reared on insects. Often feeds in the company of Ribbon Finches and Red-billed Queleas.

Breeding: Nests which are accumulations of dry grass and then lined with feathers are constructed in the drooping branches of a tree, where they resemble structures built by weavers. They are usually placed at some height from the ground. There is some doubt as to whether the birds construct the nest or utilize the abandoned nests of weavers. Eggs pale greenish white, spotted and blotched with brown and black; clutch 3-4; incubation which lasts for 10-11 days is largely the task of the female, but just before hatching the male increases his share of the work to about half; young tended by both parents; leave nest at 14-16 days, partly dependant on adults for 2 weeks or more.

Aviculture: Selected Reference CLUTCH 3-4; NESTLING PERIOD 18-19 DAYS. Nest Record Cards CLUTCH 4(ANRC); INCUBATION PERIOD 11 days (ANRC); NESTLING PERIOD 17 days (ANRC). Selected Reference ANIMAL FOOD mealworms. Diet Record Cards aphids (ADRC). Diet Record Cards WILDFOOD Guinea grass *Panicum maximum* (ADRC).

Pale Rock Sparrow

Petronia brachydactla 13cm

Description: Sexes similar. Forehead, crown, nape, mantle and back greyish; stripe over and behind eye russet brown, tail and wings ashy grey, edged black;

moustachial stripe brownish; chin and throat white; breast and belly buffish white; under tail-coverts white. Juvenile similar to adult female but paler overall.

Voice: Described by Hollom as a grasshopper-like 'zing-ling zeee' or 'zwee'.

Habitat: Stony slopes and rocky areas.

Distribution: Northern Sudan and Eritrea.

Feeding: Cereal crops, sunflower *Helianthus* barberry *Berberis,* mulberry *Morus,* strawberry *Frasaria*, cherry *Prunus*, fig *Ficus*, woad *Isatis*, gromwell *Lithospermum*, bugloss *Echium*, nightshade *Solanum*, caddisfly larvae, termites and cockroaches. Feeding data not confined to Africa.

Breeding: Nests may be sited in trees, hole or cavity in rocks and earthbanks. Also known to utilize that of martins, swallows, woodpeckers, bee-eaters and nut-hatchers. Constructed of grasses, then lined with wool, hair, paper, string and rootlets. Eggs white to whitish brown with reddish grey blotches. Nestling period 18-20.

Aviculture: No records.

Yellow spotted Petronia

Petronia xanthosterna pallida 15cm

Alternative names: Yellow-throated Sparrow.
***P.x.pyrgita* Abyssinian Sulphur-throated Rock Sparrow.**

Description: Male. Upperparts grey-brown; stripe over and behind eye buff; wings and tail ashy-brown, the former with a chestnut shoulder patch and two whitish wing-bars; throat patch yellow; chin and belly whitish; iris brown; bill horn; legs and feet dark flesh brown. Female has ground colours as male, but throat patch much paler and shoulder patch rufous. Juvenile plumage pattern basically as adult female, but mantle more or less indistinctly streaked blackish.

Males. *P.x.pyrgita* differs from *nassaica* in having upperparts lighter, less ashy brown or ashy grey.

P.x.massaica differs from *pyrgita* in having upperparts darker, more ashy brown or ashy grey.

P.x.kakamariae similar to *pyrgita*, but somewhat larger.

Voice: Described by Williams as a sparrow-like chirps but usually silent.

Habitat: Woodlands, date groves, trees near villages, gardens and cultivation.

Distribution: Senegal, Mauritania to western and central Sudan.

P.x.pyrgita Ethiopia, Somalia to northern Kenya

P.x.massaica Kenya to north-eastern Tanzania.

P.x.kakamariae southern Sudan to eastern Uganda and north-western Kenya.

Feeding: Seeds, grain, nectar and insects. Nominate race (India) recorded feeding on *lantana* berries, beetles, ants, caterpillars; on stomach contents revealed Scarab beetle *Onthophagus spinifer*, Ants *Oecophylla*

smaragdina, Weevils *Tanymecus hysipida, Myllocerus discolor* and *Geometrid* larvae. Nectar of *Bassia, Capparis, Erythrina* and *Salmalia.* Partial to rice.

Breeding: Nests are constructed in tree holes, preferably those excavated by woodpeckers, also barbets, holes in cliffs, hollows and cracks in tree trunks. The lining is a pad of grass, hair, wool and feathers. Eggs white, spotted grey-brown on uniformly mottled dark sooty brown; clutch 3-5; nest construction and incubation is exclusive to female; incubation period 13 days; nestling period 17-18 days; care of young by both parents.

Aviculture: Selected Reference CLUTCH 3-4; INCUBATION PERIOD 12-15 days; NESTLING PERIOD 14-20 days. Personal Communication CLUTCH 4; INCUBATION PERIOD 13 days; NESTLING PERIOD 16 days. Nest Record Cards CLUTCH 4,4 (ARU); INCUBATION PERIOD 12,13 days (ARU); NESTLING PERIOD 16, about 19 days (ARU). Diet Record Cards WILDFOOD leaves of Horseweed fleabane *Conyza canadensis*, seeds of Smelter's bush *Flaveria budentis* (ARU). Diet Record Card ANIMAL FOOD smooth green caterpillars (ARU).

Rock Sparrow

Petronia petronia 14cm

Alternative name: Rock Petronia.

Description: Sexes similar, Crown brown, with two dark stripes, rest of upperparts greyish brown, the mantle heavily streaked with sepia and the upper tail-coverts greyer; tail sepia, tip spotted white; lores, around eyes and upper ear-coverts buff; supercilliary stripe buffy white with a darker line above it; a yellow spot on the lower throat; breast and flanks buff-brown; underparts greyish shading to off-white in centre of belly; iris brown; bill dark horn, base pinkish; egs and feet brown. Juvenile similar to adult, but lacks yellow throat spot.

Male. *P.p.barbara* differs from the nominate race in being paler overall; bill larger.

Voice: Described by Peterson as a characteristic, squeaky 'peyi-i' varied chipping notes recall House Sparrow.

Habitat: Rocky mountain slopes, walls of ancient ruins or monuments, dry river beds and cultivation

Distribution: Morocco.

P.p.barbara Algeria and Tunisia.

Feeding: Insects, seeds, fruits and berries including caterpillars and grubs.

Breeding: Known to nest amongst colonies of House Sparrows and take over abandoned nest of a bee-eater and house martin.

Aviculture: Personal Communication CLUTCH 4-6; INCUBATION PERIOD 13 days; NESTLING PERIOD 18 day. Personal Communication WILDFOOD seeds of

Gallant Soldier *Galinsoga parviflora*, Smelter's bush *Flaveria bidentis*, leaves of Horseweed fleabane *Conyza canadensis*. Personal Communication ANIMAL FOOD butterfly/moth caterpillars, termites.

South African Rock Sparrow

Petronia superciliaris 15cm

Alternative names: African Diamond Sparrow, Yellow-throated Sparrow.

Description: Sexes similar. Forehead, crown and nape earth-brown; mantle, back and upper tail-coverts brown, streaked black; broad curved eyebrow white;

ear coverts white, tinged buff; chin, throat and upper breast buffish or greyish white; spot on centre of lower neck yellow; lower breast, belly and tail-coverts white; iris brown; bill dark horn, base pinkish; legs and feet brown. Juvenile similar to adult, but paler and lacking yellow neck spot.

Adults. *P.s.boroensis* differs from the nominate race in being paler overall, especially on the underparts.

P.s.flavigula differs from the nominate race in being much darker on the upperparts and tail.

P.s.rufitergum differs from *flavigula* in having the upperparts distinctly darker and more saturated reddish olivaceous.

Voice: Described by Williams as various chirping notes.

Habitat: Acacia savanna, exotic plantations, tall trees along streams and rivers.

Distribution: South African provinces of eastern Cape, KwaZulu-Natal.

P.s.boroensis eastern Tanzania (lowlands), northern Mozambique, southern Malawi, eastern Swaziland and north-eastern KwaZulu-Natal, and Mpumalanga provinces of South African.

P.s.flavigula south-eastern Zambia, eastern Botswana, Mozambique (Sul do Save), Zimbabwe and South Africa, in North-West, Northern Province and western Free State.

P.s.rufitergum southern Zaire, south-western Tanzania, northern Malawi, Zambia, Angola, north-western Botswana, north-eastern Namibia and the Caprivi Strip.

Feeding: Seeds, nectar and insects. Nectar of aloe *Aloe* spp., and *Loranthus* spp.

Breeding: Site a natural cavity in the tree, namely cedars and pines and in the disused holes of barbets and woodpeckers. The nest is warmly lined with grass, hair and feathers. Eggs greenish white, streaked and blotched brown; clutch 3-4, by female only; nestling period 18-19 days; young fed by both parents.

Aviculture: Selected Reference CLUTCH 3-4; INCUBATION PERIOD 12-13 days; NESTLING PERIOD 18-20 days. Nest Record Cards CLUTCH 3,4 (ARU) 4 (SAANRC); INCUBATION PERIOD 12 (ARU) 12 days (SAANRC); NESTLING PERIOD 18 (ARU) about 20 days (SAANRC). Diet Record Cards WILDFOOD seeds of Khaki weed *Tagetes minuta* (ARU), buds of Dwarf marigold *Schkuhria pinnata*. Diet Record Cards ANIMAL FOOD termites (ARU SAADRC).

Lesser Rock Sparrow

Petronia dentata 13cm

Alternative names: Bush Petronia, Bush Sparrow.

Description: Male. Headtop brownish grey; mantle and back brown; tail dark brown; sides of face and sides of neck greyish; chin and upper throat whitish, lower throat yellowish; stripe over and behind eye chestnut; breast greyish; rest of underparts greyish white; iris brown; bill black; legs and feet dark bluish grey or dark brown. Female has headtop brown; mantle and back brown, streaked black; stripe over and behind eye buff; bill horn. Juvenile resembles adult female, but yellow on lower throat faintly indicated or absent.

Male. *P.d.buchanani* differs from the nominate race in having upperparts paler.

Voice: Desribed by Mackworth-Praed & Grant as being like that of House Sparrow, but rather chirruping.

Habitat: Wadis, scattered trees and cultivation, also in clearings.

Distribution: Senegal to Ethiopia.

P.d.buchanani southern Niger.

Feeding: Insects and seeds.

Breeding: Nest in tree holes, natural or abandoned by woodpeckers. Lining consists of a pad of fine grass, some fibre, domestic animal fur and a number of feathers.

Aviculture: No records.

Scaly Weaver

Sporopipes squamifrons 10-11cm

**Alternative names: Hitler Finch,
Scaly-feathered Finch, Scaly-feathered Weaver.
S.s.pallidus Scaly fronted Weaver.**

Description: Sexes similar. Forehead and crown black, scaled white; lores, chin and bold malar stripe black; ear-coverts, nape, mantle and back light brownish grey; tail black; throat, breast and underparts white; wing-coverts and secondaries black; flight feathers dusky; iris brown; bill rose-pink; legs and feet brown. Juvenile plumage pattern similar to adult, but paler; bill horn-coloured.

Adults. *S.s.fuligescens* differs from the nominate race in being darker and more greyish on the upperparts, less sandy.

S.s.pallidus (see *Richard Howard and Alick Moore, A Complete Checklist of the Birds of the World, 1984, P. 613*).

Voice: Described by Prozesky, alarm-call a loud '*zeer-rrp*'; take-off call a soft '*zwirr-zwirr*', rapidly repeated.

Habitat: Arid scrub acacia savanna, cultivation gardens and poultry-runs.

Distribution: Southern and western Botswana, southern Angola, Namibia and northern and western Cape Province, South Africa.

S.s.fuligescens eastern and northern Botswana, Zimbabwe and Gauteng (highveld), western Free State and north-eastern Cape Province, South Africa.

S.s.pallidus Angola (Mossamedes).

Feeding: Seeds of grasses and weeds and insects.

Breeding: Nest, an oval ball of grass with a side entrance made of grass stems. Known to utilize the old nests of flycatches and shrikes. Also recorded nesting under the eaves of houses. Nest usually situated at 0,9-4, 2m above ground in a horizontal position in a thorn bush or tree, acacia mostly favoured. Eggs greenish, spotted with greyish brown; clutch 1-7, usually 3-5; incubation period 10-12 days; nestling period 13-18 days.

Aviculture: Selected Reference CLUTCH 1-7, usually 3-5; INCUBATION PERIOD 10-14 days; NESTLING PERIOD 13-18 days. Nest Record Cards 3,5,5 (SAANRC) 5 (ARU); INCUBATION PERIOD 12,13 (SAANRC) 13 days (ARU); NESTLING PERIOD 15 (ARU) 17 days (SAANRC). Diet Record Cards WILD-FOOD Seeds of Natal panic *Panicum natalanse*, Broad-leaved panic *P.deustem* Guinea grass *P.maximum*, Buffalo grass *P.stapfianum*, Red-top *Rhynchelytrum setifolium* (ARU), Hay *Chloris virgata*, Babala *Pennisetum americanum* leaves of Common dandelion *Taraxacum officinale* (SAADRC). Diet Record Cards ANIMAL FOOD termites, mealworms (ARU SAADRC), grasshoppers (ARU).

Speckle-fronted Weaver

Sporopipes frontalis 12-13cm

**Alternative names: Red-fronted Finch,
Speckle-fronted Weaver.
S.f.emini Kenya Speckled-fronted Weaver.**

Description: Sexes similar. Forehead, crown and moustachial streak black speckled with white; mantle, back and rump ashy grey; wings and tail dusky, edged with buffy white; occiput and neck pale rufous; chin white; sides of face and breast greyish; underparts dull brownish grey; iris brown; bill horn coloured; legs and feet pinkish brown. Juvenile similar to adult female, but occiput and neck tawny.

Males. *S.f.pallidior* differs from the nominate race in having upperparts paler.

S.f.emini differs from nominate in having mantle, back and rump more ashy grey.

Voice: Described by Serle *et al* as a little triling song uttered particularly when taking flight.

Habitat: Bushed grassland in low medium rainfall areas at 400-2000m; in East Africa, typically near water in semi-arid country. Also on edge of cultivation and in vicinity of human settlements.

Distribution: Senegal to eastern Ethiopia.

S.f.pallidior southern Sahara.

S.f.emini southern Sudan, north-eastern Uganda, Kenya and northern Tanzania.

Feeding: Seeds.

Breeding: Nest, a sparrow-like ball of grass, softheads being preferred, and lined with softer materials. Enters the chamber through a side entrance. Usually built in thorn trees and under eaves of houses or suspended from the end of a bough with both sexes participating in nest construction. Eggs greyish green or pale grey, with longitudinal blotches that merge with each other; clutch 3-4; incubation period 11 days; care of young by female only; nestling period 16-18 days.

Aviculture: Selected Reference CLUTCH 4; INCUBATION PERIOD 12 days; NESTLING PERIOD 21 days. Nest Record Cards 4.5 (ANRC) 5 (ARU); INCUBATION PERIOD 12,12 (ARU) about 12 days (ANRC); NESTLING PERIOD 19,21 (ARU) after 19 days (ANRC). Diet Record Cards ANIMAL FOOD termites (ARU ADRC), mealworms (ARU), aphids, wasp larvae of "grubs" (ADRC).

Grosbeak Weaver

Amblyospiza albifrons 18-19cm

Alternative names: Black Swamp Weaver, Thick-billed Weaver.
A.a.montana **Kenya Grosbeak Weaver.**
A.a.unicolor **East Coast Grosbeak Weaver, White-fronted Grosbeak.**
A.a.capitalbe **Ashanti White-fronted Grosbeak.**

Description: Male. Crown, nape, mantle, back and upper tail-coverts dark brown; tail blackish brown; frontal patch white; chin, ear-coverts, throat and breast dark brown; underparts sooty grey; primaries white as the base showing as a white wing-patch; iris brown; bill has blackish horn or dark grey; legs and feet grey to blackish. Female has crown, nape, mantle, back and upper tail-coverts olive-brown; chin, throat, breast and underparts white or creamy white, heavily streaked with dark brown; bill upper mandible greyish horn, lower mandible yellowish. Juvenile similar to adult female, but more rufous above; bill yellowish.

Males. *A.a.capitalba* differs from the nominate race in having upper breast brighter rufous.

A.a.saturata similar to *melanota*, but underparts greyish white; head and neck paler rufous.

A.a.melanota differs from the nominate in having mantle, rump and tail less brownish.

A.a.montana similar to *unicolor*, but bill stouter and larger.

A.a.unicolor differs from *melanota* in having a broader white band on forehead; upper mantle paler rufous-brown.

A.a.kasaica differs from nominate in being darker overall.

A.a.maxima differs from nominate in being darker on crown and nape; underparts more sooty grey.

A.a.woltersi differs from the nominate in being paler overall; bill less massive.

Voice: Described by Williams as a short low whistle and a bried buffling song.

Habitat: Edges of evergreen forests, exotic plantations, cultivation, reedbeds and in groves of Bugweed *Solanum mauritianum*.

Distribution: KwaZulu-Natal and Cape Province, South Africa.

A.a.capitalba Sierre Leone to Nigeria.

A.a.saturata Cameroons to Zaire.

A.a.melanota north-eastern Zaire, Ethiopia, Uganda and north-western Kenya.

A.a.montana southern Kenya, Zambia, Tanzania, northern Zimbabwe and Malawi.

A.a.unicolor eastern Kenya and eastern Tanzania.

A.a.tandae northern Angola.

A.a.kasaica Southern Zaire.

A.a.woltersi South African province of northern KwaZulu-Natal to Mozambique and eastern Zimbabwe (on Zambesi River) and south-western Zambia.

Feeding: Seeds, fruits, berries, snails and insects. Fruit of White Stinkwood *Celtis africana*, Thorny elm *Chaetcme aristata* and Dogwood *Rhamnux prinoides*. A photographic record of bird eating a frog. In Malawi recorded feeding on the seeds of conifer and termites.

Breeding: Nests in colonies of up to 50 nests in low marshy areas, each nest being slung between two upright stems of bulrush *Typha* spp., or reed *Phragmites* spp. The nest is a spherical structure of fine strips of grass, rush, sedge or palm leaves. The small circular entrance is to the side, a third of the distance from the top. Nests with large entrances are used for roosting. The building operation is carried out by the male in 2-12 days. The female assists with the arranging of materials in the nest chamber. One nest examined had an external height of 17cm, width 10cm, walls about 1,5cm thick and floor about 3cm thick. Eggs white to pink, spotted with brown, red and purple; clutch 3-5; incubation 15-16 days, by female only; nestling period 19-22 days; young fed by regurgitation, not with insects; host to Diederick Cuckoo *Chysococcyx caprius*.

Aviculture: Selected Reference CLUTCH 3-5; INCUBATION PERIOD 13-16 days; NESTLING PERIOD 19-22 days. Nest Record Cards CLUTCH 3,4 (ARU) 4 (SAANRC); INCUBATION PERIOD 14 (ARU) 13 days (SAANRC); NESTLING PERIOD 20 (ARU) about 21 days (SAANRC). Diet Record Cards WILDFOOD seeds of Paw Paw *Papaya carica* (SAADRC), Johnson grass *Sorghum halpense*, Guinea grass *Panicum maximum* (ARU). Diet Record Cards FRUIT Cape cherry *Cassina aethiopica* (SAADRC), Strawberry-guava *Psidium cattleianum* (ARU). Diet Record Cards ANIMAL FOOD termites (ARU SAADRC).

Bagafecht Weaver

Ploceus bagafecht 15cm

Alternative names: *P.b.neumanni* **Neumann's Bagafecht Weaver.**
P.b.reichenowi **Reichenow's Weaver.**
P.s.sharpii **Tanzanian Masked Weaver.**
P.b.stuhlmanni **Stuhlmann's Weaver.**

Description: Male. Forehead and crown yellow; nape yellowish green; mantle and back green, streaked blackish; rump green; tail brownish, tinged green; wings blackish, edged yellowish green; round eye, ear-coverts and chin black; sides of neck and breast yellow; belly whitish; rest of underparts yellowish; iris pale yellow; bill black; legs and feet dusky horn. Female differs from male in having forehead, crown and nape black. Juvenile similar to adult female, but upperparts dusky olive with dark streaking.

Males. *P.b.reichenowi* differs from the nominate race in having belly ashy; rump greyish, streaked black; tail green.

P.b.stuhlmanni differs from the nominate race in having upperparts golden-green; tail olive-green; underparts bright chrome yellow.

P.b. sharpii similar to *stuhlmanni* with belly pale and more lemon-yellow.

P.b.neumanni differs from *eremobius* in having underparts deeper green.

P.b.eremobius differs from the nominate in having lower breast, belly and under tail-coverts white.

P.b.emini differs from the nominate in having hindcrown to mantle black.

Voice: Described by Guggisberg as a sharp chirp; song short, chattering.

Habitat: Edges of evergreen forest, cultivation and often close to human habitations.

Distribution: Ethiopia and southern Sudan.

P.b.reichenowi Kenya and northern Tanzania.

P.b.stuhlmanni eastern Zaire, southern Uganda, western Tanzania, Zambia and Malawi.

P.b.sharpii south-western Tanzania.

P.b.neumanni Cameroon.

P.b.eremobius north-eastern Zaire and south-eastern Sudan.

P.b.emini southern Sudan and northern Uganda.

Feeding: Seeds, berries and insects.

Breeding: Nest, retort-shaped, green grass, with short spout, *neumanni* oval-shaped and unspouted. Lined with seedheads and bound to middle rib of palm, front, grass stems, eucalyptus and other low tree, bushes and sometimes thistles near the ground. In Central Africa observed attached to end of a fig *Ficus* sp., Cape Lilac and "nsambya". Breeds singly or in a small colony. Eggs pinkish white or bluish green, spotted and blotched with purple brown, rufous and lilac; clutch 2-3.

Aviculture: No records.

Bannerman's Weaver

Ploceus bannermani -cm

Description: Sexes similar. Forehead, crown, nape and sides of neck golden-yellow; face mask black; mantle, back, rump, upper tail-coverts and tail golden olive; chin, throat, breast and rest of underparts golden-yellow; iris yellow; bill black; legs and feet brown. Juvenile undescribed.

Voice: Described by Mackworth-Praed & Grant as a sharp '*pritt*'.

Habitat: Mountain forests.

Distribution: Cameroon.

Feeding: Insects.

Breeding: Not known.

Aviculture: No records.

Bates's Weaver

Ploceus batesi -cm

Description: Male. Forehead, crown, nape and ear-coverts reddish chestnut; collar and sides of neck yellow; mantle, back, rump, upper tail-coverts and tail olive-greenl; chin and throat black; breast, belly and rest of underparts golden-yellow; iris dark brown; bill black; legs and feet bluish grey. Female has forehead, crown, nape and ear-coverts black; chin and throat yellow. Juvenile similar to adult female, but head olive-green; bill pale horn.

Voice: Not known.

Habitat: Forest edges.

Distribution: Southern Cameroon.

Feeding: Insects.

Breeding: Not known.

Aviculture: No records.

Black-chinned Weaver

Ploceus nigrimentum 18cm
Alternative name: Angola Weaver.

Description: Male. Forehead and crown saffron-yellow; nape golden-yellow; mantle and back black; rump and upper tail-coverts yellow-green feathers black, edged golden yellow; tail olive-green; upper ear-coverts, chin and upper throat black; lower throat saffron; breast, belly and under tail-coverts golden-yellow; iris greenish yellow; bill black; legs and feet greyish brown. Female has forehead, crown and nape black. Juvenile not known.

Voice: Not known.

Habitat: Not known.

Distribution: Western Angola and southern Zaire.

Feeding: Not known.

Breeding: Not known.

Aviculture: No records.

Bertrand's Weaver
Ploceus bertrandi 15cm

Description: Male. Forehead and crown yellowish orange; hindneck, lores, around eye, sides of face, ear-coverts, chin and upper throat black; mantle, back and tail greenish; wings blackish, edged with green; underparts yellow, tinged with orange; iris grey; bill black; legs and feet brown. Female has entire head black. Juvenile has the head green, mixed with black; sides of face mixed with yellow and black; bill blackish horn.

Voice: Described by Brown as a noisy chattering not distinguishable from that of other weavers.

Habitat: Open woodland and bushland along rivers, edges of moist montane forest and near cultivation. In eastern Tanzania in hilly country at 900-1800m.

Distribution: Mozambique, Malawi and central Tanzania.

Feeding: Seeds, insects and their larvae.

Breeding: Built in colonies. A beautiful firmly woven nest of long broad-leaved grass with a finer lining, and an entrance on underside without porch or entrance tunnel. Nests are usually attached to the ends of boughs, low down and frequently over water.

Aviculture: No records.

Slender-billed Weaver
Ploceus pelzeini 11,5-12 cm
Alternative names: Pelzein's Weaver
P.p.monachus **Monk weaver**
P.p.tuta **Slender-billed Weaver**

Description: Male. Forehead, forecrown, sides of face, ear-coverts, chin and throat black; hindcrown, nape and sides of neck golden-yellow; mantle and back green; tail yellow, tinged green; wings dusky, edged yellow; breast and rest of underparts golden-yellow; iris brown; bill

black; legs and feet brown. Female lacks black facial adornment. Juvenile similar to adult female, but upperparts yellow, tinged green; mantle streaked dusky; bill horn.

Males. *P.p.monachus* differs from the nominate race in being smaller overall; legs and feet grey.

P.p.tuta differs from the nominate in being larger overall.

Voice: Described by Williams as a subdued chattering calls, but relatively quiet for a weaver.

Habitat: Swamp woodland and papyrus reeds.

Distribution: Uganda, Kenya, Tanzania and eastern Zaire.

P.p.monachus Ghana to Gabon and northern Angola.

P.p.tuta south-eastern Zaire.

Feeding: Seeds and insects.

Breeding: Nest, small roughly built of grass, lined with soft grassheads and a few feathers. Attached to a tree, bush or papyrus reed. Eggs pinkish white, spotted dark chocolate-brown, clutch 2-3.

Aviculture: No records.

Holub's Golden Weaver
Ploceus xanthops 17-18cm
Alternative names: P.x.jamesoni Golden Weaver, Large Golden Weaver, Olive-backed Weaver.

Description: Male. Forehead, crown, nape, sides of face and ear-coverts golden-yellow; mantle, back, rump and upper tail-coverts yellowish green; throat and upper breast golden-yellow, tinged with orange; lower breast, belly and underparts yellowish green; flight feathers blackish with yellowish edges; iris yellow; bill black; legs and feet pinkish brown. Female similar to male, but upperparts paler golden green; underparts with no orange on throat and breast. Juvenile similar to adult female, but duller.

Male. *P.x.jamesoni* differs from the nominate race in being greener, and having only the forehead yellow; ear-coverts washed with olive-green.

Voice: Described by Willis as making a harsh chrip and a prolonged swizzling.

Habitat: Rank vegetation, trees or bushes and frequently reed-beds along streams and rivers.

Distribution: North-eastern Namibia, the Caprivi Strip, north-western and northern Botswana, Angola, western and northern Zambia and Zaire, but eastern limits uncertain.

P.x.jamesoni north-eastern KwaZulu-Natal, and eastern Northern Province, South Africa to Swaziland, northern Mozambique, south-eastern Zambia and Malawi, but precise north-eastern limited not determined.

Feeding: Seeds, fruit and insects. Fruit of Sycamore fig *Ficus sycomorus*, termites.

Breeding: Nests may be solitary or in small colonies attached to the end of a branch, palm leaf or in upright reeds about 1-6m above water. Nest is a large loosely woven ball of reed blades, coarse grass or palm leaves, lined with grass inflorescenses which usually protrude through the short tubed entrance. Eggs white or pale blue; plain, speckled, spotted or blotched with reddish brown, grey and violet; clutch 2-3;, nestling period 19-22 days; young fed by both parents, mostly by female; host to Diederick Cuckoo *Chrysocossyx caprius*.

Aviculture: Nest Record Cards CLUTCH 2; INCUBATION PERIOD about 14 days; NESTLING PERIOD about 21 days (ANRC). Diet Record Cards WILDFOOD. Seeds of Guinea grass *Panicum maximum*. Diet Record Cards FRUIT Cape fig *Ficus capensis*, Common taaibos *Rhus pyroides* (ADRC). Diet Record Cards ANIMAL FOOD termites.

Orange Weaver
Ploceus aurantius 15cm
Alternative name: *P.a.rex* Uganda Orange Weaver

Description: Male. Entire head orange-yellow; black spot in front of eye; mantle, back and rump olivaceous yellow; uppertail-coverts pale-orange; tail orange-yellow, edged with olivaceous; chin and throat golden-yellow, tinged with chestnut; rest of underparts orange-yellow; iris red to reddish brown; bill blackish brown; legs and feet pale brown. Female upperparts olivaceous with indistinct dusky streaks on mantle; belly and under tail-coverts white; sides of face and chest pale yellow. Juvenile similar to adult female with bill brownish horn.

Male. *P.a.rex* differs from the nominate race in having large black spot in front of eye extending to lores; bill black.

Voice: Described by Serle *et al.* as a noisy concerted chattering at breeding colony.

Habitat: Forest edges and in reed beds.

Distribution: Senegal to Cameroon, Gabon and Zaire.

P.a.rex Uganda and north-western Tanzania

Feeding: Seeds, insects and their larvae.

Breeding: Nests are in colonies and are attached to reeds or suspended by short plaited ropes from the ends of outer boughs, usually overhanging water. Nests in all stages of construction can be observed due to the non-industrious attitudes of males to complete them at their leisure. May be observed associating in a colony of Golden-backed Weavers *Ploceus jacksoni* and Northern Brown-throated Weavers *P.castanops*. An untidy pear-shaped or spherical nest of dry grass with a small porch over the entrance which is at the side of the bottom. Lining consists of broad bladed grass. Eggs variable, greenish or bluish, spotted and blotches with various

shades of brown; clutch 3 up to 7; incubation by female only for 13-14 days; nestling period 13-16 days.

Aviculture: Selected Reference CLUTCH 2-3; INCUBATION PERIOD 17-18 days. Selected Reference WILDFOOD chickweed *Stellaria* sp., Groundsel *Senecio vulgaris*, clover *Trifolium* sp. Selected Reference ANIMAL FOOD mealworms, smooth caterpillars, earwigs, woodlice, millipedes, centipedes.

Loanga Slender-billed Weaver
Ploceus subpersonatus -cm

Description: Male. Entire head black; nape golden-yellow; mantle, back, rump and upper tail-coverts olive washed with yellow; tail yellowish green, tinged dusky; chin and throat black; breast golden-brown; belly and rest of underparts yellow washed with yellow; wings olive-green, feathers edged dusky; iris brown; bill black; legs and feet greyish brown. Female upperparts olive-green, except forehead yellow; underparts yellow washed olive brownish.

Voice: Not known.

Habitat: Coastal vegetation.

Distribution: Southern Gabon.

Feeding: Not known.

Breeding: Not known.

Aviculture: No records.

Little Masked Weaver
Ploceus luteolus 12cm
Alternative names: Little Weaver, Atlas Weaver *P.l.kavirondensis* Kavirondensis Little Weaver

Description: Male. Forehead, forecrown sides of face, ear-coverts, chin and throat black; hindcrown, nape and sides of neck yellow; mantle and back greenish yellow; upper tail-coverts yellow; tail and wings dusky, edged yellow; breast, belly and rest of underparts yellow; iris reddish brown; bill dusky horn; legs and feet flesh. Female lacks the facial adornment; underparts paler yellow. Juvenile closely resemble adult female, but paler overall.

Male. *P.l.kavirondensis* differs from the nominate race in having upperparts greener.

Voice: Described by Guggisberg as having a soft churring call and a little song interspersed with jarring notes.

Habitat: Dry woodlands, wooded and bushed grassland and cultivation at 400-1500m in East Africa.

Distribution: Senegal, Sudan and Ethiopia.

Feeding: Seeds.

Breeding: Oblong spout-like nest made of grass and unlined or lined with fine grass in the Sudan, and with hair and other soft material in Ethiopia. The nest has a tunnel entrance which goes from the lower side upwards into the bowl-shaped chamber. Eggs white; clutch 2-3.

Aviculture: Selected Reference CLUTCH 4; INCUBATION PERIOD 12 days; NESTLING PERIOD 15 days. Selected Reference ANIMAL FOOD termites.

Spectacled Weaver
Ploceus ocularis 15-16cm

**Alternative names: Bottle Weaver,
East African Spectacled Weaver
P.o.crocatus Uganda Spectacled Weaver**

Description: Male. Forehead, forecrown, sides of face and ear-coverts golden-yellow; lores, around and behind eye, chin and throat black; mantle, rump and upper tail-coverts yellow-green; tail green; wing-coverts yellow-green, flight feathers dusky edged with green; underparts golden-yellow; iris light brown; bill black; legs and feet blue-grey. Female similar to male but chin and throat golden-yellow. Juvenile like adult female, but lacks orange on face; bill horn coloured.

Males. *P.o.crocatus* differs from the nominate race in having crown more golden-yellow.

P.o.suahelicus differs from the nominate in having chestnut wash on forehead and ear-coverts stronger.

P.o.brevior (see *Hartert 1921, Novit Zool 28, P 136 Zinder (French Niger Territory)*).

Voice: Described by Skead as a pretty tripping, descending '*tee-tee-tee-tee-tee-tee*'.

Habitat: Riverine forests, on edges and in associated thickets, parks and gardens.

Distribution: Eastern Cape Province, South Africa.

P.o.suahelicus Northern Province, South Africa, northern Mozambique (Limpopo River), eastern Zimbabwe, eastern Zambia, Malawi, eastern Tanzania and Kenya (coast).

P.o.crocatus Cameroon to Ethiopia, Tanzania and northern Angola.

P.o.brevior southern Mozambique, eastern Swaziland, Mpumalanga and KwaZulu-Natal, South Africa.

Feeding: Insects, arthropods, fruit, nectar and seeds. Animal food such as spiders, millipedes, centipedes with 2 geckoes 2,5cm long being recorded. Fruit of Mulberry *Morus alba*, berries of Confetti bush *Lantana camara*, nectar of Rough-leaved commiphora *Commiphora edulis* and chicken mash. A male was observed taking 11 trips to the nest with beakfuls of bread, taken from a dustbin during a survey in KwaZulu-Natal, South Africa, 70% of the sightings were birds foraging in acacia trees spending most of the time searching the bark to obtain lepidopteran larvae on the surface and beneath the bark, and also taking spiders and the occasional large centipedes.

Breeding: The nest is a beautifully woven thin-walled ball made of green grass strands of portions stripped from broader *monocotyledonous* leafblades such as *Watsonia, Antolyza* and *Homeria* (leaves are flattened usually in two ranks, with parallel venation), reeds and palms, sinuous creeper tendrils, leaves, cow tail-hair or horsehair is sometimes incorporated, with the latter being utilized in entirely one observation. Also recorded is fishing line and nylon thread. Attached from below is a vertical entrance spout about 25-30cm long, sometimes up to 2m. Lining consists of fine grass, plant down or fine cow-tail hair. Nest building by male while female may poke at loose strands, but does not weaver, except perhaps the lining. Nests are usually attached to the end of boughs of trees, bushes, creepers or palms with Catthorn *Scutia myrtina*, African mulberry *Morus mesozygia*, Paperbark acacia *Acacia sieberana* and bougainvillea *Bougainvillea* sp. being recorded. Sited about 3-6m above ground which may overhang a dry gully or flowing stream. Eggs pinkish white or greenish, streaked and spotted with brown and grey; clutch 2-6, usually 3; incubation period 13-14 days; nestling period 17-19 days; both sexes feed the young; a Diederick Cuckoo *Chrysococcyx caprius* chick in one nest caused on average a weight loss of 8,8% to the parent birds during the nestling period.

Aviculture: Selected Reference CLUTCH 2-3; INCUBATION PERIOD 12-13 days; NESTLING PERIOD 17-19 days. Selected Reference FRUIT mulberry *Morus* sp., *Lantana camara* (no common name), Common taaibos *Rhus pyroides*, Tswana *Lantana vibrunoides*. Selected Reference ANIMAL FOOD spiders, millipedes, aphids.

Black-necked Weaver
Ploceus nigricollis 15cm

Description: Male. Forehead, crown, nape and sides of face yellow washed with chestnut; stripe through eye black; mantle, back, rump, upper tail-coverts and tail brownish black; wings brownish black, feathers edges greenish; chin and throat black; sides of neck, breast, belly and under tail-coverts golden-yellow; bill black; iris dark brown; legs and feet dusky yellow. Female has forehead, crown and nape black; mantle and back browish olive; supercilliary stripe golden-yellow; chin and throat yellow. Juvenile similar to female, but mantle and back olive-green; breast and belly pale yellow; bill horn.

Voice: Described by Guggisberg as a vibrating '*teee, teee*'.

Habitat: Forest edge and dense bush up to 1300m in East Africa.

Distribution: *P.n.brachypterus* Senegal to Nigeria, Cameroon to Sudan, Zaire, Angola, western Kenya, Uganda and Tanzania.

Feeding: Caterpillars, beetles and spiders.

Breeding: Nest, retort-shaped with entrance at end of pendulant tunnel of about 20cm long, built of grass and hangs no more than 3m above the ground. Built in clumps and Elephant grass *Hyparrhenia collina* (a perennial which is 300-1300m high and grows on or around old termite mounds), in small trees, large bushes and in African Wild Date Palms *Phoenix reclinata*. Eggs pale blue, greenish, pink or reddish white with brown, grey or mauve markings; clutch 2-3.

Aviculture: No records.

Strange Weaver
Ploceus alienus 14cm

Description: Adult. Male. Entire head and throat black; mantle, back, tail and wings green; breast and sides of lower neck chestnut; belly and underparts golden-yellow; iris brown; bill black; legs and feet greyish green. Female has entire head green; throat blackish; chest chestnut. Juvenile similar to adult female, but chin to chest yellowish green, washed with chestnut of dusky green; males have throat blackish; bill blackish horn.

Voice: Described by Hodge as the all too familiar noisy chattering not distinguishable from that of other weavers.

Habitat: Typically in the mid-stratum of forest but also in bamboo and more open country.

Distribution: Eastern Zaire and western Uganda.

Feeding: Seeds and insects.

Breeding: The nest is usually just out of reach at about 4m from the ground, suspended from a bough and composed of tendrils with a few grass blades. Eggs creamy white, thickly spotted with reddish brown and with lilac-grey undermarkings; clutch 2.

Aviculture: No records.

Black-billed Weaver
Ploceus melangaster 14cm

Description: Male. Forehead, crown and sides of face yellow; nape, mantle, back, rump, upper tail-coverts and tail black; crescent across upper breast yellow; streak through eye black; chin, throat, lower breast, belly and under tail-coverts sooty black; iris dark red; bill black; legs and feet slate-grey. Female similar to male, but chin and throat yellow. Juvenile upperparts sooty black; underparts sooty brown; bill horn.

Male. *P.m.stephanophorus* differs from the nominate race but lacks yellow crescent on upperparts.

Voice: Described by Guggisberg as being silent, but may occasionally utter a high-pitched '*chirp*'.

Habitat: Mountain undergrowth and forest canopy.

Distribution: Eastern Nigeria, western Cameroon and Fernando Pó Island.

P.m.stephanophorus southern Sudan, eastern Zaire, south-western Uganda and north-western Kenya.

Feeding: Seeds and insects.

Breeding: Nest retort-shaped, woven with grass and lined with vegetable fibres among *Lianas* hung from the branches of trees and bushes. Eggs white, spotted with grey and red; clutch 2.

Aviculture: No records.

Cape Weaver
Ploceus capensis 17-18cm

Alternative names: Rufous-masked Weaver, White-eyed Cape Weaver.

Description: Male. Forehead and crown golden-yellow, tinged with orange; nape, mantle, back, rump and upper tail-coverts yellow, streaked with olive; tail olive-green; chin, throat and ear-coverts pale yellow, tinged with orange; breast, belly and underparts golden-yellow; wings blackish, the feathers edged with yellow; iris yellow, brown or white; bill black; legs and feet flesh coloured. Female being greyish olive above lightly streaked dusky; breast and throat buffy; iris brown. Juvenile similar to adult female, but duller.

Males. *P.c.olivaceus* differs from the nominate race in having forehead, crown, chin and throat tinged with chestnut.

P.c.rubricomus differs from *olivaceus* in having the crown orange; sides of face more orange-rufous, extending to the sides of the neck; chin and fore-throat dull orange, less olive.

Voice: The fullest description of the voice of this species, that we have read, is by Skead, the male '*a-Zwit ...a-zwit ...a-zwit*', etc. rapidly repeated; flight call uttered on the ground 'swiz-swiz-swiz' etc., alarm note a deep 'chuck-chuck'; female when chased on the nest an agitated 'kaa-kaa-kaa' or 'Sh reh-shreh-shreh'.

Habitat: Any type of country with indigenous and exotic trees, cultivation, parks and gardens usually near water.

Distribution: Western Cape Province, Free State and western KwaZulu-Natal (lowlands), South Africa and Lesotho.

P.c.rubricomus Central and eastern Gauteng, northern KwaZulu-Natal, south of Northern Province and southern and central Mpumalanga, South Africa and Swaziland.

Feeding: Seeds, ovaries of flowers, nectar and insects. Nectar of *Erythrina* sp., seeds of Common hook-thorn *Acacia caffra*, Rooi-krans *A.cyclops*, Flat-crowned *Albiza adianthifolia*, fruit of Mulberry *Morus alba*; Common Taaibos *Rhus pyroides*, flower ovaries of Weeping Bottlebrush *Callisemon viminallis*, Coast erythrina *Erythrina caffra*, Red-hot-poker *Kniphofia* sp. Much artificial food and domestic scraps is eaten. Live food, namely grasshoppers, beetles, termites, caterpillars and recorded stealing "earthworms" from plovers as they were pulled from the ground.

Breeding: The males are polygamous and nest colonially in groups of up to 10 nests. A large kidney-shaped nest with short verticle entrance tube is constructed of narrow grass blades, palm leaves or pine needles. One observation revealed use of Pampas grass *Cortadera selloana*, Napier fodder *Pennisectum purpureum* and Rescue grass *Bromus unioloides*. Lined by female which may consist of seedheads, leaves and feathers. One nest contained 176 feathers, all except 2 were from white domestic poultry, the two exceptions being that of guineafowl *Numida* sp. The ingredients of one nest contained the seedheads of lovegrass *Eragrostis*, setaria *Setaria*, speargrass *Heteropogon*, dropseed *Sporobolus*, redgrass *Themeda* and Silky grass *Elyonurus argenteus* and leaves *Grevllea robusta*. Nests are attached to the outer boughs of trees, upright reeds or telephone wires, 4-10m above ground. Any nests hanging in the area at commencement of the new building season are torn down. The same twigs may well be utilized for the building of the new sites as well as using new branches. One male was observed demolishing a nest only built 3-4 days prior, only to rebuild another on the same site. Nests are used for sleeping, by breeding males and females and odd weavers during nesting season and even during the off-season. Nests provide no insulation against heat or cold, but effective in rain. Isolated nests are made by juvenile males in the breeding season, but not used. Eggs bluish green, darker at the large end; clutch 2-4; incubation period 13,5 days; nestling period 16-18 days; young fed by both sexes, mostly by female; host of Diederick Cuckoo *Chrysococcyx caprius*.

Aviculture: Selected Reference CLUTCH 2-4; INCUBATION PERIOD 13-15 days; NESTLING PERIOD 16-18 days. Nest Record Card CLUTCH 3 (ARU) 3 (ANRC); INCUBATION PERIOD 13 days (ARU); NESTLING PERIOD about 17 days (ANRC). Seeds of Guinea grass *Panicum maximum* (ARU), buds of Golden shower *Pyrostegia venusta* (ADRC). Selected Reference FRUIT nectar of Flat-flowered aloe *Aloe marlothii* African mulberry *Morus mesozygia*, *Lantana camara* (no common name), also silkworms, mealworms (ADRC).

Bocage's Weaver
Ploceus temporalis 14cm

Description: Male. Forehead, crown and nape golden-yellow, washed with greenish; ear-coverts dusky olivaceous; back and upper rump dark olive-green; mantle and upper tail-coverts greenish yellow; tail dusky yellow; wings dusky, feathers edged yellow; chin and throat dusky olive; breast, belly and rest of underparts golden-yellow; iris cream; bill black; legs and feet brown. Female upperparts olive-green indistinctly streaked dusky; underparts olivaceous yellow; bill slate. Juvenile upperparts ashy; underparts pale yelllow.

Voice: Not known.

Habitat: Not known.

Distribution: Southern Angola and north-western Zambia.

Feeding: Not known.

Breeding: Nest, retort-shaped with a wide short funnel-like entrance. Constructed of coarsely woven green grass stems and leaf strips. The nest is usually slung below the main rhachis of Raphia palm *Raphia* sp. or tail grass stems. Eggs turquoise blue; clutch 2.

Aviculture: No records.

Golden Weaver
Ploceus subaureus 16-17cm

Alternative names: Yellow Weaver, Red-eyed Yellow Weaver
P.s.aureoflavus **Smith's Golden Weaver**

Description: Male. Forehead and crown golden-yellow; mantle, back and upper tail-coverts yellowish green; ear-coverts, chin and throat pale yellow, tinged with olive; breast, belly and underparts lemon-yellow; flight feathers blackish with yellowish edges; iris red to pale orange; bill black; legs and feet pinkish brown. Female upperparts greenish grey, streaked dusky; underparts white (male similar in non-breeding dress). Juvenile similar to adult female, but paler.

Males. *P.s.togoensis* differs from the nominate race in being brighter yellow overall.

P.s.aureoflavus differs from the nominate in having the forehead, crown, sides of face, chin and throat bright saffron.

Voice: Described by Newman as making a harsh 'zik' and a soft swizzling sound.

Habitat: Dams, pans, estuaries and rivers with reedbeds and coconut palm groves.

Distribution: Eastern Cape Province, KwaZulu-Natal (coastal, midlands and north-western regions), South Africa.

P.s.togoensis north-eastern KwaZulu-Natal, South Africa to southern Mozambique.

P.s.aureoflavus Mozambique (north of Save River) to Malawi, eastern Tanzania, Kenya and Zanzibar Island.

Feeding: Seeds, fruits and insects. Seeds and fruit of Dune soap-berry *Deinbollia oblongifolia*.

Breeding: An oval ball of reed blades, grass strips and palm leaves is constructed 1-2m over water from drooping palm leaves or suspended between upright reeds. A young Fish Eagle *Haliaeetus vocifer* was trice observed in Malawi swooping down from its perch to tear off a nest from the reeds and eat the contents: a sizeable population of Lesser Masked Weavers *Ploceus intermedius* occurred in this colony. Female lines nest with grass inflorescences. Eggs white or blue, plain or spotted with brown, black or violet; clutch 2-4; host of Diedrick Cuckoo *Chrysococcyx caprius*.

Aviculture: Selected Reference CLUTCH 2-3; NESTLING PERIOD 19-22 days. Selected Reference WILDFOOD Seeds of Guinea grass *Panicum maximum*. Selected Reference FRUIT berries of Black nightshade *Solanum nigrum*. Selected Reference ANIMAL FOOD termites.

Heuglin's Masked Weaver
Ploceus heuglini 14cm

Description: Male. Forehead, crown and nape yellow; mantle and back yellowish green, spotted black; ear-coverts, chin and triangular foreneck patch black; rump bright yellow; breast, belly and under tail-coverts golden-yellow; iris pale yellow; bill black; legs and feet brown. Female upperparts pale olivaceous green, streaked dusky; underparts yellowish, except lower belly whitish; bill horn. Juvenile similar to female, but paler overall.

Voice: Described by Mackworth-Praed & Grant as a chattering call not unlike that of Village Weaver, but somewhat softer.

Habitat: Dry woodland; in East Africa mainly below 1300m.

Distribution: Senegal to north-western Kenya.

Feeding: Insects, being partial to green caterpillars found on the leaves of Madras thorn *Pithecellobium dulce* and mantids when feeding nestlings.

Breeding: Nests in mixes colonies with males ranging from 2-20, but solitary breeding occuring equally frequently. Nests are suspended from branches of tall grass. Material consists of broad leafed grasses, oil palm and bamboo leaves and occasionally includes *Morinda lucida*, *Cassia siamea* and Flamboyant *Delolix regia*. Lining consists of seeding heads of Fairy grass *Rhychelytrum repens*. Eggs dusky green or greenish blue, occasionally spotted with red; clutch 2-3; female incubates along with male being observed, feeding young on 3 occasions only.

Aviculture: Nest Record Cards CLUTCH 3 (ARU); INCUBATION PERIOD about 15 days (ARU); NESTLING PERIOD about 17 days (ARU). Diet Record Cards ANIMAL FOOD mealworms (ARU).

Golden Palm Weaver
Ploceus bojeri 14cm
Alternative names: Bojer's Weaver, Mombasa Golden Weaver

Description: Male. Forehead and crown yellow, tinged orange; nape and sides of neck golden-yellow; face mask black; mantle, back, upper tail-coverts and wings yellow, washed with olivaceous; upper throat yellow, tinged orange; lower throat, breast and belly golden-yellow, under tail-coverts paler; iris yellow bill black; legs and feet dusky white. Female upperparts green, except wings dusky with feathers edged yellow; underparts yellow; bill horn. Juvenile similar to adult female, but paler overall.

Voice: Described by Williams & Arlott as having a low-pitched weaver chattering.

Habitat: In groves of coconut palms in East Africa.

Distribution: Southern Somalia and Kenya.

Feeding: Observed feeding on cake crumbs.

Breeding: Nest, kidney-shaped and having entrance below. Attached to the top of a single down-hanging twig of a bush or palm leaf. Eggs glossy, dark olive with indistinct dark mottling; clutch 2-3.

Aviculture: No records.

Taveta Golden Weaver
Ploceus castaneiceps 14cm

Description: Male. Forehead and crown golden-yellow; nape chestnut; mantle, back, rump, upper tail-coverts and tail golden-olive; wings dusky, edged bright yellow;

chin, throat, breast, belly and under tail-coverts golden yellow; iris dark brown; bill black; legs and feet dusky. Female upperparts yellow except mantle, indistinctly streaked dusky; underparts bright yellow; bill horn. Juvenile similar to adult female, but upperparts browner; belly and flanks buffish.

Voice: Described by Guggisberg as having a rather low pitched chattering calls, interspersed with creaking song 'ee-urr-twee-twee-twee'.

Habitat: Thickets and dense riparian tangles along rivers and swamps.

Distribution: South-eastern Kenya and north-eastern Tanzania.

Feeding: Grass seeds and grain.

Breeding: Nest oval, coarsely woven from broad green strips of grass. Usually over water and suspended between two verticle reeds of grass stems. Eggs glossy, dark olive-green, often with indistinct mottling; clutch 2-3.

Aviculture: Personal Communication CLUTCH 3,3; INCUBATION PERIOD 13 days; NESTLING PERIOD 16 days. Nest Record Cards CLUTCH 3,3. Selected Reference ANIMAL FOOD mealworms. Personal Communication mealworms.

Principé Golden Weaver

Ploceus princeps 16,5cm

Alternative name: Principé Island Golden Weaver

Description: Male. Forehead, crown, nape and sides of face orange-chestnut; mantle, back, rump, upper tail-coverts yellowish green, mottled slightly; tail dark olive; wing-coverts blackish, edged yellow; chin, throat, breast and belly bright yellow; iris yellow; bill blackish horn; legs and feet pinkish brown. Female has forehead, crown, nape and sides of face yellowish green; chin pale yellow; belly white; iris greyish yellow; bill pale horn. Juvenile undescribed.

Voice: Described by Mackworth-Praed & Grant as having normal call a sharp 'zeet'.

Habitat: Coastal forests.

Distribution: Principé Island.

Feeding: Insects.

Breeding: Nests are pear-shaped, loosely woven of coarse grass or palm-leaf strips, with a finer lining and with an entrance at the bottom at one side. Attached to the ends of overhanging branches or to the tips of palm fronds. Eggs pale blue; clutch 2.

Aviculture: No records.

Brown-throated Golden Weaver

Ploceus xanthopterus 14-15cm

Alternative names: Brown-throated Weaver, Southern Brown-throated Weaver

Description: Male. Forehead, crown and nape yellow; mantle, back and upper tail-coverts yellow, tinged with green; tail yellow with dusky edges; sides of face, chin and throat chestnut; breast yellow, tinged with chestnut; belly and underparts yellow; flight feathers blackish with yellow edges; iris reddish brown; bill black; legs and feet coloured. Female has forehead, crown and nape olive; mantle and back buffy brown; throat and flanks buffy yellow; rest of underparts white. Juvenile upperparts olivaceous washed with yellow; rump buffish brown; wings dusky edged with bright yellow; underparts whitish.

Voice: Described by Maclean as a jumble of nasal twanging, buzzling, trilling and sibilant notes *zeep seep zzz swirr zeep sweeu* etc.

Habitat: In non-breeding season birds may be found in reeds but usually only at night. The day is spent away from the marshes, in woodland, thickets and adjacent grasslands.

Distribution: Northern Mozambique, north-eastern Zimbabwe and southern Malawi.

P.x.cataneigula north-eastern Namibia, the Caprivi Strip, northern Botswana, north-western Zimbabwe, south-eastern Angola and south-western Zambia.

P.x.marleyi KwaZulu-Natal, South Africa, to southern and central Mozambique.

Feeding: Seeds, berries, nectar, grain and insects. Livefood namely, moths, beetles, grasshoppers and caterpillars.

Breeding: Nests are constructed of thin strips of reed leaves. Reed or coarse grass fastened to 2-4 leaves of typha, or branches overhanging colonies of 10 to several hundred. In one observation in Malawi a male appeared to have 2-3 females and built up to 12 nests in the season; females appear to have 2 broods and new nests were constructed for second broods. One colony was built in a small acacia overhanging a garden bird bath which consisted of 20-30 nests; each day bread was placed out, and when this was stopped 4 years later the colony was abandoned which suggests they only remained because of the availability of regular food. Eggs olive-green to chocolate or blue-green, plain or spotted with brown; clutch 2-3; incubation period 14-16 days; nestling period 14-17 days; female does all the feeding of nestlings.

Aviculture: Selected Reference CLUTCH 2-3; INCUBATION PERIOD 14-16 days; NESTLING PERIOD 14-19 days. Selected Reference FRUIT berries of Black nightshade *Solanum nigrum*. Selected Reference ANI-MAL FOOD termites. Selected Reference WILDFOOD Seeds of Guinea grass *Panicum maximum*.

Northern Brown-throated Weaver

Ploceus castanops 14cm

Alternative name: Nile Brown-throated Weaver.

Description: Male. Facial mask chestnut; crown, nape and sides of face golden-yellow; mantle, back, rump, upper tail-coverts and tail yellowish green; flight feathers pale yellow; chin chestnut; breast. belly and rest of underparts golden-yellow; iris white; bill black; legs and feet dusky yellowish. Female has head, mantle and back olive-brown, streaked dusky; lores and around eye blackish; underparts yellowish buff.

Voice: Described by Williams & Arlott as having various subdued chattering calls.

Habitat: Papyrus and reedbeds and other swampy situations.

Distribution: Eastern Zaire and Uganda.

Feeding: Largely insects.

Breeding: Nest, kidney-shaped with outer basket firmly woven of grass or palm strips and with an inner lining to the chamber. One nest was incorporated with bits of hibiscus leaves. Nests hang from shrubs, trees, one being a young rubber in Uganda, and in reedbeds of Elephant grass *Hyparrhenia collina*. Eggs pinkish white or pale blue, plain or reddish brown spotting; clutch 2-3.

Aviculture: No records.

Rüppell's Weaver

Ploceus galbula 14-15cm

Distribution: Male. Facial mask and chin deep chestnut; crown, nape, sides of neck golden-yellow; mantle and rump yellow-green, streaked dusky; tail olive brown, fringed greenish yellow; wings dusky; edged yellow; iris chestnut; bill black; legs and feet dusky yellow. Female has entire head, mantle and back olive-brown, streaked blackish; rump and tail yellowish green; chin to breast buff; rest of underparts white; bill horn. Juvenile similar to adult female, but more buffish yellow on breast.

Voice: Described by Hollom *et al* as wheezy chatter which ends in insect-like hissing sounds; call dry 'cheee-cheee'.

Habitat: Palm groves, tamarisk, cultivation and wadis with acacia thorn.

Distribution: Eastern Sudan and northern Ethiopia.

Feeding: Grass seeds.

Breeding: Nests singly or colonially. Constructed of leaf strips woven into pear-shapes with side or bottom entrance, suspended from, or attached to a branch, generally acacia. Eggs pinkish, green or blue, marked with brown; clutch 2-4, usually 3.

Aviculture: No records.

Northern Masked Weaver

Ploceus taeniopterus -cm

Description: Male. Forehead and forecrown saffron; nape and sides of neck golden-yellow; face mask black; mantle, back, upper tail-coverts and tail yellowish green; rump bright yellow; wings greenish yellow, flight feathers edged pale yellow; iris reddish brown; bill black; legs and feet dusky. Female upperparts olive-buff, streaked blackish; underparts pale yellowish buff. Juvenile similar to adult female, but pale overall.

Male. *P.t.furensis* differs from the nominate race in having forehead and forecrown darker mantle bright yellow.

Voice: Described by Williams & Arlott as the usual weaver chattering.

Habitat: Lake-edge reeds bushes in East Africa.

Distribution: South-eastern Sudan and northern Uganda.

P.t.furensis western Sudan.

Feeding: Seeds of weeds, grain and insects.

Breeding: A colony breeder and oven-shaped nests suspended from the tops of reeds or branches of bushes standing in a marsh, are constructed of strips of reed blades and lined with softer grasses. Eggs sage green, blotched brown or pale green, blotched tawny, or pale coffee brown, blotched reddish brown.

Aviculture: No records.

Lesser Masked Weaver

Ploceus intermedius 14-15cm

Alternative names: Abyssinian Masked Weaver, Ethiopian Masked Weaver
P.i.cabanisii **Cabanis's Masked Weaver, Cabanis Weaver**

Description: Male. Forehead, hind-crown, sides of face and throat black; nape and sides of neck golden-yellow;

mantle, back, rump and upper tail-coverts yellowish green, with dusky centres of feathers, breast, belly and flanks yellow; wing coverts blackish with pale yellow edges; iris pale yellow to cream; bill black; legs and feet bluish grey. Female yellowish green above, streaked on mantle and back with black; iris brown; bill pinkish horn.

Males. *P.i.cabanisii* differs from the nominate race in almost lacking golden-yellow behind the black forecrown.

P.i.beattyi differs from the nominate in having chestnut wash on hindcrown darker and extending over hind-neck.

P.i.leubberti differs from *cabanisii* in lacking dusky centres to feathers of the mantle and back. Juvenile similar to adult female, but more olive-brown above.

Voice: Described by Maclean as rasping swizzling similar to that of other weavers.

Habitat: Savanna country with trees in the neighbourhood of water.

Distribution: Sudan, Ethiopia, Somalia to eastern Zaire.

P.i.cabanisii KwaZulu-Natal, Mpumalanga and Northern Province, South Africa to eastern Swaziland, Zimbabwe, Mozambique, south-eastern Zaire, Malawi and Tanzania (coast).

P.i.beattyi western Angola.

P.i.leubberti Namibia, the Caprivi Strip, northern Botswana, south-western Zimbabwe to western Angola and perhaps to south-western Zambia.

Feeding: Seeds, nectar and insects. Livefood in the form of termites, butterfly/moth larvae.

Breeding: Nests are suspended from trees at 15-18m above ground, but may also be found in bushes, reeds or palms, mostly over water, which may number 100 or more. Nests are kidney-shaped and constructed of strips of grass, reed stems of palm leaves. An untidy vertical entrance tunnel varies in length from 2,5-7,5cm. Eggs white or bluish white; clutch 2-4; young fed by both parents; host to Klaas's Cuckoo *Chrysococcyx klaas* and Diederick *Cuckoo C.caprius*.

Aviculture: Selected Reference CLUTCH 2-4. Selected Reference WILDFOOD Seeds of Spanish black-jack *Bidens bipinnata*, Guinea grass *Panicum maximum*, Broad-leaved panic *P.deustrum*, leaves of Chickweed *Stellaris media*. Selected Reference FRUIT nectar of Flat-flowered aloe *Aloe marlotthi*. Selected Reference ANIMAL FOOD mealworms, butterfly/moth larvae.

Masked Weaver
Ploceus velatus 14-16cm
Alternative names: Black-fronted Weaver, Southern Masked Weaver.
P.v.uluensis **African Masked Weaver.**
P.v.caurinus **Namaqua Masked Weaver.**

Description: Male. Hind-crown and nape yellow; fore-crown, sides of face and throat black, ending in a point; mantle, back and tail yellowish green, faintly streaked dusky; breast, belly, flanks and upper tail-coverts golden-yellow; wing-coverts and flight feathers dusky with pale yellow edges; iris red to orange-red; bill black; legs and feet brownish. Female light greyish brown, streaked heavily on mantle and back; breast buff; belly white. Juvenile similar to adult female.

Males. *P.v.uluensis* differs from the nominate race in having more black on the forehead.

P.v.finschi (see Reichenow Orn. Monatsb., 11, P. 23 Mossamedes 1903).

P.v.nigrifrons differs from the nominate in having brown wash on crown and upper breast; larger than other races.

P.v.tahatali differs from the nominate in having hind-crown, nape and mantle coppery; rump paler yellow.

P.v.shelleyi differs from *tahatali* in having hind-crown and mantle a paler greenish yellow, streaked dusky; rump and upper tail-coverts lemon-yellow.

P.v.caurinus differs from the nominate in being paler and less richly coloured on the upperparts.

Voice: Described by Newman as making prolonged sizzling sounds when breeding, plus a sharp '*zik*'.

Habitat: Any savanna situated on the edges of forest and woodland in the vicinity of water; also recorded in the waterless areas of Namibia and the Kalahari.

Distribution: North-eastern Cape, Free State, Gauteng (highveld) provinces of South Africa and Lesotho.

P.v.uluensis Sudan and Somalia to Tanzania.

P.v.finschi south-western Angola.

P.v.nigrifrons eastern Cape, Mpumalanga, northern and western KwaZulu-Natal, South Africa and western Swaziland.

P.v.tahatali Zimbabwe, south-eastern Botswana, western Mozambique, eastern Swaziland and South African provinces of northern KwaZulu-Natal and Northern Province.

P.v.shelleyi western and southern Mozambique (Save River).

P.v.caurinus southern Angola, central and northern Namibia, south-western Botswana and South African provinces of northern Cape (Gordonia and Kuruman districts).

Feeding: Seeds, fruits, nectar, ovaries of flowers, insects and grain. Seeds of dry elm eaten on the ground, stamens of African marigold *Tagetes erecta*, buds and ovaries of *Prunus* (peach and apricot) and Driedoring *Rhigozum trichotomum*, nectar of Flat-flowered aloe *Aloe marlotthi*, fruits of Common taaibos *Rhus pyroides*, Satsuma plum, Mistletoe and Puzzle bush *Ehretia rigida* and termites.

Breeding: Polygamous, each male having two or three females. Kidney-shaped nests are constructed with strips of reed or grass blades, with a vertical entrance tube of 8-12cm long hanging below. One record of a length of insulated wire being utilized to anchor nest to a branch. Breeding nests are lined with grass inflorescenes and leaves. Two observations of double-storey nests, one with single entrance, the other with two. There are transparent nests known as 'cocks nests' which have no entrance tube or lining. Nests are built at the end of branches from which leaves have been stripped, or placed between upright reeds. Nests have also been recorded strung between two wires of barbed wire fence, telephone wires and on upright pieces of bamboo. At times near the nest of a hornet (*Polistes* and *Icaria*). The alien Mesquite tree *Prosopis* spp., provide nesting sites throughout the Karoo. Eggs white, pink, pale green or blue, plain, spotted, speckled or blotched with grey and brown; laid on successive days; clutch 2-6; incubation by female except two records of males covering eggs when trapped at night; young fed by female only; Blue Waxbill *Uraeginthus angolensis* observed breeding in old weaver's nest; host to Diederick Cuckoo *Chrysococcyx caprius* and Klaas's Cuckoo *C.klaas*.

Aviculture: Selected Reference CLUTCH 2-6; INCUBATION PERIOD 12-13 days. Selected Reference WILDFOOD Seeds of Guinea grass *Panicum maximum*, Natal panic *P.natalense*, buds of Smeltersbossie *Flaveria bidentis*, Gallant soldier *Galinsoga parviflora*, leaves of Chickweed *Stellaria media*, Red garden sorrel *Oxalis latifolia*. Selected Reference FRUIT nectar of Flat-flowered aloe *Aloe marlotthi*, Common taaibos *Rhus pyroides*, Puzzle bush *Ehretia rigida*, Tswana *Lantana viburoides*. Selected Reference ANIMAL FOOD termites, fishmoths, beetle larvae, including mealworms, aphids, butterfly/moth caterpillars, also silkworms.

Katanga Masked Weaver

Ploceus kantangae -cm

Description: Male. Forehead and crown saffron; nape golden-yellow; face mask black; mantle and back yellow-green, streaked dusky; tail dusky green; flight feathers yellow; chin and upper throat black; breast yellow, tinged saffron; belly and rest of underparts golden-yellow; iris orange; bill black; legs and feet brown. Female upperparts olive-yellow, streaked dusky, except rump and tail yellow; belly white; bill horn. Juvenile similar to adult female, but paler overall.

Male. *P.k.upembae* differs from the nominate race in having bill markedly larger.

Voice: Described by Mackworth-Praed & Grant as rather harsh sizzling song in which several birds may join.

Habitat: Thick bush and waterside trees.

Distribution: North-western Zambia and south-eastern Zaire

P.k.upembae South-eastern Zaire

Breeding: The nest is a rough untidy structure of sticks, thorns and grass. The chamber is lined with finer grasses and a few feathers. Nests may be built in close proximity to villages with a record of a small colony almost touching that of a White backed Vulture *Gyps africanus*. Nests are constantly being tended in readyness for the nest season and many seasons to follow. Eggs whitish or pale green, blotched, mottled and streaked with ashy grey and brown; clutch 2-3; incubation and nestling periods unrecorded.

Feeding: Seeds, grain, locusts and other insects.

Aviculture: No records.

Tanzania Masked Weaver

Ploceus reichardi 30-40cm
Alternative name: Tanganyika Masked Weaver.

Description: Male. Forehead and forecrown saffron; mantle and back greenish yellow; rump bright yellow; tail black; wings black, coverts edged white, flight feathers edged pale yellow; face mask and chin black; breast and flanks chestnut; belly and under tail-coverts greenish yellow; iris reddish; bill blackish; legs and feet slate. Female upperparts olivaceous, except mantle streaked blackish; underparts pale yellow, except flanks buff and centre of belly white; bill horn Juvenile undescribed.

Voice: Not known.

Habitat: Swampy areas.

Distribution: South-western Tanzania.

Feeding: Not known.

Breeding: Eggs bluish or greyish green, spotted with dusky brown.

Aviculture: No records.

Vieillot's Black Weaver

Ploceus nigerrimus 18cm
Alternative name: *P.n.castaneofuscus* Chestnut and Black Weaver

Description: Male. Wholly black including bill; iris white; legs and feet blackish brown. Female upperparts olivaceous, streaked blackish on head and mantle; underparts olivaceous yellow. Juvenile similar to adult female, but upperparts browner.

Male. *P.n.castaneofuscus* (see *Richard Howard and Alick Moore, A Complete Checklist of The Birds of the World, 1984 p. 615*).

Voice: Described by Serle *et al* as a shrill and rasping sustained chattering, especially at the nest.

Habitat: Forest edges and clearings, wooded grasslands and gardens at 700-2000m in East Africa.

Distribution: Eastern Nigeria, Cameroon to western Kenya.

P.n.castaneofuscus Sierra Leone to western Nigeria.

Feeding: Seeds and insects. In Nigeria feeds of the strips of Oil Palm Nut *Elaeis guineensis* husks dropped by feeding Thomas's Tree Squirrels *Furnisciurus anerythrus*.

Breeding: Nests are round with large semi-circular entrance tube pointing downwards to the ground. Built of grass strips of palm or banana leaves of the leaves of *Grevillea* sp. and sometimes, but not always, lined with feathers. Nests in large colonies by itself or in the company of Golden-backed Weavers *Ploceus jacksoni*. Eggs blue, pale blue or greenish blue, often darker clouds at one end; clutch 2-3.

Aviculture: No records.

Weyns's Weaver
Ploceus weynsi 15cm

Description: Male. Entire head, nape, mantle and back black; rump black and green; tail green; flight feathers black, edged golden-yellow; chin, throat and upper breast black; lower breast golden-yellow; flanks chestnut; iris dark brown; bill black; legs and feet blackish. Female upperparts olivaceous green, except mantle streaked dusky; underparts greenish yellow, except flanks green; centre of belly whitish. Juvenile similar to adult female, but paler overall; bill horn.

Voice: Described by Williams & Arlott as a rather soft chirping calls.

Habitat: Forest edges and clearing and moist secondary bush at 1000-1500m in East Africa.

Distribution: Northern Zaire, southern Sudan and north-western Tanzania.

Feeding: Nectar from *Erythrina* trees.

Breeding: Not known.

Aviculture: No records.

Vitelline Masked Weaver
Ploceus vitellinus 12cm

Description: Male. Crown and nape yellow; facial mask black; mantle and back mottled black and yellow; rump and upper tail-coverts yellow; wing-coverts, edged yellow; tail olivaceous yellow; chin and throat saffron; breast, belly and rest of underparts yellow; iris brown; bill black; legs and feet dusky. Female upperparts yellowish green, except mantle streaked blackish; underparts pale yellow, except belly white. Juvenile similar to adult female, but sides of throat and breast buff.

Voice: Described by Mackworth-Praed & Grant as having a long drawn wheezy callnote.

Habitat: Acacia bush.

Distribution: Senegal to Chad and western Sudan.

Feeding: Seeds, insects and spiders.

Breeding: The nest is kidney-shaped which resembles a pear with a flatish base and tapers above to the end of single twig in a tree or bush to which it is attached. Entry is made from below. In Senegal nests were made chiefly of "spider lily" when grass was short in the breeding area. The chamber consisted of grass strands and small acacia leaves. Eggs white or pinkish white spotted brown or rufous and greenish blue, spotted brown and chocolate with mauve undermarkings; clutch 2-4.

Aviculture: Selected Reference CLUTCH 3-4; INCUBATION PERIOD 11-12 days. Nest Record Cards CLUTCH 4 (ANRC); INCUBATION PERIOD 13 days (ANRC); NESTLING PERIOD 19 days (ANRC). Diet Record Cards WILDFOOD chickweed *Stellaria* sp., Groundsel *Senecio bulgaris* (ADRC). Diet Record Cards ANIMAL FOOD termites, wasp larvae or "grubs" (ADRC).

Speke's Weaver
Ploceus spekei 15cm

Description: Male. Forehead, crown, nape and sides of neck yellow; facial mask and chin black; mantle, back, rump and upper tail-coverts olive-yellow; tail dusky olive-yellow; wings yellow, feather tipped with olive giving a mottled appearance; throat orange-yellow; breast, belly and rest of underparts yellow; iris yellowish; bill black; legs and feet dusky pink. Female upperparts ashy brown, except centre of belly white. Juvenile similar to adult female, but paler overall.

Voice: Described by Guggisberg as chattering calls, also a sharp '*teep*'.

Habitat: Open country with trees or bushes at 1200-2200m in East Africa.

Distribution: Southern Ethiopia, Somalia, Kenya and northern Tanzania.

Feeding: Seeds, insects and spiders.

Breeding: Nest, large untidy globular woven structure with short entrance spout. Built of grass strips, lined with soft grassheads, and usually attached to branches which have had their leaves stripped. Eggs blue, occasionally with a few black spots; clutch 1-3, rarely 4.

Aviculture: No records.

Fox's Weaver

Ploceus spekeoides 15cm

Description: Male. Forehead and crown yellow; face mask black; nape, mantle and back mottled black and yellow; rump yellow; flight feathers edged yellow; tail olivaceous yellow; chin black; breast, belly and rest of underparts yellow; iris yellow; bill black; legs and feet dusky red. Juvenile undescribed.

Voice: Not known.

Habitat: Wooded and bush grasslands in swampy areas.

Distribution: Nort-western to central Uganda.

Feeding: Not known.

Breeding: Not known.

Aviculture: No records.

Village Weaver

Ploceus cucullatus 15-17cm

Alternative names: Black-headed Village Weaver, Black-headed Weaver, Golden Oriole Weaver, V-marked Weaver, West African Village Weaver.
P.c.abyssinicus Abyssinian Black-headed Weaver, Ethiopian Black-headed Weaver, Great Masked Weaver.
P.c.nigriceps Layard's Black-headed Weaver, Layard's Weaver, Mottled-backed Weaver.
P.c.dilutescens Black-necked Weaver, Spotted-backed Weaver, Speckled-backed Weaver.

Description: Male. Entire head and neck forming an apex on lower neck in front; mantle, back, rump and upper tail-coverts black, feathers tipped with yellow giving a mottled appearance; tail dusky green; sides of

breast chestnut; belly and underparts golden-yellow; wing-coverts black, tipped with yellow; iris red; bill black; legs and feet purplish slate. Female has forehead, crown and nape olive; mantle, back and upper tail-coverts greyish brown; lores, ear-coverts and throat yellow; breast, belly and rest of underparts greyish white; iris brown; bill pinkish horn; legs feet brownish pink. Juvenile similar to adult female, but upperparts browner.

Males. *P.c.collaris* differs from the nominate race in having rump and upper tail-coverts yellow.

P.c.bohndorffi differs from the nominate in having less black on crown.

P.c.abyssinicus similar to *bohndorffi* but not having the golden-yellow extending to upper belly and flanks.

P.c.frobenii similar to *bohndorffi* but golden-yellow much deeper, almost chestnut wash across breast and flanks.

P.c.spilonotus differs from the nominate in having crown yellow; sides of head, throat and upper breast black.

P.c.dilutescens differs from *spilonotus* in having the forehead and crown golden-yellow. Inter-racial hybrids are common, ranging from yellow-crowned to black individuals.

P.c.paroptus differs from *nigriceps* in having deeper yellow on the underparts.

P.c.nigriceps differs from *spilonotus* in having the forehead, crown and nape black; breast, belly and underparts paler yellow.

Voice: Described by Mackworth-Praed & Grant as a sharp alarm call of 'zip'. A repeated call of 'chuck chuck' when carrying material.

Habitat: Usually near water on the banks of streams, edge of riverine forests and near human habitation.

Distribution: Senegal to Cameroon, Chad, Fernando Island.

P.c.collaris Gabon, Zaire and northern Angola.

P.c.bohndorffi northern Zaire, Uganda, Sudan and north-western Tanzania.

P.c.abyssinicus Ethiopia.

P.c.frobenni southern Zaire.

P.c.spilonotus south-eastern Cape and KwaZulu-Natal, South Africa; also introduced to Mauritius and Reunion.

P.c.dilutescens Mpumalanga, Northern Province, Free State and north-eastern KwaZulu-Natal, South Africa to Lesotho (lowlands), eastern Swaziland, southern Mozambique, southern and south-eastern Zimbabwe (lowlands) and south-eastern Botswana.

P.c.paroptus Mozambique (north to Save River) eastern and north-eastern Zambia, eastern Zaire, Malawi, southern and eastern Tanzania, coastal Kenya and south-western Somalia.

P.c.nigriceps north-eastern Namibia, the Caprivi Strip, northern Zimbabwe, northern and north-eastern Botswana, southern Angola and Zambia.

Feeding: Seeds, ovaries of flowers, nectar and insects. Seeds of *Schotia* sp., nectar of *Aloe* sp., Mexican

Blood-trumpet *Distinctus buccinatoria*. Stomach contents revealed small stones, sand grains, bits of small shell and rice; nestlings were fed grasshoppers, caterpillars, small beetles, termites and small spiders.

Breeding: Polygnous, but the degree of polygny was found to vary from different subspecies when a two week survey revealed the nominate race males averaging three females each, with *graueri* and *spilonotus* averaging only two females each. Nests are suspended from drooping branches of tall exotics such as gums or from thorn trees or upright reeds. In the Lake Chad region the following trees were utilized as nesting sites, namely Kapok tree *Ceiba pentandra*, *Hyphaenae thebaica*, *Azadirachtia indica*, *Acacia* sp and *Ficus* sp. A colony of 2000 nests were observed in Malawi mixed with Lesser Masked Weavers *Ploceus intermedius* and occupied nests occuring immediately above that of a Bateleur *Terathopius ecaudatus* a Wahlberg's Eagle *Aquila wahlbergi* and a Yellow-billed Kite *Milvus migrans*. They are made of long grass stems, reeds, sedge and palm leaves with an opening below. The outer shell is constructed by the male; the female attends to the roof thatching using tree leaves. Eggs white through light turquoise to emerald turquoise, emerald, and the emerald green, unspotted, lightly spotted heavily spotted; clutch 2-5, usually 2-3; incubation 12-13 days, by female only; nestling period 16-21 days; West African male have been found almost never helping the female to feed the nestlings, whereas *graueri* and *spilonotus* males took a very substantial share in this task; host of Diederick Cuckoo *Chrysococcyx caprius*.

Aviculture: Selected Reference CLUTCH 1-5, usually 2-3; INCUBATION PERIOD 14 days; NESTLING PERIOD 16-21 days. Nest Record Cards CLUTCH 3,3 (ARU). Diet Record Cards FRUIT nectar of *Aloe* spp., Puzzle bush *Ehretia rigida* (ARU). Selected Reference ANIMAL FOOD mealworms. Diet Record Cards termites, beetle larvae, including mealworms, aphids, butterfly/moth caterpillars, larvae or "maggots" (ARU).

Giant Weaver

Ploceus grandis 11-11,5cm

Description: Male. Entire head pale black; nape and sides of neck chestnut; mantle and back olive-yellow; rump and upper tail-coverts yellow; tail olive, edged yellow; flight feathers black, edged yellow; chin and throat pale black; breast, belly and rest of underparts yellow; flanks yellow washed with chestnut; iris golden or hazel; bill black; legs and feet brown. Female upperparts brownish olive, streaked blackish; sides of face breast buff; throat buffish brown; belly white; bill horn. Juvenile undescribed.

Voice: Not known.

Habitat: Vicinity of cocoa plantations.

Distribution: São Thomé Island.

Feeding: Not known.

Breeding: Nests kidney-shaped with opening below, untidly built but firmly woven with long coarse grass or palm strips. Suspended from branches of trees over land or water. Eggs blue; clutch 2.

Aviculture: Not known.

Clarke's Weaver

Ploceus golandi 13cm

Alternatives name: Goland's Weaver.

Description: Male. Entire head, nape, sides of face and mantle black, latter tinged greenish; rump and upper tail-coverts green, tinged blackish; tail dusky greenish, edged green; wings blackish, edged greenish; chin and throat black; breast, belly and under tail-coverts yellow, latter whitish; under wing-coverts pale yellow; iris brown; bill blackish horn; legs and feet dusky. Female upperparts bright green, except mantle streaked blackish; tail dark olive; belly and under tail-coverts buffy white. Juvenile undescribed.

Voice: Described by Williams & Arlott as a high pitched twittering.

Habitat: *Brachystegia* woodland.

Distribution: Eastern Kenya.

Feeding: Almost entirely insects. Stomach contents of a single male contained small cockchafers and other beetle remains and the larvae of butterflies and moths.

Breeding: Not known.

Aviculture: No records.

Salvadori's Weaver

Ploceus dichrocephalus -cm

Alternative names: Jubaland Weaver, Somali Yellow-backed Weaver.

Description: Male. Entire head blackish chestnut; nape and sides of neck chestnut; mantle and back olivaceous yellow; rump and upper tail-coverts yellow; tail and wings olivaceous, flight feathers edges yellow; chin and throat dusky saffron; breast and flanks yellow, tinged chestnut; belly and rest of underparts olivaceous yellow; iris brown; bill black; legs and feet dusky. Female upperparts brown, except head olivaceous yellow; superciliary stripe yellow; underparts white; flanks buff; chin and throat whitish, washed with yellow; bill, upper mandible blackish, lower horn. Juvenile similar to adult female, but crown slightly more olivaceous.

Voice: Described by Williams & Arlott as having various churring call-notes.

Habitat: Riverine *acacia* woodland adjacent to rivers.

Distribution: Southern Ethiopia, southern Somalia and north-eastern Kenya.

Feeding: Not known.

Breeding: The kidney-shaped nest is built by the male with coarse strips of reed or grass blades as an outer shell thickly lined with finer grass by the female. Nests are suspended from the dropping branches of trees and bushes and also attached to Elephant grass *Hyparrhenia collina* and papyrus sp. Eggs white, pink, brown, chocolate or various shades of green with or without brown or purplish spotting.

Aviculture: No records.

Black-headed Weaver
Ploceus melancephalus 15cm
Alternative names: Gambian Black-headed Weaver, Yellow-collared Weaver.
***P.m.dimidiatus* Uganda Yellow-collared Weaver.**

Description: Male. Entire head and upper breast black; hindneck and sides of neck golden-yellow; mantle and back olive-yellow; tail and upper tail-coverts yellow; flight feathers and wing-coverts blackish, edged yellow; lower breast, belly and underparts golden-yellow; iris brown; bill black; legs and feet flesh coloured. Female has entire head, nape, sides of face and ear-coverts olive-green; eye stripe yellowish; mantle and back earth brown streaked dusky; rump brown; upper tail-coverts greenish. Juvenile similar to adult female, but upperparts paler olive-green; underparts yellowish buff.

Males. *P.m.dimidiatus* differs from the nominate race in having underparts, tinged chestnut.

P.m.fischeri differs from the nominate in being strongly washed with chestnut on underparts.

P.m.duboisi differs from *dimidiatus* in lacking chestnut on underparts.

Voice: Described by Serle *et al.* as discordant twitterings as a '*tsssp*' call.

Habitat: Margins or rivers and reed marshes.

Distribution: Senegal to Benin, Niger and Chad.

P.m.capitalis Nigeria, southern Chad and Central African Republic.

P.m.duboisi Zaire and northern Zambia.

P.m.dimidiatus north-eastern Sudan.

P.m.fischeri Uganda, Kenya and Tanzania.

Feeding: Not known.

Breeding: Nest ball-shaped, strongly woven and without spout, lined with finer grass. In East Africa breeds in clumps of Elephant grass *Hyparrhenia collina*. In Gambia observed breeding during the rains in low bushes that fringed drainage channels. Eggs white, pink brown or green with or without brown or purplish spotting; clutch 2.

Aviculture: Personal Communication ANIMAL FOOD termites, mealworms. Diet Record Cards wasp larvae or "grubs" (ADRC).

Golden-backed Weaver
Ploceus jacksoni 15cm

Description: Male. Entire head black; mantle, back, rump and upper tail-coverts golden-yellow; tail olive, tinged dusky olive; wing-coverts olivaceous yellow, edged black; chin and throat black; breast, belly and flanks deep chestnut; under tail-coverts yellow, tinged chestnut; iris red; bill slate-grey; legs and feet dusky white. Female upperparts brown, except head olivaceous yellow; supercilliary stripe yellow; underparts white, except breast and flanks buff; bill, upper mandible blackish, lower horn. Juvenile similar to adult female, but crown more olivaceous.

Voice: Described by Williams & Arlott as having the usual weaver type calls at nesting colonies.

Habitat: River swamp or lakeside in reeds.

Distribution: Southern and eastern Sudan, western and south-western Kenya, Uganda and Tanzania.

Feeding: Seeds of grasses and weeds, grain and insects.

Breeding: Nests in colonies, often associated with Orange Weaver *Ploceus rex* and Slender-billed Weaver *P.pelzeini*. Constructs a tough, resillient nest of thin fibrous palm strips with entrance at bottom and projecting rim. Usually suspended about 60cm to 5m over water or in long grass, bushes or *acacias* growing close to rivers. Eggs turquoise-blue with pale mauve under markings; clutch 2-3.

Aviculture: No records

Cinnamon Weaver
Ploceus badius 7,5-7,8cm

Description: Male. Entire head black; mantle and back chestnut; rump golden-yellow, tinged chestnut; tail olivaceous, edged outer feathers yellow; chin, throat and upper breast black; lower breast chestnut; belly and under tail-coverts yellow; iris cinnamon-brown; bill black; legs and feet pale grey. Female upperparts buffish brown, broadly streaked black; stripe over eye and sides of face buff; throat and belly buff; bill horn.

Juvenile similar to adult female, but paler overall.

Male. *P.b.axillaris* differs from the nominate race in having hindneck black; under tail-coverts chestnut.

Voice: Not known.

Habitat: *Acacia* savanna.

Distribution: Eastern Sudan.

P.b.axillaris southern Sudan.

Feeding: Not known.

Breeding: Not known.

Chestnut Weaver

Ploceus rubiginosus 15-16cm

Alternative name: Chocolate Weaver.

Description: Male. Crown, nape, sides of face, ear-coverts, chin and throat black; hindneck, sides of neck and mantle chestnut; rump and upper tail-coverts greyish; tail blackish; wings blackish, edged with whitish; breast and underparts chestnut; iris cinnamon-brown to red; bill black (breeding) or yellowish (non breeding); legs and feet lavender grey. Female has crown greenish grey, streaked blackish; rest of underparts greyish brown (male similar in non-breeding dress). Juvenile similar to adult female, but breast streaked.

Male. *P.r.trothae* differs from the nominate race in having rump and upper tail-coverts ashy and pale chestnut.

Voice: Described by Prozesky as a loud, intense chattering at the nesting site.

Habitat: *Acacia* woodland, arid bush country; during non-breeding season also in cultivation.

Distribution: Ethiopia, Somalia, Uganda, Kenya and northern Tanzania.

P.r.trothae northern and central Namibia and south-western Angola.

Feeding: Seeds, nectar and insects.

Breeding: Nests colonially. Sex ratio about one male to five females at one nest. Nests are retort-shaped, built of green grass stems, with and entrance spout 6-7cm long. In one observation 95 separate nest entrances were counted in one single gigantic mass of dried grass. Nest lined by female with finer grass and feathers. Nests are suspended from the dropping branches of trees, mostly *acacia* and *eucalyptus*. May nest in close proximity to Masked Weavers in close-packed colonies of up to 200 or more birds. Eggs white or bluish green; clutch 3-4; incubation by female; males desert the colony before young fledge.

Aviculture: Selected Reference CLUTCH 3-4. Selected Reference WILDFOOD. Seeds of Stapf's buffalo grass *Panicum stapfianum*, Black seed panicum *P.novemnerve*; Guinea grass *P.maximum*. Selected Reference FRUIT nectar of Flat-flowered aloe *Aloe marlothii*, Bitter aloe *A.ferox*, Candelabrum aloe *A.candelabrum*, Krantz aloe *A.arborescens*. Selected Reference ANIMAL FOOD termites, beetle larvae, including mealworms, spiders.

Gold-naped Weaver

Ploceus aureonucha -cm

Description: *(see Orn. Monatsb; 28, p81 Mawabi, Belgian Congo 1920).*

Voice: Not known.

Habitat: Forest edges.

Distribution: North-eastern Zaire.

Feeding: Fruits and insects.

Aviculture: No records.

Yellow-mantled Weaver

Ploceus tricolor 15cm

Alternative name: *P.t.interscapularis* Uganda Yellow-mantled Weaver.

Description: Male. Entire head and nape black; collar across upper mantle bright yellow; lower mantle, back, rump, upper tail-coverts and tail black; breast and belly chestnut; under tail-coverts black; iris brown; bill black; legs and feet dark brown. Female. Juvenile similar to adult female, but more sooty, less brown.

Male. *P.t.interscapularis* similar to nominate race in most respects. Female upperparts dark brown, feathers edged buff; ear-coverts pale brown; chin white; breast white, spotted brown; rest of underparts whitish; lacks yellow on bend of wing.

Voice: Described by Williams & Arlott as a sharp '*tssst*' or '*chirr-it*', but usually silent.

Habitat: Forest canopy at 700-1800m in East Africa.

Distribution: Guinea to Cameroon, Gabon and Angola.

Feeding: Insects.

Breeding: Nest, retort-shaped and extremely untidy, composed of rootlets loosely woven and then lined with grass bents. Breeds at high elevations in trees and palms. Eggs pinkish white; clutch 2-3.

Aviculture: No records.

Maxwell's Black Weaver

Ploceus albinucha -cm

Alternative name: White-naped Weaver.

Description: Sexes similar. All black bird, but with distinct greyish nuchal patch on collar; lower flanks blackish brown; bill black; iris greyish; legs and feet pale brownish pink. Juvenile sooty grey overall.

Adults. *P.a.maxwell* differs from the nominate race in having underparts blackish brown; iris white to greenish yellow; nuchal patch or collar rarely visible.

P.a.holomelas differs from the nominate in having underparts blacker; lacks nuchal patch or collar.

Voice: Described by Mackworth-Praed & Grant as a running chatter at the breeding colony.

Habitat: Forest.

Distribution: Sierre Leone to Ghana.

P.a.maxwell Fernando Pó Island.

P.a.holomelas eastern Nigeria to Gabon, Central African Republic and northern Zaire.

Feeding: Fruits and insects.

Breeding: Nest built in colonies in thick foliaged forest of trees, occasionally in palms, which have been stripped of their leaves, which is the main nesting material. Grass is also used in areas where palms are scarce. Nests are kidney-shaped with an opening below with or without a spout.

Aviculture: No records.

Compact Weaver

Ploceus superciliosus 12,5cm

Description: Male. Forehead chestnut; crown yellow; nape greenish brown; face mask black; mantle and back green, streaked dusky; rump brown; tail and wings dusky, edged buffish white; chin and throat black; breast, belly and flanks yellow; under tail-coverts brown; iris dark brown; bill slate; legs and feet dusky white. Female has forehead and crown blackish green

and yellow. Juvenile similar to adult female but paler overall; bill horn.

Voice: Described by Guggisberg as a fairly melodious '*cheew-ery-cheew-ery cheew-ery*' also a single harsh '*chee*'.

Habitat: Grasslands, cultivation and open bushland and forest.

Distribution: Sierra Leone to Ethiopia, Uganda, northwestern Tanzania, western Kenya and Angola.

Feeding: Seeds and insects.

Breeding: Nest oval finely woven with entrance on side. Neatly and strongly built of grass and lined with seeding grassheads. Suspended between two reeds or tall grass stems. Eggs blue or stone-grey; clutch 3, occasionally 4.

Aviculture: No records.

Forest Weaver

Ploceus bicolor 16-19cm

Alternative name: Dark-backed Weaver.

Description: Sexes similar. Entire head pale black; mantle, back, rump, upper tail-coverts, tail and wings dark slate-grey; chin and upper throat black; lower throat, breast, belly and under tail-coverts golden-yellow; iris brown; bill bluish grey; legs and feet pinkish brown. Juvenile similar to adult, but paler with throat unbarred and flanks tinged with olive.

Adults. *P.b.tephronotus* differs from the nominate race in having mantle and back black; underparts rich golden-yellow; legs and feet greyish brown.

P.b.anclogus differs from the nominate in being paler overall.

P.b.amaurocephalus differs from the nominate in having mantle, back and rump greyish; underparts paler golden-yellow; bill less heavy and deep.

P.b.mentallis differs from the nominate in having throat golden-yellow.

P.b.kigomaensis differs from the nominate in having mantle and back considerably paler.

P.b.kersteni differs from nominate in having upperparts wholly deep black.

P.b.strictifrons differs from *kersteni* in having upperparts dusky brown, except forehead and throat feathers tipped white.

P.b.lebomboensis differs from the nominate in having forehead spotted.

P.b.sylvanus differs from *stictifrons* in being darker, more blackish on upperparts; wings and tail darker and greyer.

Voice: Described by Maclean as having high-pitched bell-like '*ting ting*' and '*zzrree*' callnotes.

Habitat: Evergreen and riverine forests.

Distribution: Eastern Cape, KwaZulu-Natal, South Africa.

P.b.tephronotus eastern Nigeria, Cameroon and Fernando Po Island.

P.b.analogus southern Cameroon.

P.b.amaurocephalus northern Angola.

P.b.mentalis southern Sudan, north-eastern Zaire, Uganda and western Kenya.

P.b.kigomaensis southern Zaire, Zambia and western Tanzania.

P.b.kersteni Somalia, eastern Kenya, and eastern Tanzania.

P.b.strictifrons Mozambique, eastern Zimbabwe, southern Malawi to eastern Tanzania.

P.b.lebomboensis Zululand Lembombo Mountains, Swaziland and Mozambique.

P.b.sylvanus Zimbabwe (highlands), Mozambique (Chirinda Forest).

Feeding: Fruits, insect and nectar of *Aloe* and *Erythrina* spp.

Breeding: Nest, woven ball of vines or grasses with long entrance funnel and lined with lichen *Usnea* sp. Suspended from drooping branches of trees or even from telephone wires at about 6-10m above ground. Eggs pinkish white, spotted with reddish olive-brown and slate; clutch 2-4, usually 3.

Aviculture: No records.

Golden-mantle Weaver
Ploceus preussi -cm
Alternative name: Congo Golden-backed Weaver.

Description: Male. Forehead and crown golden-chestnut; nape yellow; sides of face, ear-coverts, chin and upper throat black; mantle, back and upper tail-coverts golden-yellow; tail and wings black; lower throat chestnut; breast, belly and under tail-coverts golden-yellow; iris reddish brown; bill black; legs and feet brownish pink. Female has forehead black and lacks chestnut on crown and lower throat. Juvenile undescribed.

Voice: Described by Mackworth-Praed & Grant as a rather noticeable 'chee-ee'.

Habitat: Not known.

Distribution: Sierra Leone to Cameroon and Central African Republic.

Feeding: Insects.

Breeding: Nest comprises mainly of lichens bound together with palm-leaf strips and with entrance below and firmly attached to a tree branch.

Aviculture: No records.

Yellow-capped Weaver
Ploceus dorsomaculatus -cm

Description: Male. Forehead, crown and nape golden-yellow; sides of face black; mantle, back and rump half black, half yellow; tail and wings black; chin and throat golden-yellow, tinged chestnut; sides of neck black; breast, belly and rest of underparts golden-yellow; iris brownish red; bill black; legs and feet pinkish white. Female has forehead, crown and nape black; legs and feet pinkish grey.

Voice: Not known.

Habitat: Forest edges.

Distribution: Cameroon, Central African Republic, the Congo and Zaire.

Feeding: Not known.

Breeding: Not known.

Aviculture: No records.

Olive-headed Golden Weaver
Ploceus olivaceiceps 16cm
Alternative name: Olive-headed Weaver.

Description: Male. Forehead and forecrown golden-yellow; nape, mantle and back golden-yellow, tinged chestnut; tall, sides of face olive-green; throat orange-brown; breast, belly and under tail-coverts yellow; iris red; bill black; legs and feet greyish pink, tinged bluish. Female paler overall with crown, mantle and back pale olive. Juvenile similar to female, but paler, and more yellowish olive on upperparts; bill pinkish horn.

Male. *P.o.vicarius* differs from the nominate race in being slightly smaller.

Voice: Described by Maclean as a loud chattering song.

Habitat: Highland forest and forest canopy.

Distribution: North-eastern Tanzania, Malawi, south, central and northern Mozambique.

Feeding: Feeds mainly in leaf clusters and especially in tufts of *Usnea* on insects and their larvae.

Breeding: Nest singly or in small colonies in *miombo*. An oval of woven *Usnea* lichen with verticle entrance and lacking any form of spout. Nests are suspended from twig ends in protective sites. Eggs plain bright turquoise; clutch 2-3.

Aviculture: No records.

Usambara Weaver
Ploceus nicolli 14cm

Description: Male. Entire head dusky *olivaceous*; nape, mantle, back and rump dull black washed yellowish;

upper tail-coverts dull black, tinged yellow; tail slaty black; chin and throat chestnut; breast, belly and rest of underparts bright yellow; iris white; bill black; legs and feet dusky yellow. Female has entire head dusky brown; mantle black. Juvenile undescribed.

Voice: Described by Mackworth-Praed & Grant as a soft little call of '*sur-swee-ee*'.

Habitat: Forest edges.

Distribution: Tanzania.

Feeding: Insects.

Breeding: Not known.

Aviculture: Personal Communication CLUTCH 3,4. Nest Record Cards CLUTCH 3 (ANRC); INCUBATION PERIOD 14 days (ANRC); NESTLING PERIOD 17 days (ANRC). Diet Record Cards ANIMAL FOOD termites (ADRC).

Brown-capped Weaver

Ploceus insignis 14cm
Alternative name: Chestnut-capped Weaver.

Description: Male. Forehead and crown chestnut; nape, sides of face, mantle and back golden-yellow; tail, wings and ear-coverts black; throat, breast, belly and under tail-coverts golden-yellow; flanks golden-yellow, tinged chestnut; iris brown; bill slate-grey; legs and feet dusky flesh. Female has forehead, crown and nape black, streaked yellow. Juvenile has forehead, crown and nape green, streaked black; bill horn.
Male. *P.i.unicus* differs from the nominate race in having crown deeper chestnut.

Voice: Described by Williams & Arlott as being usually silent, but sometimes utters a sharp '*tssst*'.

Habitat: Mountain forests.

Distribution: Cameroon to Sudan, Angola, Zaire, Kenya and Tanzania.

P.i.unicus Fernando Pó Island.

Feeding: Insects.

Breeding: Nest, retort-shaped which lacks and ante-chamber and lining has chamber opening through a spreading funnel emerging diagonally downwards from the initial ring. The bulky structure is made of twiglets, tendrils etc., and usually hung from branches of lianas. Eggs pale blue, occasionally with faint brown spotting; clutch 2.

Aviculture: No records.

Bar-winged Weaver

Ploceus angolensis 8-8,2cm

Description: Sexes similar. Forehead, crown, nape, ear-coverts and sides of face sooty brown; mantle and

back white; rump and upper tail-coverts yellow; tail black; wing-coverts black, tipped white; chin, throat, breast and belly white; flanks and under tail-coverts white, tinged yellow; iris brown; bill black; legs and feet dusky pink. Juvenile has crown; bill grey, lower mandible pink.

Voice: Not known.

Habitat: *Brachystegia* woodland.

Distribution: Angola, north-eastern Namibia, south-eastern Zaire and northern Zambia.

Feeding: Not known.

Breeding: Not known.

Aviculture: No records.

São Thomé Weaver

Ploceus sanctaethomae -cm

Description: Male. Forehead and sides of face brownish golden-buff; crown and nape black; mantle and back dark brown, tinged olive-brown; rump lighter olive-brown; tail blackish; chin golden-buff; throat, breast and belly pale chestnut; iris chestnut-brown; bill horn; legs and feet pale brown. Female has crown and nape blackish olive-brown; rest of underparts yellow. Juvenile undescribed.

Voice: Described by Mackworth-Praed & Grant as a sharp '*chip-chip*' and a thrilling song.

Habitat: Upper levels of bushes and trees.

Distribution: São Thomé Island.

Feeding: Seeds and insects.

Breeding: Nest, retort-shaped, built of fine twiglets and leaf or stem edges and lined with lichens and other debris. More than one nest may occur in the same trees but not in colonies. Eggs elongated, pale blue or pale green.

Aviculture: No records.

Yellow-legged Malimbe

Malimbus flavipes -cm

Description: Sexes similar. Entire head black; mantle and back chestnut-brown; chin, throat, breast, wings and tail black; belly, underparts and under tail-coverts brown; iris yellow; bill black; legs and feet dusky yellow. Juvenile upperparts brownish black, chin and throat ringed with olive-yellow; underparts greyish, washed with greenish yellow; under tail-coverts yellow.

Voice: Not known.

Habitat: Tall trees in rain forest.

Distribution: North-eastern Zaire.

Feeding: Insects. In the stomach of one a small caterpillar was recovered.

Breeding: A specimen taken in September had a developed egg in its oviduct.

Aviculture: No records.

Red-crowned Malimbe
Malimbus coronatus 8,2-9,3cm

Description: Male. Crown scarlet; rest of plumage black; iris brown; bill, legs and feet black. Female black. Juvenile males have crown yellowish rufous.

Voice: Described by Mackworth-Praed & Grant as a chattering call but without the wheezy notes of other malimbe.

Habitat: Gallery forests.

Distribution: Cameroon.

Feeding: Not known.

Breeding: The nest site is at low elevations in small trees, shrubs etc. The elongated nest has a long entrance tube opening downwards. Building materials consist of vine tendrils and stems which are especially prepared before being fitted to the nest. As many as 3 males and females may assist with the construction but only one pair breed in it.

Aviculture: No records.

Black-throated Malimbe
Malimbus cassini 8,8-9cm

Description: Male. Forehead, crown, nape sides of head, chin and throat scarlet; ear-coverts, chin, mantle, back, wings and underparts black, iris brown; bill black; legs and feet greyish brown. Female black. Juvenile males have scarlet replaced with orange-red; bill horn coloured.

Voice: Not known.

Habitat: Primary forests.

Distribution: Southern Cameroon, Gabon and the Congo.

Feeding: Not known.

Breeding: The female chooses the site for the nest, initiates and leads the building activities with the assistance of 2 males. Nests usually hang 15-20m from the ground from a palm leaf, which is very neatly constructed and nearly totally transparent. The materials consist solely of palm-leaf strips with an entrance spout measuring

0,61m long and pointing downwards. Eggs white; clutch 2; incubation by both sexes.

Aviculture: No records.

Rachel's Malimbe
Malimbus racheliae 7,2-8cm

Description: Male. Forehead, crown, nape and upper throat orange-red; sides of head, breast and under tail-coverts yellow; sides of face, ear-coverts, chin, belly, mantle, back and wings black; iris red; bill black; legs and feet grey. Female black. Juvenile undescribed.

Voice: Described by Bates as a long drawn out buzzing call something like that of a Village Weaver.

Habitat: Primary forests.

Distribution: Eastern Nigeria to Gabon.

Feeding: Not known.

Breeding: The nest does not differ from that of the Red-vented Malimbe. An observation in north-eastern Gabon revealed that one nest was built by a female and 2 males, all working at the same time.

Aviculture: No records.

Red-vented Malimbe
Malimbus scutatus 15,5cm
Alternative name: Red-vented Weaver.

Description: Male. Forehead, crown, nape, sides of neck and throat scarlet; chin, around lores and ear-coverts black; under tail-coverts scarlet; rest of plumage black; iris dark brown to reddish; bill black; legs and feet blackish brown. Female lacks the scarlet adornment; rest of plumage as in male. Juvenile has scarlet adornment in males replaced with pink, in females dusky black; bill horn coloured.

Adult. *M.s.scutopartitus* differs from the nominate race in having larger scarlet breast patch.

Voice: Described by Marchant as a loud harsh, 'zee-zee-zee' or 'chit-it-zeer-zeer'.

Habitat: Oil and Raphia palms in swamp forest and often occuring in cultivation and near villages.

Distribution: Sierra Leone to Ghana.

M.s.scutopartitus southern Nigeria and western Cameroon.

Feeding: Insects and husks of oil palm nuts.

Breeding: Constructs a retort-shaped nest which is suspended between long palm fronds high up in forest canopy. The transparent looking entrance tube can reach up to 60cm in length. Materials used for the outer walls consists of tendrils, twiglets and debris with some incorporating palm fibre or even built exclusively with the latter material. The nest is adapted to withstand wind and against predators by its inaccessible siting. The female has been observed assisting in the construction of the entrance tube. Eggs white; clutch 2.

Aviculture: No records.

Ibadan Malimbe

Malimbus ibadanensis 8,9-9,9cm

Description: Male. Forehead, crown, nape, sides of neck and lower throat scarlet; ear-coverts, sides of face, chin, mantle, back, wings and underparts black; iris bluish black; bill black; legs and feet brownish black. Female has forehead and girdle from nape across the chest scarlet. Juvenile has forehead and nape pale chestnut-brown; rest of plumage dusky black.

Voice: Described by Mackworth-Praed & Grant as a high pitched mixture of tinking notes and wheezes.

Habitat: Primary forests.

Distribution: Eastern Nigeria.

Feeding: Insects, especially tailor ants.

Breeding: Not known.

Aviculture: No records.

Gray's Malimbe

Malimbus nitens 17,8cm

Alternative name: Blue-billed Malimbe, Great Blue-billed Weaver, Gray's Blue-billed Weaver.

Description: *(see J.E. Gray, 1831, Zool. Misc., 1. p.7, Sierra Leone).*

Males. *M.n.moreaui* similar to nominate race, but larger and with a distinctly heavier bill.

M.n.microrhynchus similar to nominate, but smaller and with distinctly lighter bill. Juvenile has breast and throat red; sides of head and crown black, washed reddish; breast feathers washed with grey at base.

Voice: Described by Serle *et al.* as a long drawn out 'ze-e-e-e-e'; also harsh chirping, screeching or churring calls.

Habitat: Frequents both primary and secondary growth, clusters of oil-palms and swampy country.

Distribution: Guinea to southern Nigeria.

M.m.moreaui Cameroon, Gabon and north-western Zaire.

M.n.microrhynchus north-eastern Zaire and western Uganda.

Feeding: Mostly insects, 17 stomach contents also containing 2 old palm fruits.

Breeding: Nest, retort-shaped and loosely constructed of small twiglets, rootlets and strips of palm leaf with a wide funnel like entrance some 10cm long opening downwards at an angle of 45 degrees to the verticle, wide at entrance where attached to nest. Constructed by male alone, and overhangs a forest pool or stream suspended from oil palm leaf. Nests in smaller colonies of up to 6 pairs. Eggs variable, usually whitish blotched and spotted with brown and lilac; clutch 2; female incubates alone, but males feeds the young. The male never enters the nest during this period but guards the surrounding area, harassing Red-billed Dwarf Hornbills *Tochus Camurus*, cuckoos *Crysoccyx* sp. or mobbing Gambian Sun Squirrel *Heliosciurus gambianus* or Small Green Squirrel *Paraxerus poensis*, that may approach too close to the nest.

Aviculture: No records.

Red-headed Malimbe

Malimbus rubricollis 18cm

Alternative names: Red-headed Weaver.
M.r.bartletti Barlett's Red-headed Weaver,
M.r.nigeriae Nigerian Red-headed Weaver.

Description: Male. Forehead, crown, nape and sides of neck scarlet; rest of plumage slightly glossy black; iris red to reddish brown; bill black; legs and feet blackish brown. Female has forehead and fore-crown black. Juvenile male and female paler than adults; bill horn-coloured.

Males. *M.r.barletti* differs from the nominate race in having forehead, crown, nape and sides of neck a brighter scarlet.

M.r.nigeriae differs from the nominate in having forehead, crown, nape and sides of neck reddish orange; also with a decidedly heavier bill.

M.r.rufovelatus similar to nominate, but with a decidedly heavier bill.

M.r.prcedi differs from nominate in having the forehead, crown, nape and sides of neck orange-red; iris brown.

Voice: Described by Guggisberg as a harsh chip and low, wheezy call.

Habitat: In tall forest trees at 700-1700m in East Africa, but occurs in any woodland except perhaps acacia, but most typically in the thinner types of *miombo* in Zambia.

Distribution: Eastern Nigeria to Sudan, Chad and Central African Republic.

M.r.barletti Sierra Leone to Ghana.

M.r.nigeriae Benin and western Nigeria.

M.r.rufovelatus Fernando Pó Island.

M.r.praedi northern Angola.

Feeding: Mainly insects. Stomach contents of a cuckoo nestling was small black beetles, one small spider and a snail's shell. Also berries.

Breeding: Nest, large, untidy retort-shaped with a vertically opening tube, made of twiglets and grass. One pair utilized a Msasa *Brachystegia spiciformis* as a nesting site at 5m above ground. Only the male builds by developing the initial ring first, from which specially prepared twiglets which are knotted together by short tags of bark. This is followed by the construction of the floor and sides of the chamber, the roof developing last. Of the many nests built only one will be occupied by the female. The most advanced of the other nests will be used for roosting, either by a pair or a male alone. Old nests from the previous season in the immediate area are not used at all. The female lines the nest roof with a special layer of dead leaves incorporated into the fabric. The nest gains strength from the cast-iron rigidity of the fabric when dried out, not from the flexibility of the grass whilst being exposed to the full force of wind. Birds entering the nest will have to a remarkable aerobatic sweeping down to the entrance tube and then "diving" upwards into them with closed wings. Nests are suspended from the top branches of tall trees. In Uganda 11 sites were recorded over murram pits beside roads or over the road itself, 2 were near buildings, 2 overhanging seasonal pools. The nest groups were quite solitary. Eggs pale blue clouded and zoned in a darker shade around the blunt end; clutch 2; host to Didric Cuckoo *Chrysococcyx caprius* with a record from Zambia of a chick nestling 3-4 days old which was later found dead and a second nestling 6-7 days old that was reared.

Aviculture: No records.

Red-bellied Malimbe

Malimbus erythrogaster -cm

Alternative name: Red-bellied Weaver.

Description: Male. Forehead, crown, nape, hindneck, sides of head, throat, breast, belly and underparts bright orange-vermillion; lores, ear-coverts, sides of face, chin, throat, mantle, rump, tail and wings black; iris red to brown; bill black; legs and feet brown. Female has throat red. Juvenile has entire head red except lores; underparts greyish brown; tinged with pink.

Voice: Not known.

Habitat: Frequents undergrowth, mid-stratum and canopy in Uganda.

Distribution: Eastern Nigeria to eastern Zaire.

Feeding: Not known.

Breeding: Not known.

Aviculture: Not known.

Crested Malimbe

Malimbus malimbicus 18cm

Alternative names: Congo Crested Weaver.
M.m.nigrifrons Gold Coast Crested Weaver.

Description: Male. Forehead, crown, sides of face, throat and breast, and feathers and hind-crown longish forming a sort of crest scarlet; mantle, back, rump and upper tail-coverts black; belly and underparts brownish black; iris brown; bill, legs and feet black. Female paler overall, and lacks crest. Juvenile paler overall; bill horn-coloured.

Male. *M.m.nigrifrons* differs from the nominate race in having a shorter crest; fore-crown, belly and underparts black.

Voice: Described by Williams as having a low musical whistle and various short chirping calls.

Habitat: Affecting secondary oil-palm and raphia palm bush, ranging from undergrowth to tree tops.

Distribution: Cameroon to Uganda, southern Zaire and northern Angola.

M.m.nigrifrons Sierra Leone to Nigeria.

Feeding: Largely insectivorous, but two stomach contents revealed oil-palm fruit.

Breeding: Nest, roughly woven with a short ragged spout made of tendrils, fibres, strips of broad palm leaves with very little lining, is suspended from a palm frond. The fabric is held together mainly by growth of fungus between the pieces of material acting as cement. In north-eastern Gabon 12 nests were built below, or at the tip of a rattan leaf, 3-10m above ground. Exceptional nests on a leaf of banana or *framomum*. Collected nests very rapidly disintergrated. Eggs pinkish white or greenish, heavily mottled and shaded with light brown and pale grey; clutch 2.

Aviculture: No records

Red-headed Weaver

Anaplectes melanotis 14-15cm

Alternative names: Black-eared Scarlet Weaver, Red-winged Anaplectes, Scarlet-headed Weaver

Description: Male. Entire head, neck to breast scarlet-red, streaked with black; lower mantle, back, rump and upper tail-coverts greyish; tail grey, edged orange to reddish orange; lower breast and underparts white; flight feathers dusky, edged with yellow; iris reddish; bill orange to red; legs and feet brown. Female has entire head and chin olivaceous; mantle greyish; throat and underparts white. Juvenile similar to adult female, males tinged with orange on crown and nape.

Males. *A.m jubaensis* differs from the nominate race in having underparts scarlet-red.

A.m.rubriceps differs from the nominate in having little or no black on the head; flight and tail feathers edged with yellow.

A.m.gurneyi differs from the nominate in having lores and ear-coverts black; mantle and wing-coverts more washed with olivaceous.

Voice: Described by McLachlan & Liversidge as uttering a high-pitched continuous squeaky chatter while at the nest.

Habitat: Dry savanna, though always found near water.

Distribution: Senegal to Ethiopia, Uganda and western Kenya.

A.m.jubaensis southern Somalia and north-eastern Kenya.

A.m.rubriceps KwaZulu-Natal, Northern Province, South Africa, eastern Swaziland, Zimbabwe, eastern and northern Botswana, Zambia, south-eastern Zaire, Malawi and Tanzania (coast).

A.m.gurneyi northern Namibia and southern Angola.

Feeding: Seeds, fruits, insects and spiders.

Breeding: A rough strong retort-shaped nest is made of twigs, leaf midribs, tendrils and broad leaves intertwined at the top to provide a waterproof covering. A long verticle entrance with a spout about 18-20cm long is attached. Nest construction by male, lined by female. Usually placed at the ends of drooping branches of a tree, windmill vanes or telephone wires, solitary or in small colonies. Nests are easily overlooked, but abandoned nests may survive for several seasons. In Zimbabwe 40 nests have been recorded in large Mountain acacia *Brachystegia glaucescens*. Eggs light blue, darker blue at the thick end; clutch 2-3; incubation period 11-13 days, by both sexes, mostly by female; nestling period unrecorded; host to Diederick Cuckoo *Chrysococcyx caprius*.

Aviculture: Selected Reference CLUTCH 2-3; INCUBATION PERIOD 11-13 days; NESTLING PERIOD about 17 days. Selected Reference WILDFOOD. Seeds of Guinea grass *Panicum maximum*. Selected Reference FRUIT Tree tomato *Cyphomandra betacea*, Cape ash *Ekebergia capensis*. Selected Reference ANIMAL FOOD termites, aphids and spiders.

Cardinal Quelea
Quelea cardinalis 13cm
Alternative name: Red-bib Quelea

Description: Male. Forehead, crown, ear-coverts, chin and chest crimson-red; occiput and nape streaked tawny and blackish suffused with crimson-red; hindneck, mantle and upper tail-coverts tawny with black edges to feathers; flight feathers dusky with yellow edges; breast to under tail-coverts buffish white; iris brown; bill black; legs and feet brownish flesh. Female has chin and throat pale yellowish; eye stripe buff; breast to under tail-coverts buffish; flanks streaked with brown; lacks red facial adornment. Juvenile similar to adult female, but heavily speckled on the breast.

Male. *Q.c.rhodesiae* differs from the nominate race in having the tawny and black streaked occiput clearly demarcated from crimson crown and with no red suffusion.

Voice: Described by Guggisberg as a soft 'zee-, zeet'.

Habitat: Open bush with rank grass and in cultivation.

Distribution: South-eastern Sudan, southern Ethiopia, Uganda and western Kenya.

Q.c.rhodesiae northern Mozambique (middle Zambesi River), eastern Zambia, Malawi, Tanzania and perhaps south-eastern Kenya.

Feeding: Seeds and grain.

Breeding: Nest semi-domed, with large entrance at side of top, made of fine grass. Suspended between grass stems, rarely to be found attached to a bush or tree. A nest in Malawi measured, height 150mm, width 100mm, width or entrance 30mm; bottom of entrance 80mm from bottom of nest and top 40mm from top of nest suspended at each side to a bush. No lining is added. Both sexes assist in the construction of the nest. Eggs white, blue or greenish, mottled with reddish brown; clutch 2-3; incubation period 12-13 days, by female only; nestling period 16-18 days.

Aviculture: Selected Reference CLUTCH 2-3. INCUBATION PERIOD 12-13 days; NESTLING PERIOD 16-18 days.

Red-headed Quelea

Quelea erythrops 13cm

Alternative names: Pokerhead, Red-billed Dioch, Red-headed Dioch, Red-headed Weaver.

Description: Male. Forehead, crown, nape, ear-coverts, chin and upper throat red, mantle, back, upper tail-coverts earth brown; tail earth brown, washed with black, tipped with white on outer feathers; lower throat white; breast spotted and barred with black and white; belly chestnut; flight feathers pale brown; iris brown; bill horn-coloured; legs and feet flesh-coloured. Female similar to male, but lacking the red facial adornment, except for a pale red wash on forehead, crown and nape; belly buffy. Juvenile similar to adult female, but male shows the reddish pink wash.

Voice: Described by Newman as making twittering sounds; no distinctive call.

Habitat: Affects moist grasslands situations and reed beds for breeding purposes.

Distribution: Sierra Leone, Gambia, Guinea, Liberia, east to Nigeria, São Thomé and Principé Islands, Cameroon, Chad, northern Zaire, Central African Republic, southern Sudan, Ethiopia and western Uganda.

Feeding: Seeds such as Babala *Pennisetum americanum*, grain and cultivated rice; insects fed to nestlings.

Breeding: Nest, tightly woven dome with side entrance which is more oblong than round with a short platform on the lower lip. Constructed entirely of stripped reed blades, *Typha australis* recorded at Accra Plains in Ghana and *Phragmites communis* in northern KwaZulu-Natal in South Africa. A breeding colony in West Africa numbered between 3000-5000 nests. Ten South African nests measured 90-110mm high; 70-99mm wide with an entrance of 40-45mm wide. No lining is added. In Ghana males were observed building only one transverse bridge from which females built a horizontal ring and then added the egg chamber and roof material which was used by both sexes. In South Africa the best building was done entirely by the male, although in one observation a female adjusted nest materials. Recorded associating with Red-billed Quelea *Quelea quelea* in mixed colonies in the Lake Chad region. Eggs pale blue; clutch 2-3; incubation not less than 9 days, by female only; nestling period 12-14 days; feeding of young by female only.

Aviculture: Selected Reference CLUTCH 2-3, up to 4; INCUBATION PERIOD 12-14 days; NESTLING PERIOD 21 days. Selected Reference WILDFOOD Seeds of Babala *Pennisetum americanum*, Hay *Chloris virgata*, Sudan grass *Sorghum bicolor*, Giant paspalum *Paspalum urvillei*, Common paspalum *P.dilatatum*, Broadleaved setaria *Setaria chevalieri*, Creeping setaria *S.flabellata*, Black-jack *Bidens pilosa*. Selected Reference ANIMAL FOOD mealworms and termites.

Red-billed Quelea

Quelea quelea 11-13cm

Alternative names: Black-faced Dioch, Black-fronted Dioch, Blood Bill Weaver, Common Dioch, Little Red-billed Weaver, Masked Weaver Finch, Quelea Finch, Quelea Weaver.
***Q.q.aethiopica* Sudan Dioch, Red-billed Weaver, Red-billed Dioch.**
***Q.q.spoliator* Latham's Weaver-bird, Southern Pink-billed Weaver. There is a morph of this species called Russ's Weaver.**

Description: Male. Variable forehead, sides of face and chin black, buffish or creamy white, crown, nape and throat rosy or chrome yellow; mantle, rump, wing-coverts and innermost secondaries ashy, streaked with black; tail brown, edged with yellow; underparts buffish, faintly streaked with brown; iris brown; bill red; legs and feet pinkish to orange. Female has crown, ear-coverts brownish grey; eye stripe buffish; chin and throat buffish white; bill yellowish, in non-breeding red. Juvenile similar to adult except bill pinkish horn.

Males. *Q.q.aethiopica* differs from *lathamii* in having red extending to occiput.

Q.q.lathamii differs from nominate race in having upperparts paler.

Q.q.spoliator differs from *lathamii* in having the area of the head pale buffish; underparts greyer, lacking the buffish wash.

Voice: Described by Maclean as a song mixed chattering and wheezy *'tsssrreeee'* and *'chee-chee'* notes; shrill *'chak-chak'* alarm call.

Habitat: Open savanna, thorn scrub, rank moist grass and reeds, also cultivation during crop ripening season when 500 000-600 000 to more than one million birds may arrive to feed.

Distribution: Senegal to Cameroon, Central African Republic and northern Zaire.

Q.q.aethiopica Sudan, Somalia to eastern Zaire and northern Tanzania.

Q.q.lathamii Angola, southern and eastern Zaire, Zambia, northern Namibia and South Africa in North-West, Northern Province, eastern Mpumalanga and Gauteng (except south).

Q.q.spoliator South African provinces of eastern Cape, Free State, southern Mpumalanga and northern KwaZulu-Natal; also Lesotho (lowlands), Swaziland and southern Mozambique; in non-breeding to Namibia, southern Angola, northern Botswana, Zimbabwe, Zambia and Malawi.

Feeding: Seeds, grain and insects. Seeds of Hay *Chloris virgata*, Large seed setaria *Setaria nigrirostis*, Creeping setaria *S.flabellata*, broadleaved setaria *S.chevallieri*,

Golden setaria *S.sphacelata*, Garden setaria *S.pallide-fusca*, Veld paspalum *Paspalum commersonii*, Common paspalum *P.dilataum*, Giant paspalum *P.urvillei*, Blue panic *Panicum laevigatum*, Limpopo grass *Echinochloa pyramidallis* and Wild rice *Oryza bartlii*, Coast grass *Dactyloctenium aegyptium*, Jungle rice *Echinochloa colonum*, Sorghum *purpureo-sericeum*, *Pennisetum ramosum*, *Ischaemum brachyatherum* and *Schoenfeldia gracilis* which have seeds about 2mm x 1mm in size. Cereal crops, notably wheat, sorghum, manna, millet, oats, buckwheat, rice and livefood in the form of beetles, caterpillars, grasshoppers, crickets, bugs, butterflies, ants, dragonflies, harvester termites and spiders. Flocks also feed around cattle feeding troughs, utilizing the finer portions of spilt cattle feed.

Breeding: Breeds in huge groups or small scattered colonies over a large area. The site may be in trees, bushes, rank grass or reed beds. In southern Africa the sites are in nearly all cases thorny vegetation, also use exotic *Eucalyptus* plantations. In Zambia, the Umbrella thorn *Acacia tortilis*. In South Africa, the Black thorn *Acacia mellifera*, Sweet thorn *A.karoo*, Popular *Populus deloides*, Zebrawood *Dalbergia melanoxylon*, Glory-leaved commiphora *Commiphora schimperi*, Grey-leaved saucer-berry *Cordia sinensis*, Small false mopane *Guibourtia conjugata*, Wild date palm *Phoenix reclinata* and Common reed *Phragmites communis*. In Zimbabwe Sickel bush *Dichrostachys cinerea*, Scented thorn *Acacia nilotica*, White thorn *A.polycantha*, Blue thorn. *E.erubescens*, Red thorn *A.gerradii* Umbrella thorn *A.tortillis*, Paperback acacia, *A.sieberana*, Splendid acacia *A.robusta*, Bitter albizia *Albizia amara*, Buffalo thorn *Ziziphus mucronata*, White-berry bush *Securinega virosa* and Leadwood *Combretum imberbe*. In KwaZulu-Natal, a flock of about 100 birds had made their nests in a clump of pines *Pinus* sp., constructed entirely of fresh pine needles, but nests lacked porches or linings. The nest is a small flimsy egg-shaped ball of green grass with thick walls which are pliable and are extremely tightly woven; a small porch of variable size projects above the entrance. Average measurements of 32 nests in Zimbabwe had a height of 122,2mm x width 96,3 x 103,8 depth x 38,8 entrance width and 24,3 height and 21,8 overhang. In Nigeria builds non-breeding nests of grass stems rather than of grass blades, even using leaf petioles at times. In South Africa materials consist of grass strips 20-30cm long such as Bushveld signal grass *Urochloa mosambicensis*, Milanje finger grass *Digitaria milanjiana*, Feathered chloris *Chloris virgata*, Guinea grass *Panicum maximum* and Spear grass *Heteropogon contortus*. A nest can be composed of between 600 and 700 individual pieces of grass, taking about 7-8 days to complete. Nests are sited a few centimetres apart, with some so close that their backs become woven together. A colony observation had their entrances facing away from the tree-trunks and towards the light; of 347 and 130 nests respectively 171 and 79 were facing outward, 134 and 43 along the surface of the tree slant-wise and only 42 and 8 faced

inwards. Territorial aggression ceases between neighbours once the nests are completed. Nest density in high in central Africa, a small tree may hold up to 500 nests, and a large tree up to 6 000 nests. A 50 hectare site may contain about half a million nests whilst a site of 200 hectares may contain up to 10 million nests. In southern Somalia a study was undertaken to determine the accidental death of numerous birds in a 1 5ha roosting site composed of three adjacent groves of lemon trees *Citrus acidia* and one grove of grapefruit trees *C.grandis*. Death apparently resulted from puncture wounds caused by spines on the lemon trees, probably sustained as the birds settled to roost. Eggs pale greenish or bluish white; clutch 3-5, usually 4; one brood, no attempt made to produce second clutch in same locality; incubation by female for 9,5-12 days; cared and fed by both parents; nestling period 11-14 days. In Southern Africa it has been found that queleas are attracted to roosting in stands of Sugar cane *Saccharum officinarum* and Napier fodder *Pennisetum purpureum*, the latter being planted by farmers close to their small-grain crops. The application of an avicide poison on sleeping birds at night can kill a large number in a single operation. Unfortunately numbers of non-targeted species of birds are also killed in a control operation. At a 6 hectare reed-bed in the Dichwe Lemon Forest in Zimbabwe a loss of 157 individuals from 38 species, mostly Spotted-backed Weavers *Ploceus cucullatus* and White-winged Widow *Euplectes albonotatus* were recorded.

Aviculture: Selected Reference CLUTCH 2-5; INCUBATION PERIOD 9,5-13 days; NESTLING PERIOD 11-14 days. Selected Reference WILDFOOD chickweed *Stellaria* sp., seeds of Hay *Chloris virgata*, Teff *Eragrostis tef*, Bird grass *Poa trivialis*, Popo grass *Hyparrhenia cymbaria*, Blue panic *Panicum laevifolium*, Guinea grass *P.maximum*, Lawn paspalum *Paspalum notatum*, Buffaloquick paspalum *P.distichum*, Giant paspalum *P.urvillei*, Common paspalum *P.dilatatum*, Veld paspalum *P.commersonii*, Large seed setaria *Setaria nigrirostris*, Creeping setaria *S.flabellata*, Broad-leaved setaria *S.chevalieri*, Golden setaria *S.sphacelata*, Garden stellaria *S.pallide-fusca*, fresh cut lucerne *Medicago sativa*. Selected Reference ANIMAL FOOD mealworms, mayfly nymphs, termites, spiders.

Bob-tailed Weaver
Brachycope anomala 6-6,2cm

Description: Male. Forehead and crown golden; nape brown washed with golden; sides of face black; mantle, back, rump and upper tail-coverts golden; tail black, edged yellow; chin black; throat buff; upper breast buff washed with golden; belly and rest of underparts buffish brown; iris dark brown; bill black; legs and feet pinkish brown. Female upperparts buffish brown, washed with yellow, streaked black; underparts yellow. Juvenile undescribed.

Voice: Described by Mackworth-Praed & Grant as a harsh call of 'ck-ck-ck-ck' by the male.

Habitat: Riverine growth and clearings.

Distribution: South-eastern Cameroon and the Congo.

Feeding: Seeds and insects.

Breeding: Nest, globular-shaped and sited in trees, bushes and young palms. Built of dry grass with lateral opening and lined with seeding grass heads. Eggs dark grey; clutch 2.

Aviculture: No records.

Golden Bishop
Euplectes afer 12cm

Alternative names: Golden Bishop-bird, Yellow-rumped Bishop, Yellow-crowned Bishop, Napolean Weaver.
E.a.taha **Taha Bishop-bird, Taha Weaver.**
E.a.ladoensis **Lado Taha Bishop.**

Description: Male. Forehead, crown, nape yellow; upper mantle more or less black; lower mantle, rump and upper tail-coverts yellow; band across hindneck, sides of face, ear-coverts, belly and flanks black; under tail-coverts yellow; wings and tail blackish, edged buffish; iris brown; bill black; legs and feet brown. Female had upperparts streaked blackish and greyish buff; underparts whitish, washed with buff and streaked brown on breast and flanks. Juvenile similar to adult female, but upper and underparts darker.

Males. *E.a.strictus* differs from the nominate race in having the underparts from chin to under tail-coverts black.

E.a.ladoensis differs from the nominate in having breast black, uniform with chin to belly.

Voice: Described by Serle *et al.* as a series of ringing, jingling cries.

Distribution: Senegal to Chad and Central African Republic.

E.a.ladoensis southern Sudan, Uganda, northern Kenya and northern Tanzania.

E.a.strictus Ethiopia.

E.a.taha southern Angola, Zambia, Botswana, northern Namibia, western and northern Zimbabwe, Malawi, northern Mozambique, western Swaziland, Lesotho and the South African provinces of central and eastern Gauteng, Free State, Cape, KwaZulu-Natal (interior).

Feeding: Seeds and insects. Seeds of Natal redtop *Rhynchelytrum repens*, Young fed on caterpillars.

Breeding: Constructs a neat oval nest of dried grass with an entrance at one side towards the top. The hole is covered by a porch. It is placed in short matted grass or weeds and sometimes in rice in West Africa. Male almost certainly polygamous with each male's territory measuring about 27m in diameter. Eggs white with deep green and black spots concentrated mostly at the broad end; clutch 3-4; incubation period 12-14 days; feeding and caring of young by female only.

Aviculture: Selected Reference CLUTCH 2-4; INCUBATION PERIOD 12-14 days; NESTLING PERIOD 13-21, up to 28 days. Nest Record Cards CLUTCH 3,3,4 (ARU) 4 (SAANRC) 3 (NASNRC) about 15 days (NASNRC). Seeds of Jungle rice *Echinochloa colonum* (ARU), Hay *Chloris virgata*, Garden setaria *Setaria pallide-fusca*, Natal redtop *rhynchelytrum repens*, Blue panic *Panicum laevifolium*, Bird grass *Poa trivialis* (NASDRC), Crab finger grass *Digitaria sanguinalis*. Fresh cut Lucerne *Medicago sativa* (SAADRC). Selected Reference ANIMAL FOOD mealworms, termites. Diet Record Cards mealworms, termites (ARU, SAADRC, NASDRC), earwigs (ARU), hairless caterpillars, wasp larvae or "grubs" (SAADRC), fly larvae or "maggots" (NASDRC).

Fire-fronted Bishop
Euplectes diademata 10cm

Description: Male. Forehead reddish orange; rest of head black; mantle golden yellow, streaked with black; rump and upper tail-coverts golden-yellow; tail dusky; chin, throat belly and breast black; under tail-coverts golden-yellow; underparts white; wings blackish, wing coverts and inner secondaries edged with buff, primaries edged with yellow; iris brown; bill black; legs and feet dusky yellow. Female has upperparts streaked black and buff; breast to belly white; bill horn coloured. Juvenile similar to adult female, but paler overall.

Voice: Described by Moreau as a sharp 'ze-ze' and a grasshopper-like sizzling call.

Habitat: Bushed grassland, cultivation and semi-arid plateau country with wet grassy hollows, but wanders widely.

Distribution: South-eastern Somalia, northern Kenya and north-eastern Tanzania.

Feeding: Rice.

Breeding: In small scattered colonies.

Aviculture: Selected Reference CLUTCH 3; INCUBATION PERIOD 10-12 days; NESTLING PERIOD 11-12 days. Selected Reference WILDFOOD Seeds of Blue panic *Panicum laevifolium*, Giant paspalum *Paspalum urvillei*, Hay *Chloris virgata*, Garden setaria *Setaria pallide-fusca*, Common thatch grass *Hyparrhenia hirta*. Selected Reference ANIMAL FOOD termites, spiders.

Gierow's Bishop
Euplectes gierowii 15,5cm

Alternative names: Black Bishop, Gierow's Bishop.

Description: Male. Forehead, forecrown, lores, round eyes, ear-coverts and chin black; hindcrown, nape and sides of neck orange-red; mantle yellow; rump and upper tail-coverts ashy; tail blackish; throat and upper breast orange-red; lower breast, belly and flanks black; under tail-coverts ashy; iris brown; bill black; legs and feet dusky brown. Female similar to male in non-breeding plumage by upperparts broadly streaked with buff and black; underparts yellowish buff Juvenile similar to female by paler overall.

Males. *E.g.ansorgei* differs from the nominate race in having nape orange-scarlet; mantle yellow; larger bill.

E.g.friederichseni differs from *ansorgei* in having the lower mantle and rump orange-yellow; wider collar on lower neck.

Voice: Described by West as rather nondescript chirps and twitters.

Habitat: Tall bushes grasslands, cultivation, often in patches of swampy Elephant grass which is in flower from April to May in East Africa.

Distribution: Northern Angola and south-western Zaire.

E.g.ansorgei southern Sudan, southern Ethiopia, northern Zaire and Uganda.

E.g.friederichseni south-western Kenya and northern Tanzania.

Feeding: Grass seeds and insects.

Breeding: Polygamous, having more than one female, usually 3 or 4. Breeds in colonies, a number of nests being usually built in Elephant grass *Hyparrhenia collina* being 300-1300m tall, or similar water side vegetation, and occasionally in the fork of a shrub in area where grass is scarce. The blades of Elephant grass can measure up to 400mm long and 4mm wide. These are stripped to form the outer structure of the nest, which also has a side entrance at one side near the top. Lining consists of grassheads, the stems often protruding into the porch. Eggs bluish or greenish, occasionally speckled blackish; clutch 2-5, mostly 3; incubation lasts 12-13 days and only the female broods and cares for the young; nestling period 12-14 days.

Aviculture: Nest Record Cards CLUTCH 3,3,5 (ANRC); INCUBATION PERIOD 12,13,13 (ANRC); NESTLING PERIOD 12,13,13 days (ANRC). Diet Record Cards ANIMAL FOOD termites, mealworms, smooth green caterpillars (ADRC).

Zanzibar Red Bishop
Euplectes nigroventris 10cm

Alternative names: Black-bellied Weaver, Black-bellied Grenadier, Black-bellied Bishop, Zanzibar Red Weaver.

Description: Male. Forehead, crown, nape and sides of neck orange-red; mantle, back and rump dusky red; tail blackish, edged with tawny; ear-coverts, chin, throat, breast, belly and under tail-coverts orange-red; occasionally the throat streaked with red; under tail-coverts orange; iris brown; bill black; legs and feet reddish brown. Female upperparts broadly streaked with brownish buff and black; breast and flanks streaked with dark brown; rest of underparts buffish. Juvenile similar to adult female, but has broader and paler buff edges to feathers of upperparts.

Voice: Described by West as various monotonous twittering.

Habitat: Open and bushed grassland and cultivation.

Distribution: Eastern Kenya, eastern Tanzania, northern Mozambique and the islands of Zanzibar, Manda and Kwale.

Feeding: Grass seeds, crops, mainly rice and also insects.

Breeding: Male polygamous. Small scattered colonies of no more than 16 individuals usually select dry ground areas with an abundance of suitable rank grass in which to construct their frail transparent nests. They stand no more than 2m from the ground and consist of coarse grass lined with finer grass. The oval structure sometimes contains a short porch. Eggs pale bluish, occasionally spotted with dusky brown; clutch 2-4, usually 2-3; double brooded; incubation period 12 days by female only; nestling period 13-16 days; fed by female only.

Aviculture: Nest Record Cards 3 CLUTCH (ARU) 3 (ANRC); INCUBATION PERIOD 12 (ARU) 12 days (ANRC); NESTLING PERIOD 15 (ARU) 17 days 19 (ANRC). Diet Record Cards ANIMAL FOOD termites (ARU ADRC), small spiders (ADRC).

Fire-crowned Bishop
Euplectes hordeacea 13-15cm

Alternative names: Blacik-winged Bishop, Black-winged Red Bishop, Crimson-crowned Bishop, Crimson-crowned Weaver, Red-crowned Bishop.
E.h.craspedoptera **East Coast Fire-crowned Bishop.**

Description: Male. Forehead, crown and nape red to orange; mantle reddish brown; back and upper tail-coverts red; tail black; sides of face, ear-coverts, chin and upper throat black; breast red; belly black; under tail-coverts brownish red; wings black; iris brown; bill black; legs and feet brownish. Female brownish buff, mantle streaked black; eye stripe yellow; wings and tail black. Juvenile similar to adult female, but more heavily streaked on upperparts.

Male. *E.h.craspedoptera* differs from the nominate race in having under tail-coverts white, streaked black.

Voice: Described by Mackworth-Praed & Grant as having various twittering cries, not particularly distinguishable from those of other species.

Habitat: Rank vegetation in the vicinity of streams, pans and marshes.

Distribution: Eastern Zimbabwe, Mozambique, Malawi, northern and eastern Zambia, Angola, south-eastern Congo, western Sudan to Senegal.

E.h.craspedoptera southern Sudan, south-western Ethiopia, Uganda and north-western Kenya.

Feeding: Seeds, grain and insects.

Breeding: Nests in colonies with each male having several females. The nest is constructed of green grass blades with a porch of seeding grassheads, being secured between two upright grass stems or occasionally in bushes or tall herbs. Eggs pale bluish green, plain or sparsely spotted with brown or purple; clutch 2-4, usually 3; incubation period 12-13 days; young fed by female alone; nestling period 11-14 days.

Aviculture: Personal Communication CLUTCH 4; INCUBATION PERIOD 14 days; NESTLING PERIOD 14 days. Selected Reference ANIMAL FOOD mealworms, termites.

Red Bishop
Euplectes orix 12-14cm

Alternative names: Durra Bird, Crimson Grenadier, Grenadier Weaver, Oryx Weaver, Red Bishop, Red Grenadier, Red Coffee Tink, Scarlet Bishop, Scarlet Grenadier, Southern Red Bishop.
E.o.franciscana **Little Bishop, Northern Red Bishop, Orange Bishop, Orange Weaver, West Nile Red Bishop.**
E.o.pusilla **East African Orange Bishop.**
E.o.nigrifrons **Black-fronted Red Bishop, Black Fore-headed Weaver.**
E.o.sundevalli **Bonaparte's Red Bishop, Red-crowned Grenadier, Red-crowned Bishop, Sundevall's Grenadier.**
E.o.turgidus **Clancey's Red Bishop.**

Description: Male. Forehead, forecrown, sides of face and ear-coverts black; mantle reddish brown; rump and upper tail-coverts red; tail dusky; chin and upper throat black; hindcrown, sides of neck and lower throat red; breast to belly black; under tail-coverts red; wings blackish brown; iris brown; bill black; legs and feet brownish. Female has upperparts streaked buff and dark brown; underparts white, washed buff and streaked brown on breast and flanks. Juvenile similar to adult female, but has paler buff edges to feathers of underparts.

Males. *E.o.franciscana* differs from nominate race in having back of crown extending to nape.

E.o.pusilla differs from nominate in being paler orange-red; upper and under tail-coverts not extending to tip of tail.

E.o.nigrifrons differs from nominate in having mantle darker tawny, streaked black.

E.o.sundevalli differs from *franciscana* in having the black confined to the forehead and at times also black chin.

E.o.turgidus differs from the nominate in being larger in all respects; not constantly separable on colour grounds.

Voice: Described by Maclean as a sharp '*chiz chiz*' call-notes.

Habitat: Thornveld, open grasslands and cultivated fields. Breeding takes place in reed beds of rivers, pans and dams.

Distribution: Southern Zaire, Zambia, southern Angola, north-western Zimbabwe, northern Namibia, the Caprivi Strip and northern and north-eastern Botswana.

E.o.franciscana Senegal to Ethiopia, Uganda and Kenya.

E.o.pusilla south-eastern Ethiopia and Somalia.

E.o.nigrifrons Mozambique (north of Save River), eastern Zambia, eastern Zaire, Uganda, Kenya and Tanzania.

E.o.turgidus southern Namibia, Lesotho, western Swaziland and the South African provinces of Cape, Free State, northern KwaZulu-Natal and Gauteng (highveld).

E.o.sundevalli South African provinces of KwaZulu-Natal (coast and midlands), eastern North-West, central and southern Northern Province and Mpumalanga and eastern Swaziland, Mozambique (south of Save River) and Zimbabwe (except north-west).

Feeding: Mainly seeds, flowers, grain and insects. Seeds of Garden setaria *Setaria pallide-fusca*, Blue panic *Panicum laevigatum*, Natal redtop *Rhynchelytrum repens*, Hay *Chloris virgata*, Common thatchgrass *Hyparrhenia hirta*, Giant paspalum *Paspalum urvillei*, Jungle Rice *Echinochloa cruspavonis*, Snake root *Polygonum senegalense*, *Sorghum caffrorum*, flowers of *Leonotis* sp., and *Oxymifolia* sp. on seashore. Also observed picking up Kelp fly larvae and sandhoppers *Talorchestia* from among weeds on sea shore and making occasional short sallies from the ground to catch flies in mid-air.

Breeding: This bird is polygamous, with each male having about three females. The majority of the nests are built in reeds *Phragmites* sp., in Zimbabwe, *Mauritianus*, standing in a river, dam or vlei. Also recorded in populars *Polpulus* sp., and in a field of Maize *Zea mays*, where 267 nests were counted. The nests were either attached to the flower heads of the plant or slung between the stem and a leaf. Each male constructs several oval shaped nests made of grass blades on reed stems. The entrance hole is at the top, generally with a protruding porch facing west, occasionally south-west. An old nest may be utilized after repairs. Nests are placed from 1-2-4m from the ground or water level. One nest was analysed and found to contain 340 strands of reeds and 1440 grassheads. Eggs plain bluish green; double brooded; clutch 2-5, mostly 3; incubation period 12-13 days by the female only who continues to add lining to the nest throughout incubation as well as caring and feeding the young; nestling period 12-16 days. At times young birds die before leaving the nest due to exposure from soaking rains; host to Diederick Cuckoo *Chyrsococcyx caprius* and Klaas's Cuckoo *C klaas*.

Aviculture: Selected Reference CLUTCH 2-7; INCUBATION PERIOD 12-16 days; NESTLING PERIOD 15-21 days. Nest Record Cards CLUTCH 4,5 (ARU) 4 (SAANRC); INCUBATION PERIOD 13,14 (ARU) 14 days (SAANRC); NESTLING PERIOD 13 (ARU) 12,14 days (SAANRC). Diet Record Cards WILDFOOD Seeds of Black-jack *Bidens pilosa*, Blue panic *Panicum laevifolium*, Guinea grass *P.maximum*, Garden setaria *Setaria pallide-fusca*, Golden setaria *S.sphacelata*, Broadleaved setaria *S.chevallieri*, Creeping setaria *S.flabellata*, Millet grass *S.woodii*, Tef grass *Eragrostis tef*, Natal redtop *Rhychelytrum repens*, Hay *Chloris virgata*, Common thatch grass *Hyparrhenia hirta*, Giant paspalum *Paspalum urvillei*, Common paspalum *P.dilatatum*, Veld paspalum *P.commersonii*, Lawn paspalum *P.notatum*, Buffaloquick paspalum *P.distichum*, fresh cut Lucerne *Medicago sativa* (ARU SAADRC). Selected Reference ANIMAL FOOD mealworms. Diet Record Cards termites, mealworms (ARU SAADRC), thrips-nymphs, hairless caterpillars (ARU), moths, aphids, mayfly nymphs, gnats, wasp larvae or "grubs"(SAADRC).

Golden-backed Bishop

Euplectes aurea -cm

Description: Male. Entire head and nape black mantle, back and rump orange-yellow; upper tail-coverts ashy; tail and flight feathers black, edged white and buff; under wing-coverts white; chin, throat, sides of neck, breast and upper belly black; lower belly, flanks and under tail-coverts white; iris brown; bill black; legs and feet brown. Female upperparts pale tawny broadly streaked black; stripe over eye and ear-coverts yellowish; underparts buffish white, except throat and breast buff. Juvenile similar to adult female, but washed with yellow.

Voice: Not known.

Habitat: Coastal bush.

Distribution: São Thomé Island and western Angola.

Feeding: Not known.

Breeding: Not known.

Aviculture: Selected Reference CLUTCH 2-3; INCUABTION PERIOD 13-14 days; NESTLING PERIOD 15 to after 21 days. Selected Reference WILDFOOD Seeds of Snake root *Polygonum senegalense*,

Jungle rice *Echinochloa colonum* Guinea grass *Panicum maximum*, Natal redtop *Rhynchelytrum repens*, Common paspalum *Paspalum dialatatum*, Finger grass *Digitatia eriantha*. Personal Communication ANIMAL FOOD mealworms.

Yellow-rumped Bishop

Euplectes capensis 14cm

Alternative names: Cape Bishop-bird, Transvaal Yellow Bishop-bird, Cape Widow, Yellow-rumped Widow, Yellow Bishop. *E.c.crassirostris* Black-and-Yellow Bishop, Yellow Bishop-bird, Yellow-backed Weaver, Yellow-shouldered Weaver.

Description: Male. Entire head and nape black; mantle, back, rump and wing-shoulder yellow; tail black; flight feathers black, edged buff; under wing-coverts buff; breast, belly and under tail-coverts black; iris brown; bill black; legs and feet brown. Female paler rufous brown, but head and back streaked almost black; eye stripe buff; lacks yellow on wing-shoulder, lower back and rump. Juvenile similar to adult female, but upperparts darker and underparts paler.

Males. *E.c.phoenicomera* differs from the nominate race in having wings brownish, less black.

E.c.approximans differs from the nominate in being slightly smaller.

E.c.macrorhynchus differs from the nominate in being considerably larger; bill white.

E.c.crassirostris differs from the nominate in having bill brown.

Voice: Described by Maclean as a thin '*seep*' and '*tsip*' notes.

Habitat: Tall bushed grasslands up to 2300m in East Africa.

Distribution: South-western Cape Province (east to about Plettenburg Bay), South Africa.

E.c.macrorhynchus western Cape Province (about the lower Berg River), South Africa.

E.c.phoenicomera south-eastern Nigeria, Cameroon and Fernando Pó Island.

E.c.approximans eastern Cape, Free State, KwaZulu-Natal (interior), and southern Mpumalanga provinces of South Africa to Lesotho and western Swaziland.

E.c.crassirostris in Mpumalanga and Northern Province, South Africa, north-eastern Botswana, Zimbabwe, Mozambique, Zaire, Uganda, Kenya, Tanzania, Angola, Sudan and Ethiopia,

Feeding: Seeds and insects.

Breeding: Males polygamous with 2-3 females each. Nest oval, constructed of green grass strips, with the entrance to one side at the top, with a slight porch. The lining consists of wool, feathers and seeding grassheads. This is added by the female throughout the incubation period and in the early stages of rearing the young birds. The site is usually 1-2m from the ground in matted grass or weeds. Eggs bluish white or pale green, heavily marked with blotches or streaks of dark brown or sepia; clutch 2-4; incubation period 13-16 days by female only who also feeds the nestlings; nestling period 15-16, up to 20; fed by both adults, but mostly by female.

Aviculture: Seleted Reference CLUTCH 2-4; INCUBATION PERIOD 13-16 days; NESTLING PERIOD 14-17 days. Nest Record Cards CLUTCH 3,3,4 (ANRC); INCUBATION PERIOD 14,14 (ANRC) about 13 days (SAANRC); NESTLING PERIOD 16 (ANRC) about 16 days (SAANRC). Selected Reference WILDFOOD Seeds of Hay *Chloris virgata*, Teff grass *Eragrostis tef*, Common paspalum *Paspalum dialatatum*, Buffaloquick paspalum *P.distichum*, Blue panic *Panicum laevifolium*, Guinea grass *P.maximum*, Guineafowl grass *Rottboellia exaltata*, Common thatchgrass *Hyparrhenia hirta*. Personal Communication ANIMAL FOOD mealworms, moths.

Yellow-mantled Whydah

Euplectes macrourus 18-22cm

Alternative names: Gold-backed Whydah, Yellow-backed Whydah, Yellow-backed Widow, Yellow-mantled Widow-bird, Yellow-backed Widow-bird.

Description: Male. Entire head and nape black; mantle yellow; lower rump, upper tail-coverts and tail black; wing-shoulder yellow; breast, belly and under tail-coverts black; iris brown; bill bluish grey; legs and feet black. Female brown; only wing-shoulder yellow; bill horn. Juvenile similar to female, but showing a faint wash of yellow on the underparts.

Voice: Described by Maclean as a rapid high-pitched chisisisi chisisisi chisisisi, rather insect-like.

Habitat: Rank grass in the vicinity of marshes and vleis.

Distribution: Eastern Zimbabwe, western Mozambique, Angola, Zaire, Sudan, Guinea to Senegal.

Feeding: Seeds and insects.

Breeding: The nest is situated about 15-60cm above the ground in tall grass or reeds and built of fine dry grass with a side entrance towards the top. No lining or porch is added. Eggs pale green with olive-brown or olive-grey spots or blotches; clutch 2-3; incubation by female only, who also feeds and tends to the young.

Aviculture: Selected Reference CLUTCH 2-4; INCUBATION PERIOD 12-14 days; NESTLING PERIOD 15 days. Selected Reference ANIMAL FOOD termites.

Marsh Whydah

Euplectes hartlaubi 25,5-30cm

Alternative names: Marsh Widow-bird
E.h.humerallis **Uganda Marsh Whydah.**

Description: Male. Wholly black, including long graduated tail; wing-shoulder yellow, secondaries edged buff; under wing-coverts pale buff and black; iris dark brown; bill bluish white; legs and feet black. Female upperparts broadly streaked black and brown; wing-shoulder edged pale yellow; underparts buffish, streaked brown; bill horn. Juvenile plumage pattern basically as adult female, but paler.

Males. *E.h.humerallis* differs from the nominate race in having paler buff confined to the lesser wing-coverts; tail shorter.

Voice: Not known.

Habitat: Moist grasslands, swamp edges and cultivation at 1100-1800m in East Africa.

Distribution: Angola, southern Zaire and Zambia.

E.h.humerallis Cameroon to Uganda and western Kenya.

Feeding: Seeds, berries and insects.

Breeding: A woven pouch of fine grass with side entrance, placed near the ground being attached to living grass which is bent down over and round it to form and outer shell. Eggs light bluish green, flecked or blotched with olive-brown, pale grey and lilac; clutch 2.

Aviculture: No records.

Mountain Marsh Whydah

Euplectes psammocromius -cm

Description: Male. Entire head, nape, mantle, back, upper tail-coverts and tail black; wing-shoulder yellow; wings with primary and secondary coverts pale buffy white; iris dark brown; bill bluish; legs and feet blackish. Female buffish brown, broadly streaked with wing-shoulder edged pale yellow. Juvenile similar to female but finer streaking; bill horn coloured.

Voice: Not known.

Habitat: Short thick grass bordering streams.

Distribution: South-western Tanzania, western Malawi (Nyika Plateau) and north-eastern Zambia.

Feeding: Seeds, berries and insects.

Breeding: Constructs a dome-shaped nest of fine grass loosely woven with a side entrance. Growing grasses are bent over the nest making it difficult to see at first glance. Eggs pale geen, streaked with pale lilac; clutch 2.

Aviculture: No records.

Red-collared Whydah

Euplectes ardens 24-40cm

Alternative names: Cut-throat Whydah, Cut-throat Widow-bird, Flame Whydah, Red-collared Widow, Flaming Whydah.
E.a.concolor **Black Whydah.**
E.a.laticauda **Red-naped Whydah, Long-tailed Black Whydah.**

Description: Male. Entire head, nape, mantle, back, upper tail-coverts and tail black; collar on lower neck red through orange to almost yellow; chin, throat, breast, belly and under tail-coverts black; wings-coverts black, edged whitish; iris brown; bill, legs and feet black.

Female upperparts streaked dusky and fawn; underparts white, except breast buffy. Juvenile similar to female, but upperparts broadly streaked.

E.a.concolor differs from the nominate race in lacking the collar on lower neck.

E.a.laticauda similar to *suahelicus* but have shorter tails.

E.a.suahelicus differs from the nominate in having crown and nape red to join red of foreneck and sides of neck.

Voice: Described by Mackworth-Praed & Grant as a plaintive squealing chirp, and a metallic grasshopper-like ticking song.

Habitat: Rank vegetation along streams and reeds in marshes to open savanna and cultivation.

Distribution: Eastern Cape, KwaZulu-Natal, Free State, south-eastern Gauteng, southern Northern Province, western Mpumalanga in South Africa to Lesotho, Swaziland and Mozambique.

E.a.concolor Senegal to southern Sudan, Uganda and Chad.

E.a.laticauda south-eastern Sudan and Ethiopia.

E.a.suahelicus Kenya and north-eastern Tanzania.

Feeding: Seeds and insects.

Breeding: Males polygamous with up to 3 females each. Constructs a dome of fresh green grass or reed strips which has an entrance at the top of one side, with seedheads protruding to form a slight porch. Usually placed 1-2m from the ground in reeds of grass. The female lines the nest chamber with finer grasses. Eggs bluish green, with heavy blotching and speckling of olive-brown or greyish brown; clutch 2-6, usually 3; incubation period 12-15 days by female alone, who cares and feed the young; nestling period about 16 days. Host to Diederick Cuckoo *Chrysococcyx caprius*.

Aviculture: Selected Reference CLUTCH 2-6; INCUBATION PERIOD 12-15 days; NESTLING PERIOD 147-17 days. Nest Record Cards CLUTCH 4 (ARU); INCUBATION PERIOD 14 days (ARU) NESTLING

PERIOD 16 days (ARU). Selected Reference WILD-FOOD Seeds of Hay *Chloris virgata*, Common thatchgrass *Hyparrhenia hirta*, Natal redtop *Rhynchelytrum repens*, Guinea grass *Panicum maximum*, Blue panic *P.laevifolium*, Garden setaria *Setaria pallide-fusca*, Giant paspalum *Paspalum urvillei*, Bird grass *Poa trivialis*, dandelion *Taraxacum sp.*, dock *Rumex sp.*, Sow-Thistle *Sonchus oleraceus*, Comfrey *Symphytum officinale*. Selected Reference ANIMAL FOOD mealworms. Diet Record Cards mealworms, earwigs, thrips-nymphs, termites (ARU).

Fan-tailed Whydah

Euplectes axillaris Male 17-18cm,
Female 13-14cm

Alternative names: Red-shouldered Widow.
E.a.bocagei **Bocage's Fan-tailed Whydah,**
Bocage's Whydah.
E.a.batesi **Niger Fan-tailed Whydah.**
E.a.zanzibaricus **Zanzibar Fan-tailed Widow-bird.**

Description: Male. Black including tail; wings black, shoulder red-orange, lesser coverts and under wing-coverts brown; iris brown; bill bluish; legs and feet brown. Female upperparts broadly streaked buff and black; bend of wing golden-brown, streaked blackish; underparts buffish white. Juvenile similar to adult female, but upperparts browner, feathers of wing-shoulder black, edged buff.

Males. *E.a.batesi* differs from *bocagei* in having lesser wing-coverts more reddish orange.

E.a.zanzibaricus differs from *phoeniceus* in having stouter bill.

E.a.bocagei differs from the nominate race in having primary and secondary coverts wholly brown.

E.a.quanzae differs from *bocagei* in having larger bill.

E.a.traversii differs from the nominate in having wing-shoulder orange-yellow.

E.a.phoeniceus differs from the nominate in having wing-shoulder more orange yellow.

Voice: Described by Maclean as a husky rolling rhythmic '*shreep shrik shrik wirra shreek shreek wirrily wirrily wirrily chink chink chink*', rather weak, without carrying power.

Habitat: Rank grass and cultivation, including canefields on the coast.

Distribution: Eastern Cape, KwaZulu-Natal and Mpumalanga, South Africa to Swaziland, Mozambique, eastern Zambia and Malawi.

E.a.bocagei North-western Zimbabwe, northern Botswana, north-eastern Namibia, western Zambia, southern Zaire, Angola, Cameroon and Niger.

E.a.quanzae Central Angola.

E.a.traversii northern Ethiopia.

E.a.phoeniceus southern Ethiopia, Sudan, Uganda, western Kenya and western Tanzania.

E.a.batesi Upper Volta to Upper Niger.

E.a.zanzibaricus Somalia, eastern Kenya and eastern Tanzania.

Feeding: Seeds, including rice and insects. Seeds of Bulrush *Typha latifolia*, Common Reed *Phragmites communis*, Snake root *Polygonum senegalense* and Jungle rice *Echinochloa colonum*. Livefood, namely termites and hairless caterpillars.

Breeding: Males polygamous. Constructs a loose bulky oval network of green grass. The female packs the interior with green or dried grass seedheads to form the chamber. Lining continues to be added during incubation. Average nest dimensions are 139mm high, 63.5mm wide, 176mm deep and entrance 51mm in diameter in one nest 39 strands in another 47 strands were used in the construction. Eggs bluish green or light green, speckled with brown or greyish brown; clutch 2; incubation 12-13 days, by female alone who also cares for and feeds offspring for a further 14 days after leaving the nest; nestling period 15-16 days.

Aviculture: Selected Reference CLUTCH 2-4; INCUBATION PERIOD 12-14 days; NESTLING PERIOD 12-14. Selected Reference WILDFOOD Seeds of Black-jack *Bidens pilosa*, Teff grass *Eragrostis tef*, Hay *Chloris virgata*, Common thatchgrass *Hyparrhenia hirta*, Common paspalum *Paspalum dilatatum*, Giant paspalum *P.urvillei*, Buffaloquick paspalum *P.distichum*, Finger grass *Digitaria eriantha*, Small finger grass *D.argyrograpta*, Bird grass *Poa trivialis*, dandelion *Taraxacum sp.*, dock *Rumex sp.*, Sow-Thistle *Sonchus oleraceus*, Comfrey *Symphytum officinale*. Selected Reference ANIMAL FOOD mealworms, termites, spiders, cutworms, crickets, hairless caterpillars (eg Cabbage moths), Weevils.

White-winged Whydah

Euplectes albonotatus 15-19cm

Alternative names: White-winged Widow-bird.
C.a.eques **East African White-winged**
Whydah.
C.a.asymmetrurus **Angolan White-winged**
Whydah.

Description: Male. Entire head, nape, mantle, back, upper tail-coverts and tail black; wing-shoulder yellow; greater part of primary and secondary coverts and under wing-coverts white; breast, belly and under tail-coverts black; iris brown; bill bluish grey; legs and feet blackish. Female streaked on side of breast; throat pale yellow grading to a paler yellow-brown on the breast; eye stripe yellow. Juvenile upperparts having feathers edged fawn underparts buff, except flanks darker.

Males. *E.a.eques* differs from the nominate race in having wings-shoulder cinnamon-brown.

E.a.asymmetrurus differs from the nominate in having a longer tail.

Voice: Described by Maclean as a papery rustling 'shurr', followed by 2-3 zinging 'chirps'.

Habitat: Rank grass and reedbed, but is also observed in old cultivation and dry acacia savannas.

Distribution: KwaZulu-Natal, Mpumalanga, eastern North-West, northern Gauteng and Northern Province, South Africa to Swaziland, Mozambique, Zimbabwe, eastern Botswana, Zambia, south-eastern Zaire and southern Tanzania.

S.a.eques Sudan, Tanzania and eastern Zaire.

E.a.asymmetrurus northern and north-eastern Namibia, Angola, western Zaire and Gabon.

Feeding: Grass seeds, grain, nectar and insects. Seeds of Hay *Chloris virgata*, thatchgrass *Hyparrhenia* sp. and Guineafowl grass *Rottboellia exaltata*, nectar of Flat-flowered aloe *Aloe marlothii*.

Breeding: Male polygamous with up to 4 females each. The male constructs an oval nest of coarse grass blades which usually incorporates some of the surrounding vegetation. The entrance is to one side near the top. The female assists by lining the chamber with finer dried grass. The nest is usually sited 1-1,5m above the ground. Eggs greenish blue or greenish white speckled and spotted with brown or grey; clutch 2-6, usually 2-3; incubation period 12-14 days; nestling period 11-13,5 days; host to Diederick Cuckoo *Chrysococcyx caprius*.

Aviculture: Selected Reference CLUTCH 2-4; INCUBATION PERIOD 12-14 days; NESTLING PERIOD 11-14 days. Nest Record Cards CLUTCH 3,3,4 (ANRC). Selected Reference WILDFOOD Seeds of Hay *Chloris virgata*, Common thatchgrass *Hyparrhenia hirta*, Guineafowl grass *Rottboellia exaltata*, Teff grass *Eragrostis tef*, Blue panic *Panicum laevifolium*, Guinea grass *P.maximum*, Babala grass *Pennisetum americanum*, Common paspalum *Paspalum dilatatum*, Giant paspalum *P.urvillei*, Buffaloquick paspalum *P.distichum*, Black-jack *Bidens pilosa*, dandelion *Taraxacum* sp., dock *Rumex* sp., Sow-Thistle *Sonchus oleraceus*, Comfrey *Symphytum officinale*. Diet Record Cards FRUIT nectar of Flat-flowered aloe *Aloe marlothii*, Krantz aloe *A.arborscens*. Selected Reference ANIMAL FOOD mealworms, earwigs, termites.

Long-tailed Whydah

Euplectes progne 48-60cm

Alternative names: Giant Whydah, Long-tailed Widow.

E.p.delamerei **Delamer's Giant Whydah, Delamere's Whydah.**

Description: Male. Entire head, nape, mantle, back, upper tail-coverts and tail black; wing-shoulder orange-red, median wing-coverts white to buff; under wing-coverts, breast, belly and under tail-coverts black; iris brown; bill blue-grey; legs and feet brown. Female upperparts blackish brown, feathers edged buff; ear-coverts cinnamon buff; chin white; breast white, spotted brown; rest of underparts whitish; no orange and buff band on bend of wing; primaries brown; bill dusky grey; legs and feet dusky yellow. Bill horn. Juvenile similar to adult female, but wing-shoulder buff.

Males. *E.p.delamerei* differs from the nominate race in having wing-coverts pure white.

E.p.ansorgei differs from the nominate in being generally darker and more heavily streaked (Non-breeding).

Voice: Described by Maclean as a sharp *'zik zik zik zik'* in flight display and when alarmed.

Habitat: Open grasslands, marshes and cultivation.

Distribution: Eastern Cape, KwaZulu-Natal (interior), Free State, southern North-West, Gauteng and southern Northern Province, South Africa to Lesotho, western Swaziland, south-eastern Botswana and eastern Zambia. *E.p.delamerei* eastern Kenya.

E.p.ansorgei eastern Angola and western Zambia.

Feeding: Seeds and insects. Seeds of Common paspalum *Paspalum dilatatum* and Buffaloquick paspalum *P.distichum*.

Breeding: Male polygamous with up to 6 females. The female builds a spherical nest of grass with a lining of grass seedheads. The side entrance incorporates a hood of grass stalks. The nest is placed low or on the ground, usually well concealed in a tuft of grass. Lining is added throughout the incubation until the nest is densely padded. Eggs greenish white, heavily speckled with grey and olive-brown; clutch 2-4 normally 3; incubation 14 days by female only; male roosts nearby; nestling period 17 days and only the female cares and feeds the young.

Aviculture: Selected Reference CLUTCH 2-4, normally 3; INCUBATION PERIOD 13-14 days; NESTLING

PERIOD 17-20 days. Selected Reference WILDFOOD Seeds of Hay *Chloris virgata*, Common paspalum *Paspalum dilatatum*, Buffaloquick paspalum *P.distichum*, Common thatchgrass *Hyparrhenia hirta*, Guineafowl grass *Rottboellia exaltata*, Common Reed *Phragmites communis*, dandelion *Taraxacum* sp., Fresh cut Lucerne *Medicago sativa*. Selected Reference ANIMAL FOOD mealworms, termites, grasshoppers, hairless caterpillars, moths, spiders.

Jackson's Whydah
Euplectes jacksoni Male 33-36cm, Female 14cm
Alternative names: Dancing Whydah, Jackson's Widow-bird.

Description: Male. Wholly black including long broad curved tail feathers; flight feathers, edged light brown; shoulders olive-brown to yellow; iris dark brown; bill, legs and feet bluish black. Female upperparts buff, streaked dusky; underparts buffish brown, streaked dusky on breast and flanks. Juvenile closely resembles adult female, but paler overall; bill horn.

Voice: Described by Williams & Arlott as a soft *'cheee'* uttered during display, and a brief clicking song.

Habitat: Open grassland and grazing pastures between 1500-3000m in East Africa.

Distribution: Kenya and northern Tanzania.

Feeding: Seeds and insects. Seeds of *Crambe kilimandscharica*.

Breeding: Males polygamous with up to 6 females each. Construct a rather flimsy nest of grass, lined with seedheads and has an entrance at the top on one side. Usually placed on the ground or low down in growing grass with the blades being bent over to form the woven roof. Eggs pale bluef or pale greyish green, spotted, blotched and streaked with pale brown and greyish brown; clutch 2-3.

Aviculture: Selected Reference CLUTCH 2-4; INCUBATION PERIOD 13-14 days.

Parasitic Weaver
Anomalospiza imberbis 13cm
Alternative names: Cuckoo Finch, Cuckoo Weaver

Description: Male. Forehead, sides of face and ear-coverts yellow; crown, nape, mantle, back and upper tail-coverts greenish yellow, streaked black; tail and wings grey, edged greenish yellow; flanks streaked dusky; belly and under tail-coverts yellow; iris dark brown; bill blackish; legs and feet brown. Female has forehead, crown, nape, mantle and upper tail-coverts tawny, broadly streaked black; throat and belly whitish; breast and flanks tawny, streaked dark brown. Juvenile similar to adult female, but breast distinctly streaked black; bill, upper mandible dusky, lower yellowish.

Voice: Described by Maclean as a slightly rasping *'tseep krrik krrik krrik krrik'* or *'seedle-eedle-eedle-thrush-thru'*.

Habitat: Open grasslands and cultivation.

Distribution: KwaZulu-Natal (interior), northern Province, central North-West and Mpumalanga, South Africa to Swaziland, Mozambique, Zimbabwe, Namibia, southern Angola, Uganda, Kenya, Tanzania and Ethiopia.

Feeding: Grass seeds.

Breeding: The Parasitic Weaver has a characteristic parasitic habit, laying eggs in the nests of other birds, namely Fantail Cisticila *Cisticola juncides*, Desert Cisticola *C.aridula*, Ayre's Cloud Cisticola *C.ayresii*, Pale-crowned Cloud Cisticola *C.brunnescens*, Croaking Cisticola *C.natalensis*, Le Vaillant's Cisticola *C.tinniens*, Tawny-flanked Prinia *Prinia subflava*, Black-chested Prinia *P.flavicans* and Tinking Cisticola *Cisticola rufilata*. One reference states that it almost certainly parasitic on quail finches and possibly on some sparrows. All the host's eggs are removed before laying. One or two eggs are laid, but there are two records of a Parasitic Weaver's egg being found with a complete clutch of the host's egg. Eggs described as pale blue or bluish white, marked with reddish brown and violet; incubation period 14 days; nestling period 18 days; young birds are fed by the parental host for about 10 days after leaving the nest and may remain in their company for some time.

Aviculture: Selected Reference CLUTCH 2; INCUBATION PERIOD 14 days; NESTLING PERIOD 18 days. Selected Reference WILDFOOD Seeds of Guinea grass *Panicum maximum*, Blue panic *P.laevifolium*, Broad-leaved panic *P.deustrum*. Selected Reference ANIMAL FOOD termites.

Kilombero Weaver *Ploceus burnieri*
Distribution: East-central Tanzania.

Lufira Masked Weaver *Ploceus ruweti*
Distribution: Southern Zaire.

Tai Malimbe *Malimbus ballmani*
Distribution: Tai, Ivory Coast. (see Howard, R & Moore, A. 1991. *A complete Checklist of the Birds of the World*).

Salvadori's Seedeater *Serinus xantholaema*
Distribution: Southern Ethiopia (Harrar, northern Bale and Sidamo Provinces). (see Clement C, Harris, A & Davis J 1993, *Finches & Sparrows – An Identification Guide*).

Breeding of birds

There is no fixed rule on how to be a successful bird-breeder. Successful breedings may be attributed to many factors, namely harmony between species, correct feeding and suitable housing, ideal nesting conditions and non-overcrowding. It has been demonstrated time and time again that a pair of birds which have shown no interest in breeding in one cage or aviary have produced excellent breeding results once removed to another aviary, or an aviary of another birdbreeder. This can also work in reverse; a pair of birds breeding well may suddenly stop producing when moved to new surroundings. It is wise to remove off-spring from an aviary just before showing signs of reaching adult plumage. This will eliminate the later problem of removing one of a breeding pair by mistake. If identification is necessary, then the use of coloured celluloid leg rings or mark by using dye under a wing will suffice, but birds with an unknown history can be surgically sexed. Species with anti-social tendencies should be limited to one pair per cage or aviary to avoid persecution of smaller birds on account of constant pecking and aerial chases. If the psychological well-being of each bird is taken in consideration then there is every chance of one becoming a successful bird breeder.

(1) *Round parrot cage.*

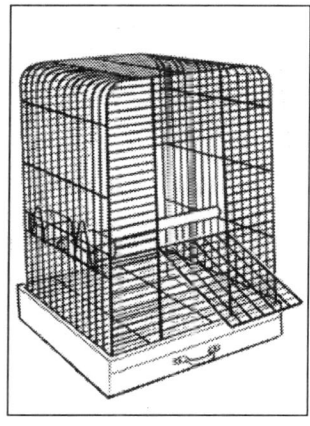

(2) *Square parrot cage.*

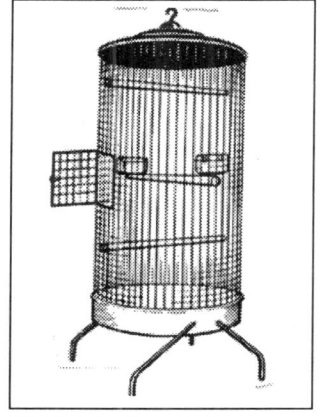

(3) *Highrise Lovebird cage.*

(1) Diameter 50cm
    Height 36cm

(2) 55cm x 55cm
    Height 85cm

(3) Diameter 45cm
    Height 91cm

Housing

In-door cages

The large parrot cage purchased from pet stores has become known as the "African Grey Parrot Cage", but is also suitable for the Cape and Jardine's Parrot. A similar cage, but square sided, is suitable for individuals of the smaller species, namely Meyer's, Brown-headed Rüppell's, Niam-Niam, Senegal, Red-bellied and Yellow-faced Parrots. Besides the reasonably priced standard designs, a wide range of expensive larger decorative cases are also available. Unfortunately difficult to obtain in Africa. One only has to browse through UK and USA publications to appreciate what is on offer to birdkeepers. Their main features include: made in a quality wrought iron, indestructible steel tubing with chrome finish (white, black, grey or beige), mounted on fancy brass-framed rubber casters, wire powder coated electrostatic finish, breeder door on side panel, bird proof button door latch, flourescent light fixture above a cage, rotating easy-access feeder cup tray holding 5 perch cups, dual front opening doors, jumbo outer and a hand sized inner door and acrylic splatter shield which protects walls and floors of the home, from seed and water while protecting birds from drafts and with many manufacturers giving up to twenty years warranty on their products. A nest box may be attached to the inside of the lovebird cage if required.

Breeding cages

A single or double breeder can be used outdoors or in birdrooms for a variety of purposes. Its many uses include:

1. Convenient standby to hold birds when no further space exists in an aviary.
2. The breeding of hybrids and mules.
3. Housing species with anti-social tendencies.
4. The isolation of young birds not able to indentify with their parents.
5. Hospitalisation.
6. Breeding of rare or delicate species.
7. Keeping birds which are to be disposed of.

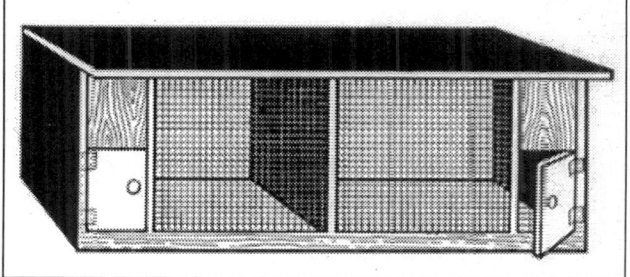

A double breeder is suitable for housing finches or waxbills.

Illustrations not drawn to scale

Each compartment should be no less than 76 x 40 x 50cm. Each door should be no wider than 15cm square, which is large enough to allow nesting boxes to be placed and removed freely. Three perches is ample, stretching from front to back. The first two, 30cm from the roof and well spaced, and the third 20cm above the floor. Cleaning can be effected by a scraper which are readily available in many sizes at your local pet or hardware store.

A single breeder for the housing of quail or lovebirds.

In the UK and USA free standing individual indoor cages that stand on casters for easy manoeuvrability can be purchased from aviary manufacturers that specialise in these types of cages. They are usually made of aluminium tubing 25 x 25mm with 14g galvanised welded mesh and with moulded nylon corners to add extra strength to the case. The measurements for parrots is about 91 x 60 x 1,8m.

Free-standing parrot cage

A set of three stackable lovebird cages each measuring about 91 x 45 x 45cm with 50mm x 12,5mm 16g welded mesh. Electricity can be installed whereby artificial light entering the cages is a good facsimile for natural light.

Stackable lovebird cages.

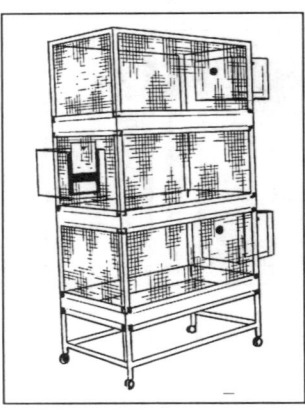

The first major break away from breeding in conventional outdoor flights came in the form of hanging cages which were made entirely of welded mesh. This new innovation was first introduced in the USA and soon spread to other parts of the world. Many variations are in existance today but the original basic design measured anything from 3,5 to 5m long and 1,2 x 1,2m. Sizes will, of course, vary considerably according to the area allocated to them. Suspension is by the use of a thick gauge wire or lightweight chains to a ceiling beam if housed indoors and to steel frames or water piping if housed outdoors. Free standing cages which are more in evidence today are supported by wattle poles, metal piping or one of the cheaper hardwoods.

The cages should be placed just far enough apart so as not to be threatened by a bird in an adjoining cage. In regions with bad weather bringing icy winds during certain times of the year, a screen in the form of a hedge may be necessary. A raised welded mesh bottom has certain advantages over free standing cages, such as not having to deal with muddy floors after heavy rains, less risk of birds being bothered with internal parasites due to eating discarded food contaminated by droppings as all debris eventually falls through the bottom of a cage. Some absorbent materials such as newspaper or wood shavings can be placed beneath the cages and then changed when necessary. Commercial birdbreeders prefer to have concrete floors which can be washed down with a hosepipe each day. The only disadvantage of these cages is that birds tend to waste more seed if food hoppers are not totally secure. New methods are being introduced from time to time with excellent results. Also during breeding, birds may become extremely anxious when one is standing in close proximity to a nestbox which may have been attached to the outside of a cage, instead of inside.

The first suspended or free standing cages were self-constructed. Today they may be purchased in standard designs or constructed to suit one's own personal needs.

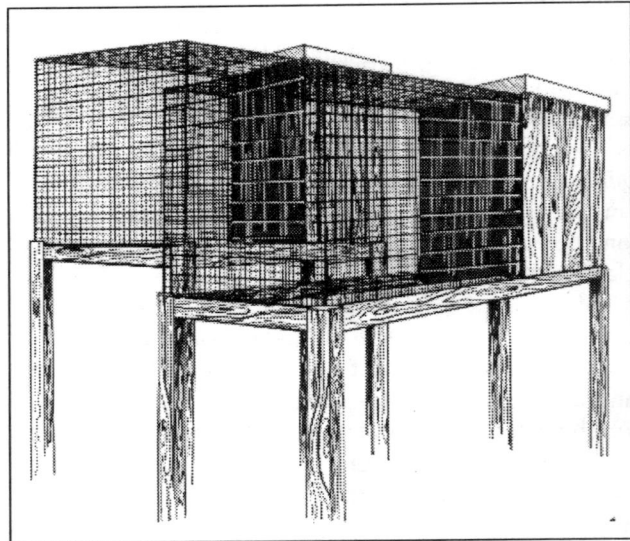

Free-standing out-door parrot cage.

Illustrations not drawn to scale

Dimensions of a manufactured design:
180m x 900mm suitable for the African Grey Parrots (nominate and *timneh*, including *Poicephalus* species.
1200mm x 600mm suitable for lovebirds.

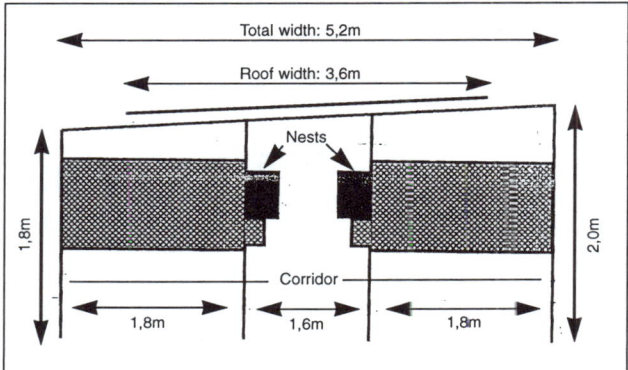

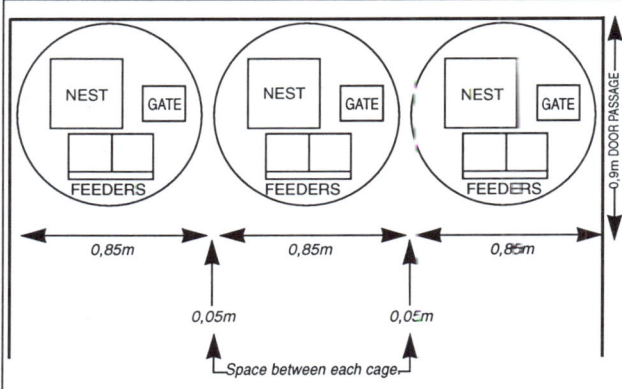

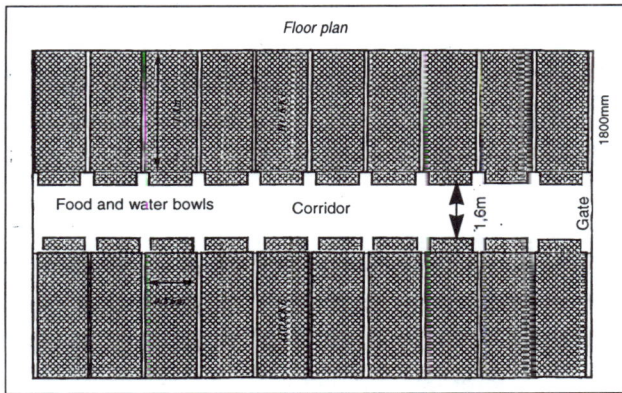

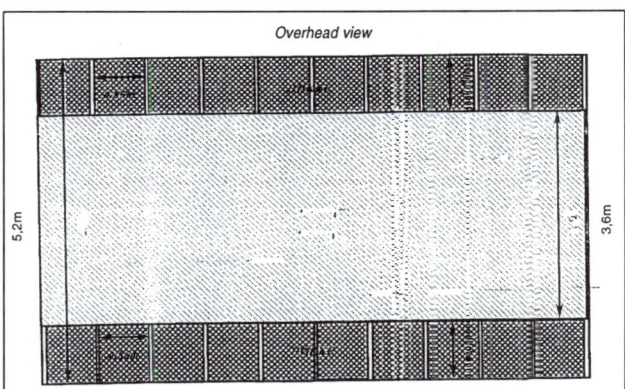

Coristo CC, PO Box 45, Hoopstad 9479, South Africa.

In more recent years research is being undertaken, especially in the USA to develop a new cage as parrot-like birds seem to prefer close proximity to each other, except in the region of nestbox positioning, then favouring complete privacy. This is referred to as the L-shaped "aviary" or suspended cage.

Aviaries
Portable aviaries

These lightweight aviaries can be purchased in most countries, but in Africa many birdkeepers construct their own. They are available in a range of sizes and most suitable for a secluded sunny spot on a verandah or sheltered spot in a garden. Unfortunately there is a drawback with larger species not having the opportunity to exercise their wings to the fullest in a restricted area of this nature.

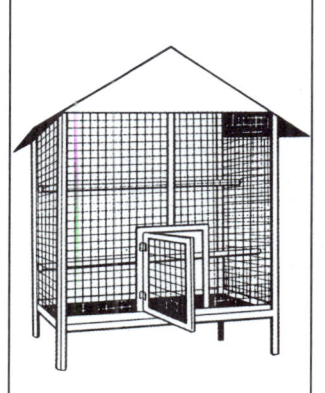

Metal construction

Length: 1,8m
Width: 0,8m
Height: 1,2m

Wooden construction

Length: 1,8m
Width: 0,8m
Height: 1,5m

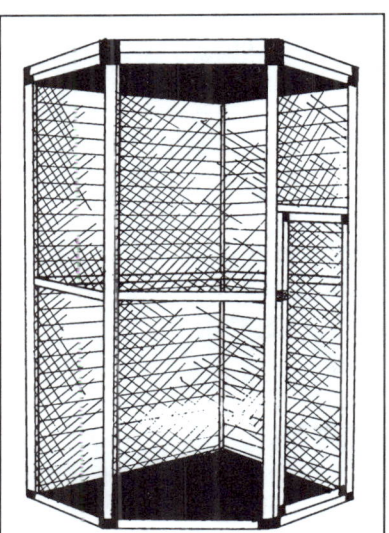

Corner flight

Height: 1,8m
Depth: (front to far corner 1,95m
Length: (Side panels 1,95m
Door height: 1,22m
Width: ,38m

Illustrations not drawn to scale

Octagonal aviaries

They are popular in large gardens and may be built to any size as the need arises. Some sort of protection against prevailing winds should be adopted in the form of a small tree, hedge or creeper to avoid ailments such as chills which occur mostly during winter.

Wooden construction

Timber 1 45cm x 45cm with tempered masonite roof, including tile felt and 2,54cm x 1,22cm 19g welded mesh attached to frame.

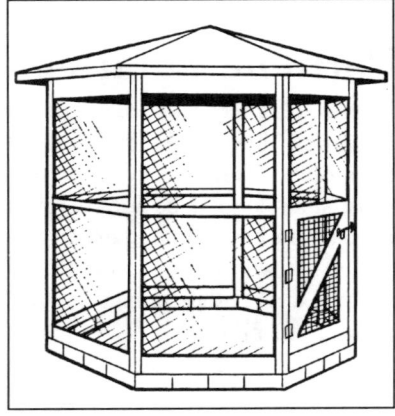

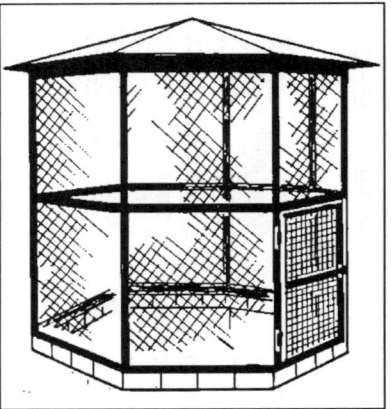

Metal construction

Height: (at apex) 2,1m

Width: 1,87m

Sleeping shelter may be attached, including an inner safety door.

Stock aviaries

A single structure may consist of an open flight or as smaller individual flights or even a combination of flights for pairs of birds.

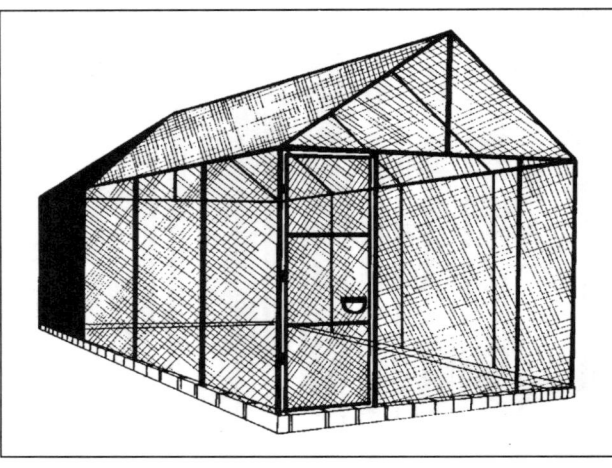

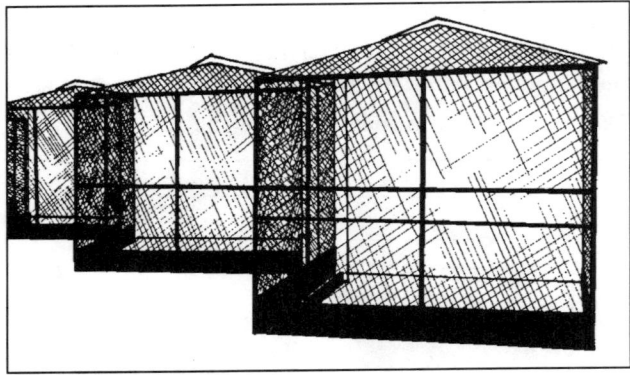

Greenhouse / Conservatory aviaries

It is useful for delicate species to be given the opportunity to prove their hardyness which will adapt well to captivity when their natural enviroment is stimulated. These warm and humid conditions can only be produced under glass or substitutes such as fibreglass and more recently the introduction of twin-wall polycarbonate sheeting which, besides being almost unbreakable, has good insulating properties as well. This latter form of covering is available in both the UK and USA. Glass has its drawbacks in that it is a fragile material with risks involved when it concerns birds. Lining the interior with wire netting will ensure effective safety against birds escaping through a broken pane.

Some difficulty will arise with atmospheric control and humidity. During cold weather condensation can become intolerable unless double glazing is installed. During hot weather the problem is now reversed, but on account of the warmer outside temperature now as well, condensation will not occur.

Backyard aviaries

In the case where space is at a minimum, a small backyard or garden aviary may be adequate for one's temporary needs. The flight and closed-in sleeping quarters is designed for countries with extreme humid summers. The illustration shows a combination of brick and wood, but many other materials can be utilised once the garage or storeroom has had its yearly spring clean.

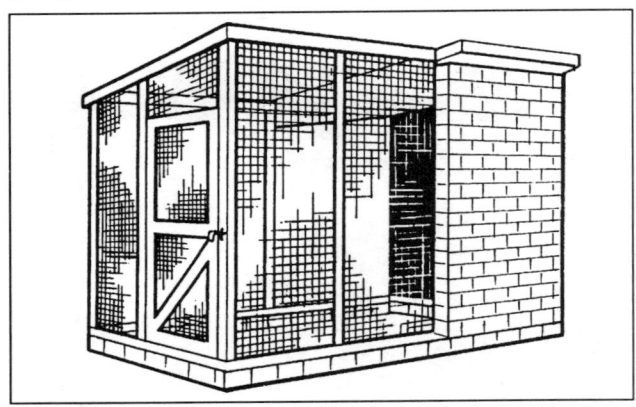

Length: 2,1m
Height: 1,8m sloping to 1,5m

Width: 0,9m
Sleeping quarters: Width: 0,9m

Illustrations not drawn to scale

Ornamental garden aviary.

Ornamental garden aviaries

A large open structure to accommodate many breeding pairs. The more roomy an aviary, provided it is not overcowded including plant life, the more useful it is likely to be. A height of no more than 3 metre is adequate in order to have some control when it is necessary to catch out birds. Width and depth will depend entirely on the numbers and sizes of species to be accommodated. Included in the structure is the sleeping quarters which runs the full width plus a 1,52 metre width roof.

Compartment aviaries

These would be primarily used to accommodate pairs of birds for the purpose of breeding. A pair of ground dwellers may also be included if the need should arise. This arrangement has worked satisfactorily as can be observed when visiting a zoo or bird garden. However, birds which suddenly show anti-social tendencies should be removed immediately before too much damage can be done.

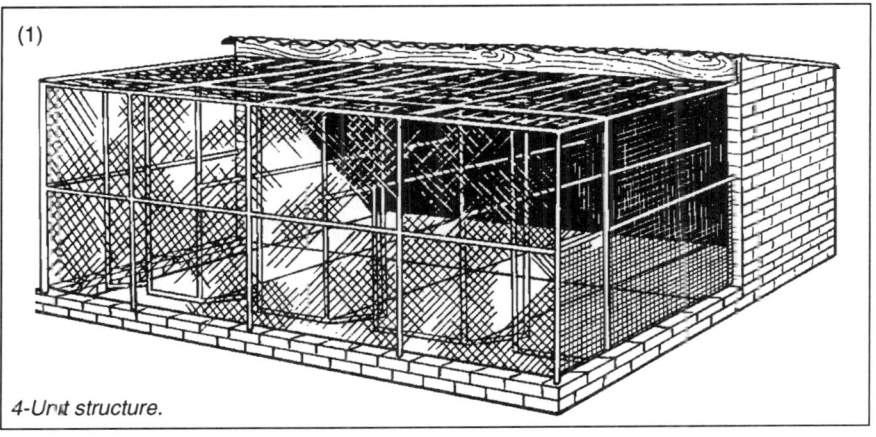

(1)

4-Unit structure.

The three, four and six-unit structures illustrated below are extremely popular in countries with tropical and sub-tropical climates. They are more open in their construction suiting the needs of birdkeepers in those regions. To give an example of suitable housing, a series of long narrow flights abutting each other has proved most successful, not only by reducing the initial cost of construction, but also economy of space as well.

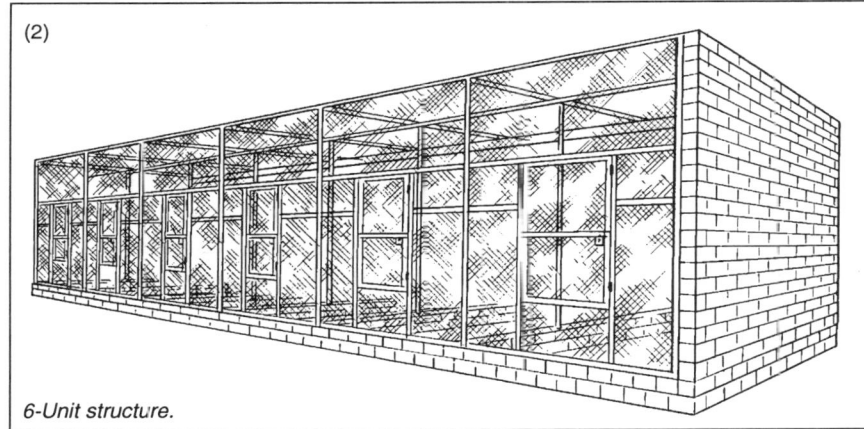

(2)

6-Unit structure.

(1) Overall measurements:
Length: 4-8m, Width: 2,7m, Height: 1,9m
Sleeping quarters: Width 0,9-1,2m
Service passage: Width: 0,7-0,9m

(2) Overall measurements:
Length: 7,3m, Width: 2,7m, Height: 1,9m
Sleeping quarters: Width: 0,9-1,2m

(3) Overall measurements:
Length: 3,7m, Width: 2,7m, Height: 1,9m
Sleeping quarters: Width: 0,9-1,2m
Service passage: Width: 0,7-0,9m

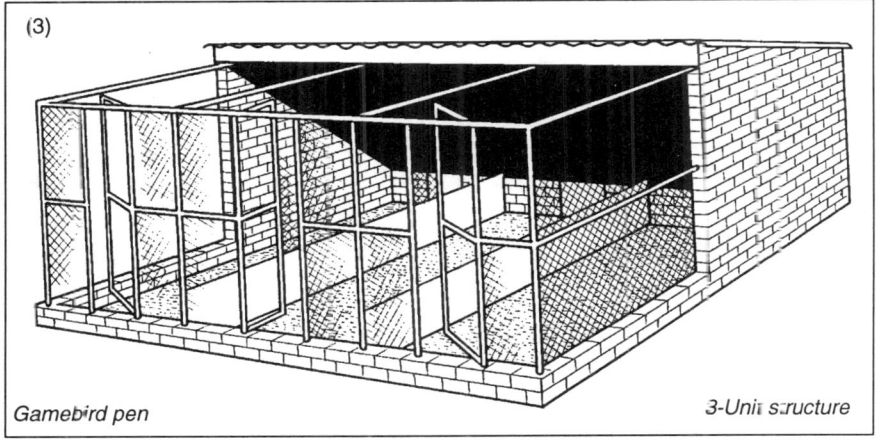

(3)

Gamebird pen

3-Unit structure

*Illustrations not drawn to scale

(1) *Overall measurements:*
Length: 3,7m, *Width*: 2,7m, *Height*: 1,9m
Sleeping quarters: *Width*: 0,9 (roof sloping to 1,2m)
Service passage: *Width*: 0,9-1,2m

The ground plan shows a door at both sides of the pens which enables entry tro each main service door.

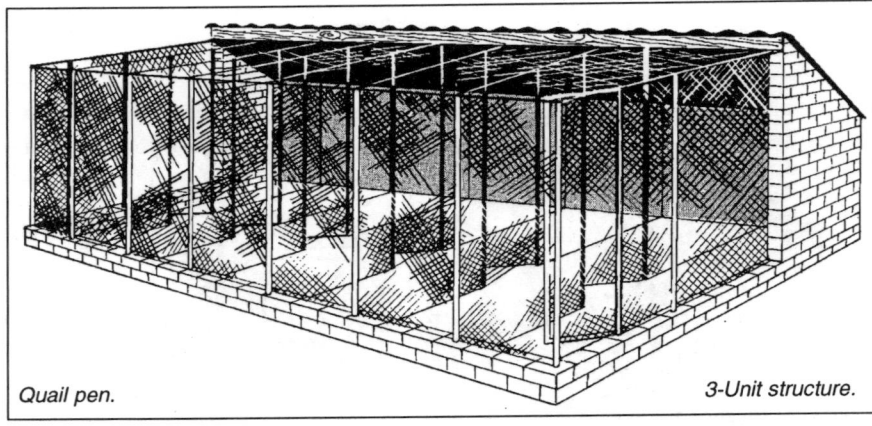

Quail pen.

3-Unit structure.

Gamebird pens

Gamebirds can be housed in open or enclosed pens, the latter preferably for costly rare species. This will ensure some control over their movements by safe-guarding them against predators and thieves. Hardboard in the form of masonite or plastic sheeting at no more than 30cm high for quail and 60cm high for larger gamebirds, should be attached to the base of the pens to prevent adults fighting each other through the wire as well as preventing young birds from escaping. Guineafowl can be allowed to wander at will, but it must be remembered that they are extremely destructive in the garden, especially if it is vegetables. As gamebirds have a habit of walking around and around the boundaries of enclosures, it would be wise to provide a dry path consisting of coarse river sand or cement which can be cleaned on a regular basis. Shade cloth or peron netting as it is known in the UK, is the best form of covering for pen tops.

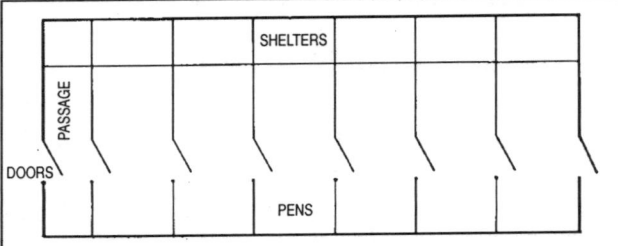

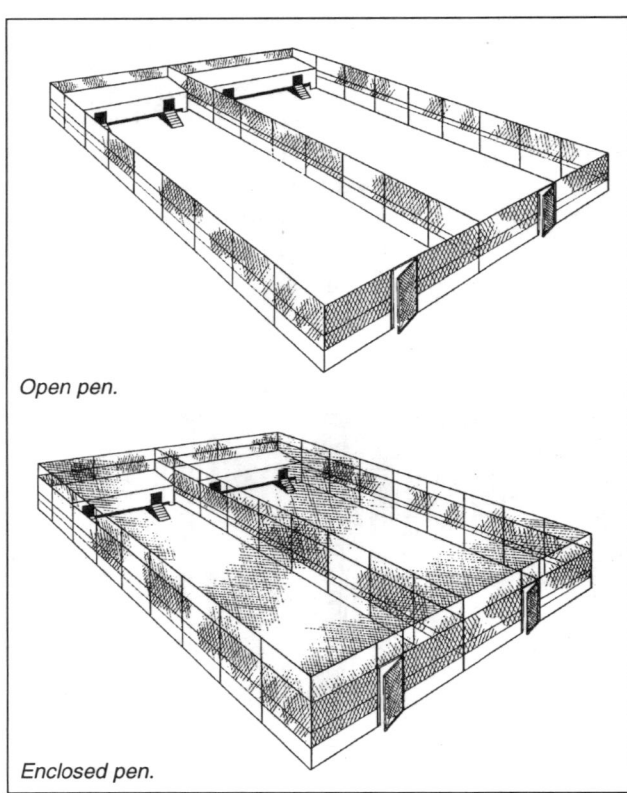

Open pen.

Enclosed pen.

Birdrooms

A birdroom is also useful in the housing of delicate species during the winter months, although it is not always necessary in many regions, which besides coastal Africa, also includes California in the USA, and some of the warmer regions of Australia. In the UK where extreme temperatures can be experienced during a winter, a birdroom may be essential to the well being of your bird collection. The object of a birdroom is to maintain a level of comfort until summer arrives, not only for the smaller species, but for parrot-like birds who are known to be susceptable to frost bite of the toes. As, when constructing the sleeping shelters, some thought must also be given to a birdroom regarding materials to be purchased and the interior layout and design. The latter with consideration for siting installation of electricity, position of seed storage bins, flight and show cages, medicine cabinet, bookshelf and most important of all, how many species or number of birds one intends to accommodate. The building materials mentioned in the construction of the exterior of the sleeping shelter will suffice for a birdroom. It will need some form or natural light through the roof which can be built of clear corrugated plastic, fibreglass sheeting or a wire-reinforced glass. A wooden floor can be made of smooth tongue-and-groove boards placed about 15cm above a concrete slab.

For the interior of a wooden framed birdroom fibreglass is placed in between the exterior and interior linings. This prevents heat entering during the summer but keeps cold out in winter. Install the electric wiring for the lighting or heating before covering the frames with hard-board panels. These panels can be made of masonite or lactonite as it is known in the UK. The latter is covered in a thin plastic coating. The roof interior can be made

*Illustrations not drawn to scale

of Rhino board or a similar fibre board, both being a thick form of compressed cardboard, will also prevent heat from escaping. The windows must be protected by removable wire netting panels for easy access to wash the panes. A protective double door to be left open if the weather should improve. Ensure that there is ample window ventilation at all times. Numerous ready made designs can be purchased if one resides in the UK or the USA. For "natural" lighting mostly recommended are flourescent strips which can be attached to a dimmer system allowing birds to settle on perches or in nest boxes before settling down for the night.

Many heat sources are available in the form of oil. gas, electric, ventilator and similar methods, but are dangerous for reasons of fire-risk and emit poisonous fumes. Most aviculturists recommend only electric tubular heaters which fit into a standard light socket. Indoor humidity can be controlled with a humidifier set at 60-70% with a temperature of 15-20 °C or a bowl of water can be left to evaporate in some part of the birdroom where the birds will not drink or knock it over.

Aviary Construction

Before proceeding with the construction one must first submit a plan of the intended aviary or birdroom,as most countries have bylaws which govern the building of such structures. This also applies to commercially built aviaries and the do-it-yourself designs which are as varied as the species one wishes to keep. Designing an aviary will depend on the site area available and the purpose for which the accomodation is required. When purchasing and aviary it is advisable to see the assembled model beforehand. The illustrations and specifications in catalogues never convey the full impact of space and size. Both the UK and USA have over two hundred designs to choose from. As with all structures and buildings, bad design features are costly and inconvenient to rectify, so it is worth considering before deciding to purchase. The choice of the site is most important to the well being of your birds as the elements can take their toll if an aviary or bank of aviaries is placed in an undesirable position. Problems which will be encountered at one time or another are cold winds, driving rain, frost, fog, drizzle or blistering heat. The floor of the night shelter can be of natural earth or concrete. In countries with hot climates, earth floors are practical. but in countries with prolonged wet conditions each year, these are impractical. To prevent any sort of contamination one should turn the soil over once or twice a year then sprinkle the surface with a coating of lime, or renew the surface layer once a year. A concrete floor, cement tiles or square paving stones can be left bare but cleaned frequently by using a scraper. An earth floor can be covered with both coarse river sand and sawdust. Before laying a concrete floor one must ensure that it slopes towards the opening, allowing water to run off. Excavate all round to a depth of 30cm for the foundations. A wall of bricks, breeze blocks or reinforced concrete is raised to a height of 20cm to form the

foundation of which the flight frames will eventually sit. Some consideration should be given to climatic conditions and insect pests, notably the termite which may occur in your region before any materials are purchased. By placing plastic damp-proofing sheet strips along the top of the walls it will prevent premature rotting if wood is to be used as a frame. The use of cresote-soaked railway sleepers which are easy to obtain since wood has been replaced with concrete in some countries, can also be used in place of other materials. Softwoods, notably pine is used mostly on account that it is relatively cheap compared to meranti or similar hardwoods which look attractive when they have been varnished. Only a hardwood will suffice for parrot-like birds. A wood thickness of 3,7cm is adequate for the majority of species, but the larger parrots will require a framework of 5cm square which should when assembled be glued and then securely screwed together. It is advisable to avoid the use of nails when working with hardwoods. If any additional weight is included in the roof construction of the flight, a larger wood thickness will have to be considered to avoid sagging. Complete panels can be purchased and rapidly assembled in less than an hour. They were recently introduced in Europe to the bird equipment market with most outlets stocking the standard size 1,8 x 0,9m and having a choice of fitted or non-fitted doors and light weight 4 x 2,5cm wooden frames. On completion of the frame treat the wood with a preservative, clear if it is to be painted with a final coat of gloss enamel paint, with black being favoured by birdkeepers in most countries. In termite regions, a coat of cresote may be applied to softwoods every six months. Other materials regularly used in aviary frame construction are round steel, angle iron, aluminium poles and galvanised water piping which can be purchased new or from a scrap metal dealer.

For the covering a choice exists between wire netting or welded mesh. The netting will of course give greater flexibility and is appreciately cheaper to purchase, but has some drawbacks in that it will in time require a coat of non-lead based paint or bitumen with additional coats from time to time to protect it from areas where rust may appear. Also branches have been known to break off during a storm or from rotting which has produced gaping holes in the roof of a flight. Unfortunately many birds have been lost in this way before the introduction of the stronger welded mesh. In the UK they are known under the following trade names; Classic wire, Monaweld, Primeweld and Twilweld. Suitable sizes and gauges are, namely 13 x 13mm 19g for waxbills and the smaller finches, 13 x 25mm 19g for the larger finches, doves, pigeons and small gamebirds and 50 x 50mm 12g for the larger gamebirds. Only welded mesh will be suitable for parrot-like birds, namely lovebirds 12,5 x 12,5mm 16g and African parrots 25 x 25mm 14g. The wire covering should be placed on the inside of a wood framework with staples being the best form of fasteners and all rough mesh edges being later covered with wood battening. Painting by means of an old roller instead of a brush will reduce this tedious task by half, as well as being less messy and a paint saving. Shade cloth, nylon or peron netting as it is known in the UK, is used mostly for the protection of fruit against insect pests and birds, has become popular in recent years as an aviary covering. Its advantages are that it is easy to handle, no maintenance, prevents at some degree excessive sunlight entering a flight and as an additional inner roof to prevent accidental escapes. They can be fitted with spring doors to ensure speedy effective closure and always made to open outwards, never inwards. In countries with low winter temperatures some precautions can be taken by partially covering over the perches in the flight with a translucent material which can be removed in the summer months. It is not recommended to cover the whole area as it will deny the birds the opportunity to bathe in the rain. The addition of overhead sprinklers can be installed to satisfy the needs of many species. During the periods of extremely prolonged poor weather a framework supported with ultraviolet-resistant plastic sheeting can also be temporarily attached to sides of a flight.

Sleeping shelters in warmer countries require the interior to remain as cool as possible, therefore they are usually constructed with fibro-cement, brick or breeze block. Substitutes being used to a lesser degree is 1cm thick tempered masonite, flat asbestos sheeting and occasionally sheet tin. In cool countries shelter designs and materials used differ in that they may also include tongued-and-grooved wood, marine plywood, treated hardboards and PVA interlocking plastic panels. All material joints must be close-fitted to avoid draughts. Besides asbestos, roofs can be made of a heavy duty exterior plywood with all joints being filled with tar, then covered with a black roof sheeting or tile felt as it is known in some countries. In the UK shingles, slate, sheet metal and ruberoid tiles are also popular. In the USA and Australia fibreglass sheeting is also utilized as a roofing material. The roof should overhang at least 30cm to prevent rain from entering the entrance of the sleeping shelter. Gutters may be installed at the back and sides to prevent eventual damage to foundations.

Understanding welded mesh

I have tried to give an insight into the properties of welded mesh that the layman will readily understand. Based upon the information presented it should be easier to make a more informed buying decision that could easily lead to considerable short and longer term savings in aviary and cage construction.

Tensile strength

The wire used in welded meshes suitable for the average birdbreeder would have a typical tensile strength of between 370 and 450 Newton/mm² and would be made from a steel containing around 3 or 4% carbon. When the wire is welded to create the mesh the strength of the weld should never be less than 50% of the tensile strength of the wire used. This is critically important if strands of wire are not to be "pulled" away by caged birds thereby creating escape or pest invasion points.

One advantage of using wire with lower tensile strengths is that the finished mesh is much easier to work with. Probably the most important variable to look for when trying to assess the strength of a welded mesh is the so called "Set Down Value".

Set Down Values

The term "set down" refers to how well the welding of the cross and longitudinal wires is carried out. In simple terms if the welding is done well then the top wire will be solidly embedded into the lower wire. If the welding is done badly then the top wire will only kiss the bottom wire or will be lightly set down. The purchaser of welded mesh can accurately determine set down values for himself if he wants to. If set down is good then the distance across a weld point will be measurably less than the sum of the diameters of two individual wires. With the help of a Vernier Micrometer applying the following formula will allow for set down value to be calculated.

$$\frac{2\text{ wires(mm)} - \text{welded wires(mm)}}{2\text{ wires(mm)}}$$

Any value less than 0,1 or 10% should be regarded as suspicious for the simple reason that weld strength is directly a function of set down value. On a quality welded mesh the set down can be observed to be food just using the naked eye. Set down should be typically not less than 13% and could even be as high as 20% for some products.

Zinc Coating

The amount, quality and application technique (eg. whether hot dip galvanised or not) of zinc galvanising will determine the life of welded mesh used in aviaries. Research work done in the UK concluded that the loss of zinc from welded mesh surfaces in rural or sparsely populated region would be around 10gms per square metre per year. In a heavily industrialised area with a heavy presence of sulphur and chlorine in the atmosphere (parts of the PWV and other coal-burning areas such as Sasolburg etc would probably fall into this classification) a zinc loss of around 50gms per sq metre per year would take place. Since a class 'C' galvanised wire according to SABS 675-1977 need only have 45gms per sq metre of zinc coating on a wire of diameter 1,6mm it can be concluded that an untreated class 'C' welded mesh in a coastal or industrialised areal will in general not last very long. Class 'A' wire is available in South Africa and would have to have a coating level of 230gms per sq metre to meet the SABS requirement. Class 'A' is normally made available as a more expensive alternative for the thicker welded meshes. It is not the standard for the lighter meshes but should be obtainable. Welded mesh is expensive and the purchaser should clarify for himself the coating level of zinc he is getting for his money. Coastal users should probably not use anything less the class 'A'. The British Standard (BS443) requires that 1,6mm welded mesh have a coating of not less than 230gms per sq metre whereas in practice British welded mesh typically has 50% more zinc than the required standard resulting from the hot dip galvanising process used.

Post galvanising

Using the right tensile strength wire getting a good set down and having sufficient zinc coating on the welded mesh will give a strong and excellent product for making aviaries if corrosion can be prevented from taking place at the many welded points. The way to prevent corrosion taking place at the welded points is to ensure that these points are very well protected from the enviromental factors such as salt, air-borne chemicals and a general combination of rust enhancing circumstances such as high temperature and moisture. The ideal way is to ensure the zinc coating is applied after welding (Post Galvanising) because in this way there is no mettalurgical imperfection at the weld point that will allow ingress of rust causing agents at this vulnerable point. If welded mesh is made from pre-galvanised wire then a black burn will be seen at each intersection. The burn is the result of zinc literally being burned away when the welding heads come down and join wires together. The very act of welding introduces a metallurgical change at the weld point which is not conducive to corrosion protection. If the weld is also not done well there is risk of oxide inclusion across the fusion boundary making the weld strength much lower than it should be. It is simple to check for post galvanising: look for the weld point being completely surrounded by zinc coating and the absence of black burn marks.

Many breeders paint their aviaries to protect the mesh from premature corrosion. This process is of course an expensive and time consumming exercise and is made totally unnecessary by using post-galvanised welded mesh.

Very light meshes

The ability to use thin high quality wire in a continuous mesh welding process (very good set downs without burning through the wire) along with a capability of hot dip galvanising the finished mesh product has made it possible to build extremely strong and rigid aviaries from 1,0mm wire mesh. These new meshes allow smaller birds to be safely kept in much lighter aviaries at a considerable cost saving (30% and more). It is when the very high quality of these thin-wire meshes is seen that it is realised that good mesh quality allows for a total re-examination of what mesh should be used for which birds. The question each bird breeder should ask himself is whether he would be able to use more economically sized meshes if weld quality and galvanising quality always came up to his expectations.

Nest boxes

While individuals of some species may wish to construct their own nests in the plant life growing in the aviary, others may wish to utilise artificial nesting receptables, especially if the plants provided are not in accordance with conditions in their natural habitat. This would apply particularly to birds which are new to an aviary environment. Birds which have bred in aviaries may change progressively from natural to artificial conditions. A suitable method to encourage aviary birds to breed is to supply as many different designs of nests as possible and to place them at different heights in the sleeping quarters as well as in an open flight in both concealed

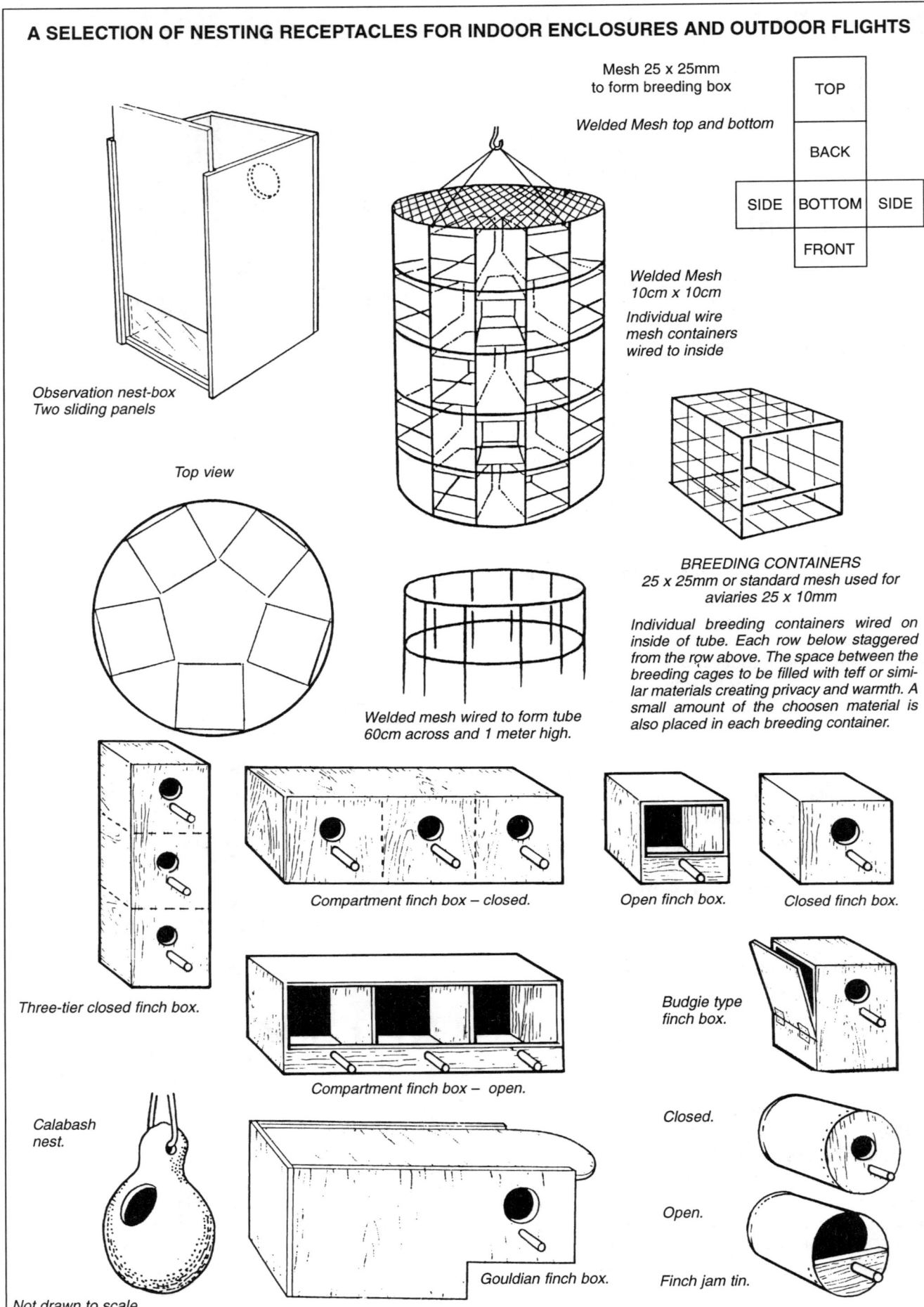

A SELECTION OF NESTING RECEPTACLES FOR INDOOR ENCLOSURES AND OUTDOOR FLIGHTS

Mesh 25 x 25mm
to form breeding box

Welded Mesh top and bottom

	TOP	
	BACK	
SIDE	BOTTOM	SIDE
	FRONT	

Welded Mesh
10cm x 10cm

Individual wire
mesh containers
wired to inside

Observation nest-box
Two sliding panels

Top view

BREEDING CONTAINERS
25 x 25mm or standard mesh used for
aviaries 25 x 10mm

Individual breeding containers wired on inside of tube. Each row below staggered from the row above. The space between the breeding cages to be filled with teff or similar materials creating privacy and warmth. A small amount of the chosen material is also placed in each breeding container.

Welded mesh wired to form tube
60cm across and 1 meter high.

Compartment finch box – closed.

Open finch box.

Closed finch box.

Three-tier closed finch box.

Compartment finch box – open.

Budgie type
finch box.

Calabash
nest.

Closed.

Open.

Gouldian finch box.

Finch jam tin.

Not drawn to scale.

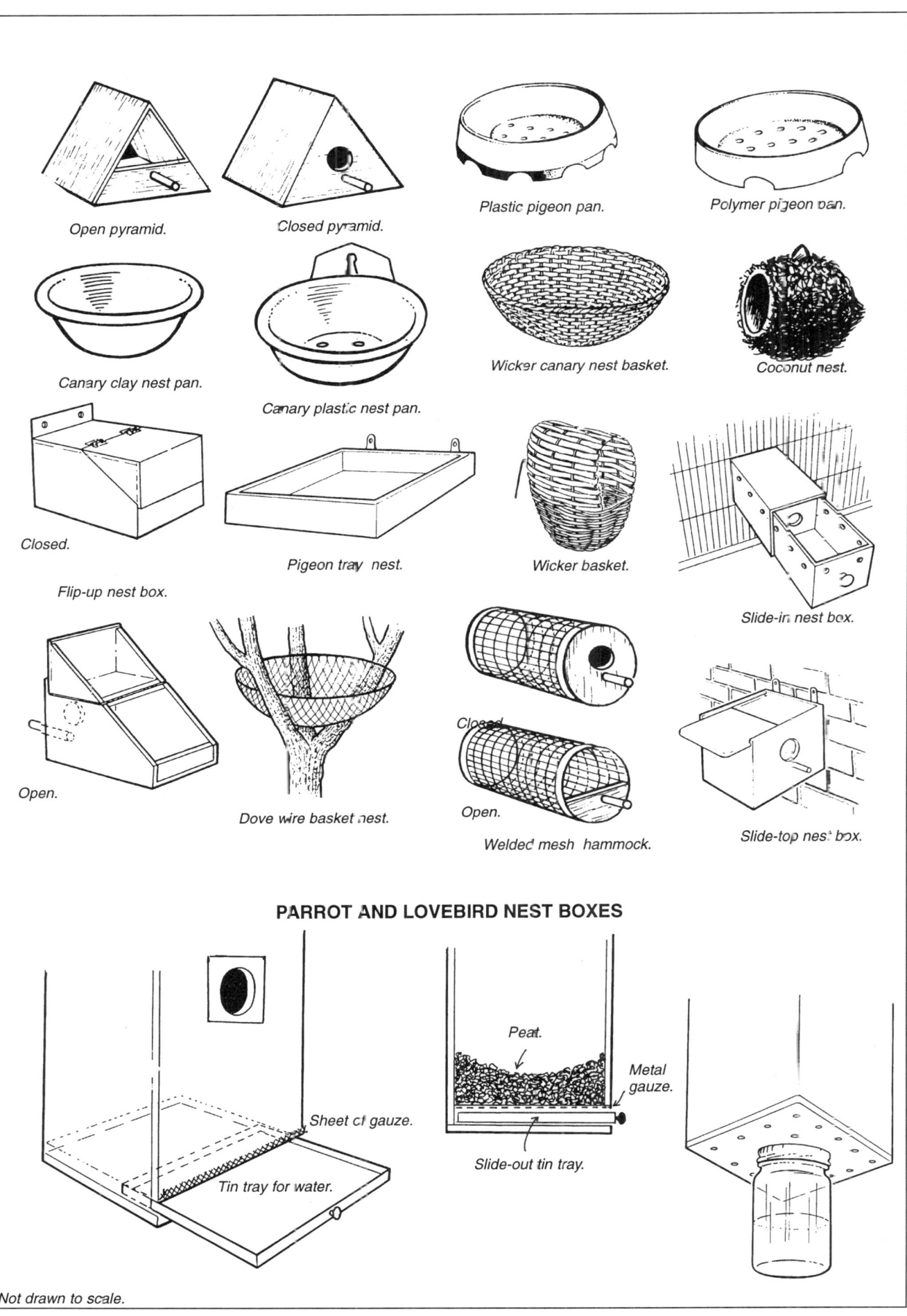

Open pyramid.

Closed pyramid.

Plastic pigeon pan.

Polymer pigeon pan.

Canary clay nest pan.

Canary plastic nest pan.

Wicker canary nest basket.

Coconut nest.

Closed.

Flip-up nest box.

Pigeon tray nest.

Wicker basket.

Slide-in nest box.

Open.

Dove wire basket nest.

Closed.

Open.

Welded mesh hammock.

Slide-top nest box.

PARROT AND LOVEBIRD NEST BOXES

Sheet of gauze.

Tin tray for water.

Peat.

Metal gauze.

Slide-out tin tray.

Not drawn to scale.

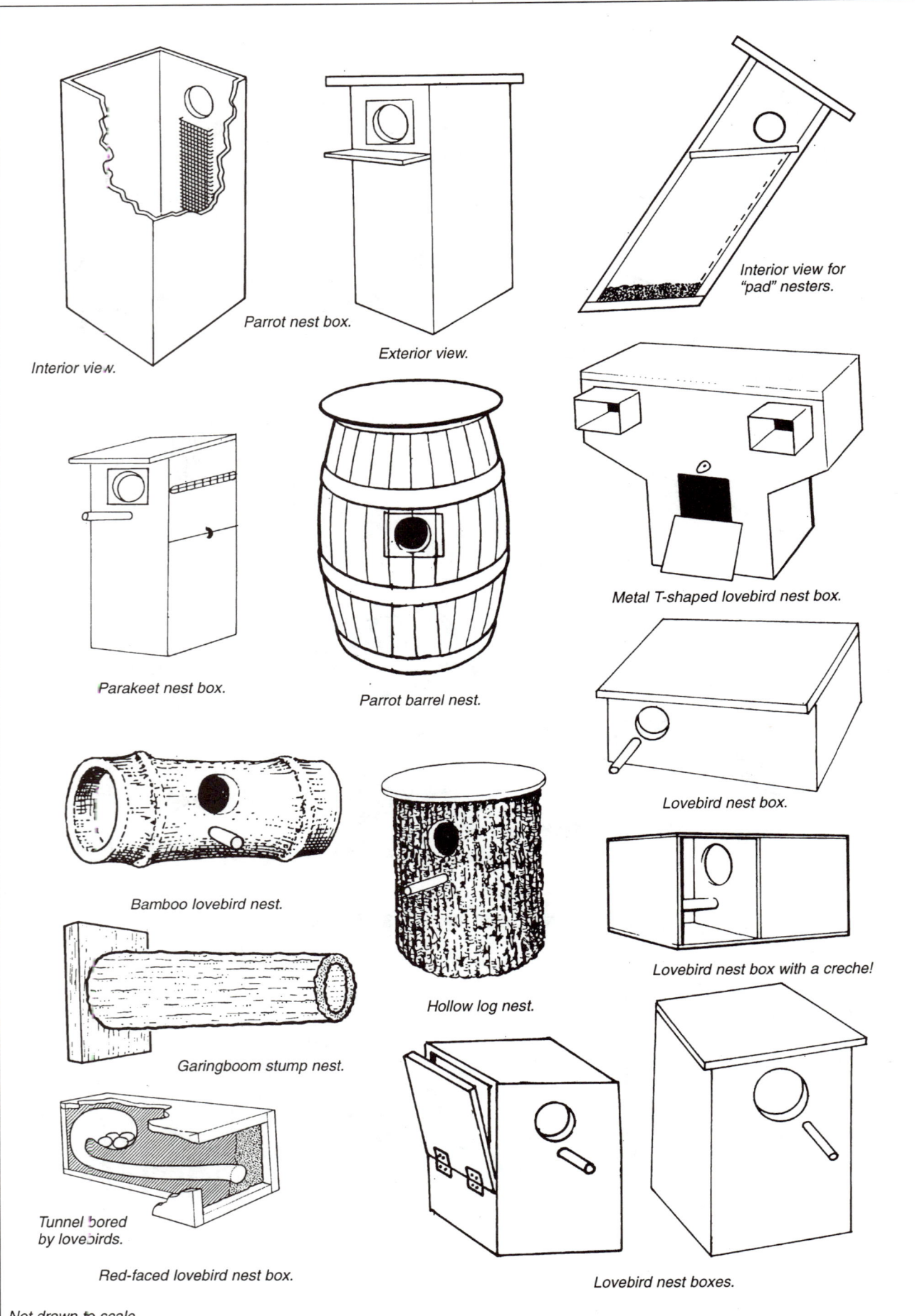

Interior view.

Parrot nest box.

Exterior view.

Interior view for "pad" nesters.

Parakeet nest box.

Parrot barrel nest.

Metal T-shaped lovebird nest box.

Lovebird nest box.

Bamboo lovebird nest.

Hollow log nest.

Lovebird nest box with a creche!

Garingboom stump nest.

Tunnel bored by lovebirds.

Red-faced lovebird nest box.

Lovebird nest boxes.

Not drawn to scale.

and exposed positions. Pet stores unfortunately have a limited selection from which to choose, namely the wicker basket, canary pan, small half-open finch, Budgerigar and Cockatiel boxes, pigeon and poultry trays, natural hollow logs, wire dove baskets and the specially designed Australian Gouldian Finch box which contains a nesting chamber below and to the side of the entrance. Metal nest-boxes, T and L-shaped, including square boxes are being advertised in the USA, and a lovebird box with a creche in the UK Successful breedings have occurred with the use of these items only, and would suffice if a wider range cannot be obtained or constructed. A handyman may wish to use bamboo, which can be cut up into segments, then break through the centre dividing membrane to form the entrance hole. In addition the trunk of a Centuary plant (Garingboom) *Agave americana* is cut up into 500mm lengths and left to dry in the sun. Once the green thread-like fibre has turned brown remove it with the use of a chisel and mallet. A piece of hardboard can be nailed to one end which are then hung up in the flight or sleeping quarters. Unfortunately it is a lengthy process but some species, especially the smaller lovebirds, have produced better results with this more natural type nest. When using a hollow log or small barrel, remember to cover the top with a piece of flat waterproof material which is to extend a few centimetres causing an overhang which will prevent water entering the entrance hole. For the finch family a nest hammock of welded mesh is packed with teff and suspended from the aviary roof. The interior consists of a vast number of small containers which are utilized as nest sites.

The placing of lovebird nest boxes at an angle of 30-45 degrees and inside the boxes below the inlet hole, is fixed a ladder or climbing perch, while on the outside below the hole, a perch or platform allows the non-incubating bird to settle, is a personal preference in its construction and hanging in position.

The flip-lid and slide-in type nest boxes can be fastened temporarily to the outside of a single or double breeder and conveniently stored away in the off-season.

Nesting materials

The wider the variety of nesting materials one supplies the birds the greater the chance of successful breedings. Grasses of which there are numerous varieties play a large part in the nest construction of many species. Grasses can be given with stems intact or alternatively the inflorescsces only in the ripe or (half-ripe) milky stage may be provided. Dried teff, lucerne, wheat straws, bits of heather, pine needles and tobacco stalks can be purchased, bound or baled, and then stored in a dry corner of an aviary or pen, from which the birds can strip the materials when required. This will ensure a continuos supply of building materials to suit the needs of all species for many seasons to come. It is not advisable to leave a bale on the floor as it often attracts mice after it has been standing for some time. Raise it up on bricks or secure it to a wall with wire which will then give one a clear view beneath the bale. Dried Flamboyant

Delonia regia midribs, a tree much favoured to add colour to the pavements of many African city streets is popular with doves and pigeons, especially feral pigeons. Dried greenfood, hamster bedding, coconut shell fibres, millet spray stems as well as hemp teasings, unpainted raffia, Congo jute, Cantana sisal (plumber's yam), carpet underfelt, pampus grass plumes and finely cut lawn grass have all been utilized as nesting materials. Many birdkeepers follow the old custom of providing some form of nesting material as a base, then allowing the birds to complete their own nests, more so with doves and pigeons. In Africa dried Curry bush *Hyperocum revolution*, Australia in Needlebush *Hakea latrostris* and UK in Heather *Calluna vulgaris* for "starter" nests to be formed. Nesting material play a major role in the breeding or parrot-like birds as it maintains humidity throughout the incubation period. Essential for successful breeding and helps to eradicate the problem known as dead-in-the-shell being observed in captive birds. In the natural state rain and mist overcome these problems. With parrots, eggs can be sprayed twice a day until nearing the date of hatching. Lovebirds require a very high humidity for hatching of their eggs by making use of palm fronds and similar plant materials in the wild. Pieces of bark and twigs of non-poisonous trees, namely willow, oak, elm, beech, hazel, elderberry and pear are popular. In Australia *Eucalyptus* bark, including that known as Jarrah (*marginata*) for wood shavings, Johnson Grass *Sorghum halepense*, Mitchell Grass *Astrelba pectinata* and bamboos are used. In Africa the leaves of Strelizia, and strangely enough, in Los Angeles, are cut up into small pieces on account of being found most suitable in place of the two previously used plants, namely the Elephant's ear *Alocasia cuprea*, a native of the West Indies and banana *Musa* spp. which were found to "powder up" in a nest box. As a substitute peat moss and strips of thick paper, obviously not newspaper as ink is poisonous, can be used. Peat moss can be soaked for a few days, then squeezed out before using. To ensure that the proper humidity is being maintained two specially designed lovebird nest boxes can be constructed or adjustments made to existing nest boxes.

In the first nest box drill small holes in the bottom as well as in the metal lid of the jar. With the use of short wide headed nails or screws attach the jar lid to the bottom of the nest box, after which the jar is filled with water and screwed into the lid. The second nest box must contain a false bottom in which a shallow tray of water can be slid in and out. A piece of fine welded mesh is to be secured above the tray on which peat moss is to be laid. Water is then added every two weeks if required. Nesting requirements for the Red-faced Lovebird would require a solid block of cork in which to excavate a tunnel that would end in a small oval chamber.

Nest linings

Try to supply the birds with as much natural materials as possible before resorting to substitutes. The inflorescences of various grass types, in particular Natal Redtop *Panicum natalensis*, are mostly favoured. If you are fortunate to live in the country, then poultry and guineafowl feathers are popular as well as the hair of domestic animals. As a substitute, short pieces of string or hessian can be cut up into pieces – no longer than 5cm – as longer pieces have caused the death of many birds by becoming entangled around their legs trapping them in the nest box or branch. Avoid cotton wool due to birds continually add extra to the nest which eventually cover the eggs or suffocate the nestlings. Untreated pine shavings for use with lovebird nest boxes has proven successful. Gamebirds collect any available material which might be in the vicinity of their nests, or they may lay on the bare ground with only their feathers as nesting material.

Nest Heating

Introduction

Birdbreeders residing in cooler regions are prevented in winter to a certain extent by the spurious cold nights, in early spring from successfully breeding certain species. Losses may be incurred in Ring-necked Parakeets and other species that breed early in the season. This problem probably arises from the fact that at the stage prior to chicks having sufficient feathers to insulate themselves from heat loss, the female becomes unable to keep them warm enough or alternatively they die of cold when she leaves the nestbox to feed.

Some birdbreeders believe that the problem can be largely overcome by installing an electric light bulb beneath the nestbox to supply heat to the chicks. This method has apparently been used successfully by a number of birdkeepers. In inexperienced hands however, it has the potential of causing heavy loss in chicks. Several incidents are known to have occurred where a nestbox including the chicks have been incinerated due to the replacing of a fused light bulb with one of a higher wattage.

Mishaps like this have been experienced in past breeding seasons on account that it is difficult to obtain information on this subject, I have been motivated to investigate the problem more closely.

The following methods were considered:

1. Attaching a heat source on the inner aspect of the floor of the nestbox.

2. Attaching a heat source in the corner on the inner aspect of one side of the nestbox.

3. Attaching heating units to the outside of the nestbox.

For several reasons which we will not discuss further we decided to use the third method. The other methods may also be effective and we do not claim that this is necessarily the best method.

However, it was found to be effective, easy to install, reasonably inexpensive and the materials for making the heater are readily available.

The anatomy of the problem

When evaluating an ordinary nestbox in terms of heating and heat loss, a number of problem areas can be identified. Each of these presents a challenge in its own unique way when a nestbox is to be heated. (*Figure on page 195 illustrates the problems involved.*)

Heat applied to the floor of the nestbox must penetrate two insulating layers, the wooden floor as well as the nesting material before reaching the chicks. The problem is further complicated by the uneven thickness of the nesting material. It is possible that the chicks may be lying directly on the bare floor or on nesting material of variable thickness. Furthermore, night temperatures vary, therefore a heat supply that is sufficient for cold nights could be excessive on slightly warmer nights. A further problem is the difficulty in obtaining information concerning the temperature at which young birds may suffer from hypothermia and the temperature necessary to ensure survival.

All nest heating systems must therefore guard against low temperatures that will result in hypothermia, as well as high temperatures that can cause death due to overheating or dehydration. This conflicting problem can be successfully resolved by the use of a thermostat to regulate the heat energy supplied to the nestbox.

The heating element used was thermostatically controlled so that we could set the temperature anywhere between 20°C and 40°C.

Temperature measurements were done by an electronic thermometer with a flexible probe which allowed us to measure the temperature in the nest at any desired location. We chose to measure the temperature at approximately 1cm beneath the surface of the nesting material.

Experiment –

For the purpose of this experiment we prepared a parakeet nestbox as follows (*see page 195*):

1. The floor of the nestbox was covered by 25mm nesting material consisting of river sand, compost and wood shavings.

2. The floor consisted of a 20mm thick compressed wood, commonly known as chipboard.

3. A hole was drilled in the side of the nestbox to a depth that would allow the sensor to be positioned at the centre of the nest box floor.

4. The floor heater had a maximum power capacity of 14 watts and was regulated to keep the bottom of the nestbox at a constant temperature of +/- 30°C.

5. The side panel heater also had a capacity of 14 watts but was uncontrolled and could only be switched on or off manually.

6. A sensor from an electronic thermometer was installed just below the surface of the nesting material and the thermometer connected to a recorder to monitor and record the temperature of the nestbox continuously.

7. A further thermometer monitored the temperature enviroment outside the nestbox.

8. The nestbox was placed outdoors whilst the recorder and thermostat were kept indoors.

The *temperature graph* below demonstrates the nest temperature variation over a period of 24 hours as well as the influence of the side panel heater on the nest temperature.

Observations:

1. With an outside ambient temperature of 0°C and a floor temperature of 30°C and without heating the side panel, the nesting material reached a temperature of 13°C.

2. With an outdoor temperature of -2°C heating the side panel resulted in the nesting material reaching a temperature of 16°C (floor still 30°C). The side panel therefore contibutes 5°C to the nest temperature when used in conjunction with the floor heater.

3. The maximum temperature recorded in the nestbox during the day (ambient temperature 16°C) was 25°C.

4. Heating of the floor only on a very cold night may be inadequate.

Observations from other experiments, the results of which are not shown in the graph, are as follows:

1. With floor heating set at 30°C and with a night temperature of -6°C the nesting material only registered 10°C. Possibly this temperature is too low to ensure survival.

2. At an outdoor temperature of -6°C, with both heaters on, the nesting material reaches 15°C.

3. The surface of the side panel heater reaches a maximum temperature of 42°C. This temperature should not endanger the chicks' lives even if they move close to the side panel. There is probably room for further improvement in the design of the side panel to slightly decrease the surface temperature.

4. If the floor heater is uncontrolled (14 watts), the floor termperature may reach up to 45°C - 50°C. This is probably too high and can be detrimental to the young birds, causing dehydration. It is probably also too high for the parents as well, which may result in them abandoning the nestbox.

Conclusions:

From the experiments described above the following can be concluded —

1. Even at a very low ambient night temperature the nestbox interior can still be kept at an acceptable temperature by supplying the correct amount of energy.

2. Floor temperature control is important.

3. Side panel heating is probably only necessary when night temperatures fall below 0°C and should be switched off during the daytime. It is advisable to connect the side panel heater to a switching thermostat that will automatically control the nestbox temperature should the outside (ambient) temperature fall below 5°C.

4. Even if the side panel heater remains on during the day, the nestbox interior should not reach unacceptably high temperatures.

Recently 14 nestboxes were fitted with heating devices as described above and placed in a number of parakeet aviaries. The nestboxes comprised a variety of sizes and sisal stumps were also used. A test run proved that the thermostat used managed the load quite comfortably. This thermostat could probably manage up to thirty nestboxes simultaneously. A small alteration to the design of the thermostat would allow for the control of a greater number of nestboxes.

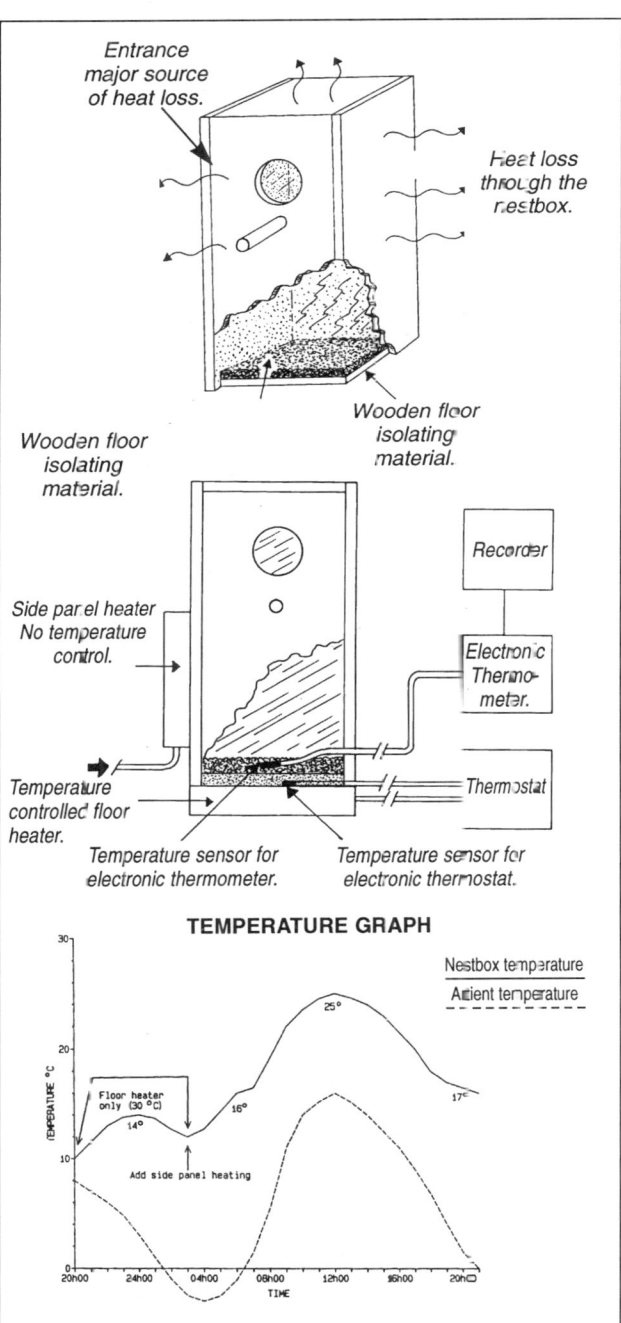

TEMPERATURE GRAPH

196

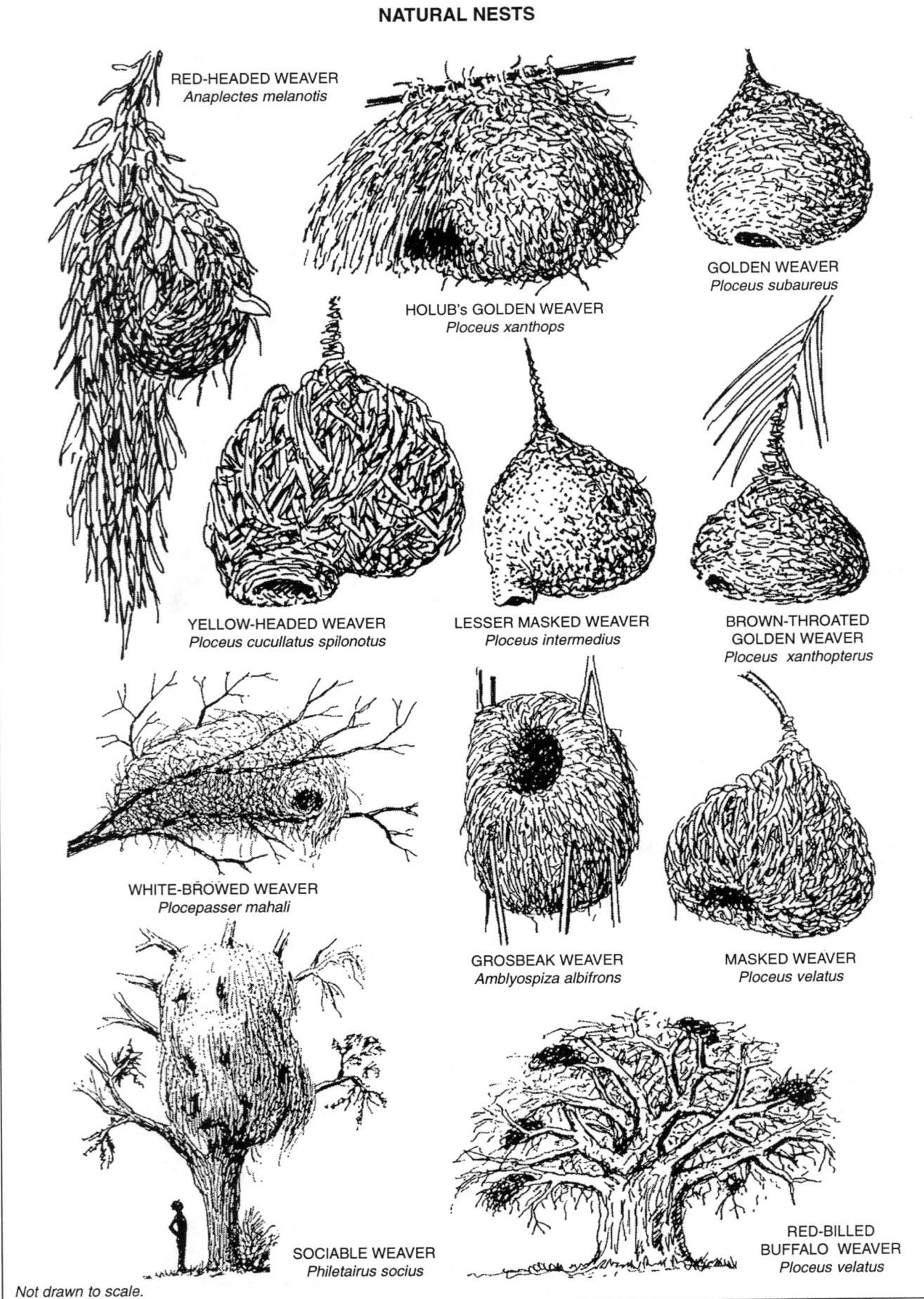

NATURAL NESTS

RED-HEADED WEAVER
Anaplectes melanotis

HOLUB's GOLDEN WEAVER
Ploceus xanthops

GOLDEN WEAVER
Ploceus subaureus

YELLOW-HEADED WEAVER
Ploceus cucullatus spilonotus

LESSER MASKED WEAVER
Ploceus intermedius

BROWN-THROATED
GOLDEN WEAVER
Ploceus xanthopterus

WHITE-BROWED WEAVER
Plocepasser mahali

GROSBEAK WEAVER
Amblyospiza albifrons

MASKED WEAVER
Ploceus velatus

SOCIABLE WEAVER
Philetairus socius

RED-BILLED
BUFFALO WEAVER
Ploceus velatus

Not drawn to scale.

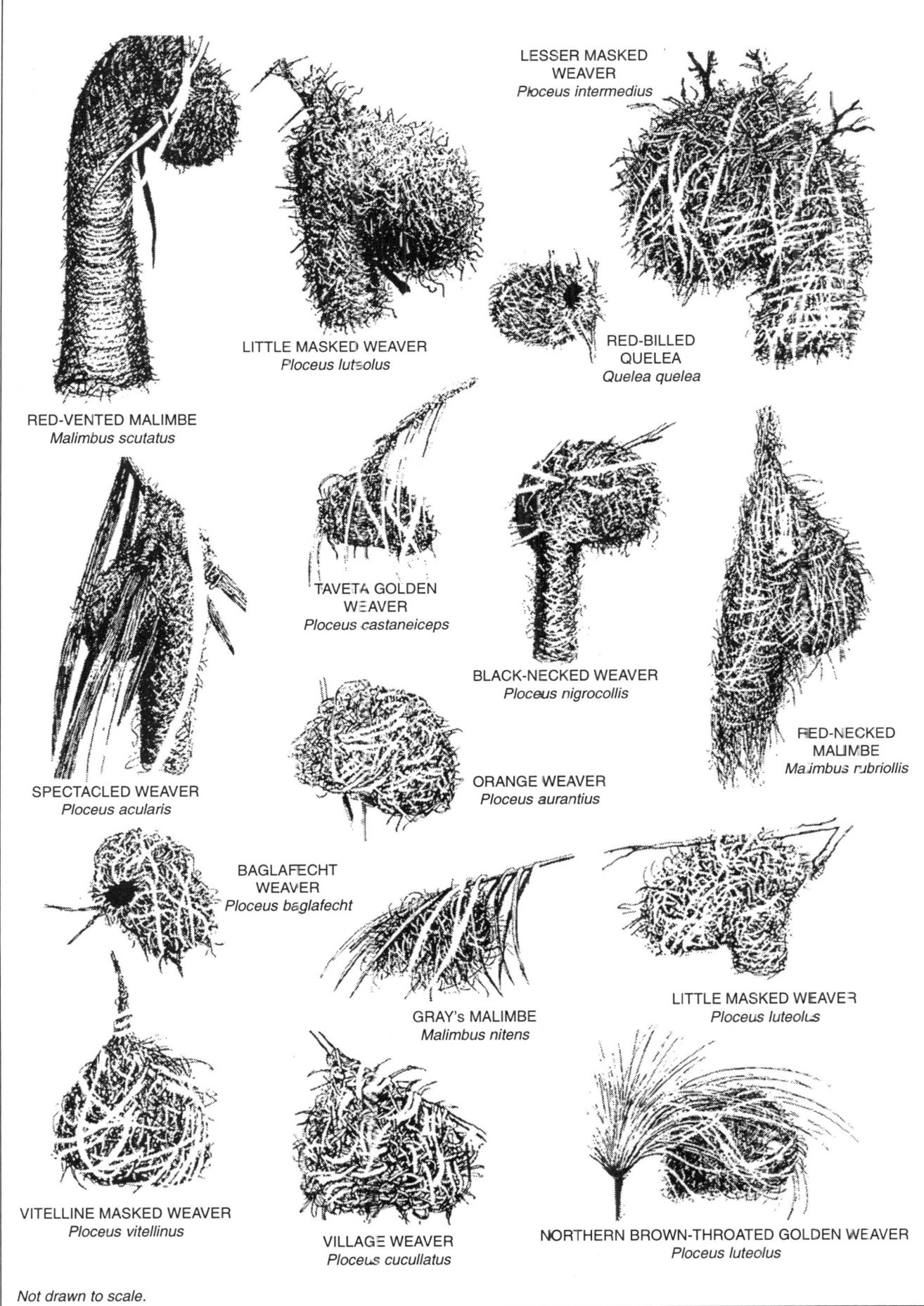

LESSER MASKED
WEAVER
Ploceus intermedius

LITTLE MASKED WEAVER
Ploceus luteolus

RED-BILLED
QUELEA
Quelea quelea

RED-VENTED MALIMBE
Malimbus scutatus

TAVETA GOLDEN
WEAVER
Ploceus castaneiceps

BLACK-NECKED WEAVER
Ploceus nigrocollis

RED-NECKED
MALIMBE
Malimbus rubriollis

SPECTACLED WEAVER
Ploceus acularis

ORANGE WEAVER
Ploceus aurantius

BAGLAFECHT
WEAVER
Ploceus baglafecht

LITTLE MASKED WEAVER
Ploceus luteolus

GRAY's MALIMBE
Malimbus nitens

VITELLINE MASKED WEAVER
Ploceus vitellinus

VILLAGE WEAVER
Ploceus cucullatus

NORTHERN BROWN-THROATED GOLDEN WEAVER
Ploceus luteolus

Not drawn to scale.

Artificial incubation and egg hatching

A birdkeeper may wish to artificially hatch eggs then raise the chicks, from the smallest waxbill to the largest gamebird. A waxbill's egg weighs less than one gram whereas the average Ostrich eggs weighs 1,3 kilograms. The incubation period of a waxbill's eggs is 12-13 days and that of an Ostrich 42 days. The quality of egg shell can vary tremendously as well, from the thick granular shell of a guineafowl to the thin and flexible shell of a parrot egg. Also the proportions of yolk to albumen can also vary tremendously, for example the yolk of a parrot egg is proportionately smaller when compared with that of a francolin egg. Factors stated above including other will influence the incubation requirements of an egg. One must bear in mind that the longer the incubation period the greater chance and time when minor incubation irregularities may influence the developing embryo.

Most of our knowledge regarding incubation arises from the requirements for successful incubation and hatching of commercially important domesticated species such as a chicken, turkey, duck, domesticated guineafowl, pheasant and quail.

It is important to be aware that the domesticated species have been selectively bred for hundreds of years and are far easier to rear after hatching than the seedeaters, that the average birdkeeper would keep in an aviary. It is also very important to realise that indigenous and exotic seedeaters which have become domesticated, all have slightly different requirements for optimal hatchability.

The availability of wild caught birds to birdkeepers are increasingly becoming more restricted through legislation. Propogation of birds in captivity is for this reason becoming most important if birdbreeders are to enjoy the great variety of birds that they presently hold in their aviaries. As the availibility of indigenous birds becomes more restricted due to bylaws, so the value of these captive birds increases. This is just one of the reasons why there has been a tremendous upsurge in the captive propogation of many species. Avicultural magazine articles and a fair number of books on the same subject have been written in recent years regarding artificial incubation of non-domesticated birds. One cannot cover all aspects of egg incubating for seedeaters in one short chapter. Readers wishing to aquire further more detailed information will have to consult works devoted entirely to this subject, as well as specialised magazine articles which occur from time to time.

Hatching a seedeater's egg may be difficult, but the greatest challenge would be the rearing of a chick.

The incubator

To successfully incubate a bird's egg, one would require an incubator. Incubators vary in sophistication from the basic still air cabinet model where manual turning of the eggs are required, to the sophisticated forced draught models where the temperature and humidity are electronically controlled. The eggs are automatically turned and the volume of air circulating through the incubator can be varied. With the upsurge in interest in artificial incubation of non-domesticated bird's eggs the sophisticated small draught model has become available to the birdkeepers at no small cost.

When purchasing an incubator one must take into consideration the following points:

1. *For size* the domesticated hen's egg was used as guide to the capacity of the incubator. 12 hen eggs and 60 hen eggs are examples of incubators that are advertised by local manufacturers.

2. *Temperature control* – the state electronic thermostat is becoming the standard heat controlling device for the incubator. The ether wafer thermostat was also very accurate. It is desirable to have a standby thermostat that operates at a slightly higher temperature than the main thermostat so that in the event of the main thermostat failing, the standby thermostat takes over and will prevent the incubator from overheating the eggs and killing the developing embryo.

3. *Humidity control* – the humidity of an incubator can be controlled by bowls of water placed in the bottom of an incubator. When sloping the bowl, a level control device can be incorporated, giving a greater or lesser water surface area for evaporation. This will in turn affect the relative humidity inside the incubator. Another method of controlling humidity was to use a wet bulb thermometer connected to a solenoid valve which will allow water to flow onto an evaporation pad as it is necessary to maintain the required wet bulb reading.

4. *Egg turning device* – method of turning an egg and the frequency of turning an egg are both important. The method of turning is to tip the end of an egg over its long axis through an arch of 90°C. This method is frequently used in large walk-in room incubators, used in the commercial poultry industry. This method will give unsatisfactory results with those eggs which have a proportionately small yolk such as duck and parrot eggs. Another method is to roll the eggs from side to side on rollers. The distance between the rollers is adjusted to accommodate eggs with a smaller or larger diameter.

Yet another method of turning eggs involves using a moving carpet. The latter moves to and fro below the bars of the egg holding tray. The eggs cannot move past the bars of the tray and the moving carpet rolls the eggs between the bars of the tray. When this method is used the eggs also sway and wobble from side to side as they rotate. This method of egg turning is regarded as being the most satifactory for hatching of difficult eggs. The turning frequency is very important whereas turning eggs two or three times a day will suffice for eggs of domesticated poultry, it is desirable to turn non-domesticated eggs once each hour. The egg turning process can be a slow continuous motion or alternatively a relatively quick motion at selected time intervals.

5. *Insulation* – The incubator temperature is generally higher than the ambient temperature. Heat is lost via convection and conduction to the exterior. The insulating quality of the materials used to make an incubator cabinet and the temperature gradient between the incubator and the immediate ambient temperature will influence the rate at which heat is lost. For example a cabinet made from wood including chipboard or cavity plastics will retain heat far better than one made of metal or a single layer of plastic.

6. *Air flow* – some incubators have non-adjustable air vents. It is an advantage to have this form of vents so that one can vary the air flow through the incubator at different times during the incubation period if desired, and with different egg types.

7. *Cleaning and fumigation* – when purchasing a small incubator it is important to establish how easy the interior of the cabinet is to clean. There is always a great deal of debris associated with the hatching of eggs, namely shell fragments, nestling and chick fluff, egg membranes and droppings. This debris is an ideal medium for the growth of bacteria which can infect chicks and unhatched eggs. The manufacturers advocate the cleaning and fumigating of an incubator between hatches. In certain small models there is no air filter between the cabinet and the compartment housing the electronics, heater and fan. In such incubators the debris associated with hatching becomes deposited in the works compartment and can interfere with the functioning of the controls.

The cleaning and fumigating between hatches may be difficult to accomplish, whereby one is likely to skimp on this very important task. Skimping on incubator hygiene is sooner or later bound to result in serious infections and loss of valuable unhatched eggs, nestling and chicks. In some models it is necessary to dismantle the compartment housing and controls for the purpose of cleaning. On reassembling the control compartment one is obliged to recalibrate the temperature controls which then take a little longer than a day to stabilise. If the parent stock are not well fed the eggs are unlikely to hatch, no matter how specialised your incubator may be.

The "Vosmar" incubator measures, 53 x 33cm high. One side forms a door which opens to the full width of the incubator and a glass window measuring 19,5 x 39,5cm long which gives good insulation and clear vision of the thermometer. Ventilator holes are provided in the bottom and top, the latter can be used as egg testers. The egg tray is supported on slides for easy removal. This model is made to withstand heat, cold and moisture without warping.

TURBOFAN INCUBATOR
Capacity: 65 poultry or 200 quail eggs.

Hovers the eggs and gently warms them until they hatch. The radiant heat tube gently warms the inside of the incubator, the air and the eggs. Thermal action of the heated air flowing out the exhaust vents in the top draws fresh air through the bottom vent. This airflow also assists the drying of chicks after they have hatched. Available with or without egg turner.

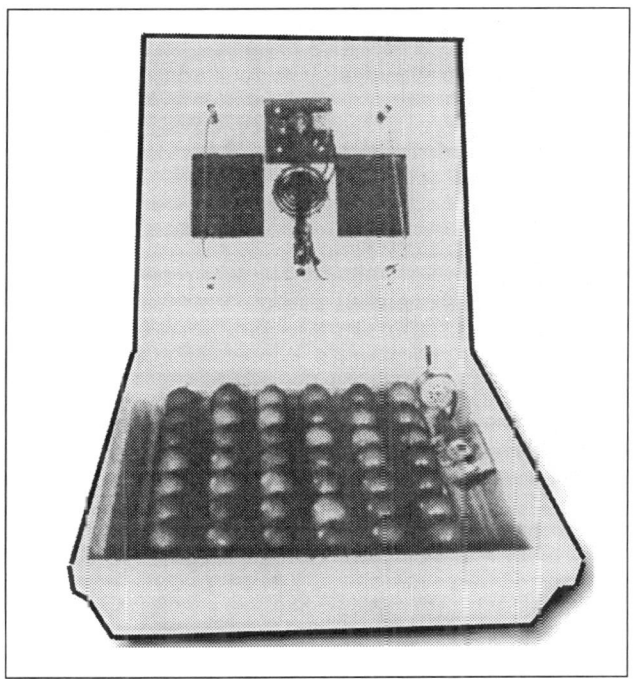

THE COMPLETE INCUBATOR AND HEATER
Capacity: 55 egg deluxe is also available in a battery operated model (12v).

Features: Extra sensitive "easy read" dial thermometer. Clean out pan. Two thermostats – in the event of one failing, a back-up would take over to prevent ruining of eggs. 220v AC-=225w heat element. Automatic electric egg Three setting trays and 1 hatching tray.

Capacity: Total ± 1200 quail eggs (set and hatch 200 / week)

± 420 large eggs (e.g. domestic fowl eggs)

± 147 Domestic goose eggs

Tray: ± 300 quail eggs

± 105 Domestic fowl/Pheasant eggs

± 37 Domestic goose eggs

VOSMAR INCUBATORS

PO Box 9692, Henopsmeer 0046, South Africa

BRINSEA Octagon ㉒ Mk III

Especially designed for parrots

The safe, simple way to hatch your eggs

• Fully automatic egg turning

• Easily cleaned, very compact

• Made from tough moulded plastic

• Humidity is controlled by a twin compartment accessible from outside the incubator

• Double glazed 'Omnitherm'

• Temperature stability ± 0,1 degree centigrade

• Fan assisted ventilation

• All round visibility

Capacity: 40-60 eggs, 24 domestic poultry eggs.

BRINSEA HUMIDITY CONTROLLER FOR INCUBATOR (with pump)

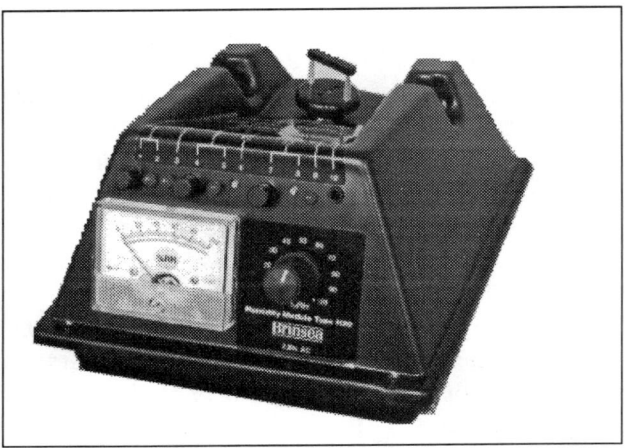

AVIAN NURSERY ICU Mk III
USA Designed

• 220v/175w

• Heavy duty ABS construction

• 5mm Sliding perspex door

• Digital thermostat control

• 1 Year guarantee

• Circulated air

• Ball bearing fan

• Filter

• Humidity tray

• Neon interior light

• Easy cleaning

• Accurate to ± 0,1°C

Agent: OWEN SANDERS
PO Box 1009, East London 5200, South Africa

Setting up the incubator

It is desirable to set the incubator and then let it operate for forty-eight hours before placing the eggs. This will allow the temperature in the interior of the incubator to stabilise.

The following points are of importance:

1. *The Incubator environment* – when using a small incubator the temperature and the relative humidity

of the interior is influenced by the surrounding ambient temperature and the relative humidity to a far greater extent than the large industrial walk-in incubators. For this reason it is important that it should be situated in a room where the ambient temperature and the relative humidity are stable.

If it is not possible to satisfy these requirements one can expect poor results even with the best of the small type incubators. A room with ambient temperature of 20° C is recommended. The air flow in the room must be satisfactory, draughts are unacceptable. Sun entering through a window which falls directly onto the incubator at certain times of each day is a recipe for a disaster-like effect, on account that the electronics of a small incubator is incapable of dealing with the external heat source arising from direct sunlight. Similarly the electronics of this incubator cannot cope with a sudden drop in ambient temperature.

2. *Incubation temperature* – Manufacturers of incubators will advocate temperatures which they have tested and found to be suitable for a particular variety of domesticated poultry eggs. For Galliforms (gamebirds), temperatures of 37,5°C to 37,8°C are advocated for the incubation of eggs and a slightly lower temperature for the hatching of eggs. Temperatures slightly lower than the above are recommended for the incubation and hatching of duck eggs, whereas a temperature as low as 36,2°C is recommended for Ostrich eggs. It is advisable to set a temperature slightly lower than the suggested setting, rather than a slightly higher temperature. When incubating the eggs of any species where one has no previous experience to draw from, one has to extrapolate from known parameters and use a calculated guess as to what would be an ideal incubation temperature. Research has revealed that a deviation of temperature by 0,5°C from the ideal temperature setting for domesticated duck eggs, for a period of three days during the incubation, can reduce the hatchibility by 50%. It goes without saying that an accurate and reliable thermometer is most important for the monitoring of the incubation temperature. Unfortunately some sophisticated incubators are supplied with thermometers of inferior quality and debatable accuracy. There are some excellent digital thermometers available now at reasonable prices. It is desirable that the calibration of any new thermometer be checked for accuracy.

3. *Humidity* – during incubation the eggs will lose weight. It is important that the correct amount is lost. The weight loss range advocated by the experts for successful hatching is between 12% and 18% with an ideal weight loss of 14%-15% from the initiation of incubation until the eternal pip, this being the time when one can observe the beak of a chick in the airspace of an egg when candling an egg. The porosity of the egg shell and the relative humidity will influence the weight loss during incubation. A relative humidity of 55% at an incubation temperature of

37,8°C should give rise to the correct weight loss during incubation. An accurate method of determining whether or not an egg is losing the correct amount of weight during incubation is to weigh the egg and then plot a graph to demonstrate the actual weight loss, then compare this with a graph that illustrates the ideal weight loss. If the loss is in excess, the humidity must be increased. Where the weight loss was inadequate the reverse holds true. The answer is that one requires an extremely accurate scale, which are usually expensive, to determine the weight loss during incubation. Readings to the second decimal point will be required for small eggs.

Monitoring eggs in the incubator

Only clean uncracked eggs with normal shape and size should be set. The temperature and the humidity must be checked on a daily basis. It must be remembered, that as the incubation progresses the eggs start producing their own heat to such an extent that it may be necessary to adjust the temperature controls to supply less heat towards the end of the incubation period. Candling of eggs must be performed every few days. Where eggs have white shells, one can determine fertility as early as the fourth day of incubation. Candling must be described as the trans-illumination of an egg with a strong light source. The early stages of embryonic development have the appearance of a spider', this resulting from the embryo from which radiate developing blood vessels. As incubation progresses an egg becomes progressively more opaque and the air cell at the broad end slowly enlarges. All fertile and addled eggs must be discarded as their presence becomes known, as they will enhance the possibility of infection.

The candling light features a high intensity prefocused lamp on the end of a 25cm flexible shaft. The new style candler lamp is recessed in a metal sleeve to fit the egg contour.

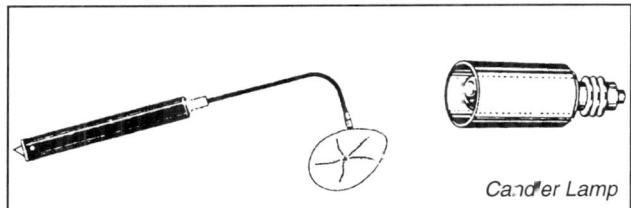

Candler Lamp

MDS Intercorporated *1640 Central Avenue, St. Petersburg FL 33712, USA.*

Candler which comes with a protective cover may be used as a handle extension (maximum length 70cm)

Egg turning for the last two days before hatching is not necessary. Where the incubation period is not known, one must discontinue turning the egg when the candling reveals that the unhatched chick's beak has broken through the egg's membranes into the airspace. The term used to describe this event is known as the internal pip. Where a separate hatcher is available, at this stage, the eggs are then transferred. Once the internal pip has occurred, it is desirable to increase the humidity so as to prevent the egg membranes from drying out during the hatching process which can vary in length from one species to another. For example the hatching process of a duck egg takes far longer than a domestic fowl egg, with quail, pigeon and dove eggs hatching particularly quicker. The term used to describe a point in the incubation process when a nestling or chick first breaks through the egg shell is known as "pipped" or as previously stated, the external pip. There is a period of resting once an egg is pipped, followed by the chick rotating inside the shell and at the same time extending the pipeline until eventually the chick pushes the top of the egg shell off and emerges.

Separate hatchers

When one is incubating more than one clutch of eggs in a given incubator, it is preferable to have a separate hatcher. This is desirable for a variety of reasons:

1. The ideal temperature for hatching is slightly lower than the incubation temperature.

2. The hatching process is very messy and one wishes to avoid contaminating the incubator with debris associated with the hatching process.

3. The humidity required during the hatching process is higher than that required in the incubation period. The controls of a hatcher must as sophisticated as that of incubators to successfully hatch eggs.

The Brooder

There are two basic categories of hatchlings, namely precocial and attricial, with both types requiring completely different brooding systems which will be discussed separately.

Brooder for precocial chicks

Examples of this catergory are the chicks of guineafowl and quail. Precocial chicks are able to run about approximately 24 hours after hatching and by so doing it is possible for them to select a temperature at which they are most comfortable. They do, however, require an external source of heat on account that they are not able to thermoregulate at this early stage. A precocial chick can be treated in a similar manner to that of a domesticated fowl's chick. A chick will require a heat source which is best served from an electric light bulb or an infra-red light bulb. The heat intensity can be controlled by the raising or lowering of the heat source.

Food is supplied in a shallow dish. Poultry rations can be used, however they have high bacterial content and initially it may be necessary to use a quality avicultural feed which has a lower bacterial count. A variety of good quality scientifically formulated feeds with a lower bacterial count is available to aviculturists. (See section on Feeding). Research in the USA has revealed that a non-domesticated chick's immune system is incapable of coping with feed that includes a high bacterial content, although even such bacteria may not necessarily cause known diseases. Water is supplied in a shallow dish in the event of a chick loosing its balance, thereby

preventing it from drowning. The size of the dish maybe in proportion to the size of the chick. As they mature and become feathered the temperature is then gradually reduced until the stage is reached when they are no longer in need of an external heat source, and then discontinued.

There are a variety of brooders manufactured for the poultry industry with models suited to birdbreeders for the raising of precocial chicks.

A very simple homemade brooder can be constructed from an old tropical fish tank or alternatively a sturdy

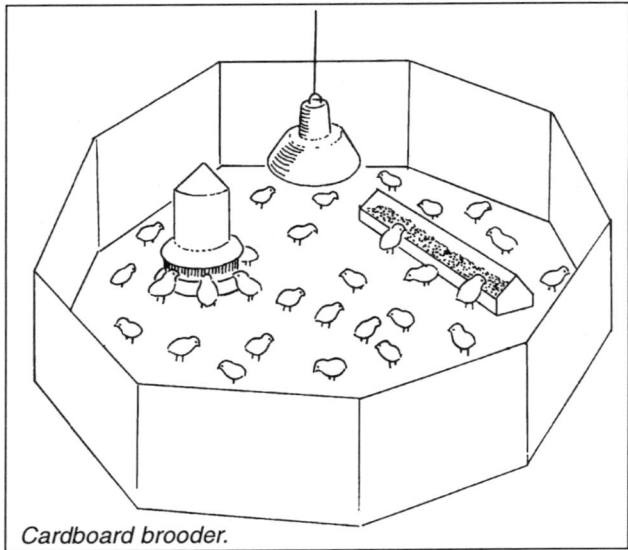

Cardboard brooder.

cardboard box. It is important to remember that precocial chicks which a birdbreeder will rear will learn to fly at an early age, being capable also of jumping great heights.

It is advisable to have a lid on the brooder so they cannot escape. As pouts grow they will require additional space by having to be moved to larger accommodation. Over crowding can give rise to vices such as feather picking and cannabilism. Once they have occured it is difficult to stop, so only with adequate quarters can it be prevented. It is also inadvisable to mix chicks of different sizes/ages in the same brooder as larger/older chicks will bully smaller/younger ones. Once a chick has been subjected to this form of stress, they can be difficult to rehabilitate.

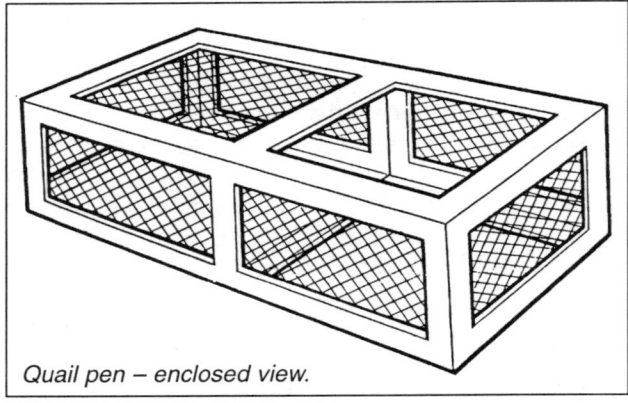

Quail pen – enclosed view.

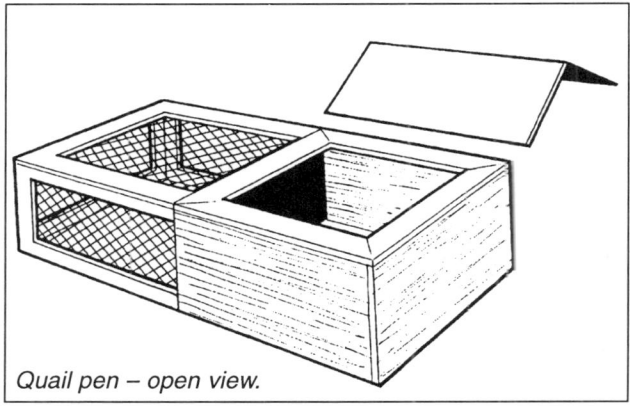

Quail pen – open view.

Overall measurements:
Length: 60cm
Width: 38cm
Height: 25cm

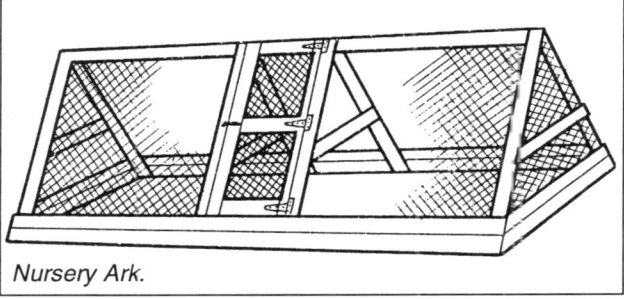

Nursery Ark.

Overall measurements:
Length: 3.3m
Width: 1,8m
Height: 1,6m

Brooders for altricial chicks

Examples are finch/waxbill or parrot chicks. This type of chick is fed in the nest by the parent bird. The finch/waxbill chick will beg for food with open mouth in the presence of the parent bird. The gape reflex is usually initiated by sound and vibration.

Parrot and dove/pigeon chicks on the other hand, do not gape. The parent bird will feed a chick by taking the beak between its own and "pumping" food between the mandibles. When dealing with altricial chicks the brooding requirements are much more sophisticated. A variety of brooder models are also available for raising of altricial chicks. These brooders are usually small with very sophisticated temperature regulating devices. Initially nestlings require a temperature of approximately 37°C. This temperature is gradually reduced as chicks begin to mature. One cannot give an exact timetable as to when and by what amount the temperature should be reduced on account of the tremendous variation in the nestling period of altricial chicks. Once wing-feathers have developed the chicks become self-thermoregulating. A chick must look comfortable, especially when handled, and if found to be cool, the temperature is too low. If a chick hyperventilates (pants) the temperature is therefore to high. Another very important aspect which one should take into consideration is humidity in the brooder. This must be kept high to prevent dehydration of the nestlings. The smaller the nestlings the greater the risk of them becoming dehydrated due to the relatively larger surface area. As with incubators, brooder hygiene is also of importance. The elevated temperatures and high humidity promote the growth of harmful bacteria, fungi and viruses. Brooders should be disinfected between different batches of nestlings/chicks.

The San Diego Zoological Society has kept records of successful incubation of a variety of birds eggs since 1980. The incubation temperature and relative humidity are recorded as well as the temperature in the hatcher and the relative humidity in the hatcher. This list of appropriate incubation temperatures for a variety of non-domesticated birds eggs is recorded in Kuehler, C. and J; Good. 1990 – Artificial Incubation of non domestic bird eggs. International Zoo Yearbook 29: pp 118-136.

The list of incubation temperatures would form a good guide as to appropriate temperatures for seed eaters.

Fostering

In the event of injury, illness or death befalling one of a pair, the eggs can be incubated safely by transferring them to another pair which had laid approximately at the same time, only if the remaining bird should refuse to continue incubating alone, then nestlings can be transferred to another nest which contains nestlings of a comparable age.

Detailed information about fostering can be obtained from a number of good specialist books listed in the reference section and available at all leading pet stores and booksellers.

Plants in the aviary

Plants serve many functions, namely perches, food, nesting sites, shelter, shade, seclusion, attracting insects and giving a pleasing natural appearance to an aviary. It is not always possible to imitate the exact natural habitat of a species, but try to recreate as best possible a similar situation with a variety of suitable plants. The final choice when purchasing will be influenced by the type and condition of the soil, size of aviary and weather conditions in the region. Climbing plants are useful for covering unsightly walls or aviary mesh, and in doing so give concealment to nesting sites, and hopefully attracting suitable insects that are drawn to the flowers which usually occur in profusion in many creeper species.

Plants can be divided into four catergories:

Trees, shrubs, creepers and ground covers. A small aviary may need only a single tree or a number of small shrubs instead, which can be planted against one side of the welded mesh. This allows ample ground space to feed. Large aviaries can have a number of trees and shrubs, one or two strong thick creepers and some ground covers, preferably seeding grass species. Great care must be taken with trees as their branches at times are inclined to break through wire netting or stretch welded mesh if allowed to grow too high if not checked regularly. The roots of trees can also be a problem at times by undermining the foundations, eventually producing cracks in the walls in which vermin will not hesitate to take full opportunity of the situation and enter the aviary to feed. Planting around the outside of an aviary is not essential but a display of flowers will enhance the area.

Suitable plants

Annual Hop	*Humulus japonicus*
Bullrush	*Typha capensis*
Bottlebrush	*Callistemon viminalis*
Blue flax	*Linum narbonese*
Box	*Buxus sempervirens*
Canary creeper	*Senecio tamoides*
Common Bamboo	*Bambusa vulgaris*
Dwarf white striped bamboo	*Arundinaria variegata*
Dwarf thrift	*Armeria vulgaris*
Dog rose	*Rosa canica*
Egyptian reed	*Cyperus papyrus*
English lavender	*Lavandula spica*
Elder	*Sambucus nigra*
English hawthorn	*Crategus monogyna*
European hornbeam	*Carpinus betulus*
European larch	*Larix decidua*
Feathertop grass	*Pennisetum villosum*
Fish tail palm	*Caryota mitis*
Foliage plant	*Elegia capesis*
Giant mountain grass	*Dryopia dives*
Grey Honey myrtle	*Melaleuca incana*
Golden privit	*Ligustrum ovalifolium aureum*
Harestail grass	*Lagurue ovatus*
Hedge bamboo	*Bambusa glaucescens*
Honeysuckle fuchsia	*Fuchsia triphylla*
Hill Banksia	*Banksia collina*
Heath-leaved Banksia	*Banksia ericifolia*
Italian woodbine	*Lonicera caprifolium*
Japanese honeysuckle	*Lonicera japonica*
Klipdagga	*Leonotis leonites*
Mountain ash	*Sorbus aucuparia*
Miscanthus	*Miscanthus giganteus*
Mock orange	*Philadelphus coronarius*
Morning glory	*Ipomoea acuminata*
Northern mountain bamboo	*Oreobambos buchwaldii*
Native wisteria	*Hardenbergia comptoniana*
Oregon holly grape	*Mahonia aquifolium*
Parlour bamboo	*Chamaedorea elegans*
Passion fruit	*Passiflora edulis*
Peach-blossom Tea-tree	*Leptospermum squarrosum*
Red-hot poker	*Kniphofia praecox*
Russian vine	*Abies alba*
Reed's Canary grass	*Phalaris canaria*
Red Ribes	*Ribes sanguineum*
Robin Red-breast shrub	*Melaleuca laterita*
Rice millet	*Oryzopsis milacea*
Sealing wax palm	*Cyrtostachys lakka*
Sugar cane	*Saccharum officinarum*
Southern mountain bamboo	*Arundinaria tessellata*
Screw pine	*Pandanus livingstonianus*
Spruce fir	*Picea excelsa*
Slender panic grass	*Paspalidium constrictum*
Snowberry	*Symphoricarpus albus*
Snowball tree	*Virburnum opulus*
Thatching reed	*Chondroprtalum tectorum*
Traveller's joy	*Clematis vitalba*
	Clematis armandii
	Clematis montana
	Clematis rubens
	Clematis spooneri
Tassel bush	*Carrya elleoptica*
Tantoon Tea-tree	*Leptospermum flavescens*
Thyme Honey myrtle	*Melaleuca thymifolia*
Umbrella thorn	*Acacia tortillis*
Umbrella sedge	*Cyperus alternifolius*
Virginia creeper	*Partheoncissus quinquefolia*
Yesterday, today and tomorrow	*Brunfelsia pauciflora*
Weeping bottlebrush	*Callistemon citrinus*
Woodbine	*Lonicera periclymenum*
	Lonicera nitida
	Lonicera yunnanensis

• The ARU does not necessarily endorse the views of contributors

Useful points when planting an aviary

1. Have ample walking space zoned by marking out intended paths before starting to plant.
2. Never over plant such as to impede the flight of the birds.
3. If possible avoid the use of delicate plants as they will be destroyed leaf by leaf by individuals of some species.
4. Use sturdy plants as they have to hold the weight of both light and heavy species.
5. Use both indigenous and exotic plants, especially those noted as being excellent seed or fruit bearers.
6. For easy access into the sleeping quarters plant only small shrubs in front of the entrance.
7. Before introducing birds into an aviary give plants ample time to take root. Slow-growing plants can be protected by covering with mist netting or welded mesh.
8. Make available suitable conditions for both arboreal and terrestrial species.
9. Avoid plants which are poisonous to birds, the whole or part thereof.
10. Where possible position natural bare perches over paths, thus preventing excreta fouling the plant life.

Detailed information on which plants contain known toxic chemicals, whether birds have been poisoned or not, can be obtained from a few excellent articles in avicultural publications including a fair number of works listed in the reference section and can be purchased from book stores or on loan from public libraries.

One may wish to despatch plants for identification to the Botanical Research Institute in your province, county or state. Please keep in mind:

1. Only send complete specimens. In the case of trees and / or large plants, leafy branches with flowers and / or fruits will be adequate.
2. Plants should never be dispatched in plastic bags on account of condensation, making them useless for identification.
3. Number the specimens if more than one is sent.

Plant species which should not be considered because they, or their derivatives, could prove poisonous

Calla lily *Zantedeschia aethiopica;* Christmas candle *Pedilanthus tithymaloides;* Cowslip *Primula veris;* Cape hyacinth *Pseudogaltonia clavata;* Cherry-Laurel *Prunus lauocerasus;* Cuckoo-pint *Arum maculatum* Common rhamnus *Rhamnus cathartius;* Common menkshood *Aconitum napellus;* Dune bush *Grotalaria spartioides;* Daffodil *Narcissus pseudonarcissus;* English yew *Taxus baccata;* Eagle Fern *Pteridium aquilinum;* Grass Chinkerinchee *Ornithogalum ornithogaloides.* Gousiekte tree *Pavetta schumanniana.* Horse chestnut *Aesculus hippocastanum.* Hemlock *Tsuga cariadensis.* Henbane *Hyoscymus niger.* Horse-tail *Equisetum ramosissimum* Honey locust *Gleditsia triphylum.* Iris *Iris* sp. Jack-in-the-Pulput *Arisama triphyllum.* Jimson wood *Dutura* sp. Kentuky coffee tree *Gymnocladus dioicus.* Kraalbos *Galenia africana.* Lord and Ladies *Arum maculatum.* Lily-of-the-valley *Convallaria majallis.* Larkshur *Consolida regalis.* Lupin *Lupinusnoot katensis.* Loo weed *Astragulus mollissimus.* May apple *Podophyllum* sp. Monkey rope *Cynanchym ellipticum.* Monkshood *Aconitum* sp. Meadow saffron *Colchicum autumnale.* Mountain-laurel *Kaimia Lalifolia.* Oak *Quercus* spp. Foxglove *Digitalis purpurea.* Pokeweed *Phytolacca amaricana.* Poison onion *Dipcadi glaucum.* Rattle bush *Crotalaria burkeana.* Rosary peas *Abrus precatorius.* Spindle tree *Euonymus europaeus.* Snowdrop *Galanthus navilis.* Snowflake *Leucolum vernum.* Star of Bethelehem *Ornithogalum thyrdcides.* St John's wort *Hypericum aethiopicum.* Transvaal chinkerinchee *Ornithogalum saundersiae.* Transvaal yellow tulp *Homeria* Spp. Australian bottle plant *Jatropha podagrica,* Crab's eye *Abrus presatorius,* Crepe myrtle *largestrowmia indica,* Marvel-of Peru *Mirabilis jalapa,* Silber lace creeper *Polgonum aubertii,* Yellow star thistle *Centaurea solistitialis,* Golden rod *Solidago viraurea,* Tung-oil *Aleurites fordii,* Red posy *Boophane disticha,* Smoke tree *Continus coggyria,* Gifboom *Acokanthera* spp., Golden trumpet vine *Allamanda cathartica,* Tennis court creeper *Araujia sericofera,* Rubber vine *Cyptostegia grandiflora.*

The ARU does not necessarily endorse the views of contributors.

Feeders

To keep seed clean and free from dampness it should be stored in containers made of china, tough plastic, hardwood, asbestos, stainless steel or any other rust-free metal. When purchasing a parrot, parakeet or lovebird cage, seed cups are provided, usually of metal, but occasionally of a tough plastic in a wide range of sizes and colours. This form of indestructable container is also suitable for parrot-type birds which are reluctant, or totally refuse to eat on or near the floor, whereby the container can be attached to the wire mesh just above a perch so as to reduce unnecessary seed scattering. The "clip-on" or "pop-out" cups are suitable for use in a double breeder or aviary with the latter needing to be attached to a hardboard or masonry surface with the use of a pair of slightly protruding screw heads. Also available is a sealed feeder that can be replenished from outside a cage and a tubular seed container that can be replenished while still attached to a cage. The food supply is visable making them an advantage over opaque ones where regular inspection is necessary. The revolving feeder has become the easest, safest and most economic method of feeding birds The unit has a pivot hinge enabling it to be turned through 180 degrees and locked in open or closed positions. Up to four extractable bowls can be installed in any type of cage or aviary. Hanging feeders are available for gamebirds with the feed openings adjusted to three positions. Slip the wire adjusting springs into the desired slots in the hopper which then locks into place, thus stopping it from slipping. The tapered body and bottom cone forces all feed types out into a pan eliminating bridging. The feeder is raised in accordance with the growth of birds, from chicks to adults. For parrot-like birds an open feeding shelf constructed of welded mesh in a wooden frame and then suspended by chairs is popular in a mixed aviary on account that falling seed drops straight onto the floor below where it can be swept up and cleaned by using a winnower.

Another form of singular feeder placed off the ground is known as a bird table. It can be placed in a flight, fixed to the top of a pole or suspended from the roof of an aviary. The base may consist of a board 35cm long and 30cm wide. Over the top is placed a sheet of flat tin, asbestos or masonite which is sloped to keep the rain out. Containers placed on the cage or aviary floor should be shallow and open, except for gamebirds. The majority of gamebird feeders are partly covered and usually contain holes through which the feed is extracted, being adopted to try and eliminate feed scattering. In the UK quail feeders give birds plenty to eat but stops them dust bathing in their food. Open containers must have seed husks blown-off regularly so birds can view the seed underneath. Free-standing self-feeders, which are more commonly known as seed hoppers, do not require such regular attention as open dishes. The hoppers come in two forms, either box-shaped with a glass front and trough or a cylinder fitted into a circular tray

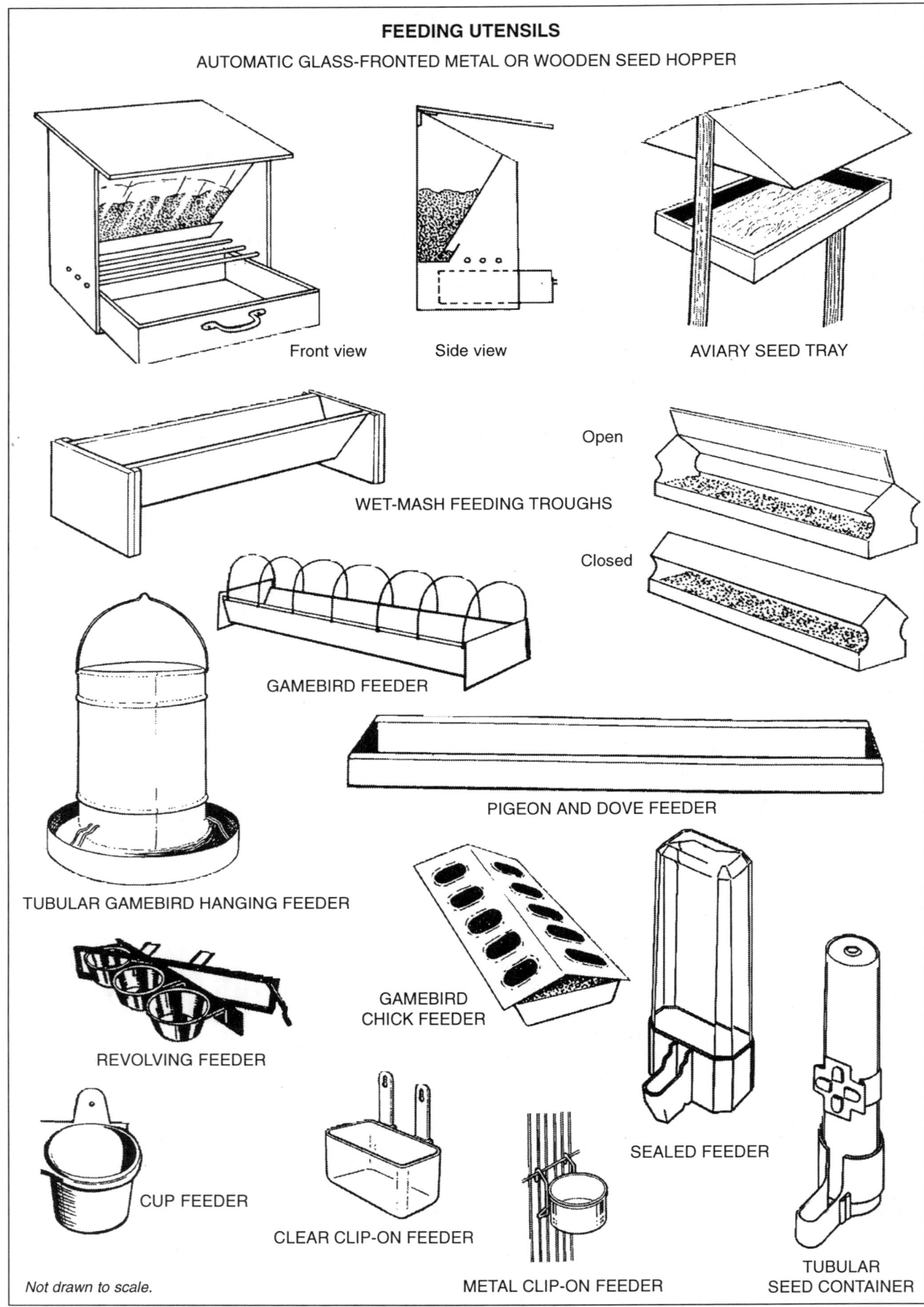

FEEDING UTENSILS
AUTOMATIC GLASS-FRONTED METAL OR WOODEN SEED HOPPER

Front view

Side view

AVIARY SEED TRAY

WET-MASH FEEDING TROUGHS

Open

Closed

GAMEBIRD FEEDER

PIGEON AND DOVE FEEDER

TUBULAR GAMEBIRD HANGING FEEDER

GAMEBIRD
CHICK FEEDER

SEALED FEEDER

REVOLVING FEEDER

CUP FEEDER

CLEAR CLIP-ON FEEDER

METAL CLIP-ON FEEDER

TUBULAR
SEED CONTAINER

Not drawn to scale.

which holds the trickling seed as the bird feeds. They should be placed in the sleeping quarters where it is light and can be viewed easily from the outside of an aviary so that checking of seed can be done regularly. This form of feeder is also available in wall-hanging models. Finally, avoid placing it below perches where it would become contaminated by the birds' own excreta.

Nutritional principles

The basic nutritional requirements of birds fall into six categories, namely carbohydrates, fats, proteins, vitamins, minerals and water. These requirements are provided in complex mixtures in most foodstuffs, but some foods ar richer in certain of them than others, and no one food provides them all, certainly not in the correct proportions. It is important, therefore, to supply a diet which is both varied and correctly balanced The following information will make it possible to plan a suitable feeding programme, and will also act as a guide to dietary correction in cases where ailments occur as a result of poor nutrition.

Carbohydrates are organic compounds made up of the elements carbon, hydrogen and oxygen (C, H and O respectively). They are the body's most accessible fuel, as immediately they are digested and absorbed they can be burnt to supply energy in the form of heat and work. This is their major use.

Fats are also C, H and O based organic compounds, but in different forms and with different properties from carbohydrates. Both solid fats and liquid fats (oils) are excellent sources of energy, but they are more than just fuels. They play several important roles in the body, including those of providing the raw materials for cell membrane structure and hormone production.

Proteins are different organic compounds from carbohydrates and fats as they contain the element nitrogen (N) in significant quantity in addition to C, H and O. They contain a certain amount of sulphur (S) as well. Proteins are the major building materials in the body. They form the major part of cell and tissue structure everywhere. Proteins are also the materials of which the body's thousands of enzymes are made, and thereby act as catalysts and controllers of metabolism in general. Young birds are developing new tissue and new enzymes all the time, and in adult birds tissue and enzyme must be repaired or replaced regularly, so proteins are a constant bodily requirement and must be provided in the diet. Food protein, when digested, is broken down to constituent amino acid "building blocks" of which there are 22 common ones. These are absorbed by the body and then built up into the particular proteins the body needs by specific reassortment of the 22 units in protein synthesis. Some food proteins are deficient in certain amino acids, so it is important for food protein to come from a variety of sources to ensure that all 22 are available to the bird as it grows and develops.

Carbohydrates, fats and proteins together constitute the major solid food requirements and, conveniently, they do all occur together in staple foods such as seeds and cereals in proportions which are quite suitable for most dietary purposes. The key to balancing these requirements lies in providing a variety of seeds and cereals acceptable to the bird in question.

Provision of the more exotic 'extras' in a bird's diet is usually for the purpose of ensuring an adequate supply of vitamins and minerals. These dietary necessities are required in much smaller amounts than are the foodstuffs described above.

Vitamins are complex organic compounds which cannot be manufactured from carbohydrates, fats or proteins in the body and thus have to be provided in the diet. They are required in extremely small amounts, but are nevertheless critically important as they have key functions in metabolism and give rise to typical deficiency symptoms if in short supply. Some vitamins are fat-soluble (e.g. vitamins A, D, E and K); these can be stored in the liver for a certain length of time and do not have to be supplied daily. The other vitamins (the B group and vitamin C) are water-soluble, cannot be stored by the body, and must be supplied continuously.

Vitamin	Food Sources	Important in
A	Yellow vegetable such as carrots	general growth and fitness
B	Whole grains, legumes, leafy greens, yeast	hatching, as well as general health
C	Fresh fruit and vegetables	skin condition and general health
D	Animal fats/oils and yeasts	bone formation, absorption of calcium and phosphorus, growth generally
E	Vegetable fats, e.g. in wheat germ, rice	fertility, healing power
K	Leafy greens, wheat bran, vegetable oils	growth, especially of nestlings

Minerals are those chemical elements which do not constitute major molecular structures in the way that C, H, O, N and S do but which are needed by the body for various purposes. Some minerals are required for use as simple inorganic salts, for example in the body fluids. These minerals (sodium, potassium, magnesium and chlorine) are needed in moderate quantity. So are the elements calcium and phosphorus which play important structural role in bone tissue as inorganic salts, as well as salts, as well as serving a number of other purposes. Other minerals are needed in much smaller quantities, and for this reason are termed "trace elements". Examples of this category of mineral are iron, iodine, manganese, molybdenum, selenium, zinc, aluminium, nickel, chromium, copper and cobalt, and there are further examples according to species. These "trace elements" are often required as minor constituents of complex organic molecules, and are incorporated into such molecule within the body during metabolism.

A varied diet automatically supplies adequate amounts of most mineral requirements, but supplements may be advisable to provide sufficient calcium, the most important mineral in quantitative terms A calcium supplement might be particularly advisable during breeding, as extra calcium is needed for incorporation into eggshell material, and nestlings have a high requirement for it during the growth of the major bones.

Water forms an essential part of all body cells and fluids and take part in metabolic reactions. The total amount of body water varies with a number of factors, but it often is as much as 90 percent of body mass. Water is lost by evaporation from lungs and skin at all times and must be replenished frequently. While some solid foods are rich in water content, liquid water, supplied separately, must supplement this source. Because of its importance, water supply is dealt with in a section of its own.

Feeding

The basic diet for most of the species mentioned in this work is a grain mixture of various seed types, divided into two categories: cereal and oil based. Good dry seed mixtures contain all the ingredients needed for a balanced diet and are available from grain merchants and pet stores. Seeds can be mixed accordingly to individual tastes of the species to be kept, or as many birdkeepers prefer, supply each type of seed on its own which will lead to less wastage in the long run. The oil seeds such as maw, rape and linseed are particularly useful during prolonged cold weather when body fat needs to be maintained.

A basic seed diet may consist of the following:

A. White millet, Golden millet, Japanese millet, Red manna (finches).

B. White millet, Golden millet, Japanese millet, Canary seed, striped Sunflower (lovebird).

C. White millet, Golden millet, Canary seed, striped Sunflower (parakeets).

D. Oats, red Maize, striped Sunflower, red grain Sorghum, unshelled Groundnuts (parrots).

E. Cracked red Maize, striped Sunflower, red grain Sorghum (doves and pigeons).

F. Sifted crushed Maize, Golden millet, White millet, Canary seed (quail).

G. Red Maize, Wheat, Barley, red grain Sorghum, striped Sunflower, shelled Groundnuts (larger gamebirds).

Composition of some common used seeds (percentages)

Seeds	Protein %	Carbohydrates %	Fats %	Minerals %
Millet	14	55-60	6	2
Canary seed	14-17	52-55	4-6	2-5
Maw	19	12	40-45	6
Rape	19-24	10	40	5
Linseed	21-24	23-26	34-36	3-6
Niger	17-21	15-22	21-23	7
Hemp	16	20-25	30	2-5
Sunflower	14-16	22	21-29	3
Safflower	14	16	28	–
Oats	11-12	53-56	4-5	2-3
Maize (yellow dent)	8-10	65-72	3-7	2
Wheat	11-14	70-80	2	2
Tares (vetch)	23	55	2	3-6
Barley	13	67	3	3-5
Rye	12	71	2	4
Brown rice	7	76	2	2
Beans	22	53	2	4
Ground nuts	26	18	47	–
Pine nuts	31	12	47	–

They vary according to the age and condition of the seeds.

Seed varieties vary from country to country. In the UK the following items are regularly advertised for sale, namely Colorado white and Dakota millet, millet sprays-French Anjou, "Rayreen" Reg. Mazagan, Moroccan, Canadian and Australian Canary seed, Chinese No. 1, Kenya white and Hungarian bold sunflower, German Rubsen rape, cress, white lettuce, chicory, French teazle seed and Gold of Pleasure. Pigeons and dove including the larger game birds may also accept Babala, white sorghum popcorn and Maple, Black Eye, Yellow, Rindo, Dunn, Cow and China peas. They can be fed whole, cracked or as compounded feeds in three major forms: dry mash, pellets and crumbles. Dry mash is supplied in a form of meal and properly balanced for a particular purpose. It is usually compounded to a formula to ensure the right combination of nutrients for each type of bird. Crumbs are very convenient to use, but usually more expensive than mash. Pelleted foods provide valuable variety alongside a seed diet. Palatability is important but persuading all birds to accept such foods may not always be successful in spite of their nutritional value. The lesser known indigenous seeds, namely Hausa, Iburua, Egyptian, Ethiopian and Saharan millets are difficult to obtain but will be enjoyed by the birds when offered to them. Sunflower seed can be purchased in black or striped, with the striped known to have a lower oil content.

A fair number of birdbreeders have eliminated sunflower from the diets because they claim that birds fed on it become lethargic and have little feather gloss; also lovebird breeders in high maize production areas in Africa have removed sunflower completely, opting for the cheaper maize. Birds new to captivity are partial to Teff and Mountain Rye including the lesser utilised feeds in the form of ground pumpkin, water melon and squash pips. Chicken mash ground Soya bean are good substitutes.

The parrot family should be offered groundnuts in the shell, the variety used for human consumption plus if available Bambara, Dika, Nitta and Oyster nuts. They must be offered the popular nuts, namely Almonds, Walnuts, Pecans, Brazils, Hazels and Cashews. In the UK Chinese Pine nuts and acorns are often mentioned in avicultural publications. In Australia they have a number of suitable indigenous species such as the Moreton Bay, Bunya-Bunya Pine, Queensland and Quandong nut. The larger parrot species enjoy cracking the stones of the Marula, peach and plum to extract the much favoured kernel with small species having to accept the leftovers. In recent years seed has become prepacked in cellophane which enables one to inspect the product before purchasing it. This eliminates the old system of purchasing seed in opaque packets from which it could not be inspected for freshness beforehand.

The grain should be shiny, clean-looking, free from mustiness, dampness or dust. Webby seed is not necessarily old or stale. This occurs when the tiny Seed Moth goes through its breeding cycle in the seed.

Grains, mashes, pellets and nuts available locally to birdkeepers

(5g, 10g, 25g and 50g packets)

Mixed fowl food	Yellow maize	Crushed maize
Sifted finely crushed maize	Grower mash	Laying mash
Laying pellets	Chick No. 1&2	Maple peas
Black-eye peas	Rondo peas	Dunn peas
Cow peas	China peas	Budgerigar seed
Plain canary	Mixed canary	Wild bird seed
Wild bird (incl Japanese millet)	Oats	White millet
Pigeon breeding pellets	Golden millet	Red manna
Special garden mixture	Wild grass seed	Babala
Buckwheat	Spray millet	Mixed millets
Japanese millet	Parrot mixture	
Special parrot mixture		
Parrot premium tropical mixture		
Parrot pellets – vitamin enriched		
Red sorghum	White sorghum	Red rape
Black rape	Maw seed	Linseed
Niger	Wheat	Barley
Pearl Barley	Lentils	Grouts
Split nuts	Shelled nuts	Unshelled nuts

(Courtesy of Sunbird Products 38/40 Wisely Road, Maydon Wharf 4001)

Avi-Plus Game Bird Starter is a fully balanced food intended for very young quail, ducks, pheasants and swans which have high protein requirements on hatching. This product should be fed for the first two to four weeks after hatching After this the normal commercial foods will be adequate.

Contains: maize, wheat, specially prepared soya, methionine, lysine, vegetable fat, salt, sugar, casein, lucerne, dicalcium phosphate, calcium carbonate, multivitamins, minerals and trace elements.

Feeding instructions: Feed as a moist mash prepared with approximately 80ml per 100ml food.

National supplier: *Avi-Products cc, PO Box 1750 Linkhills 3652.*

Soaked seed

It is necessary to have soaked seed available while young birds are being reared and for newly fledged birds who may find it difficult to digest hard seeds. The more commonly used are the oil seeds such as sunflower, rape, lettuce and the legumes (i.e. tic beans, etc) and "starch" seeds being the millets, canary, oat, wheat and sorghum. Seeds should be soaked for 18-24 hours. Also take the precaution of adding either Virkon or Vanodine to the water which will take care of any "bugs" that may be lurking in the seed. It is advisable to change the water half-way through the soaking process and prior to feeding wash it thoroughly again in fresh water.

Sprouted seed

To prepare germinated seed one needs a shallow tray made of asbestos, plastic or aluminium, a strainer, a bowl, sheets of blotting paper and plastic wrap. The bowl should be large enough to support the strainer on its rim. Fill the strainer with seed then rinse thoroughly under running water until clean. Leave the seed to soak in the bowl overnight and in the morning place in trays on blotting paper. Wrap around until small sprouts have broken through the kernels. A second method is to place well-soaked seed in a container – bottle, tupperware, etc and then leave in a warm place which will speed up germination. Within 48 hours germination will be far advanced and ready for feeding.

Avi-Med Safe Sprout

This powder is used as a fungal growth inhibitor it has no feed value and must be rinsed off well before the seed is fed to birds.

Directions for use:

Dissolve one level teaspoon (5ml) Safe Sprout in 5 litres of water. Cover seed to be soaked/sprouted with the water and allow to stand for 12 to 24 hours, depending on the type and freshness of the seed and the weather. Pour off the water and rinse the seed well. Rinse and stir the seed regularly twice a day. Keep in a cool place until the sprouts show.

Caution: Do not feed any seed that shows fungal growth or has fungal smells.

National supplier: *Avi-Products cc, PO Box 1750 Linkhills 3652*

Fruits

Many seedeaters have taken to adding fruits to their diet whenever it has been made available. In captivity it is also being used as a softfood for feeding young Bruised fruits are quite acceptable, but should never be fed in an over-ripe state. Fermenting fruits may have an alcoholic effect on the birds. Apple has become by far the most popular fruit, closely followed by the orange. Red apple (avoid green due to its high acid content) should be cut in such a way as to expose the seed cavity and pips. Orange can be cut in half and spiked on nails or bent wire. Due to the high acid content in oranges, some birdkeepers will limit the amount of this fruit, as birds has been known to lose condition if overfed. Grapes should be cut in half and also spiked. Tomatoes are favoured more when cut-up and sprinkled with a little sugar. Banana can be peeled and mixed with cubes of other fruits in a single dish, but not fed in large quantities as it may lead to over fattening, but enormous amounts have to be fed over long periods before such an effect can occur. Some species will consume only the hard seeds of the paw-paw and ignore the pulp. Mulberries and strawberries freshly picked are also a favourite with many species.

In addition one may wish to try lesser used varieties, namely peach, apricot, plum, fig, nectarine, guava, quince, pineapple, water melon, tree tomato, custard apple, prickly pear, rhubarb, pomegranate, granadilla, olive, mango, breadfruit, litchi, loquat, jackfruit, kiwifruit and cantaloupe including the lesser known varieties to southern African birdkeepers, namely akebia, akee, azarole, Barbados cherry, barberry, bearberry, Bengal quince, boysenberry, buffaloberry, carambola, carob, citange, citron, coco plum, Cornelian cherry, dewberry, durian, feijoa, goumi, hog plum, ilama, jambos, jujube, longan, mabolo, mangosteen, monstera, rosella, sapodilla, saopte, sugar apple, tamarind and wampee.

Dried fruits such as dates and figs are relished by numerous species. Berries, namely Brown ivory, *Berchemia discolour* Red ivory *B.zeyheri*, Medlar *Vangueria infrausta*, Wild raisin *Grewia caffra*, Giant raisin, *G.hexamita*, Bastard silver raisin, *G.inaeguilatera* and Peelingbark ochna *Ochna pulchara* can be stored away in jars when plentiful and fed out of season by soaking in hot water which will rehydrate them giving the appearance of raisins or currants. As an alternative to fresh fruits, canned fruits in natural juice can be used in an emergency. Indigenous fruits can be experimented with but important precautions must be adhered to, to recognise poisonous from non-poisonous fruits and berries. If one obtains fruits from a herbalist or farmer one can take their word that they are edible. It is not wise to experiment on the birds with an unknown fruit unless it is stated in some reference that birds, animals or the indigenous peoples of the region are known to feed on it, otherwise it may produce ill effects or even death. Test beforehand with the tip of your tongue touching the bare fruit. If the tongue does not experience a burning or bitter taste, bite off a small portion. After an hour if no ill-effects such as cramps or vomiting have occurred then it is assumed the fruit is edible.

Nectar

Some seedeaters will gadly accept nectar if made available, showing obvious benefits from its inclusion.

Homemade recipes vary considerably with sugar, honey or condensed milk providing ingredients common to most. In Africa one or two manufactured nectars are available with the advantage of being fortified with all the essential vitamins, and only require to be diluted with a little hot water. Allow to cool before feeding with any excess being kept in a refrigerator for up to two days only. Some species may ignore mixtures which contain meat extracts. Instead, a raw egg may be beaten up and added.

Nectar is usually given in specially designed tubular drinkers for the holding of liquids, and hung on the wire mesh by a metal clip in a shady position in an aviary.

Nectar Mixtures

Honey Eater Mix No. 1

Part A – 700mls of hot water is added to 1 dessertspoonful of Glucolin and 400g raw sugar. Mix well to dissolve.

Part B – Beat 2 eggs (yolk only) into 800mls of cold water then add 4 drops of Pentavite. Mix parts A and B together and store in a refrigerator. Use as required. *Note:* Do not keep longer than 3-4 days.

Part C – Prepare a mixture of 3 heaped dessertspoonfuls of high protein cereal to 2 heaped dessertspoonfuls of grated plain Madeira cake. Store in airtight container. To feed take part C, add A and B mixture, bring to a "gluggy" mix. This is now ready for feeding.

Honey Eater Mix No. 2

Part A – 300mls of hot water is added to 2 dessertspoonful of Complan, 2 of honey, ½ of Glucolin and 4 of a high protein cereal. Mix all the ingredients until dissolved then add 450 mls of cold water.

Part B – To part A add 1 heaped teaspoonful of protein 90 and 6 Pentavite drops. Also store in refrigerator and keep no longer than 3-4 days.

(R.Y. Hasting, Australia)

6 parts egg yolk powder
2 parts skimmed powdered milk
1 part ground wheat
1 part wheat germ
½ part fish meal
1½ part yeast
1 part casein
½ part SA 37 vitamin compound
½ part groundnut oil
1 part honey
5 parts water
Mix well and store in refrigerator.

(C. Wilson and N. Hamilton, Australia)

50g white sugar
3mg activated dried yeast
5mg plant pollen

Dilute the ingredients with 3 500 ml of boiling water which forms into a paste. Once cool add the following ingredients:

20mg spoonful Minamino
2½mg Becosym "B" group structure
2½mg fresh minced beef
Mix well and store in refrigerator.

(B.A. Peck, UK)

2 tablespoons cane syrup
1 cup Pro-Nutro
1 raw egg yolk (do not use raw egg white as this can inhibit the absorption of Biotin, which is involved in carbon dioxide fixation and in fat and protein metabolism)
½ teaspoonful multi-vitamin syrup
⅛ teaspoonful Calsup powder
1¼ litres of water
Mix well and store in refrigerator

(Dr A.N.S. Abrey, SA)

4 tablespoons brown sugar
3 tablespoons golden syrup
2 tablespoons honey
1 tablespoon Avisup soluble vitamin powder
Add adequate amount of water, mix well and store in refrigerator.

2 tablespoons brown sugar
1 tablespoon of either honey or syrup
1 teaspoon Avisup soluble vitamin powder
¼ teaspoon Bovril
1 cup plain Pro-Nutro
4 cups water water
Mix well and store in refrigerator.

(L. Saayman, SA)

6 tablespoons brown sugar
4 tablespoons golden syrup
2 drops Abidec vitamin supplement
1¼ teaspoon Bovril
1 teaspoon Haliborange
1,5 litres of hot water
Mix well and store in refrigerator.

(J. Scheepers, SA)

4 tablespoons brown sugar
4 tablespoons syrup
1 tablespoon Horlicks
1 tablespoon honey
$\frac{1}{4}$ teaspoon Bovril
Yolk of an egg

(D. Norval, SA)

1 tablespoon honey
3 tablespoons brown sugar
1 tablespoon golden syrup
$\frac{1}{8}$ teaspoon Bovril
1 teaspoon Haliborange
4-6 drops Abidec
1 litre water
Store in airtight container in refrigerator

6 tablespoonfuls brown sugar
6 tablespoons honey/syrup
1 tablespoons Vidalin
$\frac{1}{4}$ teaspoon Bovril
1 egg yolk
1 litre water
Store in airtight container in refrigerator

(T. Konigkramer, SA)

Greenfood

Fresh washed greenfood should be supplied regularly as it provides the vitamins and minerals needed to complete a balanced diet. Preferably given in limited quantities with any leftovers being removed each evening. Defrosted greens should not be supplied if a bird is to remain healthy. Some greens will be ignored by certain species while relished by others, but during breeding, birds may develop tastes for certain items which were previously refused. Supplying of home grown greenfood is by far the safest way to enable the birds to take enjoyment from a wider choice. If it is not possible to grow one's own greens, first soak in a weak solution of salt water to which a couple of drops of L.D.C. is added. A half hour later, rinse under running water whereby the greens will now be limp and insecticide free.

Dark coloured greens have a high nutritional value, namely carrot tops, spinach, young cabbage and cauliflower leaves, broccoli, peas-in-the-pod, Brussel sprouts, beetroot and onion tops, cucumber, gherkins, Swiss chard and kale. Yellow or pale greens such as lettuce, celery and watercress are often quoted as being lower in food value but this point is much debated by aviculturists. Some vegetables are termed non-greens, but are of great value to the birds, namely carrots, corn-on-the-cob, potatoes, squash, turnips, swedes yams, radishes, chillis and red peppers. All can be shredded or finely chopped to form a salad before feeding. Birdkeepers who reside by the sea can include seaweed as an additional extra. Lovebirds are partial to fresh twigs and leaves of an apple, pear, peach, blue gum and silver oak which they strip and eat. Also used to a lesser degree is sugar cane stems, pumpkin shoots, lawn clippings and fodder grasses, the latter best fed on the sod.

Scientifically composed pellets have largely replaced freshly mixed greens, especially in winter, as a convenience and to ensure a regular balanced diet. Pellets contain many ingredients and used widely for poultry, domesticated pigeons, rabbits and cattle. Dehydrated greenfood has made its appearance in recent years and is available from pet stores.

Wildfood

All parts of the plant can be fed to birds, i.e. inflorescences of seeding grasses in the half ripe "milky stage", watery stems and tips of young blades, flowering heads, leaf buds, roots and bulbs of a wide variety of weeds. Wildfoods growing on road verges, must be avoided at all costs as they may have been contaminated by animals or sprayed with weed killer. There is of course plenty of places where it can be picked with safety, namely in your own garden, in fields, on small holdings, on neglected cultivation and the edge of virgin forests. Further afield on farms where weeds are usually tolerated, therefore they grow in profusion.

Plants useful to birds (Indigenous and Exotic)

The following is a representative sample of trees, shrubs, flowers and grasses which provide food in the form of fruit, berries, nectar, blossoms, seeds, leaves, tubers and legumes.

Seeds, Blossoms, Shoots or leaves

Apple or Peru	*Nicandra physaloides*
Awnless barnyard grass	*Echinochloa colona*
Baboon thread	*Portulaca oleracea*
Barnyard grass	*Echinochloa crus-galli*
Bindura bamboo	*Oxytenanthera abyssinica*
Bitter melon	*Citrullus lantcnus*
Black wattle	*Acacia meainsii*
Blackjack	*Bidens pilosa*
Blade thorn	*Acacia fleckii*
Blue thorn acacia	*Acacia erubescens*
Blue water bush	*Cerbena bonariensis*
Bottle gourd	*Lagernaria siceraria*
Brown-rayed knapweed	*Centaurea jacea*
Buffalo-thorn	*Acacia erioloba*
Candle acacia	*Acacia hebeclada*
Cape Marigold	*Arctotheca calendula*
Cape pigweed	*Amaranthus thunbergii*
Cartwheels	*Ascepias affinis*
Castor oil plant	*Ricinus communis*
Chickweed	*Stellaria media*
Coast bean bush	*Sophora inhambanensis*
Cockscomb	*Amaranthus hybridus*
Common wild oats	*Avena futua*
Cudweed	*Gnapalium luteo-album*
Curled dock	*Rumex crispus*
Devil's thorn	*Tribulus terresiris*
Fat-hen	*Chenopodium album*
Flaky acacia	*Acacia exuvialis*
Forest bride's bush	*Pavetta lanceolata*
Garlic mustard	*Alliaria petiolata*
Gemsbok kom-kommer	*Acanthosicyos naudiniana*
Ground thistle	*Sonchus nanus*
Groundsel	*Senecia vulgaris*
Guinea grass	*Panicum maximum*

Guineafowl grass	*Rottboelie exaltata*
Horseweed fleabane	*Conyza canadensis*
Johnson grass	*Sorghum halepense*
Jungle rice	*Echinochloa colona*
Khakiweed	*Alternanthera pungens*
Korakan	*Eleusine coracane*
Little seeded canary grass	*Phalaris minor*
Maltese star thistle	*Centaurea melitensis*
Natal red-top	*Rhynchelytrum repens*
Natal wild banana	*Strelitzia nicolia*
Oat-seed grass	*Ehrharta longifora*
Pepper tree	*Combretum molle*
Pepperweed	*Lepidium africanum*
Persian milk vetch	*Astragalus edulis*
Pretty lady	*Cleome rubelia*
Ragwort	*Senecio jacobaea*
Red garden sorrel	*Oxalis latifolia*
Red heart	*Acacia nilotica*
Red-veined dock	*Rumex sanguineus*
Rescue grass	*Bromus unionloides*
Rye-grass	*Lotium perenne*
Satinflower	*Stellaria holostea*
Sharp dock	*Rumex conglomeratus*
Shepherd's tree	*Boscia albitrunca*
Slender wild oats	*Avena barbata*
Sorrel	*Rumex scutatus*
Sow-thistle	*Sonchus oleraceus*
Spanish black-jack	*Bidens bipinnata*
Spindlepod	*Cleome monophylia*
Star thistle	*Centaurea calcitrapa*
Striped wild cucumber	*Cucumis myriocarpus*
Sunbird tree	*Cordyla africana*
Swamp panicum	*Panicum subalibidum*
Tall fleabane	*Conyza sumatrensis*
Tall wild oats	*Avena sterillis*
Themeda	*Themeda triandra*
Three-throned acacia	*Acacia senegal*
Umsobo	*Solanum nigrum*
Wild barley	*Hordeummurinum*
Wild buckwheat	*Jagopyrum esculentum*
Wild cucumber	*Coccinia rehmannii*
Wild grain sorghum	*Sorghum bicolor*
Wild nemesia	*Nemesia fruticans*
Wild teasle	*Dipsacus sylvestris*
Winter wild oats	*Avena sterillis subsp.*
Yellow sorrel	*Oxalis pes-caprae*

Tubers

Aerial yam	*Dioscorea bulbifera*
Arum lily potato	*Commiphora mollis*
Bushman root	*Ceropegia multiflora*
Cape asparagus	*Aponogeton distachyos*
Cassava	*Manihot esculenta*
Greater yam	*Dioscorea alata*
Iminyela	*Sommiphora mossambicensis*
Lesser yam	*Dioscore esculenta*
Shepherd's tree	*Boscia albitrunia*
Wander's food	*Impomoea simplex*
White Guinea yam	*Dioscorea rotundata*
Yellow Guinea yam	*Discorea cayenensis*
Zulu round potato	*Solenostemon rotundifolius*

Legumes

Gemsbuck bean	*Tylosema esculentum*
Jack bean	*Canavalia ensisformis*
Kalahari pod berry	*Dialium engleranum*
Monkey bread	*Piliostgegma thonningii*
Monkey pod	*Cassia petersiana*
Sherbet tree	*Dialium schlechteri*
Sunbird tree	*Cordyla africana*

Fruit and berries

Albinsi grape	*Vitis pallida*
African cranberry	*Vacinum exul*

African ebony	*Diospyrus mespiliformis*
African holly	*Ilex mitis*
African mulberry	*Morus mesozygia*
African olive	*Vitex cienkowskii*
Akee	*Blighia sapida*
Angolan plum	*Chrysobalanus orbicularis*
Arabian wolfberry	*Lycium arabicum*
Azerolier	*Crataegus azarolus*
Baboon's breakfast	*Hexalobus monopetalas*
Baobab	*Adansonia digitata*
Bastard currant	*Ozoroa reticulata*
Bastard saffronwood	*Cassine peragua*
Batoka plum	*Flacourtia indica*
Bird plum	*Berchemia discolor*
Bird's brandy	*Lantana rugosa*
Blackberry	*Rubus ludwigii*
Blue guarri	*Euclee crispa*
Buffalo-thorn	*Ziziphus mucronata*
Bugweed	*Solanum mauritianum*
Bulungu	*Cararium edule*
Candelabra tree	*Euphorbia ingens*
Canthium	*Cararium longiflorum*
Cape beech	*Rapanee melanophloeos*
Cape chustnut	*Calodendron capense*
Cape fig	*Ficus capensis*
Cape gooseberry	*Physalis peruviana*
Cape holly	*Ilex mitis*
Cape sumach	*Colpoon compressum*
Cat-thorn	*Scutia myrtina*
Common crowberry	*Rhus pentheri*
Common spike-thorn	*Maytenus heterophylla*
Common taaibos	*Rhus phroides*
Common turkey berry	*Canthium inerme*
Curatella plum	*Parinarium curatellaefolium*
Dogwood	*Rhamnus prinoides*
Doundate	*Sarcocephalus esculentus*
Dune jackal-berry	*Diospryus rotundifolia*
Dwarf mobolo	*Parinari capensis*
Egusi	*Cucumeropsis eduis*
Ensete	*Ensete ventricosa*
False marula	*Lannea stuhlmannii*
Forest cocoa tree	*Erythroxylum pictum*
Forest milkberry	*Manikara discolor*
Giant-leaved fig	*Fisuc vogelli*
Gingerbread plum	*Parinarium macrophylla*
Hard pear	*Olinia cymosa*
Haronga	*Haronga madagas-cariensis*
Icaco plum	*Ghrysobalanus icaco*
Inkberry	*Phytolacca dodecandra*
Jacket plum	*Pappea capensis*
Jakkalsbessie	*Diospyros mespiliformis*

Nectar

African sprangletop	*Leptochloa capillacea*
Bastard cobas	*Cyphostemma juttae*
Beach salvia	*Salvia africana-lutea*
Bitter aloe	*Aloe ferox*
Black-bearded protea	*Protea lepidocarpodendron*
Blue climbing pea	*Clitoria ternatea*
Candelabra aloe	*Aloe candelabrum*
Cape Fuchsia	*Phygelius capensis*
Cape honeysuckle	*Tecomaria capensis*
Cape kaffirboom	*Erythrina caffra*
Cat-thorn	*Scutia myrtina*
Coast hibiscus	*Hibiscus tiliaceus*
Crane flower	*Strelitzia reginae*
Delphinium	*Delphinium macrocentron*
Flat-flowered aloe	*Aloe marlothii*
Golden Shower	*Pyrostegia venusta*
Hottentot white protea	*Protea lacticolor*

The ARU does not necessarily endorse the views of contributors.

Livefood

Is a principal source of animal protein needed by birds, particularly for the growth of young. Little, or in some cases, nothing is known of their livefood intake in the wild. Fortunately due to the popularity of many species, aviculturists have had the opportunity to observe or experiment with various types producing satisfactory results. It is not easy to supply a regular variety of livefood daily from a garden if one lives in a city. Living in the country is a different matter, except that this daily task might not always be possible. It is during these times that alternatives must be sought. A substitute for, or an addition to livefood is a mixture commercially known as Insectile Food which is prepacked and sold in all pet stores. The tubifex worm used by aquarists can be purchased in all countries. In Africa it is difficult to purchase any form of livefood with the exception of mealworms and silkworms which are advertised in local newspapers from time to time. The Mopane worm has recently been made available from Zimbabwe. In the UK and USA a fair selection of livefood can be purchased in the form of locusts, crickets, morio worms, live ants' cocoons, housefly, blowfly and bee larvae, red wax and whiteworms, Corsican stick insects and green aphids.

Maggots

They are the least popular method of securing livefood. In the UK they are available in three main types, namely "standard" (the larval form of the blue-bottlefly), the "squatt" (housefly) and "Pinkie" (green bottlefly). To produce one's own maggots, a box with a wire mesh lid can be hung up on a branch or pole in an out-of-the-way corner of the garden. Poultry offal or any lean meat is suitable to attract flies. Maggots can be removed with a pair of tweezers and dropped in meal, where kept for 2-3 days to rid themselves of all traces of meat. They are safe to be fed to one's birds when the black line which is visible down the centre of the body has finally disappeared. To attract fruit flies place any form of fruit inside a small, square welded mesh cage with a flip top door for easy access.

Silkworms and Mopane worms

The Mopane worm *Gonimbrasia belina* derives its name from its main food source, the tree of the same name *Colophosphermum mopane*. More commonly known is the Silkworm *Bombyx mori* which is presently being fed to birds in the early stages of their growth, have been domesticated to such an extent that they no longer occur in the wild, but are excellent as a standby in times when other livefood has been in short supply.

The Silkworm feeds predominantly on a single plant species, that of the mulberry *Morus* spp., whereas the Mopane Worm also feeds on the Marula *Sclerocarya birra*, Large num num *Carissa macrocarpa*, Karee *Rhus lancea*, Red beech *Protorhus longifolia* and Pigeonwood *Trema guineensis*. The female moth lays her eggs singly, in small batches or in clusters of several hundred. The larvae is black, specked greenish and more or less banded with a paler green, including a series of short black or dark reddish brown spines. The closely allied moth *G tyrrhea* occurs in willows, wattles, pines, poplars and oaks. These worms which weigh around 13 grams and measure around 11cm are no stranger to the indigenous people of Africa who have included them in their diet long before the white man set foot on this continent. The worms are processed into powder form and made available to birdkeepers, but at only a few outlets in Africa, making it extremely expensive to purchase.

Termites

Termites which are often misleadingly called "white ants" occur in the tropical and sub-tropical regions of the world.

Nearly 2 000 known species of which 400 occur in Africa, 55 in the USA and Canada, two in Europe and 182 in Australia.

Family 1: Mastotermitidae

A primitive Australian termite with only one living species.

Family 2: Hodotermitidae (Harvester termites)

Does damage to lawns by producing small heaps of loose soil, only 3cm or so high. They are soon blown away by wind or washed away by rain. Nests being deep make unearthing extremely difficult. They can be observed during daylight hours collecting pieces of grass.

Family 3: Kalotermitidae (Wood-inhabiting termites)

They have no connection with the soil, making their homes in felled logs, dead branches and in seasoned timber which is used for the building trade.

Family 4: Rhinotermitidae (Subterranean wood-eating termites)

Nest cavity is usually at the base of a mound, just below the surface, ranging up to 36cm in diameter and 30cm in depth. Food includes material containing cellulose, from dung and humus to sound dead wood.

Family 5: Termopsidae (Wood dwelling termites)

Requires an adequate moisture supply from the soil. Food collected from decayed wood, rooted in the ground or in contact with the soil surface.

Family 6: Termitidae

Lives in mounds constructed with soil bound together with a cement (insects' excretement) which, when dry is hard and waterproof. Major wood destroyer in buildings.

214

INSECTS AND OTHER INVERTEBRATES

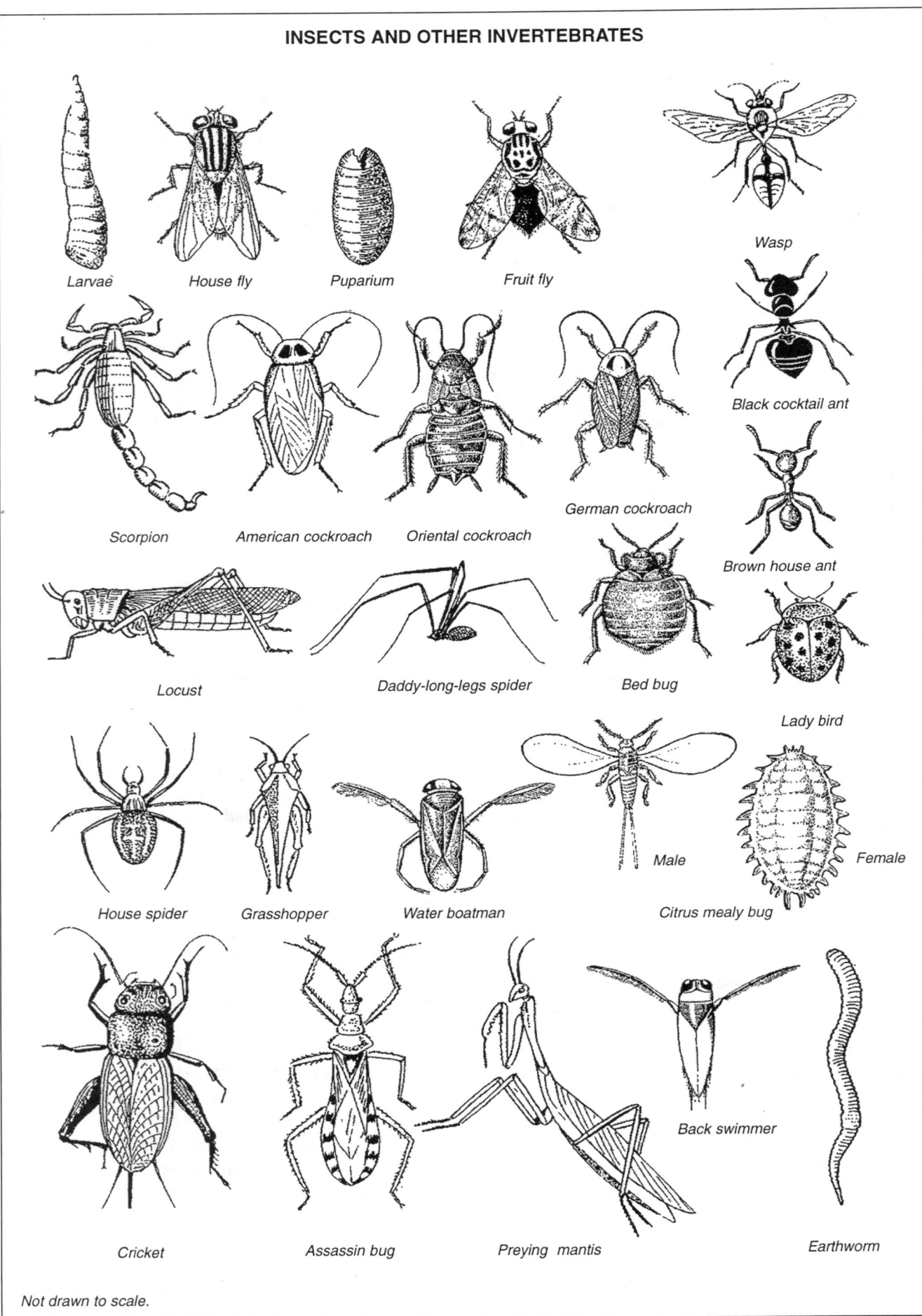

Larvae

House fly

Puparium

Fruit fly

Wasp

Black cocktail ant

Scorpion

American cockroach

Oriental cockroach

German cockroach

Brown house ant

Locust

Daddy-long-legs spider

Bed bug

Lady bird

House spider

Grasshopper

Water boatman

Male

Female

Citrus mealy bug

Cricket

Assassin bug

Preying mantis

Back swimmer

Earthworm

Not drawn to scale.

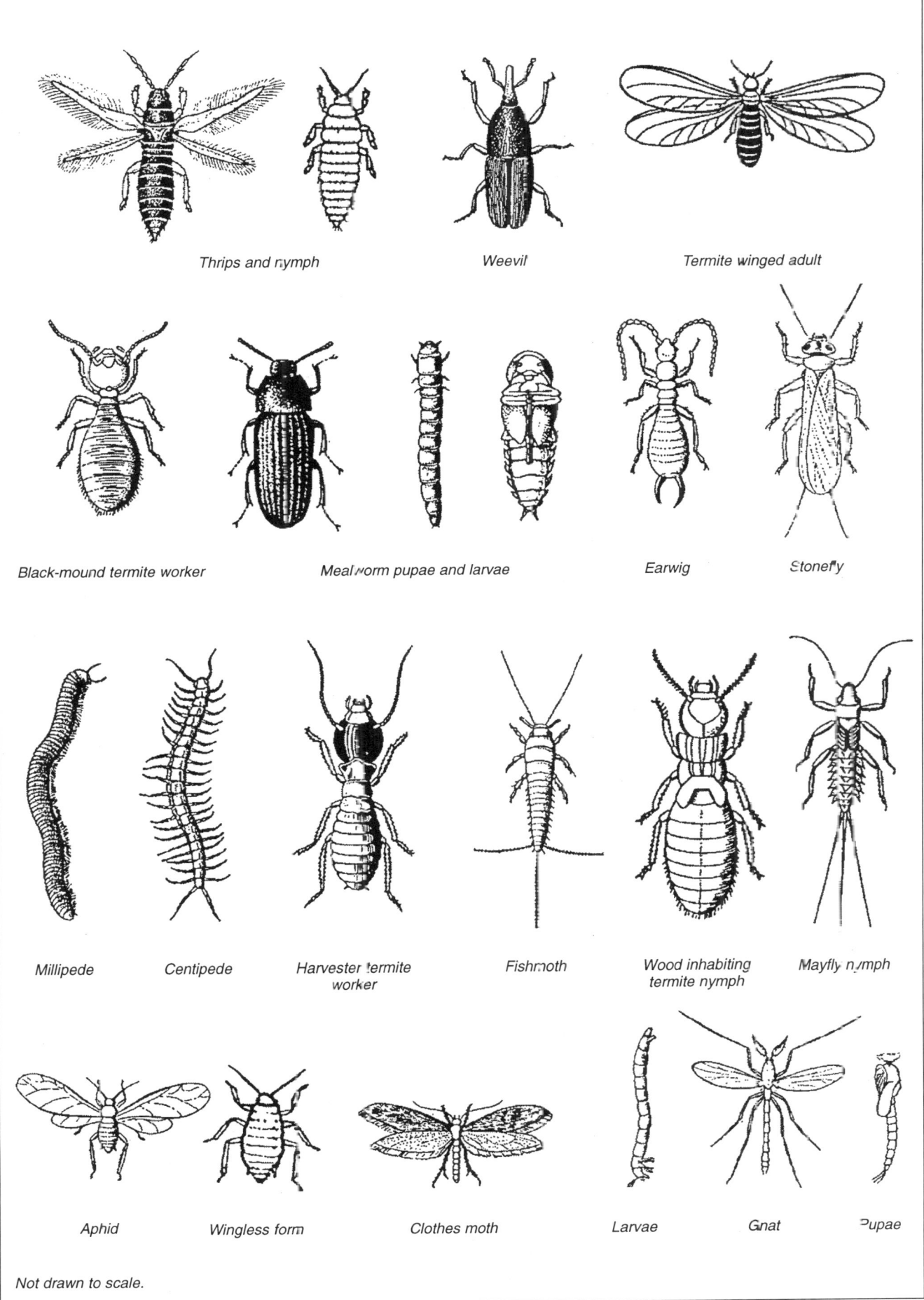

Thrips and nymph   Weevil   Termite winged adult

Black-mound termite worker   Mealworm pupae and larvae   Earwig   Stonefly

Millipede   Centipede   Harvester termite worker   Fishmoth   Wood inhabiting termite nymph   Mayfly nymph

Aphid   Wingless form   Clothes moth   Larvae   Gnat   Pupae

Not drawn to scale.

USA (northwest; became established in various towns in France, and also Hamburg in Germany).	*Rhinotermitidae* Eastern Subterranean Termite	*Reticulitermes flavipes*
USA (Florida)	Dampwood Termites	*see Prorhinoterimes*
USA (SouthWest)	*Termitidae* Soldierless Desert Termite Nasutiform Termites	
USA (South)	*Kalotermitidae* Powder-post Termites	*see Cryptotermes Calcaritermes*
USA (Florida and in Western States)	Dampwood Termites	*see Neotermes Paraneotermes*
USA (South from S. Carolina to Texas)	Drywood Termites	*see Incisitermes* and others
USA (Western and south-western states)	*Hodotermitidae* Rotten Wood Termites	
AUSTRALIA (southern Queensland, eastern NSW, Victoria, south-eastern SA and south-western WA).	*Termitidae*	Sub-family *Nasutiterminae Nasutitermes walkeri*
AUSTRALIA along coast from central QDL south-ern NSW).	*Rhinotermitidae* Clay Mound Termite	Sub-family *Coptotemitinae Coptotermes lacteus*
EUROPE (Mediterranean coast from Portugal to Greece and onto the Middle East)	*Kalotermitidae*	*Kalotermes flavicollis*
EUROPE (extends north to Bordeaux and north-ern Italy.	*Rhinotermitidae*	*Reticulitermes lucifugus*
ASIA (established from Port Elizabeth, South Africa to Mozambique)	Kalotermitidae West Indian Dry Wood Termite	*Crypotermes brevis*
South Africa	*Termitidae* Black Mound Termite	*Amitermes hastatus*
South Africa	*Hodotermitidae* Snouted Harvester Termite	*see Trinervitemes*
SA (Northern Gauteng, Namibia Zimbabwe and along Limpopo)	*Termitidae* Large Fugus Grower	*Macrotermes natalensis*
SA (Western Cape Province)	*Termitidae* Common Fungus Grower	*Termes badius*
South Africa	*Termitidae* Transvaal Fungus Grower	*Termes transvaalensis*
South Africa	*Termitidae* Lesser Fungus Grower	*Termes latericius*

When birds are fed termites they are very selective in avoiding the soldiers, but young birds or newly introduced birds may not be aware of the dangers of them becoming lodged inside the throat with tightly gripping jaws. Very little success has been achieved in trying to dislodge the head of a soldier termite which is often fatal. Fortunately they account for only 5% of the entire nest colony. After breaking open a mound it is advisable to keep the termites contained within the chambers of the broken off portions. They must be kept in a cool place as termites are only used to living in dark air-conditioned situations. They may live for a month or longer if housed in slightly damp sugar sacks. In South Africa they are kept alive for months for study purposes. A detailed account, including an illustration of an artificial nest is described by S.H. Skaife *African Insect Life* (pp 43-45). In Australia termites are stored in 100 or 200 litre drums. The drum is given a tin lid, but first cover the opening with a piece of hessian and stand in a shady area if housed outdoors. As a precaution against black ants entering under the lid, smear a layer of grease about 50-100mm around the base. Fill the drum with sand to a depth of about 100mm which should be adequate to hold small upright timber billets. It is essential to moisten the sand and the billets up to the rim to make it self-sustainable to hold a colony of termites. To encourage the termites to congregate at the top gently moisten the sand and billets around the opening. It must be remembered that not all termite species are suitable as livefood with many containing high acid levels which should be avoided at all costs. (See D.J. Borror and R.E. White, *A Field Guide to Insects of America north of Mexico;* M. Chinery, *A Field Guide to the Insects of Britain and Northern Europe;* R.D. Hughes, *Living Insects – Australia* and S.H. Skaife, *African Insect Life*).

Mealworms

Mealworms are the larval stage of the beetle *Tenebrio molitor* and an extremely valuable source of readily available livefood. The method of breeding mealworms varies very little in most countries. To start a culture one requires a wooden, asbestos or metal container. It need not be more than 60cm long x 45cm wide x 30cm high. As the wooden whisky boxes that were once easily obtainable from all liquor stores are now scarce, the asbestos container which is available from most garden outlets or the metal trunk sold in rural trading stores are ideal for the purpose. Whichever one is selected it must be able to hold a tight fitting cover to prevent beetles and young worms from escaping. For the purpose of ventilation it would be advisable to use a sheet of perforated zinc, or fine wire gauze as a cover or drill small holes in a solid lid itself. In cooler regions a container can have a 100W light bulb set in the middle beneath the lid which is thermostatically controlled at about 21°C. In the UK the Lesser mealworm or Buffalo worm *Alphitobius diaperinus* is also bred commercially.

Fill the base of a container with dry barley meal or bran, in UK also red wheat, to a height of 8cm. Some bird-keepers avoid bran as it contains phytic acid which binds calcium and so reduces their food value. Poultry chicken meal is therefore recommended. The introduction of yeast, beer or molasses is known to improve the quality of bran. Deposit the first batch of mealworms into the container and include a supply of food in the form of sliced potato, cabbage, apple, carrot or banana skin. Sacking is now placed over this with a further 8cm of bran being placed on top. Repeat this procedure until all three layers of sacking contain mealworms and are being used as adequate food supply. Another method is being used in the USA whereby chopped straw is layed 5cm deep in the base of a container. This is then covered with an old hand towel on which is placed a 4cm layer of bran. A second towel is placed over this layer followed with a further layer of bran. Food supplied is in the form of soaked bread, pieces of fruit and some greens which is adequate. The breeding stock should not be disturbed except for the addition of fresh food which will be necessary occasionally. Do not allow the bran to become damp as the entire culture could be lost. This beetle lays between 200-300 eggs which hatch in about 20 days and reach maturity after 40 days. The eggs are covered with a secretion causing them to stick to bran. New cultures can be taken from existing stock before the life cycle is completed when a mealworm changes into the pupae stage and finally into a beetle. Mealworms may be fed whole or cut-up for the smaller species, after they have turned brown, an indication that they are now fully grown, and fed raw or roasted – the latter being popular in Europe. Birdbreeders also feed half-grown worms to smaller species which are reluctant to eat the fully grown cut-up worms. When stored at 50°C – 80°C they become dormant and will keep for months.

Besides the livefood already mentioned, the following is a list of insects and arthropods which have been fed successfully to certain species, namely gnats, thrip-nymphs, fishmoths, wasp larvae or "grubs", springtails, hairless caterpillars, moths, earwigs, stoneflies, cockroaches, mantises, bugs, spiders, millipedes, ticks, centipedes, yellow and black meadow ants (misnamed "ants" eggs by the trade), slaters, vinegar flies and earthworms.

No attempt has been made to add colloquial names for animal food as it can cause considerable confusion due to the same or very similar names often being used for quite different species.

Softfoods

Softbilled birds is an avicultural term to classify them into five groups, namely omnivores, carnivores, frugivores, insectivores and nectivores.

Typical softbilled birds include louries kingfishers, hornbills, fruit pigeons, barbets, orioles, bulbuls, robins, starlings and sunbirds. Seedeaters should not be fed on dry seed alone and will require a limited amount of softfood all through the year, being much increased during the breeding season. Most birds are very specific and conservative in their eating habits by favouring certain items and showing no interest in others. After the birds have been given ample time in which to reject a newly introduced food, some degree of coaxing may be necessary. One suggestion is to sprinkle the item with a powdered nectar as an inducement. Fortunately finches, especially the *serinus* family, show great interest in anything new offered to them. For many years birdkeepers had to be satisfied with the few proprietary brands of softfoods made available to them, and these were aimed mostly at canary breeding. The high protein breakfast cereal ProNutro soon became the most popular form of softfood. This was followed in recent years by dog cubes which were moistened with water until crumbly, but never allowed to become soggy. Pelleted and powdered softfoods are a more recent innovation which are available to suit the needs of all species. Moistened leftovers must be removed each evening and a new supply given

each morning as it is quick to sour overnight. Many additional softfoods such as yoghurt, maas, bread and butter pudding, pasta, spaghetti, sponge rusks, bread spread with margarine, egg yolk, cottage cheese, putu, peanut butter, crushed biscuits etc, have been offered during the breeding season and when birds are in moult. From the local butcher bone and fishmeal can be purchased fresh being an extra item to their diet. In addition raw minced meat, white fish, bacon rind, ox heart, small pieces of boiled minced liver or kidney, domestic fowl carcass, ground prawns, shrimp and lobster can be offered.

Composition of Commercial Foods, Food Additives, Vitamin Compounds, Home Recipes and Handrearing Formulas

AVI-PLUS for Finches and Softbills is a nourishing, well balanced feed supplement for finches and softbills, containing proteins, vitamins, minerals and trace elements. It supplies your birds with essential amino acids, vitamins, minerals and trace elements, which may be partly or totally absent in a pure seed diet. When birds breed, they will eat more and the well balanced food value ensures that the baby birds grow well and feather perfectly. It is made from pre-cooked, processed ingredients manufactured and passed for human consumption. This ensures maximum digestability and minimum bacteria content, protecting precious baby birds against unnecessary infections. No additions to this diet are recommended (eg eggs) except mixed seeds, fruit and vegetables.

Contains: Maize, wheat, specially prepared soya, sugar, salt, dicalcium phosphate, calcium carbonate, casein, vegetable fat, lysine, methionine, multivitamins, minerals and trace elements.

Feeding instructions: Add 80ml cold water to 100ml Avi-Plus. Mix well to a moist, crumbly texture. Add chopped greens, fruit and soaked or sprouted seed as required.

Recommended daily allowances to be fed in conjunction with a well balanced seed mix.

Out of breeding season: 1 heaped teaspoonful per pair of finches every second day.

In breeding season: 1 heaped teaspoonful per pair of finches daily or twice daily, increase amount according to number of young fed. Larger birds require more food depending on their size.

AVI-PLUS Handrearing: Parakeet has been formulated with syringe feeding in mind. It is highly digestible and when water is added to a creamy consistency, it passes easily through a syringe and crop needle. Because of its digestibility it is recommended for feeding nestling birds from the age of 7 to 10 days after hatching, onwards.

It is completely compatible with Avi-Plus Handrearing: Parrot and in no way replaces Avi-Plus Handrearing: Parrot.

It has a lower percentage protein than Avi-Plus Handrearing: Parrot and this will make it more suitable for rearing smaller species like lovebirds, cockatiels, grass parakeets and rosellas among others. It can also be used for larger parrots once they are over the maximum growth rate on their growth chart. Avi-Plus Handrearing: Parakeet can be mixed with Avi-Plus Handrearing: Parrot where a breeder feels an intermediate nutritional level is required.

It contains proteins and amino acids in the proportions shown to be most suitable for avian species. The carbohydrates have been cooked to ensure complete digestibility and unsaturated as well as saturated vegetable fats have been added at optimal levels as shown by research.

Like Avi-Plus Handrearing: Parrot, is the best quality food for your nestling birds.

Contains: wheat, maize, barley, specially prepared soya, casein, whole egg, dicalcium phosphate, calcium carbonate, lysine, methionine, vegetable fat, salt, sugar, multivitamins, minerals and trace elements.

DIRECTIONS:

1. Mix to a creamy consistency with boiled, cooled water.
2. Warm to 38°C to 40°C
3. Feed only enough to comfortably fill the crop.

AVI-PLUS Handrearing: Parrot is intended for parrot type birds that are removed from the nest for handrearing from about two weeks of age. In order to protect the health of your young birds all the ingredients used are manufactured for human consumption. The product does not require the addition of any further foodstuffs. It was formulated to assist the busy aviculturist by having an instant formula that would suit the majority of nestling parrots. The ease of preparing the food means that most time can be spent on caring for your other birds and their needs.

It has all the necessary proteins, amino acids, vitamins, minerals and trace elements for the development of the young parrot. Calcium and phosphorus have been balanced in the correct ratio so no further additions are recommended.

N.B.: The addition of any other foodstuffs will cause an imbalance between the essential ingredients eg. the proteins, vitamins, minerals and trace elements.

Contains: wheat, maize, barley, specially prepared soya, casein, whole egg, dicalcium phosphate, calcium carbonate, lysine, methionine, vegetable fat, salt, sugar, multivitamins, minerals and trace elements.

Method: To one measure add approximately two measures of cooled boiled water (ie 10g No. 2 to 40g water), enough to give a creamy texture that will flow from the spoon. (The amount of water depends on the age of the parrot and the temperature at which he is kept). Warm the feed to 30°C-40°C, and feed with a specially bent spoon or syringe.

National supplier: Avi-Products cc,
PO Box 1758, Linkhills 3652

POULTRY MULTI-VITAMIN Supplement

Composition: Vitamin A-D3-E-K-B2 (Riboflavin)-B1 (Thiamine)-B6 (Pyrodoxine-B-C (Ascorbic Acid)-Panthothenic Acid-Potassium and Sodium (as salts)

Salisbury SA Veterinary (Pty) Ltd,
PO Box 1785, Kempton Park 1620

PIGEON MULTI-VITAMIN Supplement

Composition: Vitamin A-B1 (Thiamine)-B2 (Riboflavin)-D3-E-B6 (Pyridoxine)-B12-Niasien-Calsium CA-Pantothenic Acid and Manganese

Exceder, PO Box 58119,
Newville 2114

ABIDEC-Multi-vitamin Supplement

Vitamin A-D-B1-B2-B6-C and Nicotin

Parke-Davis Research Labs — a division of
Warner-Lambert SA (Pty) Ltd,
241 Main Road, Retreat 7945

GEVRIL Multi-vitamin supplement

Composition: Vitamin A-D-B-B2-B6-B12-C-E-Niacin-Ca-pantoth-Fe-fumar-L-lyusine-Calcium-Iron-Magnesium-Potassium-Copper and Choline bitartrate.

Lederle — a division of
SA Cyanamid (Pty) Ltd,
52 Electron Avenue, Isando 1600

BEEFEE TABS Nutritional supplement

Composition: Vitamin A1-B1-B2-B12-B6-D3-Folic Acid-Nicotinamide-Calcium-Phosphorus-Copper Manganese-Cob alt-Iron-Fluoride-Zinc and Protein

Centaur Labs (Pty) Ltd,
36 Durban Street, Johannesburg 2001

WHEAT GRASS POWDER

Promotes healthy digestive tract, top condition, better health, optimum fertility and brighter colour. Used together with Earthrise Spirulina when hand-feeding parrot chicks (100 and 500 gram packs)

Agents: Lakeview Farm,
PO Box 6, St Lucia 3936

EARTHRISE SPIRULINA

A remarkable food supplement to condition breeding birds and handreared chicks. (100 and 500 gram packs)

Agents: Lakeview Farm,
PO Box 6, St Lucia 3936

HI-ENERGY SPIRULINA

A highly acceptable blend of nature's own health and vitality products. The scientifically formulated supplement is made up from Spirulina platesis, sun dried Kelp, Soy Protein, powdered dried skim milk, Siberian

Ginseng, Fructose and charcoal. It is one of the most concentrated sources of pure food and nutrition known – high in protein, high in carbohydrates, yet low in fat. Promotes healthy feather growth adding lustere and sheen. Kelp is the most abundant supplier of natural minerals. It contains over 20 different kinds of minerals including many difficult to find, but important trace minerals. Ginseng has been used for thousands of years in the East where it is known to strengthen the heart and nervous system and build up health, vitality, a resistance to disease and promotes fertility. Skimmed milk and Soy protein are both complete proteins. Easy digestable Fructose introduces instant energy, is sweeter than sugar making this product highly palatable and acceptable to most species of birds. (100 and 500 gram packs).

Agents: Lakeview Farm, PO Box 6, St Lucia 3936

CALSUP POWDER

Provides calcium in balanced, easy assimilated form with 1-25g measures daily sprinkled on food

Composition: Vitamin A-D3-E-Calcium Gluconate-Calcium Phosphate Dibasic-Calcium-Lactate-Calcium Glycerophosphate and Iron (as ferrous Fumarate) in a liver/yeast base.

Centaur Labs (Pty) Ltd,
36 Durban Street, Johannesburg 2001

AVI-SUP Soluble multivitamin

Feeding recommendations: Especially formulated containing 13 essential vitamins in the proportions that suit most avian species. When used regularly as a dietary supplement it will promote the general good health of your birds all year round.

Readily dissolve in water and the concentration is such that it is easy to measure the correct amount using the usual household measuring spoon.

1. Add 1 rounded teaspoon (5g) vitamin powder to one litre of water.

2. Mix thoroughly.

3. Can also be used in liquid nectar foods.

Sold in 100g or 350g bottles and in 1kg plastic buckets.

Caution: Not for human consumption. Store in a cool dry place. Do not store in direct sunlight.

Natonal Supplier: Avi-Products cc
PO Box 1758, Linkhills 3652

AVI-CAL – A Calcium supplement

The calcium/phosphate ratio has been adjusted so that when fed with a supplement or soft food and a mixed seed diet, adequate levels of calcium and phosphorus will be available in the correct ratio for most purposes, i.e. egg laying and rearing chicks. It is most easily fed with "softfood", to which it must be added before moistening.

Directions:

1. One to two heaped teaspoons to one kilogram of softfood on dry weight.

2. Mix thoroughly with the softfood before moistening.

3. Can be used in conjunction with Avid-sup multivitamins and Avi-plus feed supplements.

Composition per 1000g
Calcium 262g
Phosphorus 135g
Avi-Products cc, PO Box 1758 Linkh lls 3652

PIET SCHOEMAN's ELIXIR – Vitamin supplement for pigeons.

Composition: Each 5ml contains Cyanocobalamine (Vitamin B12) 35 mg.

Allvet (Pty) Ltd, PO Box 1825, Honeydew 2040.

AVI-PLUS PARROT BIX

(For parrots and parakeets). Contain proteins, vitamins, minerals and trace elements that may be partially or wholly absent from a pure seed diet. The well balanced nutritional value of Avi-plus parrot bix ensures that chicks grow well and feather beautifully. For your breeding birds the pellets supply dicalcium phosphate and lime for egg shell formation, as well as ten other minerals and trace elements. They also supply proteins and vitamin E – among thirteen other vitamins – to ensure maximum fertility.

The Bix are easy to feed, especially with greens, fruit, soaked seeds or boiled beans and maize. Because of their size they can be conveniently mixed with sunflower and other seeds in a self feeder for the birds to help themselves over weekends or while you are away.

Contains: maize, wheat, specially prepared soya, casein, vegetable fats, dicalcium phosphate, calcium carbonate, salt, sugar, lysine, methionine, multivitamins, minerals and trace elements.

Feeding instructions:

For softfood mix one part of Bix with two parts of soaked seeds or cooked seeds (eg. maize and peas) and one part chopped greens and fruit.

For dry feeding with dry seeds mix one part of Bix with four parts of seed mixture including sunflower.
1kg, 5kg and 10kg packs.

AVI-MOULT

Is a multivitamin and amino acid supplement designed for cage birds and aviary birds during the moult.

When the birds are moulting their bodies have to produce a complete covering of feathers within three to six weeks. Although we always think of feathers as being so light, they are on average 6% to 7% of the bird's body weight and in some cases this is the same weight as the bird's skeleton! This means that the bird's system is under some stress during this time, particularly if the essential amino acids most required for moulting are limited in their diet.

Most seeds are low in two of the essential amino acids most needed for forming feathers, i.e. lysine and methionine. This means that a supplementary source of these amino acids is essential to ensure a complete successful moult. The well balanced multivitamins also help keep the bird in excellent physical health enabling the feathers to grow smoothly and continuously and leaving no marks and feather breaks.

Feeding instructions: Add one rounded teaspoonful (5g) to one litre of water. Mix well. Mix a fresh amount daily during moulting time. Stop once moulting is complete.

Caution: Not for human consumption. Store in a cool dark place. Do not store in direct sunlight. Keep out of reach of children.

Avi-Products cc, PO Box 1758 Linkhills 3652.

AVI-STRESS – Multivitamins and Electrolytes

Feeding recommendations: Avi-Stress is a combination of Vitamins and Electrolytes specially formulated to assist birds that have undergone stress as a result of travelling or handling. The electrolytes help restore the essential salt balance in the blood serum. The multivitamins in Avi-Stress and in particular the Vitamin C ensure that a suitable level of essential vitamins be maintained, as during stress the bird's normal intake of vitamins may be insufficient.

Directions: Add one rounded teaspoon (5g) Avi-Stress to 1 litre drinking water. Treat for three to five days.

Caution: Use only as directed. Mix fresh quantity daily. Store in a cool dry place away from direct sunlight.

Avi-Products cc, PO Box 1758 Linkhills 3652.

PHENIX STRESSPAC – for vitamin and glucose supplementation during periods of stress

During breeding and growth in case of low resistance and during moulting and after treatment of diseases.

Composition: Vitamin A-D3-E-K3-B1-B2-B6-B12-C (Glucose)-Nicotinamide-Calcium-Pantothenate and Folic Acid.

Phenix SA (Pty) Ltd, PO Box 1825 Honeydew 2040.

AVI-PLUS PARROT AND PARAKEET FOOD SUPPLEMENT

Contains proteins, vitamins, minerals and trace elements that may be partially or wholly absent from a pure seed diet. The well-balanced nutritional value ensures that chicks grow well and feather beautifully. It is manufactured from pre-cooked, processed ingredients intended for human consumption, which guarantees maximum digestion and minimal bacterial content and protects the chicks from unnecessary infections.

Contains: Maize, wheat, specially prepared soya, casein, vegetable fats, dicalcium phosphate, calcium carbonate, salt, sugar, lysine, methionine, multivitamins, minerals and trace elements.

Feeding instructions: To 100ml add 80ml cold water. Mix well. Add chopped greens, fruit and soaked seeds as required. Recommended daily allowances to be fed in conjunction with a well balanced seed mix:

Small birds, e.g. Lovebirds – 1 heaped teaspoon per bird.
Medium birds, e.g. Ringnecks – 2 heaped teaspoons per bird.
Parrots, e.g. African Greys – 1 heaped tablespoon per bird.

Breeding birds will require more food, depending on the number of young they are feeding.

Avi-Products cc, PO Box 1758 Linkhills 3652.

Home Recipes

3 cups biscuit and egg rearing food
3 cups wheat germ
3 cups Hi-Pro softfood mix
1½ cups ground sunflower kernels
1 tablespoonful ground kelp (seaweed)
1 tablespoonful linseed
1 tablespoonful soya bean flour
6 tablespoonfuls of the above ingredients is mixed with a slice of insectivorous cake which is first crumbled.
4 tablespoonfuls sprouted seed is then added which aerates the mixture, keeping it crumbly, not allowing it to become too wet.
(K. Sietas, Australia)

2 parts whole wheat brown bread
2 parts ProNutro (dampened with milk)
Add once a week a multi-vitamin / mineral supplement
Add twice a week Calsup
Mix thoroughly and give fresh daily.
(Dr W.D. Russell, SA)

3 Cups Putu (African indigenous name for maize meal) boiled in water until it has evaporated, causing it to form into lumps similar to that of dry porridge.
Add water or milk and give fresh daily.
(A. Joao, Mozambique)

14 parts dried crumbs
2 parts dried skimmed milk
1 part bran
1 part wheat germ (not oil) 1 part groundnut oil
1 part sunflower oil
1 part iodized salt
1 part dried egg yolk
(L. Goodman, SA)

5 hard boiled eggs (mashed)
¼ cup ProNutro
¼ teaspoonful Marmite
1 tablespoonful sunflower oil
½ teaspoonful wheat germ oil
Mix well and store in refrigerator.
(N. Grobler, SA)

Sunflower seed, groundnuts, well cooked maize and rice, raw green peas and potatoes, hard boiled egg yolk, uncut, uncooked spaghetti, ProNutro are mixed with water using a blender and the occasional meat from a bone may be included.
(P. Pascoe, SA)

4 Raw eggs
1½ cups Canary Rearing food
1 Ox heart, minus fat
2 teaspoonfuls Glucose
1 teaspoonful Calcium
1 teaspoonful Cod liver oil
1 teaspoonful Vidalin
Mix well and then store in refrigerator.
(T. Konigkramer, SA)

500g shelled groundnuts
3 cups ProNutro
3 cups chicken rearing mash
2 cups Mini Chunk dog biscuits
2 hard boiled eggs
½ tin Butch chicken or beef dog food
2 tablespoonfuls honey
40 drops Abidec
Mix well and then store in refrigerator.
(T. Konigkramer, SA)

1 cup flour
1 cup bread crumbs
Add ½ cup milk to moisten
1 cup raisins
1 cup groundnut butter
Mix the above ingredients and then bake at 350°C for one hour or until it is brown.

(A. Black, Australia)

1 tablespoonful honey / glucose
Vitamin syrup
Thick maize meal porridge
Given fresh daily.

(D. Pringle, SA)

1 part whole wheat brown bread
1 part ProNutro
Wheat germ oil (10 drops to each part of the above mixed ingredients)
Add water and give fresh daily.

(N. Grobler, SA)

½ cup Avisup canary rearing food
½ cup Nyoni rearing food
1 cup sprouted seed
Mix above ingredients then add –
1 tablespoonful Avisup Trace Elements
1 tablespoonful multi-vitamin powder
1 tablespoonful SMA powder
Mix above ingredients then add –
1 grated carrot
1 hard boiled egg (mashed)
1 grated apple
Chopped spinach / chard
Twice weekly add 1 tablespoonful Cod liver oil
Mix thoroughly and give fresh daily

E.A. Clewlow, SA)

140g fish meal
140g bone meal
140g soya bean flour
280g shrimp meal
340 honey
450g lentil meal
2 teaspoonfuls multi-vitamin powder
Mix thoroughly and give fresh daily.

(A Miller, UK)

450g self-raising flour
450g granulated sugar
6 eggs (including shells)
907g honey
250ml rosehip syrup
450g beef dripping
907g groundnuts
907g cheese
450g raisins or sultanas
450g soya bean meal
1 tablespoonful Phillips yeast mixture.
Mix flour, sugar and the eggs together forming a batter. Pour mixture into a baking tin and bake in an oven for about 1¼ hours at 177 °C / Gas Mark 3, until completely hard. When cool, grind into a fine flour. Now grind the groundnuts, cheese, raisins or sultanas in a blender, later adding a canary rearing food. Mix all the ingredients well and store in a large container. Finally heat the honey and at the same time melt the beef dripping. Add the rosehip syrup and pour the contents over the mixture already in the container. When cool, add the soya bean meal and Phillips yeast mixture. Mix thoroughly before feeding.

(R.E. Oxley, UK)

Oxheart
2½ cups Avi-Plus Finch and Softbill Mix
2 tablespoonfuls glucose
2 teaspoonfuls Calsub a or Di-Calcium Phosphate
1 teaspoonful Avi-Plus Multi-Vitamins
½ teaspoonful Cod liver oil
1½ -2 cups of water
Add one oxheart, with fat removed first, then mince very finely. Mix thoroughly before feeding.

(A. Green, SA)

3 parts monkey chow (ground in blender)
1 part baby strained vegetables / fruit
(paw paw or banana) and enzymes (a proteinaceous catalyst produced by living organisms and acting on one or more specific substrates)

(T. Silva, USA)

1 part racing pigeon mix
1 part red beans
1 part lentils
1 part rice
Grind above ingredients into a powder
Add cat chow and sufficient water
Cook in oven for 15 minutes
Add baby strained peas
Small portion of apple sauce
D. Calcium Phosphate

(J. Warner, SA)

1 hard boiled egg
1 small grated carrot
1 small shredded lettuce / carrot tops
Sprinkling of iodized salt
3 tablespoonfuls ProNutro
3 tablespoonfuls canary rearing food
1 tablespoonful sunflower oil
Mix thoroughly and give fresh daily.

(E.A. Clewlow, SA).

Substitutes for insectile or livefoods
(a)
7 parts fine biscuit meal
1 part dried milk powder
1 part wheat germ (not oil)
1 part white fish
(b)
2 parts fine biscuit or baby rusk
1 part shrimp meal or dried flies
1 part dried egg yolk
1 part honey
1 part wheat germ (not oil)
1 part sunflower oil

(L. Goodman, SA)

Softbill Paste
340g paste
340 pea meal
114g coarse oatmeal
28g olive oil
28g moist sugar
57g honey
Stir thoroughly until dissolved, then add 1 cup of crushed hemp seed and a gill of maw seed.

(C.D. Farrar, SA)

4 tablespoonfuls brown sugar
4 tablespoonfuls syrup
1 tablespoonful of Horlicks
1 tablespoonful of honey
¼ tablespoonful Bovril
Yolk of egg

(D. Norval, SA)

Insectivorous cake
750g self-raising flour
500g cottage cheese
250g raw sugar
250g cooking margarine
3 tablespoonfuls vegetable oil
7 eggs, including shells
Blend the margarine, eggs, sugar and vegetable oil together, then add the flour and mix well in a blender, after which the cottage cheese is added. Pour the mixture into shallow cake tins and bake in the oven at 160°C for 1½ hours.

(C. Percival, Australia)

Grit

A supply of fresh grit must always be on hand for birds to ingest as it acts as a grinding agent in the organ called the gizzard, which is a small, tough-skinned chamber, corrugated on the inside and situated below the stomach. Powerful muscles produce a squeezing motion which grinds down the food to a fine pulp, and then passes it on to the duodenum. The lack of grit causes indigestion which is indicated by almost constant eating. The most common form of grit is coarse river sand, used in the building trade. One problem with this sand is that it may carry parasitic roundworms of the nemotode type. Worms and eggs are eliminated if the sand is sterilised by heating in an oven at 160°C for an hour. The sand can be provided in shallow dishes or it can be used as a floor covering in the sleeping quarters, being scattered on the concrete slab. If one is fortunate to live on the coast, sea sand can be used, this having a high salt content. "Health" grit as it is commercially known, furnishes various important minerals and is obtainable from your local pet store or supermarket. Crushed oyster shell is popular, giving a source of lime and iodine including cuttlefish bone, the white chalky-looking skeleton of the cuttlefish, charcoal, well rinsed old mortar and limestone. The latter having calcium which is necessary for bone formation and egg shell production. Freshly baked eggshell is a valuable adjunt to grit and should be made available regularly. "Iodine nibbles" are also useful for the same purpose.

Grit Cake recipe

Crushed charcoal
Coarse salt / sea or river sand
Flower of sulphur powder
Iodine
Shellgrit
Red sand
Few dog pellets (crushed)

Mix thoroughly with sufficient water to form a thick "dough". Pour ingredients into containers to form the shape of "cakes" then allow to dry in the sun for a few days.

(J. Vermeulen, SA)

Waterers

Drinking and bathing utensils come in a wide variety of sizes and colours and constructed in a vast number of materials. They vary from household food containers such as tuna and sardine tins, tupperware, wet tray retainers for flower pots and motor tyres cut in half, enabling both halves to be used. Unfortunately very few suitable drinking utensils are manufactured for the aviary bird market, therefore alternatives have to be found. Poultry equipment dealers supply founts with those holding a capacity of one to three litres being adequate. They also supply the very useful siphon drinker which has had a certain amount of success with exotic dove and pigeon breeders. The specially designed homer pigeon drinker with its umbrella-like cover allows birds easy access to the bowl and the water remains clean and cool. They generally hold a capacity of one or two litres. Cylindrical fountains operate on a vacuum principle and sit on the ground for gamebird chicks and raised on legs to 18cm for adult birds. The cylinder is constructed so that it is easily filled without spilling. The drinking vessel provides ample space for ground dwelling chicks. Plastic tubular drinkers which can be used for water or nectar are available for attaching to show or breeding cages. An automatic watering system allows a drinking valve to be easily operated by most straight and hooked-billed species and provides a continuous supply of clean water.

Bird baths usually consist of concrete, asbestos, zinc or a light galvanised iron, especially in point of durability. The shallow depth varies from 2,5cm-7,6cm with birds preferring to flutter about rather than become submerged in deep water. Stepping stones can be secured to the bottom for nervous birds wishing to enter the bath. Some species prefer to bath under a gentle spray of water which can be generated from a sprinkler system fixed to an aviary roof. Parrot-like birds enjoy a bath with the use of a garden hose.

Water

Water has been left till last, but it is as important as food. A constant supply of fresh clean drinking water must be available at all times because birds have no salivary glands, which makes digesting dry seeds a formidable task. The majority of birdkeepers today accept local tap water, but newly acquired birds, especially those having been recently trapped, then exported, should be weaned on rain water for a week, after which it can be diluted gradually with tap water.

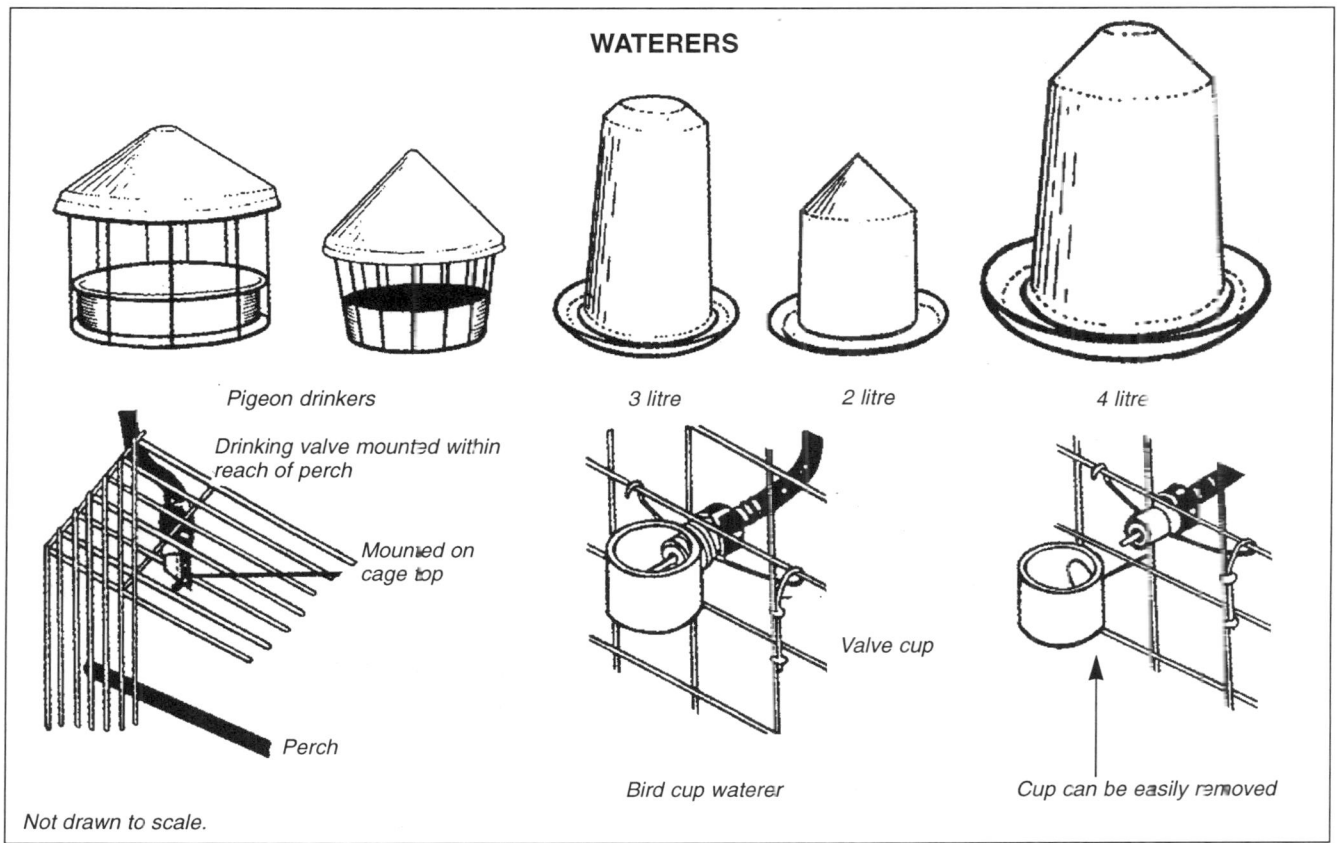

WATERERS

Pigeon drinkers

3 litre

2 litre

4 litre

Drinking valve mounted within reach of perch

Mounted on cage top

Perch

Valve cup

Cup can be easily removed

Bird cup waterer

Not drawn to scale.

Ailments and Diseases

We wish to point out that sometimes birds die while seemingly in perfect health. This generally occurs in old birds. More often old age is accompanied by short breath, baldness, weak flight, etc. In younger birds symptoms associated with most illnesses may include loose droppings, puffy feathers, weight loss, head constantly tucked under the feathers and lack of interest in food. A sick bird should be isolated as soon as possible and placed in a hospital cage. If it has no external injuries, isolation under warm conditions with tempting food provided may place it on the road to recovery. Detailed information about the ailments and diseases of birds can be obtained from a number of good specialist books listed in the reference section and are available at all leading pet and book stores.

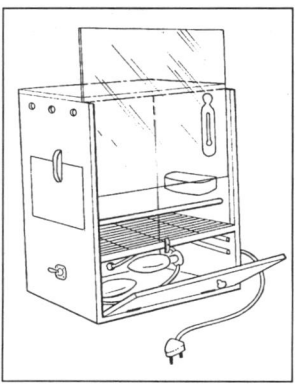

A hospital cage is usually box-shaped with a glass-front which is able to slide up and down in the groove provided. A false bottom contains two 40-watt electric light bulbs and a switch to control the amount of heat being emitted as required. One may wish to construct your own cage with wood or galvanised sheet tin with measurements usually 30 x 45cm high x 30 x 45cm wide x 20 x 25cm long. A perch should be fixed about 8cm off the floor. Easy access can be gained to seed and water pots situated in each side of the cage. A new heater for sick birds comes in the form of a heating platform measuring 38 x 38cm x 12,7mm and made of a grey high impact proof acrylic and placed underneath a show cage which will remain at about 65°C at all times.

Composition of medications and modes of treatment

CALSUBA – 170g pack
Hypercalcaemia resulting from hyperthyroidism, milk-alkali syndrome and due to increased ionisation of calcium in acidosis.
Group Laboratories SA (Pty) Ltd, 21 Wrench Road, Isando 1600.

SPARTRIX tablets
For treatment of Trichomonas gallinae (canker) in pigeons.
Composition: Each 270g tablet contains 10g Carnidazole.
Janssen Pharmaceutica (Pty) Ltd, 15th Road, Halfway House 1685.

L-SPARTAKON tablets
For the treatment of large roundworm Ascaridia columbae and hairworm Capillaria obsignata infestations in pigeons.
Janssen Pharmaceutica (Pty) Ltd, 15th Road, Halfway House 1685.

LONGSTIM – 200g
For the prevention of mycoplasmosis and bacterial infections of the respiratory tract (slime-in-the-throat) of pigeons.
Contains Amoxycllin trihidrate 5%m/m Tylosir tartrate.
Medpet 1081 Pretorius Street, Hatfield 0083, Pretoria.

TERRAMYCIN – 200g pack
For the treatment of bacterial respiratory disease.

Antibiotic for oral administration in the drinking water. 55mg per gram Oxetracycline hydrochloride.

Pitzer Laboratories (Pty) Ltd 102 Rivonia Road, Sandton 2199.

AVIVET – 100g pack

An aid in the treatment of respiratory tract infections in pigeons and cage birds.

Composition: Amoxycillin – Vitamin B1-B2-B6-B12 and Niacin.

Allvet (Pty) Ltd, P.O. Box 1825, Honeydew 2040.

VITALYTE

For oral electrolytes replacement in the drinking water when suffering from dehydration or diarrhoea, including stress situations.

Dosage – 1 level measure (5kg) per 5 litres drinking water.

Composition: Vitamin A, E, D3, K3, Pantothenic Acid-Thiamine-Potassium Acetate and Dextgrose

C E Industries (Pty) Ltd t/a Panvet, 7 Derrick Road, Spartan, Kempton Park, 1620.

AVI-MOULT – 100g and 350g packs

A vitamin, lysine and methionine preparation that can be given in drinking water before and during the moulting period to relieve stress and enhance healthy new feather growth.

Shady Streams Bird Farm P.O. Box 899, Hillcrest 3650.

FOLIGLOBIN – 30 tablets

Coated iron for controlled release for rapid and effective haemoglobin response.

Composition: FE sulphur-Folic Acid-Ascorbia Acid-Cyanocabalmin.

Pharmaceutical Enterprises (Pty) Ltd, Howard Studios, Howard Drive, Pinelands 7405.

BAYTRIL 10% oral solution for chickens

Composition: Each 1ml contains 100mg Enrofloxacin. Benzyl alcohol as preservative; 1,355mm.

Inhibits the bacterial enzyme DNA-gyrase, which is essential for bacterial replication, transcription and recombination. Therapy of bacterial infections due to coli-bacillosis, fowl cholera, infectious coryza and salmonellosis of broiler chickens, growing pullets, broiler and layer breeder birds as well as prophylaxis and an aid in therapy of mycoplasmal infections, due to *Maycoplasma gallisepticum* and *M.synoviae*.

Bayer Animal Health Division, 27 Wrench Road, Isando 1600.

MINAMINO SYRUP – 200ml pack

Composition: Amino Acids-Alanine-Arginine-Aspartic Acid-Glutamic Acid-Glycine-Histidine-Isoleucine-Leucine-Lysine-Methionine-Phenylalanine-Proline-Tryptophan-Threonine-Tyrosine-Valine-Vitamin B1-B2-B6-B12 and Nicotinamide.

Minerals: Green Ferric Ammonium Citrate-Manganese sulphate and Copper sulphate.

Biologicals: Soluble liver, spleen and gastric mucosa extract.

Preservatives: Methyl hydroxybenzoate and Propyl hydroxybenzoate.

Lagamed (Pty) Ltd, 17 Eastern Service Road, Eastgate Ext 8, Sandton.

SULFAZINE 16%

For the treatment of Coccidiosis and Coryza (croup) in poultry.

Milborrow Animal Health Division of the Premier Pharmaceutical Co. Ltd, P.O. Box 334, Isando 1600.

VIRKON – 50g pack

The ultimate virucidal disinfectant for safe effective control of all known types of virus, bacteria, fungi, yeasts and moulds. Proven effective against all 15 virus families. "One step" cleaning and disinfection of all surfaces, equipment, utensils and cages.

Antec International, UK patent-obtainable locally from your pharmacy.

TRICHO PLUS

For the prevention and treatment of trichomonosis and Spironucleus infections (hexamitosis) in pigeons and doves. Also used for the treatment of trichomonosis, cochlosomosis and giardiosis in cage birds.

Composition: Contains 200mg of ronidazole per sachet.

Indications:

(a) Pigeons – trichomonosis and spironucleus infections (hexamitosis).

(b) Cage birds – trichomonosis, giardiosis and cochiosomosis

Administration and dosage:

Pigeons: Curative treatment:

Dissolve 1 sachet in 2 litres of drinking water (daily ration for 40 pigeons). Administer fresh daily.

A trichomonosis treatment normally lasts five days, while a Spironuceus infection needs a 7 to 10 day treatment. In case of severe infections, it is often necessary to treat the birds for a further five days.

Cage birds: Dissolve 1 sachet into 4 litres of drinking water (daily ration for 100 birds). Renew the solution daily. A normal treatment lasts 5 days. In case of cochlosomosis a second treatment is recommended 2 days after the first one has ended. In severe cases of trichomonosis, prolong the treatment for another 5 days.

Adverse effects: None.

Remarks: May be safely used during reproduction. Not toxic for young pigeons and cage birds.

Medpet 1081 Pretorius Street, Hatfield, 0083.

DOXYBIOTIC

An aid in the prevention of bacterial infections in pigeons and cage birds.

Composition: Doxycycline Vitamine A-B1-B2-B 6-E-K-Lactose and Dextrose

Directions for use: Add 5g (1 heaped measure – included) to 1 litre of drinking water for 5-7 consecutive days. Change medicated water daily.

Medpet 1081 Pretorius Street, Hatfield 0083.

KARBA-DUST – 500g pack

Insecticide dusting powder for home gardens and animal use. Red mites and tampans on poultry and cage birds.

Dust all poultry houses thoroughly and pay attention to the floor, perches, nest materials, cracks in walls and in woodwork.

Efekto, P.O. Box 912-787, Silverton 0127.

The Bird Breeder and Medication

Basic Principles

Birdbreeders are often obliged to give their birds some form of medication. However, we often do not have effective contact with an avian veterinarian to give us advice and are left to our own judgement to diagnose the problem and administer medication. The choice of medication and determining the correct dosage involves many aspects of which the average birdkeeper is unaware. A number of general basic principles that are relevant to the use of medication are therefore discussed hereunder.

When considering the use of medicines there are certain principles which must be adhered to:

All medicines must be regarded as potentially poisonous. Therefore if administered incorrectly, the bird may die or suffer serious effects. I will attempt to bring to the attention of birdkeepers some important aspects regarding medication and its effects so that in future one may use medicines with far greater insight and responsibility.

This chapter is not meant to help diagnose illnesses or assist in the choosing of medication for each individual case, but rather to bring to your attention some basic principles regarding medicine and its uses. The correct diagnosis and treatment of sick birds must, where possible, be made in consultation with or under the guidance of a veterinarian who is knowledgeable in avian diseases.

The fate of medication in the body

Attention will be devoted to medication that must reach the blood stream to become effective, that is it must be absorbed and distributed by the blood to its site of action. Other groups of medication are applied to the skin and have an effect without reaching the blood stream and will not be discussed. The fate of medication in the body is illustrated below.

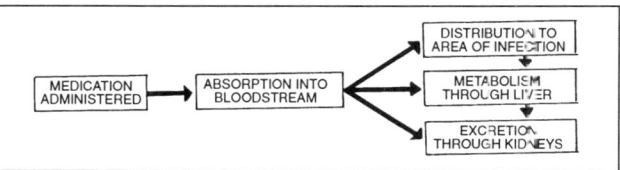

Absorption

In all methods of administration, with the exception of intravenous injections a process of absorption is required for the medicine to reach the blood stream, and in turn reach the area where it is to elicit its effect. Once it has reached the bloodstream the route of administration no longer influences the effectiveness of the medication.

The process of absorption is the area where a medicine can be "lost". When medicine is given orally it can be absorbed from the crop (proventilulus), gizzards (ventriculous) or the small intestine. Not all medicines are absorbed equally well from these areas and diseases of the intestinal tract can influence the process of absorption. If the digestive tract is not functioning well absorption will be slow and incomplete. When a bird has diarrhoea the medication will pass through the digestive tract very quickly and minimal absorption will occur.

Another problem to be borne in mind is that there is often a lack of information regarding how intestinal absorption varies in specific species of birds. One must then therefore depend on information applicable to poultry and other domesticated animals.

Such information is not necessarily always relevant because different bird species do not necessarily absorb and metabolise medication in the same way.

Other factors that may play a role is the age of a bird (older the bird the less absorption), the blood supply to the intestinal tract, the presence of food in the crop and a possible presence also of parasites, like worms or coccidia. It is therefore clear that several factors influence the rate as well as the completeness of the absorption of medicines. These factors must always be taken into consideration when considering the oral dosage.

Distribution

After a medicine reaches the blood stream it is transported by the blood to every part of the body. In this way the medicine reaches the areas where it is to be effective. The pattern of distribution of a specific medication is determined by its chemical characteristics. When selecting a medicine for a specific condition or to treat a particular organ a knowledge of the chemical characteristics of the medicine and its distribution pattern is of fundamental importance. For example, to treat a urinary tract infection a medicine must be chosen that reaches and passes through the kidneys virtually unchanged.

Metabolism (Chemical change)

The metabolism of medicines occurs mainly in the liver and is to do with the body trying to get rid of the medication. The metabolism of medicines involves changing the medicines to more water soluble compounds that can easily be passed out via the kidneys. Not all medicines however are metabolised. Some are excreted via the kidneys without having been changed. Knowledge of the metabolic pattern becomes very important when a bird suffers from e.g. liver complaint or an illness which influences the effectiveness with which the bird can metabolise medicines. In such cases use medicines that are not, or only to a small degree metabolised in the liver.

Excretion

The important organs for the excretion of medicines and their metabolites are the kidneys. When a bird's kidneys are affected by an illness or are weakened as a result of a lack of fluids (dehydration), the excretion of medicines becomes slower than expected and therefore dangerous concentrations may build up the body. Dehydration can lead to some medicines (or their metabolites) becoming so concentrated that when being excreted by the kidneys, crystals can form with fatal consequences. Some of the sulfonamide group of antibiotics are prone to this phenomenom.

Dosage

Dosages and Methods of Dosing

One major problem that confronts a birdkeeper is how to treat a bird when one does not have expert advice on medicines and on how to calculate the correct dosage. Most medicines that are available to birdkeepers are formulated for use by humans or large animals.

The following example acts as a guide to the problem that confronts a birdkeeper when one has to treat a bird with medicines formulated for human use.

Imagine that a medicine is available as a syrup or suspension and the dosage for an adult of 75kg is 10ml or 2 teaspoonful measures. The dosage for a bird which weighs 150 grams can be calculated as follows:

Mass of person = 75kg (75 000g)
Dosage for person = 10ml
Mass of bird = 150g
Dosage for bird = 150/75000 x 10 = 0,02ml.

The bird will receive a half drop of the medication. When medication, as stated in the example above, is made available in liquid form it is still possible to measure the correct dosage by using a 0,5ml syringe which is obtainable from a pharmacy. If it only comes in tablet form, dosage calculation is more problematical.

One 500mg tablet is the recommended dosage for a 75kg person. The dosage for a 150g bird is calculated as follows:
Dosage for bird 150/75000 x 500 = 1mg.

A bird will require 1/500th of a tablet. The correct dosage can be measured as follows:

1. Grind the tablet to a fine powder.
2. Add powdered tablet to 500ml glucose or sugar.
3. Mix ingredients thoroughly.
4. Add 1ml of the mixture to a fine commercial softfood.
5. Administer the mixture directly into the crop with a syringe and crop needle.

Always bear in mind that the above dosage is not necessarily correct, because a bird's physiology, absorption, metabolism and excretion patterns often differ from those of humans. The dosage should be calculated bearing this fact in mind.

The correct dosages for birds are not readily available, therefore we suggest one should discuss dosages with a veterinarian. As a general rule it is probably safe to state that a bird would require a larger dosage based on mass than the corresponding human dosage.

Overdosing

One can deduct from the above discussion that the dangers of overdosing are high. It has been suggested that birdkeepers suffer more losses as a result of incorrectly using medications, rather than from the ailment they are trying to treat. I must therefore emphasize that whenever one is to administer medicine to a bird, great care should be taken to ensure the correct dosage.

Methods of dosing

1. Add to drinking water or food.
2. Administer directly into crop.
3. By way of injection.

Birdkeepers may argue as to the best method of dosing birds. It is important that the correct method to be adopted in relation to the type of illness which has to be treated.

Dosing via drinking water

Adding medicines to the drinking water is regarded as one of the less effective methods of dosing on account of the following reasons:

1. There is no control over the bird's intake.
2. Some medicines when diluted deteriorate quickly when exposed to light, e.g. Tetracycline antibiotics lose their effectiveness as a medication within a few hours when added to water.
3. A sick bird may refuse the intake of water whereas another which has a temperature, will consume far more water than usual. This can result in an overdose.
4. Some birds are able to go without water for longer periods than others, therefore it is difficult to observe if the medication has been taken over the given time. A good knowledge of the eating and drinking habits of the birds in your aviaries can lead to an effective dosing programme especially in respect to the preventative treatment of healthy birds. The removal of the drinking water from an aviary of seedeaters as well as softfood, including fruit, for the softbills, will induce them to drink the medicated water when reintroduced some time later.

The removal of water must be done with circumspection, closely supervised and only with species that will tolerate such action. Finches, for instance, may die if they do not have constant access to water.

Dosage via the crop

Direct dosing into the crop is the second most effective method of administering medication. Matters that will require attention are as follows:

1. Sterilized crop needles of a suitable size for all the species that are to be dosed must be available and used.
2. The crop needle must be securely attached to the syringe so that it will not become detached and lodge itself in the crop of the bird.
3. Only administer a volume which the bird's crop can accommodate.

The following volumes are useful as a guideline:
Ring-necked Parakeet +/- 2ml, Grey Parrot +/- 5ml.

Injection

Dosing by injection is the most effective manner of administering medication provided that the medicine is injectable and that the equipment is sterilised. The correct technique must be adhered to, with some medications being injected under the skin, while others must be injected into the muscle and the third method being the intravenous injection. Once again, it is advisable to consult a veterinarian before attempting intravenous injections.

Concentration of medication in the bloodstream

Most medicines must first reach the blood stream before they can have any effect and must also be present in the correct concentration (Figure 1).

Figure 1

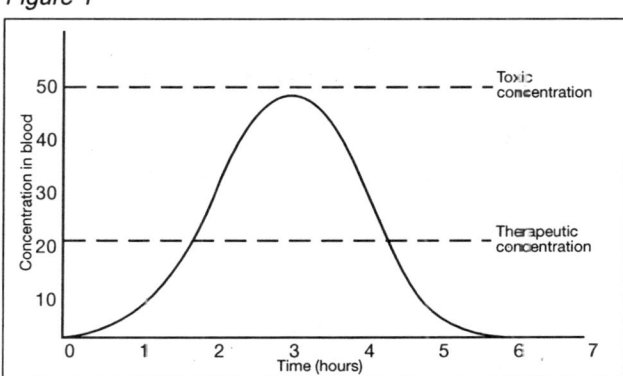

The illustration shows clearly that a medicine must reach a certain concentration in the bloodstream before it can be effective. The so called THERAPEUTIC CONCEN-TRATION must be reached. It is however also clear that the concentration must not be too high because a TOXIC CONCENTRATION is then reached which will lead to unwanted side-effects. The medication shown here would only be effective between one and four hours after dosing. When the dosage is too low the following situation occurs (Figure 2).

Figure 2

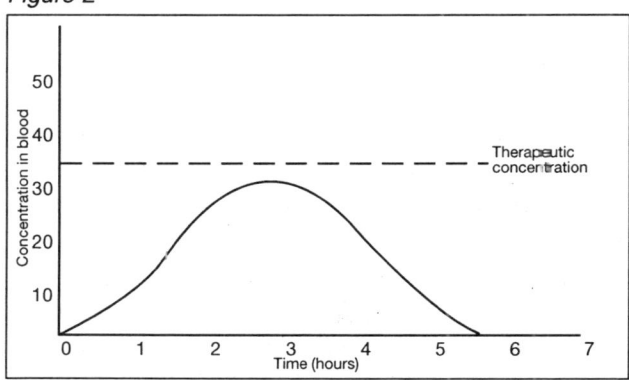

When medication is administered in this manner it cannot make any sort of contribution to combating diseases for which it was intended. When the dose is too large, the situation as depicted (in Figure 3) may occur.

Figure 3

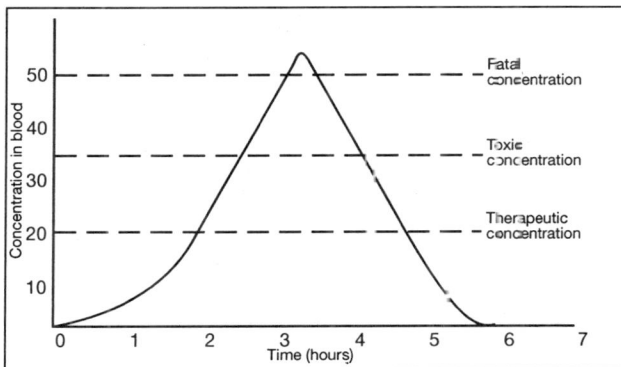

If a large difference should exist between the therapeutic and toxic concentration, a medicine is then regarded as safe and the accurate calculation and administration of the dosage is less important. In the case of a number of medicines the difference between the therapeutic and the toxic concentrations is not very high and therefore the correct dosage must be determined with care.

Using the above as a guideline, some antibiotic medicines (Penicillin) can be regarded as safe while others (Vancomycin) must be regarded as dangerous. This information is not generally made available to birdkeepers, therefore it is better that one regards all medicines as potentially dangerous and treat them as such. When a prescription requires medication to be given with a specific dosage every 6 to 8 hourly intervals as an example, it is most important that these instructions be followed. The reason is that some medications are only effective if the therapeutic concentration is maintained for a certain period of time.

In figure 4 it is clear that the medicine only reached the therapeutic concentration after a few consecutive doses. The medicine maintains its effect as long as it is given at the correct time, but loses its effect soon after dosage is stopped.

Figure 4

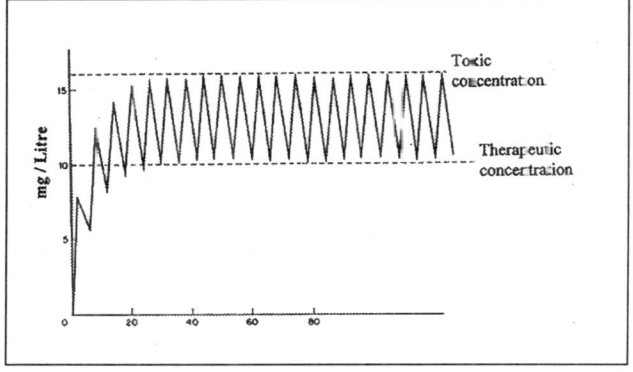

If the correct dosage is given but the time intervals are not correct, the following will happen. (Figure 5).

Figure 5

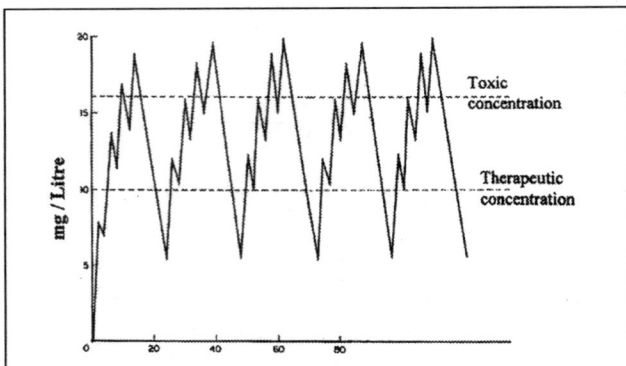

The therapeutic concentration is only maintained periodically and the treatment is therefore less effective than it should be.

Dosage amount by mouth vs dosage amount by injection

The required oral dosage of a medication differs to that administered by injection. When a medicine is given orally, only part of the dosage is absorbed to reach the bloodstream. The absorption process is also often very slow so that the concentration in the blood is lower than would be following an injection.

After an oral dosage a certain amount of medication is always "lost". The amount that is lost depends on factors such as the formulation of the medication (a syrup is better absorbed than a tablet), the presence of food in the crop as well as the health/condition of the bird. As a rule an oral dosage should be larger than a dosage by injection to give rise to the same blood concentration. In conclusion it is important that the correct medication, dosage, route and time interval be adhered to, to achieve the desired therapeutic effect.

Antibiotics

History

The term "antibiotic" comes from a similar term "antibiosis" which is defined as a chemical compound secreted by one living organism and being used by the organism to kill another living organism.

The use of antibiotics has a long history and it is known that the Chinese used moulds that grew on sour milk and soya beans some 2500 years ago for the treatment of infected wounds. In the Bible we find prescriptions for the use of moulds that grow on decaying wood. Certain traditional home remedies also made use of the mucor that grows on jam for the treatment of infected wounds.

The examples mentioned make use of antibiotics which are produced by the relevant moulds. The basis for modern antibiotic therapy was laid down in 1877 when two French scientists, Pasteur and Joubert observed that splenic fever (anthrax) bacteria grew well in a sterile environment and poorly in an environment where other bacteria were present.

The modern era of chemotherapy really was initiated with the discovery of the first "sulpha" drug known as sulphanilamide in 1936 and the discovery of Penicillin in 1941. Their discoveries resulted in health authorities at the time, predicting that illnesses that occurred as a result of bacterial infection would be erradicated in a few years. However, it soon became evident that this prediction would not come true. Presently we are experiencing an enormous increase in the number of antibiotics. This indicates that we are still fighting a losing battle against bacterial infections.

This observation alone should cause us to think seriously about using antibiotic medication and make us realise that antibiotics must be used with great care and responsibility.

Bacteria, parasites and infection

A parasite may be defined as an organism which lives together with another living organism (the host organism) which provides the parasite with a suitable environment for it to obtain nutrition and live and reproduce. The term parasite is used to describe a large number or organisms varying in size from microscopic bacteria and fungi to large roundworms and tapeworms. Parasites frequently live together with their host without the host suffering any ill effects. The more successful the parasite host relationship the less negative influence experienced by the host. In such a situation the infection is termed latent of sub-clinical. Where the balanced relationship between the host and parasite is disturbed, the parasite causes damage to the host and host manifests signs of illness. It is important to realise that several bacteria that can cause illnesses are normally present in the host, be it man, animal or bird. Other parasites need to penetrate the body from the surrounding environment to cause an infection. Where conditions arise which allow the normally resident potentially pathogenic bacteria to multiply excessively or where external organisms gain access and multiply excessively, the host becomes ill.

Why do bacteria cause illnesses?

Bacteria release chemical substances which are toxic to the host. Where the number of bacteria is low the toxins do not affect the host adversely.

The following examples can be used to demonstrate how toxic substances affect the host's physiology:

1. *Staphylococcus infection (food poisoning)*

The toxin released by this organism is very stable and can withstand temperatures of 100 °C for 30 minutes, therefore boiling food that has gone off will not make it safe for human consumption. The toxins are absorbed in the stomach and transported to the brain and the central nervous system. The toxins affect the nerves that control the movement of the digestive system and cause excessive contraction of the intestinal wall. This causes diarrhoea and will result in the loss of fluids and electrolites and eventually this may result in the death of the infected host.

2. **Streptococcus (the organism causing throat infections)**
Some streptococci produce toxins which dissolve red blood cells and tissue cells. This may be fatal to the host.

3. **Botulism (This illness is a form of food poisoning and is caused by the bacterium Clostridium botulinum)**
The toxins produced by the organisms are transported to the nervous system and affect those nerves that control the respiratory muscles and prevent the release of their neuro-trasmitter acetyl choline. Paralysis of the respiratory system results, and this is followed by death of the host.

The above examples will give some idea how certain toxins can affect the host adversely.

Definition and characteristics of antibiotics

Antibiotics are traditionally regarded as chemical compounds that are manufactured by a variety of micro-organisms and that are able to inhibit the growth of other micro-organisms or destroy those other organisms. Nowadays a number of antibiotics are being manufactured in the laboratory and the original definition is no longer correct. There are a number of such antibiotics on the market with their number increasing yearly. Antibiotics differ greatly in regard to their physical, chemical and pharmocological character and also regarding their spectrum of activity and working mechanisms.

The ideal antibiotic must have the following characteristics:

1. Be effective against a variety of micro-organisms.
2. Be selective against the pathogenic organisms and not negatively influence the patient.
3. Destroy bacteria rather than inhibit their growth.
4. Not allow resistant bacteria to develop.
5. Be safe even when large doses are administered.
6. Give rise to few or no side effects.
7. Not adversely affect the important organs of the body.
8. Be stable in dry form as well as in solution.
9. Administerable by different routes, namely by injection or orally.
10. Effective blood concentrations must be reached quickly and maintained for a long period.
11. Be inexpensive and easy to manufacture.

When reviewing the points mentioned above, it is clear that an ideal antibiotic would be very difficult to manufacture at present and the antibiotics available have one or more of the abovementioned shortcomings

and as a result there are dangers involved in their use. One must be aware of the dangers of antibiotics at all times.

How do antibiotics work?

Different antibiotics effect micro-organisms in different ways. The following examples will demonstrate some of the modes in which antibiotics work:

1. The organism's cell wall is affected and weakened thereby causing the death of the organism.
2. The reproductive mechanism or mechanism for its existence protein synthesis of the organism is affected.
3. The antibiotic closely resembles one of the chemical compounds being used by the organism for its existence. If the organism use this chemical compound in any part of its biochemical process, the said process is disrupted to such an extent that the organism dies.

Living organisms constantly come into contact with a variety of micro-organisms. Should these micro-organism gain access to the body and the immune system of that organ is functioning well, the defence mechanism of the organisms is activated to destroy the invading organism Should the invasive micro-organism multiply, the defence mechanism of the host will be activated to operate at an increased level. Only when the defence mechanism becomes overwhelmed does an infection occur which needs to be treated.

Misuse of antibiotics and the consequences thereof

Antibiotics can be misused in a number of ways:

1. Treatment of untreatable infections. Viral infections do not respond to treatment with antibiotics, therefore treatment is of no value. The administration of an antibiotic during a viral infection can only be of value if a secondary bacterial infection has occured or is in the process of developing.

2. Treatment with the incorrect medication. No individual antibiotic is effective against all kinds of harmful micro-organisms. If an infection is present it is necessary to make a tentative diagnosis as to what type of bacteria might be present so as to facilitate the choice of the correct antibiotic. Initially one would choose a broad spectrum antibiotic. It is important that birdkeepers consult a veterinarian before administering antibiotics to a bird.

Correct use of antibiotics

The correct use of antibiotics is based on the following principles:

1. Identify the pathogenic organism or make a tentative diagnosis of the bacteria involved. It is probably correct to say that antibiotics are often used by birdkeepers without their really knowing what ailment

the bird is suffering from. One has little chance of success if a wild guess is made regarding the antibiotic chosen.

2. Having made a diagnosis, an antibiotic must be chosen that will selectively destroy the diagnosed organism or group of organisms.

3. Administer the correct dose via the correct route at the correct intervals for the required period of the treatment.

4. Continue with the treatment even though the symptoms may show signs of subsiding, for the prescribed period of treatment.

5. If no signs of improvement should occur consult your local veterinarian.

The original diagnosis may have to be revised and a different medication prescribed.

Preventative treatment

It is important to remember that an antibiotic cannot prevent a bird from acquiring an infection and can only be of value if the infection is already present. Preventative dosing will not increase the bird's immunity to infection, the opposite being the case. Remember that the normal bacterial population of a human/ animal/bird forms an important defence mechanism against harmful bacteria. Unconsidered preventative treatment often disturbs these mechanisms and creates ideal conditions for the introduction of an infection. It can also lead to the development of resistant types of micro-organisms which can result in the outbreak of an infection that is difficult to treat.

There is, however, instances where preventative treatment can be effective and of great value if approached correctly.

For example, if one suspects that a bird has been in contact with, or in danger of being infected with a specific organism, or if one suspects that the bird is already infected without showing any symptoms, then preventative treatment can be useful.

In cases as described above where the number of micro-organisms are still reasonably low a single dosage of the bacteriocidal antibiotic in the correct dosage will often be all that is required to reduce the number of organisms to the level where the body's defence mechanism can prevent further infection. Examples of situations where preventative treatment can be used effectively are as follows:

1. One bird in a group shows symptoms of diarrhoea. Diagnose the possible cause and remove the sick bird from the aviary. The aviary must be disinfected and the infected bird treated with an antibiotic which is effective to combat the infection. Treatment of the rest of the birds in the group may be indicated.

2. One or more birds may show signs of having coccidiosis infection (This is confirmed microscopically).

Because the coccidiosis parasite can easily spread from aviary to aviary, remove all sick birds and disinfect their quarters. Treat the rest of the birds.

3. Birds, especially wild caught, often have subclinical Psittacosis infection when subjected to the stress of being caught, transported and then kept in a new environment, the Psittacosis infection may become visible. Treatment of the ill bird as well as other birds in the same consignment is indicated.

The misuse of new antibiotics

New more powerful antibiotics appear regularly on the market and resourceful birdkeepers acquire them in the hope that they will solve their disease problems.

The new medications are with good reason under strict control and are only used in selected cases and under strict guidance. If a birdkeeper acquires such medication it would be very short sighted to use it at the first opportunity. It may achieve short term advantages but at the same time there is a danger of having to suffer losses in the future as a result of the development of resistant strains of micro-organisms that are for practical purposes untreatable. If such a situation arises it can have disastrous implications, not only for the particular birdkeeper, but also for the birdkeepers in general.

Resistance to antibiotics

The discovery of antibiotics as it has been observed, did not lead to the complete irradication of infectious diseases.

Both the human and animal populations sill have members dying of bacterial and other infections. In practice we find that when a new antibiotic is initially used it is effective, but gradually with the passage of time its effectiveness becomes less and eventually it has to be replaced by a new antibiotic. Resistance to antibiotics has been in evidence for some time and has become a problem for doctors and veterinarians treating infections. The development of resistance is a complicated subject as resistance can occur in different ways and also differ from medication to medication and from organism to organism.

Knowledge of the mechanism by which resistance can originate may lead to a better understanding of the problem and hopefully birdkeepers will then use antibiotics with greater responsibility.

Resistance can originate in two ways:

1. **Mutation**

Micro-organisms as is the case with all forms of life, are subject to natural genetic mutations. When taking into consideration that the lifespan of an organism is short and that tremendously large numbers are involved in an infection, it is clear that the chances for the spontaneous development of a resistant mutation is fairly large. The degree of resistance of such mutations can of course differ. Some resistance mutations merely need a higher concentration of antibiotics before they are destroyed, while other mutations can be totally resistant to the antibiotic in question. Such a new micro-organism is genetically stable and can reproduce. As long as no interference occurs in the composition of a micro-organism population the resistant mutants will not cause a problem as they only make up a very small part of the total population. They are also no more dangerous that the original strain, and under normal circumstances the body's natural defence mechanisms which keep the organism under control.

2. Selection

Just imagine that an infection has occurred in a human or a bird and is treated with an antibiotic.

The susceptible organisms are quickly irradicated and only a small quantity of resistant organisms remain behind and rapidly increase in numbers. The patient's normal bacteriological inhabitants are now replaced with a resistant strain of the organism. One must bear in mind that humans/animals carry bacteria that can lead to illnesses but that the body's normal defence mechanisms keep the number of these organisms down. If a situation should arise which causes the number of bacteria to increase quickly resulting in an infection which has to be treated we find that the antibiotic that was previously effective is no longer effective, or that a larger dosage is now necessary to bring the infection under control. When the original infection was treated the initial dosage was probably too low. The blood concentration of the medicine was such that only the most susceptible bacteria were irradicated. The suboptimal dosage thus permitted a resistant strain to develop. If antibiotics are correctly used this scenario is exceptional. The development of resistant strains adversely effect future antibiotic therapy.

3. Super infections

These are a variation on the theme of resistance as discussed above.

It has already been pointed out that a normal healthy human/animal carries a large variety of micro-organisms. These include non-dangerous bacteria and fungi as well as potentially dangerous organisms. Normally the non-dangerous organisms are present in tremendous numbers and as the dangerous organisms have to compete for nutrients the non-pathogenic organisms remain dominant and the number of dangerous organisms remain low.

In all humans/animals there are special relationships between the different types of micro-organisms (bacteria, fungi etc.). The composition of the population is such that both the organisms and the host have the best chance of survival. This is advantageous to both the host and resident bacteria and fungi. When the host has been treated with antibiotics the following changes can result.

(a) The unwanted organism is destroyed.
(b) Non-pathogenic organisms are also destroyed.
(c) The medication that destroys bacteria does not destroy the fungi.

When treatment with an antibiotic is continued for a prolonged period one may find that the composition of the micro-organisms' population is changed with an organism that is normally kept under control, proliferating out of proportion.

By treating one infection, and possibly with success, an ideal condition has been created for the occurrence of a second non-related infection.

An example would be as follows:
A bacterial infection such as diarrhoea is treated, but the treatment is continued for a long period. A fungal infection now makes an appearance or suddenly a lung infection develops. Such super infections are often difficult to treat and therefore must be avoided at all costs.

Vermin

Vermin can contaminate food, frighten adult birds off their eggs and kill nestlings and roosting birds at night. If cats, owls and other noctural predators are likely to disturb roosting birds, they are best kept at bay by using a false roof of wire mesh placed about 5cm above the actual aviary top. An electronic fence is an ideal low-cost device for teaching cats that they are not welcome and when coming into contact with the wire receive a limited electric shock. It is both practical and humane. The contents of a unit usually consists of two each DC Input cables and Fench connector cables with clips, 5 each cable tiles and screw eyes, a silicone rubber tube and nuts and washers.

In the UK Regency Lofts have eradicated the problem with an ultrasonic deterrent in the form of a defender cat/rodent repeller. It produces ultrasonic sound (above the level of human hearing) by irritating and repelling cats and rodents, but will not harm dogs.

The manufacturer claims a 99% success rate but due to deafness and persistence of some animals, will not accept liability for loss of birds or animals.

Also available is the Dazer, hand-held cat repeller which is battery powered, and the Pet Chaser which will get rid of rats, mice, other disease-carrying pests and insects.

Unfortunately this sophisticated method of eradicating pests is not well practiced in Africa. Simpler methods such as a two-compartment box-trap can be constructed at home or an elaborate trap can be purchased with the following features: spring-loaded latch on a single gravity door, treadle located beyond centre point to ensure a positive catch. The traps can be placed in an aviary, but do not use poisons with an arsenic or cyanide base if placed on the outside, particularly if children play in the immediate vicinity.

RAT AND MOUSE TRAPS

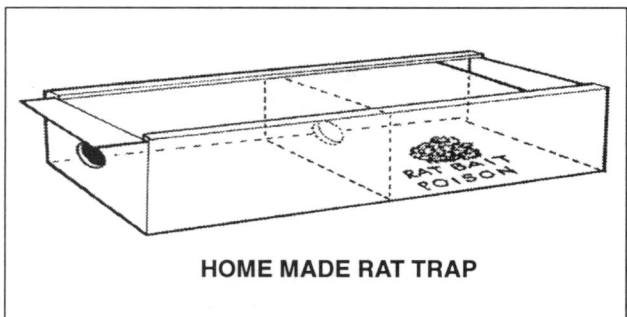

HOME MADE RAT TRAP

Suitable poisons are obtainable from one's local pharmacy or supermarket. Racumin is endorsed by the Poisons Working Group in view of the reduced risk of secondary poisoning and available in wax blocks, ready-to-use-bait, liquid bait and tracking powder. A simple method of catching mice is to place a large empty jar in the soil with the screw top being level with the ground, but beforehand a 15mm hole is to be drilled in the top. Fill the jar with a sweet liquid such as watered down honey, or instead of a liquid, a variety of baits can be used.

For example, cheese and other cheese-based products can be used. With this method mice can die from drowning or be captured alive. Raptors are not only pests in rural areas with young birds looking for easy prey, but also in urban areas where it is illegal to shoot, capture or poison them.

A Goshawk trap is being used by zoos and bird gardens to entice a bird into the trap with a dead bird or animal and then release it elsewhere.

Shrews, ganets, weasels and stoats do not only catch birds on the outside of an aviary, but find the most undetected holes in which to enter a flight. They cause havoc with numerous losses encountered in a very short period. Fortunately traps are manufactured to capture these animals humanely.

Snakes are difficult at most times to control, especially the house species. These snakes are the main culprits who seem to slip through wire mesh regardless of the gauges used in aviary construction. If a snake is suspected of hiding in an aviary, check all disused nest boxes and also in the sleeping quarters behind any dry bush or bales of teff stored here. Best wait until dusk, when snakes usually become restless, then attempt to lodge it from its hiding place with a stick and a good torch.

Ringing and Banding

As a rule, indigenous species, especially imported birds, are rarely closed rung or seamless banded as it is alternatively known in the USA, thus making it difficult when purchasing stock to guess their ages. However, today many birdbreeders specialising in doves and pigeons, carry closed rings, very similar to that of homing pigeons which carry the year of hatching.

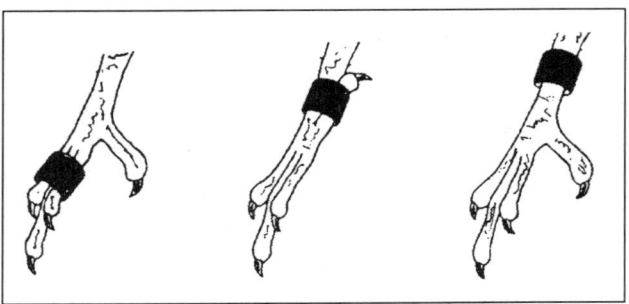

These aluminium rings have raised serial numbers and letters. They are fitted to the legs to identify a particular club or association. As growth rates differ, each species is rung at a different age. It is important to ring young birds at the right time, otherwise complications will arrise. A little vaseline can be used as a lubricant if ringing was left a little late. Before proceeding with the ringing of nestlings, be sure to order the correct sizes beforehand. The rings are available in size numbers 1-21, which caters for all species.

The actual ringing of nestlings is not a difficult procedure. Even though it may sound a little tricky to a newcomer, with a little practice, there is really nothing to it. Gently, but with a little firmness to the nestling's body and using one's left hand, take the ring with lettering displayed right side up, slide the ring over the front three toes and over the fourth toe which is held against the back of the leg. Split plastic rings which are available in numerous plain and striped colours may be attached to, or removed from a bird's leg at any given time. They are mostly used for identifying breeding pairs, in which a male can be rung on the left leg with one colour, and a female on the right leg with another colour, or vice versa. Black numbered rings on a white base are most legible, at some distance, which avoids having to handle the birds too often. Placing this form of ring on a bird is made simple with the use of an applicator which is supplied free when ordering rings.

Catching and Handling

Catching by netting of birds in an aviary is common practice, but first attempts are extremely difficult. Birds are extremely wary and nervous when the aviary in which they are housed is approached too closely, especially larger gamebirds, including pigeons and doves with the latter species whose immediate reaction to someone entering the aviary is to rush headlong into the open in search of a higher perch, but others crash their way through the undergrowth only to become entangled in branches causing some to drop through to the ground. This may lead to disfigurements to any bird from scalping of the head to other damages such as a fractured skull or a broken neck. Fortunately, this occurrence is very much reduced with species such as finches and weavers who escape by moving quickly through the foliage or by hanging on the far end of the aviary mesh.

Before any attempt at catching is made, the following important factors should be adhered to:

1. Select the correct size net which will depend solely on the species to be caught, remembering the larger the bird, the deeper the pocket. Ensure that the circular wire rim is well padded with foam rubber or medical cotton to prevent injury, problems such as head, wings and feet becoming entangled.

2. Move calmly into position where one is able to use the arm fully extended without becoming entangled in the plant life.

3. Select a clear area of wire mesh at the far end of the flight to catch the birds against.

4. Slowly advance towards a bird, then with a quick twist of the wrist bring the net in contact with the wire mesh. Hopefully the catching attempt is successful. The more experienced birdkeepers also catch birds in mid-air by scooping them into a net while in the flight path, mostly with the help of a colleague. When catching in cages, first remove most or all the perches which will make it much easier as finch-like birds will now be confined to hanging on the wire or settling on the ground, the latter position is difficult when catching birds. Catching by hand has been observed in large aviaries at night when a bird is removed from its perch or nestbox by merely shining a torch into its face, blinding it momentarily. A small lightweight step-ladder may be required or a permanent strong ladder / perch can be incorporated into the design of the aviary. Once a bird has been removed from the net, handhold it tightly to prevent feather loss caused from wriggling, but not tight enough to restrict normal breathing.

5. If one has doves or pigeons in one's collection the accepted correct method of holding them is by placing the thumb across the lower back, the fingers and palm around the lower belly and folded wings, the feet passed between first and second fingers. The other hand is placed beneath the breast. A little practice will make perfect. This method was developed by Homer Pigeon fanciers The method of catching ground dwelling birds is by using a small trap about 1 x 0,75m x 0,50m and made of 5 x 4cm pine, covered with 50mm aperture welded mesh. A sliding door at the one end is shut once a bird has entered the cage. Removal is by a trap door in the top. The old method of trapping in an aviary is still being practised which consists of a welded mesh cage and a flip down door which is operated by a long piece of string. This simple trap will not injure birds if handled carefully and prevents stress as a bird can be removed quickly.

Aviary Photography

Photography has become important in recent years. With more and more birdbreeders writing articles and submitting them for publication, with editors requesting records of their findings in the form of photographs or mostly colour transparencies.

It is not necessary to go to the additional expense of building an extra flight or a specially designed box as an outdoor studio. The service passages attached to many aviaries are ideal for this purpose. The length of a passage that serves four or more flights is adequate for both small and large species. A piece of hardboard such as masonite can be painted with blue PVA paint, giving the effect of a clear sky or with browns and greens to depict undergrowth. These backdrops can be hung on the inside welded mesh at the far end of a passage. Natural perches can be fastened tightly across the full width. The height of a branch is very important because if placed too close to the roof the welded mesh pattern shadow will be thrown over the bird as well as the perch. Shadow problems can be eradicated by covering the roof with a sheet of dark material, plastic or canvas. With the disposal of natural light an alternative source can be found with the use of flash or video lighting. The near-end door of the service passage must have a small circular hole cut in it to allow a camera lens to be inserted. Attach potato sacking or a similar material to the outside of the passage where the hole was previously cut which now acts as a hide. Doves, pigeons, lovebirds and parrots are usually easy subjects to photograph as once they have found the perch, or a wide board which may be needed for large pigeons, they remain quite motionless for at least two minutes — ample time in which to take at least one photograph before they show signs of becoming restless. The smallest of bird species are always extremely active, hopping from the ground to the perch or hanging on the wire mesh. This is where the autofocus lens takes all the frustration out of bird photography. For the larger species a zoom lens is adequate and also has an advantage over fixed lenses in that it gives greater latitudes which are essential with the wide range of bird sizes.

Following overleaf, interesting places where birds can be viewed and photographed.

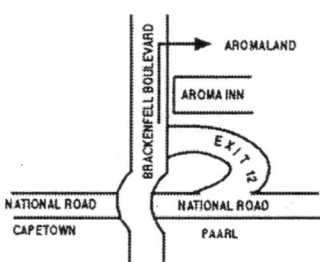

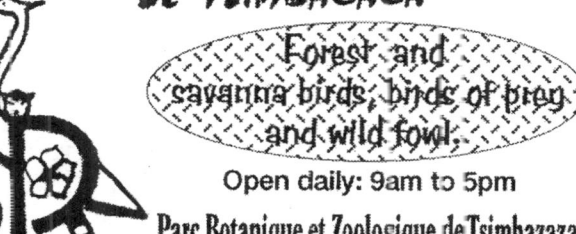
ERRATA and CORRIGENDA

It is regretted that this species was omitted from page 58.

Peach-faced Lovebird

Agapornis roseicollis 15-18cm

Alternate names: Rose-faced lovebird, Rosy-necked Lovebird, Rosy-faced Lovebird, Rosy-ringed Lovebird.
A.r.catumbella Angolan Peach-faced Lovebird, Red-headed Peach-faced Lovebird.

Description: Sexes similar. General plumage bright grass green, more yellow on underside; forehead red; sides of the head and throat salmon-pink; flights blackish, wing-coverts with innermost secondaries and under wing-coverts bluish green; rump and upper tail-coverts sky blue; tail green with outer feathers orange-red towards the base and with a black sub-terminal bar; under tail-coverts green; eye dark brown; indistinct narrow white periophthalmic ring; bill yellowish with a black tip; legs and feet grey. Juvenile has forehead pale red; sides of face to lower neck paler; bill yellowish and streaked with black on the upper mandible.

Adults. *A.r.catumbella* differs from the nominate race in having deeper red on forehead; cheeks and throat more heavily suffused with red.

Voice: Described by Forshaw as a shrill metallic *'skreek'* repeated several times in quick succession.

Habitat: Dry woodland, usually near water.

Distribution: North-western Cape Province, South Africa to Namibia. *A.r.catumbella* south-western Angola

feeding: Seeds, flowers, berries, including ripening grain. Seeds of *Albizia* spp. and *Acacia* spp.

Breeding: This lovebird breeds in holes in walls, in rock crevices, under the eaves of buildings, but more often in the communal nests of the Sociable Weaver *Philetairus socius*. Also suspected of breeding in the nests of the Whitebrowed Sparrow Weaver *Plocepasser mahali*, where the Sociable Weaver is absent. Recorded utilising a swallow's nest in the eaves of a house. Material is carried to the nest by the female tucked amongst the feathers of the lower back rump. Eggs dull white, rounded; clutch 4-8; Incubation period 23 days, by female alone; nestling period 43 days; nestling fed by both parents, but more by male than female.

Aviculture: Selected Reference CLUTCH 3-7; INCUBATION PERIOD 21-23 days; NESTLING PERIOD 38-44 days. Personal Communication CLUTCH 3,4,4,6; INCUBATION PERIOD 21,21,22,23; NESTLING PERIOD 37,38,43 days. Nest Record Cards CLUTCH 4,4,5,6 (SAANRC) 4,5 (NASNRC) 4,4 (ARU); INCUBATION PERIOD 22,23 days (SAANRC) 21,23 days (ARU); NESTLING PERIOD 39,42,44 days (SAANRC) 41,42 (ARU). Diet Record Cards WILD-FOOD. Unripe heads of Finger millet *Eleusine coracana*, sunflower *Helianthus* sp., Rescue grass *Bromus unioloides*, fresh cut Lucerne *Medicago sativa*, leaves of Silver oak *Grevillea robusta*, Morning glory *Ipomoea acuminata*, White flowering gum *Eucalyptus calophylla*, Red flowering gum *E.ficifolia*, flowers of Weeping boer-bean *Schotia brachypetala*, *Gladiolus* sp. chickweed *Stellaria* spp., (SAADRC, ARU, NASDRC). Personal Communication Twigs of willow Salix, poplar *Populas*, maple *Acer*, Sycamore, *A.pseudoplatanus*, *Eucalyptus*, *Banksia Hakea*, *Acacia* and *Callistemon*.

Distribution Maps

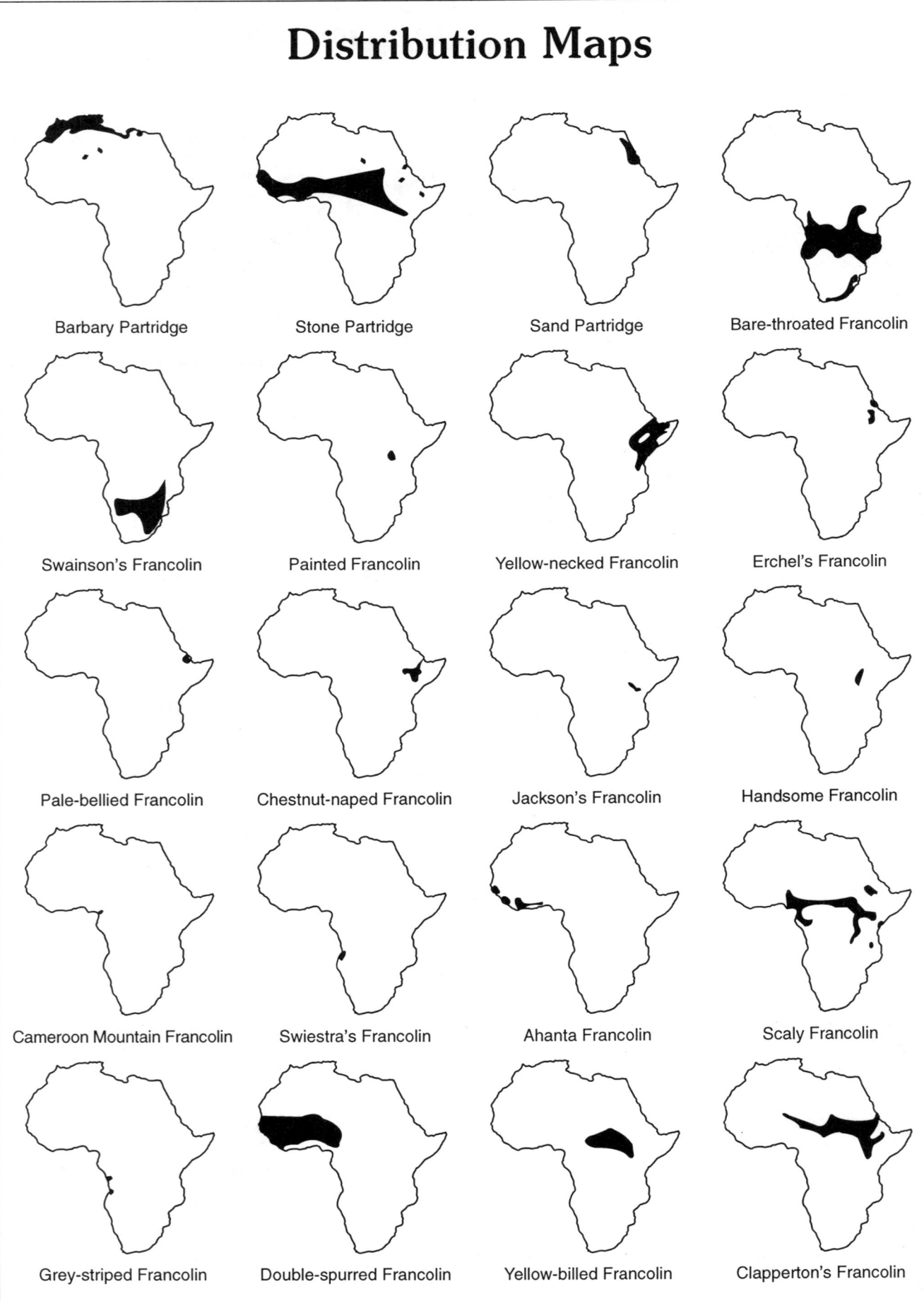

Barbary Partridge

Stone Partridge

Sand Partridge

Bare-throated Francolin

Swainson's Francolin

Painted Francolin

Yellow-necked Francolin

Erchel's Francolin

Pale-bellied Francolin

Chestnut-naped Francolin

Jackson's Francolin

Handsome Francolin

Cameroon Mountain Francolin

Swiestra's Francolin

Ahanta Francolin

Scaly Francolin

Grey-striped Francolin

Double-spurred Francolin

Yellow-billed Francolin

Clapperton's Francolin

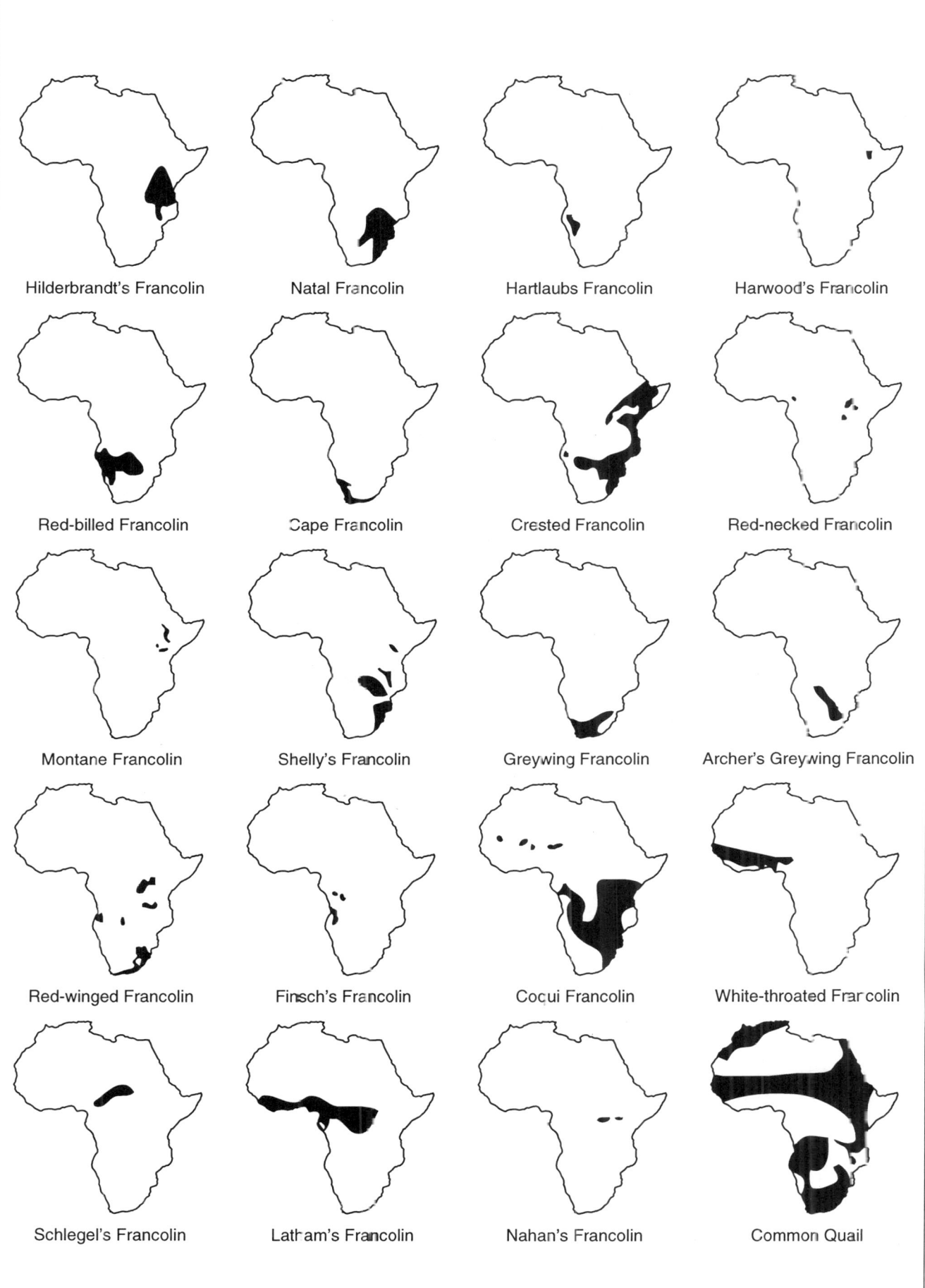

Hilderbrandt's Francolin

Natal Francolin

Hartlaubs Francolin

Harwood's Francolin

Red-billed Francolin

Cape Francolin

Crested Francolin

Red-necked Francolin

Montane Francolin

Shelly's Francolin

Greywing Francolin

Archer's Greywing Francolin

Red-winged Francolin

Finsch's Francolin

Coqui Francolin

White-throated Francolin

Schlegel's Francolin

Latham's Francolin

Nahan's Francolin

Common Quail

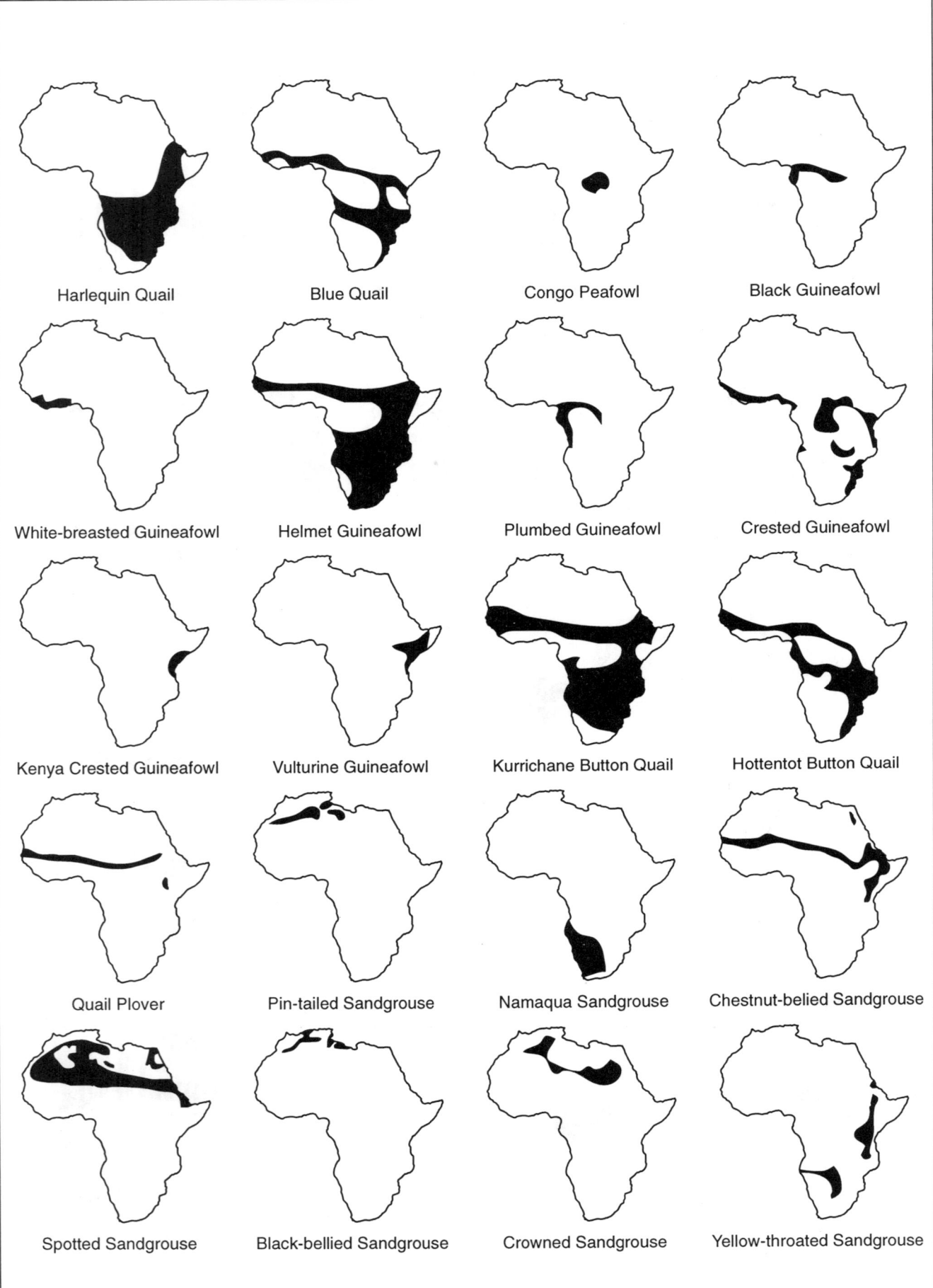

Harlequin Quail

Blue Quail

Congo Peafowl

Black Guineafowl

White-breasted Guineafowl

Helmet Guineafowl

Plumbed Guineafowl

Crested Guineafowl

Kenya Crested Guineafowl

Vulturine Guineafowl

Kurrichane Button Quail

Hottentot Button Quail

Quail Plover

Pin-tailed Sandgrouse

Namaqua Sandgrouse

Chestnut-belied Sandgrouse

Spotted Sandgrouse

Black-bellied Sandgrouse

Crowned Sandgrouse

Yellow-throated Sandgrouse

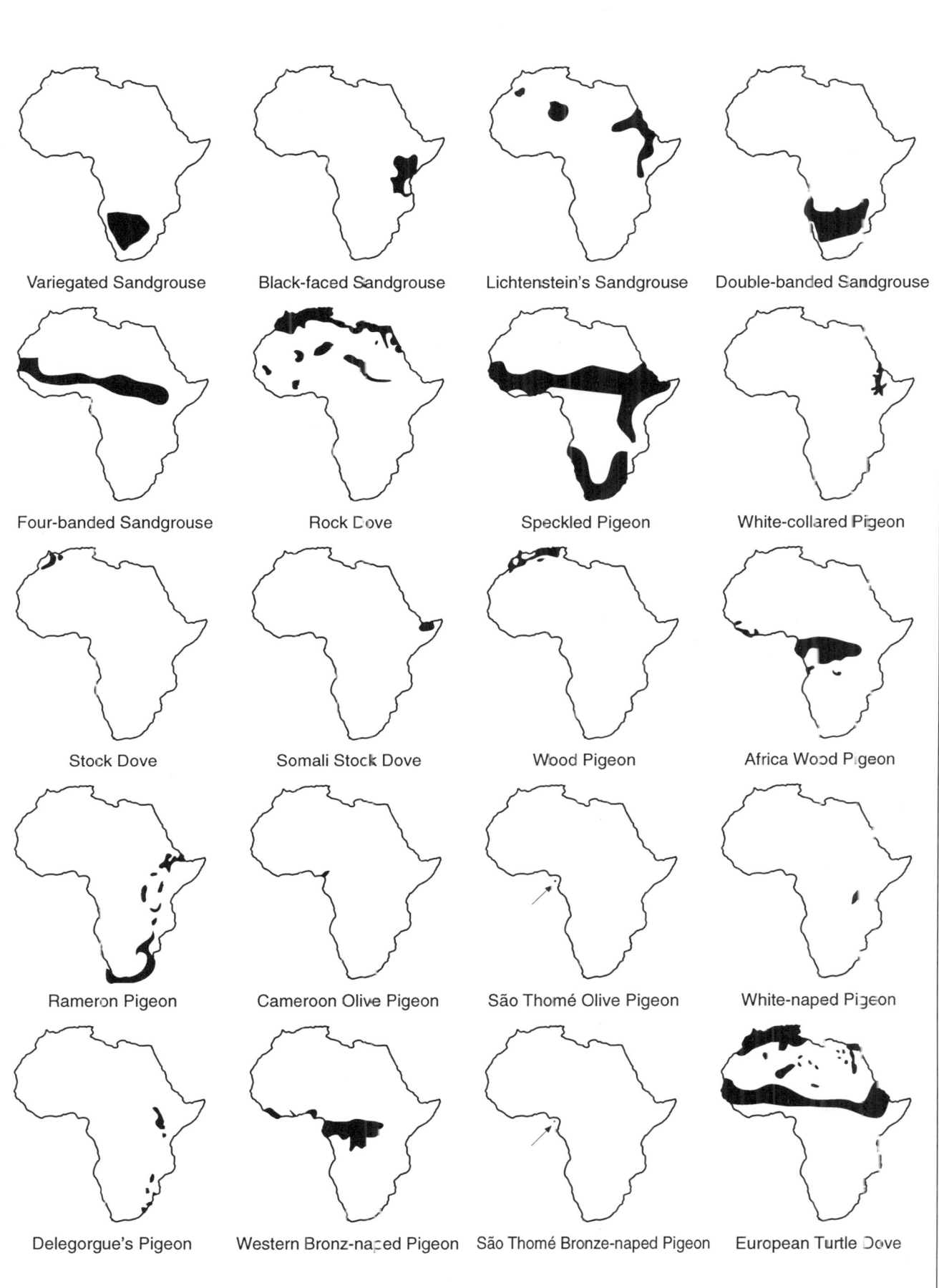

Variegated Sandgrouse

Black-faced Sandgrouse

Lichtenstein's Sandgrouse

Double-banded Sandgrouse

Four-banded Sandgrouse

Rock Dove

Speckled Pigeon

White-collared Pigeon

Stock Dove

Somali Stock Dove

Wood Pigeon

Africa Wood Pigeon

Rameron Pigeon

Cameroon Olive Pigeon

São Thomé Olive Pigeon

White-naped Pigeon

Delegorgue's Pigeon

Western Bronz-naped Pigeon

São Thomé Bronze-naped Pigeon

European Turtle Dove

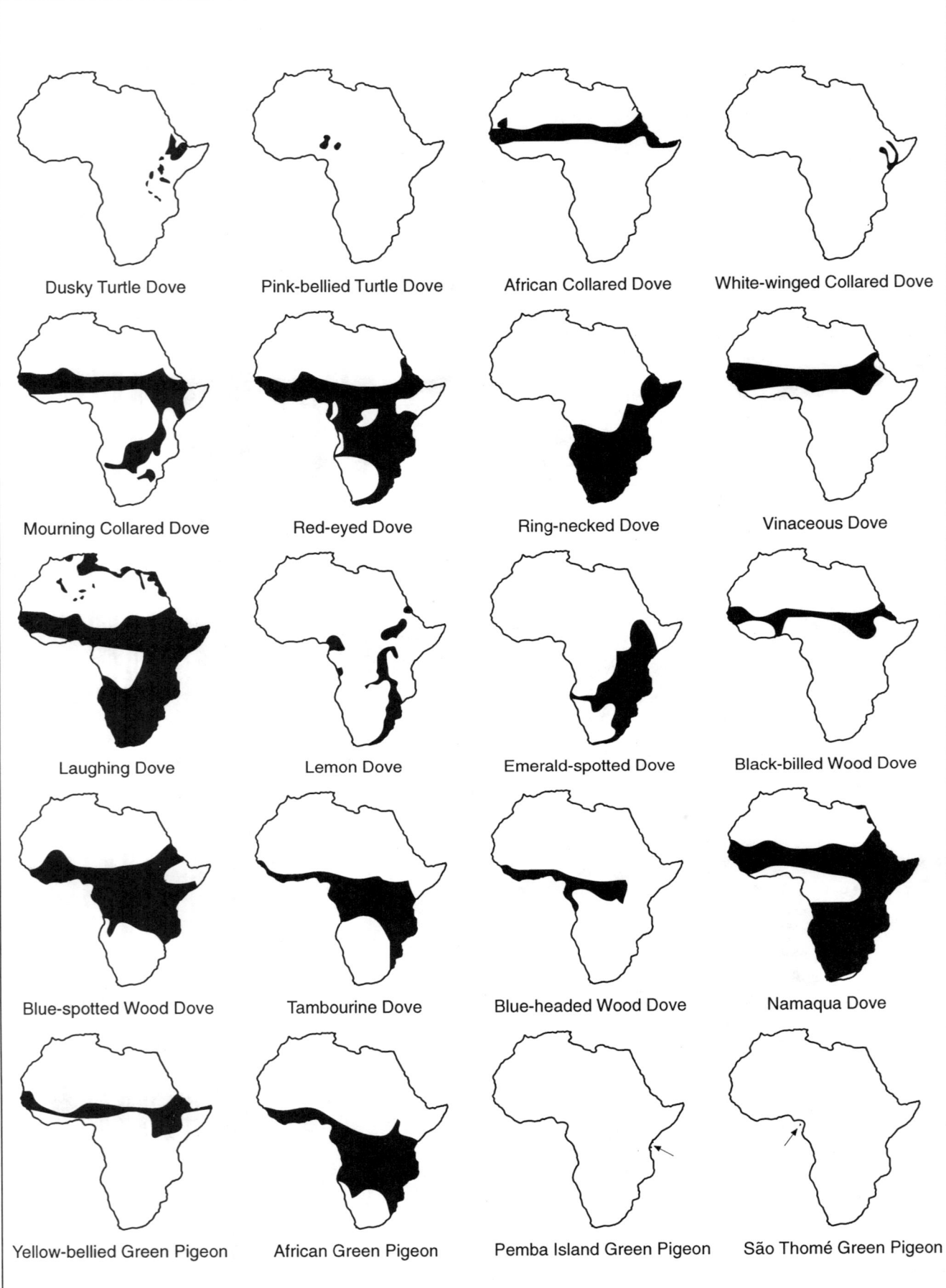

Dusky Turtle Dove

Pink-bellied Turtle Dove

African Collared Dove

White-winged Collared Dove

Mourning Collared Dove

Red-eyed Dove

Ring-necked Dove

Vinaceous Dove

Laughing Dove

Lemon Dove

Emerald-spotted Dove

Black-billed Wood Dove

Blue-spotted Wood Dove

Tambourine Dove

Blue-headed Wood Dove

Namaqua Dove

Yellow-bellied Green Pigeon

African Green Pigeon

Pemba Island Green Pigeon

São Thomé Green Pigeon

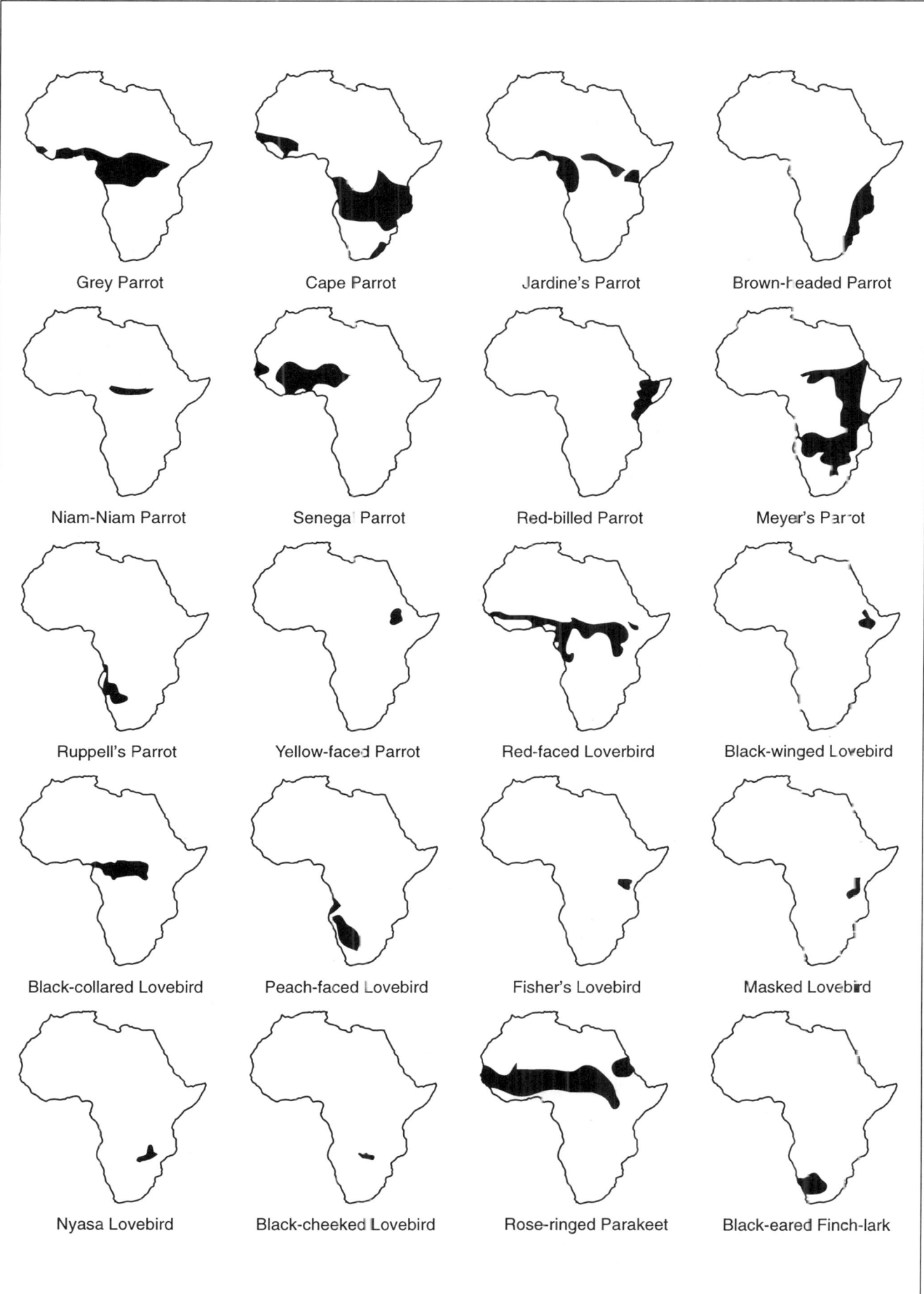

Grey Parrot

Cape Parrot

Jardine's Parrot

Brown-headed Parrot

Niam-Niam Parrot

Senegal Parrot

Red-billed Parrot

Meyer's Parrot

Ruppell's Parrot

Yellow-faced Parrot

Red-faced Loverbird

Black-winged Lovebird

Black-collared Lovebird

Peach-faced Lovebird

Fisher's Lovebird

Masked Lovebird

Nyasa Lovebird

Black-cheeked Lovebird

Rose-ringed Parakeet

Black-eared Finch-lark

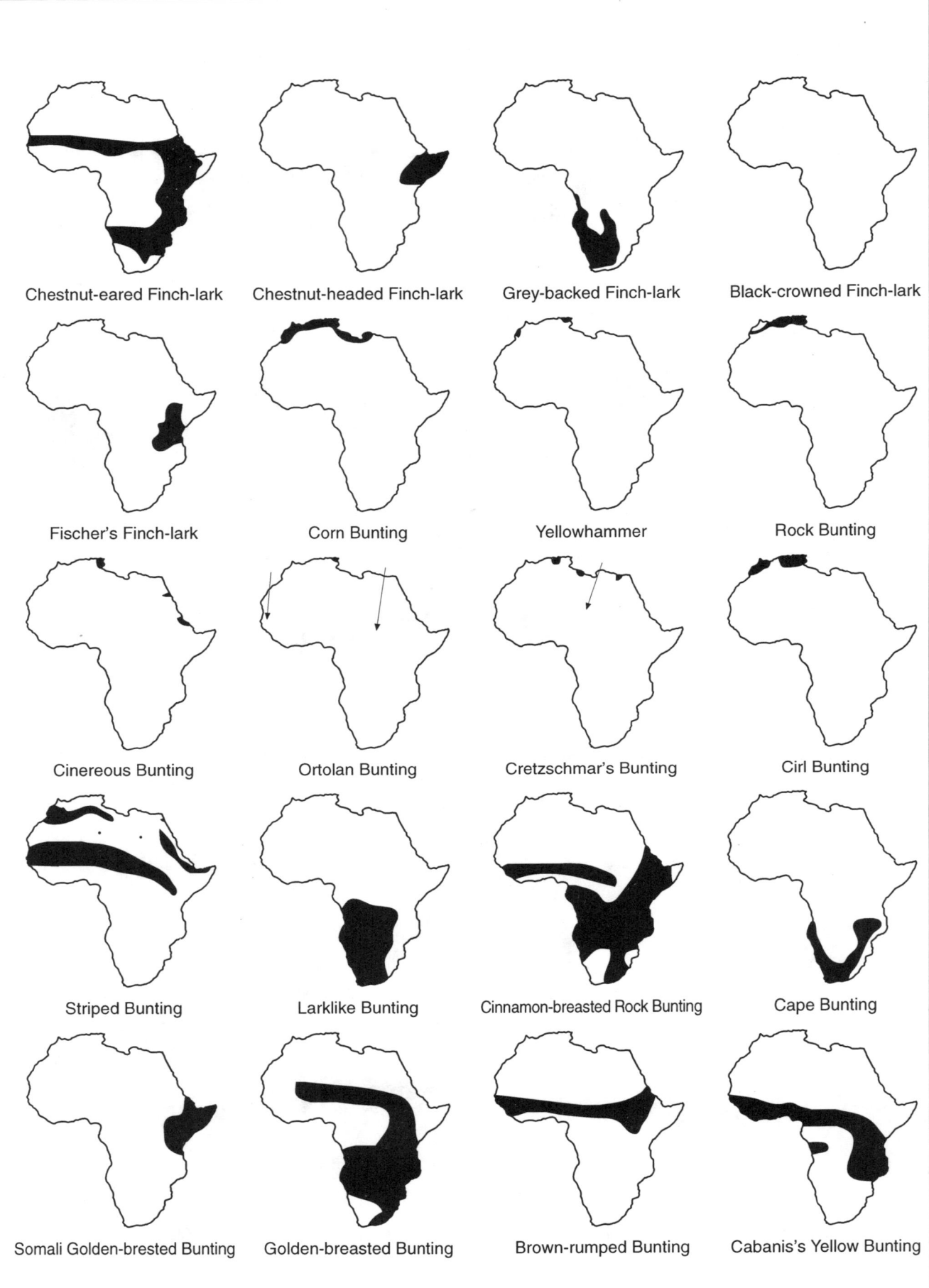

Chestnut-eared Finch-lark

Chestnut-headed Finch-lark

Grey-backed Finch-lark

Black-crowned Finch-lark

Fischer's Finch-lark

Corn Bunting

Yellowhammer

Rock Bunting

Cinereous Bunting

Ortolan Bunting

Cretzschmar's Bunting

Cirl Bunting

Striped Bunting

Larklike Bunting

Cinnamon-breasted Rock Bunting

Cape Bunting

Somali Golden-brested Bunting

Golden-breasted Bunting

Brown-rumped Bunting

Cabanis's Yellow Bunting

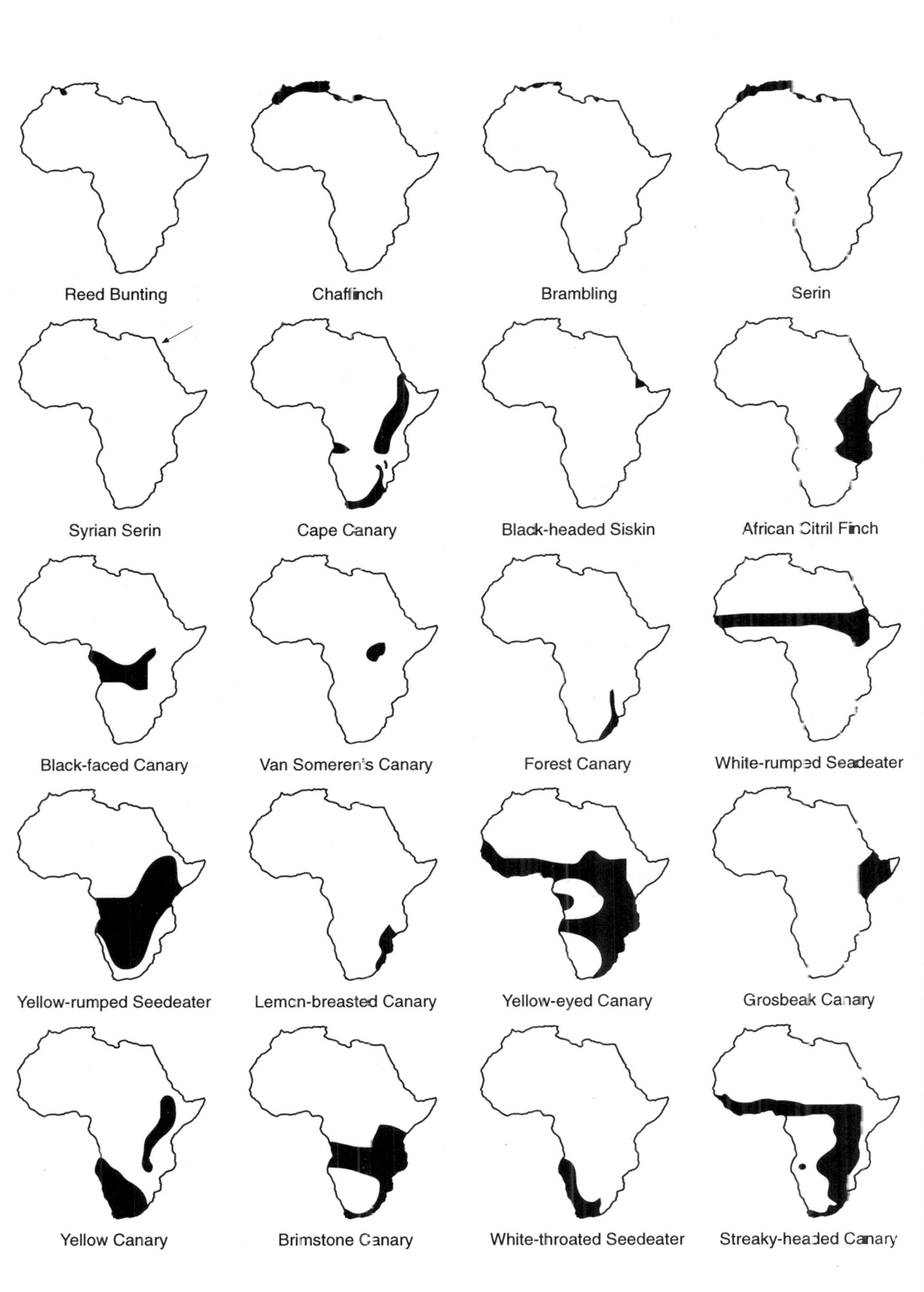

Reed Bunting

Chaffinch

Brambling

Serin

Syrian Serin

Cape Canary

Black-headed Siskin

African Citril Finch

Black-faced Canary

Van Someren's Canary

Forest Canary

White-rumped Seedeater

Yellow-rumped Seedeater

Lemon-breasted Canary

Yellow-eyed Canary

Grosbeak Canary

Yellow Canary

Brimstone Canary

White-throated Seedeater

Streaky-headed Canary

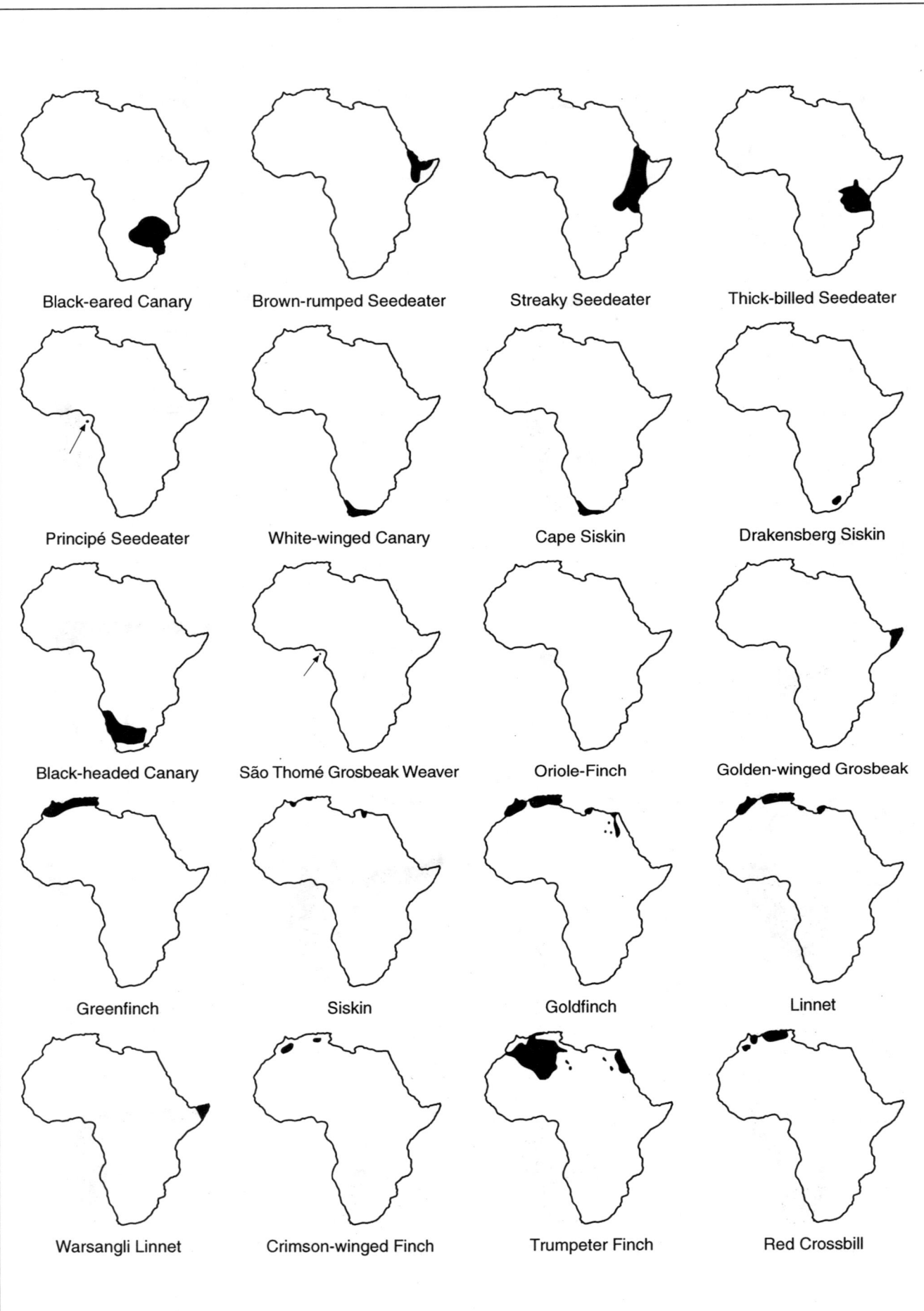

Black-eared Canary

Brown-rumped Seedeater

Streaky Seedeater

Thick-billed Seedeater

Principé Seedeater

White-winged Canary

Cape Siskin

Drakensberg Siskin

Black-headed Canary

São Thomé Grosbeak Weaver

Oriole-Finch

Golden-winged Grosbeak

Greenfinch

Siskin

Goldfinch

Linnet

Warsangli Linnet

Crimson-winged Finch

Trumpeter Finch

Red Crossbill

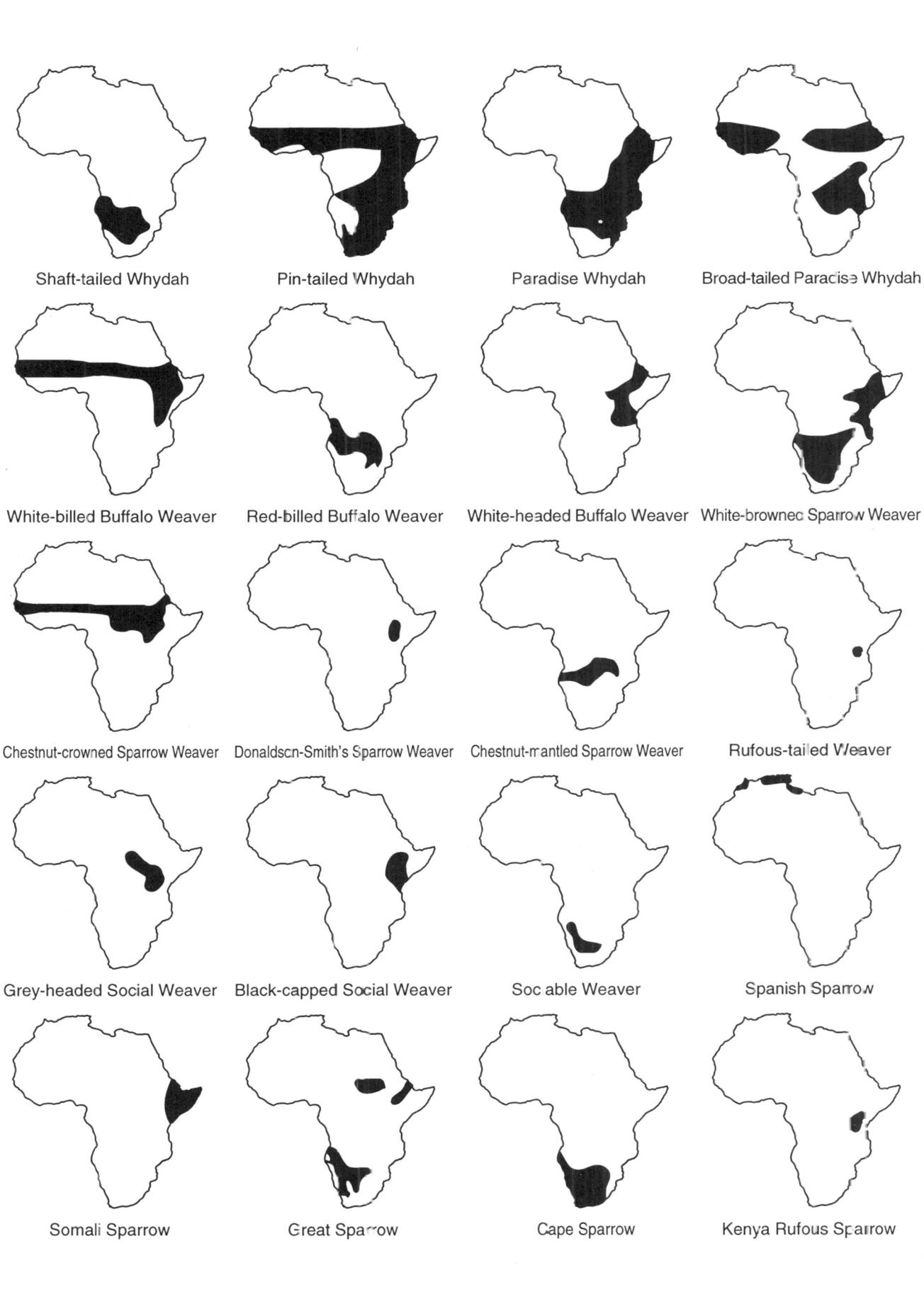

Shaft-tailed Whydah	Pin-tailed Whydah	Paradise Whydah	Broad-tailed Paradise Whydah
White-billed Buffalo Weaver	Red-billed Buffalo Weaver	White-headed Buffalo Weaver	White-browned Sparrow Weaver
Chestnut-crowned Sparrow Weaver	Donaldson-Smith's Sparrow Weaver	Chestnut-mantled Sparrow Weaver	Rufous-tailed Weaver
Grey-headed Social Weaver	Black-capped Social Weaver	Sociable Weaver	Spanish Sparrow
Somali Sparrow	Great Sparrow	Cape Sparrow	Kenya Rufous Sparrow

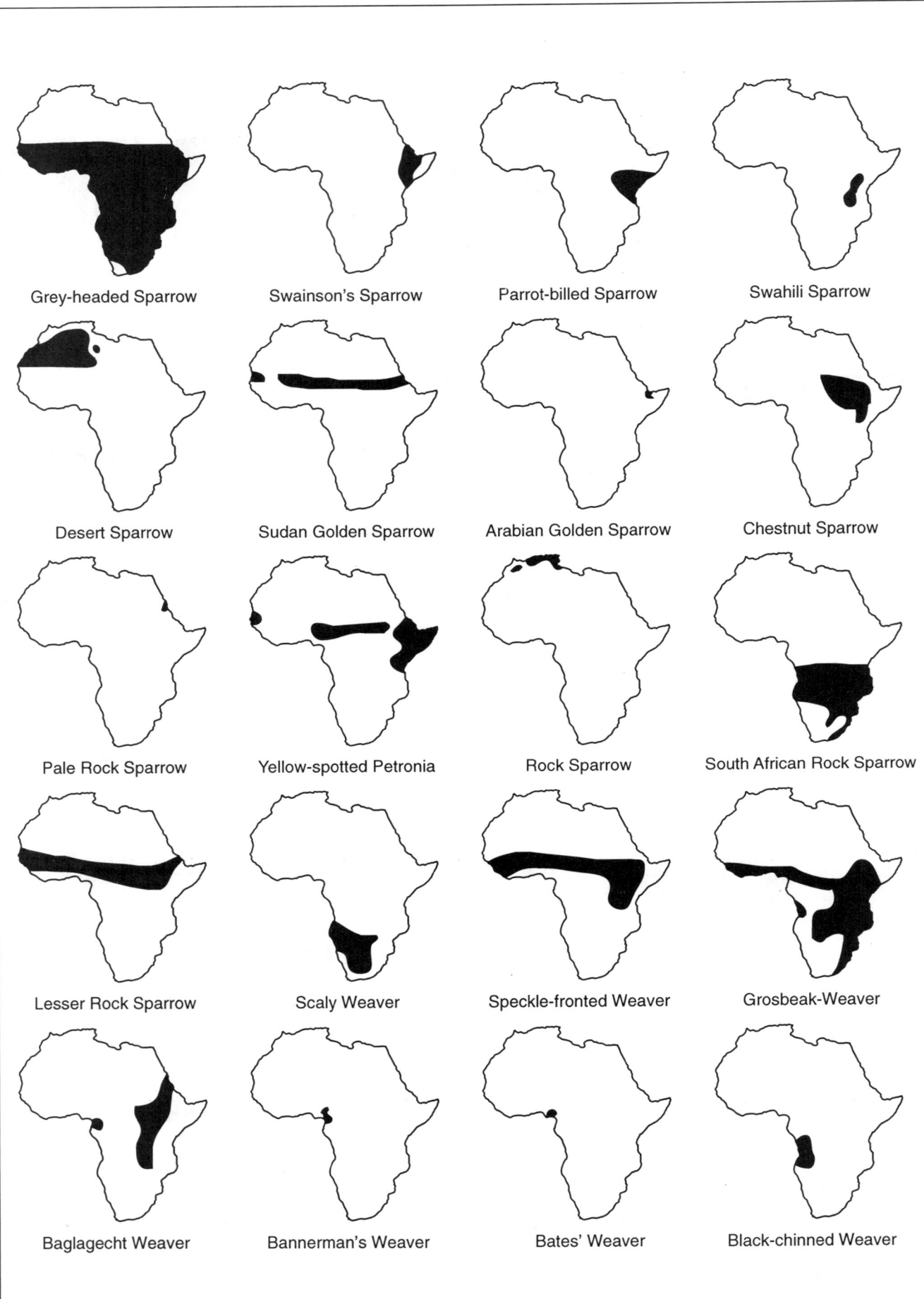

Grey-headed Sparrow

Swainson's Sparrow

Parrot-billed Sparrow

Swahili Sparrow

Desert Sparrow

Sudan Golden Sparrow

Arabian Golden Sparrow

Chestnut Sparrow

Pale Rock Sparrow

Yellow-spotted Petronia

Rock Sparrow

South African Rock Sparrow

Lesser Rock Sparrow

Scaly Weaver

Speckle-fronted Weaver

Grosbeak-Weaver

Baglagecht Weaver

Bannerman's Weaver

Bates' Weaver

Black-chinned Weaver

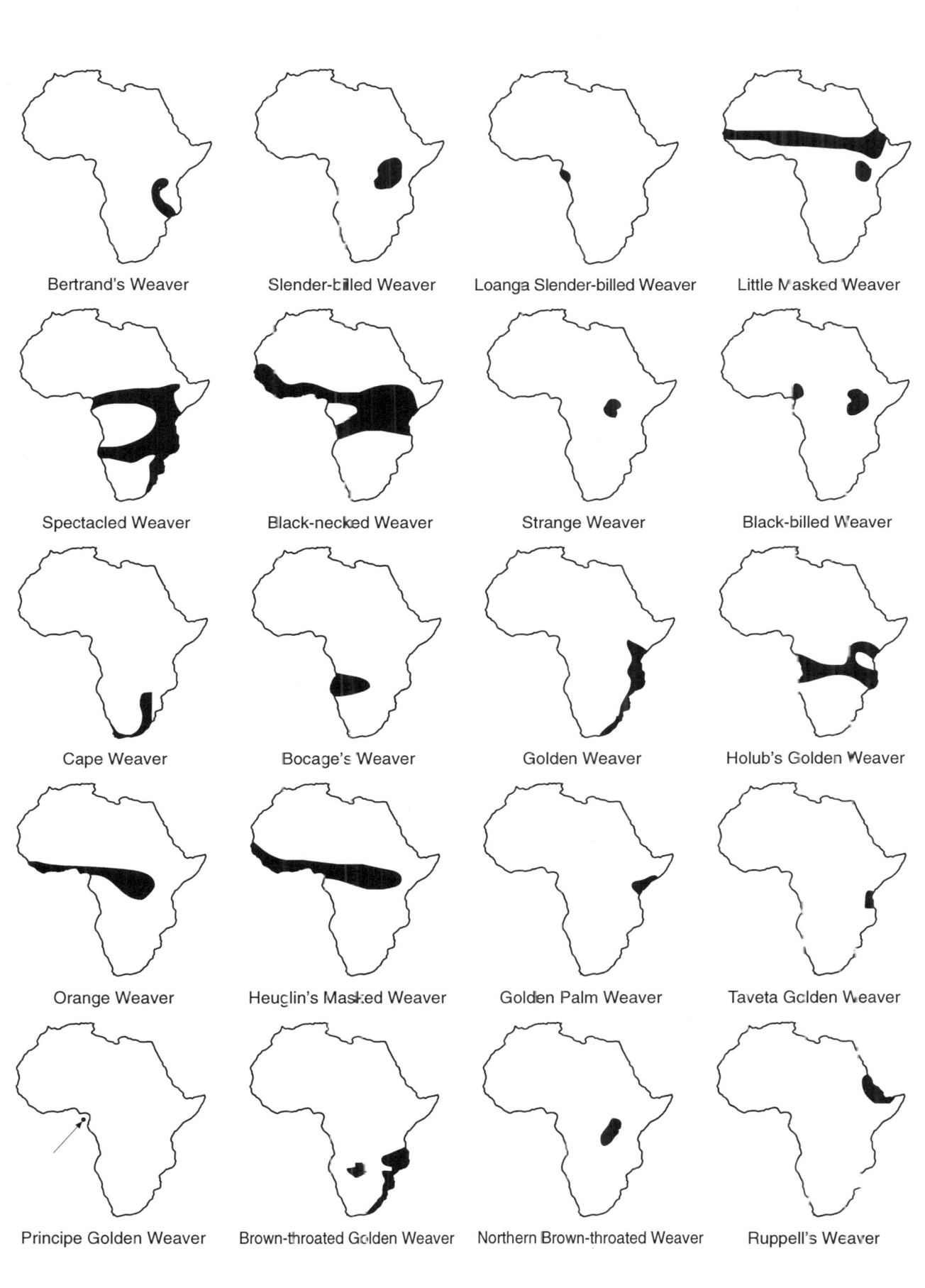

Bertrand's Weaver

Slender-billed Weaver

Loanga Slender-billed Weaver

Little Masked Weaver

Spectacled Weaver

Black-necked Weaver

Strange Weaver

Black-billed Weaver

Cape Weaver

Bocage's Weaver

Golden Weaver

Holub's Golden Weaver

Orange Weaver

Heuglin's Masked Weaver

Golden Palm Weaver

Taveta Golden Weaver

Principe Golden Weaver

Brown-throated Golden Weaver

Northern Brown-throated Weaver

Ruppell's Weaver

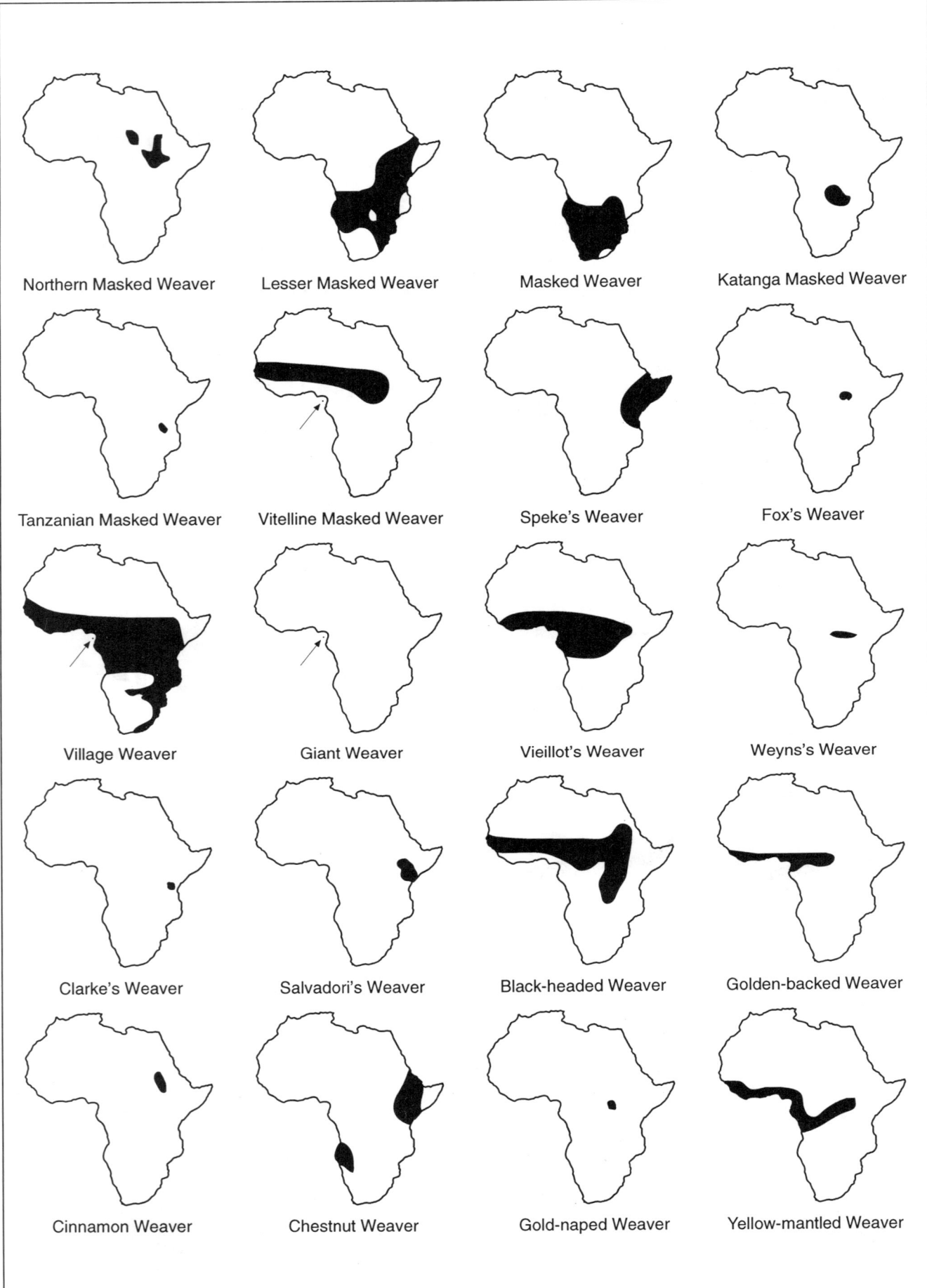

Northern Masked Weaver

Lesser Masked Weaver

Masked Weaver

Katanga Masked Weaver

Tanzanian Masked Weaver

Vitelline Masked Weaver

Speke's Weaver

Fox's Weaver

Village Weaver

Giant Weaver

Vieillot's Weaver

Weyns's Weaver

Clarke's Weaver

Salvadori's Weaver

Black-headed Weaver

Golden-backed Weaver

Cinnamon Weaver

Chestnut Weaver

Gold-naped Weaver

Yellow-mantled Weaver

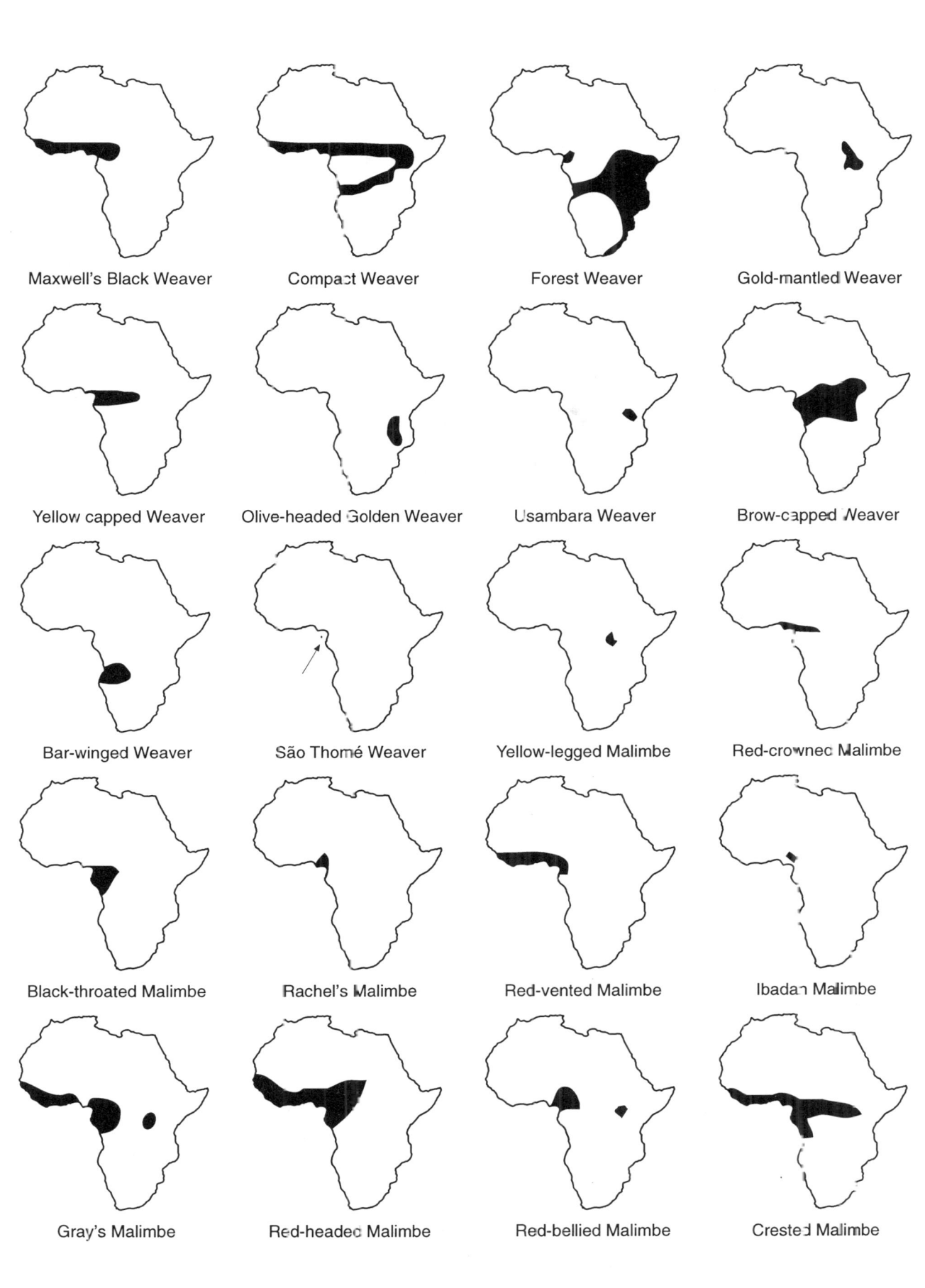

Maxwell's Black Weaver

Compact Weaver

Forest Weaver

Gold-mantled Weaver

Yellow capped Weaver

Olive-headed Golden Weaver

Usambara Weaver

Brow-capped Weaver

Bar-winged Weaver

São Thomé Weaver

Yellow-legged Malimbe

Red-crowned Malimbe

Black-throated Malimbe

Rachel's Malimbe

Red-vented Malimbe

Ibadan Malimbe

Gray's Malimbe

Red-headed Malimbe

Red-bellied Malimbe

Crested Malimbe

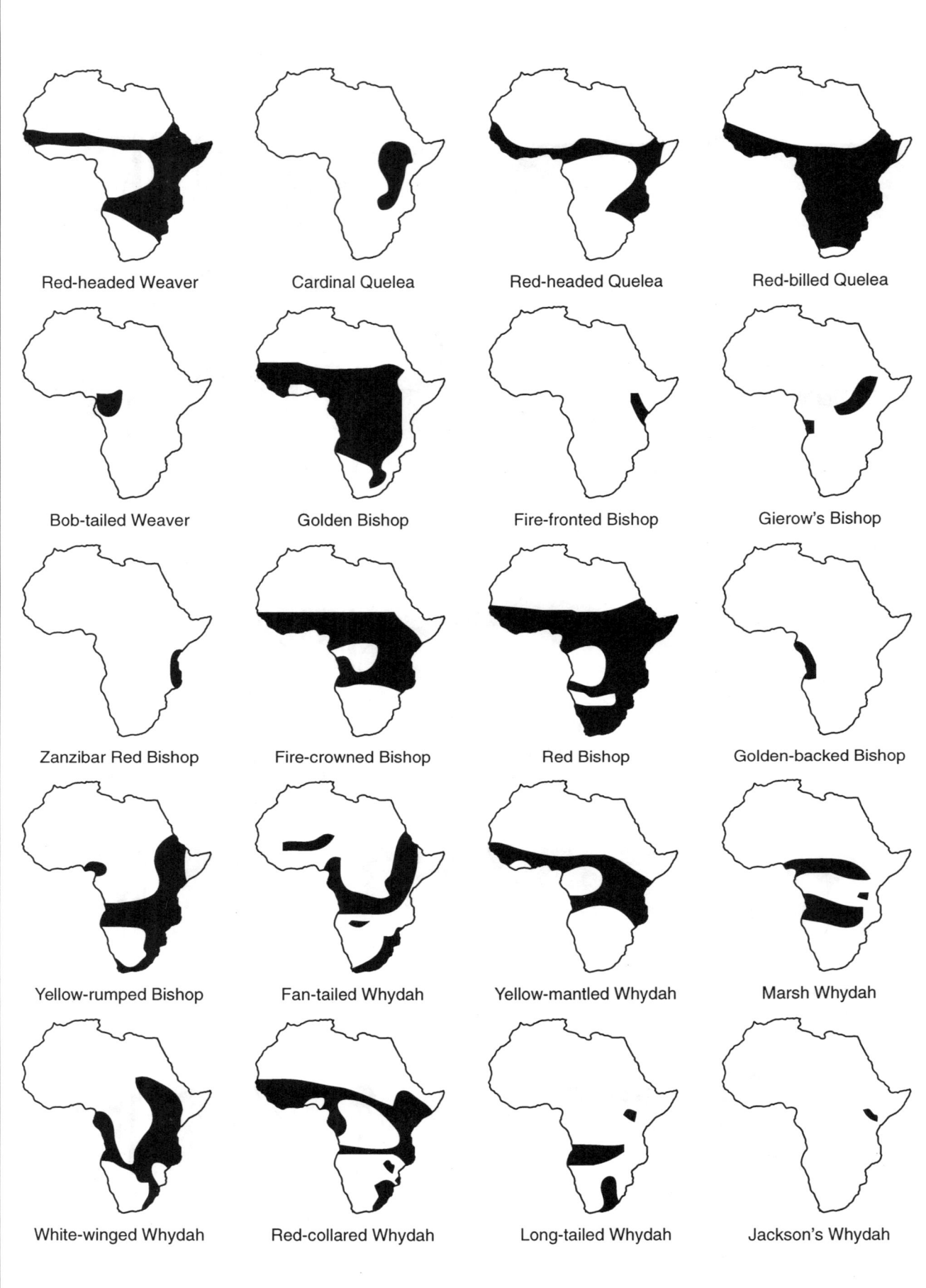

Red-headed Weaver

Cardinal Quelea

Red-headed Quelea

Red-billed Quelea

Bob-tailed Weaver

Golden Bishop

Fire-fronted Bishop

Gierow's Bishop

Zanzibar Red Bishop

Fire-crowned Bishop

Red Bishop

Golden-backed Bishop

Yellow-rumped Bishop

Fan-tailed Whydah

Yellow-mantled Whydah

Marsh Whydah

White-winged Whydah

Red-collared Whydah

Long-tailed Whydah

Jackson's Whydah

Parasitic Weaver

?rences

J, D. 1979, Lovebirds, Their care and breeding, K.R. td. England.

he Complete Cage & Aviary Birds Handbook, Pelham td, London.

Birdkeeper's Guide to Pet Birds Salamander Books Ltd,

. Birdkeeper's Guide to Parrots and Macaws. Salamander .td, London.

S.D. RIPLEY 1969, Handbook of the Birds of India and i, Oxford University Press, Bombay India.

N BROWNE, A.F., 1979, The Incubation Book, SA ing Company Limited, England. Aden, 4 volumes, Gurney kson, London.

G. & E.M. GODMAN, 1937-61, The Birds of British and and the Gulf of Aden, 4 volumes, Gurney and i, London.

L. & I.F. KEYMER, 1975 Bird Diseases Bailliere Tindall, n.

BORN, C., 1978, Die Papageien, Albrecht Philler Verslag, i, Germany.

& J.E. MISKELL 1983, Birds of Somalia and their habitat and distribution, Ornithological Sub Committee, EANHS, i, Kenya.

.W. 19--, Native Trees of Australia, W.A. Hamer Publishers, urne, Australia.

. TILFORD, T. & WOOLHAM, F. 1974, Aviary Birds in , Blandford Press, Dorset, England.

D. 1972, A Treasury of Australian Wildflowers, Published by . Smith Pty Ltd., Sydney, Australia.

MAN, D.A. 1953, The Birds of West and Equatorial Africa, imes, Oliver and Boyd, Edinburgh, Scotland.

, A. 1963, Aves de la isla de Fernando Po Editorial Coculsa, d, Spain.

G.L. 1930, Handbook of the Birds of West Africa, Bale and Danielson, London.

1934, Birds of the Southern Sahara and adjoining countries in French West Africa, Part 3.

BATES, H.J. & R.L. BUSENBARK 1963, Finches and Soft-billed Birds, T.F.H. Publications Inc. Neptune City, USA.

BAXTER, E. 1989, Nutritional value of seeds, Queensland Aviculture Vol. 16, No. 4, pp 15.

BEDFORD, DUKE OF 1969 Parrots and Parrot-like Birds, T.F.H. Publications Inc. Neptune City, USA.

BELSHAW, R.H.H. 1985, Guinea Fowl of the World, Published by Nimrod Book Services, England.

BENSON, C.W. & C.M.N. WHITE, 1957, Checklist of the Birds of Northern Rhodesia, Government Printer, Lusaka, Zambia.

F.M. BENSON 1977, Bird of Malawi, Montford Press, Limbe, Malawi.

BROOKE, R.K. DOWSETT, R.J. & M.P.S. IRWIN 1973, The Birds of Zambia, Collins, London.

BERNDT, R.M.W. 1959, Natur geschichte der Vogel Franckh'sche Verlagshandlung, Stuttgart, Germany.

BICE, C.W. 1955, Millets for Cage Birds, All-Pets Magazine, London.

BIEFELD, H. 1984, Atlas Prachtfinken, Published by Horst Muller Verlag, Walsrode, Germany.

BLOMBERRY, A. & T. RODD 1982, Palms, Angus & Robertson Publishers, Australia.

1980, Australian Native Plants, Angus & Robertson Publishers.

BLUNDELL, M. 1987, Collins Guide to the Wild Flowers of East Africa, Collins, London.

BOETTICHER, H. VON 1959, Papageien. Ziemsen-Verlag Wittenburg, Germany.

BOOSEY, E.J. 1962, Foreign Bird Keeping 2rd ed Life Books, London.

BRICKELL, N. 1986, Introduction to Southern African Cage and Aviary Birds, Volume 1. Nadine Publishers, South Hills, Johannesburg.

1989, Introduction to Southern African Cage and Aviary Birds, Volume 2. Avicultural Research Unit, Durban.

BRITTON, P.L. (ed) 1980, Birds of East Africa their habitat, status and distribution EANHS, Nairobi, Kenya.

BROCKMAN, C.F. 1986, A Field Guide to Identification of Trees of North America Golden Press, New York, USA.

BROCKMANN, J & W LANTERMAN 1981, Agaporniden, Stuttgart Verlag E. Ulmer.

BROOKE, R.K. 1984, South African Red Data Book - Birds, South African National Scientific Programme Report No 97.

BROUK, B. 1975, Plants consumed by man, Academic Press, London.

BROWN, L.H. & P.L. BRITTON 1980, The Breeding Seasons of East African Birds, EAHNS, Nairobi, Kenya.

BROWN, R.W. 1956, Composition of Scientific Works, Reese Press, New Jersey, USA.

BRYANT, A.T. 1907, A Description of Native Foodstuffs and their Preparation, Times Printing and Publishing Co , PMB.

BUNDY, G. 1976, The Birds of Libya: An Annotated checklist, British Ornithological Union, London.

BUTLER, A.G. 1901, Foreign Birds of Cage & Aviary Volumes 1 & 2, Feathered World, London.

CAVE, F.O. & J.D. MACDONALD 1955, Birds of the Sudan, Oliver and Boyd, Endinburgh, Scotland.

CHIPPENDALE, G.M. 1957-9, Poisonous Plants of the Northern Territory Part 2 & 3 Northern Territory Administration, Animal Husbandry Branch, Australia.

CHRISTIE, I. 1985, Birds a guide to a mixed collection, Bok Books International South Africa.

CHVAPIL, S. 1983, Hamlyn Colour Guides - Ornamental Birds, Hamlyn Publishing, Middlesex, England.

CLANCEY, P.A. 1964, The Birds of Natal and Zululand, Oliver and Boyd, Edinburgh.

1886 The Birds of Southern Mozambique African Bird Book Publishing, Westville, South Africa. 1967, Gamebirds of Southern Africa, Purnell, Cape Town.

1971, A Handlist of the Birds of Southern Mozambique, Lorenco Marques.

1985, The Rare Birds of Southern Africa, Winchester Press, Johannesburg.

(eds), 1980, S.A.O.S. Checklist of Southern African Birds. Southern African Ornithological Society, Pretoria.

CLAUSEN, L. 1989, Plumhead Finch Aidemosyne modesta Aviary Bird Journal (Australia) pp 2-6.

COATES PALGRAVE, K. 1957, Trees of Central Africa, National Publication Trust of Rhodesia.

1977, Trees of Southern Africa, C. Struik, Cape Town.

COLE, B.H. 1985, Avian Medicine and Surgery, Blackwell Scientific Publications, England.

COLLAR, N.J. AND S.N. STUART 1985, Threatened Birds of Africa and its islands, ICBP Bird Red Data Book 3rd ed Int. Council for Bird Preservation, Cambridge, England.

CRAMP, S. & SIMMONS. K.E.L. (eds) 1977-88, The Birds of the Western Palearctic, Volumes 1-5, Oxford University Press, England.

& PERRINS, C.M (eds) 1994. The Birds of the Wstern Palearctic. Vol viii and ix. Oxford University Press.

CRIBB, A.B. & J.W. CRIBB 1976, Wildfood of Australia, Fontana, London.

CURTIS, W.M. 1956, The Student's Flora of Tasmania, Government Printer, Hobart, Tasmania.

DALE, I.R. & P.J. GREENWAY 1961, Kenya Trees and Shrubs, Buchanan's Estate, Nairobi.

DALZIEL, J. 1937, The useful plants of West Tropical Africa, Hutchinson & Dalziel, London.

DANNHAUSER, C.S. 1980, Key to the most important veld grasses of the western Transvaal and northern Free State. Department of Agriculture and Fisheries, Pretoria.

DE JONGH, S.A. (ed) 1979, Common names of Insects. Plants Protection Research Institute.

DE ROUGEMONT, G.M. 1989, A Field Guide to the Crops of Britain and Europe, Collins, London.

DECOTEAU 1982, Exhibition Birds, T.F.H. Publications Inc. Ltd. Neptune City, USA.

1980, Wild Pigeons and Doves, T.F.H. Publications Inc. Ltd, Neptune City, USA.

DILIGER, W.C. 1960, The Comparative Ethology of the African Parrot Genus Agapornis Z. Tierpyschologie 17, pp. 649-685.

DORLING, M. 1981, Ducks, Wild Ducks and Geese for Profit, Howard Timmins, Cape Town.

DORST, J. & P. DANDELOT 1972, A Field Guide to the Large Mammals of Africa, Collins, London.

DOUGLAS, J.S. 1978, Alternative Foods - A World Guide to Lesser Known Edible Plants, Pelham Books, London.

DUGGAN, E. (ed) 1983, Illustrated Guide to the Game Park & Nature Reserves of Southern Africa, Readers Digest, Cape Town.

EDWARDS, D. et al. (ed) 1989, The Revised Edition of Finch Breeders Handbook, Volume 2, The Foreigns, A Queensland Finch Society Inc. Handbook, Australia.

ETCHECOPAR, R.L. & HUE 1967, The Birds of North Africa, Oliver and Boyd, Edinburgh, Scotland.

FARRELL, D.J. & P. STAPLETON (ed) 1985, Duck Production Science The World Practice. Sponsored by Australian Development Assistance Bureau.

FELTWELL, R. 1980, Small-Scale Poultry Keeping. Faber and Faber Limited, London.

FITTER, R. & A. FITTER 1984, Collins Guide to the Grasses, Sedges, Rushes, and Ferns of Britain and Northern Europe, Collins, London.

FLOWERS, M.L. & F. FLOWERS 19--, Finches, their Care and Breeding, Birdhaven Publishing Co. USA.

FORBES-WATSON, A.D. 1971, Skeleton Checklist of East African Birds, Nairobi, Kenya.

FORSHAW, J.M. 1973, Parrots of the World, Landsdowne Press, England.

FOX, F.W. & NORWOOD YOUNG, M.E. 1983, Food from the Veld, Delta Books(Pty) Ltd, Johannesburg.

GALLERSTEIN, G.A. 1984, Bird Owners Home Health and Care Handbook, T.F.H. Inc. Ltd., Neptune City, USA.

GARWOOD, P. 1990, Birds just love this cake for their young, Queensland Aviculture, Vol. 17, No. 6, p37.

GERRITS, H.A. 1961, Pheasants - Incubation, their care in the aviary, Blandford Press, Dorset, England.

GERSTENFELD, S.L. 1978, The Bird Care Book, Addison-Wesley Publishing Co., California, USA.

GIBBS, R.G.E., L. WATSON, M. KOEKEMOER, L. SMOOK, N.P. BARKER, H.M. ANDERSON & M.J. DALLWITZ 1990, Grasses of Southern Africa, Memoirs of the Botanical Survey of South Africa.

GILL, L. 1959, First Guide to South African Birds, Maskew Miller, Cape Town.

GLUE, D. (ed) 1982, The Garden Bird Book, Macmillan, London.

GOODMAN, L. 1980, The Aviculturist's Handbook, Juta & Sons Ltd., Johannesburg.

GOODWIN, D. 1970, Pigeons and Doves of the World, British Museum (Natural History), Cornell University Press, England.

1982, Estrildid Finches of the World, British Museum (Natural History), Oxford University Press, England.

GOS, M.W. 1981, DOVES, T.F., H. Publications Inc. Ltd. Neptune City, USA.

GRANDBANT, K. 1985, Weeds of the Crops and Gardens in Southern Africa Seal Publishing (Pty) Ltd, Johannesburg.

GRAF, A.B. 1963, Exotica, Roehres Publishing Co., New Jersey, USA.

GRAHL, W.DE 1974, Papageien unserer Erde, Hamburg, Germany.

GREENE, W.T. 1887, Parrots in Captivity, Volumes 1-3, George Bell and Sons, London.

GROUNDS, R. 1979, Ornamental Grasses, Pelham Books Ltd., London.

GROW, O. 1972, Modern Waterfowl Management & Breeding Guide, Published by American Bantam Association, USA.

GRUSON, E.S. 1978, A Checklist of the Birds of the World, Collins, London.

GRZIMEK, H.C.B. 1972-73, Animal Life Encyclopedia, Volumes 6,7 & 8, Van Nostrand and Reinhold, New York, USA.

GUGGISBERG, C.A.W. 1986, Birds of East Africa, Volume 2, Mount Kenya Sundries Ltd. Nairobi.

GUILLARMOD, J.A. 1971, Flora of Lesotho, Germany.

HADFIELD, J. & Z. GILBERT 19--, Down-to-earth Fruit & Vegetable Gardening in South Africa, Stuikhof Publishers (Pty) Ltd., Cape Town.

M. HALL, B.P. & R.E. MOREAU 1970, Atlas of Speciation of African Passerine Birds, British Museum of Natural History, London.

HAMPE, H. 1957, Die unzertrennlichen Pfungstadt, Germany.

HARDY, E. 1952, A-Z Pigeon Guide, Burke Publishing Co. Ltd. London.

HARPER, D. 1986, Pets, Birds for Home and Garden, Salamander Books Ltd, London.

HARRIS, T.Y. 1948, Australian Plants for the Garden, Angus & Robertson, Sydney.

HAYWARD, J. 1979, Lovebirds and their colour mutations, Blandford Press, Dorset, London.

HEIDENRICH 1982, Diseases of Parrots, T.F.H. Publications Inc. Ltd., Neptune City, USA.

HEINZEI, H., R. FITTER AND J. PARSLOW 1974, The Birds of Britain and Europe with North Africa and the Middle East, Collins, London.

HEMY, C. 1988, Growing vegetables in South Africa, Southern Book Publishers, Johannesburg.

HEYWOOD, V.H.E. 1978, Flowering Plants of the World, Oxford University Press, England.

HILL, C.R. 1969, Pet Library's Pigeon Guide, The Pet Library (London) Ltd. England.

HOESCH, W. 1955, Die Vogelwelt Sudwesafrikas, John Meinert, Windhoek, Namibia.

HOLLOM, P.A.D., R.F. PORTER, S. CHRISTENSEN, and I. WILLIS 1988, Birds of the Middle East and North Africa, T. & A.D. Poyser Ltd., England.

HOLM, Le Roy, G, D.L. PLUCKETT, J.V. PANCHO & J.P. HERBERGER, 1977, The World's Worst Weeds, The University of Hawaii.

HOLMES, S. 1986, Henderson's Dictionary of Biological Terms, Longman's Group, London.

HOSIE, R.C. 1969, Native Trees of Canada, Canadian Forestry Service, Queens Printer, Ottawa.

HOWARD, R. & A. MOORE 1984, A Complete Checklist of the Birds of the World, Macmillan, London.

HUTSON, H.P.W. and D.A. BANNERMAN 1931, The Birds of Northern Nigeria, Part 3, London.

HYDE, D.O. 1974, Raising Wild Ducks in Captivity, Published by E. Dutton & Co., New York.

IMMELMAN, K. 1972, Australian Finches, Angus & Robertson, Sydney.

IRWIN, M.S. 1983, The Birds of Zimbabwe, Quest Publishing, Salisbury, Zimbabwe.

IVENS, G.W., MOODY, K. & J.K. EGUNJOBI, 1978, West African Weeds, Oxford University Press, Ibadan, Nigeria.

JACKSON, F.J. 1938, The Birds of Kenya Colony and the Uganda Protectorate 3 volumes, Gurney & Jackson, London.

JAEGER, E.C. 1944, A source book of Biological Names and Terms, Charles C. Thomas, Illinois, USA.

JARRET, H.R. 1962, Africa, MacDonald and Evans Ltd, London.

JENNINGS, G. 1985, Beginner's Guide to Parrots, Paradise Press, London.

JOHNS, L. & V. STEVENSON, 1979, The Complete Book of Fruit, Angus & Robertson Publishers, Sydney.

JOHNSON-DELANEY, C.A. 1990, Choosing Safe Plants Bird Talk, Vol 8, No 3, pp 40-44.

JOUBERT, J.J. 1987, The Broiler Potential of Helmeted Guineafowl, Partial proceedings of the Gamebird Symposium, Pretoria, pp 168-171.

KNUTSON, K. 1975, Wild Plants you can eat. Dolphin Books, New York, USA.

LANTERMANN, W. 19--, The New Parrot Handbook Barrons Woodbury, New York, USA.

LE VAILANT, F. 1970, "Travels into the interior parts of Africa by way of the Cape of Good Hope in the years" 1780-85.

LEGENDRE, M. 1958, Oiseaux exotiques de cage, Paris, France.
1971, Colombes Pigeons, Et Tourterelles Editions N Boubee & Cie, Paris, France.

LEVI, W.N. 1945, The Pigeon, R.L. Bryan Co. Columbia, USA.

LICHTENSTADT, S. 1898, Zwerg-und Zierpapage Modes Verlag, Berlin, Germany.

LINT, K.C. & A.M. LINT, 1981, Diets for Birds in Captivity, Blandford Press, Poole, Dorset.

LOCKLEY, R.M. 1961, The Pan Book of Cage Birds, Pan Books Ltd, London.

LONDT J.G.H. 1984, A Beginner's Guide to Insects, The Wildlife Society of Southern Africa, Durban.

LONG, J.L. 1981, Introduced Birds of the World David & Charles, London.

LOW, R 1980, Parrots their care and breeding, Blandford Press Ltd., England.
1984, Endangered Parrots, Blandford Press, Dorset, England.

LUKE, L.P. 1952, Lovebirds and Parrotlets, Cage Birds, London and A. SILVER 19--, Aviaries Birdrooms and Cages, Cage Birds, London.

MACKWORTH-PRAED C.W. and C.H.B. GRANT 1970, Birds of West-central and Western Africa, Longmans Green and Co. Ltd. London.
1962, Birds of the Southern Third of Africa, Longmans Green and Co. Ltd. London.
1952, Birds of Eastern and North-eastern Africa, Longmans Green and Co. Ltd. London.

MACLEAN, G.L. 1985, Roberts' Birds of Southern Africa, John Voelcker Bird Book Fund, Cape Town.

MARTIN, R.M. 1983, The Dictionary of Aviculture, B.T. Batesford Ltd., England.
1986, Cage and Aviary Birds, Collins, London.

MASTERFIELD G.B. M. WALLIS, S.G. HARRISON and B.E. NICHOLSON 1969, The Oxford Book of Food Plants, Oxford University Press, London.

McLAGHLAN, G.R. & R. LIVERSIDGE 1978, Roberts Birds of South Africa, CNA, Cape Town.

MEINERTZHAGEN, R. 1930, Nicoll's Birds of Egypt, 2 volumes, Hugh Rees, London.

MESSENT, P.R. 19--, Introduction to Diseases in Cage Birds, Published by Isles d'Avon Ltd, England.

MULLER, M.A.N. 1984, Grasses of South West Africa/Namibia, The Directorate of Agriculture and Forestry, Windhoek.

NAETHER, C. & VRIENDS, M.M. 1978, Building an Aviary, T.F.H. Publications, Inc. Ltd, Neptune City, N.J.
1979 Raising Doves and Pigeons, David McKay Company Inc. New York, USA.

NELSON, B. 1973, Azraq: desert oasis, Allen Lane, London.

NICOLAI, J. 1981, Breeding Birds at Home, T.F.H. Publications Inc. Ltd, Neptune City, USA.

OXLEY, R.E. 1982, Management Methods of a back-garden collection, Avicultural Magazine, Vol. 88, No 4, pp. 239-243.

PALGRAVE, K.C. 1967, Trees of Central Africa, National Publication Trust of Zimbabwe.
1988, Trees of Southern Africa, Struik Publishers, Cape Town.

PALMER, E. 1983, A Field Guide to the Trees of Southern Africa, Collins, London.

PARADISE, P.R. 1979, African Grey Parrot, T.F.H. Publications Inc. Ltd, Neptune City, USA.

PARKER, H.H. 1959, Aviculture in South Africa, Afrikaans Pers, Johannesburg.

PEARCE, D.W. 1983, Aviary Design and Construction, Blandford Press, Dorset, England.

PERCIVAL, C. 1985, Softbilled Birds, 3rd National Avicultural Convention, Victorian Avicultural Council, Melbourne.

PETERS, J.L. 1931-70, Checklist of the Birds of the World, Harvard University Press, Massachusetts, USA.

PIENAAR, K. 1984, The South African What Flower is That, C. Struik, Cape Town.

PINTER, H. 1979, Handbuch der Papageienkunde Franchk'sche Verlagshandlung, Stuttgart, Germany.

POPENOE, W. 1924, Manual of Tropical and Sub-tropical Fruits, Macmillan Co. New York, USA.

PRIEST, C. 1934, The Birds of Southern Rhodesia, William Clowes and Sons Ltd, England.

PROZESKY, O.P.M. 1976, A Field Guide to the Birds of Southern Africa, Collins, London.

RAMSAY, W. 1923, The Birds of Europe and North Africa, Edinburgh, Scotland.

REITZ, J.B. de V (ed) 1972, A Guide to the National Parks, Game and Nature Reserves of Southern Africa, S.A. Nature Foundations, Stellenbosch.

RESTALL, R.L. 1975, Finches and other Seed-eating birds. Faber and Faber, London.

RISDON, D.H.S. 1953, Foreign Birds for Beginners, Cage Birds, London.

ROBBINS, G.E.S. 1981, Quail, Their Breeding and Management, Published by World Pheasant Association, England.

1984, Partridges Their Breeding and Managementy, Published by Boyell Press, England.

ROBERTS, B.R. & J.H. FOURIE 1985, Common Grasses of the Northern Cape, Northern Cape Livestock, Co-operative Limited, Vryburg.

1973, Common Grasses of the Orange Free State, The Orange Free State Provincial Administration, Bloemfontein.

ROBILLER, F. 1986, Lexikon der Vogelhalthung Leipzig, Germany.

ROBILLER, L. 1974, Cage and Aviary Birds, Almark Publishing Co. London.

ROGERS, C.H. 1986, Encyclopedia of Cage and Aviary Birds, Penham Books, London.

ROOTS, C. 1975, Exotic Birds, Cassell, London.

ROWAN, M.K. 1984, The Doves, Parrots, Louries & Cuckoos of Southern Africa, David Philip, Cape Town.

RUTGERS, A & K.A. NORRIS, 1972, Encyclopedia of Aviculture, Vol. 2, Blandford Press, London.

1977, Encyclopedia of Aviculture, Vol. 3, Blandford Press, London.

RUTGERS, A. 1976, The Handbook of Foreign Birds, Volume 2, Blandford Press, Dorset, England.

1977, The Handbook of Foreign Birds, Volume 1, Blandford Press, Dorset, England.

SCHOLTZ, C.H. & E. HOLM, 1985, Insects of Southern Africa, Butterworth Publishers (Pty) Ltd, Durban.

SIETAS, K. 1990, Lecture Notes on Feeding Birds, Queensland Aviculture, Vol. 17, No 4, pp 40-41.

SERLE, W., G.J. MOREL and W. HARTWIG 1977, A Fieldguide to the Birds of West Africa, Collins, London.

SHEPHARD, M. 1989, Aviculture in Australia, keeping and breeding aviary birds, Black Cockatoo Press, Victoria.

SILVA, T. and B. KOTLAR 1981, Breeding Lovebirds, T.F.H. Publications Inc. Ltd, Neptune City, USA.

SKAIFE, S.H. 1953, African Insect Life, Longmans Green & Co. London.

SKEAD, C.J. (ed) 1960, The Canaries, Seedeaters and Buntings of Southern Africa, CNA, Johannesburg.

SMITH, A.G. 19--, Parrot Eggs. A.F.A. Watchbird, Vol. 18, No 4.

SMITH, C.A. 1966, Common Names of South African Plants, Department of Agricultural Technical Services, Pretoria.

SMITH, G.A. 1979, Lovebirds and Related Parrots, T.F.H. Publications Inc. Ltd. USA.

SMITH, L.J. 1987, The Rearing of Gamebird Chicks in Captivity, Partial Proceedings of Gamebird Symposium, Pretoria, pp. 41-42.

SMITHERS, REAY H.N. 1983, The Mammals of the Southern African Sub-region, The University of Pretoria.

SNOW, D.W. (ed) 1978, An atlas of speciation in African non-passerine birds, British Museum of Natural History, London.

SODERBERG, P.M. 19--, Waxbills, Weavers and Whydahs, T.F.H. Publications Inc. Ltd. Neptune City, USA.

1977, All About Lovebirds, T.F.H. Publications Inc. Ltd. Neptune City, USA.

STEINBACHER, G. 1959, Cage and Garden Birds, B.T. Batsford Ltd, London.

STEYN, D.L. 1934, The toxicology of plants in South Africa, Published by Central News Agency, Johannesburg.

STRINGER, M. 1977, Identification of Cage and Aviary Birds, Arco Publishing Inc., New York, USA.

STROUD, R. 1964, Diseases of Birds, T.F.H. Publications Inc. Ltd. Neptune City, USA.

STURTEVANT, E.L. 1972, Edible Wild Plants of the World, New York, USA.

STOMBERG, J. 19--, A Guide to Better Hatching. Stromberg Publishing Company, Minnesota, USA.

TAINTON, N.M. BRANSBY, D.I. & P. DEV. BOOYSEN, 1976, Common Veld and Pasture Grasses of Natal, Shuter & Schooter, Pietermaritzburg.

TEITLER, R. 1984, Starting right with Lovebirds, T.F.H. Publications Inc. Ltd. Neptune City, USA.

THOMSEN, P. and P. JACOBSEN, 1979, The Birds of Tunisia: an annotated checklist, Jelling Aps. Denmark.

TOLLEFSON, C.I. 1969, Nutrition & Diseases of cage and aviary birds, Lea & Febiger, Philadelphia, USA.

TRAYLOR, M.A. 1962, Notes on the birds of Angola, Publicacoes culturais Cimpanhia de diamentes de Angola.

TROLLOPE, J. 1983, The Care and Breeding of Seed-eating Birds, Blandford Press, London.

URBAN, E. 1966, Shell Guide to Ethiopian Birds, Addis Ababa, Eto Publications.

HILARY FRY, C and S. KEITH, 1988, The Birds of Africa, Vol. 2, 1983, Academic Press, London.

VAHRMEIJER, J. 1981, Poisonous Plants of Southern Africa that cause stock losses, Tafelberg Publishers Limited, Cape Town.

VAN TYNE, J. and A.B. BERGER 1959, Fundamentals of Ornithology, John Wiley and Sons Inc. New York, USA.

VANE, E.N.T. 1958, Guide to Lovebirds and Parrotlets, Iliffe Books Ltd., England.

VICKERY, M.L. 1979, Plant Products of Tropical Africa, Macmillian Press, Ltd, London.

VILMORIN-ANDRIEUX 19--, Dasgrosse Buch der Vogel in kafig und Voliere, Munchen, Germany.

VRIENDS, M.M. 19--, The Vegetable Garden, John Murray Publishers, California, USA.

1974, Het Sierparkietenboek, Amsterdam, Holland.

1978, Encyclopedia of Lovebirds and other Dwarf Parrots, T.F.H. Publications Inc. Ltd. Neptune City, Usa.

1979, Parakeets, of the World, T.F.H. Publications Inc. Ltd. Neptune City, USA.

1981, Starting an aviary, T.F.H. Publications Inc. Ltd. Neptune City, USA.

1983, Papegaaien en Parkieten Best, The Netherlands: Zuid Boekproducties.

1984, The Macdonald Encyclopedia of Cage and Aviary Birds, Macdonald and Co. Publishers, London.

1985, Breeding Cage and Aviary Birds, Howell Book House Inc., New York, USA.

1986, Lovebirds, Barrow's Educational Series, Woodbury, New York, USA.

1987, The Complete Book of Finches, Howell Book House, Inc., New York, USA.

VRIENDS, T. 1985, cage and Aviary Birds, Ward Lock Ltd. London.

WALRAVEN, C. 1984, Onze Papegaai be Regenboog, Amsterdam, Holland.

WALSH, B. 1986, B.B.B. Aviary Bird Journal (Australia) pp 312-313.

WALTERSON, M. 1980, The Complete Birds of the World, David & Charles, Newton Abbot, England.

WATT, J.M. & M.G. BRYER-BRANDWYK, 1962, Medicinal & Poisonous Plants of Southern and Eastern Africa, Livingstone Publishers, London.

WHITE, C.M.N. 1963, A Revised Checklist of African Flycatchers, Tits, Tree Creepers, Sunbirds, White-eyes, Honey-eaters, Buntings, Finches, Weavers and Waxbills, Government Printer, Lusaka, Zambia.

WILLIAMS, J.G. 1973, A Fieldguide to the Birds of East and Central Africa, Collins, London.

1976, A Fieldguide to the National Parks of East Africa, Collins, London.

1980, A Fieldguide to the Birds of East Africa, Collins, London.

WILSON, C. & N. HAMILTON, 1986, Breeding the Western Spinebill Acanthorhynchus superciliosus, Av culture Magazine, Vol 90, No 1, pp 1-10.

WINTERBOTTOM, J.M. 1971, Priest's Eggs of Southern African Birds, Winchester Press, Johannesburg.

WOOLHAM, F. 1987, The Handbook of Aviculture, Blandford Press, Dorset, England.

WRIGHT, M. 1984, The Complete Handbook of Garden Plants, Michael Joseph, Rainbird Publishing Group Ltd. England.

WURST, I. 1980, Soft egg-food, Bird Keeping in Australia.

YEALLAND, J.J. 1971, Cage Birds in Colour. H.F. & G. Witherby Ltd. London.

ZIMMERMAN, D.A. Turner, D.A. & D.J. Pearson 1996, Birds of Kenya and Northern Tanzania Russel Friedman Books cc, Halfway House, South Africa.

ANRC Aviculturist's Nest Record Card; ARU Avicultura Research Unit; NASNRC Natal Avicultural Society Nest Record Card; SAANRC South African Aviculturist's Nest Record Card; SAADRC South African Aviculturist's Diet Record Card; NASDRC Natal Avicultural Society Diet Record Card; ADRC Aviculturist's Diet Record Card.

Information was obtained from articles by the following authors:

Abs, M.; Acocks, J.P.H.; Adams, P.J.; Adlersparre A.; Ager, B.E.S.; Alderson, R.; Alderton, D.; Alexander, B.; Alexander, C.J.; Allan, D.; Allen, G.H.; Allen, R.; Allen, W.A.; Amadon, D.; Anderson, M.; Andres, R.J.; Angus, A.; Anon; Appert, O.; Arageus, A.; Archer, G.; Armstrong, E.M.; Ash, J.S.; Ashley-Maberly, C.; Aspinwall, D.R.; Attenburg, W.; Attwell, R.I.G.; Averin, Y.; Avery, M.L.; Baars, W.; Baggs, R.J.; Blaikie, W.B.; Bailey, D.; Bain, W.; Bannerman, D.A.; Bannerman, E.A.; Bannister, S.; Baptista, L.F.; Barber, R.M.; Barnicoat, F.; Barnley, F.; Barnley, T.; Barns, T.A.; Barnwick, E.; Barrena, R.P.; Barrena R.P.; Barrett, R.; Basilo, A.; Bass, J. Mrs; Bassett, J.S.; Batchelor, G.R.; Bates, R.S.P.; Bauling, T.; Baxter, E.; Beason, R.C.; Bechinger, F.; Bede, P.; Belskaya, G.S.; Belcher, C.F.; Bell, H.L.; Bell, J.; Bell, R.; Belshae, R.H.H.; Bennett, G. Benson, C.W.; Benson, F.H.; Benson, F.M.; Berard, R.; Bergman, G.; Bernasek, O.; Bernis, F.; Berriman, R.; Berruti, A.; Berry, G.; Berry, R.J.; Betham, R.M.; Bethell, F.E.; Bevan, G.; Bielfeld, H.; Bigalke, R.C.; Bishop, H.; Black, B.; Black, H.L.; Blackburn, H.; Blanchet, A.; Blane, S.; Bleksley, C.H.; Blome, R.; Blondel, J.; Blynn, D.; Boardmann, J. Mrs; Boardmann, J.; Bocage, J.A.; Boch, W.J.; Boehme, R.L.; Boenig, K.G.; Bolster, R.C.; Bond, A.C. Boosey, E.J.; Booyse, E.; Bortoli, L.; Boshoff, A.F.; Botes, P.J.; Boughen, D.; Boughton-Leigh, P.W.T.; Bourassa, J.B.; Bourke, D.; Bourliere, F.; Bourquin, O.; Bouvier, A.; Bowden,J.; Bowen, W.W.; Bowland, A.; Boyer, H.J.; Braby, M.E.; Bracegirdle, J.; Bradbury, R.; Braine, J.W.S.; Braine, S.G.; Brickell, N.I.; Bright, H.E.; Broadley, D.G.; Broekhuysen, G.J.; Bromet, H.; Bromley, F.C.; Brooke, R.; Brooker, A.; Brooks, D.J.; Brooksbank, A.; Brossett, A. Brown, A.; Brown, D.J.; Brown, D.W.; Brown, G.K.; Brown, P.; Brown, R.E.B.; Bruggers, R.L.; Brunel, J.; Bub, H.; Buchan, J.; Buchanan, D.R.C.; Buckingham, R.; Buckle, M.G.; Budde, H.; Bulman, J.F.H.; Bump, G.; Bunning, J.; Burkard, B.; Burkard, R.; Burton, R.W.; Butler, A.G.; Butler, E.A.; Cade, T.C.; Cade, T.J.; Calder, D.R.; Callaghan, E.; Cameron, D.; Campbell, A.E.; Campbell, H.; Candy, M.; Cannon, C.E.; Cardwell, P.J.; Carpenter, R.; Casado, M.A.; Castell, P.; Cawkett, E.M.; Cayley, N.W.; Charlton, D.O.; Channing, A.; Chapin, J.P.; Chapman, F.M.; Chappuis, C.; Chappuls, C.; Cheesman, R.E.;

Chessman, R.E.; Chittenden, H.N.; Chivapil, S.; Chubb, E.C.; Cleland, J.B.;Clement, J.; Clewlow, E.A; Clinning C.F.; Coelho, A.; Coetzee, E.; Colebrook-Robjent, J.F.R.; Coles, D.; Collar, N.; Collar, N.J.; Collias, E.; Collias, E.C.; Collias, N.E.; Collins, D.; Collins, J.; Collins, R.; Colston, P.R.; Compertz, T.; Conacher, G.D.; Cooper, J.; Cotterell, R.; Coupe, M.F.; Courtenay-Latimer Miss; Cox, G.W.; Craig, A.J.F.K.; Crick, H.Q.P.; Crook, J.H.; Cross, K.; Cullen, P.A.; Cummings, S.C.; Cummings, W.D.; Cunningham, J.M.; Currie, M.H.; Curry-Lindahl, K.; Cyrus, D.; De Camara-Smeets. Dale, D.; Dalton, F.J.; Danzel, A.B.; Dathe, H.; David, J.H.M.; Davidson, D.C.; Davies, C.G.; Davis, G.; Day, D.; Day, E.; De Grahl, W.; De Swart, D.; Dean, W.R.J.; Deckert, G.; Decoux, A.; Dekeyser, P.L.; Delacour, J.; Delius, J.D.; Delmee, E.; Dennison, V. Mrs; Dennison, D.; Descarpentris, A.; Deskert, H.; Desmond, T.; Dhaepens, F.C.; Dilger W.C.; Dilks, P.J.; Disney, H.J.; Dodd, K.; Dodwell, G.T.; Dolgushin, A.; Dommer, B.P.; Dorn, J.; Dorrofield, D.C.; Downey, S.; Dowsett, R.J.; Drake, K.; Dresser, H.E.; Drost, R.; Dudley, E.P.V.; Duve, G.; Earle, R.A.; Eckl, G.; Edmonds, J.A.; Eisentraut, M.; Eisner, E.; Eisner, E.A.; Elgood, J.H.; Elliot, C.C.H.; Ellis, M.; Elwell, N.; Emlen, J.T. Emslie, J.; Endes, M.; Erard, C.; Erickson, W.A.; Etchecopar, R.D.; Evans, Evans, S.M.; S.M.; Evard, C.; Everitt, C.; Ewers, S.L.; Exell, W.A.; Fairbairn W.A.; Falkiner, S.; Farrand, J.; Farrar, R.; Farthing, M.; Faruq, S.A.; Fent, R.; Ferguson-Lees, I.F.; Festa, E.; Fillmer, H.R.; Finn, F.; Finney, A.C.; Finsch, O.; Flieg, M.C.; Flint, V.E.; Flugel, G.T.; Forbes, W.A.; Ford, A.H.; Ford, N.; For-Shaw, J.M.; Fowle, R.K.; Frampton, P.; Frampton, T.; Fraser, M.; Freeman, J.A.; Friedmann, H.; Frisch, O.; Fritz, H.; Fry, C.H.; Grace, K.; Gallagher, M.; Gallagher, M.D.; Ganya, I.M.; Garland, I.; Garrick, R.; Garwood, P. Mrs; Garwood, P.; Gass, M.C.I.; Gaugris, Y.; Garvrn, V.F.; George, F. George, U.; Feriach, R.; Germain, M.; German, O. Geyr von Schweppenburg, H.; Gibb, J.N.; Gibson, L.; Gibson, T.; Gill, E.L.; Gill, H.B.; Gillet, H.; Gillman, C.; Gilpin, H.G.B.; Ginn, P.; Glutz von Blotzheim, U.N.; Glutz, U.N.; Godfrey, R.; Godan E.M.; Goger, R.; Gooders, J.; Goodwin, D.; Gordge, K.G.; Gore, M.E.J.; Goriup, P. Grabrandt, C.; Graib, C.L.; Granbrandt, K.; Grannersberger, K.; Grant, M.; Gray, J.T.; Gray, J.Y.T.; Green, A.; Green, R.E.; Greenway, K.W.; Greenway, P.J.; Greenwayk, W.; Greghorn, C.; Greig-Smith, P.A.; Griffiths, A.; Grimes, L.G.; Grobler, J.H.; Grobler, J.J.; Grobler, N.; Grobs, S.A.; Grote, H.; Groves, R.H.; Grubbe, O.; Grzimek, B.; Guichard, G.; Gush, R.D.; Guttinger, H.R.; Haagner, C.; Haagner, C.H.; Hack, D.; Haeflin, H.; Hald, E.; Hall, D. Mrs; Hall, M.F.; Hallack, M.H.; Hamed, Hamilton, N.; D.M.; Hampe, H.; Hammer, D.B.; Hanson, B.; Hadingham, G; Harland, K.C.; Harman, I.; Hazrper, D; Harris, F.; Harris, R.; Harrison, C J.O.; Hartert, E.; Hartlaub, G.; Harwin, R.W.; Hatch, W.R.; Haun, M.; Hay, P.; Hayward J.; Hazel, S.S.; Hearnshaw, J.; Heath-Stubbs. B. Mrs; Heath-Stubbs, B.; Hegazi, E.M.; Heim de Balsac, H.; Heinrich, G.; Henstock, J.H.; Henze, I.; Herroelen, P.; Heslop, I.R.P.; Heston, J.; Heuglin van M.T.A.D.; Hewitt, J. Miss; Hick, U.; Hieronymus, P.; Hill, R.; Hill, R.; Hinseley, S.A.; Hitchins, P.M.; Hockey, D.J.; Hockey, P.A.R.; Hodges, M.; M. Hodkinson, J.B.; Hoesch, W. Holbek, F.; Holcombe, L.C.; Holder, J.; Holman, F.C.; Hopkirs, D.W.; Hopkinson, E.; Horner, I.F.; Horner, J.; Horstkotte, E.; Hosken, J.H.; Hough, B. Miss; Hough, B.; Hough, R.; Howard, W.E.; Howell, N.S.; Hubbard, M.M.; Hue, F.; Hume, A.O.; Hunter, C.; Hunter, C.H.; Huntley, B. (the late); Hurry, C.; Hurry, L.; Hustler, Hutton, R.; K.; Immelman, G.; Immelmann, K.; Inbar, R.; Irwin, M.P.S.; Isaacson, A.J.; Isakov, Y.A.; Isert, G.; Isert, H.H.; Jackson, F.J.; Jackson, H.D.; Jackson, J.R.; Jacobsen, P.; Jaeger, M.M.; James, H.W.; James, P.; Jansen, R.A.C.; Jardine, W.; Jarman, H.; Jarvis, J.F.; Jarvis, M.J.; Jefferies, R.; Jenkins, C.F.H.; Jenkins, J.; Jenson, M.K.; Jenson, R.A.C.; Johns, B.E.; Johnson, F.; Johnson, H.H.; Johnson, M.E.; Johnson, P.; Johnson, S.; Jojo, W.B.; Jones, M.A.; Jones, P.J.; Jones, T.; Joseph, C.A.N.; Jubb, R.A.; Jury, E.T.; Kalchreuter, H.; Kannwischer K.; Kapzynski, B.; Karl, F.; Keigh, S.; Kekiiva, A.F.; Kemp, A.C.; Kemp, M. Miss; Kere, A.; Kessner, E.; King, M.; King, S.; Kingsley, C.; Kingston, R.; Kleefisch, T.; Klerk, W.; Kloot, T.; Knoblauch, D.; Koenig, A.; Koffan, K.; Kondo, K.; Kostin, Y.V.; Kovaccvic, J.; Kuhrer, K.; Kujawa, W.; Kunkel, P.; Kunze, H.D.; Kuznetsov, A.A.; L'Homme, L; Laburn, R.J.; Lacey, H.; Lack, D.;

Lageese, J.; Lambert, M.; Lamm, D.W.; Lane, A.A.; Lang, E.; Langberg, W.; Lange, E.M.; Langfelt, W.; Lawson, P.C.; Lawson, W.J.; Laycock, H.; Laycock, L.T.; Lea, A.M.; Lee, A.J.; Lendrum, A.L.; Lewek, T.; Lewis, D.M.; Lewis, J.G.; Lewis, M.; Line, L.J.; Lippens, L; Lippert, W.; Lipscomb, C.G.; Lister, U.G.; Little, J. Miss; Lofts, D.; Loots, R.P.; Louette, M.; Louw, G.W.; Lovel, T.W.I.; Low, R. Mrs; Low, R.: Lowe, J.R.; Lowe, R.; Ludwig, H.; Lynch, G.C.; Lynes, H.; Macdonald, I.A.W.; Macdonald, M.A.; Mackowicz, R.; Maclatchy, A.; Maclean, G.L.; Macleod, J.G.R.; Madge, S.G.; Malbrant, R.; Malherbe, A.; Malherbe, E.; Manning, A.F.; Mansfield, D.N.; Manson, P.D.; Marchant, S.; Marcus, M.B.; Markus, M.; Marler, P. Marriage, A.W.; Marshall, A.J.; Marshall, H.W.; Marshall, P.J.; Marshall, W.; Marten, K.; Martin, K.; Martin, J. Martin, R.; Masterson, A.N.B.; Matsinger, H.; Mayaud, D.; McCulloch, D.; McCulloch, E.M. Mrs; McCullock, K.; McKay, R.; McLachlan, G.D.; Mclean, S.; McLelland, V.S.; McMahon, L.; Meade-Waldo, E.G.; Meadows, B.S.; Meeklenburg, B.S.; Meeklenburg, A.F.; Medvedev, S.I.; Meinertzhagen, R.; Memtis, M.T.; Mendelsohn, J. Dr.; Mentis, M.T.; Mentz, H.; Meyer, H.F.; Meyer, J.J.; Middlemiss, E.; Middleton, E.; Miles, H.M.; Millar, R.; Milstein, R. le S.; Milatein, P.; Miskell, J.; Miskell, J.E.; Mitchell, P.; Mitsch, H.; Moeed, A.; Mogg, A.O.D.; Moller, A.P.; Moore, P.; Moreau, R.E.; Morel, G.: Morel, M.Y.; Morgan, J.H.; Morgan-Davies, A.M.; Morony, J.E.; Morphew, J.; Morris, D.; Morrison, B.; Mortimer, G.S.; Mostert, D.J.; Moynihan, M.; Mikherjee, A.K.; Mullard, B.; Mullee, D.; Muller, M.; Mungure, S.A.; Munz, K.; Murray, R.W.; Murshid, A.A.; Musil, A.; Myburgh, N.; Myer, E. Mrs; Myres, J.G.; Nadler, T.: Neethling, J.; Neff, R.; Nelson, R.; Nethersole, C.; Neuby Varty, B.V.; Neumann, O.; Neuzig, K.; Newby, J.E.; Newman, K.; Newman, T.H.; Nicholls, E.G.; Nichols, G.; Nicholson, E.; Nicolai, J.; Nielson, A.V.; Neithammer, G.; Niven, C.; Niven, J.; Norris, C.A.; North, A.J.; Norse, A.D.; O'Gorman, G.; Oatley, T.; Oatley, T.B.; Olioso, G.; Oppenborn, G.; Orcutt, F.S.; Oren, D.C.; Osborne, D.G.; Oschadleus, D.; Otton, J.; Oxley, R.E.; Page, W.T.; Panjain, H.A.; Palfery, J.: Panjain, H.A.; Park, P.O.; Parker, S.A.; Pascoe, P.; Pasture, G.; Paton, D.C.; Pattern, G.; Patterson, H.; Payn, W.H.; Payne, K.; Payne, P.B.; Payne, R.B.; Pearson, D.J.; Pearson, R.J.; Pearson, T.B.; Peck, A.; Peck, B.; Pek, L.V.; Peltet, A.; Penry, E.H.; Pensold, R.; Pepler, D.; Pepler, E.; Percival, C.; Pereyra, J.A.; Perkins, S.; Perreau, G.A.; Perry, D.G.C.; Perry, M.; Peters, J.L.; Petersen, G.; Pfeffer, P.; Phillips, R.: Pialek, W.; Pickles, H.; Pickles, S.; Pickup, S.G., Mrs; Pitman, C.R.S.; Pitwell, L.R.; Plowes, D.C.H.; Peacock, T.W.; Pohland, E.; Pohland, E.; Poltimore, L.; Poltimore, L; Ponweiser, H.; Pope, J.; Pope, W.A.; Porter, O.; Porter, S.; Potts, G.R.; Prestwich, A.A.; Price, D.M.: Miss; Prigogine, A.; Proebsting, F.; Prizibram, H.; Quine, D.; Rabbich, H.B.; Radtke, G.A.; Rand, L.; Randall, L., Mrs; Rantzau, C.; Rattigan, G.E.; Raymond, W.D.B.; Read, J.; Read, M.E.; Reed, R.A.; Reichenow, A.; Restall, R.L.; Richardson, D.; Ride, W.D.L.; Riney, T.; Robbins, G.F.S.; Roberts, T.: Robson, O. Mrs; Robertson, H.A.; Robin, A.P.; Robin, R.; Robinson, E.; Robson, N.E.; Rochat, K.; Roche, J.; Rogers, M.J.; Rohloff, P.: Roles, D.G.; Roots, C.; Rose, M.; Roselaar, C.S.; Rothschild Lord; Rowan, M.K. Mrs; Row, L; Row, P. Mrs; Rowles, R.A.: Rowntree, M.H.; Ruschin, H.W.; Russ, K.; Russell, C.: Rustamov, A.K.; Rutgers, A.; Ryaboy, V.F.; Rydzewski, W.: Safriel, U.N.; Safar, P.M.; Sage, B.L.; Salt, F.W.; Salvadori, F.B.; Sarkin, R.; Saunders, D.A.; Saunderson, C.; Schassmann, A.; Scheeder, F.; Scheepers, J.; Scheimer, C.W.; Scherterlei, K.; Schifter, H.; Schlater, W.L.; Schmidt, R.K.; Schonwetter, M.; Schwartz, E.R.; Schwarz, H.; Schweiger, C.; Sclater, G.E.; Sclater, W.L.; Scott, A.J.; Scott, D.; Sedgwick, E.H.; Seely, M.K.; Sellar, P.J.; Serle, W.; Shannon, G.R.; Shaw, P.; Shephard, J.B.; Shephard, M.; Sheton, J.B.; Shillinglaw, S.N.; Shirt, D.B.; Shishkin, V.W.: Sindel, S.; Shore-Bailey, W.; Shotter, R.A.; Shuel, R.; Sieberer, O.; Siegried, W.R.; Silva, T.; Silver, A.; Silzer, M.; Siman, H.Y.; Simms, C.; Simpson, C.S.; Siroki, Z.; Skead, C.J.; Skead, D.M.; Sladen, A.G.L.; Sluyter, F.: Smith, B. Mrs; Smith, D.A.: Smith, E.J.; Smith, G.A.; Smith, K.D.; Smithers, R.H.N.; Smook, C.; Smythe, A.B.; Snow, D.W.; Sopper, E.; Spenkelink Van Schaik, J.L.; St Quintin, W.H.; Stamps, D.A.; Stanford, J.K.; Stannard, J.: Stanton, J.E.L.; Stehle, W.; Stein, O.; Steinbacher, J.; Steinbascher, K.: Steiner, H.; Steinhagen, R.; Stephens, J.M.; Steyn, P.; Stilwell, M.W.; Stoodley, A.A.; Stoodley, A.A.J.; Storr, G.M.; Stresemann, E.; Stringer, R.: Strutt, J.; Stuart, S.N.; Stunnell, J.; Sudhaus, W.; Sudworth, G.B.; Summers-Smith, D.; Sushkin, P.P.; Swanepoel, W.; Taibel, A.; Taibel, A.M.; Tait, C.C.; Taka-Tsukasa, N.: Tarboton, W.; Tarboton, W.R.; Taylor, I. Mrs; Taylor, J.; Taylor, J.S.; Taylor, R.H.; Teschemaker, W.E.; Them, P.; Thiollay, J.M.; Thomas, A.; Thomas, D.I.; Thompson, T.R.H.; Thomsen, P.; Thorpe, H.; Thuron, L.; Ticehurst, C.B.; Tidball, E.: Tiley I.; Timmis, W.H.; Todd, W.W.; Tohme, G.: Townsend, D.: Traylor, M.A.; Tree, A.J.; Tristram, H.B.; Troppope, J.; Tucker, B.; Turbott, C.; Tuxford, T.; Tweddle, C.: Tweddle, D.; Tweddle, S.C.; Tyler, H.; Underhill, H.; Uys, C.J.; Valverde, J.A.; Van Baelen, E.: Van Breda, N.D.: Van der Eyssen, M.; Van der Merwe, G.; Van Eyk, W.; Van Niekerk, J.H.; Van Nierop, F.; Van Rooyen, J.C.; Van Rooyen, S.V.; Van Someren, G.R.C.; Van Someren, V.G.; Vaughn, J.H.; Veal, A.R.W.; Veldman, M.; Venter, P.; Venter, P.S.: Verheijen, J.A.; Verheyen, R.: Verheyen, W.N.; Vermaak, C.T.; Vernon, C.J.; Vesey-Fitzgerald, D.F.; Victoria, J.K.; Villiers, A.; Vincent, A.W.; Vincent, W.; Von Maltitz, M.; Von Schwind, H.: Voorus, K.H.; Vorster, R.; Vriends, M.M.; Vurkard, R.: Wahlen, W.; Walker, H.O.; Walker, M.A.; Wallace, D.I.M.; Wallis, H.M.; Wallis, R.; Wallis, E.S.: Ward, P.; Warncke, K.; Watson, T.; Wevv, C.S.; Webb, L.V.R.; Weekes, J.T.; Weissenbacher, B.K.H.; Welch, G.; Welch, H.J., Wells, D.R.: Westood, N.J.; Whitaker, J.I.S.; White, D.: Whitmore, G.E.: Whittaker, L.; Wytbrow, C.: Wildeboer, H. Dr.; Wilkins, J.C.: Wille, H.; Williams, F.; Williams, K.; Williams, T.M.; Wilson, C.; K.J.; Wilson, R.I.; Winterbottom, J.; Wintle, C.C.: Witt, C.R.: Wolff-0Metternich< G.F.: Wolters, H.E.; Wood, D.: Woohall, P.E.; Woodcock, M.W.; Woods, P.J.E.; Woolham, F.; Wostendick, U.; Wright, A. Dr; Wurst, I.; Yanney-Ewusie, J.; Yeomans, R.; Zedlityz, O.; Zeh, A.; Zeuner, F.E.: Ziswiler, V.; Zottman, T.M.; Zurcher, E.

Publications consulted were:

Academy of Natural Sciences, Philadelphia Journal, USA; African Wildlife (Official publication of the Wildlife Society of Southern Africa); Agapornis Journal (Journal of the African Lovebird Society of Victoria, Aust); Albatross (Branch magazine of Southern Africa Ornithological Society); American Cage Bird Magazine, USA; American Cage-Bird, USA; American Museum Notivates (Publication of the American Museum of Natural History; Annals of the Carnegie Museum, USA; Annals of the Transvaal Museum, RSA; Ardca (Tijdschrift der Nederlandse Ornithologigishe Unie); Arnoldia (Publication of the National Museums of Zimbabwe; Auk (The American Ornithologist's Union, USA); Australian Bird Watcher (The Bird Observers' Cluyyb); Australian Birdkeeper, Aust; Australian Birds (New South Wales Field Ornithologist's Club); Australian Corella (Australian Bird Study Association); Aviary Topics (Monthly Journal of Avicultural Society, RSA); Avicultural Bulletin (Avicultural Society of America Inc); Avicultural Bulletin, USA; Avicultural Magazine (The Journal of the Avicultural Society, UK); Avizandum, RSA; Beitrage zur Fortpfianzumgsbiologue der Vogel; Biology Gabon, WA; Bird Keeper, UK; Bird Notes (Journal of the Foreign Bird Club, UK); Bird Talk, USA; Bird World, USA; Birds Monthly Illustrated, (UK); Black Lechwe (Magazine of the Wildlife Conservation Society of Zambia); Bokmakierie (General Interest Magazine of the Southern African Ornithological Society); Boletim de Sociedade Broteriana; Bonner Zoologische Beitage, Germany; Bonner Zoologische Beitrage; Botanic Survey Memoir, RSA; Bulletin du Jardin Botaniquado l'Etat, Bruxelles; Bulletin of National Herbium of New South Wales, Aust; Bulletin of Niger Ornithological Society; Bulletin of the Comparative Zoology, Harvard, USA; Bulletin of the Zambian Ornithological Society; Cage and Aviary Birds, (UK); Celmisia (New Zealand Journal of Botany); Condor, USA; Der Ornithologische Beobachter (Societe sulusse pour l'etude des oiseaux et leur protec-tion, FR); Die Giefiederete Welt, (Germany); Durban Museum Notitates (Miscellaneous Taxonomic notes on African Birds, RSA); East African Natural History Society Bulletin; Fauna and Flora; Fieldiana Zoology, USA; Finch News, Aust; Flora of Tropical East Africa, UK; Flora of Tropical West Africa, UK; Flora Zambesiaca, UK; Foreign Birds (The Magazine of Foreign Bird League, UK); Ghana

Journal of Science; Honeyguide (Magazine of the Ornithological Association of Zimbabwe); Ibis (Journal of the British Ornithologists Union, UK); International Zoo News, UK; Internation Zoo Year Book, UK; Journal East African Natural History Society; Journal for Ornothologie Auftrage der Deutschen Ornithologischen Geselischaft; Journal of the East Africa and Uganda Natural History Society; Klubnuus (Magazine of the Bloemfontein Cage Bird Society, RSA); Le Monde de Oiseaux, France; London Zoo Reports (Occasional Republications, UK); Los Angeles County Museum, Contributions to Science, USA; Magazine of the Avicultural Council of Southern Africa; Magazine of the Parrot Society, UK; Malimbus (Journal of the West African Ornithological Society); Miscellaneous Data on the keeping of Cage and Aviary Birds (Research magazine of Natal Avicultural Society, RSA); Nigerian Field Bulletin (Nigerian Ornithological Society); Occasional Papers of the National Museums of Zimbabwe; Ornithological Monographs, publication of the American Ornithologists' Union; Oryx (Journal of the Fauna Preservation Society); Ostrich (The Journal of the Southern African Ornithological Society); Pet Business World-Pet Industry News, UK; Postilla (Publications of the Peabody Museum of Natural History, Yale University, USA); Poultry World, UK; Proceedings of the Zoological Society of London; Psitta Scene (Published by the World Parrot Trust, USA); Puka (Occasional Papers of the Department of Wildlife, Fisheries and National Parks, Zambia); Queensland Aviculture (Official publication of the Avicultural Society of Queensland In. Aust); Rand Aves (Publication of the Rand Avicultural Society, RSA); Report of Netherlands Ornithological, Mauritanian Expedition, None Groningen, Holland; Revue de Zoologie et de Botanique Africane, Revue Zoologigque et Botanique Africaine; Rhodesian Agricultural Journal, Zim; Safring News, RSA; San Diego Bird Breeders Journal, USA; Sandgrouse, UK; Society of Malawi Journal; South African National Science Programme Reports; Targanyika Notes and Records, Tanzania; Tasmanian Bird Report The Bird Observers Association of Tasmania); The A.F.A. Watchbird, USA; The African Ark, USA; The Australian Birdwatcher (Publication of the Observers Club); The Canary and the Finch Journal, USA; The Emu (Royal Australian Ornithologists Union); The Lammergeyer (Journal of the Natal Parks Board, RSA); The Rhodesia Science News (The Journal of the Association of Scientific Societies in Zimbabwe); The Sunbird (Queensland Ornithological Society, Aust); University of Natal Wildlife Society Newsletter, RSA; Witwatersrand Bird Club News (Branch Magazine of Southern Africa Ornithological Society); World Pheasant Association Journal, UK; Zambia Museum Journal; Zambia Museums Papers; Zeitschrift des Kolner Zoo, Zoologischer Garden, Germany; Zoo Federation News (Published by National Federation of Zoological Gardens of Great Britain and Ireland); Zoonooz (Publication of San Diego Zoological Society, USA).

Note:
It has not been possible to illustrate with colour plates all bird species listed in this work, so we suggest for identification purposes consult the suggested standard ornithological reference books or video tapes on each region.

Field Guides
SOUTHERN AFRICA
Field Companion to Roberts' Birds of Southern Africa by G.L. Maclean
The Birds Around Us by R. Liversidge
Sasol Birds of Southern Africa by I. Sinclair, P. Hockey and W. Tarboton
Newman's Birds of Southern Africa by K. Newman
Ian Sinclair's Field Guide to the Birds of Southern Africa by Ian Sinclair

Large format publications
The Complete Book of Southern African Birds by P.J. Ginn, W.G. McIlleron and P. le Milstein (Eds)
The Birds of Africa by E.K. Urban, C. Hillary Fry and S. Keith (Eds) (5 volumes, two still in preparation)

EASTERN AFRICA
Collins illustrated checklist – Birds of Eastern Africa by B van Perlo
Collins Safari Guide – Common Birds of East Africa by D. Hoskins and D. Withers
Birds of East Africa by C.A.W. Guggisberg (2 volumes)
A Fieldguide to the Birds of East Africa by J G. Williams and N. Arlott
Birds of Kenya and northern Tanzania (including majority of species in southern Ethiopia, Somalia and Sudan by D.A. Zimmermann, D.A. Turner and D.J. Pearson

WESTERN AFRICA
A Field Guide to the Birds of West Africa by G.J Morel and W. Hartwig

NORTHERN AFRICA
Birds of Europe with North Africa by L. Jonsson

Bird Monographs and Family Studies
Munias and Mannikins by R. Restall
Finches and Sparrows an identification guide by P. Clement, A. Harris and J. Davis

Video Tapes
SOUTHERN AFRICA
Gibbon's Birds of Southern Africa (316 species featured) by G. Gibbon
Birds of the Kruger National Park (250 species featured) by G. Gibbon
Newman's Birds: An Introduction (100 species featured) by K. Newman
An Introduction to Garden Birds of SA by J. Wehner and J. Bruce-Brand
An Introduction to Water Birds of SA by J. Wehner and J. Bruce-Brand

Available from all leading bookstores.

Index